"TRUE STORIES OF WORLD WAR II MAKE FICTION PALE BY COMPARISON!"

—Associated Press

"A terrible toll of man and ships, no other type of United States warship suffered so many casualties—but at what a cost to the enemy!"

—Norfolk Virginian-Pilot

"WITHOUT DESTROYERS AND DESTROYER ESCORTS, THE WINNING OF NAVAL CAMPAIGNS IN WORLD WAR II WOULD HAVE BEEN IMPOSSIBLE . . . Ranging the globe, the pitching and rolling 'cans' fought wherever there was combat . . . A wealth of historical material, wonderfully accurate and complete!"

—The New York Times

TIN CANS

THE TRUE STORY OF THE FIGHTING DESTROYERS OF WORLD WAR II

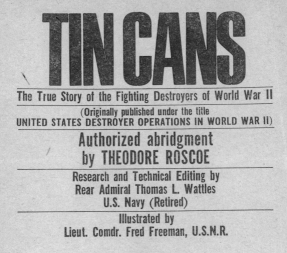

TIN CANS

The True Story of the Fighting Destroyers of World War II

(Originally published under the title
UNITED STATES DESTROYER OPERATIONS IN WORLD WAR II)

Authorized abridgment
by THEODORE ROSCOE

Research and Technical Editing by
Rear Admiral Thomas L. Wattles
U.S. Navy (Retired)

Illustrated by
Lieut. Comdr. Fred Freeman, U.S.N.R.

BANTAM BOOKS · TORONTO · NEW YORK · LONDON

. . . To the Destroyermen of the United
States Navy, Past, Present, and Future . . .

TIN CANS: THE TRUE STORY OF
THE FIGHTING DESTROYERS OF WORLD WAR II
Originally published under the title
UNITED STATES DESTROYER OPERATIONS IN WORLD WAR II
A Bantam Book / published by arrangement with
The United States Naval Institute

PRINTING HISTORY
U.S. Naval Institute edition published December 1953
2nd printing ... December 1957
Bantam edition published February 1960
2nd printing .... July 1960
3rd printing .... November 1968

Bantam Books are published by Bantam Books, Inc., a subsidiary
of Grosset & Dunlap, Inc. Its trade-mark, consisting of the words
"Bantam Books" and the portrayal of a bantam, is registered in the
United States Patent Office and in other countries. Marca Registrada.
Bantam Books, Inc., 271 Madison Avenue, New York, N.Y. 10016.

Contents

☆ ☆ ☆

None of them knew the colour of the sky.

Their eyes glanced level,

and were fastened upon the waves that swept toward them.

These waves were of the hue of slate, save for the tops,

which were of foaming white,

and all of the men knew the colours of the sea.

The horizon narrowed and widened, and dipped and rose,

and at all times its edge

was jagged with waves that seemed thrust up in points like rocks.

Many a man ought to have a bathtub larger than the boat

which here rode upon the sea.

These waves were most wrongfully and barbarously abrupt and tall,

and each froth-top

was a problem in small-boat navigation . . .

STEPHEN CRANE, *The Open Boat*

Foreword

☆ ☆ ☆

U.S. destroyer operations in World War II presents the dramatic story of the United States Navy's Destroyer Service —the story of the DD's and DE's and the destroyermen that waged and won the greatest sea, anti-submarine, and surface-air battles in naval history.

This volume is not the official operational history, nor is it a formal history in the academic sense. Many aspects of destroyer warfare which would normally go unrecorded in a purely historical account are discussed in this text. Some of the technical features of destroyer work are herein detailed to explain the technological "how" which is linked with the "who, when, where, what and why" of destroyer missions and combat actions.

Featured in the following chapters are every major and a multitude of minor destroyer battles, missions, and undertakings—the actions and activities which engaged the destroyers and destroyer-escorts of DesLant and DesPac during World War II. The veteran destroyerman and the destroyermen of tomorrow will cherish the achievements of the Destroyer Service recounted in this volume. The uninitiated layman and landsman will find them thrilling.

The historical narrative serves as a background against which destroyers and destroyer escorts are silhouetted in many roles—the DE as convoy escort and sub-hunter extraordinary; the DD as jack-of-all-trades and master of all: scout, A/S vessel, screen for larger warship, bombardment ship, rescue vessel, blockade runner, transport, supply ship, radar picket, and all-around fighting ship capable of trading blows with everything from enemy submarine to battleship, enemy coastal battery to dive bomber. Threaded through the narrative are discussions of destroyer tactics, with special emphasis on A/S (anti-submarine) tactics and anti-aircraft tactics—subjects of particular interest to all destroyermen, and highly significant in the light of recent developments.

Destroyer losses and failures are recounted in this volume as well as destroyer gains and successes. Unless one bows to Napoleon's definition of history as "a fiction agreed upon," mistakes must be recorded, if only in the interest of veracity.

Altogether serious errors were remarkably few—amazingly few when one considers the global scope of the destroyer effort, the number of ships involved, and the hazardous circumstances of their involvement—but those few major errors are herein reported for their instructive worth. So is the story of the wretched torpedo performance caused by a defective torpedo—a weapon's failure which hampered the Navy's destroyer effort, even as it hamstrung the Navy's submarine effort, from the start of World War II until the torpedo's belated correction in 1943.

This volume, however, is not to be considered a textbook on any aspect of destroyer warfare. A type history, it presents a comprehensive picture of destroyer operations—the record of a service, and a summary of its achievements—the story of a war effort composed of, by, and for the destroyermen of the United States Navy.

The book is based on material drawn from action reports, ship diaries, and war records researched by Rear Admiral Thomas L. Wattles, USN (Ret.), a veteran destroyer officer who saw action in Atlantic, Mediterranean, and Pacific theaters. Additional material was drawn by author and researcher from contemporary news and periodical accounts, and from authoritative reference works. Statistical data and ship- and submarine-sinking assessments are from the compilations of the United States Strategic Bombing Survey, the Joint Army-Navy Assessment Committee, and *The U. S. Navy at War, Official Reports,* by Fleet Admiral Ernest J. King, USN.

The manuscript's preparation was generously aided by critical comment from a number of destroyer officers, including Vice Admiral Walden L. Ainsworth, USN (Ret.); Rear Admiral E. T. Woolridge, USN (ComDesLant, 1949); Rear Admiral Arleigh A. Burke, USN; Rear Admiral Ralph Earle, Jr., USN; and Captain J. W. Boulware, USN, and Lieutenant Commander John J. Hession, USNR. Miss Loretta McCrindle, and Miss Barbara Gilmore, of the Office of Naval History, appreciably aided the research effort. Original publication was suggested and sponsored by Captain J. B. Rooney, USN, Captain H. P. Rice, USN, Captain A. L. Renken, USN, and Captain G. W. Pressey, USN, all of the Training Division, Bureau of Naval Personnel.

Introduction

☆ ☆ ☆

Nearly one hundred and fifty years ago, Lord Nelson, chasing a phantom Villeneuve across countless leagues of the Atlantic, fiercely complained, "When I die, you will find this want of frigates graven upon my heart." By World War II the lifting sail of these fast, light ships had given way to the airplane for the primary service of reconnaissance, but the complaints of the Admirals were much the same. When at grips with the enemy on the sea, under the sea, or in the air, no Task Force Commander ever had enough destroyers.

In war, the strength of the offensive is as the strength of the line of communications—the service of supply. In the pages to follow will be found the saga of the small ships whose unwearied watch brought thousands of our youth safely to distant shores to form for the assault; whose guns blazed the way across the beach for them; and whose youth then returned to the weary watch to escort yet more ships to distant shores with those thousands of tons of supplies required to make the assault successful.

And these small ships with the lethal punch were versatile; no job was too small, no task too great. Many types were evolved for special duties, principal among these being destroyer escorts, designed to meet and defeat the submarine menace. And defeat it they did. And, with the changes war itself must bring, the character of the first-line destroyer itself was changed. Thus the Carrier Task Force became our greatest offensive weapon, and its screening a major destroyer mission; thus the enemy threat from the air overshadowed all else, and the destroyer bristled with anti-aircraft guns.

Finally, as the war in the Pacific entered its latter stages, the once proud Japanese Navy had disappeared from the surface of the sea; there were no targets left for torpedoes, so for us the torpedo boat as such ceased to exist. In her place was still the destroyer, now to fight its greatest battle as the radar picket in the battle for Okinawa.

The ring-down of the curtain at Okinawa—the end of the show—brought the most bitter naval battle of the war to the destroyer, and ended in victory for the radar picket.

Our soldiers and marines went ashore standing up; the bitter battle for them lay ahead, but an unbroken line of supply was to insure their victory. The real victory came first to the small ships who held the line—but at what cost! At the end of six weeks our losses in ships sunk and severely damaged on the picket line were greater than the total number of United States destroyers in commission at the beginning of the war. Our naval casualties in killed and missing—the men who would never come home—were greater than those of the combined Army and Marine forces on shore. But—the last despairing effort of the *Kamikaze* was defeated—the line held —the work horse of the Fleet had proved once more a thoroughbred.

Many of the readers of the following pages will be those who served in Industry on the home front—the source of supply which made possible the winning of the War. They will take pride in reading of the men who went down to the sea in small ships to help keep the supply lines open. And then there will be the soldiers—who varied the monotony of their progress overseas by watching the destroyers knife their zigzag course in search of the preying submarine. They may well take pride in reading about what the sailors went through to get the Army over there.

And, lastly, there will be those of that half million officers and men, Regular and Reserve, who joined the war to live and sweat, fight and die, in these small ships. They held their heads high, with fierce pride. They became the soul and spirit of the Destroyer Navy. Of them we may all be very, very proud.

WALDEN L. AINSWORTH
Vice Admiral, U.S. Navy, (Retired)
COMMANDER DESTROYERS
PACIFIC FLEET
July 1942 to January 1943
October 1944 to July 1945

PART ONE

Little Ships into Action

☆ ☆ ☆

Give me a fast ship
for I intend to go in harm's way.

JOHN PAUL JONES

Chapter 1

Destroyers and Destroyermen

☆ ☆ ☆

Here Come the Small Boys!

Night, and a sea lathered with storm. A small gray ship, her bows streaming spume, fights her way across the heaving slopes and sinking valleys of water. Off in the blowing murk another vessel rides the sea—a low-lying craft that slides through the waves like a gliding shark. Suddenly the little gray ship spears the blackness with a shaft of light that reveals the second craft in dim silhouette. At once the little gray ship charges, rolling her beam ends under. There is a crash, the shock of collision. Pinned together, the two vessels wrestle in the storm; then the shark, wounded, burrows into the sea. In her wake, the small gray ship releases a tumble of iron cylinders. Lightning flashes beneath the waves, and there is thunder down under. Some time later a deep-sea blast is heard. The little ship steams away. She is USS BORIE, and she has just killed a German submarine. . . .

On the other side of the world, equatorial ocean. And three little ships advancing across blue water. Abruptly they pause, circle about, spatter the surface with darts that dig into the water like needles. And presently the surface is rumpled by explosions—up comes a dark blot of oil, scraps of rubbish, a bit of flotsam. The three little ships sail on. They are USS ENGLAND, USS GEORGE, and USS RABY, conducting one of the greatest submarine hunts in naval history.

Another scene: a group of American escort-carriers steaming along in the early morning of a dangerous day. Salt wind, and a pastel twilight; then sunrise painting the open sea. And now on the horizon appear enemy masts: four battleships, eight cruisers, eleven destroyers—dragons wanting nothing better than to get their teeth into baby flat-tops. Planes take

2

to the sky like angered bees. Guns rumble, and the ocean's surface is splashed by shells. And as the carrier group wheels to escape, a little gray ship—the USS JOHNSTON—swerves about and makes a dash straight for the oncoming leviathans.

The little ship's guns are blazing, her torpedoes streak the water like an opening fan. Behind her, other little gray ships are coming—HOEL and HEERMANN, JOHN C. BUTLER, DENNIS, RAYMOND, and SAMUEL B. ROBERTS.

SMALL BOYS *comes a crackling order by voice radio.* SMALL BOYS ON MY STARBOARD QUARTER INTERPOSE WITH SMOKE BETWEEN MEN AND ENEMY CRUISERS

"Small boys," Admiral Sprague called them. But those little gray ships did a man-size job. They, and scores like them. They were the destroyers and the destroyer-escorts of the United States Navy.

Some called them "cans." They meant the word for a noun. But the destroyers changed it to a verb. "Can" meaning "Wilco," and "able to do."

And they did. . . .

The destroyers took punishment—no other type of United States warship suffered as many combat casualties. From all causes, 71 American DD's and 11 DE's—a total of 82 "small boys"—were lost during the war. But if American DD's and DE's took punishment, they dealt it out in overwhelming reprisal. In battle areas that ranged from North Atlantic to South Pacific, from Mediterranean to Bering Sea, they sank over 100 Axis submarines, destroyed at least as many of the enemy's surface warships, demolished thousands of tons of enemy supply vessels, transports, and auxiliary craft, and shot down scores of enemy planes. The wholesale damage inflicted by their innumerable shore bombardments defies accurate statistical assessment. Nor could adding machines total the value of anti-submarine sweeps that cleared the way for Allied merchant shipping and troop transports—or the value of destroyer screens which time and again successfully thwarted enemy attack on the aircraft carriers, battleships, and cruisers of the United States Atlantic and Pacific Fleets.

Steel ships and steel men, the Navy's Destroyer Forces made valiant history in World War II.

This is their story.

Chapter 2

The Modern DD

☆ ☆ ☆

Thunder Before Storm (1930-1938)

"There won't be another war," optimists said. "No nation can afford one." But—

In 1931 a Japanese army swept into Manchuria. In 1934 Adolf Hitler became full-fledged dictator of Germany. By 1938 Europe was a vast powder mine; the League of Nations was tottering; the democratic world was facing a deadly crisis.

The World War II DD

At time of war's outbreak in Europe, the U.S. Navy's destroyer (DD) fleet was largely composed of the BENSON and BRISTOL (or LIVERMORE) classes, such destroyers as those of the PORTER and CRAVEN classes, and the husky FLETCHER class. The latter remained the fleet-destroyer heavyweight until 1944 when new destroyers of the ALLEN M. SUMNER class were commissioned. Biggest of American DD's to steam into action were the GEARING class destroyers which appeared in 1945.

Destroyer Group Organization

During World War II the Navy's destroyers were attached to the Navy's fleets—Atlantic, Pacific, Asiatic—came directly under the control of the various Fleet commanders. When attached to Spruance's Fifth Fleet, or Halsey's Third Fleet, or Kinkaid's Seventh (Southwest Pacific) Fleet, or Ingram's South Atlantic Fleet, they were operationally controlled by the subordinate Fleet commanders.

For administrative purposes, two main destroyer-force commands were organized. Destroyers assigned to the Atlantic Fleet were designated "Destroyers, Atlantic Fleet" (DesLant). Those assigned to the Pacific Fleet were designated "Destroyers, Pacific Fleet" (DesPac.).

The administrative heads of these two destroyer "forces" were known as Type Commanders. They kept track of the destroyers attached to the various Fleets. And from the "ship pool" they furnished destroyers when wanted for such operations as convoy escort duty, a "hunter-killer" campaign, or service with the local defense forces of a sea frontier. They were in over-all charge of all DD personnel. They advised on strategy and tactics. They recommended new battle gear and improvements of old. They requisitioned facilities, matériel, and equipment. They sponsored new training activities, and were in charge of training new DD's and of "refresher training" for veteran ships. They pushed ship construction. They broke bottlenecks. Many of the destroyer successes recounted in this history were spark-plugged by the officers who served as ComDesLant and ComDesPac. This is the roster:

COMDESLANT	*Date in Command*
Rear Admiral F. L. Reichmuth	*As of Oct. 1941*
Rear Admiral A. S. Carpender	*Dec. 22,1941*
Rear Admiral O. C. Badger	*June 3, 1942*
Rear Admiral M. L. Deyo	*Dec. 15, 1942*
Rear Admiral J. Cary Jones	*Jan 1, 1944*
Rear Admiral O. M. Read	*Sept. 20, 1944*
Rear Admiral F. E. Beatty	*Oct. 6, 1945*

COMDESPAC	
Rear Admiral M. F. Draemel	*As of Sept. 1940*
Rear Admiral R. A. Theobald	*Dec. 31, 1941*
Rear Admiral W. L. Ainsworth	*July 4, 1942*
Rear Admiral M. S. Tisdale	*Jan. 8, 1943*
Rear Admiral J. L. Kauffman	*Jan. 2, 1944*
Rear Admiral W. L. Ainsworth	*Oct. 31, 1944*
Rear Admiral W. H. P. Blandy	*July 13, 1945*

The largest destroyer group within the Fleet setup is the flotilla. The word, defined as "A fleet of small ships, or a small fleet," applies destroyer-wise, either way.

At the beginning of the war there were two Destroyer Flotillas in the Pacific. They were commanded by Rear Admiral R. A. Theobald (ComDesFlot One), and Rear Admiral M. F. Draemel (ComDesFlot Two).

Destroyers were also grouped in Task Flotillas. The Destroyer Task Flotilla is composed of two or more destroyer squadrons. Destroyer squadrons are composed of two (occasionally three) destroyer divisions. There is no standard size for the squadron; no set number of ships in the division. The average squadron contained nine destroyers—a division composed of five, and a division of four. However, the destroyer squadron (DesRon) may contain two full divisions and two units of a third division. A destroyer division (DesDiv) may contain four, five, or six DD's.

A World War II newcomer was the Escort Division (CortDiv), which was composed of destroyer-escorts.

Comparable to military field commanders, destroyer squadron and division commanders were combat leaders who fought the war on the front line—often enough, behind the enemy's lines. Tactical officers, they led their ships into action and quarterbacked the destroyer team-play.

Destroyer Guns

Largest caliber on the American DD of World War II was the 5-inch 38 which was housed in a movable mount. The average destroyer (medium size) carried four such guns, the FLETCHER class carried five, and the larger SUMNER and GEARING classes, which came later, carried six of them in three twin mounts.

Hydraulic machinery moved the mount in train (to left or right), and it also elevated or depressed the gun.

Such lighter guns as the 20-mm. and the 40-mm. stood in open "gun tubs." These "tubs" were stationary and served as shields only.

The 5-inch 38's composed the destroyer's main battery. The lighter automatic guns—the 20-mm. Oerlikon and the powerful 40-mm., designed after the Swedish Bofors—composed the secondary battery.

The 40-mm. is the Navy's largest machine-gun.

For a while U.S. destroyers carried 1.1-inch anti-aircraft guns. This gun proved an expensive "bust," and it was discarded early in the war.

The 5-inch 38-caliber, the destroyer's main-battery weapon, is a dual-purpose, semi-automatic, rapid-fire gun good for an anti-aircraft barrage, for salvos at surface targets, and for shore bombardment. In its movable, enclosed mount, it possesses such features as high-speed power drives for train and elevation, a hydraulic rammer which loads the gun, local handwheel control and remote director control, a firing key for electrical firing, a foot mechanism for percussion firing, a sight mechanism which contains three telescopes, and a set of instruments which receive fire-control directions transmitted from a remote gun-director.

Shooting at a surface target, this big gun can throw a 54-

pound projectile a good 18,000 yards. Its maximum aerial range is over six miles! The gun fires an average of 15 rounds per minute, and crack destroyer gun crews obtained a rate of fire as high as 22 rounds per minute.

The single-mount 5-inch 38 and the twin-mount 5-inch 38 are both moved in train and elevation by hydraulic power drives. Automatic (remote) control from a director system is accomplished by means of electric signals transmitted to mechanisms which control the mount's hydraulic machinery, and the gun is serviced by means of power-driven powder and projectile hoists equipped with automatic fuse-setting devices for adjusting the fuse on a projectile according to order.

Torpedoes and Tube Mounts

The torpedoes carried into World War II by American destroyers were complicated weapons. Various models were used, but the best in service at war's beginning were 21-inchers (21 inches in diameter) propelled by the air-alcohol-water, superheated gas-turbine system. This torpedo weighed 2,215 pounds when readied for a warshot, and cost about $10,000.

By a complex set of mechanisms the torpedo, once launched, maneuvered itself to run at a pre-selected depth and steered itself to the target. The 21-incher could maintain a speed of 46 knots for a run of 4,500 yards. In effect, it operated as a miniature self-guiding submarine carrying an explosive charge of about 500 pounds of T.N.T. to the bull's-eye. (In later models the charge was increased to 1,100 pounds of torpex.) There was only one trouble with this remarkable engine of destruction. Too often it flubbed the dub and missed the mark.

The fault lay chiefly in a defective exploder device attached to the warhead. Adopted by the Navy and issued to the Destroyer Service late in 1941, this exploder mechanism was a "Buck Rogers" affair which was supposed to detonate the warhead when the torpedo came within the target's ship's field of magnetic influence.

Unfortunately the magnetic exploder was a "bust." Highly sensitized, it frequently "prematured"—blew up at a point near the target, but too far from the hull to wreak damage. Flooding was another common fault of this exploder. After months of painful error, the U.S. Navy abandoned the device. (On July 24, 1943, Admiral Nimitz, Commander-in-Chief Pacific Fleet, ordered ComDesPac to inactivate magnetic exploders on all torpedoes.)

In other respects the American torpedo was below par. The Japanese had the jump on this deadly weapon. During the war, they showed up with a 24-inch torpedo which had a speed of 49.2 knots and a range of almost 6,000 yards, and was armed with a warhead containing 1,210 pounds of explosive—over twice the charge of the American 21-incher. Before war's end the Japanese produced a torpedo with a range of 22,000 yards. These oxygen-driven monsters were practically "wakeless."

By comparison, the American torpedo was a poor "fish." But the torpedomen in the U.S. Destroyer Service made the best and the most of it. After the Battle for Leyte, U.S. destroyers had little opportunity to make torpedo attacks. Perhaps the chief reason was dearth of enemy targets—the Pacific was all but "fished out" by that date. But the DD itself had changed character. Originally designed as a torpedo vessel, the destroyer had assumed new and more important roles as a sub-hunter, gunfighter, and AA vessel on radar watch.

Standard torpedo launching-gear on American destroyers consisted of tube mounts located on deck amidships. On old destroyers the mounts were placed on the port and the starboard side of the ship. New destroyers usually carried the tube mounts on the center line. The modern mount was quintuple—a battery of five individual tubes. The mounts revolved automatically, were trained by director-control, and were fired by remote control. Torpedoes could be fired individually or in salvo.

Coming of Radar

It was in the field of electronic detection gear—radar and sonar—that the advantage was all on the American (and Allied) side. Radar, in particular. The Germans were never able to cope with it, and the Japanese never caught up with it.

The first American search radar set went to sea in April 1937 on the United States destroyer LEARY. Installed by the Naval Research Laboratory, the set was a "hush-hush" item if there ever was one. By the autumn of 1941, installations were spreading through the Fleet, and American destroyers were slated to receive their share. Pioneering, destroyer LEARY could take a bow for making the first radar contact on a U-boat in American naval history. The date was November 19, 1941. But it was not until the summer of 1942 that most of the Navy's warships were furnished with radar of one kind or another. The improved, long-range SG ("Sugar George") model, designed for use against ships only, was not distributed until the autumn of that year. The destroyer that carried search radar in 1941 considered itself lucky.

Operating with radar, scouting destroyers could cover an

area many leagues larger than those covered by scouts dependent on 20-20 vision and binoculars.

With the single exception of the atom bomb, radar was perhaps the most amazing development of World War II.

Combat Information Center (The C.I.C.)

With all kinds of information coming in on all sorts of instruments from all points of the compass, the warship on the receiving end was swamped with vital intelligence. The need for a coordinating center, a sort of information clearing-house on board ship, became imperative. In order to assemble, evaluate and disseminate all this data continually arriving via radio, visual means, radar, and sonar, a central "brain" was needed. In consequence, the Combat Information Center (C.I.C.) was organized early in the war.

The C.I.C. was not a mechanical brain, although switchboards, computers, and other contrivances were in the set-up. It was simply an agency for collecting and evaluating incoming information, fitting the various items into their respective places in the tactical scheme of things, and relaying same to appropriate control stations on the ship, or to neighboring vessels.

In short, the Combat Information Center was comparable to a military field headquarters, which received and digested dozens of reports, maintained an over-all picture of the constantly shifting battle scene, and sent various forces into action.

In destroyers the charthouse originally served as the information collection center. As the C.I.C. organization developed, so did the need for space, and the center was soon provided with its own room. The C.I.C. was manned by a team of officers and men trained for this complex activity. Size and composition of the team varied according to the ship and the information-gathering equipment available. In charge of the C.I.C. was the ship's Executive Officer.

Second World War

On September 1, 1939, Hitler touched off the Armageddon that was to kill millions of people. World War II was begun.

On September 3, 1939, England and France, honoring treaty commitments, declared war on Nazi Germany. Twelve hours later the British passenger liner ATHENIA with many Americans aboard was torpedoed and sunk by a U-boat off northwest Ireland with the loss of 112 passengers, including many women and children. The Battle of the Atlantic was on.

On September 8, 1939, President Roosevelt issued a proclamation of limited national emergency to *"safeguard and enforce"* the neutrality of the United States, and to *"strengthen our national defenses."* Empowered to do so by the Neutrality Act, the President forbade American shipping to enter the war zones, which included the North Sea, the Bay of Biscay, and the waters around the British Isles to a line some 350 miles west of Ireland.

On September 14, 1939, the Navy Department announced that 40 of the 110 destroyers in "mothballs" would be recommissioned for neutrality-patrol duty. That same day the USS MUSTIN—60th destroyer built since 1934—was commissioned.

History Repeats

The German seizure of Norway in the spring of 1940 put U-boat bases on Britain's northern flank. Seizure of Holland and Belgium installed them on the Channel. When France collapsed in June 1940, Germany became an Atlantic power. Italy's "backstab" entry into the war at that time placed the Axis athwart the Mediterranean. British shipping losses promptly mounted to an alarming figure.

But it was the *Rudeltaktik,* or wolfpack, that sank Britain's hopes of holding the Atlantic line. The wolfpack was the creation of Admiral Karl Doenitz, keen and ruthless commander of the German U-boat Force. Instead of trying to clamp a blockade on the British Isles, the new idea was to cut Britain's shipping lanes in the open Atlantic. Simply move the U-boats to mid-ocean where they would be beyond range of Allied land-based aircraft. Work the subs in teams—packs of eight or nine. Mass attack, always stronger than individual, could scatter the convoy's defenses, force the escorts to disperse. Then the stalking subs could strike in through the tattered screen.

The *Rudeltaktik* called for surface attacks at night. Convoys spotted in daytime were reported by the sub which made contact. Doenitz's headquarters would then order the nearest pack to converge on the convoy and lie in ambush. After dark the pack would strike. Thus the U-boat could take advantage of night's cover and of the high speed of a surface run under Diesel-engine power.

Deprived of air cover, the convoy in mid-ocean was bereft of one of its strongest defenses. Protection was entirely up to the escort vessels guarding the ship-train. "Asdic," the British submarine-detection device, was not enough. Deck guns and depth charges were not enough. At the outset the British were caught short of escort vessels. And at Dunkerque in May

1940 the British suffered staggering destroyer casualties—ten destroyers sunk and 75 disabled.

In May 1940 Winston Churchill sent a cable to Franklin D. Roosevelt. WE URGENTLY NEED DESTROYERS. So Roosevelt agreed to swap 50 old DD's for naval bases in the Bahamas and West Indies.

Chapter 3

Destroyers "Short of War"

(Opening Gun, 1941)

☆ ☆ ☆

Storm Approaches America

Late in January, 1941, U.S. Army and Navy leaders met with British military and naval representatives in Washington to discuss plans for collaboration and to decide over-all strategy to be employed in the event of American involvement in a global war.

By the end of March a number of British-American agreements had been reached. With regard to the European aggressors, it was decided that the United States would pursue a policy of "belligerent neutrality" and conduct various "short of war" operations which included Atlantic Safety Belt patrols, the defense of Greenland, and joint protection of shipping to or from the waters of the Eastern Atlantic war zone. It was also decided that if worldwide war exploded, the Allies would hold the line in the Pacific and concentrate on first defeating Nazi Germany as Global Enemy No. 1.

By the spring of 1941 the DD's of DesLant were engaged in "short-of-war" activities just a chalkline this side of open conflict. Readying for escort-of-convoy operations, the Navy in March organized a support force for Atlantic duty to be commanded by Rear Admiral A. L. Bristol, Jr. (flagship PRAIRIE), composed of destroyers, Navy aircraft, and accompanying tenders. The Support Force destroyer roster is listed on the opposite page.

In March Hitler had extended U-boat activities by proclaiming that Iceland and its surrounding waters were now in the war zone. The U-boats' successes in the North Atlantic impelled Admiral Stark to warn on April 4, *"The situation is obviously critical. . . . In my opinion, it is hopeless except as we take strong measures to save it."*

DESTROYER SQUADRON 7
Capt. J. L. Kauffman

PLUNKETT	Lt. Comdr. P. G. Hale
(Flagship DesRon 7.)	
NIBLACK	Lt. Comdr. E. R. Durgin
BENSON	Lt. Comdr. A. L. Pleasants, Jr.
GLEAVES	Lt. Comdr. E. H. Pierce
MAYO	Lt. Comdr. C. D. Emory
MADISON	Lt. Comdr. T. E. Boyce
LANDSDALE	Lt. Comdr. John Connor
HILARY P. JONES	Lt. Comdr. S. R. Clark
CHARLES F. HUGHES	Lt. Comdr. G. L. Menocal

DESTROYER SQUADRON 30
Capt. M. Y. Cohen

DALLAS	Lt. Comdr. H. B. Bell
(Flagship DesRon 30.)	
ELLIS	Lt. Comdr. J. M. Kennaday
BERNADOU	Lt. Comdr. G. C. Wright
COLE	Lt. Comdr. W. L. Dyer
DUPONT	Lt. Comdr. E. M. Waldron
GREER	Lt. Comdr. Forrest Close
TARBELL	Lt. Comdr. S. D. Willingham
UPSHUR	Lt. Comdr. W. K. Romoser
LEA	Lt. Comdr. C. Broussard

DESTROYER SQUADRON 31
Capt. Wilder D. Baker

MACLEISH	Lt. Comdr. A. C. Wood
(Flagship DesRon 31.)	
BAINBRIDGE	Lt. Comdr. E. P. Creehan
OVERTON	Lt. Comdr. J. B. Stefanac
STURTEVANT	Lt. Comdr. W. S. Howard, Jr.
REUBEN JAMES	Lt. Comdr. H. L. Edwards
MCCORMICK	Lt. Comdr. J. H. Lewis
BROOME	Lt. Comdr. T. E. Fraser
SIMPSON	Lt. Comdr. F. D. McCorkle
TRUXTON	Lt. Comdr. H. B. Heneberger

In his ultimatum regarding Iceland, Hitler had stretched the war zone across Denmark Strait to the three-mile limit of Greenland. On April 9, 1941, the United States, at Denmark's behest, agreed to assume responsibility for the protection of Greenland until Denmark was free of the Nazi yoke. The Navy projected a Greenland Patrol (and laid plans for Iceland). But while these plans and projects were on paper, the U-boats were at sea. That April nearly 600,000 tons of British-controlled shipping went down to submarine fire.

On May 24 the British battle cruiser HOOD was sunk by the new German battleship BISMARCK. Although British warships and aircraft trapped and sank the BISMARCK three days later, the destruction of HOOD in the waters between Iceland and Greenland left an icy pall over the North Atlantic.

On May 27, the day BISMARCK was blasted under, President Roosevelt declared an "Unlimited National Emergency." Broadcasting to the nation, he warned: *"The war is approaching the brink of the Western Hemisphere itself. It is coming very close to home. . . . It would be suicide to wait until they* [the aggressors] *are in our front yard. . . . We have, accordingly, extended our patrol in North and South Atlantic waters."*

The Navy was bending every effort to build a protective fence along the eastern border of that Atlantic front yard—a fence whose pickets would be mostly destroyers—extending from Greenland's frosty waters to the tropic seas of Brazil.

"Short-of-War" Bases

Newfoundland, a huge land mass with ragged coasts separated from the Canadian mainland by the Gulf of St. Lawrence and the Strait of Belle Isle, is North America's nearest approach to Europe. As such, it was the "jumping-off place" for Allied convoys bound for Britain. In 1940 the Navy selected the harbor of Argentia, deeply recessed in the Avalon Peninsula, as an advanced base for convoy escorts. By the autumn of '41 it was serving as "headquarters" for the destroyers of the Support Force.

The destroyermen found Argentia anything but Snug Harbor. Flailed by winter storms, the bay was a rough anchorage; the frost-bitten village provided little for the entertainment of weary bluejackets. But Navy tenders were there to rejuvenate tired DD's. And Argentia would look like Paradise to destroyers after North Atlantic convoy hauls to such ocean rendezvous areas as "Eastomp" (long. 22 E), "Westomp" (long. 52 W) and "Momp" (an oceanic area about midway between the British Isles and Canada, where convoy escorts peeled off for the run to Iceland or made rendezvous with eastbound or westbound ship trains).

Even so, Argentia remained a cheerless Paradise. Casco Bay in Maine was a pleasure resort by comparison. Selected for a destroyer base in the summer of 1941, Casco Bay ("Base Sail" to destroyermen) soon boomed with DD business.

Bermuda seemed like a holiday for the DD's that made this balmy landfall in the Gulf Stream. There, the Navy located its largest base installations on a site opposite Hamilton Island.

Working out of the Bermuda base, a powerful task group under Admiral Cook's command was presently engaged in conducting the Central Atlantic Neutrality Patrol. Extension of the "Western Hemisphere" to this mid-ocean parallel was a move to counter Nazi contemplation of the Azores Islands as target for a German grab.

Neutrality patrols in the Caribbean Area also kept the destroyermen alert, if not on tenterhooks. By Lend-Lease arrangement the Navy had acquired such West Indies bases as Kingston, Jamaica, and Port-of-Spain, Trinidad. In addition to San Juan, Puerto Rico, and Guantanamo, Cuba, they were key bastions of the Caribbean defense.

The U-boats had already invaded the Caribbean to rake Dutch Curaçao with shellfire and commit other depredations. And a nasty situation had developed in the French West Indies where the collapse of France had left "Vichy" Admiral Georges Robert in control of Martinique and Guadeloupe. Under Robert's command was a French West Indies Fleet which included the aircraft carrier BÉARN, the training cruiser JEANNE D'ARC, light cruiser EMILE BERTIN, and some smaller warships.

To keep an eye on this doubtful "Vichy" squadron, the U.S. Navy in 1940 established a special patrol which operated out of San Juan, Puerto Rico. The patrol was originally conducted by Destroyer Squadron 2 and 12 VP planes, under command of Captain W. L. Ainsworth in MOFFETT.

Destroyers to Iceland (NIBLACK *and* CHARLES F. HUGHES *in Action*)

President Roosevelt's answer to Hitler's Icelandic war zone ultimatum was a quiet directive to Admiral Stark ordering the Navy to reconnoiter the approaches to Iceland. The United States had no intention of allowing Hitler to extend his dominion to an island so strategically placed across the northern trans-Atlantic routes.

Hence the President's reconnaissance directive, and an order that sent an American destroyer steaming northward to conduct the special mission. The destroyer chosen for this sensitive task was the USS NIBLACK (Lieutenant Commander E. R. Durgin), flying the pennant of Commander D. L. Ryan, ComDesDiv 13.

NIBLACK was on her way early in April, 1941. The North Atlantic run proved uneventful until the 10th, and on that date things happened. Nearing Iceland, the destroyers sighted three lifeboats in the surface haze—survivors of a torpedoed Dutch merchantman! Durgin and company promptly went into action as lifesavers. They accomplished the rescue nimbly, the destroyer maneuvering with expert precision to pick up each boatload of exhausted seamen.

As the last of the bedraggled survivors were coming up the ship's side, NIBLACK's sonar instruments registered a submarine contact. The range was closing; apparently the U-boat was boring in to launch an attack. Durgin rushed NIBLACK's crew to General Quarters, and Division Commander Ryan ordered a depth-charge salvo.

Over went the ashcans, a booming "embarrassing pattern" that evidently embarrassed the sub to the point of a hasty retirement. These seem to have been the first depth charges fired in anger by American destroyermen in World War II.

NIBLACK's reconnaissance mission, and observation flights by Navy planes, pioneered the way for the American occupation of Iceland, a move to forestall possible German occupation. On July 1 U.S. Marines steamed from Argentia. Destination: Reykjavik.

For this major operation the Navy had assembled the first American Naval Task Force organized for foreign service. Designated TF 19, under command of Rear Admiral D. McD. LeBreton, the force consisted of 25 American ships. The Marines were carried by four naval transports. The escort included two battleships, two cruisers, and nine destroyers.

The formation embraced an "Inner" and "Outer" destroyer screen. The DD's in the Outer Screen were ELLIS, BERNADOU, UPSHUR, LEA and BUCK. Those in the Inner Screen: PLUNKETT, NIBLACK, BENSON, GLEAVES, MAYO, CHARLES F. HUGHES, LANSDALE, HILARY P. JONES. The DD's in the Outer Screen were positioned some 10,000 yards ahead of the main body. Patrolling out in front, the four old "four-pipers" and BUCK led the parade. No one knew what sort of reception committee might be waiting at the gates of Denmark Strait.

However, on July 7 the task force reached Reykjavik in one piece—with the exception of a destroyer which had left the formation to perform a rescue feat that was as thrilling as any Hollywood drama. The destroyer was the CHARLES F. HUGHES with Lieutenant Commander C. L. Menocal, commanding officer, and Commander F. O. Kirtland, ComDesDiv 14, on her bridge.

The drama began on June 5 when ten American women, members of the Harvard Unit of Red Cross nurses, set sail from New Orleans for England on the Norwegian motorship VIGRID.

On the 23rd the VIGRID, slowed by engine trouble, dropped

out of the convoy. That night a roaming wolfpack scented the disabled ship, and at 0735 the following morning the helpless vessel was torpedoed.

Crowded into four lifeboats, 37 seamen and the ten American nurses were adrift on the lonely ocean.

The next day the survivors glimpsed a convoy . . . and suffered the harrowing disappointment of seeing the ships steam on over the horizon.

The survivors decided to proceed in independent groups. Two of the lifeboats set a course for Ireland, and one of this pair was finally rescued by a British naval vessel. The other two lifeboats set a northwesterly course for Greenland. They chose a gruelling alternative. The little boats were overtaken by a storm that turned the voyage into a nightmare. The hardtack petered out. The water ration dwindled. One night one of the boats disappeared. The remaining lifeboat clung stubbornly to existence.

In this last boat there were 14 survivors, including VIGRID's captain and four of the Red Cross nurses. "We thought help would never come." That was the outlook by July 5 when the water ration was reduced to two swallows a day, the food ration to half a biscuit. But that evening the help was there— destroyer CHARLES F. HUGHES coming out of the dusk, big as an ocean liner, big as a hospital.

When the survivors were safe on board, the destroyermen conducted a search for the other lifeboat, but the North Atlantic vastness refused to relinquish the missing.

When the HUGHES arrived at Reykjavik on July 8, she found Task Force 19 crowding the harbor, the Marines going ashore, and the situation better than well in hand. And Reykjavik had acquired an American name—"Rinky Dink."

Attack on USS GREER

In March 1941 Hitler had proclaimed the seas off Iceland a danger zone for Allied and neutral shipping. The zone became far more dangerous in June when Hitler hurled Germany into war with the Soviet Union, and the Allies extended Lend-Lease to Russia. In the ocean southeast of Cape Farewell one merchantman after another had since been blown to the bottom by sharpshooting U-boats. "Torpedo Junction" the seamen called it—an apt name for North Atlantic waters where the wolfpacks waited to meet the east-bound Allied convoys.

The United States destroyer GREER was not steaming with a convoy when she neared "Torpedo Junction" on the morning of September 4, 1941. Flying the pennant of Commander G. W. Johnson, ComDesDiv 61, the GREER was proceeding independently, Argentia to Reykjavik, with mail and supplies for the American Icelandic base.

The DD was an old "four-piper," one of the 1200-ton flush-deckers recommissioned for Atlantic patrol in September 1939. Her captain, Lieutenant Commander L. H. Frost, had been in command just one month.

Heading for Iceland, GREER was deep in the submarine danger zone at daybreak, September 4. She was about 175 miles from Reykjavik, with the clock at 0840, when she was approached by a British patrol plane which flashed a U-boat warning. A German sub had been spotted about ten miles distant, directly in GREER's path. The destroyer acknowledged the warning, and the plane winged back to the spot where the enemy had been sighted.

Frost stepped up speed to 20 knots, sounded General Quarters, and sent the DD ahead on a fast zigzag. When the destroyer reached the submarine's reported position, the Commanding Officer slowed speed to 10 knots (to accommodate sonar work), and the destroyer's "pinging" gear went into action. The submerged U-boat was presently detected— at a point about 150 miles southwest of Reykjavik—and GREER had a submarine on her hands. Or, to sharpen the metaphor, she had a tiger by the tail.

For the destroyermen, the situation was peculiar, to say the least. On the one hand, the United States was not at war with Nazi Germany; on the other, "belligerent neutrality" wasn't peace. Concerning a meeting between a U.S. naval vessel and a German U-boat, the Navy's operational plan was ambiguous. Could the destroyer fire upon the sub, or must she wait for the sub to open fire? Without express authority to shoot, the destroyermen could only hold on, and keep their fingers crossed. Which is what GREER's destroyermen did.

They held on. For the next two hours GREER maintained sonar contact with the U-boat, and reported the submarine's position, course, and speed to all ships and planes within radio range. Frost kept the destroyer's bow pointed at the undersea menace, moving his ship this way and that as the sub maneuvered to evade. At 1000 the British patrol plane inquired if GREER was going to attack. The Commanding Officer was compelled to signal negative. At 1032 the British plane swooped down and dropped four random depth charges. Then the pilot signaled he was returning to base to refuel.

"There she goes," one of the destroyermen said. "Now what!"

From the bridge came an order that held GREER hard on the submarine's tail. The destroyer would continue to hold on.

But sooner or later an annoyed tiger was bound to turn. When?

The U-boat turned at 1240, and headed straight for the American destroyer. GREER's sonar instruments registered the closing range. Then the destroyer's lookouts sighted a discoloration and disturbance of the water a few hundred yards off to starboard. They did not see a periscope, but at 1248 they sighted the impulse bubble of a fired torpedo. The U-boat had let fly!

The destroyer seemed to leap at the warning cry, *"Torpedo!"* Frost sent his ship in a swing to evade, and a moment later the foaming wake was sighted sizzling through the water about 100 yards astern.

Exactly two minutes after the shot was fired, Commander Johnson, acting with the authority of Division Commander, ordered GREER to counterattack. Counterattack she did, steaming forward on the warpath to try for the submerged foe with a pattern of eight depth charges that boomed overside at 1256.

At 1258 another torpedo was sighted racing for the destroyer on collision course. Frost called for a hard turn to port; the destroyer swung to the left; the lethal "fish" missed the mark by a good 300 yards.

Contact was lost in the turmoil of exploding depth charges and evasion maneuvers, but GREER's sonar crew regained it at 1312, a few minutes after Division Commander Johnson ordered the search resumed. At 1315 a British plane skimmed across the seascape, and dropped two smoke pots on the spot where GREER had dumped her depth charges. Probing for the target with sonar fingers, the destroyer continued the sub-hunt, and the U-boat apparently went deep to evade. GREER was still searching when the British destroyer I-26 arrived on the scene at 1415.

The British destroyermen asked the Americans if they desired to conduct a coordinated search. Division Commander Johnson replied in the negative, and the British DD departed after dropping a random depth charge.

At 1512 GREER made sonar contact which was evaluated as "submarine," and the destroyermen delivered another attack. Eleven depth charges thundered down into the sea, but results were evidently zero. No oil slick, no debris, no sign of a shattered U-boat. GREER went on with the search until 1840 when she received orders from Iceland to proceed to her destination.

In a memo to Admiral Stark, Chief of Naval Operations, President Roosevelt advised, *"I think it is essential that . . . two facts be made to stand out so clearly that they cannot be separated by any hostile press—first, that two hours elapsed between the bombing of the submarine by the British plane and the firing of the first torpedo by the submarine; and second, that no weapon was fired by the GREER until after the torpedo attack began."*

Three days after the GREER episode, the American merchantman STEEL SEAFARER was bombed and sunk in the Red Sea by Nazi aircraft. On September 11, President Roosevelt made an historic radio address. Broadcasting to the world from the White House, he declared:

"Upon our naval and air patrol—now operating in large numbers over a vast expanse of the Atlantic Ocean—falls the duty of maintaining the American policy of Freedom of the Seas . . .

"From now on, if German or Italian vessels enter the waters, the protection of which is necessary for American defense, they do so at their own peril. . . ."

Spoken one week after GREER's brush with the U-boat, this was the famous "shoot on sight" order which untied the hands of United States forces defending Western Hemisphere waters. From that hour on the United States was involved in a *de facto* naval war with Nazi Germany. The war was undeclared, but the term *"de facto"* means actual, or patently existing.

Translation by USS GREER.

Torpedoing of USS KEARNY

As was to be expected, even a limited naval war with Nazi Germany could not be waged without casualties. And American destroyermen escorting convoys to and from "Momp" were aware that a showdown was in the making.

For the USS KEARNY it came early in the morning of October 17, 1941.

KEARNY was one of the new 1630-ton destroyers launched in 1940—a five-million-dollar warship, powered by engines that could drive her at close to 40 knots. Her fire-control apparatus, sonar devices, and weapons were the latest thing on the sea. Her crew was a smartly-trained team. Her captain, Lieutenant Commander A. L. Danis, ran a taut ship. Yet expert crew and the best detection gear and weapons proved unavailing when death stalked.

Destiny beckoned to KEARNY while she was at Reykjavik in company with an American destroyer division which had made the Iceland run. Her sortie was in response to a distress call from a convoy which had floundered into a wolfpack ambush about 400 miles south of Iceland. This Convoy, SC-48, sailed from Canada on October 10. Plagued by bad weather and breakdowns, the train of 50 merchantmen had experienced tough going. By October 15, eleven stragglers, among them the Convoy Commodore's flagship, had dropped out. The convoy could do no better than 7½ knots. The escort, consisting of four Canadian corvettes and the Canadian destroyer COLUMBIA, was unable to cope with the wolfpack that struck during the night. Three ships had gone down, torpedoed, when the call for help reached Reykjavik.

The Navy answered by dispatching four destroyers to the scene of action. Under group command of Captain L. H. Thebaud, ComDesRon 27, the DD quartet included PLUNKETT (Lieutenant Commander W. A. Graham) flying Captain Thebaud's pennant; LIVERMORE (Lieutenant Commander V. Huber) flying the pennant of Commander H. B. Broadfoot, ComDesDiv 21; DECATUR (Lieutenant Commander J. C. Sowell); and KEARNY.

The old "four-piper" GREER, the British warship BROADWATER, and the Free French corvette LOBELIA were also dispatched from various nearby areas to the battle scene. Convoy SC-48 was in dire need of all the aid that could be rushed. When Captain Thebaud's destroyer group arrived shortly before sundown of the 16th, the Canadian escorts were literally staggering with exhaustion, the merchantmen were panicky, and the U-boats were in the offing biding their time for another strike.

PLUNKETT, LIVERMORE, DECATUR, and KEARNY took station to shield the nine-column formation, and the convoy crawled forward through a dusk as gray as apprehension. In conformance with prevailing doctrine, the American destroyers were positioned 1,000 to 1,500 yards from the convoy. As DesLant leaders were to learn, such a screen was too tight. Obviously if escorts hugged a convoy, stalking submarines were permitted to come within close range of the ships. While attaining short torpedo-range, the U-boats could fire from positions beyond range of the destroyer's sound gear. Thus a tight screen gave submarines a decided edge. The mauling dealt convoy SC-48 was a case in point.

As night spread its black wing over the seascape, the wolfpack closed in. About two hours before midnight, a merchantman was torpedoed. A burst of orange flame, thudding explosions, and frantic signals sent the convoy milling. Dropping helter-skelter depth charges and firing starshells, the escorts broke up the attack, but they failed to discourage, much less demolish, the assailant.

With the clock nearing 2315 the U-boats struck again. This time torpedoes, ploughing into the center of the convoy, blasted two more merchantmen to the bottom.

About three hours later (around 0200 in the morning of

October 17) the wolfpackers struck a third time. Unleashing a series of three swift attacks, they sent torpedoes ripping through the convoy like chain-lightning. Four merchant vessels were fatally hit. And it was during this tumult of fire, water, and explosion that KEARNY was struck by an undersea thunderbolt.

Her crew at General Quarters, the destroyer was advancing into the fray at 15 knots, lookouts straining for a glimpse of U-boats running with decks awash. Pyrotechnics arched and flared in the night, illuminating the seascape with frenzied fireworks. Tinted smoke bulged over the carcasses of sinking ships. Some 1,200 yards from the KEARNY a torpedoed tanker was burning. A belch of flame from the tanker shed a sudden gush of light across the scene. The glare silhouetted a British corvette maneuvering in to pick up survivors, and it also silhouetted KEARNY as she commenced a port swing and dropped "embarrassing charges."

The destroyermen were rolling ashcans from the racks to drive off subs which might be astern. Sighting the corvette which was cutting across her bow, KEARNY slowed to avoid collision. And at that moment a U-boat lurking somewhere ahead drew a bead on the destroyer. Three torpedoes were aimed at the DD—murderous fingers reaching for KEARNY's bow. Stretching across fire-lit water, the rushing wakes were unseen.

Executing the turn to port, the destroyer swung, heeling. A torpedo whipped through the water just ahead. As the lookouts stared in shock, another hissed by astern. Then, as men braced themselves on the canted deck, the ship was rocked by a stunning explosion.

Struck on the starboard side by a torpedo, KEARNY was hard hit. The war head caught her at the turn of the bilge, smashing into the No. 1 fireroom. Vented forward and upward, the explosion wrecked the fireroom, ruptured the forward bulkhead of the boiler-room, burst the deck overhead, ripped off the starboard bridge-wing, knocked the forward funnel acock-bill, and damaged the deckhouse. Four men were flung overside by the blast. Seven were scalded in the flooded boiler-room. Others, bleeding, scorched, wounded by flying debris, were felled on deck or snared in the mangle below. Drowning the dead, the sea plunged in through the rent in KEARNY's side. Jammed open, the steam siren poured raw sound from its throat.

The ship came out of a stagger, steadied on, and slowly regained headway.

As was usually the case with battle damage, initial injuries developed a host of successive complications. KEARNY suffered her share of these. But expert damage control and ship-handling held her on an even keel, and about ten minutes after the torpedo smash she was able to steam at 10 knots.

A Very flare brought an American destroyer to KEARNY's aid—the old "four-stacker" GREER (Lieutenant Commander L. H. Frost). It was a dramatic coincidence: the first American DD to be shot at by a Nazi U-boat, running to assist the first American destroyer to be struck by a Nazi torpedo.

Lieutenant Commander Danis informed GREER that the injured destroyer could make Iceland. GREER was directed to search for the four men hurled into the sea by the torpedo explosion. The old flush-decker combed the area, but the missing men were not to be recovered. Later that morning an urgent call for blood plasma brought a Catalina winging down from Iceland with plasma from the cruiser WICHITA.

With a yawning hole in her side, KEARNY steamed to Iceland under her own power. There she was turned over to the Navy repair ship VULCAN. A few months later she was off the "binnacle list" and once more ready for active duty.

But the *de facto* Battle of the Atlantic collected its death toll. Cost to the USS KEARNY: 11 killed, 24 wounded.

Loss of USS REUBEN JAMES

They called her *"The Rube"*—a nickname that expressed the affection of American destroyermen for a DD which bore one of the proudest names in the U.S. Navy—a name that harked back to the Tripolitan Wars and a battle with the Barbary pirates.

She was far from modern as ships go; some of her gear verged on the obsolete, but she got around with an agility that won her favor of the task force commander. Her captain, Lieutenant Commander H. L. ("Tex") Edwards, had been a champion mat-man at the Naval Academy and a wrestler on the Olympic team. The crew were worthy of both her name and her captain.

From Iceland she was dispatched to the States to engage in escort-of-convoy duty. And so came a day in the latter part of October when REUBEN JAMES headed out into the North Atlantic as one of a group of five destroyers (under Commander R. E. Webb in BENSON) screening eastbound convoy HX-156—a ship-train freighting Lend-Lease goods to the British Isles.

The convoy of 44 merchantmen made a slow 8.8 knots through the late October seas. REUBEN JAMES steamed on the port beam of the formation, abreast of the last ship in column. Destroyers HILARY P. JONES (Lieutenant Commander S. R. Clark) and BENSON (Lieutenant Commander A. L.

Pleasants) were positioned on the port bow and starboard bow, respectively. Destroyer TARBELL (Lieutenant Commander S. D. Willingham) was positioned off the starboard beam abreast of the last ship in column. These escorts were stationed some 3,000 yards from the convoy's body. Destroyer NIBLACK (Lieutenant Commander E. R. Durgin) covered the convoy's rear, and patrolled about 1,000 yards astern. NIBLACK was the only one of the group equipped with radar.

There was tension in the ocean air. The escorts had heard of the KEARNY incident; all hands were aware the convoy was in wolfpack water. But the voyage during that last week of October was proving uneventful. Routine steaming. Nothing to report. Nothing—until the morning of the 31st.

On that date the convoy was in the "Momp" area, about 600 miles west of Ireland. Night was dissolving into a faint suggestion of day, and the convoy was marching steadily eastward in good formation, not zigzagging, while the escorts rode herd in their assigned positions, dipping along in the swinging seas. The hazy dark-before-dawn revealed no hint of impending disaster. The hint came on a gust of ocean wind, invisible, about 0525, when a guardship picked up a "foreign" radio transmission close aboard.

Afterward there was a question concerning REUBEN JAMES' exact position at this crucial moment—whether she was maintaining station or had begun daylight patrol. Whatever the circumstance, she was about 2,000 yards on the convoy's flank, and on the point of turning to investigate the direction-finder bearing when (time: 0539) she was struck by an unseen torpedo.

The war head hit her on the port side near No. 1 stack. A sheet of fire flagged skyward. Blending with the torpedo explosion, a stupendous blast almost lifted the destroyer from the water. Evidently the torpedo-burst exploded the forward magazine, for the ensuing blast amputated the destroyer's entire forward section, which carried away aft of the No. 3 stack.

Crew members were hurled overside like straws in a gust of scrap iron. Seamen who had been asleep in their bunks found themselves swimming in a nightmare of flotsam and black oil. Clinging to life jackets and balsa floats, the survivors stared aghast at the hulk which was all that remained of the REUBEN JAMES. For about five minutes the stern section remained afloat, a jagged segment in the debris-littered sea. Then this section sank, rumbling and roaring as it went down. The thunder came from exploding depth charges—blasts that killed some of the swimmers who had survived the torpedoing.

The men clung to the slippery rafts, dazed, sick with shock, trying to shout encouragement to one another.

Help comes slowly in the hour of disaster—yet the rescuers were on the way at top speed. Destroyers NIBLACK and HILARY P. JONES were dispatched to the scene to search for survivors. Blazing oil and pitiless sea almost frustrated the rescue ships. Only 45 REUBEN JAMES men, including one chief petty officer, were recovered. About 115 of the destroyer's complement had perished in the torpedoing or drowned in the icy water. Lieutenant Commander Edwards went down with his ship. So did every other officer of the ship's company.

The killer submarine was neither sighted nor detected by any of the escorts or ships in the convoy before the strike.

One question, however, was definitely answered. The attacks on GREER and KEARNY might conceivably have been the work of hotheaded submarine commanders. But the attack on REUBEN JAMES was obviously deliberate. Manifestly the Nazis were dedicated to an all-out war with the United States; the U-boats had been passed the word.

On November 1, 1941—within 36 hours of the REUBEN JAMES sinking—President Roosevelt, as authorized by act of Congress, transferred the Coast Guard to the Navy. Thereafter the USCG was to operate as part of the USN until returned to the Treasury Department by Executive Order.

Aroused by the thunder of torpedo-fire, Congress voted the following week to amend the Neutrality Act. Two amendments were passed. The first permitted the arming of American merchantmen so that they might defend themselves against attack. The second abolished the restriction which denied European waters to American shipping. The Navy could now convoy Lend-Lease goods to ports in the United Kingdom.

Many Americans continued to believe that the nation was at peace. But in the autumn of 1941, weeks before Pearl Harbor, American Navy men were fighting the Battle of the Atlantic.

The destroyer REUBEN JAMES was the first United States warship lost in World War II.

What Ship Is That? (Destroyermen Aid Capture of Suspected "Slaver")

Early in 1820 the United States sloop-of-war CYANE, under a Captain Trenchard, arrived in the waters off darkest Africa to inaugurate a new American naval patrol. The previous year Congress had passed a law forbidding the importation of Negro slaves. Whereas most American skippers were ready to abandon the nefarious traffic, there were criminal elements equally ready to indulge in slave smuggling. It was to stop this felonious game at the outset that the Navy established the African Patrol.

That a suspected slaver would turn up in the South Atlantic in November 1941 was a phenomenon expected by no modern naval authority.

The surprise was in the making on November 6, when three ships approached a point about 657 miles from Recife, Brazil. Steaming in company as Task Group 3.6, on patrol, the United States light cruiser OMAHA (Captain T. E. Chandler) and destroyer SOMERS (Commander J. C. Metzel) were heading in for Recife. Steaming independently, the third vessel, a motorship whose stern bore the name SS WILLMOTO of Philadelphia, was heading northward.

OMAHA and SOMERS were surprised to sight WILLMOTO— a darkened ship with American flags painted large on her sides —and they changed course to intercept and investigate. For her part WILLMOTO was apparently surprised to encounter the American cruiser and destroyer. She ran up code flags spelling out her name. But when hailed, she did not answer.

OMAHA and SOMERS closed in for a sharper scrutiny. Stars and Stripes flew above the freighter's taffrail—why her silence?

A destroyer lookout eyed a shipmate on SOMERS' bridge. "There's something queer about that bucket!"

OMAHA's captain thought so too. The steamer was signalled to lie to and await a boarding party. Then, as the cruiser's launch set out for the enigmatic vessel, a confetti of flags appeared on the freighter's halyards. The message constituted another surprise. AM SINKING SEND BOATS.

Captain Chandler had already sent a boat. As OMAHA's launch drew alongside, the boarding party saw WILLMOTO's crew abandoning. The shouting merchant seamen did not sound like Philadelphians, although they might have been Pennsylvania Dutch.

"They were Dutch, all right," a Navy man described afterwards. "But they weren't from Pennsylvania, and they weren't from Holland."

While the boarders were clambering up to the WILLMOTO's deck, two muffled explosions sounded in the vessel's hold. Demolition charges! Tendrils of smoke reeled from the hatches. Lieutenant G. K. Carmichael and visiting bluejackets made a dash for ladders going below. Quick work took care of the damage, and instead of settling to the bottom, the motor-ship remained stolidly on the surface. Another surprise, and an unpleasant one for Captain Gerhart Loers, the vessel's skipper.

It now appeared that Loers was a German. Equally Teutonic were the mates, and other crew members. The WILL-

MOTO was the ODENWALD sailing under false colors—a blockade-runner. En route to Germany from Japan, she was laden with general cargo, the bulk of which consisted of some 3,800 tons of rubber.

German ship, cargo, captain, and crew were escorted to Port of Spain, Trinidad, by cruiser OMAHA and destroyer SOMERS. Since the United States was not officially at war with Nazi Germany there was some doubt as to the legality of the prize capture.

However, one good euphemism deserves another. And the "short-of-war" technicality invited a very fine bit of counter casuistry. Harking back to the old days of "blackbirding," Commander Task Group 3.6 reported that ODENWALD had been captured as a "suspected slaver"!

War Declared!

On December 8, 1941, the United States Government declared war on Japan. On December 11, Germany and Italy declared war on the United States, and Congress promptly returned the compliment. This was *it!*

But to the forces of DesLant, "it" was only so much anti-climax. The official declaration of war found the U.S. Navy's destroyermen already fighting the Atlantic Battle with their gloves off. In the war from that hour when a Nazi U-boat took a shot at GREER, they had long since dispensed with formalities. And after the KEARNY and REUBEN JAMES torpedoings, the only gloves in evidence in the DesLant Force had been those on the hands of the "hot shell" men.

Chapter 4

Pacific Explosion

☆ ☆ ☆

DesPac, December 7

The Samauri sword of Damocles that fell on December 7, 1941, plunging the United States into a two-ocean war, was aimed at decapitating the U.S. Pacific Fleet at Pearl Harbor and leaving the United States Navy impotent, if not dead, in the Pacific.

Destroyers fought the enemy from the first alarm. In fact, a DesPac destroyer transmitted the first alarm a few minutes after the approaching Executioner was detected —almost four hours before the deadly blow was delivered.

On December 7, 1941, there were 54 destroyers on duty with the Pacific Fleet. About half of these destroyers were at sea when the Japanese raiders struck at Oahu.

At anchor or docked in Pearl Harbor on December 7 were eight battleships, nine cruisers, some twenty-nine destroyers, five submarines, a hospital ship, and the usual complement of tenders, tugs, fleet oilers, repair ships, and auxiliaries.

Many sailors were ashore on week-end liberty and leave, and most of the ships were manned by skeleton forces. The usual routine. Honolulu drifted off to sleep Saturday night with no thought of the nightmare to come. The clock ticked somnolently into Sunday—a day that began as any other day. That is to say, it began peacefully for the Americans. Japan had already gone to war.

Closing in on Hawaii like an assassin in the night was a Japanese Carrier Force. The Japanese did not know the exact location of the ships in the harbor, but cunning Intelligence work had provided them with a fair idea of what they would find in East Loch and anchored off Ford Island. Marked for special attention was "Battleship Row." Also marked for attention were the Oahu airfields.

Ahead of Admiral Nagumo's carriers prowled an Advance

Expeditionary Force of I-boats, to lie off the harbor entrance and ambush any warships which attempted to escape the December 7 slaughter. For a minor mission, several of these large subs were to release midget submarines which had been trained for special work in the target area. The midgets were to reconnoiter the entrance channel, and if possible enter the harbor. In one of the more amazing feats of modern submarining, a Jap midget did succeed in entering the harbor and circuiting Ford Island in the very heart of the great naval base—a daredevil exploit comparable to the undetected prowl of a Bengal tiger around Times Square. The "baby sub" apparently got in at 0430, circled the island counter-clockwise, and got out an hour later. It was eventually captured, complete with chart showing the route of its incredible junket. Not the least incredible feature of this nocturnal invasion was the fact that it occurred *after* another midget had been spotted and sunk off the harbor entrance.

The opening shot at Pearl Harbor was fired by the destroyer WARD. Here is the story—

WARD *and* CONDOR *Kill Midget*

On December 5, 1941, destroyer WARD steamed out of Pearl Harbor to patrol the waters outside the harbor entrance.

WARD was an old "four-piper" of World War I vintage. Her guns were old-fashioned 4-inch 50's; she had to strain to make 30 knots.

At 0300 in the morning of December 7, WARD was heading into Pearl Harbor on the homestretch of her patrol. The patrol had been singularly uneventful—a fact which pleased Lieutenant W. W. Outerbridge, her skipper, as this was his first command. It also pleased the officers of WARD's crew, who were Naval Reservists and eager to show their skills. As for the men in WARD, the ship's company was typical of that blend of professional Navy man and civilian-in-uniform which was to man the United States Fleet's destroyers and destroyer-escorts during World War II.

About 0357 Ensign L. F. Platt, USNR, reported to Lieutenant Outerbridge that WARD had just received a blinker message from the minesweeper CONDOR. CONDOR had sighted something which resembled the periscope of a submarine.

The minesweeper had spotted this suspicious "stick" skulking through the dark water at 0350. At that time the CONDOR was conducting sweeping operations approximately one and three-quarter miles southwest of the Pearl Harbor entrance buoys.

Outerbridge sent the WARD to General Quarters. For about an hour WARD searched the area. Her lookouts saw nothing;

her sonar detected nothing. Circling across the seascape, she approached CONDOR and Outerbridge spoke the minesweeper over TBS (radio-telephone).

The talk between the two ships was intercepted by a naval radio station on Oahu. The radio mentor copied the dialogue, which went somewhat as follows: WHAT WAS THE APPROXIMATE DISTANCE AND COURSE OF THE SUBMARINE SIGHTED? Answer: THE COURSE WAS ABOUT 020 MAGNETIC AND SOME 1,000 YARDS FROM THE HARBOR ENTRANCE. Question: DO YOU HAVE ANY ADDITIONAL INFORMATION? Answer: NO ADDITIONAL IN-FORMATION. Question: WHEN WAS THE LAST TIME YOU SAW THE SUBMARINE? Answer: APPROXIMATELY 0350, AND IT WAS APPARENTLY HEADING FOR THE ENTRANCE.

WARD's skipper was about convinced that the little mine-sweeper had sighted a "phantom." He gave the word to secure, and returned to his bunk. At 0637 he was awakened by Lieutenant (jg) O. W. Goepner, USNR, Officer of the Deck. *"Captain! Quick! Come out on the bridge!"*

Outerbridge hit the deck with both feet. On the bridge he found excited men pointing at a vessel which was towing a lighter into the entrance channel. The vessel was the target ship ANTARES. Not an unusual sight. But the spectacle of *a small submarine* trailing the ANTARES was *most* unusual.

Outerbridge immediately sent WARD steaming toward the queer little sub. In the dim morning light the submarine's silhouette was positively identified as "stranger." These were restricted waters for foreign submarining, and as soon as the destroyer's guns could be brought to bear, Outerbridge ordered the crews to open fire. The range was about 100 yards when the bow gun flashed and roared. The first United States shot in the Pacific War was fired at 0645.

That No. 1 shot from WARD's No. 1 gun missed the under-sized conning tower. But her second shot, fired from her No. 3 gun at a range of 75 yards, slammed into the base of the conning tower with a dazzling flash. The little sub heeled over, slowed, and began to sink. The destroyer passed ahead and Outerbridge shouted an order which started the "ashcans" rolling. Chief Torpedoman W. C. Maskzawitz adjusted the depth settings with deft precision and released the first charge directly under the midget's nose. In all, four charges were dropped. The sub swam squarely into the explosions, and went down in 1,200 feet of water. American destroyermen had killed their first Jap submersible.

The kill was timed at 0645. Outerbridge immediately notified "Com 14" at Pearl Harbor. WE HAVE ATTACKED, FIRED UPON, AND DROPPED DEPTH CHARGES UPON SUBMARINE OPERATING IN DEFENSIVE SEA AREA!

After waiting several minutes, he spoke to the Naval Radio

Station at Bishop's Point to check the communication. About 0712 the Bishop's Point operator acknowledged the dispatch.

But somehow the message evaporated in the misty dawnlight over Pearl. As old Navy men phrase it, "Someone always fails to get the word." This time the commanders at Pearl Harbor failed to get it. Neither Com14 nor Commander-in-Chief Pacific received the word in time. Apparently no one took it seriously. As CinPac later stated,

During the previous year there had been several reports of submarine contacts, all of which turned out to be false.

It was the old story of "Wolf! Wolf!"

Back on board the WARD the lookouts saw oil swilling to the surface where the invader sub had gone down. The destroyermen searched the area. Someone spotted a fishing craft sailing out in the sunrise across restricted water. WARD steamed over to investigate this trespasser. The craft proved to be a motor-driven sampan from Honolulu, with a Jap crew. The vessel hove to as WARD came up, and the destroyermen turned her over to a Coast Guard cutter which took the suspicious sampan into custody. With every nerve quivering, the WARD continued to search the harbor entrance, and while she was so doing her lookouts sighted a large number of aircraft over Pearl. Some columns of black smoke climbed into the morning sky over the Harbor. Heavy-footed explosions echoed across the water.

The United States was in the throes of World War II.

Destroyers Versus Pearl Raiders

One of the first destroyers to open fire on the Japs at Pearl Harbor was the BAGLEY (Lieutenant Commander G. A. Sinclair). She was moored in Berth B-22 at the Navy Yard for repairs to her starboard bilge keel. Her crew raced to General Quarters at the time a torpedo-bomber flung a "fish" into the battleship OKLAHOMA.

BAGLEY's AA gunners broomed the sky with flak. Other ships in the harbor were doing the same. A number of Jap planes stunted away trailing smoke.

BAGLEY was taken to sea by Lieutenant P. W. Cann, whose quick-thinking sortie doubtless saved the ship from severe punishment. She operated in the off-shore patrol area until she returned to the Harbor on December 9.

In Berth X-9, East Loch, on the morning of December 7 were destroyers SELFRIDGE, CASE, TUCKER, REID, and CONYNGHAM. About four minutes before morning colors, the Officer of the Deck on board SELFRIDGE saw a Jap plane launch a torpedo at cruiser RALEIGH. He sounded General Quarters, and at about 0758 SELFRIDGE's machine-gunners opened .50 caliber fire on Jap planes. At 1000 she pulled out of the nest, and headed seaward. She was presently followed by CASE, TUCKER, and REID. CONYNGHAM, undergoing tender overhaul, did not get out of the berth until that evening. All four ships in SELFRIDGE's wake opened fire on the attacking aircraft.

Destroyer HULL sounded General Quarters at 0757. If the Japs had a glimpse of the sailor at HULL's gangway shooting at them with a .45 pistol, they saw a typical American destroyerman doing his best with equipment available.

When all hell exploded in the Harbor, destroyers HENLEY, PATTERSON, and RALPH TALBOT were moored to Buoy X-11 in East Loch. Through a freakish error HENLEY's crew was at battle stations when the first Jap planes appeared in the sky—someone had sounded General Quarters instead of Quarters for Muster. The green hand who made this mistake inadvertently gave his ship a chance to fire the first destroyer shot at the rampaging Japanese.

At 0830 HENLEY shoved off from the buoy. While she was slipping her chain, a heavy bomb struck the water about 150 yards on the port bow. Just as she cleared the nest she received a signal, "Submarine in Harbor!" Directly ahead of her the MACDONOUGH dropped depth charges. Swerving to side-step this action, HENLEY raced on out of the entrance channel, the third ship to sortie. After she rounded Hospital Point she was strafed by a light bomber. Her machine-gunners lashed at the plane with .50 calibers. Outside the Harbor she made sonar contact with what may have been a midget submarine. Two depth charges were dropped, but results could not be determined.

As desperate a sortie as any at Pearl was made by destroyer BLUE. About 85 per cent of her regular crew were on board when the Jap raiders struck. Seated in the wardroom at that fatal hour were Ensigns N. F. Asher, M. J. Moldfasky, USNR, J. P. Wolfe, USNR, and R. S. Scott, USNR. These four were the only officers on board. Assuming temporary command, Ensign Asher rushed the crew to battle stations. BLUE's gunners opened fire with main batteries and machine-guns as the Japs roared over. At 0847 she got under way. She maintained a furious fire while negotiating the difficult channel. By 0910 the ship had passed the entrance buoys and was proceeding to her patrol station.

At 0950 her sonar registered a contact. BLUE made two depth-charge attacks. On her first run she dropped four charges; on the second she dropped two. A large oil slick and thick cluster of bubbles appeared on the surface. It seems probable that BLUE abolished one of the five midget submarines spawned by the Jap I-boat Expeditionary Force operating off Pearl Harbor.

Another midget submarine was probably sunk off the harbor entrance by destroyer HELM (Lieutenant Commander C. E. Carroll). HELM was under way when the attack exploded the Sunday quiet. She was steaming in West Loch when Jap torpedo-planes raced in over Barber's Point. Flying low, the planes skimmed over the Loch, and HELM was strafed but not hit. At 0813 the ship galloped past the gate vessel and on out to sea.

At 0817 HELM's lookouts sighted the conning tower of a sub not far from the No. 1 entrance buoy. The sub submerged before the destroyermen could shoot. At 0819 the conning tower reappeared. HELM fired at the sub at 0820. Probably damaged, the sub again submerged. At 0821 a torpedo passed close under HELM's stern. This was probably a parting shot from a midget submerging for the last time.

HELM continued a search for the little undersea boat, but the vessel had apparently gone for good. Jap aircraft attacked the hunting destroyer. At 0915 she battled a Jap fighter which tried to get her with two bombs. One burst in the water 50 yards off the HELM's port bow, and one exploded 20 yards off her starboard bow. Power steering went out; her gyro was injured; her sonar went out of commission. It was 15 minutes before the bridge could regain steering control. Shaken up though she was, HELM went on with her patrol until 1215, at which time she received orders to join cruiser DETROIT.

Destroyer AYLWIN, rocked by a bomb which fell about 75 yards off her starboard bow, got under way at 0858. In precipitous departure she left her anchor chain and stern wire at the buoys. With guns blazing she stood out the channel. Senior officer on board AYLWIN was Ensign Stanley Caplan, USNR, who was ably seconded by Ensign H. C. Anderson, USNR. AYLWIN's regular Commanding Officer, Lieutenant Commander R. H. Rodgers, was at home in Honolulu when the fireworks began. Racing to Pearl Harbor, he secured a motor launch and with other AYLWIN officers chased the destroyer to sea. ComDesRon 1 would not permit a transfer at sea, so Rodgers and the others boarded the destroyer CHEW and remained with that ship until the following day. Commending the handling of AYLWIN during and after the sortie, Lieutenant Commander Rodgers wrote: *"The conduct of Ensign S. Caplan, USNR . . . in taking command for 33 hours during war operations of the severest kind, is considered outstanding."*

Meantime, destroyer MONAGHAN was having it out with the

midget submarine that attacked the CURTISS. At 0827 she was ordered by cruiser DETROIT to sortie, and about the same time she was directed over the TBS to establish offshore patrol with DesDiv 2. As she was maneuvering away from the nest she noticed that CURTISS was flying a submarine-alarm signal. This was hardly reported before MONAGHAN'S lookouts sighted a midget conning tower about 250 yards from CURTISS.

The midget was under fire from the seaplane tender and the minesweeper TANGIER. Lieutenant Commander W. P. Burford squared away to ram, and at 0837 MONAGHAN rushed at the sub. The midget fired a torpedo which missed. MONAGHAN did not miss. A slight shock shivered the ship as she passed over the sub. She dropped two depth charges which raised a haystack of water and brought the midget thrashing to the surface. As the sub rolled over and sank, MONAGHAN backed emergency to avoid collision with a derrick moored off Beckoning Point. It took some jockeying, but at 0847 she swung out into the channel to steam out of the Harbor astern of destroyer DALE.

So, singly and severally, the DesPac DD's sortied from the furnace of Pearl Harbor and fought their way out to sea.

Behind them the sortiing DesPac destroyers left a fleet which had been blasted to ruin. Three heavy cruisers and three light cruisers had gotten out; these and the destroyers which escaped the cauldron were about all that was left of the surface force which had been trapped in the Harbor. They, and the carriers at sea, and the Pacific Submarine Force, would be compelled to hold the line from the Aleutians to Australia.

Manila Strike (Destroyers Asiatic)

Like a delayed-action bomb, the Japanese strike at Manila exploded on December 10.

Compared with the Juggernaut forces of the Japanese Imperial Navy bearing down on the Philippines, the defending American Asiatic Fleet was little more than a squadron.

As of December, 1941, the Asiatic Fleet consisted of the heavy cruiser HOUSTON (flagship of Admiral Thomas C. Hart, Commander in Chief), light cruisers MARBLEHEAD and BOISE, 13 venerable destroyers of the 1917-18 class, and 29 submarines. Ordered to defend the hundreds of miles of coastline and the myriad miles of sea from northern Luzon to southern Mindanao, Admiral Hart's naval forces were presented with an impossible mission. Beaten at the start, the Asiatic Fleet could only retreat.

Composing DesRon 29, under leadership of Captain H. V.

Wiley, whose broad command pennant was in destroyer
PAUL JONES (Lieutenant Commander J. J. Hourihan), were
DesDivs 50, 57, and 58. The ships and commanders are listed
below.

DESDIV 50
Comdr. P. H. Talbot

PEARY	*Comdr. H. H. Keith*
POPE	*Lt. Comdr. W. C. Blinn*
FORD	*Lt. Comdr. J. E. Cooper*
PILLSBURY	*Lt. Comdr. H. C. Pound*

DESDIV 57
Comdr. E. M. Crouch

WHIPPLE	*Lt. Comdr. E. S. Karpe*
ALDEN	*Lt. Comdr. L. E. Coley*
JOHN D. EDWARDS	*Comdr. H. E. Eccles*
EDSALL	*Lt. J. J. Nix*

DESDIV 58
Comdr. T. H. Binford

STEWART	*Lt. Comdr. H. P. Smith*
PARROTT	*Lt. Comdr. E. N. Parker*
BULMER	*Comdr. L. J. Manees*
BARKER	*Comdr. L. J. McGlone*

At the beginning of December Admiral Hart's ships were
disposed in various areas of the Philippine Archipelago. Flying
the flag of Vice Admiral W. A. Glassford, cruiser HOUSTON
was at Iloilo in the central Philippines. BOISE was at Cebu.
MARBLEHEAD and destroyers PAUL JONES, STEWART, BARKER,
BULMER, and PARROTT had been ordered to Tarakan, Borneo,
to loiter off that possible target island. Tender BLACK HAWK
and destroyers WHIPPLE, ALDEN, J. D. EDWARDS, and EDSALL
had steamed to Balikpapan, Borneo, another potential target
for the Japanese.

In drydock at Cavite were destroyers PEARY and PILLSBURY,
undergoing overhaul after a collision some weeks before.
Repairs were almost concluded by December 10: a few more
hours and the ships would have been ready to go. The other
two destroyers of DesRon 29—POPE and JOHN D. FORD—
were patrolling in the Manila area when the first air raid
struck Manila Bay the afternoon of the 10th.

The Cavite raid was not a carbon copy of the Pearl Harbor
massacre; there were fewer ships corraled for the slaughter.
But the Japs smashed the Cavite docks and Navy Yard into
junk, and pulverized the junk into rubble. Cavite's 3-inch
AA batteries barked in frenzy, but they failed to bite the

high-level bombers. The defenders could only sit and take it while the ships tried to get out. Among others, destroyer PILLSBURY made a fast getaway. And destroyer PEARY, badly mauled, escaped only by the grace of Providence and a brave little minesweeper named WHIPPOORWILL.

Retreat to the Malay Barrier

Not long after the shattering of Cavite, Admiral Hart ordered a general retirement to Soerabaja, Java. Among the last ships to leave Manila Bay were destroyers PEARY and PILLSBURY, steaming down the Bay on the 27th of December.

PILLSBURY made the voyage to Soerabaja without incident. PEARY'S road was thorny. The day before she sortied, Jap aircraft almost got her again off Cavite. They tagged her a second time when she ran into Compomanes Bay on the island of Negroes. The next day they trailed her down into the Celebes Sea. As she ran on south she was harried by enemy torpedo-planes. Then, as she raced into Molucca Passage, she was attacked through error by Lockheed Hudsons of the Royal Australian Air Force. On the last day of 1941 the destroyer staggered into Ambon, her decks fire-scarred, her crew exhausted.

So the Asiatic Fleet and its destroyer complement pulled out of the Philippines. On January 1, 1942, the Japanese conquerors paraded into Manila. The Asiatic Fleet, retiring to the Netherlands East Indies, prepared to make a stand at the Malay Barrier. In that first month of the New Year Admiral Hart's forces became part of the ABDA (American-British-Dutch-Australian) Fleet committed to the defense of Indonesia.

PART TWO

Shield and Spearhead

☆ ☆ ☆

Who's there, besides foul weather?
KING LEAR

Chapter 5

Destroying the Submarine

(Destroyer A/S Weapons, Methods, and Tactics)

☆ ☆ ☆

U-Boat Killer

Fighting in the forefront of the World War I U-boat battle, the DD showed its mettle offensively as a sub-hunter, and defensively as a convoy protector. By the end of that war its reputation as an A/S (anti-submarine) vessel was fully established. But as is so often the case with generalities, the broad statement (and it was made) that the submarine had met its match in the modern destroyer was subject to a great deal of qualification. Naval engineers and designers worked overtime to improve the undersea boat. The U-boat (true also of Allied submarines) entered World War II as a highly modernized war vessel, a submarine as far ahead of the World War I variety as the modern Ford was ahead of the Model T.

The Diesel-electric powered U-boat of 1939 was rugged, deepgoing, fast. It packed a stunning punch. Its torpedoes were deadlier than the "tin fish" of World War I. Its cruising range was far more extensive. It was possessed of extraordinary stamina.

The DD steamed into the Battle of the Atlantic equipped with marvelous new detection devices. And it was in this field of detection that the destroyer achieved an immediate superiority in the game of hide-and-seek with the undersea foe. But it was not enough to tag the enemy. He then had to be downed. New A/S ammunition was demanded.

The Depth Charge

The ashcan-type depth charges commonly used by American destroyermen in World War II resembled 25 and 50 gallon oil drums in size and shape and contained explosive charges of 300 or 600 pounds of TNT. On the deck of a ship these depth charges were harmless enough, but when the firing mechanism was activated by hydrostatic pressure they became weapons. The firing mechanism was located in a central tube and was, in essence, a bellows which was operated by water pressure. By the adjustment of an external pointer mechanism the ashcan could be set to fire at various depths below the surface.

It was not necessary to hit the submarine with an ashcan (or with a teardrop) depth charge. The blast of an ashcan close aboard may crush the submarine's hull or deal the submersible a jolt that starts fatal leakage or wrecks the interior machinery.

The sub-hunter, however, was usually shooting blindly at a moving target—a target he tracked by sound. But sound contact was sporadic, and at close range it was lost. Moreover, the evading submarine could escape in "depth" as well as "plane." Sonar contact could not give the hunter a submersible's exact depth, and many an attack failed because the depth charges were set too shallow or too deep.

Of course, the speed at which the attack could be delivered, once the target was within range, was a most important factor. Primarily this depended on the launching or projecting gear. Much also depended on the sinking speed of the depth charge.

Drop a can of beans into a pond, and the chances are it will sink at an erratic tangent and hit bottom some distance from the point where you dropped it, especially if there's any current in the pond. Now drop a pear-shaped sinker of the same weight, and you will see the sinker go down much more rapidly, heavy-end first, and on a fairly straight line from your hand. Obviously a streamlined depth charge shaped like a pear or a teardrop would have several advantages over one with ordinary cylindrical shape. So destroyermen were presented with the new "teardrop" design.

No submarine lingered long in the vicinity when a destroyer was weeping these teardrops. So far as the sub was concerned, the DD's tears were wholly crocodile.

Depth-Charge Launching Gear

Three types of depth-charge launching gear were used by destroyers during World War II.

The old-type ashcan was originally sent on its way by the simple principle of "roll out the barrel." A track of flanged rails was set on an incline at the ship's stern. Hoist the ashcan on to the rails, and let 'er go.

Improvements created the "depth-charge release gear" in use by 1918 and employed by United States destroyers in

World War II. The gear consisted of a track (called a "rack") down which the depth charge rolled on an incline, a framework in which the ready ashcans were all set to roll, and a hydraulic control which unleashed the depth charge at a release trap, permitting the ashcan to drop astern.

Because charges which were stern-dropped could be spaced along only one axis of a pattern, some sort of projector was called for to widen the pattern's area. So the "Y" gun was invented. Produced in 1918, this apparatus lobbed two depth charges out over the water. The depth charge was placed in a saddle or "arbor," atop this gear, and was fired overside by an explosive charge.

The Y-gun permitted an advantageous distribution of depth charges lobbed to port or starboard of the vessel's beam, and it tossed the lethal charge a good distance from the ship. It was made obsolescent, however, by the modern K-gun.

Installed in most American destroyers by 1942, the K-gun was a much-used projector during the battle against Hitler's U-boats. This depth-charge thrower had a single, stubby barrel with a fast-operating breech mechanism and a comparatively simple firing system. The depth charge was placed in a tray-like arbor which sat in the K-gun's mortar-type barrel. When the gun was fired, the ashcan went flying.

K-guns were mounted in pairs, one on either side of the ship. As many could be installed topside as seemed feasible, and additional projectors expanded the area under fire and bettered the depth-charge pattern.

Hedgehog

Early in 1942, Captain Paul Hammond, USNR, serving on the U.S. Naval Attaché staff in London, had an opportunity to inspect the designs for a new A/S weapon. The weapon operated on an entirely novel charge-projecting principle. It consisted of a steel cradle in which were planted four rows of spike-like spigots. (Hence the name "hedgehog.") In effect, this projector worked as a rocket-firer.

The apparatus fired 24 projectiles, lobbing them a considerable distance. Lobbed into the sea, they sank swiftly, shooting down through the water like a school of barracuda— steel barracuda with deadly snouts.

The hedgehog projectile, however, had to make a direct hit to explode. Contact explosion was a virtue rather than a limitation. Heretofore the destroyermen had never been certain of a hit. The conventional depth charge exploded when it reached the pre-set depth, and the hunters on the surface did not know at the time whether the blast was a bull's-eye or a miss that was as good as a mile. But hedgehog explosion assured them the target had suffered damage.

The direct-hit feature was not the weapon's only virtue. Because hedgehog projectiles were thrown ahead of the ship, the weapon could frequently be fired before sound contact with the submarine was broken. In other words, the A/S craft could be "on the beam" when it opened fire with hedgehog—the destroyermen were not shooting more or less blindly, as in the case with ashcans and teardrops.

The weighty hedgehog projector had a mule-kick recoil, and it was unsuitable for small anti-submarine vessels. So a smaller launcher capable of firing six rocket projectiles was designed. This weapon was called "mousetrap." Mousetrap packed a potent punch—its 65-pound rocket loaded with torpex was the same size and had the same explosive content as the hedgehog projectile. But, although employed with success by the British, mousetrap did not feature in many American A/S actions during World War II.

Sonar and Radar

After the U-boats almost sank England in 1914, the British bent every effort to the creation of instruments which could detect the submerged submarine. Eventually they produced the hydrophone—a sensitive listening device which could pick up the sound of a moving submarine. Installed on the bottom of a ship, the instrument conveyed to the operator's earphones the whisper of the U-boat's propellers and the general location of the sub.

Between wars, electronic scientists labored to overcome some of the hydrophone's shortcomings. Both the British and the American Navies produced sound gear capable of indicating the submerged submarine's range. This supersonic electronic gear functioned in a performance known as "echo-ranging." The British named the device "Asdic." The Americans had a word for it—"Sonar"—from "Sound-Navigation-Ranging."

The electronic workings of sonar are too complex for brief discussion, and the scientific "how" must be hastily by-passed for a descriptive "what." The sonar gear is housed in a "dome" or container on the ship's bottom. The operator may employ the gear in two ways: as "listening gear" to pick up the sound of a submarine's propeller or internal machinery, or as "echo-ranging gear" to locate the submarine and give an accurate indication of its range.

Echo-ranging is defined as the process of determining the bearing and distance of a submerged object by sending out a directional sound signal and receiving the echo on a directional sound device. The time it takes for the "ping" to return (echo) gives the target range and the "ping's" line of travel gives the bearing on the target.

Then sonar contact could not be continuously maintained even when once established. For example, a destroyer might make sonar contact at 1015—lose it at 1016—regain it at 1030—hold it until 1045—then lose in again at 100-yard range in the last lap of an attack. Further, the crashing disturbance of a depth charge exploding served to deafen the echo-ranging gear temporarily, and water where depth charges exploded provided a mask behind which the submarine could hide. Under some circumstances contact might be permanently lost.

So the game of hide-and-seek was not all in the hunter's favor. And the submarine was far from obsolete as it torpedoed its deadly way through the two-ocean war.

American destroyers were experimenting with echo-ranging devices as early as 1934. Destroyers RATHBURN, WATERS, TALBOT, and DENT and two submarines were the first United States naval vessels to carry echo-ranging equipment. By September 1939, some 60 DD's in the United States Fleet were sonar-equipped. And at this time the Navy was opening the first of its Sound Schools where sonarmen ("ping jockeys") and A/S crews were trained.

One of the busiest schools was the subchaser school organized at Miami. Officially titled the Submarine Chaser Training Center, its express mission was the schooling of officers and men for the "Donald Duck" service. As the subchasers were to be officered by Reservists, many of them with little or no sea experience, a strenuous curriculum was in order.

The school was commissioned at Miami on March 26, 1942. On April 8 Commander E. F. McDaniel, veteran destroyerman just in from rough North Atlantic duty in USS LIVERMORE, took over as schoolmaster. He was a flinty teacher, but an expert on the subject from "ashcan" to "pigboat," and the student body appreciated an educator who knew his stuff.

By the end of 1943 over 10,000 officers and 37,000 enlisted men had learned the ins and outs of submarine-chasing at Miami's famous SCTC. Looking back, they would revere the Miami Subchaser School with the affection of "old grads" for Alma Mater. To scores and hundreds of destroyermen the Training Center on Biscayne Bay was "McDaniel's Academy" —an expression of regard for the officer who had turned a "Donald Duck" kindergarten into an A/S university.

Radar Versus Submarines

The manifest value of radar as a submarine-detector gave

it a high priority on the "must" list for A/S warfare.

By August 1942 most of the combat ships in the Atlantic Fleet were equipped with radar sets, and the gear had been distributed to the naval forces in the Pacific. The SG (Sugar George) microwave radar— an improved "surface radar" that presented a brighter and more easily identified "pip"—was issued to the Navy's fighting forces in the autumn of 1942. In 1943 came microwave radar for aircraft. But as aircraft were teaming up with destroyers on the submarine hunt, anything which aided the aviator in turn aided the destroyerman. And microwave radar was the bane of the U-boat. The Germans tried all manner of tricks in their effort to frustrate search radar. They sent up decoy balloons which trailed tinfoil streamers which created a "false target." They attempted to develop a "black U-boat" which would absorb radar beams. They tried to "jam" the airwaves. *Nicht gut!* Nor could German search receivers detect this new S-brand radar. Even the hard-to-catch *Schnorkel* stack was vulnerable. After the war German Submarine Admiral Doenitz blamed two things for the U-boat's defeat. One: short-sightedness on the part of Hitler, who failed to provide the German Navy with a sufficient number of submarines. Two: long-sightedness on the part of search radar.

"Huff-Duff"

Early in the war the Royal Navy developed a method for determining the general location of U-boats at long range. The principle was fairly obvious—just intercept the submarine's radio transmissions and then obtain cross-bearings by means of high-frequency direction-finders stationed along the coast.

High-frequency direction-finders (HF/DF, or "Huff-Duff") did not translate intercepted messages. Huff-Duff merely established the whereabouts of the transmitting submarine, and temporarily fixed its position.

The Huff-Duff detection device gave convoys a chance for evasive routing, and it informed escorts on the location of "submarine water." Later in the war, Huff-Duff information obtained by shore stations put many a hunter-killer group on the track of a U-boat or a submarine concentration.

Destroyer A/S Tactics (The Hold Down)

The Navy's Destroyer Forces devised doctrines to meet most given situations of A/S warfare and designed combat maneuvers which were more or less standarized, like the opening gambits of chess. For example:

An A/S vessel (call it a destroyer) is serving as a convoy escort in the screen in front of a convoy. Suddenly the DD picks up a sound contact, or sights a periscope "feather" dead ahead. Immediate action is required to prevent the sub from getting off an accurate torpedo salvo. So the destroyer flashes a warning over the TBS (voice radio) and launches an attack to force the enemy to break off his approach and "go deep."

The sub thus driven down cannot fix a periscope eye on the advancing convoy to draw a bead for a torpedo shot. Nor can it follow the maneuvers of the warned convoy, which may swiftly execute a radical course-change to side-step the line of fire.

When the convoy is out of danger, the defending escort (assisted by another escort, if one can be spared from the screen) may take the offensive in an effort to develop the contact and launch attacks to kill the sub. Otherwise, and according to the dictates of circumstance, the escort will rejoin the convoy screen and resume normal patrolling.

A submarine detected at the convoy's rear might invite a similar gambit—an attack to drive the enemy under, and some depth-charging to make him keep his periscope-head down, thereby frustrating torpedo fire and subsequent tracking of the convoy.

Aware of playing "it" in this deadly game of tag, the submerged enemy employed strenuous and crafty evasive measures to escape the hunters. Trapping a sub which had "gone deep" to elude pursuit was never an easy task.

Frequently employed by DD's, DE's, and other sub-hunters (including aircraft), the *hold-down tactic* was designed to keep a submarine submerged to the point of suffocation, desperation, or exhaustion. At which extremity the submariners would be literally forced to come up and fight it out on the surface —a climax which usually spelled disaster for the embattled submarine.

The tactic might be essayed by a single A/S vessel, by subchaser and aircraft, or by a large group of hunter-killers acting cooperatively. Naturally, the more numerous the A/S craft, the better the odds on their side. But there were instances in World War II wherein a single A/S vessel successfully "held down" an enemy submarine to the point of its forced exposure and destruction.

Convoy Escort Duty

The typical ocean convoy, consisting of 40 to 70 merchant ships, steamed in a rectangular formation of nine to fourteen columns. The columns were spaced 1,000 yards apart, and the ships in column were spaced at 600-yard intervals. An eleven-column convoy, therefore, presented a frontage of five nautical miles and had a depth of one and a half miles or more, depending upon the number of ships placed in column.

The escorts formed a screen on the periphery of the convoy. They were, of course, stationed in positions carefully calculated to provide the best protection for the convoy.

To strike at the convoy, a submarine had to pass through the screen undetected and attack at a range short enough to ensure a hit, or else fire a torpedo from a position outside the screen—a so-called "browning shot." If the escort vessels were drawn in to form a tight screen, the sub had a better chance of hitting with a browning shot (for the obvious reason that if the escorts closely hugged the convoy, the attacking sub could make a nearer approach). On the other hand, if the escorts were stationed far out, the sub was more likely to penetrate the screen undetected. To reduce the sub's chance to a minimum, screening diagrams were scientifically designed to place the escorts at such distances that a sub's chance of penetrating the screen was on a par with its chance of making a hit with a browning shot.

Chapter 6

DesLant into Battle (Part I)

☆ ☆ ☆

Dual Mission, Atlantic

After formal declaration of war, the United States Navy was confronted in the Atlantic with a dual problem.

Trans-Atlantic convoying and defense of home-coast shipping were the priority tasks at once assigned to the Navy's Atlantic forces; tasks which principally featured escort-of-convoy duty and offensive anti-submarine warfare.

Destroyers, therefore, were what was called for. Escorts by profession, and submarine-hunters by design. Already the Navy's DD's were swinging along on North Atlantic convoy runs. Already they had traded blows with Hitler's wolfpacks. Now they were to escort North Atlantic convoys all the way to Londonderry, Northern Ireland. The Atlantic Battle was to be all-out.

Not many U-boats were contacted in the North Atlantic during the weeks immediately following the war declaration. The slack-off suggested a realignment of wolfpack forces, a revision of U-boat strategy, rather than defeat and retreat. The Nazi U-boat Force was gathering muscle for an offensive.

Onslaught on ON-67 (DD's versus Wolfpack)

One of the tough convoy-wolfpack battles fought in the first quarter of 1942 involved the American destroyers EDISON, NICHOLSON, LEA, and BERNADOU. The quartet comprised the ocean escort for Convoy ON-67, west-bound for Halifax from the United Kingdom. In charge of the escort was EDISON's skipper, Commander A. C. Murdaugh.

If flaws showed up in the performance of the escorts, the cause was deficient equipment and unfamiliarity with modern A/S techniques; NICHOLSON's was the only radar which worked consistently, and BERNADOU was just out of "mothballs."

Leaving Hvalfjordur, Iceland, on February 16, Murdaugh's destroyer group picked up the convoy three days later at the ocean rendezvous point called "Momp."

The convoy consisted of 35 ships steaming in 8-column formation. Falling in, the American destroyers relieved the British escorts, with the exception of HMCS ALGOMA, the latter being directed to stay with the convoy as long as her fuel permitted.

The hours of February 19 and 20 were uneventful. Morning of the 21st the convoy, on course 204°, was smoking badly. With visibility about 10 miles, the billowing smudge was as obvious as an Indian signal. Fog set in around noon—perfect cover for stalking enemies. And as the convoy advanced through thickening vapor, EDISON's sonar picked up a contact.

The echo was indistinct, a "doubtful." But at 1730 the rescue ship TOWARD picked up a submarine's signal on her "Huff-Duff" gear. Bearing 107°. But after searching for about an hour, LEA reported "no contact," and resumed her station.

Evidently LEA's search should have been more persistent. For an enemy was in the vicinity. At 0305 the following morning a U-boat attacked the left rear flank of the convoy.

At this hour the escorts were patrolling in night formation, with LEA and BERNADOU shifted to the convoy's forward flanks. Striking at the exposed rear flank, the submarine was undetected. Apparently it fired from outside the screen. The long-range "browning shots" struck home. Thunder boomed in the night. Mushrooming smoke and orange fire, two ships staggered to a halt, hard hit.

NICHOLSON fell back to join TOWARD and ALGOMA in picking up survivors. The rescue vessel's big dip net featured in this life-saving detail, as did her special hospital facilities. The destroyermen, grim and determined, hauled their own share of shivering merchant seamen from the brine.

Daylight of February 22 revealed a seascape devoid of submarines. There were no attacks that night.

Nevertheless, the enemy kept the convoy under surveillance. At 1210 next day EDISON once more picked up sound contact, a sharp one that definitely spelled "submarine." Murdaugh ordered attack on the sub, which was directly ahead of column 8. A pattern of five depth charges rumbled under the sea. Due to interference from the convoy, the DD was unable to regain contact. But EDISON searched the vicinity until the convoy was over the horizon, then rejoined at 25 knots.

During the afternoon, BERNADOU picked up a sound contact at 1615, twelve miles on the convoy's port beam. Lieutenant Commander Braddy tried for the target with two depth-charge patterns. The contact evaporated.

These sporadic contacts suggested a wolfpack in the convoy

area, and Murdaugh bent every effort to avoid ambush. But in spite of evasive course changes and utmost vigilance and precaution, the U-boats got in.

The first strike came at 0030 in the morning of February 24th. Thereafter successive attacks were made until 0645. The convoy was beset from both quarters by five or six sharpshooting submarines. Four merchantmen were torpedoed. Two of the damaged vessels kept on going. Two went to the bottom.

During this onslaught, "snowflake" illumination was used by the convoy to give the Armed Guard on the merchant vessels a chance to spot surfaced U-boats. But the brilliant light failed to silhouette any targets for the deck-gunners.

While the battle was at its climax, the convoy's course was radically shifted to 285°. Meantime, offensive screening operations were extended and intensified.

Early that afternoon the rescue ship TOWARD picked up foreign signals on her "Huff-Duff." Running 15 miles ahead to investigate the direction-finder bearing, NICHOLSON sighted two surfaced submarines. The destroyer staged a single-handed double play, forcing the two U-boats to dive, and keeping them down under until after dark.

The wolfpack closed in hungrily at dusk. Following their favorite *Rudeltaktik,* the U-boats surfaced after dark to run ahead for high-speed lunges at the advancing convoy. Not long after nightfall EDISON picked up a sound contact on the convoy's starboard bow. Then the lookouts sighted a U-boat silhouette slinking through the moonlight. The silhouette slid out of sight before the deck-gunners could get in a shot, but EDISON's depth charges went overside in the water where the U-boat submerged.

After six depth-charge attacks the destroyermen were unable to regain contact. Murdaugh held the DD in the vicinity for a thorough search before ordering her to resume her station in the screen. Then, while rejoining the convoy at 0205 in the morning of the 25th, EDISON spotted another submarine.

This U-boat was close aboard—200 yards!—and nearly abeam. A barely glimpsed spectre in the gloom, it faded into the water before EDISON could turn to ram, and before the destroyer's main battery could be brought to bear. So spectral was this submarine that EDISON's sonar gear was unable to pick it up. The destroyermen dropped one depth charge on the vanished target, after which EDISON patrolled between the convoy and the point of submergence until dawn.

As a result of these A/S efforts, no attacks were made on the convoy during the night of February 24-25. But daylight did not dispel the submarine peril. Fog surged across the seascape at 1410, and with its onset the ranging escorts were recalled. The screen was reforming when TOWARD's "Huff-Duff" picked up another suspicious signal. BERNADOU, running down the direction-finder bearing, established sound contact at 1459. She dropped a pattern of seven depth charges on this unseen target, and searched the vicinity until dark.

Fog wallowed around the ships throughout that night (February 25-26), and morning brought rough seas. Daylight also brought the Coast Guard cutter SPENCER (Commander E. H. Fritzsche, USCG) toiling up through the heavy weather to join the convoy as a welcome reinforcement. Convoy ON-67 was now well along on the home stretch, and the last lap of the westward voyage proved uneventful.

For the destroyermen in Commander Murdaugh's unit, however, the voyage had been sufficiently trying. The convoy's merchant crews had also endured their portion of ordeal. Four ships sunk and two damaged by torpedo fire were eventful enough for any convoy's log.

Loss of USS TRUXTUN

Captained by Lieutenant Commander Ralph Hickox, TRUXTUN, in company with the destroyer WILKES (Commander J. D. Kelsey) was escorting the Navy cargo vessel POLLUX from Portland, Maine, to Argentia. The night of February 17-18 brought a tumultuous winter gale—foaming waters and a snowstorm that reduced visibility to zero. Blindfolded, the little convoy bucked its way through white midnight, the ships rolling their beam ends under.

But wicked February seas off Newfoundland were the rule rather than the exception. And the convoy, heading for Placentia Bay early in the morning of the 18th, was given no intimation of impending disaster. TRUXTUN apparently had no warning. Steaming on the southwest side of Ferryland Point, she was unable to determine that in the blizzarding gale the convoy had gone off course. If booming surf were heard by the lookouts, or churning breakers were glimpsed, the menace was detected too late.

At 0410 TRUXTUN struck with a crash. Hard aground, she was immediately assailed by furious seas that pounded her with catapult force. Waves plunged across her listing decks, swept her superstructure, and shouldered her across jagged rocks. Wrenched beyond endurance, her frames buckled; her plates caved, letting in the icy flood.

Then, before TRUXTUN could warn them, both the POLLUX and WILKES ran aground. At once the freighter's plight was as desperate as the destroyers'; however, WILKES backed clear with comparatively light damage.

Blizzard and wild seas prevented WILKES from aiding the grounded ships or their men. TRUXTUN broke up soon after

she went aground, and valiant destroyermen went down with
the wreckage to succumb to freezing wind and wave. Some of
her crew were rescued from the waters by the courageous work
of Newfoundland natives who risked their lives in small boats
and on the icy cliffs ashore. Only a few of TRUXTUN's crew
survived; among those lost was the destroyer's captain. POL-
LUX's crew was able to reach the shore over booms and lines
carried through raging seas by brave men, but the ship herself
did not long survive.

The tragedy tells a story well known to veteran Navy men—
the story of the age-old conflict between mariner and storm.
In this battle for mastery, the sea asks no quarter, and it gives
none. Neither do the men who go down to the sea in warships.

U-Boats Off Atlantic Coast (DD's on Roving Patrol)

The day after Nazi Germany declared war on the United
States, German Admiral Raeder conferred with Adolf Hitler.
The outcome of this meeting of master minds was a decision
to open a U-boat campaign against American coastwise shipping. So a U-boat squadron was readied for Operations *Paukenschlag*.

Paukenschlag means "Roll on the Drums." Very military.
Fortunately for the United States, the U-boat Force could not
begin this drumming immediately. Only six U-boats (500-ton-
ners) were immediately available for the trans-Atlantic invasion. By February 1942 several more were added to the
drum-squad.

The din began on January 12, 1942—a torpedo blast that
sent a British merchantman sloughing to the bottom some 300
miles off Cape Cod. Two days later, the Panamanian tanker
NORNESS was downed off Cape Hatteras. On the 15th, the
British oiler COIMBRA went down. On the 18th, the American
tanker ALLAN JACKSON. On the 19th, a Latvian merchantman
and the American freighter CITY OF ATLANTA. Then six more
tankers went down, one after the other, in the coastal waters
between New York and Cape Hatteras. Before the year's first
month was out, 14 ships were blown to the bottom off America's Eastern Seaboard.

To stiffen the defenses, Vice Admiral A. A. Andrews asked
for 15 destroyers to undertake roving anti-submarine patrols,
and in February 1942 he was allocated seven destroyers on
temporary detail.

Among the destroyers which engaged in these A/S patrols
were JACOB JONES, ROPER, HAMBLETON, and EMMONS. The
employment of single DD's on such patrols was soon proven
fatally ineffective.

Loss of USS JACOB JONES

The disaster which befell the second JACOB JONES clearly pointed to the fatal futility of employing lone destroyers on roving anti-submarine patrols. It was such a mission that took JACOB JONES down to the Delaware Capes. U-boats had become so bold in this area that ships had been torpedoed within sight of watchers on the beach. A sludge of oily flotsam scummed the Jersey shore. At Cape May the bodies of drowned merchant seamen came in with the dark tide. In those waters, patrolling alone, JACOB JONES was in dire peril. Her captain, Lieutenant Commander H. D. Black, Jr., had been instructed to hunt Nazi submarines.

It was a case of the hunter becoming the hunted. The U-boats were there. They saw her first.

Early in the morning of February 28, 1942, JACOB JONES was steaming on a southerly course, speed 15 knots, her wake a broad, bright avenue trailing astern on the calm, moonlit sea. Scanning the seascape with binoculars, the lookouts saw no ominous sign.

At some moment between 0400 and the ensuing hour, a U-boat began its stealthy approach. Perhaps it had been stalking for some time. Perhaps luck had placed it directly in the destroyer's track. Whatever the circumstance, the enemy readied the torpedoes and crouched in ambush. Then, at 0500—

Two (perhaps three) shattering explosions sent the destroyer reeling. The blasts hurled sleeping men from their bunks, and others, not asleep, were killed instantly.

General Alarm! Bluejackets racing topside to man battle stations. Flame leaping through passageways and water plunging into compartments. Surging smoke; spurting steam; a smell of scorched metal, burning oil, and fuming chemicals.

The men in JACOB JONES fought a losing fight to save their ship.

Mortally stricken, the torpedoed destroyer listed over on her side. She remained afloat for about an hour while the flood poured in and fire ravaged her internally. Some 35 men got clear of the sinking vessel. She went down at 0600.

As she sank, her depth charges exploded, hurling debris high in the air. All except 11 men were killed by this final blasting. Few destroyers suffered heavier casualties in the war. Not a single officer survived the JACOB JONES disaster.

ROPER *Kills* U-85 *(First Blood)*

Companion of JACOB JONES in Destroyer Division 54 was the destroyer ROPER, flagship of Division Commander S. C. Norton, and captained by Lieutenant Commander H. W. Howe. Like JACOB JONES, she was an old four-stacker with the salt of years of sea duty on her record. In company with JACOB JONES she had served at the Key West Sound School as a schoolship to provide novice Sound crews with sea-going sonar training. She was among the first American destroyers to carry radar.

The sinking of JACOB JONES had come as a shock to the other DD's of DesDiv 54, and the destroyermen in ROPER had hungered for a crack at the undersea enemy. Their chance came sooner than expected.

On the night of April 13-14, ROPER was steaming south from Norfolk. She was moving at 18 knots, and she had just put Wimble Shoal Light astern when (time: 0006) a "pip" flickered across her radar screen. With the range at 2,700 yards, ROPER's skipper stepped up speed to 20 knots to close in.

The target vessel appeared to be zigzagging, ROPER's Sound operator heard rapidly turning propellers, and obtained range and bearings which coincided with those obtained by radar. At 2,100 yards the wake of a small vessel was discerned. ROPER's skipper was cautious; in coastal waters there was always a chance of contacting a friendly vessel, perhaps a convoy "stray." Then, with the range closed to 700 yards, the wake of a torpedo was sighted. The lethal ribbon streaked through the water, and passed close aboard the destroyer's port side.

Lieutenant Commander Howe seemed determined not to fire until he saw the whites of this enemy's eyes. At 300 yards he shot the ray of a 24-inch searchlight pointblank at the stranger—a German submarine.

With the gray silhouette positively identified, Howe ordered ROPER's gunners to open fire. A 3-incher blazed. Machine-guns lashed at the target. A shell smote the U-boat at the waterline under the conning tower. Smoke and debris spurted skyward. A whip of bullets cut down the Germans huddled at a gun mount. The sea surged over the submarine's settling stern. Attacking on sonar contact, ROPER hammered down the submarine with a barrage of 11 depth charges.

Twenty-nine bodies were recovered the following morning. They were identified as crewmen of the U-85.

The U-85 was the first German submarine sunk in World War II by a United States man-of-war.

ICARUS *Kills* U-352

This is Coast Guard history.

The story is included in the present text (as are some others featuring the USCG) because the Coast Guardsmen were a bulwark of the American home-sea defense, and their A/S operations were geared to those of the DesLant Force. Early in the war they were frequently called upon to pinch-hit for the Navy's destroyermen. They were stalwart pinch-hitters. Case in point, the U-boat killing by the cutter ICARUS.

Subject for execution was the new 500-ton U-352 on a maiden cruise that sent her trespassing in the shallow waters off Cape Lookout. The submarine commander was another Doenitz-picked expert, Herr Kapitan Leutnant Hellmut Rathke. Lieutenant Commander Maurice Jester, USCG, was the Coast Guard skipper who trumped this Nazi ace.

Patrolling off Cape Lookout, ICARUS picked up the submarine contact on her sonar gear at 1625 in the afternoon of May 9, 1942. When the cutter maneuvered for an attack position, brash Kapitan Rathke fired a torpedo. The torpedo missed, and the U-boat found itself with too few fathoms for deep evasion.

Down came the Coast Guard's depth charges—explosions hammering the U-boat's pressure hull like pile drivers pounding on a boiler. After a number of close blasts the U-boat was in trouble. When the blasts came even closer, the submarine captain's nerves frazzled out, and he decided to abandon. The U-boat broached on the rise; the crew fought its way out of the conning tower; the submarine, scuttled, went down for the last time.

Running in to capture survivors, ICARUS fished 33 submariners from the water, among them Kapitan Leutnant Rathke. The cutter took this haul to Charleston, S.C., where the Navy was able to report the destruction of the fourth U-boat downed on the Eastern Sea Frontier since the war's outbreak.

Four U-boats. Slim recompense for the 87 merchant ships already torpedoed and sunk off America's Atlantic Coast by the *Paukenschlag* raiders. But the U-boats downed by destroyer ROPER and Coast Guard cutter ICARUS were merely the leaders of a long hit parade.

Chapter 7

DesLant into Battle (Part II)

☆ ☆ ☆

Loss of USS STURTEVANT

About one o'clock in the afternoon of April 26, 1942, the destroyer STURTEVANT (Lieutenant Commander C. L. Weigle) stood out of Key West. Her orders: to rendezvous with a convoy off Southwest Pass in the Gulf waters at the mouth of the Mississippi River.

At 1515, STURTEVANT was about eight miles north of the Marquesas Keys. She was drumming along at good speed, her bow knifing through warm seas, when a sudden, shattering explosion heaved her up by the stern. The ship shuddered, wallowed in a billow of smoke, and was rocked by a second shattering blast.

Stunned officers and men thought the destroyer had been torpedoed. Below decks they fought flood and flame while lookouts and gun crews topside strained their eyes for a glimpse of periscopes or torpedo wakes.

The damage was not to be controlled, for ruptured plates buckled, the sea rushed in, and vital machinery was deluged. Nor were the gun crews given a shot at a stalking U-boat. STURTEVANT had not been torpedoed. She had run headlong into a newly planted minefield—American mines!

Mortally stricken, the destroyer went down—the third destroyer of Captain W. D. Baker's original Squadron 31 to be lost through unexpected disaster, the first two being REUBEN JAMES and TRUXTUN. One hundred and thirty-seven STURTEVANT survivors were taken to Key West by small craft. Casualty list: *"Three dead, 12 missing."*

Always in mined water there was this risk. For the mine, an impartial weapon, may strike friend or foe, alike. The field in question had been planted only the day before STURTEVANT sailed.

STURTEVANT's Commanding Officer said he had not been

given advance information about this new minefield.

Navy men had a maxim for such cases. "Somebody always fails to get the word."

THETIS *Kills* U-157

On June 10 the U-157 attacked a merchantman in the Old Bahama Channel off the north coast of Cuba. The following morning the submarine was detected and bombed by an Army observation plane, and sighted by a Pan-American plane. Meanwhile Admiral Kauffman had rushed his killer groups into action. From Key West a group of PC's raced to patrol Nicholas Channel. From Miami another PC group sped to Santarem Channel. The NOA (Lieutenant Commander B. N. Wev) was sent to Old Bahama Channel; GREER (Lieutenant Commander L. H. Frost) to that channel's eastern entrance; DAHLGREN (Lieutenant Commander R. W. Cavenagh) to a point about midway between Matanzas, Cuba, and Andros Island.

On June 12 the U-boat was radar-detected by an Army observation plane off the Florida Keys. The plane missed with an attack, and a defective radio prevented prompt report of the contact. However, early in the morning of the 13th an observation plane was dispatched to the submarine's predicted position. So were DAHLGREN, NOA, and a bevy of PC's. The plane sighted the U-boat, which immediately submerged. Ensued a game of hide-and-seek, with four more Army planes and the Coast Guard cutter THETIS (Lieutenant [jg] N. C. McCormick, USCG) arriving to participate.

THETIS and her Coast Guardsmen led the attack. At 1550 of that afternoon they obtained sound contact on the submarine, and dropped seven depth charges on the target. A spew of oil rose to the surface. The five PC's in the vicinity followed through with depth-charge salvos. There was thunder down under, and within the next twelve hours the depths gave up a mass of splintered deck gratings and two pair of trousers labeled *"Fabrikken am Deutsch."* U-157 had gone beyond the reach of mortal contacting.

The sinking of U-157 was significant. A demonstration of coordinated A/S effort by air and surface craft, it certified the value of such teamwork, and emphasized the urgent need. It showed the shape of things to come—the "hunter-killer" groups of the future.

Destroyer Patrols Off Panama

It was reasonable to assume that German periscopes would be eyeing the approaches to the Canal.

On June 9 the Nazi invader struck. Laden with Army stores for the Canal Zone, the cargo vessel MERRIMACK was ambushed and torpedoed near Cozumel Island off Yucatan. BORIE (Lieutenant Commander P. R. Osborn) was not far from the area. She had been escorting two British ships to Key West, and now she was ordered to hunt for the sub and the MERRIMACK's survivors. A week later she found the survivors—eight emaciated figures on a raft—but the sub got away.

Meantime, two cargo ships were torpedo-sunk off Swan Island; three vessels were downed in the waters off Old Providence and St. Andrews; and a merchantman under escort of gunboat ERIE was torpedoed within 85 miles of the Canal entrance. All this in two days' time (June 9-10) while BORIE was busy in the Yucatan area, and BARRY, GOFF, and TATTNALL were on off-shore patrol. Then on the 13th two cargo ships were torpedoed and sunk at the very entrance of the Canal.

The raid put the Canal Zone in an uproar. Cristobal was closed to Caribbean-bound traffic while Admiral Van Hook assembled a task group to hunt down the invader.

The submarine responsible for this five-day blitz was the U-159. An Army plane spotted her in the sea 80 miles north of Colon, and the hunters were rushed to that vicinity. The Task Group included the destroyers EDISON (Lieutenant Commander W. R. Headden) and BARRY (Lieutenant Commander L. K. Reynolds), the former having just arrived at Cristobal with a Navy tanker. Several Navy aircraft and an Army plane joined the hunt.

EDISON and BARRY made a coordinated search for the U-boat, but except for bringing in survivors the search was without success. The U-159 went on her merry way.

Then on June 17 a British tanker was sunk by the shell-fire of two U-boats that ambushed her within 75 miles of Cristobal. Not long after that two merchantmen were downed off Santa Marta, Venezuela. And on June 24 a surfaced U-boat waylaid the schooner RESOLUTE between St. Andrews and Old Providence.

The RESOLUTE was crowded with island passengers. Without ado the U-boat closed to machine-gun range and opened fire, slaughtering the women and children who stood screaming on the schooner's deck.

By any definition, this was murder. Only the appearance of a patrol plane interrupted the massacre, but the submerging U-boat left in her wake a sufficient flotsam of bloody work. The Caribbean had not seen anything like this since the days of Blackbeard and bloodthirsty pirates.

The U.S. Navy was determined to end this murderous

onslaught. It mustered at Cristobal every A/S vessel available. Before these A/S forces could counter-attack, a U-boat glided into the Costa Rican harbor of Puerto Limon, and fired a deadly spread of torpedoes at a freighter alongside the wharf. Something had to be done quickly. And it was. By Army and Navy aircraft, and the destroyer LANSDOWNE.

LANSDOWNE *and Aircraft Kill* U-153

The submarine raider at Puerto Limon was the U-153. Not as smart as the skipper of U-159, her captain allowed her to suffer a bombing by Army patrol planes which sighted her on June 6. Apparently the damage was not extensive, but it must have been hampering. Only July 11 the U-153 attacked the net-tender MIMOSA off Almirante. She missed with a spread of five torpedoes, three of which passed under the net-tender. Then she was slow on the getaway.

At 0355 in the following morning, a PBY picked up the sub by radar. The plane dropped flares and straddled the U-boat with four depth charges. Undoubtedly hurt, the submarine went deep.

PC-458 (the EVELYN R.) was ordered to the scene. So was another Navy plane. PC and PBY trailed and bombed the Nazi sub for better than 10 hours.

Enter the destroyer LANSDOWNE (Lieutenant Commander W. R. Smedberg III), dispatched from Cristobal, where she had arrived as a convoy escort. Ordered to join the sub-hunt at top speed, she reached the scene at 1830 in the evening of the 13th.

LANSDOWNE relieved little PC-458, and set to work to get a bead on the target. Within a quarter of an hour after taking over, the DD picked up a sharp sound contact. The destroyermen raced to battle stations. Smedberg maneuvered his ship into attack position. A brisk run. A pattern of 11 depth charges appropriately laid. Thunder under the sea. Then up came a great spreading swell of oil that carpeted the near-by seascape.

LANSDOWNE probed the area with detection gear. Sound instruments could obtain no answering echo from water 1500 fathoms deep. A night of radar searching found nothing on the surface. But next day oil was still rising from the depths.

U-153 was 1500 fathoms down. The Nazi blitz on Panama Canal traffic was over.

Murder on the Murmansk Run (DD's versus Luftwaffe)

This has been called the "grimmest convoy battle of the entire war." Certainly few convoys were given such punishment as was dealt Convoy PQ-17—Iceland-Archangel. None suffered a worse ordeal.

The men who manned this Iceland-to-Archangel convoy did not anticipate a delightful excursion. The Murmansk Run had already acquired an evil reputation for bad weather, angry seas, and angrier Nazi attacks. The flanking Norwegian coast was a littoral of U-boat lairs, and alive with Luftwaffe hives. And the run to Archangel was even more perilous, in that it extended the Murmansk journey by a long haul down the White Sea.

The men of Convoy PQ-17 were fully aware of the hazards. Confidence was encouraged, however, by the fact that the ships sailed from Iceland under guard of one of the largest escort forces yet assembled in those waters. And powerful support and covering forces supplemented the escort. Convoy PQ-17 was a big ship-train. It was carrying some seven hundred million dollars' worth of munitions for besieged Russia.

The convoy of 33 merchant vessels (22 of them American) sailed from Reykjavik on June 27, 1942. Responsible for the escortage, the Royal Navy provided six destroyers, two flak ships, two submarines, and eleven smaller craft.

The Allied Support Force under Rear Admiral L. H. K. Hamilton, RN, sailed from Seidisfjord, Iceland, on July 1 to join the convoy in Denmark Strait. The Support Force consisted of British cruisers LONDON and NORFOLK, American cruisers WICHITA and TUSCALOOSA, and a screen which contained three destroyers. Two of the destroyers were American —the WAINWRIGHT (Lieutenant Commander R. H. Gibbs) and ROWAN (Lieutenant Commander B. R. Harrison). The former was flagship of Captain D. P. Moon, ComDesRon 8. The third destroyer was HMS SOMALI.

The Allied Covering Force, under Admiral Sir John Tovey, had sailed from Scapa Flow the previous day. This task force was to operate in the waters between Iceland and Spitzbergen, where it would shield Convoy PQ-17 from a possible thrust by the German warships based at Alten Fjord. It was also responsible for the safe return of a westbound convoy. The force included a British battleship, an American battleship, a British aircraft carrier, three British cruisers, a squadron of British DD's and corvettes, and American destroyers MAYRANT (Commander E. A. Taylor), flagship of Commander C. C. Hartman, ComDesDiv 16, and RHIND (Lieutenant Commander H. T. Read). As it eventuated, this powerful task group was diverted to an area far distant from the convoy, hence was unable to lend PQ-17 any direct assistance.

The Nazis knew about the big munitions convoy, its

make-up, even its sailing date. Thus informed, the German Admiralty set in motion an operation they called "Knight's Gambit." Plan was to send a battle force led by TIRPITZ out of Alten Fjord to menace the convoy as it simultaneously came under the fire of U-boats and land-based bombers. But as soon as German air scouts reported the presence of the Allied Covering Force off Spitzbergen, TIRPITZ was ordered back into her lair. To that extent Admiral Tovey's Covering Force aided the convoy.

The bulk of the convoy's surface defense was up to Admiral Hamilton's Support Force. Then there were the convoy's escort screen and the Naval Armed Guard. But, as will be seen, the escort screen dissolved. As for the Armed Guard, the gunners were stouter than their weapons. But one ship (Panama registry) carried a 4-inch 50-caliber gun. Only three of the American merchantmen were armed with 3-inch AA's. The rest carried .50-caliber and .30-caliber machine guns. Naturally these merchantmen depended on the accompanying warships for security.

The convoy's route skirted northern Iceland, took a north-by-east tack, went past Jan Mayen Island, continued northward toward Spitzbergen and Bear Island, then swung southeast through the Barents Sea to skirt the Kola Peninsula and enter the White Sea. On July 1 a Nazi reconnaisance plane approached the convoy and was shot down. The Germans made their first attack on July 2, U-boats and long-range torpedo-bombers striking at the convoy near Jan Mayen Island. Operating with Support Force, American destroyermen were promptly engaged in countering these opening moves of "Knight's Gambit."

The battle exploded just as the destroyer ROWAN, only recently dispatched to join the convoy for fueling, reached the area. The six attacking U-boats were driven off by the convoy's escorts. An umbrella of anti-aircraft fire frustrated the four attacking planes. Scorching the sky with their A/A batteries, ROWAN's destroyermen helped to raise the umbrella. Then one of her sharpshooting gun crews got a Swastika in the sights, and down came a Luftwaffe specimen. Score one for the USS ROWAN.

Later that day, ROWAN came under fire. Another quartet of German planes. Another torpedo attack. And one of the torpedo-planes struck at ROWAN. Sighting two oncoming wakes, the destroyer's lookouts cried the warning in time. Commander Harrison maneuvered to avoid, and the vengeful "fish" failed to find the mark.

So far so good—but for Convoy PQ-17 that was only a beginning. The following afternoon 26 German planes attacked the ship-train. Low clouds screened the convoy, and the bombing went amiss. But the next day, July 4, brought more fireworks.

It was a Fourth of July that American merchant seamen in the convoy would never forget. Neither would the Britishers who manned the six DD's in the convoy's escort—destroyers KEPPEL, OFFA, LEDBURY, WILTON, FURY, and LEAMINGTON (ex-USS EVANS).

It started early in the morning when a Heinkel roared out of a fog bank to stab a torpedo into a Liberty ship. Fatally hit, the SS CHRISTOPHER NEWPORT had to be abandoned and sunk.

Then came a group of attacking Heinkels. Bombs and torpedoes—zigzagging ships—three Heinkels shot down. Sweating destroyermen and Armed Guard gunners breathed a sigh of relief when that assault was broken up. But it was only the second round.

Round Three began about 1647—a slam-bang attack that knocked two merchantmen out of the convoy. In the vortex of this action was the American destroyer WAINWRIGHT, flagship of Captain Moon, the Support Force screen commander.

Earlier that afternoon the WAINWRIGHT had been directed to leave the Support Force formation and join the convoy train to take on fuel from the British tanker ALDERSDALE. The destroyer was approaching the convoy when six torpedoplanes raced in to strike at the merchantmen. WAINWRIGHT's anti-aircraft guns added weight to an aerial barrage that dispersed the enemy. At 1700, shooting at long range, her marksmen drove off still another torpedo-plane.

Determined to dig this thorn out of their side, the Germans now concentrated on the American DD. Down through the overcast roared a flock of dive-bombers. By ordering hard right rudder and top speed, the destroyer's skipper, Lieutenant Commander Gibbs, got her out from under the blasting.

At 1820 the Germans resumed the attack, some 25 Heinkels coming over the horizon. Sweeping in from the southward, the German planes formed two attack groups—one aimed to strike the convoy's starboard quarter, the other circling to strike the starboard bow. Captain Moon immediately sent WAINWRIGHT to an ahead position to meet the bow attack. Steaming out through the escort screen, the DD opened long-range fire on the planes closing the starboard quarter, then raked the Heinkels coming in on the convoy's bow. WAINWRIGHT's gunners put up a shield that compelled the bow attackers to let fly at long range. When the bombers dropped their torpedoes WAINWRIGHT went hard right to parallel and comb the tracks.

Thanks to WAINWRIGHT, then, the torpedoes dropped by the bow group missed the convoy. On the convoy's starboard quarter, where there was no destroyer defense, some of the Heinkels got in. Liberty ship WILLIAM HOOPER was torpedoed. The crew abandoned without orders, and the derelict, left to burn, had to be sunk by an escort. A torpedo struck the Russian tanker AZERBAIDJAN, but her damage-controlmen kept her going.

Not a devastating score for the Luftwaffe. Although destroyer WAINWRIGHT was severely strafed, the enemy's aim was poor. No man had been injured on the American DD, and she had damaged several Heinkels in return. So Convoy PQ-17 was holding her own on that Fourth of July.

However, at that stage of the run the convoy had reached that point on the route to Russia just south of Spitzbergen. There were many miles of the Murmansk highway remaining. And at that critical point the British Admiralty sent to the convoy Support Force a fatal dispatch ordering Admiral Hamilton's warships to quit the convoy area.

Hamilton transmitted the crucial message: CRUISER FORCE WITHDRAW TO WESTWARD AT HIGH SPEED OWING TO THREAT FROM SURFACE SHIPS CONVOY IS TO DISPERSE AND PROCEED TO RUSSIAN PORTS X CONVOY IS TO SCATTER.

American officers in the Support Force stared at the signals in unbelief. Their departure would leave the convoy defenseless. Left to fend for themselves, the merchantmen would be set-ups for air and submarine attack. "I know you will be as distressed as I am," Admiral Hamilton informed the American cruiser TUSCALOOSA, "at having to leave that fine collection of ships to find their own way to harbor."

The order was, in effect, a death warrant for Convoy PQ-17. Tragically enough, it was based on misinformation which led the British Admiralty to believe that the battleship TIRPITZ, the pocket battleship SCHEER, and eight German destroyers had sortied to intercept the convoy.

Actually on that evening of July 4 the German warships were in Alten Fjord. They did not move until July 5. Then, with TIRPITZ, SCHEER, the heavy cruiser HIPPER, and seven destroyers, German Admiral Carls made a brief run up the Norwegian coast, dodging back to base on the 6th.

A flounder by the German Admiral; a blunder by the British—two overly wary antagonists. It can be said for the latter that they hoped to lure the German warships westward, and thus decoy them away from Convoy PQ-17. However, the withdrawal of the Support Force left the Allied convoy hopelessly exposed. So urgent was the word from London that the convoy's screen commander, although not directed to do so, ordered the six British DD's of the screen to cover the Support Force as it headed westward. The deserted merchantmen were left to play a desperate game of run-sheep-run.

Because destroyers WAINWRIGHT and ROWAN, operating with the Support Force, were withdrawn from the area, the convoy's death-battle with German submarines and aircraft has no direct relation to destroyer history. Yet the battle merits a brief account in this text as an unforgettable illustration of what could happen to a convoy bereft of the DD's defensive arm.

In compliance with orders, the merchantmen scattered and set out singly and in little groups, heading in the general direction of North Russia. They ran into arctic snowstorms. They encountered ice floes. They lost their way in dense fog. And in this limbo they were caught by U-boats and Junker bombers.

On July 5 the tanker CARLTON, steaming independently, was torpedoed and sunk by a U-boat. That same afternoon a flight of Junkers bombed and sank the cargo ship WASHINGTON, two accompanying British freighters, and the Dutch freighter PAULUS POTTER.

On July 6 the Russian ship OLOPANA, answering the WASHINGTON's S-O-S, was torpedoed and sunk. A few hours later three Junker dive-bombers found and downed the freighter FAIRFIELD CITY off Nova Zembla.

With FAIRFIELD CITY was the Liberty ship DANIEL MORGAN. The German bombers pounded the MORGAN from pillar to post. Late that night the mangled vessel was sunk by a U-boat. MORGAN's valiant Navy gun crew was rescued by the Soviet tanker DONBASS.

On July 9 the Liberty ship SAMUEL CHASE was leading a remnant group of merchantmen along the coast of Nova Zembla. Junkers struck at the ships, and down went the SS HOOSIER and the SS EL CAPITAN. The SAMUEL CHASE received a savage flogging. Her courageous gun crew managed to shoot down two Junkers, but the ship was nearly wrecked.

The sea between Murmansk and Nova Zembla became an inferno. The ships ran this way and that, seeking cover in fog, haven in unknown coastal waters. Several of the merchantmen went aground. And fog offered little protection from stalking submarines.

The U-boats torpedoed and sank the ALCOA RANGER, the HONOMU, the JOHN WITHERSPOON. Merchantmen PAN ATLANTIC, PAN-KRAFT, and PETER KERR were sunk by dive-bombers. The British fleet oiler ALDERSDALE was bombed and sunk. So were British merchantmen EARLSTON, EMPIRE BYRON, BOLTON CASTLE, HARTLEBURY. Finally the rescue ship ZAAFARAN, severely damaged by dive-bombers, was scuttled by her crew.

The last battered remnants of the convoy staggered into

Archangel on July 25. When the final count was in, 11 of the convoy's 33 ships were on hand. The other 22 had been sunk. Of the 22 American merchantmen that started with the convoy, only eight survived. The tonnage loss was stupendous—millions of dollars' worth of cargo. Loss of life was proportionately high—the icy waters and lonely reaches of the Barents Sea did not abet rescue. Not only did this massacre deprive the Russians of urgently needed war supplies, but it left a costly hole in Allied shipping and severely strained the morale of the merchant service.

The Germans were jubilant over the success of "Knight's Gambit." But they might have noted their win was by way of a fool's-mate—the result of blunders an opponent is unlikely to repeat.

Never again would a group of American merchantmen be left on their own to run a gantlet through submarine-infested seas.

Atlantic Summary, January-July '42

"It was rugged going," a destroyerman said. The official consensus, reduced to the vernacular.

Submarine Admiral Doenitz to Adolf Hitler (June 15, 1942): *"I foresee vast possibilities through a rapid increase in the number of U-boats and the use of supply submarines."* And to a German war correspondent (summer of 1942): *"Our submarines are operating close inshore along the coast of the United States of America, so that bathers and sometimes entire coastal cities are witnesses to that drama of war, whose visual climaxes are constituted by the red glorioles of blazing tankers."*

Chapter 8

Ordeal of DesRon 29

(The Battle for the Malay Barrier)

☆ ☆ ☆

EDSALL *and Corvettes Kill* 1-124
(First Blood)

A good many depth charges had been dropped in the Pacific by the third week in January 1942. They jolted Japanese nerves, but so far as is known they did little damage to the Emperor's submarines. On the DD agenda the reckoning was overdue.

First honors fell to the USS EDSALL. One of the Asiatic Fleet veterans of DesRon 29, she was one of that valiant squadron of oldsters bearing the brunt of the Japanese onslaught on Indonesia. It was fair reward that one of these old grayhounds should participate in the first major submarine kill for American destroyers in the Pacific.

The scene: off Port Darwin, the "ghost town" emergency naval base on the north coast of Australia. There, on the morning of January 20, 1942, the destroyer EDSALL, captained by Lieutenant Joshua J. Nix, member of an escort group conducting a convoy into Darwin, picked up sound contact with an enemy sub.

The destroyer could not abandon the convoy to race off on a submarine hunt. But as she steamed into Darwin with the ship-train, her call brought a group of Australian corvettes to the scene. The invading sub was promptly made "it" in a deadly game of tag.

That afternoon the EDSALL was dispatched from Port Darwin to join the game. She was off at 1633. That evening, at 1900, she formed a scouting line just northwest of Melville Island with her companion "four-piper" ALDEN (Lieutenant Commander L. E. Coley).

Three Australian corvettes—His Majesty's Australian ships DELORAINE, LITHGOW, and KATOOMBA—were at that time

64

maneuvering around the spot where the sub had been first contacted by EDSALL.

Heading for the scene of action, EDSALL's sonar "put the finger" on the sub at 1929. The destroyermen endured a four-minute wait while HMAS DELORAINE made a depth-charge run over the target. Then EDSALL laid a thunderous pattern in DELORAINE's wake.

The sea boomed and boiled and bubbled. Up came a flood of oil and an effervescent, murky swirl which bore evidence that a large Jap submarine had been erased from the Imperial Navy's roster. And destroyer EDSALL and corvette DELORAINE could each paint a Rising Sun naval flag on the ship's "scoreboard."

Final inquest (autopsy might be a better term) was made by divers of the USS HOLLAND. Going down at lat. 12-05 S., long. 130-06 E., they boarded the remains of the Japanese submarine I-124. For American destroyers in the Pacific she was No. 1 on the "Hit Parade."

Abdafloat Versus Japanese Juggernaut

As had been related, the Allies in the Asiatics organized the ABDA Command on January 15, 1942.

Lacking air cover, the ABDA naval forces were hopelessly handicapped.

Figures best summarize the ABDAFLOAT-Japanese armada disparity. In fact, the story of the Allied naval defeat in the Philippines, Malaya, and the Netherlands East Indies is contained in the following statistical table:

ABDAFLOAT		*JAPANESE SOUTHWEST PACIFIC FORCE*
Battleships	*0*	2
Aircraft carriers	*0*	5
Light carriers	*0*	1
Heavy cruisers	*2*	14
Light cruisers	*7*	5
Destroyers	*23*	43
*Submarines**	*46*	*(Unknown)†*

* *(Effort cancelled by faulty torpedo)*   † *(But operating with the best torpedo in the Pacific)*

The odds were so overwhelming as to be impossible. Asiatic Fleet, Dutch, and British squadrons could not count on reinforcements for months to come, if at all. Neither could ABDAFLOAT count on overhaul or refits. This meant that a badly crippled ship must either retire in disablement, or fight on as best she could, although seriously lamed.

Finally there was the language handicap. Most of the American naval officers could not speak three words of Dutch; nor were they able to read the Dutch charts and sailing instructions. Communication errors and misunderstandings plagued the ABDA forces from the first.

Yet in spite of the odds and handicaps, ABDAFLOAT fought several of the great battles of the Pacific War. In those desperate battles for the Malay Barrier, American destroyers—the old "four-pipers" of Captain Wiley's DesRon 29—participated in a manner that assumes heroic proportions.

The Battle of Balikpapan

Aside from their strategic value, the Dutch islands of Indonesia were rich with economic treasure, not the least of which was "liquid gold." The wells of Tarakan Island, off the northeast coast of Borneo, gushed oil of unusual purity. To capture these liquid gold mines, the Japanese Central Force stormed down through the Celebes Sea. Tarakan was handily taken on January 11. On the 21st the invaders headed down Makassar Strait to seize Balikpapan.

As Balikpapan on Makassar Strait lay to the north and east of Bali, the Japanese advance was in "American territory." In consequence Admiral Hart, in operational command of ABDAFLOAT, ordered Admiral Glassford's Striking Force to intercept the Japs in Makassar Strait.

When the order to move arrived (on the morning of January 20), Admiral Glassford's force was fueling in Koepang Bay, Timor, at the eastern end of the Netherlands Indies Archipelago. As originally organized, Glassford's Striking Force contained the light cruisers BOISE and MARBLEHEAD, and eight destroyers of DesRon 29. But the entire force was not on hand. In company with HOUSTON, destroyers WHIPPLE and JOHN D. EDWARDS were escorting a convoy to Torres Straits. Destroyers ALDEN and EDSALL were also on convoy duty. And several DD's were undergoing repair. So only the two light cruisers and no more than six destroyers were available to Glassford. And as it turned out, only four of the destroyers—JOHN D. FORD, POPE, PARROTT, and PAUL JONES—led by Commander P. H. Talbot, ComDesDiv 59, with his pennant in the FORD, would be available for the crack at Balikpapan.

The destroyers were fed fuel by the MARBLEHEAD. And then, with his abbreviated force, Admiral Glassford set out for the Strait of Makassar. The ships steamed westward across the Savu Sea, then swung northward to slip through Sape Strait between Komodo and Soembawa Islands.

Here Glassford's force received its first setback at the hands

of Chance and Blunder, those capricious war-gods given
to upsetting the best laid plans of mice and men-of-war. In
Sape Strait there was (by Chance) a pinnacle rock which
reared from the water like an upthrust dagger. It caught the
light cruiser BOISE as she steamed through the strait, and
gave her a wicked slash along the keel. With her bottom laid
open, BOISE had to head for the nearest port. The little force
was minus one light cruiser, plus the destroyer required to
escort her to port.

Meantime, MARBLEHEAD had been slowed by a turbine
casualty which cut her speed to 15 knots. Admiral Glassford
in BOISE ordered both cruisers into Wararoda Bay, Soembawa.
And so another DD was detached to screen this cruiser. That
reduced the Striking Force group to four destroyers—the four
old "four-pipers" under Commander Talbot. Doggedly this
little quartet steamed on through Sape Strait, then headed
across the Flores Sea for Cape Mandar, Celebes, at the southern end of Makassar Strait. Four tired old "cans" of World
War I manufacture advancing to hit a Jap invasion force
which contained some 12 destroyers and several armed
auxiliaries. Not to mention Admiral Nishimura's light cruiser
NAKA.

Odds notwithstanding, Talbot led his four destroyers northward up Makassar Strait during the afternoon of January 23.
Making 25 knots. About an hour after sunset, with the ships'
clocks at 1930, Talbot headed the ships for Balikpapan,
Borneo.

Commander Talbot passed the word over the TBS: TORPEDO
ATTACK. USE OWN DISCRETION IN ATTACKING INDEPENDENTLY
WHEN TARGETS ARE LOCATED. . . . WHEN ALL TORPS FIRED,
CLOSE WITH ALL GUNS. . . . USE INITIATIVE AND DETERMINA-
TION.

As the little column started an oblique run across the
Strait, speed was stepped up to 27 knots. Through the dark-
ness the four old-timers galloped—flagship JOHN D. FORD
(Lieutenant Commander J. E. Cooper); POPE (Lieutenant
Commander W. C. Blinn); PARROTT (Lieutenant Commander
E. N. Parker); PAUL JONES (Lieutenant Commander J. J.
Hourihan).

At midnight the ships were still racing through the blackout; the sea had calmed, and the destroyers were moving on
a beeline.

Presently FORD's lookouts sighted the firelight of a couple
of burning Jap transports, handiwork of Dutch airmen who
had attacked the invader the previous afternoon. Then Balikpapan came to view under a sky flushed crimson. The whole
shoreline was an angry smolder. The Dutch had blown up
the local refineries. Against this netherworldish glow, Japanese

transports were intermittently silhouetted; for a moment, a ship would be seen, then it would be screened by a surge of smoke. But the smoke which screened the herd of transports also served to screen the approaching American destroyers. And the old "four-pipers" were not detected.

So Chance, capricious as always, provided DesDiv 59 with a break at Balikpapan. It was a destroyerman's set-up—the anchored transports; the smoke-smudge which screened the attacking DD's; the fiery shoreline which just silhouetted the targets.

Suddenly a searchlight stabbed from the darkness on FORD's starboard bow. A Jap destroyer, one of four crossing the American column from starboard to port, blinked a challenge at the American DD's. Talbot ordered a swift course-change, and the column kept on going. Another course change put it back on the "main line" for Balikpapan.

Talbot led his ships in on the attack with a high-speed dash. Their opening strike was aimed at a line of transports anchored about five miles off the entrance of Balikpapan Harbor. PARROTT was the first to loose her torpedoes. She launched at close range—a spread of three. The three missed.

Lieutenant Commander Parker ordered a slight turn to port. About two minutes after the first torpedo salvo, PARROTT fired a brace of five torpedoes at a target some 1,000 yards to starboard. She was shooting, so to speak, at the broadside of a barn. All five torpedoes missed.

Simultaneously FORD let fly at an anchored transport. Another miss.

End-ship in the column, PAUL JONES fired a torpedo at 0257, shooting at a vague silhouette which loomed up in the smoke as a destroyer or a cruiser. As it eventuated, the vessel was a small minesweeper. And that torpedo also missed!

So Blunder once more reared its ugly head to bedevil this force. Ten torpedo shots at "sitting duck" targets, and not a single hit! Critics there were who later suggested that the old "four-pipers" were moving too fast for accurate marksmanship. But evidence indicates that it was the torpedoes that failed, and not the destroyermen.

And now the chance for surprise was lost; the punch was "telegraphed"; the enemy was sounding the alarm. Among the Japanese ships all was hue, cry, and confusion. In the oily smoke-fog, Jap patrol craft began to dash this way and that. Signals twinkled, and there was some aimless shooting. Meanwhile (time: 0300) Commander Talbot brought his column circling around for another run past the line of transports. As the DD's started the loop, PARROTT fired three torpedoes at a ship dimly glimpsed on her port bow. This time the torpedoes found the mark. The transport, SOMANOURA MARU, blew up with a night-shaking blast. Out of Balikpapan Bay, pell-mell, came Japanese Admiral Nishimura's destroyer squadron. This pack of modern DD's should have dealt Talbot's old quartet a homicidal thrashing. They did nothing of the kind. Somehow convinced that his transports were under submarine attack, Nishimura led his destroyer squadron steaming out into Makassar Strait to conduct a vigorous sub-hunt.

While the befuddled Admiral's destroyers searched for a sub that wasn't there, Talbot's "four-pipers" ran riot through the Jap transport fleet.

Highballing on the back track, destroyer POPE at 0306 launched a spread of five torpedoes at a silhouetted target. Two minutes later PARROTT fired a torpedo salvo at the same ship, and PAUL JONES unleashed a salvo two minutes after that. Another dazzling eruption illumined the night, and down went the 7,000-ton transport TATSUKAMI MARU.

The column raced southward, then swung hard right to clip through the southern end of the anchorage. At 0319 POPE and PARROTT loosed simultaneous torpedo salvos at what looked like a Jap destroyer off to port. The shots demolished a small patrol boat.

At 0322 FORD and PAUL JONES launched single torpedoes at the dim silhouette of a good-sized transport. A ruffle of froth at her stern, the vessel was under way, and she managed to dodge the "fish." Talbot brought the column circling around this target, and PAUL JONES fired a killing torpedo at 0325. Victim was the 5,000-ton KURETAKE MARU.

Once more the column headed northward on a dash paralleling the transport line. Then Talbot ordered an abrupt turn to westward to begin a long run that would take the speeding DD's through an inner line of transports.

As the column began the long westward loop, all four DD's opened fire with their deck guns. POPE and PARROTT and PAUL JONES were out of torpedoes. FORD was retaining her final salvo for fat targets.

By now POPE, PARROTT, and PAUL JONES reported "all torpedoes expended." Giving the other three destroyers orders to proceed independently with gunfire, Talbot directed the FORD to attack again with her remaining torpedoes.

The following excerpt from the account by FORD's Gunnery Officer describes this final round.

"Down on the bridge I heard 'Fire ten!' Just two torpedoes left. Now only the POPE was left astern of us. We fired our last two torpedoes at a group of three transports. Now I knew the stage was mine. Many a time I had fired at target rafts, but this was the real thing. 'Commence firing!' rang in my earphones. I was ready, but how different this was from peacetime firings! I could still remember the sonorous argu-

ments of the publications I had studied at the Naval Academy over the relation effectiveness of searchlights and starshells. I didn't use either, nor did we use any of the complicated fire-control apparatus installed. This was draw-shooting at its best. As targets loomed out of the dark at ranges of 500 to 1,500 yards, we trained on and let go a salvo or two, sights set at their lower limits, using the illumination furnished by burning ships. Finally we sighted a transport far enough away to let us get in three salvos before we had passed it. The projectile explosions were tremendous. Deck-plates and debris flew in all directions. When we last saw her she was on end, slipping slowing under. . . .

"One more transport we mauled badly, then there was nothing left to shoot at. On the bridge I heard our Division Commander give the order to withdraw. Back aft the blowers began to whine even louder as the Chief Engineer squeezed the last ounce of speed out of the old boat. Later I learned we were making almost 32 knots, faster than the FORD had gone since her trials. In the east the sky was growing uncomfortably bright. Astern of us the sky was also bright, but from the fires of burning ships. . . ."

Apparently one of those ships was the transport ASAHI MARU, damaged and set ablaze by FORD's gunnery. Another seems to have been the TSURUGA MARU, a 7,000-tonner torpedoed and sunk in the last-round foray.

So ended the Battle of Balikpapan.

Behind them Talbot's destroyers left wreckage and total destruction. On the bottom off Balikpapan Bay lay four Japanese transports: The cargoman KURETAKE MARU, 5,175 tons; and passenger-cargomen TSURUGA MARU, 6,988 tons; TATSUKAMI MARU, 7,064 tons; SOMANOURA MARU, 3,519 tons. With them lay Japanese patrol craft PC-37, 750 tons. Altogether 23,496 tons of enemy shipping.

In the flame light of later torpedoings, this tonnage might appear insignificant. But in January 1942 the torpedoings by Talbot's destroyers created the one bright spot in the Southwest Pacific War picture.

ABDA Setbacks

The destroyermen in Captain Wiley's DesRon 29 were delighted by the Balikpapan victory, but they knew what they were up against. The 13 Asiatic Fleet "four-pipers" serving with ABDAFLOAT were orphans of the storm. Already Soerabaja, provisional headquarters of the Asiatic Fleet on the north coast of Java, was menaced by the Jap advance on Borneo. On the south coast of Java the port of Tjilatjap (pronounced Chillachap) offered a few basing facilities but scarcely enough. The Jap thrust into the Bismarck Archipelago directly threatened the security of Darwin, Australia. About the only front-line base the destroyers could count on was the tender BLACK HAWK. And that overworked ship would soon be as bare of supplies as Mother Hubbard's cupboard.

It was a bitter cup of Java, off the Malay Barrier in February 1942. Caught without air cover, cruisers HOUSTON and MARBLEHEAD were savagely mauled by Jap aircraft. With HOUSTON badly damaged, and MARBLEHEAD out of the campaign, the battle for the Malay Barrier was a back-to-the-wall fight. As though the odds were not sufficiently adverse, a Dutch destroyer piled up on a reef during the night of February 14. On the 15th, American DD's BARKER and BULMER were disabled by Jap aircraft off Bangka. And that same day, destroyer PEARY was lost.

Loss of USS PEARY

Early in the morning of February 15, 1942, the USS HOUSTON and destroyer PEARY escorted a convoy out of Port Darwin, Australia. Destination: Timor, at the eastern end of the Netherlands East Indies.

Meanwhile ABDA Headquarters had received word that a strong Japanese Carrier Force was at that time somewhere in the Banda Sea or the Flores Sea. The onslaught on the Allied convoy verified this information. With Jap carrier aircraft in striking range, the convoy's situation was extremely hazardous, and the effort to reinforce Timor was too little and too late. Captain Rooks was ordered to return the convoy to Port Darwin.

The ships entered Darwin Harbor in the morning of February 18. The crews heaved sighs of relief. But as it eventuated, the convoy had retired into a trap.

Outside Darwin that night destroyer PEARY picked up a submarine contact. Lieutenant Commander J. M. Bermingham and company conducted the usual vigorous search. The Jap submarine escaped. The long game of hide-and-seek diminished PEARY's fuel supply. She was ordered back to Darwin to "top off" (refuel), while cruiser HOUSTON was to proceed westward independently.

For HOUSTON it was a reprieve; for PEARY, a death sentence. In the morning of February 19, a great flock of Japanese bombers came droning over the horizon. Darwin had no radar warning. Warehouses, docks, the local airport—the town itself was practically blown to rubble. Nearly every ship in the harbor was destroyed.

Army transport MAUNA LOA took two bombs down an open

hatch, and sank with a rush. Struck by about 20 bombs and blasted by an aerial torpedo, Army transport MEIGS went down in 18 fathoms. The troopship TULAGI was severely damaged. Punctured by a near miss, the PORTMAR was beached. Hard hit, the Brazilian DON ISIDORO was gutted by fire after escaping from the harbor mouth. Answering the Brazilian's distress call, a coastal steamer was bombed and sunk. SS ADMIRAL HALSTEAD, American freighter loaded with high-octane gasoline, was sunk. Two Australian corvettes were blown to the bottom.

In the vortex of this cataclysm the ex-destroyer PRESTON and the destroyer PEARY fought their hearts out to beat back the enemy. At the start of the raid the two old "four-stackers" had headed for the harbor mouth, PRESTON in the lead. Three bombs hit PRESTON. The ship was thrashed by flying iron; her skipper Lieutenant Commander Etheridge Grant was blown overboard. The PRESTON, however, was not downed. She remained afloat and firing to the last—one of the few vessels to survive the blasting of Darwin.

Less fortunate was the USS PEARY. She was zigzagging as best she could in the cluttered harbor, and holding up her end of the anti-aircraft barrage, when the bombers dived. She was staggered by two savage hits. One blast wrecked her fantail, demolishing the depth charge racks, shearing off the propeller guards, and flooding the steering-engine room. The other bomb, an incendiary, crashed into the galley and left the ship in flames.

Even then she continued to fight. She was fighting at the last when, at 1300, she broke up and sank in a pall of smoke and fire. A witness reported that a .30-caliber and a .50 caliber machine-gun were blazing away as PEARY's shattered remains went under.

About 80 of the crew, and PEARY's captain, Lieutenant Commander Bermingham, went down with the ship. Only one officer, Lieutenant W. J. Catlett, Jr., survived. Lieutenant Catlett was the Engineer Officer.

Chapter 9

Ordeal of DesRon 29

(Retreat to Australia)

☆ ☆ ☆

The Battle of Badoeng Strait

In mid-February the Japanese flag flew over Borneo, the Celebes and the Moluccas. The invaders landed on Sumatra. Singapore crashed on the 15th. Storming eastward, the Japs bore down on Bali. ABDA naval forces in the Java Sea were morsels in the jaws of the Japanese dragon.

Defense was up to Dutch Rear Admiral Karel Doorman.

Doorman was unable to collect a force strong enough to prevent the Japs from landing on Bali. However, he determined to strike at the invasion shipping in the roadstead off the Bali beachheads. His plan called for a three-wave attack. With Dutch cruisers DE RUYTER and JAVA he would lead the ABDA warships out of Tjilatjap for a gunfire and torpedo attack on the enemy ships off Bali. DE RUYTER and her group would then retire through Lombok Strait. That would be the first wave.

The second wave would come from Soerabaja—the light cruiser TROMP (Commander J. B. de Meester, RNN) and American destroyers STEWART, PARROTT, EDWARDS, and PILLSBURY. This group would attack the Bali invasion ships about three hours after the initial strike.

As a mop-up wave, a small group of Dutch PT boats would then slough into the Japanese force, to finish off the residue. On paper, at least, this made a nice finale to a feasible-looking plan.

But American Admiral William O. Glassford, serving as Commander U.S. Naval Forces Southwest Pacific, had his doubts. So did a number of American destroyer officers. An attack by successive echelons would be one of decreasing surprise. Also Doorman was counting heavily on gunfire. The old "four-pipers" were not too strong in that department, and night gun-actions were likely to be haphazard for ships without surface radar.

Nevertheless, at 2200 in the evening of February 18 the DE RUYTER group got under way. And at the very take-off, in the narrow harbor mouth of Tjilatjap, the Dutch destroyer KORTENAER ran aground. This left only the Dutch destroyer PIET HIEN, and the Americans FORD and POPE, to screen the two Dutch cruisers.

The two old "four-pipers," under leadership of Lieutenant Commander E. N. Parker in FORD, were in turn led by the modern PIET HIEN. As the ships headed eastward in the night, FORD and POPE moved out in front to form a Sound screen ahead of the cruisers.

The group approached the southeast coast of Bali at 2100 in the evening of February 19. In attack formation DE RUYTER led, with JAVA astern. Far astern of the cruisers PIET HIEN led the destroyer column.

About 2200 the group steamed northward into Badoeng Strait, the narrow waterway between Bali and Nusa Besar, a fragment of island lying in Lombok Strait. The enemy ships were in Badoeng Strait, hugging the Bali shore—one transport, the SASAGO MARU, and Japanese destroyers ASASHIO and OSHIO. The bulk of the Jap invasion convoy had already left Bali.

Not much of a catch, one MARU and two DD's. But snaring even the prizes proved unexpectedly difficult.

JAVA opened fire at 2225. The Japs answered with a searchlight sweep, star shell, and gunnery. In the first exchange of shots, JAVA was hit on the stern, but only slightly damaged.

Next, destroyer PIET HIEN, coming within range, opened fire with her guns and unleashed a torpedo. Then, swerving on a sudden zigzag to starboard, she laid down a screen of smoke. This move baffled the American destroyers, trying to follow PIET HIEN's maneuvers. Upping their speed to 28 knots, FORD and POPE ploughed through the smoke and fell in 1,000 yards astern of the Dutch DD. She then led the column on a sharp veer to port. As FORD executed this tight turn, her lookouts spotted the Jap transport steaming northwestward and a Jap warship heading northeast.

The warship was OSHIO, her guns smoking from the exchange of shots with Dutch cruiser JAVA. As PIET HIEN and the two Americans raced on a westward loop, they opened fire on the Jap silhouettes. Shells struck the Jap transport. The Jap DD evaded. Both FORD and POPE flung torpedoes at the transport, and a burst of orange fire suggested a hit.

But the transport was not fatally hurt. And a moment later PIET HIEN was engulfed in a volcanic burst of flames. Either struck by a deadly gun-salvo or a torpedo from the Jap destroyer ASASHIO, the Dutch destroyer was left dead in the water, sinking.

FORD and POPE now were plunged into a raging gun battle with ASASHIO and OSHIO. The Dutch cruisers, according to plan, had steamed on northward out of Badoeng Strait, but the American destroyers found it impossible to follow. Trading hammer-and-tongs gunnery with ASASHIO, hard-pressed FORD (Lieutenant Commander J. E. Cooper), was driven southward. POPE (Lieutenant Commander W. C. Blinn) trailed FORD. The OSHIO bore down with blazing guns, and for about six minutes the seascape was livid with shellfire.

Division Commander Parker headed the two old "four-stackers" over toward Nusa Besar island. The American DD's were out of portside torpedoes, and Parker wanted to bring the starboard torpedoes into action. As FORD and POPE swung across Badoeng Strait, they crossed OSHIO's bow, and the Jap destroyer hurled a stream of shells at the American ships. While FORD laid a wall of smoke to cover her, POPE replied to OSHIO's fire with five starboard torpedoes. The entire spread missed. Were they "deep-runners" or dumb-headed duds?

It was time to disengage, and at 2310 the American destroyers were hightailing southward in column, POPE in the lead—as Navy men phrase it, "getting the hell out of there." Behind them, the Japs were still firing furiously. As it happened, ASASHIO had come up unexpectedly—perhaps through a drift of FORD's smoke—and OSHIO took her for another enemy. The two Jap DD's were shooting savagely at each other as the two American hauled south out of Badoeng Strait and struck westward for Tjilatjap.

And now the hour had arrived for the second Striking Force wave to wash through Badoeng Strait. Light cruiser TROMP and American destroyers STEWART (Lieutenant Commander H. P. Smith) flagship of Commander T. H. Binford, ComDesDiv 58, PARROTT (Lieutenant J. N. Hughes), EDWARDS (Commander H. E. Eccles), and PILLSBURY (Lieutenant Commander H. C. Pound) were on the way.

Binford's four destroyers had made a fast run along the coast of southern Java to join TROMP at the appointed rendezvous. Dutch Commander de Meester in TROMP headed the group for Bali on schedule. Binford attempted to communicate with FORD and POPE by radio. But STEWART's operator was unable to obtain an answer, and Binford could not find out how the first wave fared.

About midnight off Bali, the Dutch group commander in TROMP formed the attack column. STEWART was placed in the lead. The other "four-pipers" trailed Binford's flagship, and TROMP brought up the rear. The DD's were to open with a torpedo attack; the Dutch cruiser was to follow through with heavy gunfire.

Steaming at 25 knots, the column entered Badoeng Strait at 0135 in the morning of February 20. The Bali shoreline was misty, and the Jap ships, twinkling signals at each other, appeared as wraithlike silhouettes in the haze. Out in the clear, under radiant stars, the little ABDA force was exposed. To hit fast and first, Binford ordered an immediate torpedo barrage.

Time: 0136. Both STEWART and PARROTT let go with spreads of six torpedoes. PILLSBURY fired three. Launched from portside tubes, the torpedoes streaked across the water. The destroyermen ticked off the seconds, listening for detonations. Nothing. All fifteen missed.

The enemy, warned, wheeled to do battle.

Charging to meet the oncoming Americans, the two Jap destroyers, ASASHIO and OSHIO, rushed at STEWART's port beam. Glimpsing enemy bows, STEWART flashed on a searchlight, fired torpedoes, and hurled shellfire at 0143. Behind her, EDWARDS tried a torpedo salvo. Two torpedoes leapt away, and missed. Two others jammed in the tubes.

The Japs replied with furious gunnery, promptly straddling Binford's old "four-pipers." At 0146 STEWART got it from a ricochetting projectile—one man killed; Executive Officer Lieutenant C. B. Smiley agonizingly wounded. Then a shell smashed into her steering-engine room, flooding the steering machinery.

After she was hit, Binford swung STEWART to starboard, leading the column northeastward. On the turn PARROTT and PILLSBURY came within paint-width of colliding. The close shave threw PILLSBURY out of the column. But all four "four-pipers" continued to race northeastward up Badoeng Strait. And now TROMP joined the gun battle. The Jap destroyers had rounded on de Meester's cruiser, and the Dutchman answered their fire by hitting OSHIO with a shell that killed about seven of her bridge personnel. TROMP sustained some ten hits in return, and was sorely hurt.

After the exchange with the Dutch light cruiser, OSHIO and ASASHIO lost contact. But the battle was not yet over. As the ABDA group steamed northward toward the Lombok Strait exit, two more Jap destroyers were heard from.

The newcomers were units of Admiral Kubo's Bali Force which had previously entered the area to support the Bali invasion. Dispatched to Badoeng Strait by Kubo when he received word of Doorman's attack, these DD's—IJN ARASHIO and IJN MICHISHIO—made a fast dash southward to the scene of action. Wherewith they came butting into Badoeng Strait just as Binford's destroyers and TROMP were retiring.

At the northern entrance of Badoeng Strait the opposing

ships practically met head-on. Time: 0219. ARASHIO and
MICHISHIO fired pointblank at STEWART and EDWARDS. Ensued a lightning exchange of shells, oaths, more shells, torpedoes. Then PILLSBURY, out of column and racing up on
the enemy's port hand, struck MICHISHIO with a staggering
main-battery salvo. As the Jap destroyer veered from the
shock, EDWARDS caught her from starboard with a solid shell-
hit. Finally TROMP struck her in passing. MICHISHIO sloughed
to a halt, 96 of her crew dead, dying, or wounded.

The four American destroyers and TROMP sprinted on out
into Lombok Strait. PARROTT's sprint was rudely interrupted
when her steering control jammed with her rudder swinging
her left. The ship was steaming at 28 knots toward a nest of
rocks, and Lieutenant Hughes and crew did some sweating as
the engines were ordered full speed astern.

Luckily Kubo was too far distant to intercept. And Chance
again took an amazing hand in the proceedings. Earlier that
evening FORD had jettisoned a motor-whaleboat, and into that
castaway craft crawled 33 survivors of the Dutch destroyer
PIET HIEN. Then PARROTT jettisoned a drum of gasoline. The
Dutch survivors picked that up, too, and motorboated safely
back to Java!

But although the ABDA ships had dealt damage to destroyers OSHIO and ASASHIO, and had given MICHISHIO a fiery
thrashing, they made no dent in the Bali invasion. And the
raid was a costly one—PIET HIEN sunk, TROMP badly damaged, and the old "four-piper" STEWART disabled. After
Badoeng Strait the ABDA naval forces sailed into desperate
seas of misfortune.

Loss of USS STEWART *(and a Remarkable Resurrection)*

With her steering gear disabled by a 5-inch shell-hit, the
USS STEWART steamed out of the Battle of Badoeng Strait,
and made it into Soerabaja. She was badly in need of routine
repairs. With her were destroyers EDWARDS, PILLSBURY, and
PARROTT, and the battered Dutch light cruiser TROMP. And a
drydock was to be had. The one made available—a 15,000-
ton-lift floating drydock owned by a private shipyard—seemed
luck too good to be true.

It was. Everything in Soerabaja was at sixes and sevens at
the time. At the shipyards, both Dutch and native workmen
refused to work on Sunday. Moreover, spare parts, tools, all
sorts of necessary equipment, could not be begged or bor-
rowed. And finally the dockers and yardhands were panicked
by the constant enemy air-raids.

Under such conditions workmanship was sloppy and slip-
shod. When placed in drydock STEWART was not properly

positioned on the keel blocks. Nor was she correctly shored up. As the dock began to lift, the destroyer keeled over on her port side, like a beached whale.

Before the destroyer could be righted and floated, Japanese aircraft struck Soerabaja a devastating smash, and the prostrate STEWART was hit by a bomb. That settled it. There was no chance of repairing the thrice-damaged ship. Soerabaja was fast becoming untenable. One after another the ABDA ships were ordered to leave. By March 1, 1942, the evacuation was almost complete. Of the American warships which had been at Soerabaja, only helpless STEWART remained.

To prevent her capture by the invading Japanese, demolition crews rigged their high explosives in the vessel. These were set off on March 2. So it was reported that the USS STEWART met her end at Soerabaja on March 2, 1942. The Navy was satisfied that STEWART would never be seen at sea again.

The enemy swarmed over the Malay Barrier and stormed down into the Solomons. And then one fine day some American airmen were surprised to see an American warship steaming deep within the heart of the Greater East Asia Co-Prosperity Sphere.

The first aviators to see her looked again. And other aviators saw her, and looked twice. She was an American by all that was holy in the silhouette book!

She was seen here. And she was seen there. She was seen hull down, and she was seen coming over the horizon. And always she was seen behind the Japanese lines, cruising inside their territory.

And so the legend grew. A spectral yet corporeal American destroyer, a sort of living apparition, was operating behind the enemy's lines.

Somehow she was never torpedoed. Somehow she was never blasted and sunk. Not even at the last when United States and Allied forces were closing in on Japan, and crushing Japanese harbors and naval shipping under avalanches of shells and bombs.

So there was something uncanny about this man-of-war. She was found on October 15, 1945, by the American occupation forces in Japan. She was located in a residual huddle of Japanese shipping in the Kure-Hiroshima Area, the very heart of the enemy homeland. Then it was that she was identified as the former USS STEWART, the old "four-piper" lost in March, 1942, at Soerabaja.

It would seem the demolition party detailed to destroy the STEWART on that date had failed in the mission. Or perhaps the old destroyer was just plain indestructible. At any rate she had been salvaged and resuscitated by the invading Japanese, who gave her a "raked" stack and tripod mast, and sent her to sea as PATROL VESSEL 102.

On October 28, 1945, the ex-STEWART was taken over by a United States Navy prize crew at Hiro Wan. On November 3, 1945, she was ordered to the United States.

But the destroyermen had a name for the vessel. They called her "RAMP," for "Recovered Allied Military Personnel."

The Battle of the Java Sea

On February 27 Admiral Kondo's Southern Striking Force closed in on Java for the kill.

Doorman's force at this date consisted of flagship DE RUYTER, heavy cruisers HOUSTON and EXETER, light cruisers JAVA and PERTH, Dutch destroyers WITTE DE WITH and KORTENAER, British destroyers JUPITER, ELECTRA, and ENCOUNTER, and the American "four-pipers" EDWARDS, ALDEN, FORD, and PAUL JONES. To refuel the destroyers and give the exhausted officers and men a few hours in port, Admiral Doorman led his ABDA ships into Soerabaja on the afternoon of February 27.

But there was to be no rest for the weary. The ships were hardly through the minefield in the outer entrance to the harbor before Doorman received from Admiral Helfrich orders to attack a large Japanese naval force detected off Bawean Island about 100 miles north of Soerabaja. With no time to devise an attack plan, Doorman turned his ships "about face" with the message, *"Am proceeding to intercept enemy unit. Follow me."*

Almost as soon as Doorman's force was away from Soerabaja, the Allied ships came under air attack. At 1600 Doorman radioed an urgent appeal for fighter cover. He was crying into an empty barrel. At Soerabaja there were no more than eight land-based fighter planes, and the Dutch Air Commander was holding them for shore defense.

Running northwestward in the Java Sea, Doorman's column shook off the first aerial onslaught. Then it encountered the large Japanese naval force which was covering an invasion convoy. The showdown battle was on.

The Jap warships sighted were those of Rear Admiral Takagi's Eastern Covering Group: heavy cruisers NACHI and HAGURO, light cruiser JINTSU (Rear Admiral Tanaka), and seven destroyers. This group, glimpsed to the northwest, was supported by a second which came over the horizon due north—Read Admiral Nishimura's Eastern Attack Group, containing light cruiser NAKA and seven destroyers.

Totaling two heavy cruisers, two light cruisers, and 14 DD's, the enemy force was almost matched in size and weight by Doorman's Striking Force. But the ABDA ships lacked air cover. Moreover, they were without spotting planes; contemplating a night action on the 26th, Doorman had unshipped the several cruiser-carried planes, and left them ashore. NACHI and HAGURO used seaplane spotters during the ensuing action.

Steaming northwestward, the Jap ships were crossing the ABDA formation's bows when contact was made. Doorman had his cruisers in column, flagship DE RUYTER followed by EXETER, HOUSTON, PERTH, and JAVA. Ahead of the column screened the three British destroyers. Destroyers JUPITER and ENCOUNTER were on either side of ELECTRA. The two Dutch destroyers and four American were on the port side and to the rear of the cruiser column—a disposition which was to prove highly disadvantageous. For Doorman swung the formation to westward soon after the enemy was sighted. The Japs also bore to the west, roughly paralleling the Allied course. The Dutch DD's and the American destroyers were thus left on the disengaged side of the ABDA formation, a decidedly unfavorable position from which to launch a torpedo attack.

Doorman had ordered a flank speed of 26 knots, as he was striving to close the range to bring his cruiser's 6-inch batteries into action. Dutch destroyer KORTENAER, panting with boiler trouble, could make no better than 24 knots. The American destroyers had been instructed not to pass the Dutch DD's in their lead, and so the whole destroyer column was slowed.

At 1616 Takagi's heavy cruisers opened fire at extreme range (about 28,000 yards), hurling salvos at USS HOUSTON and HMS EXETER. The Allied heavies replied a moment later.

Then light cruiser JINTSU joined the fray, closing to 18,000 yards to fire at the British van destroyers. With three spotting planes in the air, the Jap fire was hot and accurate. Six- and eight-inch splashes doused the ABDA cruisers. At 1631 Doorman's flagship was pierced by an 8-inch dud which smashed into her auxiliary engine-room.

The Japs had been racing at top speed, evidently bent on crossing Doorman's T. In an effort to avoid that tactical trump, Doorman swung his formation more to the west. For a few minutes the opposing forces steamed on courses almost parallel, firing as they ran.

By this time the American destroyers, baffled by confused orders, had put on enough speed to bring them abreast of flagship DE RUYTER. They were still on the disengaged side of the ABDA formation, too far away to launch torpedoes or fire at the Jap ships. And as the old "four-pipers" pulled like

Roman chariots to maintain this assigned position, they raced in column in the following order: JOHN D. EDWARDS (Commander H. E. Eccles) flying the pennant of Commander T. H. Binford, ComDesDiv 58; ALDEN (Lieutenant Commander L. E. Coley); JOHN D. FORD (Lieutenant Commander J. E. Cooper) flying the pennant of Lieutenant Commander E. N. Parker, ComDesDiv 59; and PAUL JONES (Lieutenant Commander J. J. Hourihan).

At 1632 the Japs unleashed a torpedo attack on the ABDA cruisers. The spreads missed. The Jap destroyers laid dense smoke screens and closed the range, and launched more torpedoes. No hits. But at 1708 an 8-inch shell struck British heavy cruiser EXETER, and burst in a powder chamber. The savage explosion staggered the ship, and as she slowed abruptly, the cruisers behind her swerved off course in confusion. A few minutes later the Dutch destroyer KORTENAER, not far from the EDWARDS, was torpedoed.

"There was a heavy whitish explosion flinging debris 100 feet in the air," the captain of EDWARDS noted in this action report. "KORTENAER *heeled away over and yawed. . . . She poised momentarily and then turned turtle and folded up like a jackknife. . . . Men were blown high in the air. . . . No survivors could be seen in the water."*

With Japanese armor-piercing shells and super-powerful torpedoes on target, and the Allied formation broken, the ABDA force was in desperate trouble. Doorman swung his flagship in a wide arc, striving to realign his disordered formation. An order was transmitted to the British DD's, directing them to cover injured EXETER, and counterattack. Leading an attack on Jap cruiser JINTSU, the British destroyer ELECTRA was fatally struck by a blizzard of shells. Battered and burning, ELECTRA settled in a shroud of steam and smoke.

Now, at twilight, the whole seascape was fogged with the smoke of explosions, shellfire, and conflagration. The surface was littered with debris and streaked with oil. Intermittently the wakes of torpedo spreads came tracking through the water. The Allied destroyermen thought Jap submarines had entered the battle—another antagonist to worry about.

Two ships down, and as yet no visible damage to the enemy. Doorman finally jockeyed his cruisers into ragged formation, and swung them southward to escape torpedo broadsides and sharpshooting gunnery. Then, at 1806, he ordered the American destroyers to counterattack. DE RUYTER's radio had gone bad, and HOUSTON's TBS was out of kilter, so the order was flashed by blinker.

At once Division Commander Binford turned EDWARDS, ALDEN, FORD, and PAUL JONES northward to carry out the attack. As the destroyers were wheeling to face the foe,

Doorman flashed a countermanding order: CANCEL COUNTER-ATTACK.

The American destroyers were now (at last) positioned between the ABDA cruisers and the enemy. Commander Binford wondered if he were reading Doorman's signals aright. Came a third message: COVER MY RETIREMENT.

One method for covering a retirement was a sharp counterattack. With no time for crossword puzzles, Commander Binford ordered a strike at the oncoming enemy. Plunging northward through the smoke they had been laying, the American destroyers sighted Jap ships about 22,000 yards off to starboard.

Binford called for torpedoes—starboard salvos to be fired at 10,000-yard range. This was a long-range fire, but if he sent the old "four-pipers" any closer to the Jap cruisers, the Japs would massacre them.

After the firing of starboard salvos, Binford ordered reverse course, and EDWARDS, ALDEN, FORD, and PAUL JONES fired portside torpedoes. All torpedoes missed.

But the destroyers did something with their old 4-inch guns. The Jap destroyer ASAGUMO got a shell through her hull above the water line, and stopped dead with paralyzed engines. ALDEN's captain, Lieutenant Commander Coley, thought he saw a hit on one Jap warship's superstructure.

With torpedoes expended, Binford turned the American destroyers southward. At 1831 he caught a blinker message from Admiral Doorman: FOLLOW ME.

Binford stepped up speed to keep on the trail of the ABDA cruisers. The dusk was blackening, and the big guns had gone silent.

Doorman was trying to locate and intercept the convoy. For about an hour the ABDA force ran northward through the night. At 1930 enemy aircraft swooped overhead to drop parachute flares over the Allied cruisers. DE RUYTER's lookouts sighted Jap ships to port. Cruisers HOUSTON and PERTH opened fire, and the Japs answered with torpedo salvos.

Doorman swung his ships eastward and doubled back on a run south. The ABDA formation was trailed by enemy float planes which dropped more flares. By 2100 the Allied cruiser column was nearing shoal water just off the Java coast at a point about 50 miles west of Soerabaja. At this point Doorman made a sharp turn to the west. Out of torpedoes, low on fuel, and on the verge of engine breakdown, the American destroyer division dropped out of the race, and headed eastward for Soerabaja. As Binford reported it:

"Realizing that I had no more torpedoes and that further contact with the enemy would be useless, since my speed and

gunpowder were less than anything I would encounter. . . . I retired to Soerabaja."

A Jap plane trailed the exhausted "four-pipers," and dropped a flare on them as they maneuvered through the Soerabaja minefield. Silhouetted by this fiery chrysanthemum, the old grayhounds panted into the harbor.

Steaming on westward, Doorman led the diminished ABDA force into wholesale disaster. At 2125 the British destroyer JUPITER was ripped apart by a tremendous blast. Apparently she was sunk by a friendly mine.

Then, heading northward, the ABDA cruisers ran headlong into Jap cruisers NACHI and HAGURO. In bright moonlight both sides opened fire. Then the Japs launched torpedoes. Both DE RUYTER and JAVA were fatally blasted. By midnight it was all over. Doorman ordered cruisers HOUSTON and PERTH to retire to Batavia. Battered cruiser EXETER and destroyer ENCOUNTER made their way to Soerabaja. The Battle of the Java Sea was finished. And so was the Allied effort to hold the Netherlands East Indies.

If any scintilla of satisfaction could be dredged from the battle's Slough of Despond, it was the fact that one of Binford's old "four-pipers" fired the only damaging shot—a hit on Jap DD ASAGUMO.

In retiring to Soerabaja, EDWARDS, ALDEN, FORD, and PAUL JONES escaped a gruesome aftermath. Able to fuel, they were promptly dispatched by Admiral Glassford to Australia. As will be seen, they were more fortunate than their squadron mate POPE, ordered to proceed at a later date. By the time she left Soerabaja (evening of February 28) the Java Sea had become a molten crucible.

Cruisers USS HOUSTON and HMAS PERTH were caught by the enemy on the last night of February while attempting to escape the crucible through Soenda Strait between Java and Sumatra. Fighting to the last gun, both cruisers were hammered to the bottom.

HOUSTON's destruction was not the only heartbreaking sequel to the Java Sea defeat. Elsewhere the battered old-timers of DesRon 29 were overwhelmed by the conquering enemy.

Loss of USS EDSALL

In an effort to rush reinforcements to Java, American aircraft tender LANGLEY had been sunk during the afternoon of February 27, 1942. Her survivors had been picked up by escorting destroyers WHIPPLE (Lieutenant Commander E. S. Karpe) and EDSALL (Lieutenant J. J. Nix).

To relieve the two old "four-pipers" of LANGLEY's men,

the Navy oiler PECOS, Ceylon-bound from Tjilatjap, was directed to make rendezvous with EDSALL and WHIPPLE at a point off Christmas Island.

The destroyers met the tanker at the appointed spot on the morning of the 28th. The LANGLEY survivors were about to be transferred to PECOS when a flight of Jap land-based bombers came winging down from Java. Riding in WHIPPLE, Commander E. M. Crouch, ComDesDiv 57, ordered the ships on a southward run that took them out of range. The following day (March 1) the LANGLEY men were put on board PECOS, and the tanker parted company with the destroyers.

But about two hours after she separated from the destroyers, PECOS sighted (and was sighted by) a Jap aircraft-carrier plane. The tankermen knew they were in for it.

Two hours later (time: 1145) the enemy struck. Over the horizon came the bombers, three of them, to blast the tanker with a Japanese *blitz*.

The PECOS went under at 1548.

Casualties in the PECOS-LANGLEY disaster were heavy. The combined losses of both ships numbered about 50 men, and some 150 wounded. WHIPPLE rescued, and safely delivered in Freemantle, some 220.

Perhaps fatalities would have been fewer had the destroyer EDSALL too been able to answer PECOS' distress call. Where at that time was the EDSALL?

No one knows.

After parting company with PECOS and WHIPPLE on the morning of March 1, EDSALL headed in a northeasterly direction. Lieutenant Joshua J. Nix and his brave company went over the horizon—and into oblivion.

Was this lonely "four-piper" attacked and sunk by Jap carrier planes off the coast of Java—the same SORYU aircraft that bombed PECOS? That was the original supposition.

But after war's end, Navy investigators uncovered conflicting information. Interrogated by officers of the United States Naval Technical Mission to Japan, a number of Japanese naval officers stated that the EDSALL was overhauled and attacked by two battleships of Kondo's division and two cruisers of the Japanese Light Cruiser Squadron. A pair of SORYU bombers joined the onslaught. The American destroyer fought a hopeless action against this overwhelming force— an action that ended on the afternoon of March 1, 1942. According to this testimony (and reports in the War Diary of Japanese Battleship Division 3) EDSALL was finally sunk by gunfire from the battleships HIEI and KIRISHIMA.

A somber cloud of mystery veiled the destroyer's final hour. Of her crew of some 150 officers and men, there were no survivors. Not one of her company was mentioned in Japanese records, or located in a Japanese prison camp. It is seldom that a surface ship's entire complement is lost without trace. Such a casualty toll is usually associated with the loss of a submarine. Or it may be attributed to ruthless massacre.

It was not until the spring of 1952 that details of EDSALL's end came to light. On a dim strip of film taken by Japanese cruiser ASHIGARA—the cruiser firing pointblank at the trapped little ship. In grim shadow-drama she went down before the eyes of shocked investigators, who were subsequently led by the ASHIGARA clue to a forgotten South Pacific cemetery. There they found the graves of five unidentifiable destroyermen who had been prisoners of war—the sole survivors of EDSALL. Apparently they had been beheaded.

The EDSALL's tragedy was to have a counterpart in the loss of the destroyer PILLSBURY.

Loss of USS PILLSBURY

Out of torpedoes and in need of repair, destroyers PILLSBURY and PARROTT, withdrawn from the ABDA Striking Force, were still at Tjilatjap on the fatal morning of March 1 when Admiral Helfrich ordered the evacuation. At once Admiral Glassford directed all American naval vessels to leave the threatened harbor and clear for Exmouth Gulf, Australia.

PILLSBURY (Lieutenant Commander H. C. Pound) and PARROTT (Lieutenant J. N. Hughes) moved out with a nondescript little flotilla.

At best speed the ships headed southeastward into the morning light—a thousand miles to go to Australia and "down under." Only the two little minesweepers, the converted yacht, schooner LANIKAI, gunboat TULSA, and the destroyer PARROTT made it.

Somewhere off the Java Coast the USS PILLSBURY, U.S. gunboat ASHEVILLE, and Australian gunboat YARRA were overtaken by the warships of Admiral Kondo. Somewhere in that area of the Indian Ocean the American destroyer and the two gunboats fought their last battle against the mighty enemy which had driven the United States Asiatic Fleet out of the Philippines, and had shattered the ABDA fleet.

It is believed that PILLSBURY and ASHEVILLE, in a desperate night action, were sunk by three cruisers of the Japanese Fourth Cruiser Squadron and two destroyers of the Japanese Fourth Destroyer Division. Details of this battle are wholly lacking. After leaving Tjilatjap, PILLSBURY and ASHEVILLE steamed into oblivion deeper than that which enfolded

EDSALL. And scraps of information concerning them uncovered by the U.S. Naval Technical Mission after the war were vague and discrepant.

The gunboat and the old "four-piper" were blotted out. All hands were lost with ASHEVILLE. All hands were lost with PILLSBURY.

It is possible that in each case they went down in a ship smothered under a tempest of 8-inch shellfire. More probable that some of the crew members got overside, and were left adrift on life rafts and debris—overlooked (or ignored) by the rampaging enemy. No man was recovered.

Sinking of USS PILLSBURY raised American destroyer fatalities to three DD's lost in that disastrous Java evacuation. And still another DesRon 29 destroyer was to go down in the maelstrom. The old "four-piper" POPE.

Loss of USS POPE

POPE got away from Soerabaja in the evening of February 28, 1942. She slipped out through the minefields with HM cruiser EXETER and the British destroyer ENCOUNTER.

Rear Admiral A. F. E. Palliser, RN, had chosen the route for EXETER and her escorts. The crippled cruiser and the two DD's were ordered to pass to the east of Bawean Island, then head westward for a daylight run down the Java Sea to Sunda Strait. It was hoped the group could make an after-dark transit of this strait between Java and Sumatra, and thus escape into the Indian Ocean for a dash to Ceylon. It was a slim chance.

At 0750 the lookouts spotted two large warships bearing down on them from south-southwest.

In dazzling tropical daylight the fugitive Allied ships, in the middle of the Java Sea, were as exposed as a caravan in mid-desert. The enemy showed up as two heavy cruisers (CA's) accompanied by a destroyer. The CA's were the Imperial Navy's NACHI and HAGURO, under command of Rear Admiral T. Takagi—part of the force commanded by Vice Admiral Takahashi. The three Jap warships headed for EXETER, POPE, and ENCOUNTER.

EXETER's Captain O. L. Gordon, RN, ordered a northwesterly course-change, but escape in that direction was blocked. Northwest of the Allied ships, and racing to cut them off, was Admiral Takahashi's flagship group—heavy cruisers ASHIGARA and MYOKO, and three destroyers.

At 1020 the Allied ships opened fire on NACHI and HAGURO. IJN NACHI replied with her 8-inchers. With four heavy cruisers bearing down, a getaway to the westward was impossible. Captain Gordon swung his little group hard right on a radical course change, and they raced eastward along the Borneo coast.

There was no haven for the three Allied ships. No refuge. EXETER, POPE, and ENCOUNTER were trapped.

Unable to make better than 26 knots, they were soon overhauled by Takahashi's cruisers. As POPE and ENCOUNTER spread a screen of smoke in her wake. HMS EXETER exchanged shots with the enemy CA's. Thunder rolled across the brilliant sea, followed by the smash of bursting shells. The Jap closed the range to 18,000 yards—14,000 yards—near and nearer. EXETER's salvos were not hitting; her fire-control was out of kilter. Directed by a Jap spotter plane, Takahashi's gunners began to straddle, then to hit the British cruiser.

With the clocks approaching 1110, EXETER loosed a torpedo spread at ASHIGARA and MYOKO. About five minutes later POPE fired four torpedoes at these Japs. The long-range torpedo shots missed. Their guns blazing, a couple of Jap destroyers came racing in on EXETER's starboard. Covering the cruiser, USS POPE and HMS ENCOUNTER exchanged a blistering fire with these DD's. But the gun duel was hopelessly one-sided. About 1120 a shell smashed into one of EXETER's boiler-rooms. As she staggered in a haze of smoke and steam, all power lost, her main-battery and secondary-battery gun controls gave out. With her big guns silenced, she slowed to four knots.

Captain Gordon ordered ENCOUNTER and POPE to run for it. The British and the American destroyer kept on going. As Jap shells pounded the stricken EXETER and Jap torpedoes reached for her in a murderous fan, Captain Gordon ordered his cruisermen to abandon. They had just gone overside when a torpedo—one of the 18 fired by the Jap destroyers—struck EXETER a mortal smash. The British cruiser capsized and went down.

A few minutes later HMS ENCOUNTER received a fatal hit. She, too, was abandoned to sink under a tempest of smoke and fire. That left USS POPE, alone, in a sea of enemies.

And for a moment it looked as though Fate might deal valor the fair rewards. About 1145 an opaque rainsquall swept the seascape ahead. Commander W. C. Blinn called upon his engineers to force the last possible turn out of the turbines. Unreeling a wall of smoke behind her, the old DD dashed for the cloudburst. Enemy shells sent up geysers around her, and explosions thundered in her wake. Somehow she made it.

The rainsquall blotted her from sight; gave her a breathing spell. As she panted along through the squall, her crew had time to rush ammunition to depleted handling rooms and ready boxes; her Damage Control Officer, Lieutenant R. H. Antrim, was able to manage a few emergency repairs. He could do nothing for the brick walls of No. 3 boiler, which had collapsed from concussion; otherwise he found the battle damage fairly light.

On the bridge, Blinn was heartened to see the enemy had faded out astern. POPE emerged from the rainsquall, raced across a patch of open sea, and plunged into a second downpour. Maybe they could elude pursuit; keep going east along the coast of Borneo, then, after nightfall, race south, and sprint through Lombok Strait.

But luck was not in the cards for POPE. When the second rainsquall dissolved, POPE was once more exposed under a noonday sky of tropic blue. The Borneo sun glared mercilessly down—and so did the pilot of a cruiser-carried Japanese plane.

The Jap spotter sent out a call. The call was answered by six dive-bombers from the carrier RYUJO, at that time about 100 miles due west. At 1230 the dive-bombers had the target in their sights. The hour had struck for USS POPE.

She squared away to fight with her single 3-inch anti-aircraft gun. The rackety old weapon held the Japs off for 75 rounds. Then its recoil system jammed; it would not return to battery.

At 1250 Commander Blinn ordered the crew overside. Officers and bluejackets quit the ship in good order, taking their assigned places in the destroyer's motor whaleboat and on life rafts. Finally the demolition crew abandoned.

Just as all hands stood clear, a pattern of shells splashed around the doomed vessel. The Jap cruisers had overhauled her again. So it was a cruiser salvo which sent the old "four-piper" under. An 8-inch shell found the mark, delivered the killing blow. In a shroud of smoke and steam the USS POPE went down by the stern.

Winging low across the water, a Jap seaplane skimmed over the motor whaleboat. Enraged, several of the survivors opened fire on the plane with a Browning automatic. The shooting gave the Japs an excuse to strafe the survivors, and they made the most of it. For about 30 minutes the angered seaplane and companion aircraft stunted over the whaleboat and the rafts, lashing at them with machine-gun fire. By some miracle, no one was killed.

And miraculously enough, no one of POPE's crew had been killed in the murderous battle with Takahashi's cruiser force and the RYUJO's bombers. The assailed destroyer did not suffer a single fatality through enemy action. Only one member of the crew was lost—a man killed by a demolition charge.

The miracle was to persist. Throughout the afternoon of March 1—and the following day, and the day after that—for nearly three days, the little clutter of rafts and the whaleboat carrying the POPE survivors were adrift on the Java Sea. Not an officer or man succumbed to this ordeal. On the third night of it, a Japanese destroyer hove over the horizon. All hands were picked up—151, including Commander Blinn.

Made prisoners of war, the POPE survivors were treated with fair consideration by the Jap destroyer's crew. They were landed at Makassar City, Celebes; then transferred to a former Dutch concentration camp where conditions were somewhat improved. Commander Blinn, along with a number of officers from POPE, EXETER, ENCOUNTER, and PERTH, was eventually shipped to Japan. Of the 151 POPE survivors, 27 men died in Java or Celebes during the war. Malnutrition.

Destroyer POPE was awarded a Presidential Unit Citation. But accolades hardly measure the valor of such a captain and crew.

The battle fought by the old "four-piper" brought the curtain down on the ABDAFLOAT effort. When Takahashi's cruisers opened fire on her at the last, the USS POPE was the last Allied man-of-war on the Java Sea.

Chapter 10

Pacific Stand

☆ ☆ ☆

Holding the Pacific Line

Japanese chauvinists had a grandiose term for it—*"Hakko Ichiu."* Which means "bringing the eight corners of the world under one roof."

Erecting a Japanese pagoda-roof over just the Orient was going to be a job. One corner of the imperial edifice could be anchored in Manchuria, perhaps, and another might be anchored in Burma or Malaya. But Japan's grand strategists were baffled by the oceanic side of the structure. How far eastward should it extend? Could Australia be appropriated for a bastion? Could Hawaii be taken for a mid-ocean cornerstone?

Admiral Isoroku Yamamoto advocated an interesting plan. It was aggressive, colorful, complex enough to be militarily impressive, and just plausible enough to make it seem feasible and worthwhile. The Admiral stuck a thumbtack in Midway Island. He stuck another far to the north in the Aleutians. On a blueprint it was all so easy.

The American and Allied strategists on their part produced some down-to-earth plans designed to frustrate "Hakko Ichiu."

The United States Pacific Fleet was to carry out two primary missions. First, it was to hold the line of an Allied defense frontier which extended from Dutch Harbor in the Aleutians to Midway in the Central Pacific, from Midway to Samoa in the South Pacific, and from Samoa through the Fijis to the New Hebrides lying east of the Solomons. Second, the Pacific Fleet was to maintain a United States-Australia supply line which extended from the American west coast to Hawaii, from Hawaii to the Samoan group, and from Samoa to Australia.

This side of the world is nearly all sea. So the defense and maintenance of those long, thin lines across miles of open ocean was up to the U.S. Navy—a dual mission to stagger the imagination of any naval strategist. Look at those shipping routes! Look at those vast expanses of salt water. Destroyers were demanded, and at once. Destroyers to guard the convoys; destroyers to screen the task groups; destroyers to patrol off Dutch Harbor and Midway, off Oahu and Samoa; destroyers to guard the waters off eastern Australia, and the sea lanes down under. And to fight an all-out anti-submarine war—this last a primary mission of DesPac (Destroyers Pacific).

The South, Central, and North Pacific—that was a large order. But the destroyermen notched in their belts, spat on their hands, and pitched in.

JARVIS *and* LONG *Down* I-23

On January 28, 1942, an enemy submarine was detected in the waters off Pearl Harbor. The destroyer JARVIS (Commander W. R. Thayer) and destroyer-minesweepers LONG, TREVER, and ELLIOT were soon hot on the undersea marauder's trail.

At 1447 JARVIS picked up sound contact. She presently lost it—regained it—lost it—picked it up once more—lost it again. But at 1710 the ex-destroyer LONG (Lieutenant Commander W. S. Veeder) tagged the sub with an echo-ranging "ping." Five minutes later JARVIS reestablished contact. JARVIS and LONG then teamed up to deliver a joint attack. At 1721 the destroyer dropped a booming depth-charge pattern. The old destroyer-sweeper followed through with a pattern at 1724.

An hour later both ships were once more on target, maneuvering in for a second go. Over went the successive patterns; the sea absorbed the charges; then, at 1839, two delayed explosions rumbled up from down under.

That evening the destroyermen, combing the surface for evidence, sighted dark patches of oil. JARVIS and LONG had disposed of the Japanese submarine I-23. As one of Captain K. Imaizumi's group, she had been with Admiral Nagumo's fleet in the great raid on Pearl Harbor. Her January visit was by way of a return to the scene of the crime. Only this time crime did not pay.

Battle of the Coral Sea

From January to May 1942 the mid-Pacific front was like a volcano quietly boiling. No monster explosion, but the Jap advance spreading like lava, and a major eruption in the making.

During this ominous prelude to a showdown, DesPac destroyers served in Halsey's ENTERPRISE task force staging pioneer raids on the Marshalls, the Gilberts and Wake Island. They steamed with carrier LEXINGTON projecting a strike at Rabaul—the Jap advance base in the Bismarcks. They escorted carrier HORNET in the Doolittle "Shangri La" air strike that stunned Tokyo in mid-April.

Some memorable "cans" were in on these early missions. Mark the names of a few. BLUE, HUGHES, SIMS, WALKE, MEREDITH, MCCALL, RALPH TALBOT, BALCH, MAURY, BAGLEY, HULL, DALE, PATTERSON. They fired a few shots and smacked some Jap planes. Sparring. The big fight was coming.

It came when the Japs decided to seize the Solomons and eastern New Guinea flanking Australia. And sent carriers SHOKAKU, ZUIKAKU and light carrier SHOHO to the area.

A convoy loaded with Imperial Marines steamed into Tulagi Harbor in the Solomons on the 4th of May. The invaders were unaware of the fact, but they were touching off the showdown sea-air engagement which was to halt the Japanese juggernaut in the South Pacific Entering Tulagi, the Jap Marines lit the fuse to the Battle of the Coral Sea.

Equally unaware of the drama impending were the American destroyermen serving in MORRIS, PERKINS, HAMMANN, ANDERSON, WALKE, and SIMS, at that date operating in the Coral Sea with Admiral Fletcher's Task Force 17—a formidable force built of carrier YORKTOWN and cruisers ASTORIA, CHESTER, PORTLAND, and CHICAGO.

Also in the Coral Sea was Task Force 11 (Rear Admiral Aubrey W. Fitch), containing the aircraft carrier LEXINGTON, cruisers MINNEAPOLIS and NEW ORLEANS, and destroyers PHELPS, DEWEY, AYLWIN, FARRAGUT, and MONAGHAN.

The YORKTOWN and LEXINGTON forces were fueling when word had come on May 2 that the Japs were mustering strength for a drive on Port Moresby at the southern tip of New Guinea just a jump away from Australia.

Admiral Fletcher gathered his forces in the Coral Sea to combat the enemy drive. At this juncture Task Force 11 combined with Task Force 17. Fletcher organized the force in three combatant groups:—an Attack Group of cruisers and destroyers to engage the enemy's surface forces; a Support Group of cruisers and destroyers to cover the carriers; and an Air Group composed of YORKTOWN, LEXINGTON, and destroyer screen. A fueling and a search group complemented the combatant groups.

Informed on some of the movements of Inoue's ships, and deducing others, Admiral Fletcher headed the Allied task force in a northwesterly direction. On the evening of the 6th he detached the tanker NEOSHO and her escorting de-

stroyer Sims, ordering them over the southward horizon. The
following morning he dispatched Admiral Crace's Support
Group, plus destroyer Farragut, to Jomard Passage in the
Louisiades to block the Jap vanguard there. With the rest of
his force, he continued northward.

He was huntingq big game, and he found it. About 0845
that morning of May 7 American scouting planes spotted a
portion of the Jap Occupation Force north of Misima Island
in the Louisiades. And the portion spotted was a sizable one.
It included several transports and the light carrier Shoho.

Mistakenly the Shoho was identified as a large carrier,
and the scouts thought they saw a second carrier in this
vanguard. Hoping for a crack at Shokaku, the "York" and
"Lex" airmen took off at rocket speed. Because of an incor-
rectly coded contact report, some 92 American planes were
sent winging northwestward. A report from Australian land-
based aircraft eventually steered them to the waters off
Misima Island where they located the targets at about 1130.

The few Zero fighters that rose to intercept were brushed
aside as though they were flies. While Shoho reeled in frantic
circles, trying to escape destruction, the "York" and "Lex"
dive-bombers plastered the flat-top with an explosive rain
that left the ship a listing, burning Ark.

The demolishment of Shoho and the appearance of Allied
warships near Jomard Passage induced Admiral Inoue to call
off the Port Moresby expedition. The remnant Occupation
Force was already retiring northward. The Shokaku-Zuikaku
Striking Force was farther from home, however. Having
rounded the eastern end of the Solomons chain, it was by this
time well south of Guadalcanal. And while aircraft from
Yorktown and Lexington had been flying destruction to
the Japanese carrier Shoho, planes from Shokaku and
Zuikaku had been dealing death to the destroyer Sims.

Loss of USS Sims

During the night of May 6-7 the Japanese Striking Force
with Shokaku and Zuikaku had run steadily southward in the
Coral Sea to a point about 250 miles due south of Guadalcanal. And as misty daylight sifted through the overcast, the
Jap carriers launched scouting planes to search for the Allied
force reported in the area. These planes spotted Sims and
Neosho, ships detached and sent southward, presumably out
of reach of the enemy.

After the war it was learned that the Jap scouts identified
Neosho as a carrier—all that was needed to bring from
Shokaku and Zuikaku a flock of fighters and bombers 70
strong. When the first wave roared over the horizon the

American destroyermen and tankermen knew they were in for it.

In the opening attack, Jap marksmanship was lacklustre. About 0910 a bomb intended for SIMS landed in the water a goodly yardage to port, and showered her with nothing but brine. The destroyer and the tanker dodged and dashed out from under the assault.

Twenty minutes later 16 high-level bombers attacked in two waves. Again, no hits. But at 1130 a flight of 24 dive-bombers came hurtling down from the ceiling, and SIMS was plunged into what was to be her final battle.

Her anti-aircraft guns rattled, slammed and crashed. Flame splattered the sky, and into the sea fell a tattered plane. Then the dive-bombers were on top of the destroyer. Several of them were gunned out of the air; two or three, unable to pull out of screaming power dives, were blasted into extinction by their own bombs. But SIMS took three back-breaking hits. Not long after the third direct hit, she broke in two and sank in a pall of smoke and steam. Only 14 of her crew survived the sinking. Lost with the rest was SIMS' Commanding Officer, Lieutenant Commander W. M. Hyman.

The Battle of the Coral Sea (Continued)

Destroyer SIMS was not alone in her agony. Struck by a spate of bombs and a burning plane, the tanker NEOSHO was reduced to a floating wreck. A helpless derelict, she drifted for four days before she was located by the destroyer HENLEY (Commander Robert Hall Smith), dispatched on the 8th to the rescue. After the tankermen and SIMS survivors were taken off, HENLEY sank NEOSHO's charred hulk with a pair of torpedoes. All told, she rescued 14 destroyermen and 109 tanker sailors.

Some 176 of NEOSHO's crew were fatalities. Sixty-eight had abandoned ship on a float fashioned of four life rafts fastened together. For ten days this wretched party was adrift. When destroyer HELM (Lieutenant Commander C. E. Carroll) finally located the float, only four men were found alive.

In the meantime the Battle of the Coral Sea thundered on to its climax. On the afternoon of May 7 Admiral Crace's Support Group, which included destroyers PERKINS, WALKE, and FARRAGUT, was attacked south of the Louisiades where it had been sent to block Jomard Passage.

By late afternoon of the 7th it became apparent that the numerous aerial "pips" showing up on carrier radar screens must be planes from a Jap carrier force near at hand. American Wildcats, boring through the cloudy ceiling, intercepted some Zeros and carrier-type dive-bombers. The SHOKAKU-ZUIKAKU force was at that hour no more than 30 miles distant!

Admiral Fitch urged a night attack by cruisers and destroyers—strike in the dark. His proposal was vetoed by Admiral Fletcher, who directed that an all-out air assault be made the following morning. To this end Fletcher ordered the American Air Group southward to widen the range. Simultaneously the Jap carrier force made a northward run. However, the Jap force reversed course early in the morning of May 8. By daybreak the Jap carriers had reached a point about 250 miles southwest of Guadalcanal. Farther to the southwest, the American Air Group was some 170 miles distant from the Jap.

The enemy, under a front of clouds, had the better position; YORKTOWN and LEXINGTON were steaming beneath sunny skies. Both forces sent out scout planes at dawn. Japanese and American carriers were soon detected by the competing scouts, and at 0900 the opposing carriers launched attack squadrons. From the "YORK" and the "LEX" a total of 82 planes took off; some 70 soared away from SHOKAKU and ZUIKAKU. These enemy squadrons passed each other without making contact, and both were on target at about 1100 of that morning.

Planes from YORKTOWN pounded on SHOKAKU and disabled her with a blasting. "LEX" planes dealt ZUIKAKU a clawing that laid this second carrier up for a month.

While the planes from YORKTOWN and LEXINGTON were hammering at the Jap flat-tops, aircraft from SHOKAKU and ZUIKAKU were concentrating their heaviest onslaught on LEXINGTON, the larger of the two American carriers. Maneuvering to evade the attacks, YORKTOWN and LEXINGTON took divergent courses which led them three or four miles apart. Bulk of the cruiser escort (ASTORIA, PORTLAND, and CHESTER) went with YORKTOWN, drawing with it destroyers RUSSELL, PHELPS, HAMMANN, and AYLWIN. This left LEXINGTON to bear the battle's brunt with cruisers MINNEAPOLIS and NEW ORLEANS, and destroyers MORRIS, ANDERSON, and DEWEY.

Skillful ship-handling brought YORKTOWN unscathed through three torpedo attacks. But her crew was fighting painful battle damage when the final attack was over.

Less fortunate was the LEXINGTON. In spite of masterful maneuvering by Captain F. C. ("Ted") Sherman, the great carrier, assailed by torpedo-planes from port and starboard, took two portside hits. Then dive-bombers whistled down to puncture the ship with near misses and stagger her with two direct hits. A 1,000-pound bomb smashed the port forward battery, and another bomb exploded inside the carrier's funnel. Severely wounded, the "Lex" carried on. A sudden series of explosions shook the damaged carrier and touched off raging internal fires.

That danger was more than apparent to the captain and crew of Morris. Alongside the huge smoke-hazed carrier, the little DD was nuzzling a rumbling volcano. Nevertheless Commander Jarrett and his destroyermen coolly went about their business, passing lines through the billowing smudge, and taking aboard the carriermen who came down the ship's side.

At 1707 Admiral Fitch ordered Captain Sherman to abandon. Admiral Kinkaid, placed in charge of rescue operations, sent destroyers Anderson (Lieutenant Commander Ginder) and Hammann (Commander True) to join Morris alongside the carrier and take off survivors. Cruisers Minneapolis and New Orleans also moved in to stand by.

It took adroit conning to maneuver alongside this floating Vesuvius. The water around was crowded with rafts and swimmers. On a thread-like maze of lines men were sliding down the ship's side. Jockeying this way and that, destroyers Morris, Anderson, and Hammann had to move with the precision of figure skaters to avoid colliding with rafts, the burning carrier, and each other.

At 1720 Admiral Kinkaid ordered destroyer Hammann around to the carrier's starboard side to rescue swimmers and men on rafts. By expert conning, Commander True worked his destroyer through the clotted sea without upsetting rafts or running down swimmers, and Ensigns T. E. Krepski and R. L. Holton shoved off in Hammann's boats to snatch drowning officers and bluejackets from the seething water.

Having picked up nearly 100 men, Hammann was just backing clear, her deck crowded with survivors, when a tremendous explosion in Lexington showered the destroyer with firebrands. The debris fouled Hammann's circulating pumps, slowing her back-up. But no one was injured.

About 1800 Captain Sherman with a few last-standers quit the ship. They were the last to leave. Of the Lexington's complement of nearly 3,000, all but 26 officers and 190 men survived the gruelling ordeal of battle, inferno, and abandonment. So far as could be determined, not a carrierman was drowned in the maelstrom overside.

At 1853 the destroyer Phelps (Lieutenant Commander Beck) was directed to sink the Lexington with torpedo fire. Five torpedoes were shot at the abandoned carrier; four exploded against her smoldering hull. About an hour later the great ship listed over and went down to the accompaniment of last tremendous explosions.

The Battle of the Coral Sea signaled a tidal turn in the

South Pacific. The Japanese drive below the equator had been stopped.

Battle-cost to the Allies was heavy—carrier LEXINGTON, destroyer SIMS, fleet oiler NEOSHO; YORKTOWN badly damaged; death toll of 543 officers and men.

But the Japanese paid for their eastward trespassing with the light carrier SHOHO, destroyer KIKUZUKI; SHOKAKU crippled; ZUIKAKU's wings plucked; OKINASHIMA disabled; death toll of some 900 officers and men. "Hakko Ichiu" was proving costly.

The Battle of Midway

The Jap drive at Midway was planned as a haymaker to break America's mid-Pacific line. Yamamoto's armada included 10 battleships, 5 carriers, some 18 cruisers, 57 destroyers, 3 seaplane tenders, and various auxiliaries. A number of submarines operated with this immense fleet, and it was supported by aircraft from the Marshall Islands and the Marianas.

The Admiral assumed that he could capture Midway almost without a fight. He knew that LEXINGTON and YORKTOWN had been plastered with bombs; it seemed possible that both carriers had been sunk. The Admiral was also informed that carriers HORNET and ENTERPRISE were in the South Pacific, and that SARATOGA in Puget Sound was still undergoing repair. With all American aircraft carriers in the Pacific thus accounted for, it appeared easy for KAGA, AKAGI, HIRYU and SORYU, plus light carrier ZUIHO and the battleships and cruisers, to wipe out anything that stood between them and Midway.

Yamamoto's information was far from accurate. YORKTOWN was neither sunk nor damaged beyond the possibility of high-speed repairs. ENTERPRISE and HORNET were not so far afield in the South Pacific that they could not steam to the Midway area by the third day in June. Still, three carriers, one of them shaky from an emergency repair job, were heavily outnumbered by five.

Admiral Nimitz was unable to scrape up any battleships for Midway's defense. In addition to the three carriers, just eight cruisers, 16 destroyers, and a couple of fleet oilers completed the American surface force at Midway. A total of some 33 United States ships facing the Japanese armada of 100!

Two big advantages the Americans had. Nimitz knew that Yamamoto was coming. Knew it from carefully assembled fragments of information, reports from here and there. So the Japanese lunge at Midway was robbed of surprise.

The other American advantage was radar. Not all of the

ships had it, but enough of them, including the carriers, were so equipped. Whereas the Japs did not begin to install radar in any of their ships until the following August.

Exploding on June 3, 1942, and ending on June 6, the Battle of Midway was a long-range air engagement, similar to the Battle of the Coral Sea. A detailed account of this stupendous carrier duel—one of the crucial naval battles of all time, and perhaps the decisive battle of the Pacific War—cannot be included in this destroyer history. But briefly—things did not go according to Yamamoto's plans. Nimitz was not deceived by an Aleutian strike made on the morning of June 3. That same morning the Jap armada was spotted 700 miles off Midway by an air scout. Then, an American submarine sighted the Japanese Occupation Force. On the night of the 3rd, the armada was hit by planes from Midway.

About dawn of June 4 Jap air scouts sighted the ENTER-PRISE-HORNET-YORKTOWN threat on the horizon. The word was flashed to the Jap Striking Force. Carriers KAGA, AKAGI, HIRYU, and SORYU were promptly headed northeastward to intercept the American carriers.

Wild air battles exploded over the Japanese Striking Force as planes from HORNET, ENTERPRISE and YORKTOWN attacked.

While KAGA, AKAGI, and SORYU were transformed from carriers into catafalques, YORKTOWN, some 200 miles away, was attacked. YORKTOWN spotted the attackers on her radar screen, and a dozen of her fighters soared to meet the foe.

YORKTOWN was hit, but her damage-controlmen soon had fires and wreckage in hand. Within two hours the carrier was capable of 20 knots, and her planes were returning to her flight deck. Suddenly the radar screen picked up another flock of enemy "bogies." Up went YORKTOWN fighters to intercept, but before they could do so, the Japs were within striking range of the flat-top.

These were torpedo-planes from HIRYU—some 16 or so—escorted by the usual cordon of vicious Zeros. They ran into a curtain of fire from the AA guns of the carrier and of destroyers HAMMANN, RUSSELL, MORRIS, ANDERSON, and HUGHES. In less than six minutes all 16 torpedo-planes were consumed as so much confetti tossed into a furnace.

But before they died, four of them slipped torpedoes into the water within range of YORKTOWN. Striking her on her port side amidships, two of the torpedoes blew huge holes in the carrier's hull, jolting her with immense explosions that left her listing and reeling. With white smoke gushing from her stacks, the great flat-top swung in a helpless circle, her lights blown out, her flight deck canted, the ocean pouring in below decks.

The guardian destroyers closed in around her. YORKTOWN's damage-controlmen could do nothing to stem the inrushing flood. The port list increased to an angle that threatened an imminent overturn. Fearing his ship would capsize at any moment, Captain Elliott Buckmaster gave the order to abandon. The destroyers moved forward to pick up the men who came sliding down the carrier's tilted deck.

As for YORKTOWN, she remained stubbornly afloat. Presently she was on a tow line tethered to the American mine-sweeper VIREO, dispatched to haul her home to Pearl Harbor. Two destroyers arrived on the scene that afternoon to assist the smoldering carrier—USS GWIN (Commander Higgins) and USS MONAGHAN (Lieutenant Commander Burford).

Yamamoto still had at hand his Main Body—six battleships, light carrier ZUIHO, a cruiser division, and a squadron of destroyers. Led by mighty super-battleship YAMATO, this force would have been facing two weary American carrier groups whose air complements were sorely depleted and whose surface crews were ready to drop from exhaustion. But Yamamoto was unwilling to risk his Main Body, much less his own carcass, and at 2200 on June 4 he ordered his forces to retire.

By the time GWIN's salvage party boarded YORKTOWN the residue of Yamamoto's armada was fleeing westward, pursued by American planes. This denouement permitted the dispatch of more destroyers to the aid of YORKTOWN. That night Captain Buckmaster arrived on the scene with BALCH (Lieutenant Commander Tiemroth), BENHAM (Lieutenant Commander Worthington), and HAMMANN (Commander True), the DD's under command of Captain Sauer in BALCH. With the coming of daylight (June 6) a salvage crew boarded the smoldering YORKTOWN.

Captain Buckmaster believed his ship could be saved, and he sent HAMMANN in on the starboard side of the drifting vessel to assist the fire-fighters and to furnish power for fire-fighting apparatus. One gang went to work pumping out some flooded compartments and flooding others to shift the water below decks and bring the ship on even keel. Another gang fought the fires. Others labored at repairs.

By early afternoon the salvage work was showing results. YORKTOWN's list had been reduced. HAMMANN, secured alongside, was steadily pumping, and the carrier's internal fires were being smothered. At 1530 they were winning the fight. At 1535 all was lost.

"Torpedo!"

Four watery lightning-streaks sped into view on YORKTOWN's starboard side. Two torpedoes hit her directly below her island, smashing through the hull as though it were eggshell. And one torpedo struck the HAMMANN. An enormous cloud of smoke billowed skyward, and the two ships, side by side, were mortally stricken.

The time was 1536.

The Battle of Midway had exploded its aftermath.

Loss of USS HAMMANN

The submarine that torpedoed YORKTOWN and HAMMANN in the afternoon of June 6 was the I-168. Executing an unquestionably daring attack, she struck the deadliest blow the Japs were able to deal to the United States surface forces at Midway.

HAMMANN did not go down alone. At 0701 the following morning, YORKTOWN capsized and sank. These were the only United States men-of-war lost in the Battle of Midway—one aircraft carrier, and one destroyer.

The battle cost the Imperial Japanese Navy four aircraft carriers and a couple of cruisers.

PART THREE

Holding the Oceanic Front

☆ ☆ ☆

But here are men who fought in gallant actions
As gallantly as ever heroes fought. . . .

BYRON

Chapter 11

Convoy Escorts versus Wolfpacks

(July-December 1942)

☆ ☆ ☆

All-Out U-Boat Drive

In the summer and autumn of 1942 the U-boats stepped up the offensive against Atlantic shipping. They struck at every convoy that crossed in August 1942. They turned the Murmansk Run into a murder relay. They harried the sea lanes from Labrador to Brazil.

Attacking Atlantic shipping on all fronts, the wolfpacks sank some 88 Allied vessels in September 1942. Much of this tonnage went down in areas under American control. But American escorts were still short of A/S equipment, training, and experience.

One of the heavy losers that autumn was North Atlantic Convoy SC-100. Ambushed during a three-day storm, and attacked by a pack that numbered at least seven U-boats, the 24-ship convoy had to fight tempest as well as torpedoes. The running battle began on September 20, and ended two nights later. The escorts, among them United States Coast Guard cutters SPENCER and CAMPBELL, under command of Captain P. R. Heineman, put up a vigorous defense. But the convoy was unable to keep formation in the storm. Four ships, two of them stragglers, were struck and downed by torpedo salvos.

The cutters sighted the U-boats, but were unable to overhaul, and the enemy escaped in high seas. Apparently the U-boats employed *Pillenwerfer* to thwart sonar contact.

Not long after the attack on Convoy SC-100, westbound Convoy ON-127 was ambushed. Seven ships were torpedoed and sunk in the battle that ensued.

Although troop convoys were priority targets for U-boat torpedoes, they escaped submarine attack because of two factors: speed and strong escortage. Deprived of these, the troopers were as vulnerable to wolfpack assault as any other type of shipping. Late in the summer of 1942, Convoy SG-6, impeded by slow ships and insufficient escort was hard hit at the cost of Army transport CHATHAM.

However, from July until the last of December 1942, troop convoys crossed to Britain in a steady procession. They were escorted by Task Force 37 (Rear Admiral L. C. Davidson) composed of cruiser PHILADELPHIA, battleship NEW YORK, and six to twelve destroyers, and Task Force 38 (Captain C. F. Bryant, Jr.) consisting of battleship ARKANSAS, cruiser BROOKLYN, and seven to eleven DD's. Anywhere from eight to fifteen transports were in convoy. Not a ship was torpedoed.

Two serious voyage disasters marred the record, however. The first was visited upon Task Force 37, and resulted in calamitous destroyer casualties. The second ruined a large transport in a convoy escorted by Task Force 38.

Loss of USS INGRAHAM

The disaster which overtook the destroyer INGRAHAM furnishes a striking example of the fatal chain-of-events sometimes unleashed by a trivial happenstance or minor incident.

At 0623 in the morning of August 22, 1942, eastbound convoy AT-20, under escort of Task Force 37, was standing seaward from Halifax Harbor. There were ten ships in the troop convoy. Accompanying PHILADELPHIA and NEW YORK, nine destroyers made up the escort group. Screen Commander was Captain J. B. Heffernan with his pennant in the destroyer BUCK.

At 2205 the flag destroyer BUCK received orders over TBS (voice radio) from Commander Task Force 37 to go close aboard the LETITIA and escort her to her proper station 1000 yards on cruiser PHILADELPHIA's starboard beam. The smother was so opaque that BUCK, running on radar ranges and bearings, was ordered to use her bull horn to direct LETITIA to her proper station as she shifted position in the shuffled screen.

At 2225, as BUCK was crossing through the column, a ship loomed out of the fog only 30 yards from the destroyer's beam. The lookout's shout was drowned by a grinding crash as the transport AWATEA rammed BUCK in the starboard quarter. The transport's steep bow almost sheared off the destroyer's fantail. Dislodged from its arbor, a 300-pound depth charge hurtled from a K-gun and exploded near BUCK's churning propellers. BUCK reeled away, dragging a wrecked stern.

A moment later the damaged destroyer heard a thunderous explosion—a tremendous blast that tinted the fog off to starboard where the fleet oiler CHEMUNG (Commander J. J. Twomey) had been steaming. BUCK's bridge personnel and

Screen Commander Heffernan thought the CHEMUNG had been torpedoed.

The eruption, however, was that of a destroyer blowing up. Disaster had ricochetted to strike the USS INGRAHAM as her captain, Commander W. M. Haynsworth, maneuvered her through the BUCK-AWATEA collision, INGRAHAM had steamed directly across the bow of the CHEMUNG, and the fleet oiler had run into the destroyer headlong.

The destroyer's entire crew was nearly immolated, only ten men and one officer escaped the bursting warship. Commander Haynsworth was lost with the others.

The destroyer BRISTOL was directed to escort the injured ships back to port. Convoy AT-20 continued eastward. Altogether, it had been ravaged as though by a wolfpack battle. Destroyer INGRAHAM sunk with heavy casualties. Destroyer BUCK severely damaged. Tanker CHEMUNG badly damaged. Transport AWATEA crippled and forced to turn back. Four ships, plus destroyer BRISTOL (necessarily detached), deleted from the convoy at one stroke. And perhaps none of it would have occurred if an inexperienced sonar man had not mistaken a school of porpoises for an enemy submarine.

Fire At Sea! (Escorts to the Rescue of Transport WAKEFIELD)

Naturally, the best accident "insurance" is the prevention that stops trouble before it starts. Next best is the prompt alarm and immediate response by well-trained trouble shooters and rescue crews. Catastrophes result when accidents are allowed to get out of hand through blunder.

Fire, for example. On board transport WAKEFIELD, the ex-luxury liner MANHATTAN. Under captaincy of Commander H. G. Bradbury, USCG, she was making the westward passage, United Kingdom to New York, as a member of Convoy TA-18, escorted by Task Force 38 (Captain C. F. Bryant, Jr.).

WAKEFIELD was crowded to capacity with some 1,000 civilian construction workers from camps in the British Isles. Fire broke out late in the afternoon of September 3, 1942, when the convoy was little more than a day's run out of New York.

At 1830 lookouts on the escorting cruiser BROOKLYN saw a cloud of gray smoke surge from WAKEFIELD's superstructure, directly below the bridge. WAKEFIELD hoisted the signal, "I am on fire!" and turned to port to clear the formation and put the fire to leeward. Task Force Commander Bryant ordered destroyers MAYO and NIBLACK to screen the burning ship. He then slowed the convoy to maneuver in WAKEFIELD's vicinity.

Meantime, the destroyer MAYO (Lieutenant Commander F. S. Habecker) obtained permission to leave her patrol station on WAKEFIELD's flank and also go to the transport's assistance. Clouds of hot smoke and steam gushed from the liner's leeward side, and the flames amidships had driven several hundred passengers to the ship's bow. Some twice that number were congregated on her after decks. Fortunately the sea was calm; the liner lolled on easy ground swells, and MAYO, closing in at 1900, was able to come alongside.

First to reach the WAKEFIELD, the destroyer sidled under the liner's port bow and grappled for rope ladders which had been lowered to serve as gangways from ship to ship. WAKEFIELD's passengers swayed nimbly across to the destroyer's deck. In 17 minutes MAYO took off 247 men.

Cruiser BROOKLYN reached the burning ship at 1907, maneuvering to bring her starboard bow alongside WAKEFIELD's port quarter. Three lines were tossed from BROOKLYN's forward deck to the transport's after deck, and WAKEFIELD's abandon-ship nets were hauled over by the cruisermen. At 1927 the cruiser cast off with some 800 of WAKEFIELD's passengers. About 300 men remained on board the liner, whose captain believed the fire could be brought under control.

But as MAYO and BROOKLYN headed away, stack-high towers of flame swirled up from the liner's superstructure. The Task Force Commander ordered BROOKLYN to stand by as MAYO, crowded to capacity, rejoined the convoy and the destroyer MADISON (Commander W. B. Ammon) left formation to cover the cruiser.

With the fire now going like a volcano, WAKEFIELD's captain gave the order to abandon, and signalled BROOKLYN to come alongside her stern.

MADISON moved in on the liner's port bow. In a few minutes the destroyer picked up 80 men from the drifting lifeboats. The rest of WAKEFIELD's crew scrambled across the nets to BROOKLYN's forward deck.

As a fire-rescue feat this cooperative performance by cruiser and destroyers was tops. Operations had gone without a hitch. That over 1,400 men had been snatched from the inferno without a single fatality speaks well for the Navy's training and discipline.

And by way of an epilogue, WAKEFIELD herself was subsequently saved. Destroyer MADISON stood by the abandoned liner until noon of September 5. Early in the morning of the 5th, destroyers RADFORD and MURPHY arrived from Halifax. A few hours later two tugs arrived from Portland, escorted by Coast Guard cutter CAMPBELL. By the 7th several more vessels were on the job, and WAKEFIELD was towed into Halifax on the 8th. Then the fire was finally overcome, and by spring of 1944 the transport was back in service again.

INGHAM *Kills* U-626 *(One Depth Charge, One Sub!)*

The last U-boat destroyed by American agency in 1942 fell prey to a United States Coast Guard cutter on December 15. And the manner of that destruction was exemplary.

Killer was the cutter INGHAM (Commander G. E. McCabe, USCG). The episode can only be told as a short story, for brevity is its very essence.

INGHAM was one of three escorts screening the Iceland section of North Atlantic Convoy ONS-152. In company with destroyers BABBITT and LEARY, the cutter was herding the ships from Iceland toward a rendezvous with the main convoy. At 1045 in the morning of the 15th INGHAM scouted ahead in search of the big ship-train. At 1235 she made a sonar contact which could only be classified as "doubtful." McCabe directed a run over the spot; the cutter dropped one 600-pound depth charge. At 1247 INGHAM "secured" and returned to her patrol station with the Iceland group. Later that afternoon the rendezvous with the main convoy was achieved without incident.

INGHAM's Coast Guardsmen were not given to boastful announcements. Nobody believed a kill had been made, but postwar examination of German records divulged the fact. INGHAM had dropped her 600-pounder at lat. 56-46 N, long. 27-12 W. And in that position, on that specific date, the U-626 had gone out of existence.

That a cutter could sink a submarine with a single depth charge seemed fantastic. But in this case the phantasy proved real. As a DesLant sailor described it afterwards in short-story form, "INGHAM made a hole in one."

Apotheosis of Admiral Doenitz

During the 12 months of 1942 almost 1,000 ships had gone down to torpedo fire in Atlantic and Arctic Areas for a grand total of nearly 6,000,000 tons. By way of reprisal, Allied A/S forces destroyed 82 U-boats. (Of these, United States A/S forces accounted for only 18.) The year's summary, then, was On January 30, 1943, he promoted Admiral Doenitz to Grand not so bright on the American side of the picture.

Hitler was hugely pleased with the U-boat accomplishment. Admiral, and made him Commander in Chief of the German Navy. But nemesis in the form of A/S warfare would eventually "demote" the Grand Admiral.

Chapter 12

Destroyers to North Africa

(DD's in Operation Torch)

☆ ☆ ☆

Play Ball!

When France collapsed under the mighty treads of the Nazi *Wehrmacht,* Hitler gloated, and French Marshal Henri Pétain came into power as head of the Vichy Government. That was in 1940. And even as Hitler exulted, British war leaders determined to prevent Algeria and French Morocco from falling into the conqueror's clutch. Upshot came after America's entry into the war. "Operation Torch"—the counter-invasion of North Africa.

"Operation Torch" presented the Western Naval Task Force with a three-element job. It was to transport Patton's army, some 37,000 strong, across the Atlantic to French Morocco. It was to land these troops on beachheads on Morocco's Atlantic seaboard, and support a campaign to capture Casablanca—a port which would give the American forces a base for a steamroller drive across North Africa to Tunis. And it was to aid in the establishment in French Morocco of a striking force which could assure Allied control of the Straits of Gibraltar.

The transport task, a matter of convoying, was well within the Navy's experience. But the landing of a large army called for use of the Navy's new amphibious technique in an outsize effort.

For if the Vichy French chose to resist the landings, they could put up some fierce opposition.

Under the invasion plan for Morocco, destroyers of the DesLant Force were to screen the troop convoys of the Western Task Force on the Atlantic crossing; they were to add their guns to the fire-support effort during and after the seizure of the Moroccan beachheads; and they were to feature as special-missioners in the amphibious program. Shore

107

bombardments, anti-aircraft gunnery, A/S work, and special missions—DesLant DD's were to serve as the right hand holding the "Torch." D-Day was set for November 8, 1942.

Admiral Hewitt's Western Naval Task Force 34 contained some 102 vessels.

For landing operations the Force was organized in four task groups: the Southern Attack Group, assigned to the Safi area; the Northern Attack Group, assigned to the Mehdia area; the Center Attack Group, assigned to the Fedala-Casablanca area; and the Covering Group to support the Center Attack Group in the Casablanca area.

Battleships MASSACHUSETTS, NEW YORK, and TEXAS, the five carriers, seven cruisers, numerous destroyers, mine vessels, and auxiliaries were variously attached to these groups.

By the evening of November 6 the Western Task Force was in African coastal waters. Favorable weather and sea reports were received on November 7, and the attack groups squared away for the November 8 deadline.

Stealthily the assigned Attack Groups and the Covering Group closed in on the objective beaches of Mehdia and Fedala. If the Vichy French opened fire, the Americans were to answer with every weapon available. The signal for action was the code phrase "Play ball!"

At 0600 in the morning of November 7 the Southern Attack Group, detached from the main body of the Western Task Force, headed southward on a course for Safi, French Morocco. There, too, the Americans would play ball.

The Attack on Safi (Task Group 34.10 Takes the Field)

By nightfall of November 7 the Southern Attack Group was a few miles out from Safi, whose twinkling lights seemed strangely unsuspecting and peaceful.

But Admiral Davidson was taking no chances. Two coastal batteries of naval guns guarded Safi to the north, and an army battery of 155 mm. guns was located south of the port. A local garrison of Foreign Legionnaires and Moroccan Tirailleurs could be quickly reinforced by troops from Marrakech in the interior. Safi could explode in the face of the American amphibs, and Davidson disposed his forces to counter such an explosion.

While the transports quietly approached a pre-determined transport area off Safi breakwater, PHILADELPHIA and NEW YORK steamed to stations where their guns could trade shells with the coastal batteries. Destroyers MERVINE, BEATTY, and KNIGHT moved to positions where they could cover the landings with close-in-fire-support.

So clock and calendar moved silently into November 8,

D-Day. H-Hour was set for 0400. Thirty minutes before H-Hour two odd-looking ships peeled away from the transport group and headed in to Safi harbor. They were the transformed "four-pipers" BERNADOU and COLE. The game was about to begin.

BERNADOU *and* COLE *in Double Play*

On board the two assault destroyers the volunteer crews stood at battle stations, the lookouts straining their eyes to see ahead, the gunners in hair-trigger readiness at their mounts.

Both BERNADOU and COLE were carrying assault troops trained for special shore jobs. The troops included K and L Companies of the 47th Infantry. Mission: to land these troops inside Safi harbor where they were to seize harbor installations and shipping and prevent the destruction or damaging of local port facilities. BERNADOU's shock troops were to go to the beach. COLE's were to capture the mole with its loading cranes and marine machinery—an objective of vital importance, as the transport LAKEHURST was laden with tanks which were too heavy to send ashore through the shallows, and COLE's crews were to ready the mole for the unloading of these big tanks.

Behind the two assault destroyers chugged a procession of troop-crowded landing craft. Ahead was a little scout boat.

Then at 0410 the invaders were sighted, and a flickering light challenged BERNADOU as she approached the long breakwater. Her skipper, Lieutenant Commander R. E. Braddy, Jr., answered with a reply which seemed to satisfy the harbor watch, and the DD continued her quiet advance toward the land end of the breakwater.

But at 0428, just as BERNADOU rounded the bell buoy off the north end of the dim mole, a shore battery suddenly blurted flame. The crash of French 75's was overtoned by the metallic stutter of machine-guns and the crackle of rifle fire. As salvos and volleys swept the harbor, Braddy snatched the TBS and passed the signal. "Play Ball!" BERNADOU's six 3-inchers and five 20 mm. guns let out a roar. The game was on.

Bad luck at the start. The destroyermen had been equipped with a magnificent pyrotechnic extravaganza which was to have made an aerial burst over the harbor. The item was a parachute flare which, when fired aloft, would unfurl an American flag. The parachute would then drift over Safi, with the flare illumining the Stars and Stripes. It was believed this dramatic display might have an agreeable influence on the sentimental French.

Instead, gun-flame jabbed the darkness, and both BERNADOU and COLE were straddled by salvos. Firing pointblank at the flashes, range 1,500 yards, BERNADOU's gunners answered with a hot barrage. Destroyer MERVINE also opened up on this target, which was identified as the Batterie des Passes some 2,000 yards north of Safi. Apparently BERNADOU's 3-inchers registered a direct hit. About six minutes after the firing began, the Batterie des Passes was silenced.

The invasion ships then came under fire of the Batterie Railleuse—four 130 mm. naval rifles emplaced on a headland about three miles northwest of Safi. These big enemy guns lobbed some heavy salvos into the harbor before they were knocked out. Battleship NEW YORK, cruiser PHILADELPHIA, and destroyers MERVINE and BEATTY were straddled, but not hit. An answering salvo temporarily silenced this coastal battery, and it was finally muzzled about 0715.

Meantime the landings went forward in the pre-dawn dark. At 0430 BERNADOU's bows touched land and her load of assault troops went overside on Green Beach. The special troops carried by COLE (Lieutenant Commander G. G. Palmer) landed on the merchandise pier where they handily seized the loading cranes. Going alongside the enemy dock, COLE tide up with the precision of an excursion boat discharging holiday passengers at a beach resort. The ship came through the Safi adventure without a scratch, but one of her men was shot through the lungs. (He returned to duty a month later.) BERNADOU, deliberately run up on the beach, suffered only minor damage.

In recognition of sterling amphibious work, BERNADOU and COLE were each awarded a Presidential Unit Citation.

Attack on Mehdia (Task Group 34.8 Takes the Field)

The fortified harbor of Mehdia lies at the mouth of the Oued Sebou, a sultry river which is navigable for some distance inland. Nine miles upstream is Port Lyautey with its airfield. This airfield was the prize in the Mehdia package.

Mission of Task Group 34.8 was to land the Army forces at Mehdia, provide fire-support for military operations if necessary, and and in the seizure of the airfield at Port Lyautey. The airfield's defenses were known to be sketchy—a few anti-aircraft and mobile guns. If assault forces could get upstream, Port Lyautey should be easy to take. But getting upstream was the rub. The Sebou River was shallow, sluggish, and meandering. A sullen stone fort guarded the estuary. The approaches to Mehdia on the south bank were under the guns of a battery of French 75's and a 138.6 mm. battery. Not far to the south, the Moroccan capital of Rabat contained a sizable garrison which could be rushed to Mehdia's defense.

The clocks were at 2321 when the group reached attack position. Three main beachheads (altogether there were five beaches) had been marked for the Mehdia landings. One lay three miles below the river mouth; another was located four miles north of the estuary; the third hugged the jetty on the south side of the entrance channel. While assault troops seized Mehdia, destroyer DALLAS was to steam up the Sebou to Port Lyautey with a Ranger Detachment on special mission to capture the Lyautey airfield.

H-Hour for Mehdia was set for 0400 in the morning of November 8. By 0100 the transport area was a-bustle with landing craft. Troops were going over ships' sides on cargo nets, and clambering down to bull-nosed LCP's. Jeeps and war gear were being stowed on blunt little ferries. Army Rangers, disembarked from transport SUSAN B. ANTHONY, crossed the water to board destroyer DALLAS. The sea was as smooth as undulant velvet under a night sky in which contented clouds were pastured. Mehdia slept.

At 0411 fire-support destroyers KEARNY, ROE, and ERICSSON took their respective stations. KEARNY (Commander A. H. Oswald) was positioned on the north side of the Sebou estuary. Lieutenant Commander Nolan maneuvered ROE into her assigned place south of the river mouth. ERICSSON (Lieutenant Commander C. M. Jensen) was stationed offshore in the backfield.

Landing operations, delayed, did not begin until about 0500. At that hour the first assault waves on their way in to the beaches passed the fire-support DD's. Before the watch at Mehdia woke up, the troops had landed on the target beachheads. Then the amphibs were spotted by a searchlight which speared down from the fort above Mehdia. A rash of rifle fire broke out along the dim parapets.

Navy Versus French Foreign Legion

The fort which crowned the native Kasbah proved a stumbling block to the American forces. It was an old-time affair garrisoned by Foreign Legionnaires, but its 138 mm. batteries badgered the landing craft and kept the channel under fire.

But every hour of delay undermined the invasion effort, so DALLAS was ordered to start upriver, fort or no fort. A heavy barrage finally silenced the guns on the Kasbah heights, but another stumbling block barred DALLAS' advance. A net and a large boom had been stretched across the river entrance. Working in darkness slashed by enemy rifle fire from the river bank, a Navy crew from one of the transports hacked down the net and partly cleared the channel. About noon, DALLAS steamed in and tried to ram the boom.

Another stymie! The boom was cut on the north side where the channel was too shallow for DALLAS. She had to ram the cable in deeper water, and in trying to do so, she ran aground. While she was struggling like a mired carabao, the Kasbah guns opened fire. A big shell raised a geyser dead ahead, and a near miss aft lifted her stern out of the muck. Lunging at 18 knots, she struck the cable midway between two floats, and brushed it aside. So DALLAS "lowered the boom" on the famed French Foreign Legion.

Attack on Port Lyautey (DALLAS *Steals a Base*)

The river still lay ahead. And not only did the river meander around a score of bends convenient for ambush, but its channel was as shallow as a dishpan, and lumpy with shifting mud bars.

While Lieutenant Commander Robert Brodie, Jr., the skipper, looked after things in general, Lieutenant John N. Ferguson, Jr., the destroyer's "Exec," did the navigating across the treacherous entrance bar. Thereafter the DALLAS was piloted by René Malavergne, a Free French volunteer, who had been chief pilot on the Sebou before the war, and who knew every inch of the tricky channel.

Slowly, warily, DALLAS advanced up the waterway. The banks closed in and the French opened fire. While 75 mm. shells splashed close aboard, and machine-gun bullets zipped across the bow, the river bed grabbed at the destroyer's keel. She scraped bottom most of the way to Port Lyautey, her propellers churning chocolate mud. But in spite of mud under keel and gunfire from the Sebou's banks, she made Port Lyautey without damage or personnel casualties.

As at Safi, casualties were astonishingly light. Not a ship in action in the Mehdia area suffered a damaging hit, and the only man harmed by all the shooting was the bluejacket injured when a plane strafed destroyer KEARNY.

Attack on Fedala (Task Group 34.9 in Action)

Timed to coincide with the Safi and Mehdia operations, the move on Fedala in the Casablanca area began late in the evening of November 7 when the Center Attack Group of the Western Task Force approached Cape Fedala. Commanded by Captain R. R. M. Emmet, the Center Attack Group contained three cruisers, carriers RANGER and SUWANNEE, and destroyers WILKES, SWANSON, LUDLOW, MURPHY, BRISTOL, WOOLSEY, EDISON, TILLMAN, BOYLE, ROWAN, ELLY-

SON, FORREST, FITCH, HOBSON, and CORRY. Fifteen transports and cargo vessels were in the convoy, and minesweepers steamed in the van. The big assignment was to land about 20,000 Army troops on the beaches of Fedala, and to furnish whatever fire-support was necessary.

Fedala was a fortified strongpoint covering the approaches to Casablanca Harbor about a dozen miles distant. Powerful French batteries guarded the little port. With all guns going, the French could raise a considerable storm at this Moroccan beach resort.

Destroyers WILKES, SWANSON, LUDLOW, and MURPHY were among the first invasion ships at Fedala to come under fire.

At 0620 the "Play Ball!" signal was spoken, and the ships of Task Group 34.9 bore down on the offensive. One minute after the signal was flashed, MURPHY reported that she was being straddled, and requested fire-support from cruiser BROOKLYN. SWANSON joined in the bombardment of the Blondin battery at 0645. The big coastal guns of this stronghold flung booming salvos at the American cruiser and the DD's, and about the time SWANSON trained her guns on this enemy, MURPHY was hit.

The shell thunderbolted into MURPHY's after engine-room. Three men were slain by the explosion; seven were wounded. An excerpt from MURPHY's War Damage Report states:

> Immediate damage-control measures taken by the ship consisted in stuffing the exterior hole with a mattress, flooding magazines, and steam-smothering the engine-room. The Engineer Officer, Lieutenant Commander Robert W. Curtis, in utter disregard of his own safety entered the engine-room after it had filled with steam and smoke and had risen to an insufferable temperature; he tripped the still-running generator and thereby took electrical power off the arcing switchboard; thereafter he endeavored to insure that none of his men remained below.

Pounded by shells from BROOKLYN, SWANSON, LUDLOW, and MURPHY, the Blondin guns were finally silenced. In the meantime destroyers WILKES, SWANSON, LUDLOW, BRISTOL, EDISON, and BOYLE traded intermittent salvos with the coastal guns at Fedala.

Naval gunnery was ended in the Fedala area at 1140 when the Army forces ashore signalled for a cease fire.

Although naval casualties were heavier at Fedala than at Safi and Mehdia, the local fighting for the beachheads was soonest ended.

The big-league match on D-Day was at Casablanca.

Attack on Casablanca (Task Group 34.1 plays Ball)

The mission of the Western Task Force Covering Group was to hold the French fleet at bay in Casablanca Harbor and give such support to the landings as might be required. Commanded by Rear Admiral R. C. Giffen, the Covering Group contained flag battleship MASSACHUSETTS, cruisers TUSCALOOSA and WICHITA, and destroyers WAINWRIGHT, MAYRANT, RHIND, and JENKINS.

If the French at Casablanca showed fight, MASSACHUSETTS was to take care of the coastal battery at Point El Hank and knock out the immobilized French battleship JEAN BART. The cruisers were to bombard the Table d'Aoukasha and El Hank shore batteries and attend to the French submarines or other naval vessels that might attempt a sortie from Casablanca. The destroyers, units of Captain Moon's DesRon 8, were to provide an A/S screen for the heavy ships; to hunt down enemy submarines; to put an anti-aircraft defense if needed; and to fire at such enemy warships and shore targets as would be designated.

The shooting began at daylight when the French opened fire. El Hank roared salvos at the American naval vessels. Then JEAN BART commenced firing from her berth in Casablanca Harbor. Hurled at 10-mile range, the French battleship's 15-inch projectiles threw up geysers ahead of the MASSACHUSETTS.

The destroyers maintained their screening stations under this enemy fire—a nerve-wracking experience, as the DD's were unable to return the long-range shots. And then at 0815, while the big guns were roaring, the French ships came out. They were destroyer leaders MILAN and ALBATROSS, and destroyers FRONDEUR, FOUGUEUX, BRESTOIS, and BOULONNAIS.

The Frenchmen headed for the American anchorage at Fedala. AUGUSTA, BROOKLYN, and destroyers of the Attack Group off Fedala moved southward to intervene.

Destroyers WILKES, SWANSON, BRISTOL, and BOYLE engaged the French destroyers.

Punctured and set afire by shell hits from Wilkes, the MILAN was driven in to the beach. BOULONNAIS, staggered by a hit that wrecked her steering gear, was sunk by salvos from MASSACHUSETTS. Multiple hits from MASSACHUSETTS and TUSCALOOSA sent the destroyer FOUGUEUX to the bottom.

The action became a furious melee when the light cruiser PRIMAGUET and more French destroyers steamed out at 1000 to engage the American ships. Rocked by a tornado of fire, destroyers BRESTOIS and FRONDEUR were fatally hit. One by one the Frenchmen were driven into port or disabled. Of the ships that steamed out of Casablanca, only a single destroyer, the ALCYON, survived the unfortunate sortie.

There remained a number of French submarines and the battleship JEAN BART in Casablanca Harbor. Stubborn Vichyite Vice Admiral F. C. Michelier refused an armistice until the afternoon of November 1, when the JEAN BART had been beaten into silence and American assault troops were at Casablanca's gates.

But it was the Nazis who made the final play in the Casablanca area. Striking in the wake of the French surrender, Axis submarines slashed at American invasion shipping along the Moroccan coast. Within a two-day period immediately following the Casablanca armistice, four United States transports were sunk off Fedala, and three other American ships, including the destroyer HAMBLETON, were torpedoed.

Torpedoing of USS HAMBLETON

HOSTILITIES IN FRENCH MOROCCO HAVE CEASED BE ESPECIALLY VIGILANT AGAINST AXIS SUBMARINES

To American naval forces at Safi, Mehdia, Fedala, and off Casablanca the foregoing message with its explicit warning was broadcast shortly after the French capitulated. All A/S screens were alerted, and lookouts kept a sharp watch for tell-tale periscope "feathers."

Somehow the enemy subs got in. At Fedala Roads their torpedoes struck the Western Task Force a ferocious smash, and the American invasion fleet suffered its only losses off Morocco. The subs were the U-173 and the U-130, members of the wolfpack concentration which had missed the invasion fleet in the Atlantic. Now they had caught up.

Down went the transports JOSEPH HEWES, HUGH L. SCOTT, EDWARD RUTLEDGE, and TASKER H. BLISS.

Destroyer HAMBLETON (Commander Forrest Close), flagship of DesDiv 19, was struck early in the evening of November 11, just after JOSEPH HEWES and WINOOSKI were torpedoed.

Here it is in the official language of the destroyer's War Damage Report:

HAMBLETON absorbed a tremendous amount of damage. Her survival was possible because of the general excellence of the damager-control measures, adequate stability characteristics, and the ruggedness of her hull. Favorable weather conditions and the proximity of a port were important factors. Temporary repairs at Casablanca not only were ingenious but also were soundly conceived and executed.

HAMBLETON was placed in the floating drydock at Casablanca on January 19, 1943. The "ingenious" repairs in reference consisted of removing all structure between frames 87 and 116, moving the stern section forward 38 feet, and then connecting the bow and sterrn by a fairing section 12¾ feet long. That these repairs were "soundly conceived and executed" was evidenced by the fact that the repair plan required the minimum docking time of all schemes proposed, and the surgical engineering put HAMBLETON back on her feet. The work was completed on May 8, 1943, and the following day she steamed out of Casablanca and headed for home. With only the port propeller to go on, she made the Atlantic crossing in good time, arriving at Boston Navy Yard on June 26. There she underwent permanent repairs and alterations, and she was back in service on November 15, 1943. Remarkable recovery for a ship which had been literally truncated, shortened, sewed together again, and sent home with one amputated propeller.

Some people like to talk about their operations. Veteran destroyermen talk about HAMBLETON's.

WOOLSEY, SWANSON *and* QUICK *down* U-173

During the forenoon of November 16, destroyers WOOLSEY (Commander B. L. Austin), SWANSON (Lieutenant Commander L. M. Markham), and QUICK (Lieutenant Commander R. B. Nickerson) were patrolling as units of the A/S screen off Casablanca. Then at 1135 WOOLSEY's sonar registered sudden contact with an underwater target, range 700 yards. The echo, coming in "sharp and firm," called for an urgent attack. With neither time nor space to draw a bead on the target ahead, Commander Austin swung the destroyer to deliver a starboard K-gun broadside.

An upwelling of oil which spread a lush black carpet across a considerable yardage of the ocean's surface. Large air bubbles came popping up like little balloons. Interested observers on board the WOOLSEY expressed an elated opinion. The consensus was: "We got her!"

But you never could tell from a first gush of oil and air. Here was a case in point. After WOOLSEY launched her urgent attack, the target was traced on the move. By 1149 the sub had made a complete circle and was now back on its original course, traveling at snail's pace.

At 1149, then WOOLSEY attacked again. This time the destroyer flailed the sea with a pattern of four depth charges. For 15 minutes the oil and air continued to rise. To WOOLSEY it looked like the death throes of a stricken submersible.

Contact with the target was regained at 1214. The sub was lying inert. Commander Austin conned WOOLSEY directly over the target, and four more depth charges were dropped. They must have landed on the sub's conning tower—if it still had a conning tower—but the only evidence of a hit was another display of violent bubbling.

SWANSON and QUICK stepped in to deliver the death blow to the undersea enemy. Taking over the contact, SWANSON dropped two depth-charge patterns on the spot where the bubbles continued to rise. The explosions produced still more bubbles. Finally QUICK, with a positive signature on her ASMD (Anti-Submarine Magnetic Detector), maneuvered in to drop a single charge set for bottom explosion. If the enemy submarines had been "blowing bubbles" for the purposes of trickery, that final blast put an end to the game.

This submarine kill had several unique features. Unusual was the fact that SWANSON and QUICK thought they were attacking some "sunken hull." It was a "sunken hull," all right. But WOOLSEY was the only DD certain that the contact was a sub, and, as Nazi records disclosed, she made the most of that certainty.

The submarine downed by WOOLSEY, SWANSON, and QUICK was the U-173, the very U-boat which had sunk the HEWES, damaged the WINOOSKI, and all but sunk the HAMBLETON.

North African Drive

On November 10, 1942, Vichy Admiral Jean Darlan, Commander-in-Chief of French North African forces, was induced to abandon his pro-Nazi position and switch to the Allied side. On the 11th Hitler's armies swept into Vichy France, and most of the former Vichy holdouts in North Africa promptly joined the Allies. Not long after the Nazis marched into southern France, French Navy commanders scuttled the residual fleet at Toulon. Already the light of "Operation Torch" was falling across Europe.

Chapter 13

Destroyer Warfare in the Aleutians

☆ ☆ ☆

The Birthplace of Bad Weather

On June 6-7, 1942, the Japanese landed on the Aleutian Islands. It was the first time American soil had been trod by a foreign army since the War of 1812.

United States military leaders had been fully aware that the Japanese might make a lunge into the Aleutians. Anticipating an attack on those strategically valuable islands, the War Department and the Navy Department had pushed the construction of naval and air bases at Dutch Harbor, Kodiak, and other Aleutian strongpoints. U.S. submarines began patrols through the Aleutian Archipelago.

Navigation in those waters was an adventure in peril; many of the island approaches were uncharted, channels were blocked with saw-toothed reefs, and bays were ulcerous with shoals and submerged rocks. Crazy currents and racing tide rips coiled and swirled through the archipelago. When the islands weren't smothered in fog, they were whipped by screeching "williwaws" that kicked up monstrous seas and reduced visibility to "less than zero." A calm and sunny morning could deteriorate by noon to a foaming, ship-smashing norther. Nightfall might bring a black sleet storm, or a blinding, featherbed blizzard. With good reason the native Aleuts had named this wild archipelago "The Birthplace of Bad Weather."

Contrary to the initial impression made on the American public by the move, the Japanese High Command was not planning an invasion of continental Alaska.

According to the postwar testimony of Captain Taisuke Ito, staff officer of the Imperial Fifth Fleet:

The primary objective of the Aleutian Operation was to

occupy Adak as a northern base for patrol planes, which, in conjunction with Midway, could cover the northern approach across the Pacific to Japan. When the Battle of Midway went unfavorably, Admiral Yamamoto was against occupying any of the Aleutian Islands. However, Vice Admiral Hosogaya, Commander Fifth Fleet, argued strongly for the occupation of Kiska as a position from which to neutralize Dutch Harbor and prevent an advance toward Japan via the Aleutian Islands.

Both invader and defender fought a gruelling war with the weather.

Kiska Bombardment

Late in July a U.S. task group set out to bombard the invader's positions on Kiska. The striking force contained heavy cruisers INDIANAPOLIS and LOUISVILLE and light cruisers NASHVILLE, ST. LOUIS and HONOLULU. Four destroyers screened. The DD's were CASE, REID, GRIDLEY and McCALL.

Dense fogs slowed the advance and endangered the ships. But at length they were off Vega Bay.

Tons of steel were hurled into Kiska Harbor, but the American spotting planes could neither verify hits nor ascertain damage done to military installations. Fog!

Suddenly lookouts spied a feather on the water, the serpent's-head of a Jap periscope. Submarine! The lookouts flashed the alarm, and the American light cruisers executed an emergency turn to avoid torpedo attack. The turn brought the light cruisers squarely across the bows of heavy cruisers INDIANAPOLIS and LOUISVILLE, forcing the heavies to cease fire abruptly and turn hard right. With this maneuver the bombardment was broken off. All units except the CA's had completed their regular bombardment schedule.

Behind the whole Kiska bombardment operation hovered a doubtful question mark. Admiral W. W. Smith concluded in a critical report:

The bombardment of Kiska by a surface force of heavy ships is of questionable value unless followed by landing of troops. Results to be expected by indirect bombardment do not balance the risk to heavy ships under difficult conditions of approach in mineable waters, where enemy destroyers and submarines may be encountered in low visibility. . . .

Radio Tokyo, with its usual penchant for exaggeration, announced that a tremendous gun duel had been fought between an American fleet and Kiska's shore batteries. The fleet (declared Radio Tokyo) had been driven off.

But it was not the Japs but the Aleutians themselves that frustrated the American task group—with fog.

REID *and Aircraft Kill* RO-61

On the morning of August 31, the destroyer REID (Lieutenant Commander H. H. McIlhenny) was about ten miles southeast of Cape North, Atka, proceeding to conduct an anti-submarine patrol off the Nazan Bay harbor entrance.

At 0930 a Navy PBY droned into view out of nowhere. The plane—a unit of PatWing 4—raced toward the REID and signalled "Sub!" McIlhenny sent the crew to battle stations, and REID dashed into action.

The PBY led the DD to the target, a Jap submarine which had suffered from a bombing by the airmen. The plane dropped a smoke float on the oil slick left by the damaged sub, and REID steamed to the spot to try for the underwater bull's-eye.

The destroyer established sonar contact and McIlhenny ordered a depth-charge attack. Overside went the TNT, and up came the thunder. There was no sign of debris, and the "ping jockey" (sonar operator) reported the sub was still down there.

A depth-charge barrage was dropped at 1219. After the first charge was dropped, the fathometer indicated REID was passing over the sub. The barrage brought the enemy floundering to the surface. The submarine broached at a sharp angle, then lolled helplessly in the sea, her bow slanted skyward, stern under water. Frantic seamen fought their way out of the conning tower as REID's gunners opened fire with 5-inch 38-caliber and 20 mm. batteries.

The destroyer marksmen riddled the submarine's conning tower, and punched shells through the up-angled bow. After about eight minutes of this sharp-shooting, the sub capsized and sank by the stern. Seventeen survivors were counted in the swirling sea; the destroyermen were able to rescue but five.

The shivering submariners identified their demolished boat as RO-61. The obliteration of this undersea invader was remarked by a veteran destroyer-force commander as *"an excellent example of cooperation between a DD and a plane."*

Loss of USS WORDEN

Late in 1942, Admiral Nimitz projected an advance on Kiska. The move called for the preliminary seizure of Amchitka Island. Occupation of Amchitka was scheduled for mid-January 1943.

D-Day was set for January 12. Landings were to be made on the beaches of Constantine Harbor. Troops were carried by the Coast Guard transport ARTHUR MIDDLETON. And the destroyer WORDEN (Commander W. G. Pogue) was assigned to transport from Adak Island and land at Amchitka the Advance Security Detail of the Army.

The night of January 11-12 was as black as anthracite, the weather clearing and calming after a storm. Closing the harbor entrance, the destroyermen obtained a glimpse of outlying rocks and headland. Radar checked the picture, and the DD started in. After ticklish maneuvering between a great bed of kelp and a cluster of rocks, WORDEN managed the hazardous approach on the beach without misadventure, and quietly anchored off shore. In the darkness before the subarctic dawn she lowered her boats and landed the Army detachment. By 0720 of the 12th the last man was on the beach, and the destroyermen were congratulating themselves on a mission handily accomplished.

About 0730 WORDEN was once more under way, heading seaward. The bridge watch was vigilant. The lookouts scanned the water for signs of treachery. No man on watch was asleep on his feet. But the island was to exact a toll of these visitors, vigilance despite.

The destroyer was almost free of the bay's embrace when there was a crash, a grinding snarl under the keel, and the ship was snagged by a jagged rock. She tore free from the clutch of this concealed snare, only to find herself trapped in a nest of rocks, with an outcropping of granite directly abeam. WORDEN had apparently been set to northwestward when she ran into this mist-veiled trap. She had hit hard, under the engine-room. Water spurted through her torn bottom-plates, and the engine-room spaces flooded rapidly.

With power lost, the ravaged DD drifted at the mercy of ground swells which drove her into a nest of rocks.

Rescue operations were as hazardous as they were urgent. Whaleboats from DEWEY and the landing boats from the transport MIDDLETON came sweeping through the shoals to pick up WORDEN's survivors. In the furious water a number of the destroyermen were injured. Several were drowned. Rabid seas continued to pound the stranded destroyer. At 1225 the ship's hull broke in two, and she sprawled on the rocks, a halved carcass.

By evening a williwaw was blowing full force.

The same storm, followed by a blinding blizzard, swamped landing craft and disabled small boats. When the blizzard swirled off into Aleutian oblivion and the weather finally cleared to visibility, the date was January 17. The rocky teeth in the mouth of Constantine Harbor were bare. The WORDEN wreckage had been swallowed.

Battle of the Komandorskis

> *Unique in the naval history of the Pacific War, the Aleutian campaign provided at the Komandorski battle the only conventional daylight gun duel between opposing surface forces in which air attack was not made.*
>
> *The Campaigns of the Pacific War*

As suggested by the foregoing statement, the Battle of the Komandorski Islands was an old-fashioned naval engagement, a hammer-and-tongs shooting match between ships.

Commanded by Rear Admiral C. H. ("Sock") McMorris, Task Group 16.6 was composed of the heavy cruiser SALT LAKE CITY, the light cruiser RICHMOND and the four destroyers of DesRon 14 under Captain R. S. Riggs. The DD's were BAILEY (Lieutenant Commander J. C. Atkeson), COGHLAN (Commander B. F. Tompkins), DALE (Commander A. L. Rorschach), and MONAGHAN (Lieutenant Commander P. H. Horn). Admiral McMorris had his flag in RICHMOND, and Captain Riggs rode in BAILEY.

During the third week in March, 1943, this task group was patrolling the seas west of Attu. To the majority of the crews the waters off Attu must have resembled the freezing approaches to World's End.

But Admiral McMorris and the other Aleutian veterans in TG 16.6 were aware that the Attu area could prove hotter than it looked. Sooner or later the Japs would have to send supplies to their Attu and Kiska garrisons or the invading forces would lose their toehold on that tenebrous archipelago and meet defeat through the simple process of starvation.

The Japanese were well aware of the task group's presence in the area. Given a fairly comprehensive idea of the opposition to be contended with, Vice Admiral Moshiro Hosogaya, commander of the Japanese Fifth Fleet, prepared to shatter the blockade with a superior naval force.

Hosogaya's plan to run a large convoy through to Attu was carefully laid. Three transports were assigned to the convoy. For the escort force Admiral Hosogaya mustered all the Fifth Fleet units available. The force included the heavy cruisers NACHI (flagship) and MAYA, the light cruisers TAMA and ABUKUMA, and the destroyers WAKABA, HATSUSHIMO, IKAZUCHI, INAZUMA, and USUGUMO. As is apparent from the line-up, the cruisers of this formidable fleet outnumbered McMorris's cruiser force two to one. The Japanese destroyer force was one up on the American. The Jap warships were not equipped with radar, but this lack was at least partially offset by three spotter planes carried by NACHI and by decidedly preponderant fire-power.

Morning of March 26. The Japanese ships, steaming in single column on a northerly heading, were led by NACHI in the following order: MAYA, TAMA, ABUKUMA, WAKABA, HATSUSHIMO, IKAZUCHI, ASAKA MARU, SAKITO MARU, INAZUMA. Sunrise was still some time away when Commander Miura on NACHI's bridge turned his glasses southward and glimpsed a mast on the gilded horizon.

The mast sighted by Miura was that of the USS COGHLAN. McMorris's force had been steaming on a scouting line, the ships some six miles apart. Farthest north was the destroyer COGHLAN. Light cruiser RICHMOND was next in the formation. Then came destroyers BAILEY and DALE, heavy cruiser SALT LAKE CITY, and destroyer MONAGHAN.

McMorris promptly changed course to parallel the enemy's. He was determined to maintain contact, but he wanted to avoid closing the range until his group was better concentrated and the situation had clarified.

By 0820 RICHMOND's bridge personnel could count ten Jap vessels in the convoy, but the cruiser silhouettes were not yet identifiable. As Admiral McMorris phrased it, he *"still felt that a Roman holiday was in prospect."* A few minutes later the two Jap heavy and two light cruisers were identified. *"The situation had now clarified,"* Admiral McMorris stated in his battle report. And he went on to note, *". . . but it had also radically and unpleasantly changed."*

It seemed that the prospects of a Roman holiday remained, but there was a question as to who might do the celebrating. Even as that doubt arose on RICHMOND's bridge, it was apparent that the Jap warships were steaming eastward to come between the American task group and its base. Obviously the Japanese fleet was intent on closing the range and giving battle.

"Sock" McMorris prepared to slug it out, long odds or no. He set a course to pursue the fleeing Jap transports. There was a chance that the Japanese might divide their forces in an effort to cover the retreating *marus*. The American task group closed up, RICHMOND and SALT LAKE CITY in column with the flagship leading, van destroyers BAILEY and COGHLAN off the light cruiser's port bow, and DALE and MONAGHAN off the heavy cruiser's starboard quarter. Determinedly the task group started a chase to overhaul the fugitive merchantmen, but the Japanese fleet commander was not tricked by the stratagem. Instead of dividing forces the Jap warships closed up and bore down for concentrated attack.

NACHI opened fire at 0840, range approximately ten miles. The Jap gunners were promptly on target, their salvos soon straddling the RICHMOND. But the blast of the opening salvo wrecked the two Zero spotting planes on NACHI's starboard catapult. In consequence, the spotters had to be jettisoned, and the Zero reconnaissance plane on the port catapult was the only one that managed to take off. Throughout the engagement, this seaplane served as a spotter. It was (according to postwar testimony by NACHI's Commander Miura) the only Jap aircraft in the battle area. The Americans had no spotters in the air.

Shortly after her opening salvo, NACHI and MAYA launched torpedoes. All ran wide of the mark.

Meantime RICHMOND and her consorts opened up a few seconds after NACHI's introductory salvo. The Americans gave as good as they got, and the gun duel went hot and heavy for the first quarter of an hour. MAYA shook RICHMOND with straddles, then turned her weapons on SALT LAKE CITY, the only American warship capable of trading heavyweight punches with the Japanese CA's. SALT LAKE CITY's 8-inchers volleyed and thundered as the range decreased and the Jap cruisers drove the American forces westward. The gunners on SALT LAKE CITY were not old salts, but they were seasoned enough to score hits on the enemy.

But SALT LAKE CITY was soon struck and damaged. The blow staggered the heavy cruiser, left her with a list, and inaugurated a series of troubles that seriously hampered her thereafter.

By way of reprisal, NACHI was hit and the light cruiser TAMA struck. The American gunners scored several more hits on Hosogaya's flagship, and by 0950 NACHI was showing the signs of painful damage. In post-war testimony, the Japanese waxed eloquent concerning the American destroyers' gunnery. *"Their shells,"* said Miura, *"landed aboard like rain."*

The Japs redoubled their efforts to demolish SALT LAKE CITY, and they made her the target of a relentless and murderous barrage. "Overs" and "shorts" splashed around the covering DD's, and the destroyermen could hear the big ones rushing through the air like invisible express trains. To add to her difficulties, SALT LAKE CITY was badgered by steering casualties.

Light cruiser ABUKUMA and the DD's WAKABA, HATSUSHIMO, IKAZUCHI, and INAZUMA had closed on the starboard quarter. Between 1105 and noon, the Jap cruisers and two of the Jap destroyers launched torpedoes, but the range was extreme, and the "fish" failed to hit. Within that hour, MAYA, NACHI, and ABUKUMA got off a total of 16 torpedo shots; DD's WAKABA and HATSUSHIMO fired twelve.

If Captain Riggs and his destroyermen had been tight-nerved, they were afforded no relaxation. At 1146 the Jap cruisers resumed the attack on SALT LAKE CITY. And at 1154 the cruiser's engines shuddered to a stop. Salt water in the oil booster line to the boilers. As her boilers went out and she slowed to a drift, it looked like "curtains" for the American cruiser.

Now DesRon 14 was called upon to save the imperiled day. From Admiral McMorris the order went to Captain Riggs—DesRon 14 was to launch an immediate torpedo attack; one DD would remain behind to screen SALT LAKE CITY. Squadron Commander Riggs relayed the order to his little force. DALE would screen the cruiser. BAILEY, COGHLAN, and MONAGHAN would execute the attack. Captain Riggs concluded the order with a directive, brusque and sharp:

"Get the big boys!"

The three DD's pointed their bows at the Japanese Fifth Fleet and start a run for the enemy cruisers. At the rushing DD's the Jap heavy cruisers hurled a hurricane of 8-inch projectiles. Dodging and weaving, the destroyers raced forward through the exploding storm. NACHI's bridge personnel stared at the oncoming "cans" in awe and unbelief. In postwar testimony Commander Miura expressed admiration for the destroyer charge, and went on to declare, *"I do not know how a ship could live through the concentration of fire that was brought to bear on the leading destroyer."*

The three DD's were literally *"smothered with shell splashes."* Onward they raced, rushing in to launch their torpedoes. Driving in, COGHLAN fired furiously at the heavy cruiser MAYA. Little BAILEY and MONAGHAN hurled 5-inchers at the bellowing NACHI. The latter was ripped by several 5-inch hits.

But in making their sacrifice play, the DD's of Task Group 16.6 could not escape punishment. Zigzagging through a murderous pattern of shell splashes, van destroyer BAILEY was staggered by four successive hits. The first 8-incher pierced her like a bullet going through cardboard, and exploded in the galley passageway, wrecking the provision issuing room. One officer and three bluejackets were killed by the explosion, and another man, mortally wounded, died a short time later.

In the next moment NACHI's big guns punched another shell into BAILEY. This projectile holed the destroyer's hull at the forward fireroom, waterline level. A fast-working repair crew plugged the hole, and the fire-and-bilge pump ousted the flood.

Then came a third hit, holing the destroyer at the forward engine-room. Water gushed into the ship, and it was necessary to secure and abandon the flooded compartment. Forward boilers No. 1 and No. 2 were secured. When shift was made from main to emergency feed—the steam supply from boilers No. 3 and No. 4 being temporarily suspended— BAILEY came to a four-minute stop. She went ahead at 15 knots, and when main feed was restored, about ten minutes later, she built up to 18 knots on one engine, and dodged away through the shell-tornado.

On the assailed destroyer's bridge, Captain Riggs ordered the torpedoes fired. Lieutenant Commander Atkeson voiced the "Torpedoes away!" The fanning wakes were sighted, and MAYA maneuvered to evade the deadly war heads. But cruiser NACHI was flailed by a succession of 5-inch hits.

BAILEY could deal it out, but she was also taking it. All hands sighed with relief when she finally came through the shell storm.

Miraculously, her team-mate MONAGHAN emerged from the scorching combat unscathed. COGHLAN, too, was singularly favored by Fortune. With four casualties, none fatal, COGH-LAN plunged through the tempest of 8-inch fire. Worst hurt of the three attacking destroyers, BAILEY limped out of it with all hands preparing to make a last-ditch stand.

But the Japanese did not follow through to easy victory. Convinced that an air attack was imminent, Admiral Hoso-gaya gave the order to retire.

American destroyermen stared in unbelief.

"Damned if they're not heading for the horizon!"

Chapter 14

Solomons Crucible

(The Guadalcanal Campaign)
(Part 1)

☆ ☆ ☆

Green Hell in Molten Sea

In the Southwest Pacific the war had raged for 8 months. General Mac-Arthur wanted to strike directly at Rabaul, the enemy's Bismarck citadel. Navy strategists dissented. They pointed out that Rabaul was a powerhouse which could only be crushed by a large-scale offensive, and in the summer of 1942 the Navy had neither the ships nor men available for such an offensive.

That the Navy's strategists were right in their estimates of Japanese strength was soon evident from the ferocious conflict which exploded at Guadalcanal. "Operation Watchtower," the Allied counter-offensive designed to expel the Japs from the Solomon Islands, proved a gruelling, murderous struggle.

Code name for Guadalcanal was "Cactus." An exceedingly apt name. The Japs were dug in when the Marines got there. The Marines dug them out and hurled them back, capturing their air field and renaming it Henderson. The Japs dug in again, just west of the Manatanikau River. Down from Rabaul then rushed supply convoys—ship trains that came to be known as the "Tokyo Express." Their midarchipelago route was dubbed the "Slot." The USN would fight a desperate battle to plug that waterway.

It was remarked that destroyers were particularly beset in the crucible. During the seven months of the Guadalcanal Campaign, more United States destroyers were lost than any other type of combatant ship engaged. Fourteen American DD's went down in the Solomons. And another—ominous beginning—was lost at the very outset at Espiritu Santo.

Loss of USS TUCKER

On August 4, 1942, the destroyer TUCKER (Lieutenant Commander W. R. Terrell) was leading the cargo ship NIRA LUCKENBACH into harbor at Espiritu Santo in the New Hebrides.

As she was heading into the western entrance, she was suddenly staggered by a shocking blast that sent a sheet of fire up her side and left her wallowing with a broken back, her hull almost torn in two at the No. 1 stack.

The entire steaming watch in the forward fireroom perished, and dazed men with bleeding hands and faces came stumbling topside from other compartments. Most of the destroyermen below decks managed to get out, but the USS TUCKER was finished.

The broken destroyer gradually settled, a slowly folding jacknife. The crew abandoned, and near-by rescue vessels quickly recovered the survivors. Nothing could be done for the ship. The stern section of the wreck sank the following morning. A diving party scuttled and sank the jagged bow.

TUCKER's loss was a blow to the DesPac Force, at that date trying to muster every available ship for the Guadalcanal showdown. Bad enough if she had been downed by the enemy, it was worse to have her downed, as was the case, by a friendly mine.

Entering Espiritu Santo, the hapless destroyer had steamed straight into the jaws of a minefield. Investigation disclosed that TUCKER had been given no information on the field. Again somebody had failed to send the word.

Destroyers to Guadalcanal (Opening "Operation Watchtower")

The opening move in "Operation Watchtower" called for simultaneous Marine landings at Lunga Point on Guadalcanal, and on Tulagi and Gavutu islands in the embrace of Florida Island almost due north across Savo Sound. Landings were to be made by troops of the reinforced First Marine Division, 19,500 strong. They were to be carried to the beachheads by 23 transports screened by five American and three Australian cruisers, and accompanying destroyers. An Air Support Force, built around aircraft carriers SARATOGA, ENTERPRISE, and WASP, screened by battleship NORTH CAROLINA and numerous cruisers and destroyers, was to dominate the sky.

By the afternoon of the 8th the enemy's unfinished airstrip at Lunga Point was in Marine possession, and the Japs on

Guadalcanal were nowhere to be seen. Almost immediately the Americans ran into a nightmare, one of the worst of the entire Pacific campaign. This Solomons nightmare materialized on the evening of August 8 in the near vicinity of Savo Island barring the entrance to Tulagi and Lunga Roads.

The Battle of Savo Island (A Tragedy of Errors)

Word of the Marine landings in the Solomons reached Japanese headquarters at Rabaul about 0700 in the morning of August 7. Admiral Mikawa, Commander Eighth Japanese Fleet and Outer South Seas Force, promptly mustered his warship strength for a strike at the Allied invasion shipping. Late that afternoon he led a hastily assembled cruiser squadron out of Rabaul. This force consisted of heavy cruisers CHOKAI (flagship), AOBA, FURUTAKA, KINUGASA, and KAKO; light cruisers YUBARI and TENRYU; and destroyer YUNAGI, the only Jap DD then available in the area for battle duty.

Well aware that he was up against superior forces, Mikawa planned a fast hit-and-run strike to set the Allies back on their heels and clear the way across Savo Sound for a convoy of six troopships to be rushed from Rabaul to reinforce the Imperial Guadalcanal garrison. Mikawa timed the strike for the early hours of August 9. To reach the target in time, the run down through the Solomons archipelago had to be made during daylight of the 8th.

At the outset several B-17's of MacArthur's command sighted the cruisers on the move in St. George's Channel. The movement was reported, but the ships were too close to Rabaul for any indication of their intentions, and the report, due to slow transmission, was delayed.

This snail-paced report was the first error in a series destined to make Savo a name no Navy man likes to remember. Less reprehensible than the delay, but equally disastrous, was inaccurate identification of the enemy ships as *"three cruisers, three destroyers, and two seaplane tenders or gunboats."*

Because the airmen reported "two seaplane tenders" with the advancing Japanese force, Admiral Turner assumed the enemy contemplated an air, rather than a surface, strike. On Santa Isabel Island, 155 miles northwest of Savo, there was a bay perfectly suited for a seaplane base. Logic suggested the enemy force would put in there.

As for American carrier planes, Admiral Fletcher had precipitately withdrawn his carrier force from the Guadalcanal area in the evening of August 8, reporting to Admiral

Ghormley that his ships were low on fuel and his fighter-strength dangerously reduced.

At the very hour that Fletcher's carriers were retiring, Mikawa's cruisers were steaming down the "Slot" toward Savo Sound. By midnight of the 8th, the Jap ships, unde-tected since that morning, were at a point about 35 miles from Savo Island.

Meanwhile Admiral Crutchley disposed his screening forces in positions calculated to cover the Guadalcanal and Tulagi beachheads. Savo Sound had been divided into three sectors. A Northern, a Southern, and an Eastern Force were stationed in the respective sectors. The Northern Force was stationed inside a triangle immediately to the east of Savo Island, the Southern Force occupied a trapezoid to the south of Savo, and the Eastern Force operated in an area east of a line which extended from the western tip of Florida Island to Lunga Point.

Positioned to block the waters between Savo and Florida, the Northern Force consisted of U.S. cruisers VINCENNES, ASTORIA, and QUINCY, and destroyers HELM and WILSON. This force was under command of Captain F. L. Riefkohl in VINCENNES.

The Southern Force contained the Australian cruisers AUSTRALIA and CANBERRA, the USS CHICAGO, and destroyers PATTERSON and BAGLEY. Admiral Crutchley in AUSTRALIA was in immediate command of this force.

The Eastern Force, positioned below Florida Island, was composed of light cruisers SAN JUAN and HMAS HOBART, and destroyers MONSSEN and BUCHANAN. It was commanded by Rear Admiral Norman Scott whose flag was in SAN JUAN.

At Lunga Roads was Admiral Turner in flag transport MCCAWLEY, with 19 troop and supply ships which were to be unloaded that night, some at Guadalcanal, some at Tulagi.

An enemy trying to slip around Savo Island and get into the Sound for a crack at Tulagi or Lunga Roads would al-most certainly be intercepted by the Northern or Southern Forces on patrol.

To tighten the guard, two picket destroyers were assigned to sentry beats outside the western entrances. Destroyer RALPH TALBOT patrolled a line to the northwest of Savo Island; destroyer BLUE patrolled a line to the southwest. Both RALPH TALBOT and BLUE carried SC radar. It was as-sumed that, making radar sweeps, they could detect and report any enemy forces which might attempt to pass north or south of Savo Island.

Analysts have since pointed out that the disposition con-tained a number of serious flaws; that the picket screen of only two destroyers was weak; that their older-style SC radars had a reliable range of no more than 10 miles; and that when each destroyer was at the far end of her patrol line, the "center" was not covered. Admiral Scott's flagship SAN JUAN, the only ship with the new SG surface radar, was located far in the eastern backfield.

Again, the picket destroyers were not stationed far enough west to give the forces to the east of Savo Island adequate preliminary warning in the event of a contact. Finally, the Allied cruiser groups were too far apart to support each other if an engagement developed.

So the stage was set and the curtain was rising on what some historians consider the Navy's worst performance of the war. Moving toward Savo Island were five Jap heavy cruisers, two light cruisers, and a single destroyer—eight ships in all. Available for the defense of Savo Sound were four United States heavy cruisers and a U.S. light cruiser, two Australian heavy cruisers and a light, and eight United States destroyers —a total of 16 ships. The Japs had the advantage of initiative. But the Allies had what should have been the overwhelming advantage of radar.

The night was sultry, overcast, and murky, with visibility varying between 4,000 and 12,000 yards. About half an hour before midnight a steamy rain-squall swept southeastward from Savo Island, drawing a watery curtain between the Northern Force and the Southern. All Allied ships were held at Condition II of readiness—half the crew on watch, the other half "in the sack," sleeping in exhaustion. Around 2345 when the mid-watch was pulling itself together to go on duty, there was the drone of planes in the sky.

The planes were Jap scouts catapulted from the approaching cruisers to search the Sound ahead. One was glimpsed and identified by destroyer RALPH TALBOT. Her skipper, Lieutenant Commander J. W. Callahan, immediately broadcast the alarm over TBS. WARNING WARNING PLANE OVER SAVO HEADED EAST.

To the southward, destroyer BLUE heard this alarm, and made radar contact with a plane. Cruiser QUINCY also made a radar contact, but thought nothing of it. And cruiser VINCENNES sighted aircraft, but her captain assumed they were Allied because their running lights were on. None of the ships in the Sound opened fire on the Jap scouts, and in consequence they were able to work without hindrance and to furnish Mikawa with a good picture of the Allied naval disposition.

But why had RALPH TALBOT's alarm been ignored?

Another of those bad breaks. The destroyer's voice radio

was short-range, and weather conditions created static. The original alarm did not get through to Admiral Turner, only 20 miles away in flagship McCAWLEY. As a result, the senior commands failed to obtain the word.

Certainly everything conspired to favor the oncoming Japs. With the Allied cruiser forces located, and a fair idea of the shipping at Lunga Point and Tulagi, Admiral Mikawa squared away to strike. With his warships in an extended column—CHOKAI in the lead, followed by heavy cruisers, light cruisers, and destroyer YUNAGI as "tail-end Charlie"— he set a course to pass south of Savo Island, and ordered a high-speed advance on Guadalcanal.

Now occurred a break which was utterly fantastic. As the Japs came highballing down the track in the early morning of August 9, destroyer BLUE (the southern picket) was steaming toward the southwest end of her beat. Simultaneously, RALPH TALBOT (the northern picket) was beating well along in the opposite direction. Both ships had their fantails toward the approaching enemy. And apparently the destroyer lookouts, relying heavily on the radar watch, were concentrating on the waters ahead, and neglecting the waters aft.

At 0554 CHOKAI's lookouts sighted the BLUE. She was then about 5½ miles distant, and the Jap cruisermen were certain CHOKAI had been sighted in return. Pressing onward, the Japs trained their guns on the American destroyer and held their breaths. Then they relaxed. The American destroyer moved ploddingly away, paying no apparent attention. Racing on at about 25 knots, the Japanese cruiser squadron passed with some 500 yards of the BLUE—and remained undetected!

Mikawa, however, could not believe his luck. With every reason to think BLUE must have seen and reported him, he abruptly ordered a course-change to pass north of Savo Island. Then, as the column swung northward, CHOKAI's lookouts spied—or thought they spied—another destroyer. This could only have been the RALPH TALBOT. But according to her log, she was then about ten miles away. Yet the lookouts did report a ship, and Mikawa swung the column back on its original south-of-Savo course. Needless to add, RALPH TALBOT's lookouts did not see the Japanese ships.

So both of the American picket destroyers missed the enemy. Because of unfavorable atmospheric conditions and the background "interference" of Savo Island, the SC radars failed to pick up the Japanese column, and the eight Jap ships went by as though they wore invisible cloaks.

Mikawa's column entered the passage between Savo Island and Guadalcanal. And at 0134 the Jap lookouts sighted a third destroyer, range 3,00 yards, off the south coast of Savo

Island, heading westward. Once again the Japs enjoyed fantastic luck. For this DD was the USS JARVIS, badly damaged during the previous day's air raid. As will be seen, she was off Savo at that hour by mere accident, and if she sighted the enemy, she had no means for communicating the alarm. Passing south of her, the Jap ships were safe. Mikawa detached the destroyer YUNAGI to protect his rear from BLUE and JARVIS. The column raced on through the passage. The foxes were in the hen-house!

At 0136 CHOKAI's lookouts glimpsed two destroyers directly ahead. These were PATTERSON and BAGLEY, screening cruisers CANBERRA and CHICAGO of the Southern Force.

On the port bow of CANBERRA, destroyer PATTERSON (Commander F. R. Walker) was the first Allied ship to sight the Japs. Instantly she radioed the alarm: *"Warning! Warning! Strange ships entering the harbor!"* But the time was 0143. Already the Jap cruisers had launched torpedoes. And now brilliant flares, dropped by Jap float planes, illumined the anchorage off Lunga Point and silhouetted CANBERRA and CHICAGO. Simultaneously CHOKAI and two other Jap cruisers opened fire.

A rain of shells fell on HMAS CANBERRA, and at the same time two torpedoes smashed into her starboard side. In an instant she was swaddled in flames and listing to starboard, disabled.

After flashing a repeat warning by blinker, PATTERSON's skipper had swung the destroyer hard left to bring her batteries to bear. The gunners fired starshell; then Commander Walker ordered a torpedo spread. The torpedo order went unheard, but the DD's guns opened up with a roar. An answering salvo smashed her No. 4 gun, put another gun out of action, and started a fire. The blaze was soon extinguished, and PATTERSON's guns kept on shooting as long as the enemy ships were in sight.

On CANBERRA's starboard bow, destroyer BAGLEY (Lieutenant Commander G. A. Sinclair) swung hard left to fire a starboard torpedo salvo at the enemy cruisers. So sudden was the attack that the torpedoes could not be readied for this salvo. BAGLEY continued to circle until the port torpedoes were brought to bear. The salvo was fired, but by that time the Jap cruisers were beyond range.

While BAGLEY's torpedomen were striving to insert primers into the starboard "fish," the Jap cruisers had turned northward and flung torpedoes at CHICAGO. At 0147 a torpedo smashed home, shearing off some of CHICAGO's bow. Her gunners fired starshells; the starshells were squibs. Unable to see any targets, CHICAGO floundered in uncertainty; then she spotted an enemy searchlight ahead. The light was from destroyer YUNAGI. CHICAGO opened fire; the Jap destroyermen snapped off their light. The damaged American cruiser ran blindly westward, and so on out of the battle.

Having dealt with the Allied Southern Force, the Jap cruiser column split up, racing northeastward. The split-up—unintentional, as the ships fell out of formation—left CHOKAI, AOBA, KAKO, and KINUGASA in column to the east of YUBARI, TENRYU, and FURUTAKA. Running on roughly parallel courses, the two Jap groups had the fabulous fortune to catch Captain Riefkohl's Northern Force betwixt and between.

The Northern Force had been steaming between Savo Island and Florida Island, following the legs of a square or "box patrol." The three American cruisers were in column, VINCENNES leading QUINCY and ASTORIA. Destroyers HELM (Lieutenant Commander C. E. Carroll) and WILSON (Lieutenant Commander W. H. Price) were screening ahead of VINCENNES.

Moving at 10 knots, the American ships were turning the southern corner of the square, and heading northwestward, when CHOKAI saw them and opened fire with torpedoes and shells. A moment later AOBA caught cruiser QUINCY smack on the quarter with a glaring searchlight. AOBA opened fire. Blazing guns, whistling projectiles, and dazzling searchlights stunned the Americans. General Quarters had been sounded, but battle stations were not yet fully manned. Gun-flashes had been seen far to southward, but Captain Riefkohl had assumed CHICAGO was shooting at aircraft. To add to the night's confusion, CHICAGO had failed to warn the Northern Force about the enemy cruisers.

So Riefkohl's force suddenly found itself in a battle that exploded like a bolt from the black. Within a few minutes all three American cruisers suffered multiple hits. Riddled, ASTORIA burst into an inferno. Caught between the CHOKAI column and the inside Jap column, the QUINCY was soon shot into hopeless wreckage. Torpedoes and shells smashed into VINCENNES. Disabled and burning, the three American cruisers fought back. Their shells hit CHOKAI, AOBA, and KINUGASA, but the Japs, getting off with minor damage, left destruction in their wake.

For the American destroyers with the Northern Force the battle was a hellish scramble of blind-man's-buff. The enemy was here, there, and yonder, and the American cruisers were in the line of fire. Destroyer WILSON hurled some shots at CHOKAI, but her 5-inchers could not reach Mikawa's flagship. Bewildered in the melee, destroyer HELM had difficulty distinguishing friend from foe. She fired four rounds of 5-inch, then took off in pursuit of what proved to be a friendly ship—perhaps destroyer RALPH TALBOT. The Jap cruisers paid scant attention to WILSON and HELM; Mikawa was concentrating on American heavies.

By 0220 the Jap admiral was satisfied that he had done a *banzai* job. Ordering a withdrawal, he swung CHOKAI north-westward. The two Jap columns, going around Savo Island counter-clockwise, headed for Rabaul. Behind them they left the USS VINCENNES, ASTORIA, and QUINCY, and HMAS CANBERRA all sinking.

But there was one more target up ahead. Squarely in the path of the inside Japanese column was the picket destroyer RALPH TALBOT.

Damaging of USS RALPH TALBOT

When RALPH TALBOT heard the alarm broadcast by destroyer PATTERSON, Lieutenant Commander Callahan headed his picket DD southwestward at top speed. Distant flashings in Savo Sound resembled the faraway flares of a thunderstorm, but the destroyermen knew a battle when they saw one.

The baleful flashings came closer. Then the glow of burning ships flushed the overcast. And then, about 0217, the blue-white ray of a searchlight swept across the water and focussed on RALPH TALBOT. An instant later she was target for a rain of shells that fell close aboard and showered her with colored splashes. A hit wrecked her No. 1 torpedo tube and killed two men. Callahan's hair went up. Those colored splashes were like American dye. He flashed recognition signals, and shouted the word over TBS. The firing abruptly stopped.

This first cluster of salvos may have been American, or they may have come from the Jap light cruiser TENRYU, at that time swinging northwestward around Savo Island. In any case RALPH TALBOT was passing dead ahead of the YUBARI-TENRYU-FURUTAKA column, like a Ford crossing the main line in front of the Limited Express. YUBARI now switched on her searchlights, and RALPH TALBOT was in for it.

Fire was opened at 3,300 yards, Japs and American destroyermen letting go in unison. YUBARI's gunners found the mark. The destroyermen fired four torpedoes, which missed, and they may have hit the cruiser with a shell or two. YUBARI's light went out, and the enemy ships raced by, their skippers doubtless thinking they had demolished another American vessel.

With flames pouring from her charthouse, her power and steering control gone, and her hull listing 20°, RALPH TALBOT was badly hurt. But she was far from demolished. A friendly rainsquall swept over her like a benison. Valiantly battling the damage, her engineers regained pressure in the after boilers, and she limped close in to Savo Island. There the fire was extinguished, the list taken off, and temporary repairs were made. Eventually, with 12 of her crew dead, two missing, and 23 wounded, she hobbled into port at Tulagi.

Savo Aftermath ("Ironbottom Bay")

The Japanese departure did not end the shooting.

About 0300 of that hectic morning of August 9 destroyer PATTERSON was ordered by CHICAGO's Captain H. D. Bode to go to the assistance of disabled CANBERRA. As PATTERSON jockeyed alongside the burning Australian cruiser, the latter's ammunition began to explode. And it was not until about 0400 that Walker and his destroyermen were able to aid the Australians in fighting the inferno.

It was soon evident that the fires could not be controlled in time for the cruiser to retire that morning with Admiral Turner's forces. The order was given to abandon. While the "Aussies" were going overside, an unidentified vessel came up out of the west in the darkness at 0510. PATTERSON challenged, and received no answer. After two more unanswered challenges, PATTERSON put a light on the stranger. The other opened fire. After an exchange of several salvos, Commander Walker thought he recognized CHICAGO's silhouette. Hurriedly he sent up emergency recognition signals. The stranger was indeed CHICAGO, and the gun duel was called off.

Destroyer BLUE came up at 0622 to aid CANBERRA, and she and PATTERSON took off the 680 Australian survivors, who were carried to the transport anchorage at Guadalcanal. About 0800, to prevent possible enemy capture, CANBERRA was torpedo-sunk by destroyer ELLET.

A flaming funeral pyre, cruiser QUINCY had capsized and sunk at 0235. Fifteen minutes later, the fire-gutted VINCENNES rolled over and went down. Some of the survivors of these two cruisers were picked up by destroyers BAGLEY and HELM.

BAGLEY also rescued some cruisermen from the ASTORIA, going bow-to-bow alongside the burning ship to take off sailors who were trapped on her forecastle. A little later the plucky destroyermen edged up to remove a party from the cruiser's fantail.

As ASTORIA remained afloat, 300 of her crew went back aboard to fight the fire. By daylight she was under tow of a minesweeper, and destroyer WILSON was on hand to aid the fire-fighting. Late in the morning WILSON and BAGLEY were relieved by destroyer BUCHANAN, whose men pitched into the ship-saving effort. But ASTORIA was too far gone to be saved. By noon her main deck was awash; the cruisermen abandoned; and at 1215 the ship capsized and sank.

To the Japanese forces at Savo the Fates had presented a stupendous victory. At the cost of minor damage to CHOKAI, AOBA, and KINUGASA, and an insignificant scratch on KAKO, the Jap warships had sent three United States heavy cruisers to the bottom; had fatally disabled an Australian heavy cruiser; and had left an American destroyer sorely crippled. Some 111 Japs had been killed or wounded. The American death toll totaled 1,023 officers and men. And 709 Americans were wounded.

By the hard-hit Navy, Savo Sound—graveyard of warships —would always be remembered as "Ironbottom Bay." And the Battle of Savo Island would be grimly remembered as a horror of fouled-up communications, fuddled tactics, mistaken moves, and atrocious breaks.

Facing the issue squarely, the Navy lost no time in conducting an investigation to find out what went wrong. Among other things, the Navy learned it needed more training for night surface actions.

Meantime the Japs indirectly scored another Savo killing by sinking the American destroyer JARVIS.

Loss of USS JARVIS

JARVIS (Lieutenant Commander W. W. Graham, Jr.) was one of the destroyers screening the transport group at Lunga Roads when the Jap planes lashed at this shipping in the noon hour of August 8, 1942.

The transports were under way, and the ships maneuvered radically to dodge bombs and torpedoes. But some of the enemy bombers got in through the AA barrage. And a moment after the transport GEORGE F. ELLIOT was hit by a crash-diving plane, JARVIS was struck by a torpedo.

Fourteen destroyermen were killed, and seven were badly wounded in the explosion which ripped a ragged hole in the destroyer's hull. When the air attack was over, DEWEY moved in to assist the disabled vessels. She took the burning transport in tow (beyond salvage, this ship had to be sunk later) after towing JARVIS inshore.

Examination showed the destroyer's injuries had not left her entirely crippled; her engines were not wrecked, and Lieutenant Commander Graham was certain she could make port under her own steam. As the destroyer tender DOBBIN was at that time stationed in Sydney, Graham determined to lose no time in getting there with JARVIS so that she might be repaired and sent back into action as soon as possible.

This was a brave decision for Graham to make, for the ship would have to run a long gantlet in skirting Guadalcanal, and the severe damage she had suffered would reduce her speed. But the officers under him were undobutedly eager to try it. As the hull was leaking, everything topside that could be jettisoned was thrown overside—boats and rafts included —to save weight. The engines were tested, and their performance was satisfactory.

Admiral Turner had dispatched a message directing the destroyer to stand by for an escort and then to depart by an eastern channel. Apparently Lieutenant Commander Graham never received these orders. So crippled JARVIS limped straight into the Battle of Savo Island.

At 0250 in the morning of August 9, the destroyer BLUE, on picket duty off Savo, glimpsed the JARVIS rounding Cape Esperance to the southwest. BLUE closed the range to identify the silhouette, and in so doing was diverted from the savage conflict at that hour raging in the Sound.

BLUE noted that JARVIS was limping along at 8 knots, and trailing a long slick of oil. Satisfied as to the lamed ship's identity, the picket destroyer turned away at 0325. JARVIS passed out of sight, gamely going it alone.

Not long after daybreak JARVIS was sighted by a scout plane from SARATOGA southwest of Guadalcanal at lat. 9-42 S, long. 158-59 E. The destroyer was in bad shape, down by the head and trailing oil. As she had passed through the thick of the Savo battle, analysts who studied that wild engagement concluded she could have been hit by fire from CHICAGO—a possibility, as she was within range of the cruiser's guns. And YUNAGI may have disabled JARVIS. For the Jap DD reported an attack on a "light cruiser" heading westward—undoubtedly JARVIS.

In any event, the SARATOGA scout plane was the last friendly eye to see the ship. JARVIS was never heard from again. It was presumed she foundered, and her fate remained a mystery until Japanese records were inspected after the war. The records disclosed that JARVIS was attacked and sunk by torpedo-bombers of the Japanese 25th Air Flotilla at 1300 in the afternoon of August 9, 1942.

Acting on word from YUNAGI that the damaged ship was in the area, the Jap planes combed the seascape and found the target. The aviators reported that they took her for a "light cruiser," and their onslaught was devastating. Lieutenant Commander Graham and his men were doomed. All hands—some 247—were lost with the ship.

Loss *of* USS BLUE

If any ship seemed to steam under an unlucky star, it was BLUE. At Savo Island she had missed a Japanese squadron only 500 yards distant. Again, she had been diverted from the scene of action by contact with crippled destroyer JARVIS. She was the only ship within 15 miles of Savo which did not fire a shot in that sorry battle.

Now, as though following some course predetermined by destiny, she approached the climax of an ill-starred career. It was the evening of August 21, 1942.

At that date and time destroyer BLUE (Commander H. N. Williams) was steaming in company with destroyers HENLEY and HELM as escort for supply ships FOMALHAUT and ALHENA bound for Guadalcanal.

Indispensable Strait had been transited safely, and the convoy was off Tiavu Point at the eastern reaches of Lengo Channel when BLUE's "final orders" came. They came by way of a dispatch from Admiral Turner directing the BLUE and destroyer HENLEY (Lieutenant Commander E. K. Van Swearingen) to leave the convoy and race ahead to Savo Sound where they were to intercept enemy naval forces bear-down on Lunga Point.

The two DD's peeled off as ordered, and sprinted at top speed for "Ironbottom Bay." By mid-watch, August 22, they were in that dark body of water. At 0324, when the destroyers were near the center of Savo Sound, BLUE's radar and sonar instruments registered contact with an unidentified target. But the contact petered out; in the moonless dark nothing was seen; at 0346 the DD's slowed to 10 knots and patrolled at cautious pace, the lookouts tense and watchful.

Another suspicious radar and sonar contact was picked up by BLUE at 0355. She was then steaming eastward, about 400 yards ahead of HENLEY, and her electronic detection gear indicated the target as 5,000 yards distant on the starboard beam—a high-speed vessel of some sort, doing anywhere from "20 to 50" knots. HENLEY also made radar contact with this target, and off across the water a creamy wake was sighted. Was the vessel foe or friend?

Neither destroyer took a positive or offensive action. Continuing on her course at unchanged speed, BLUE brought her guns and torpedo tubes to bear, but she held her fire. HENLEY, too, held her fire. The range closed to 3,200 yards as the high-speed "stranger" approached. The stranger was a Jap DD.

At 0359, shocked lookouts on board BLUE suddenly saw a spread of phosphorescent wakes reaching through the water

toward their destroyer's stern. Compliments of Jap DD
Kamikaze.

"*Torpedo!*"

The cry was drowned out by the roar of exploding war
heads. Flame enveloped BLUE's stern; men, guns, and gear
were flung skyward; and the destroyer reeled to a halt dragging a shattered fantail.

HENLEY steamed forward to guard the paralyzed destroyer.
At daylight she took BLUE in tow. Ensued a gruelling haul to
Tulagi.

It was a sad destroyer BLUE that crawled at rope's end
toward the harbor—eight dead and 22 wounded among her
complement, and nothing to show but her battle scars. Then
even the Tulagi haul was to go for naught. As a large Japanese force was approaching Guadalcanal that night, Destroyer
Division Commander Robert Hall Smith recommended that
BLUE be scuttled to prevent possible capture. Admiral Turner
issued the order, and BLUE was sent to the bottom of "Ironbottom Bay."

GAMBLE *Kills* I-123

Operating with the Jap fleet in the Solomons arena was an
Advance Expeditionary Force of submarines. This undersea
contingent contained I-9, I-11, I-17, I-19, I-26, I-31, I-174,
and I-175. With it were three submarines of Mikawa's command—I-121, I-123, and RO-34. In August the I-boats began
to rear their ugly periscope heads in the waters east of
Guadalcanal.

It remained for an old "four-piper," an ex-DD, to wipe out
the first of the subs that went down in the enemy's Guadalcanal offensive. The old-timer was the USS GAMBLE. Converted into a destroyer-minelayer, GAMBLE was on duty off
Guadalcanal as an A/S vessel. At 0805 in the morning of
August 29, her lookouts sighted the conning tower of a large
submarine some 9,000 yards distant.

GAMBLE's skipper, Lieutenant Commander S. N. Tackney,
snapped the crew into action. Though the old "four-piper"
had taken up mine-planting as a vocation, she still carried
depth-charge gear. She attacked the sub with "ashcans" at
0844, and kept at it for the next three hours.

After her last attack, made at 1147, a large quantity of oil
surged to the surface, bearing in its dark tide the splintered
remnants of deck planking. The kill was eventually verified by
Japanese records opened for post-war inspection. In the bloodstained waters off Guadalcanal, GAMBLE had sunk I-123.

"SARA" *Blasted!* WASP *Sunk!*

GAMBLE's killing of I-123, and the damage dealt I-9 and I-17, removed three Japanese subs from the seas off Guadalcanal. But other I-boats remained in the area. And while Japanese destroyers and troop convoys continued to reinforce the Imperial Army on Guadalcanal, and Jap aircraft hammered at Allied convoys bound for Lunga Point, the I-boats tried to set up an undersea blockade.

The day before GAMBLE sank I-123, airmen from the U.S. carrier WASP sighted and drove off an I-boat in the carrier's vicinity. Then, at 0746, the following morning, destroyer MACDONOUGH (Lieutenant Commander E. V. Dennett), screening on "SARA's" starboard bow, made an urgent sonar contact dead ahead.

The contact was hardly reported to the bridge before MACDONOUGH's lookouts sighted a periscope close aboard. By the time it took to get a shout out of a dry throat, the cobra-headed thing was only 30 feet from the destroyer's bow. In one split second (0746) the destroyermen hoisted the submarine warning signal; in another they shouted the word over TBS, "Torpedoes heading for carrier!"; and in another they dropped two depth charges. In the excitement, someone forgot to apply depth settings. And as the futile charge splashed into the water, something rasped like a giant piece of sandpaper aaginst MACDONOUGH's hull. She had literally rubbed elbows with the Jap submarine.

Meantime, the sub—the I-26—had launched a spread of six "fish" at the SARATOGA. One of these jumped out of the water astern of MACDONOUGH. The others raced on toward the target.

With hard right rudder and a burst of speed, Captain D. C. Ramsey strove to swing the great ship to comb the wakes. It was like trying to move the Flatiron Building at moment's notice. One minute ticked away. Then another. Then came the big jolt as a torpedo smashed into the starboard side of the flattop abreast of the island, and a geyser erupted against the sky. *Boom!* Stabbed by a submarine at the very start of the war, "SARA" had been nailed again.

Luckily the blast did not cause severe structural damage. With eleven of the crew injured and Admiral Fletcher wounded, the big carrier limped off for Tongatabu.

Early in the afternoon of September 15, while carriers WASP and HORNET were escorting an Allied reinforcement convoy to Guadalcanal, two Jap I-boats slipped through the screen. As WASP was making a routine turn, her lookouts sighted torpedo wakes to starboard. Before Captain F. P.

Sherman could swing the ship, two Japanese "fish" hit her. A third torpedo glanced off the hull, and a fourth passed under the keel of destroyer LANSDOWNE.

WASP was fatally blasted. The explosions tossed her planes in the air as though they were jackstraws. Fire burst from ruptured gasoline lines. Ready ammunition began to go off, and the ship assumed a dangerous starboard list. About half an hour after she was hit, a monstrous eruption shattered the ship internally, and Captain Sherman was soon compelled to order her abandonment. That evening the flaming hulk was sunk by torpedoes from destroyer LANSDOWNE. Some 193 of the carrier's crew of 2,247 had perished in the molten ship.

The submarine which torpedoed WASP was the I-19. With her was the I-15. And so the HORNET had a close call. She was about five miles northeast of WASP when the latter was struck. And within a few minutes of that blasting, torpedoes were racing toward HORNET.

Destroyer LANSDOWNE had voiced the alarm over TBS, but the word did not reach all of the ships in HORNET's screen. Lookouts on destroyer MUSTIN, on HORNET's port bow, were suddenly shocked by the sight of a torpedo wake. The deadly "fish" skimmed under MUSTIN's keel as the destroyermen stared, aghast. Then, seconds later, it smashed into battleship NORTH CAROLINA, some 500 yards away.

The blast killed five men in the battleship, and blew an enormous underwater hole in her port side. But the big "wagon" kept right on going at 25 knots, and eventually she steamed into port under her own power.

About two minutes after NORTH CAROLINA was slugged, a torpedo slammed into destroyer O'BRIEN. The blast did not kill her, but it left her badly crippled. And her disablement eventually caused her untimely death.

The convoy carrying the 7th Marine Regiment reached Guadalcanal in safety. But the sinking of WASP at a time when ENTERPRISE and SARATOGA were on the binnacle list was a major disaster. HORNET was now the only Allied aircraft carrier left in the South Pacific.

Loss of USS O'BRIEN

The blow that struck O'BRIEN laid open her stem, leaving a tremendous gash from keel to hawsepipe—a jagged hole that forced the vessel to veer and shudder violently, slowing the ship.

O'BRIEN staggered as the shock vibrated her hull, wrenched her framework, jolted her internal machinery, and threw men headlong against bulkheads. Fortunately the blast did not start a fire, and the damage-controlmen were able to cope with the flooding. O'BRIEN's skipper, Commander T. Burrowes, reported that the engines were still running; the ship could do 15 knots.

At 1600 of that afternoon O'BRIEN was directed to proceed independently to Espiritu Santo, and she succeeded in making port the following day.

After emergency repairs at Espiritu, O'BRIEN limped on to Nouméa, where she was worked on by a tender. The tendermen patched her up, and a naval constructor signed her out as capable of a run to the States. She set out with destroyer LANG and an oiler.

In the morning of October 19, 1942, when the home-bound group was off Samoa, O'BRIEN suffered something like a spasmodic seizure. While in this spasm, she began to break up. Literally she came apart at the seams. Deep fractures developed in the shell plating of the forward engine-room; a longitudinal crack opened in her hull; her keel snapped; and she pulled apart like a worn-out bushel basket.

Happily all hands got off in time, and there were no casualties.

The wreckage sank at 0759, and the hard-pressed Fleet had lost another destroyer.

Battle of Cape Esperance

In spite of numerous wrecks caused by Marine Corps bombers, the "Tokyo Express" continued to run down the "Slot" with depressing regularity. By the end of September, 1942, some 26,000 Imperial troops and a Jap naval contingent of 3,500 men were facing the Marines at Lunga Point. In the vicinity of Bougainville pagoda-masted warships were clustered in herds. Another Guadalcanal showdown was brewing.

At Nouméa 6,000 American soldiers prepared to embark for "Cactus." The HORNET task force took up a covering position to the west of Guadalcanal. A task force headed by battleship WASHINGTON moved into the seascape east of Malaita. For further protection Admiral Ghormley dispatched a newly-organized cruiser force from Espiritu Santo to the waters south of Guadalcanal, to cover the convoy's left flank. As it happened this force, with code name "Task Force Sugar," was to shoulder most of the protection burden.

Under command of Rear Admiral Norman Scott, Task Force Sugar consisted of heavy cruisers SAN FRANCISCO (flagship) and SALT LAKE CITY, light cruisers BOISE and HELENA, and the following destroyers:

FARENHOLT   *Comdr. E. T. Seaward*
                     Flying the pennant of
              Capt. R. G. Tobin, COMDESRON 12
BUCHANAN   *Comdr. R. E. Wilson*
LAFFEY   *Lt. Comdr. W. E. Hank*
DUNCAN   *Comdr. E. B. Taylor*
MCCALLA   *Comdr. W. G. Cooper*

The force stood out of Espiritu Santo on October 7 and set a course toward Rennel Island. After getting there they cruised off the southwest coast of Guadalcanal for two more days. Then, in the afternoon of October 11, scouting aircraft sighted a Jap "express" coming down the "Slot" about 210 miles from Guadalcanal. To intercept, Admiral Scott led his ships around the western end of the island to Cape Esperance where they could cover the entry to Savo Sound.

At 2325 U.S. cruiser HELENA made radar contact with the oncoming enemy. But HELENA let 15 minutes elapse before reporting this contact. She was carrying new SG radar gear, and her captain evidently wanted to confirm the contact. However, at 2330 a SAN FRANCISCO search plane sighted enemy ships approaching Cape Esperance, and Scott knew the foe was in the immediate offing.

Task Force Sugar was at that time off the west coast of Savo Island, heading northeastward. The ships were in column with destroyers FARENHOLT, DUNCAN, and LAFFEY in the van, followed by SAN FRANCISCO, BOISE, SALT LAKE CITY, HELENA, BUCHANAN, and MCCALLA, in that order. Intending to block the passage between Savo and Cape Esperance, Admiral Scott called for the column to reverse course.

The order "Left to course 230 degrees!" was voiced over the TBS. Led by flagship SAN FRANCISCO, the cruisers smartly executed the maneuver, as did rear destroyers BUCHANAN and MCCALLA. But van destroyers FARENHOLT, DUNCAN, and LAFFEY, supposed to swing out as a separate column to regain head position, made a belated swing. They were thus left in the rear of the southbound cruiser column.

Squadron Commander Tobin now led the three DD's in a race down the starboard flank of the cruiser column in an effort to regain the van. But the battle exploded before Tobin's destroyers could get into the lead. FARENHOLT and LAFFEY were well abreast of the cruiser column when HELENA (time: 2346) opened fire on a target she had tracked by radar and then sighted some 5,000 yards to starboard.

The gunnery from HELENA was touched off by another of those freakish "breaks." When the HELENA, having made definite radar contact, requested permission to open fire, Admiral Scott's reply was, "Roger!" He meant he'd received the message. But HELENA's captain took the acknowledgment for permission to open fire.

Scott's captains had been supposed to open fire on their own discretion. But the Admiral doubtless would have restrained the cruiser guns until the destroyer situation cleared. Captain Tobin had advised him that the three destroyers were coming up to starboard, but Scott could not discern their exact position. And with the DD's somewhere between the American cruiser column and the enemy, their position was precarious, to say the least.

Moreover, DUNCAN had sheared out of line astern of FARENHOLT. While swinging on the hairpin turn, she had made radar contact wth the enemy. Assuming that FARENHOLT was heading for the enemy, DUNCAN's Commanding Officer sent the DD on a westward run toward the target. LAFFEY was apparently following FARENHOLT on a course parallel to the cruiser column when HELENA's guns opened up. Then the other cruisers let go. Tobin's disrupted destroyer column was right in the line of fire.

But the Japs were in an even worse position.

Steaming along without benefit of radar, Admiral Goto's cruiser column was making a beeline for Savo Island just as Admiral Scott's cruiser column executed its hairpin turn. Scott's column capped the Japanese "T" with a roaring broadside that sent a torrent of projectiles crashing around flagship AOBA. In that same burst of fire FURUTAKA was hard hit, and destroyer MURAKUMO was struck. Then, afraid that his cruisers were firing on Tobin's destroyers, Admiral Scott ordered a cease fire.

At this juncture Goto might have recovered somewhat, but he swung his ships on a column right, intending to reverse course—a fatal move which exposed each ship in turn to American fire. Some of Scott's captains did not hear the cease-fire order, and as AOBA made the turn a smacking salvo wrecked her bridge. It also wrecked Admiral Goto, who fell mortally wounded.

Admiral Scott now spoke with Tobin over the TBS, attempting to locate destroyers FARENHOLT, DUNCAN, and LAFFEY. Tobin informed him that the three DD's were coming up to starboard. Scott ordered them to flash recognition signals. When they did so, he ordered his cruisers to resume fire.

Destroyer DUNCAN had already been hit in. As has been related, she had made a single-handed dash toward the enemy force. When the Jap column turned right, DUNCAN found herself less than a mile from IJN FURUTAKA. Lieutenant Commander E. B. Taylor realized his ship was between two fires, and he did some desperate conning to bring his torpedo batteries to bear on FURUTAKA while dodging Jap and American shells.

For a starter DUNCAN shelled the Jap cruiser, then she shifted fire to an oncoming Jap destroyer (apparently MURAKUMO), then she fired two fast torpedo shots at FURUTAKA. At the same time she took hits which disabled her gun director, toppled her forward stack, and ignited the powder in her No. 2 handling room. A moment later DUNCAN was struck by what was evidently an American salvo. With her lights blown out, she staggered off in mortal disablement.

About the time DUNCAN was disabled, destroyer FARENHOLT was hard hit by what were probably American shells. A shot in the fireroom opened a leak in the main steam line of her No. 1 boiler, releasing a murderous jet which threatened to skin the crew alive. FARENHOLT's skipper, Lieutenant Commander E. T. Seaward, urged the fireroom watch to hold out as long as possible before it secured and abandoned. From the water tender in charge came the stalwart reply, *"We'll steam her into Tokyo!"*

Eventually she made Espiritu Santo under her own power.

In the meantime Admiral Scott had headed his cruiser column on a northwesterly course in an effort to maintain contact with the retiring enemy. Then BOISE picked up a radar "pip" and snapped on a searchlight. The American force now concentrated on KINUGASA, lashing her with shellfire as she fled northwestward. By 0200 the battle was over. Scott pulled his ships together, and sent destroyer MCCALLA out to round up and assist the cripples.

BOISE's cruisermen fought the ship's battle-damage with a determination that quenched flames and had her engines doing 20 knots by 0240. At that hour, too, destroyer FARENHOLT was going on her own steam. But destroyer DUNCAN—the only American ship to die in the engagement—was going down.

Loss of USS DUNCAN

DUNCAN was mortally wounded when she reeled out of the battle around midnight. The ship's superstructnre was a shambles. Everywhere lay the dead—in the shattered charthouse, on the bridge, in smoke-choked passageways and blasted compartments, and on the burning forecastle. But her engines were still pounding and the ship was circling blindly at 15 knots.

After a futile attempt to communicate with the crew aft,

her captain, Lieutenant Commander E. B. Taylor, ordered the bridge abandoned. When the wounded were let down to rafts, the Commanding Officer and the others went over. DUNCAN circled off across the seascape, a burning death-ship.

But there were still living men in that floating inferno—men topside and below decks who did not know the skipper had gone overside, or who thought everyone on the bridge had perished. Making his way to the after conning station, Ensign Frank A. Andrews succeeded in communicating with the Engineer Officer, Lieutenant H. R. Kabat. Assuming command as senior officer on board, Kabat ordered Ensign Andrews to beach the ship. Aided by Chief Torpedoman Boyd, Andrews strove to head the destroyer for Savo Island, to run her aground. Before they could get her inshore, the destroyer's bow was gutted by fire, and the engineers had to abandon the forward engine-room. Gradually the ship lost power and slowed to a stop.

About 0200 the ammunition began to explode, and the surviving members of the crew leapt overboard. Clinging to powder cans, rubbish, anything that could keep them afloat, they swam away from the bursting destroyer. Her fiery hull was presently sighted by destroyer McCALLA (Lieutenant Commander W. G. Cooper), hunting for BOISE to the west of Savo Island.

DUNCAN's survivors were in dire need of help. A school of sharks had caught the scent of blood. Around the huddle of floats and swimmers, the dark water had come alive with cruising dorsal fins and the gleam of slippery, white fish-bellies. Men and fish were engaged in a dreadful scuffling when the McCALLA party arrived on the scene. Rifle-fire broke up the shark attack only in time.

At daybreak destroyer McCALLA returned to search for survivors, and in a short time most of the living were picked up. A total of 195 officers and men were rescued. Most of the dead—some 48 or 50 of the crew—went down with the USS DUNCAN.

Loss of USS MEREDITH

For sheer horror the destruction of the DesPac destroyer MEREDITH surpassed anything thus far endured by destroyer-men in that Solomons war of nightmares.

Her last voyage began in mid-October when she set out from Espiritu Santo with a gasoline convoy bound for Guadalcanal. By that date the aviation fuel shortage in General Vandegrift's camp had become extremely critical. So an emergency convoy was scraped together—attack cargomen

BELLATRIX and ALCHIBA, PT-boat tender JAMESTOWN, and fleet tug (former minesweeper) VIREO, with destroyers NICHO-LAS (Commander W. D. Brown) and MEREDITH (Commander H. E. Hubbard) for escort. Each cargoman towed a barge loaded with 1,000 barrels of gasoline and 500 quarter-ton bombs.

On October 15 the ships were off San Cristobal Island, a day's run from their objective. Daylight brought a Japanese scout plane, a mosquito hovering against the sky. It hovered long enough to make a gratifying inspection of the convoy; then it flew over the western horizon. The destroyermen knew what was coming. At 0608, in accordance with a dispatch from Ghormley, the barge towed by BELLATRIX was shifted to VIREO. NICHOLAS then shepherded the two cargo ships and JAMESTOWN in a hasty retirement. MEREDITH and VIREO trudged steadily forward.

At 1050 the "bogie" attack came—a pair of Jap planes pouncing on the destroyer and the tug. The planes made two assaults; were twice beaten off by crack-shooting AA gunners. Then MEREDITH received word that two enemy warships were in her vicinity, and Commander Hubbard ordered VIREO to reverse course.

It was soon apparent that the tug VIREO, panting in an effort to make 14 knots, would have to be abandoned or would fall prey to the nearing enemy. At noon Commander Hubbard ordered the tug's crew to quit the vessel. MEREDITH picked up the VIREO crew, and drew off to sink the tug by torpedo fire. The destroyermen were squaring away to fire the torpedo shot when (time: 1215)a flight of 27 Japanese planes from the carrier ZUIKAKU roared across the sky.

Caught in a thundering, screaming blizzard of bombs, tor-pedoes, and machine-gun fire, the MEREDITH was literally torn to fragments. Her desperate gunners shot down three planes. But the destroyer was a shambles, and the wreckage sank in a trice. And the MEREDITH survivors struggled in a sea of smoke, blood, burning flotsam, and flaming oil.

On the rafts lay men who were wounded beyond hope and beyond the soothing lenitive of opiates—men with charred bodies, with crushed features, with riddled limbs. The strong supported the weak, and the maimed tried to comfort the blind. Among those dying on the rafts was MEREDITH's cap-tain, Commander Harry E. Hubbard. At the Naval Academy in 1925 he had graduated at the head of his class.

There was not enough room on the rafts, and those who were able remained in the water, clinging to lifelines. When a wounded man died, a swimmer would take his place on the gratings. And so there was a final horror—sharks.

Attracted by the scent of blood, a school of sharks trailed the drifting rafts, and glided in to nip and slash at the swimmers hanging to the lifelines. Kicking and stabbing, the destroyermen fought them off. On one occasion a shark slithered aboard a listing raft to attack a bleeding man. Ensued a ghastly scrimmage in which the shark gnashed a bite of flesh from the victim's thigh before he was driven overside.

For three days and nights the Purgatory persisted. At last, on October 18, the survivors were sighted and picked up by destroyers GRAYSON and GWIN, and the tug SEMINOLE. A ghostly 73 destroyermen were recovered. Some 185 of MEREDITH's crew had perished. Of the VIREO crew, 51 were lost. The gasoline convoy never reached Guadalcanal.

Chapter 15

Solomons Crucible

(The Guadalcanal Campaign)
(Part 2)

☆ ☆ ☆

Battle of Santa Cruz Islands

As of mid-October, 1942, the fierce Guadalcanal campaign had cost Des-Pac six destroyers: five downed in action, one sunk by a friendly mine. The six DD's were sorely missed by a Force straining every rivet to meet the pressures of supply and demand.

New destroyers were coming into the South Pacific—FLETCHER-class ships manned by well-trained men— but as yet they couldn't keep pace with the reserves from Tokyo. Yamamoto was now for pitching every available Jap warship into the crucible, and he had available in the South Pacific five aircraft carriers, five battleships, 14 cruisers, and 44 destroyers. On the Allied side in the South Pacific were two carriers, two battleships, nine cruisers and 24 destroyers— 37 warships against 68. "Operation Watchtower," the Allied effort to gain control of the Solomons area, had reached a crisis. And now, in a crucial four weeks' time, the Navy lost an aircraft carrier, two cruisers, and eight destroyers—seven of the latter in a battle which raged for three days. But the Japs were thrown back with a jolt which ripped their grip from Guadalcanal.

The first American destroyer lost in this Solomons tidal turn was the USS PORTER. She was sunk in the Battle of Santa Cruz Islands, and she went down in company with aircraft carrier HORNET.

Loss of USS PORTER

Death came for PORTER (Lieutenant Commander D. G. Roberts) at 1003 in the morning of October 26, 1942. Flagship of Captain C. P. Cecil, ComDesRon 5, the destroyer was working in the ENTERPRISE screen when enemy planes attacked Task Force 61 off the Santa Cruz Islands.

By mid-morning HORNET had been blasted, and the ENTER-PRISE screen was waiting with cocked guns for a glimpse of Jap aircraft. At 0958 a flight of "bogies" was reported about 30 miles away. PORTER's gunners tightened the chinstraps of their helmets and waited grimly.

At 1000 Roberts stopped his ship to pick up the pilot and gunner of an ENTERPRISE plane which had been shot down close aboard. The destroyermen were engaged in this rescue act when (time: 1002) a torpedo rushed through the sea 50 yards ahead of the ship. The alarm sent a shock through the destroyer. Then, before she could make an evasive swing, a second torpedo was sighted, lunging at the ship's port beam.

An ENTERPRISE pilot saw the deadly wake and came down in a power dive, lacing the water with machinegun lead in an attempt to blast the warhead. The "fish" beat the gun. Crashing into PORTER amidships, the torpedo exploded with a blast that wiped out both firerooms and instantly killed 11 destroyermen. PORTER staggered to a halt with steam pouring out of her wrecked boilers and oil spewing from her side.

At 1015 the enemy planes attacked ENTERPRISE. PORTER's gunners flailed at the flying "meatballs" while her damage-controlmen battled chaos below decks. Meantime, destroyer SHAW (Commander Wilber G. Jones), maneuvering to screen her disabled sister, made sonar contact with the submarine. Dropping depth charges, SHAW attacked furiously. But the undersea killer escaped.

At 1055 PORTER's predicament was seen as hopeless, and SHAW was ordered alongside to take off the crew. Circling away, SHAW then pumped gunfire into the half-sunk ship to speed her journey to the bottom. She took her dead down with her. Four of the nine men who had been wounded in the torpedo blast subsequently died.

The submarine responsible for this sinking was the I-21. But the score was soon to be evened as an American destroyer downed one of the I-21's sisters.

SOUTHARD *Kills* I-172

It was early in the morning of November 10, 1942, and the I-172 was enjoying a breather on the surface near Cape Recherché, San Cristobal. The fresh night air was invigorating, and the batteries were charging beautifully, and wrist watches made in Japan timed the hour as 0230. Perched atop the conning tower, the Jap lookouts scanned the dark seascape. Perhaps the lookouts were sleepy. At any rate the night was suddenly smashed by a flash of flame, a crescendo whistle, and the blast of an exploding salvo. I-172 was under fire.

The sub had been sighted at 0231 by the USS SOUTHARD, an old "four-stacker" which had been pressed into South Pacific service as a minesweeper. Skippered by Lieutenant Commander J. G. Tennent, III, the ex-DD was en route to Aola Bay, Guadalcanal, with ammunition and rations for a Marine Raider Battalion.

When SOUTHARD opened fire, the enemy sub made haste to submerge. But the old destroyer went after the target with sweeping sonar gear, and soon picked up the contact. At 0242 she attacked with depth charges.

Lieutenant Commander Tennent maneuvered SOUTHARD in for the kill. At 1003 the submarine's conning tower heaved up, and the destroyermen opened fire at 2,000 yards. A salvo crashed into the conning tower; the I-boat rolled at the blast, then thrust her bow toward the sky and plunged to the bottom to stay.

The Battle of Guadalcanal (November 13)

The three-day naval engagement, which came to be called the Battle of Guadalcanal, began on Friday, November 13, 1942. Friday the 13th. For the DesPac Force that was truly an unlucky day. Before it was two hours old, four American destroyers were sunk in combat, with heavy loss of life, and three were barbarously damaged.

Driven rabid by their inability to wipe out the American front on Guadalcanal, the Japanese War Lords had planned a supreme effort to regain the island.

The tip-off came when Admiral Halsey received word that Japanese war-shipping was concentrating at Truk, at Rabaul, and at various points in the upper Solomons. The shipping off Buin, Bougainville, and the Bismarcks was not for any run-of-the-mill "Tokyo Express." Something big was coming down the "Slot." And something bigger was coming down from Truk. To meet the threat some 6,000 additional Army troops and Marines were dispatched "special delivery" from Espiritu Santo and Nouméa to Guadalcanal. Admiral R. K. Turner's Amphibious Force warships did the delivering.

The convoy moved in two contingents. The first contingent was composed of three attack cargo ships under escort of a force commanded by Rear Admiral Norman Scott. This force consisted of flag cruiser ATLANTA, and the destroyers AARON WARD, FLETCHER, LARDNER, and McCALLA, under Captain R. G. Tobin, ComDesRon 12, in AARON WARD. The contingent left Espiritu Santo on November 9 and reached Lunga Roads on the 11th.

The second contingent, commanded by Admiral Turner, contained four transports, including flagship McCAWLEY, under escort of a task group composed of two cruisers and three destroyers. These ships left Nouméa on the 8th. When it arrived off San Cristobal Island on the 11th the convoy was joined by three more cruisers and five destroyers. All of the warships with Turner's contingent were units of Task Group 67.4, a Support Group under command of Rear Admiral Daniel J. Callaghan in flag cruiser SAN FRANCISCO.

Turner knew his forces in Savo Sound were heavily outweighed and outnumbered. Yet something had to be done to prevent a blasting of Henderson Field by the oncoming enemy battleships. To Callaghan's Support Group fell the defense of Guadalcanal.

In the twilight of November 12 Turner led his transports eastward, back toward Espiritu Santo. His ships were to be escorted to Espiritu by destroyers BUCHANAN (damaged), SHAW and McCALLA (low on fuel), and old-timers SOUTHARD and HOVEY (minesweepers). Callaghan's warships screened the convoy through Lengo Channel, then turned back to re-enter Savo Sound and cover the approaches to Lunga Point. The opening moves of this back-to-the-wall defense were left up to Admiral Callaghan.

The odds against Callaghan's force were long. The Japanese Striking Force which was advancing on Savo Sound included battleships HIEI and KIRISHIMA, light cruiser NAGARA, and 14 DD's. Somewhere behind it were two aircraft carriers, and up the "Slot" was a large transport group containing 12 DD's.

Against the Jap Striking Force and its potential reinforcements, the American force included heavy cruisers SAN FRANCISCO (flagship) and PORTLAND; light cruiser HELENA, anti-aircraft (AA) cruisers JUNEAU and ATLANTA, and eight DD's. The destroyers are listed below.

Two heavy cruisers and three light cruisers against two battleships and a light cruiser. Eight destroyers against 14. So stood the American Support Group against the Japanese Striking Force. It was going to be a battle in which brains would have to make up for brawn.

Steaming westward through Lengo Channel in total darkness, the Support Group was strung out in a long serpentine column. In the van were destroyers CUSHING, LAFFEY, STERETT, and O'BANNON. They were followed by cruisers ATLANTA, SAN FRANCISCO, PORTLAND, HELENA, and JUNEAU, in that order. Destroyers AARON WARD, BARTON, MONSSEN, and FLETCHER brought up the rear. This sort of column had been favorably employed by Admiral Scott in the Battle of Cape Esperance. But on the present occasion the alignment, in respect to radar work, could have been better. Three cruisers and two destroyers which carried the new SG surface radar had been given rear positions.

In command of the Japanese Striking Force, Vice Admiral Hiroaki Abe himself committed one or two errors in judgment on the eve of battle. He had been informed that a group of American warships were in the vicinity of Lunga Point, but he chose to assume that these men-of-war had retired eastward at sundown. And since his mission was to destroy Henderson Field, he loaded his guns with bombardment ammunition for that purpose and single-mindedly pressed forward into Savo Sound.

Early in the morning on Friday, November 13—a "Black Friday"—Callaghan's column was off Lunga Roads. Simultaneously the Japanese Striking Force steamed into the passage south of Savo Island. Americans and Japs were driving through the night on what amounted to a collision course.

At 0124 cruiser HELENA made radar contact with the enemy at 27,000 yards. Three minutes later Admiral Callaghan ordered his column to make a starboard turn which headed it straight for the enemy. In the meantime, destroyer O'BANNON made contact, and her skipper reported it over the TBS. As the range closed swiftly, the American TBS system became jammed with calls—a babel of range-and-bearing data, tactical orders, and requests for information. Once again the American communications apparatus was haywire, and the ships were plunged into battle with voice radios shouting in confusion.

Division Commander Stokes in lead destroyer CUSHING was straining his eyes on the darkness ahead. At 0141 Stokes suddenly sighted two Jap destroyers silhouetted in the starshine. They were I.J.N. YUDACHI and HARUSAME, screening ahead of Abe's battleship group. They were cutting directly across CUSHING's bow at a scant range of 3,000 yards.

CUSHING immediately radioed the word, and her skipper ordered a left turn to avoid headlong collision with the foe and to bring torpedo tubes to bear. The abrupt turn threw the rest of the van out of line, and cruiser ATLANTA had to sheer hard left to avoid ramming the turning DD's.

Callaghan's voice crackled over the TBS: WHAT ARE YOU DOING.

ATLANTA's captain answered: AVOIDING OUR OWN DESTROYERS.

Again the TBS circuit was jammed with inquiries from the other American ships—Where were the targets?—Should they open fire? Commander Stokes finally broke into the TBS clamor with a request to open torpedo fire.

Stokes was granted permission, but the word came too late. Destroyers YUDACHI and HARUSAME had not waited for this delayed-action order, and they were now beyond CUSHING's range. From Callaghan the answer finally came at 0145, "Stand by to open fire!" Five tense minutes ticked by, then at

0150, a Jap searchlight flung its ray across the water and focussed squarely on cruiser ATLANTA.

With the range at 1,600 yards, the American cruiser opened fire. The Japs answered with a rain of salvos that were murderously accurate. Landing on ATLANTA's bridge, a heavy shell exploded with a blast that killed Admiral Norman Scott and felled the sailors around him right and left. Only one member of his staff survived this homicidal blow.

At this crucial moment Admiral Callaghan issued the order, *"Odd ships commence fire to starboard, even ships to port!"* Unfortunately some of the ships could not find targets on the designated hand, and the order did not allow for selective firing on vessels which were within range.

Results were chaotic. The American column ploughed headlong into the Japanese formation; both the American and the Japanese formations broke completely. All chance for a battle of maneuver went with the wind. What ensued was a knockdown and dragout battle in every sense of the term—a conflict as wild as the Savo Island fray.

ATLANTA, the target for a sledgehammer fire from the Japs, was the first American ship battered out of action. Shortly after Admiral Scott was killed the ship was struck by one or more Japanese torpedoes. The blast almost heaved her out of the water. Listing and afire, she stumbled to a halt, ruinously damaged.

But the first American ship to go down was the destroyer BARTON.

Loss of USS BARTON

BARTON (Lieutenant Commander D. H. Fox was one of the rear destroyers in the American column which floundered into the Japanese formation. In the ensuing free-for-all, BARTON remained in combat for a brief seven minutes. The doom which overtook her struck with terrible suddenness, and she was gone with most of her crew as though in a flash, leaving in her wake little more than the memory of a good ship manned by brave destroyermen.

At 0148 she heard the baffling order, "Odd-numbered ships fire to starboard, even-numbered ships fire to port." Simultaneously, searchlights blazed from near-by vessels and BARTON pitched in as best she could. She launched four port torpedoes at a fast-moving target, and made an abrupt stop to avoid collision. As her propellers were churning, bringing her to a halt, she was struck by two torpedoes.

The first torpedo blasted BARTON's forward fireroom. Hitting her a split second later, the second torpedo smashed into the forward engine-room. Torn in two, the ship went down almost instantly, drowning 90 per cent of her crew.

Lost with the ship was her captain, Lieutenant Commander D. H. Fox.

Destroyers Versus Battleships

Japanese Admiral Abe sent battleship HIEI booming south-eastward toward the center of Savo Sound. KIRISHIMA, some 800 yards on the port quarter, came on firing. With his formation gone helterskelter, Admiral Abe pushed forward. As his flagship advanced he was astounded to discover she was under destroyer fire. At first he could not believe it, but such was the case. U.S. destroyers CUSHING, LAFFEY, STERETT, and O'BANNON were launching individual attacks on the bellowing battleship. The battleship struck back in berserk fury.

HIEI was an old-timer, vintage of 1916. But like her companion, KIRISHIMA, she weighed 31,000 tons, carried thick armor, and packed 14-inch guns.

A destroyer's chances against any battleship are somewhat comparable to those of a pistolman armed with a .22 against a foe armed with an elephant rifle. The destroyermen knew their best chance lay in torpedo fire, and they maneuvered desperately to hit with "fish."

CUSHING and LAFFEY paid for valor with their lives.

Loss of USS CUSHING

Deprived of a chance to hit the Jap destroyers she had sighted at 0141, CUSHING's gunners were bursting with impatience when the order to open fire finally came. It was then too late to torpedo the targets she had lined up, but by that time targets were everywhere in the offing, and she fired several fast salvos at another Jap destroyer glimpsed to starboard.

Then the melee broke around her, and the night became livid with gun flashes, the splattering incandescence of star-shells, and the huge twinkle of explosions. Gusts of orange fire flared from torpedo hits, and red smoke billowed from burning hulls.

Several shells struck CUSHING amidships, and the blasting knocked out her power lines and slowed her to a crawl. Her Captain, Lieutenant Commander E. N. Parker, conned her as best he could, the helmsman steering by hand. On the bridge Division Commander T. M. Stokes was trying to make order out of chaos and keep tabs on his scattered van division.

At 0154 Parker sighted the Japanese battleship HIEI looming up on the port beam. Parker swung his destroyer to the right to unleash a torpedo salvo. By the time CUSHING made her slow-motion turn, IJN HIEI was only 1,000 yards away.

Parker gave the order, and six torpedoes, fired by local control, went leaping at the monster target. But HIEI's lookouts must have seen them coming, for the big ship swung her prow to the left and lumbered westward, disappearing in the smoke-haze.

At this juncture CUSHING, having steadily lost way, drifted to a stop and stood dead in the water, paralyzed. Then, as the ship remained glued to the spot, an enemy searchlight struck her in the face.

An instant later CUSHING was rocked by a deluge of enemy shells. At 0220 Lieutenant Commander Parker ordered the burning vessel abandoned. The shells were still hailing down as the CUSHING men went overside.

Looking back across the water, the survivors saw CUSHING drift away in a cloud of fire and bright smoke. In that inferno six officers and some 53 men were lost.

The destroyer burned throughout the morning. A redhot stove in a tide of debris, she remained afloat until late that afternoon. About 1700 the heat reached her magazines, and she blew up and sank.

Loss of USS LAFFEY

In the group of van destroyers leading the American column into the Battle of Guadalcanal, the USS LAFFEY was the second ship in line. She was steaming in CUSHING's wake when the flag destroyer sighted the enemy, and she followed CUSHING's abrupt left turn into battle.

About the same time that CUSHING sighted the battleship HIEI, LAFFEY's lookouts saw the Jap behemoth ploughing up out of the night. White foam curled at the battleship's prow and her Oriental clipper bow towered against the stars like a cliff—an overhanging cliff advancing on LAFFEY with the speed of an avalanche.

LAFFEY's skipper ordered an abrupt swing which was made just in time to avert a collision. As the destroyer swung, two torpedoes were unleashed at the Japanese battlewagon. Both "fish" were seen to hit—and leap from the water at the battleship's bulge like playful bass. Fired at very close range, they had not had time to arm.

The HIEI crossed LAFFEY's stern almost within pistol shot. Gritting their teeth, the destroyer gunners lashed at the great ship's bridge with all weapons that could bear. Ropes of 20 mm. and 1.1-inch fire flogged the Japanese pagoda, perhaps killing some of Admiral Abe's sailors and smashing some of HIEI's glass.

The battleship answered with a roar. Two 14-inch salvos smote LAFFEY, and almost simultaneously she was struck in the stern by a torpedo. The big shells demolished LAFFEY's power plant; the torpedo blast flooded her after compartments. Out of control, listing, she lay like a trampled basket in the middle of a crowded street. As a pillar of flame surged up amidships, her captain gave the command, *"Abandon ship!"*

The LAFFEY men went overside in good order. But as the survivors took their places on the rafts and the swimmers were adjusting kapok jackets, the destroyer's fantail with its depth charges blew up like a monstrous bomb. Showered with fire and wreckage, many of the survivors in the water were killed. The ruptured vessel sank immediately, pulling others of the crew down with her.

LAFFEY's casualties were excruciatingly heavy; nearly all of her crew were lost. Her captain, Lieutenant Commander W. E. Hank, went down with the destroyer.

STERETT *and* O'BANNON *Versus Battleship* HIEI

Destroyer STERETT, third in line in the van group, was one of the odd-numbered ships in the American column. Her captain, Commander J. G. Coward, strove to obey Admiral Callaghan's firing order, and STERETT's guns opened up on a Japanese warship glimpsed to starboard, range 4,000 yards.

Off to port destroyers CUSHING and LAFFEY were engaged in a death struggle with the mighty HIEI. But STERETT's skipper had his orders, and he kept up a rapid starboard fire for at least three minutes. Then a spate of Jap shells struck STERETT. Momentarily out of control, the damaged ship swerved drunkenly. Only quick work on the part of destroyer O'BANNON, maneuvering astern of STERETT, prevented a collision.

Steering by means of the engines, Coward succeeded in bringing his ship into position for a torpedo attack on the HIEI. At a close range of 2,000 yards STERETT fired four torpedoes at the leviathan. Maybe they missed, or maybe they failed to arm and misfired.

While STERETT was thus striking at the Jap battlewagon, O'BANNON, sheering off to avoid Coward's injured destroyer, came right under the eye of the enemy Goliath. Commander E. R. Wilkinson promptly ordered his O'BANNON gunners to shoot the works at the HIEI. She was no more than 1,200 yards on the port bow when the destroyer opened fire.

Valiantly the 5-inchers blazed at the enormous target. And the Japanese giant was so close to little O'BANNON that her bellowing turret guns could not be depressed to draw a bead on the barking destroyer. For her part O'BANNON was shooting at the broad side of a barn. Shellfire spattered the great ship's pagoda, lighting her up like a carnival float. Then, as the destroyer gunners were pumping it in, a bewildering command came from Admiral Callaghan: CEASE FIRING OWN SHIPS.

Believing that the SAN FRANCISCO was mistakenly firing into the ATLANTA, Admiral Callaghan had ordered the cease fire presumably only for that ship; but whether or not this order had been intended for the flagship alone, it went out over TBS to all ships of the Force.

Some of the American ships received the word, some of them didn't. With HIEI's 14-inchers tearing through the air over his ship, Wilkinson ordered his gunners to hold their fire. But the Jap battleship was sliding by. Snapping into action, Wilkinson swung O'BANNON to bring her torpedoes batteries to bear, and unleashed two "fish" at the HIEI. The wakes ribboned straight for the mark, but apparently the "fish" ran deep or failed to explode. O'BANNON turned away to avoid collision with destroyer LAFFEY, lying helpless in her path.

O'BANNON's sailors flung life-jackets to the LAFFEY men as Wilkinson swung his ship hard over to steer clear of the sinking destroyer. The shout "Torpedo!" was raised by lookouts who sighted sizzling wakes ahead, and O'BANNON made another radical turn. Seconds later a huge underseas blast shook the maneuvering destroyer. Across the water, LAFFEY had blown up.

Around O'BANNON all of Savo Sound seemed to be blowing up too. Unable to distinguish one ship from another, Wilkinson headed his destroyer southeastward in an effort to get his bearings and to identify enemy targets. So O'BANNON steamed out of the holocaust—one of the war's few destroyers to survive a pitched battle with a battleship.

STERETT—another DAVID—took a severe beating after her round with HIEI. With radar shot away and steering gear out of commission, she was left to fight her way through a crowd of HIEI's screen destroyers. The ship was subjected to a tempestuous shelling which knocked out all but two of her guns, set her ready-service powder afire, and turned her superstructure into an incinerator.

But her engines were pounding steadily, and by sporadic slowdowns to keep the wind from fanning the flames and flank-speed sprints to get the ship out of enemy range, Commander Coward brought her into the clear.

"Another example of the fighting spirit of the men in our destroyer force," Admiral Halsey commented.

Loss of USS MONSSEN

Destroyer MONSSEN (Lieutenant Commander C. E. Mc-Combs) had been next to last ship in the American column. She was directly astern of the BARTON when that destroyer, first to go down in the melee battle, was fatally torpedoed.

Searchlights were blazing, shells were crashing, and BARTON was going down before MONSSEN could grasp the situation.

Then MONSSEN herself was under fire. A torpedo wake whisked through the water and passed under her keel. Maneuvering at high speed to evade, McCombs sent his ship racing ahead. Tragically enough, she plowed through a drift of flotsam from BARTON, killing unseen swimmers. Everywhere the darkness was exploding, and the flashes of fire and livid shell bursts created a kaleidoscopic play of glare and shadows that frustrated the lookouts.

But HIEI's silhouette was now plainly in view on MONS-SEN's bow, about 4,000 yards to starboard. McCombs swung the destroyer, and five torpedoes were fired at the looming battlewagon. Simultaneously her gunners were hurling 5-inch salvos at enemy ships dimly seen to port, and her 20 mm. batteries were flailing at a destroyer no more than a quarter mile distant to starboard.

Suddenly a swarm of starshells burst over MONSSEN, bathing her with brilliant light. Believing they had been fired by a friendly vessel which had fallen out of column, Commander McCombs flashed MONSSEN's recognition signals. Instantly a pair of searchlights fastened upon the destroyer. Within a matter of seconds she was reeling under a torrent of Japanese shells. A spread of torpedoes raced at her. The torpedoes missed, but the shells slammed home with deadly accuracy.

Altogether some 37 shells, at least three of them major caliber, struck the destroyer. When the firing subsided she was a total wreck, enveloped in searing flames.

The ship was abandoned at 0220. Trapped on the mangled bridge, the Commanding Officer and others of the conning party were compelled to leap overside from the rail. All were seriously injured.

Fighting their way out of the wreckage topside and the hell below, other officers and bluejackets escaped. But all too few survived this ship-slaughter. Clinging to life rafts and debris, the survivors in the water watched the flames chew their way through the abandoned ship. Then someone heard a cry for help. There were living men in that fiery ruin!

The cry reached across the water like an appealing hand. And it was grasped by a Bos'n's Mate and two seamen who contrived to put their raft alongside the ship at daylight. By that time the vessel was a crematorium. But men were trapped in the interior of that furnace. And C. C. Storey, Boatswain's Mate Second, and L. F. Spurgeon, Gunner's Mate Second, and J. G. Hughes, Fireman First, boarded the death-ship to get them.

Eight wounded men and their valiant rescuers got away with little time to spare. About noon of that day the MONSSEN blew up and sank.

Down Go the Big Guns (Death of the HIEI)

"We want the big ones—!" The voice was Admiral Callaghan's, broadcast by radiotelephone from the bridge of flagship SAN FRANCISCO. The destroyers were already flailing at battleship HIEI, and IJN KIRISHIMA was due appropriate attention. The American cruisers turned their guns on both battlewagons. Then the column broke up as it stormed into the Japanese formation. Shells, apparently from SAN FRANCISCO, slashed into disabled ATLANTA, and Callaghan's abrupt cease-fire order crackled over the TBS.

As the cruisers checked their fire, a volley of Jap salvos came whining across the sky.

Pinpointed by enemy ships on both sides, SAN FRANCISCO was hit more than a dozen times by major caliber projectiles, most of them 14-inch from HIEI, with whom she was closely engaged. One heavy shell killed Admiral Callaghan and most of his staff; another killed Captain Cassin Young; others wiped out most of the ship's bridge personnel.

ATLANTA, too, was damaged and afire, out of action. But the other cruisers—PORTLAND, HELENA, and JUNEAU—still struck furiously at the enemy. And then in almost no time only PORTLAND and HELENA of the American cruisers were left fighting, for as JUNEAU waded into action with her guns going, she was savagely stabbed by a torpedo. Had Admiral Abe but known it, this was the moment to deliver his knockout—when only two United States cruisers and three or four destroyers stood between his battleships and Guadalcanal.

But the Japanese commander himself was confused by the violence of the American attack and the tactical turmoil. Ships were everywhere, American cruisers where American destroyers should be, and American destroyers on HIEI's flank where Japanese destroyers should have been. They were even shooting at the battleship with machine-guns!

To the neat little admiral all this must have seemed sheer delirium. And so, at about 0200 he ordered HIEI and KIRISHIMA to turn homeward. KIRISHIMA made the swing ahead of HIEI, came back in a long loop to lob a few shells at the American ships, then retired around the north coast of Savo Island. Behind her she left destroyer YUDACHI exploding like a fireworks display and battleship HIEI fighting off the American cruisers. KIRISHIMA received only one scratch in that night's engagement: she was grazed by an 8-inch shell.

HIEI, slow on the northward turn, and heavily hit by SAN FRANCISCO, had run into another blistering fire. Altogether, about 50 shells struck her in the superstructure. Badly damaged, Abe's battleship made a half-circle turn below Savo, and went staggering northward along the east coast of the island.

The fighting in the Sound was almost over. But for the Americans the worst was to come as a sequel.

Only cruiser HELENA and destroyer FLETCHER had emerged from the night's madness without injury. As the ships headed southeastward through Indispensable Strait, pace was set at 18 knots to accommodate the cripples. Destroyer O'BANNON, with damaged sonar gear but otherwise sound in wind and limb, was sent ahead to get off a radio message to Admiral Halsey. FLETCHER and limping STERETT were positioned 4,000 yards in front of the cruisers to serve as a screen.

About 0950 STERETT made sudden sonar contact with an enemy submarine. Gamely she went after the unseen foe, dumping depth charges in an urgent attack. Commander Coward was unable to determine the results, and the ships could not wait to conduct a prolonged hunt.

They steamed into a deadly trap. Time: about 1100. Bridge personnel on SAN FRANCISCO glimpsed torpedo wakes racing across their bow, close ahead. The "FRISCO" men had no means of radioing the alarm, nor time to turn their ship away. Limping on "FRISCO's" starboard bow, cruiser JUNEAU was right in line for the shot.

At 1101 one of the torpedoes smashed into JUNEAU's port side. The blast was utterly cataclysmic. Literally the ship was blown to fragments. When the mountains of fire and smoke dissolved, there was nothing but a few bits of flotsam where the ship had been. Only ten of JUNEAU's men survived. Some 700 of her crew perished in the disaster.

This savage blow, struck by the I-26, was not the final echo of that battle of the 13th. In Savo Sound, where there was mopping up to do, the Americans would strike the final blows.

After the Japanese retirement there had still remained on the field the cruiser PORTLAND (unable to steer), destroyer AARON WARD (unable to steam), cruiser ATLANTA (a charred wreck), and the fiery carcasses of CUSHING, MONSSEN, and IJN YUDACHI. On the north side of Savo, HIEI was halted by an internal collapse, with destroyer YUKIKAZE squatting in near-by attendance.

Daybreak revealed Savo Sound as a steaming, debris-strewn sea in which the dead and dying vessels lay like flies in a pan of glue. In that cluttered seascape nothing moved. The water was motionless; on its yellow surface the ships remained fixed.

And now one of the vessels comes to life—the PORTLAND. Having halted for a moment to attempt a repair, she steams in a circle that brings her within range of the Jap destroyer YUDACHI. The hulk blows up and vanishes from the scene, a heartening display to American sailors watching from rafts.

Farther north, another sign of life on the water; the tug BOBOLINK from Tulagi steams into the scene. She has come to tow out the destroyer AARON WARD.

This stir of activity awakens the battleship HIEI. Thirteen miles distant, the wounded Japanese giant lets out a gruff roar.

The thunder from HIEI awakens Marine Corps aircraft which come winging across "Ironbottom Bay" with a vengeance. It is curtains, now, for Admiral Abe's flagship.

By evening of the 13th most of the battle wreckage had been cleared from Savo Sound; the hulks were on the floor of "Ironbottom Bay," and a cleanly tide was sweeping rubbish and bodies in to the beaches of Savo Island and Cape Esperance.

But the naval battle for Guadalcanal was not yet over.

Chapter 16

Solomons Crucible

(The Guadalcanal Campaign)
(Part 3)

☆ ☆ ☆

The Battle of Guadalcanal (November 14-15)

Fuming at Truk, Yamamoto ordered full speed ahead on the Guadalcanal offensive.

A cruiser squadron from Rabaul was rushed down the track to Guadalcanal. It was thrown back by Navy airmen. Then a reinforcing "Tokyo Express" was wrecked in the "Slot."

Meantime, up north of Florida Island, another striking force was getting set for a crack at Henderson Field. This force—it was designated a Bombardment Group—was under command of Vice Admiral Kondo. It contained the heavy cruisers ATAGO (Kondo's flagship) and TAKAO, battleship KIRISHMA, two light cruisers, and a squadron of nine destroyers. Kondo's left flank was covered by a Screening Group composed of the light cruiser SENDAI and three destroyers. Air cover from the backfield was provided by a carrier group containing JUNYO and HIYO, battleships KONGO and HARUNA, heavy cruiser TONE, and screening destroyers.

Kondo's ships were sighted and reported by American planes and the submarine TROUT. Admiral Halsey sent a dispatch to the ENTERPRISE force, ordering battleships WASHINGTON and SOUTH DAKOTA and four destroyers to leave the carrier's screen. They were to steam hell-for-leather to intercept Kondo's warships and the remnants of the wrecked "Tokyo Express" approaching Savo Sound.

This interception force was under tactical command of Rear Admiral W. A. ("Ching") Lee in the WASHINGTON. The four destroyers were the USS WALKE (Commander T. E. Fraser), BENHAM (Lieutenant Commander J. B. Taylor), GWIN (Lieutenant Commander J. B. Fellows), and PRESTON (Commander M. C. Stormes).

The six American warships raced for Savo with bones in their teeth. By that evening of November 14 they were off the western end of Guadalcanal making a clockwise swing around Savo Island.

Lee was confident his big battleships could stop Kondo's cruisers and IJN KIRISHIMA. At the same time he knew his interception force was burdened with several disadvantages. This was a new, unpracticed team going into action. The four destroyers were without a division commander. The force was strictly improvised for an emergency mission. And improvisation to counter planning is always hazardous.

However, the risk had to be taken, and Lee accepted it boldly. His ships were in an extended column with destroyers WALKE, BENHAM, PRESTON, and GWIN in the van some 4,000 to 5,000 yards ahead of battleships WASHINGTON and SOUTH DAKOTA.

They were all inside Savo Sound by 2215. The water was as still as stagnation. It was silent—too silent. Where was the enemy?

He had been coming down from the north, far distant on the American column's beam. But not so far abeam that lookouts on board IJN SENDAI had not been able to discern through their excellent Japanese binoculars the silhouettes of Lee's ships to the southward. SENDAI had flashed the word to flagship ATAGO, and Admiral Kondo had lost no time in deploying his ships for battle.

The SENDAI group, split up in two sections, forked southward to cover the east and west side of Savo Island. Cruiser NAGARA and four destroyers were ordered to make a dash to the south of Savo and enter the Sound from the west. With his flank covered by the SENDAI group and his advance screened by the NAGARA group, Kondo would swing his big bombardment warships around the west side of Savo to strike at the Americans when opportunity presented. Kondo had the initiative, but he lacked accurate information. SENDAI had described the American force as *"two cruisers and four destroyers."*

For his part Admiral Lee had no current information. Unaware that enemy ships were trailing him into Savo Sound, he headed his southbound column on a beeline for Lunga Point.

Not far from the Guadalcanal coast Lee turned his column sharp right to follow the coastline toward Cape Esperance. The column was steaming due west when, at 2300, battleship WASHINGTON's radar picked up the Japanese scout group coming down the east side of Savo Island.

By radar, and then by telescope, WASHINGTON tracked the enemy. At 2317, she opened fire on the SENDAI. The Jap light cruiser and her destroyer companion fled. But destroyers AYANAMI and URANAMI, coming around the southwest coast of Savo, pressed forward. So did NAGARA and her consorts. Gunfire exploded as these ships encountered Lee's van destroyers. In the cyclonic battle which followed, three of those American destroyers went down fighting.

Exeunt PRESTON, WALKE, and BENHAM.

Loss of USS PRESTON

Leading the American column that morning of November 15, destroyer WALKE opened fire at 2322 on enemy ships detected 15,000 yards to starboard. BENHAM and PRESTON, next in line, quickly followed suit. Last in the destroyer line, GWIN fired starshells at the target detected by WASHINGTON.

The enemy just south of Savo returned shot for shot. The island in the background gave the Jap ships radar sanctuary and blurred their silhouettes. Firing at flashes, the American destroyermen scored a number of hits, but the Jap salvos came faster and harder.

Destroyer PRESTON was not the first American destroyer hit in this action, but she was first to receive a critical blow. Five minutes after the shooting started, her superstructure was burning fiercely, a torch for the enemy marksmen.

Those marksmen were manning the guns of the NAGARA. Virtually undetected, this Jap cruiser had closed in on Lee's column to strike at the van destroyers. Almost at pointblank range she opened fire on PRESTON.

Raked by gunfire, PRESTON rolled and shook under successive hits. Her gunners hurled steel at NAGARA, but the cruiser's salvos ripped the vitals out of the destroyer before she could punch home a solid blow. By 2336 she was listing heavily to starboard and settling by the stern. Her captain, Commander M. C. Stormes, gave the order to abandon.

As the men were going overside, the ship rolled over on her beam, then slowly capsized and went down stern first. Commander Stormes was lost with the ship. About 131 of her survivors were picked up by the destroyer MEADE.

Loss of USS WALKE

Spearheading the American column, WALKE opened fire at 2322 on a Jap ship glimpsed against the dark foreshore of Savo Island. As Chief Fire Controlman R. P. Spearman recalled the encounter:

We opened up with a range of around 14,000 yards, but the ranges came down very fast. I don't remember what it was when we ended up, but I know it was pointblank. The

Gunnery Officer said, "We'll take the bridge off that ship!"
so we went through 250 rounds into that bridge.

About ten minutes after she opened fire, WALKE was hit
by a number of heavy shells, probably from cruiser NAGARA.
Then she was struck by a torpedo. The explosion hurled her
No. 2 gun a hundred feet in the air, slung men far out across
the water, and tore away the entire forecastle. Bridge and
after section were left foundering. At 2343 Commander Fraser
ordered his sinking craft abandoned.

Only two life rafts could be launched, and many of the
survivors going overside were compelled to tread water. They
were swimming in oil, and splashing through flotsam when
WALKE's stern section went under. As the fantail sank, depth
charges which had been reported on "safe" began to explode.
Many swimmers were slain by this blasting.

Lost with WALKE were some 75 of her crew. Among them
was her skipper, Commander Thomas E. Fraser.

Loss of USS BENHAM

Third American destroyer to go down in that battle of
November 15, 1942, the BENHAM (Lieutenant Commander
John B. Taylor) was in position 300 yards astern of WALKE.
She opened fire on the target WALKE had sighted, then shifted
to another enemy silhouette which emerged from Savo's
shadowy shoreline.

Lieutenant Commander Taylor kept the guns going, but
held his torpedoes in reserve for an opportune attack. Before
the opportunity developed, BENHAM was hit by a torpedo.

The blow was struck at 2338. An enormous geyser deluged
the destroyer's prow, and a portion of her bow disintegrated.
The blast heaved BENHAM over to port, then she rolled back
on her starboard beam. Then, shuddering and shaking, she
came back to even keel, and steadied.

Destroyer WALKE was in flames by this time, and PRESTON
was sinking. BENHAM's skipper thought his ship might be able
to aid the distressed vessels. BENHAM couldn't make it. Although the crew stemmed the flood up forward, damage was
progressive and cumulative. By 0100 the ship was fighting to
keep under way, and Taylor was eventually forced to report
that her condition was worsening. Admiral Lee then dispatched destroyer GWIN to escort the struggling BENHAM to
Espiritu Santo.

About 0300 GWIN joined her west of Guadalcanal, and the
two ships started the "long voyage home" at 12 knots. The
effort was too much for BENHAM. About 1500 in that afternoon of the 15th, when the ships were off the south coast of

Guadalcanal, she began to break up. GWIN took off Taylor and his weary crew. The sinking destroyer was hurried under by GWIN's guns.

No lives were lost with the BENHAM. Miraculously enough, in the ferocious action off Savo only seven of her crew had been injured.

Tassafaronga Backlash

Tassafaronga was an anti-climax. It shouldn't have happened. It was a lacerating slash from a badly wounded tiger wasting strength in an effort to hold untenable ground.

In this instance the tiger was personified by Rear Admiral Raizo Tanaka, a very tough, very capable little man. Admiral Turner's counterpart, he was charged with the delivery of reinforcements and supplies to the Japanese front in the Lower Solomons. He won the nickname of "Tenacious Tanaka" for driving the battered remnants of the "Tokyo Express" through to Tassafaronga while Savo Sound still echoed the shots of the Battle of Guadalcanal.

Tassafaronga had grown hot for Japanese shipping. Anyone but Tanaka might have despaired of landing perishable Jap cargo at this torrid terminal.

But Tanaka came up with a cool scheme. Run high-speed destroyers down to Tassafaronga at night, and toss the goods overside in watertight drums which would drift in on the tide to shallows where small craft and swimmers could recover the stuff. If a number of such runs were successfully made, the garrison could be supplied for a time.

The upshot of Tanaka's scheme was the Battle of Tassafaronga, which occurred late in the evening of November 30, 1942. From coast watchers, submarines, scouting aircraft, and other sources, Admiral Halsey learned that the enemy was going to make another attempt to reinforce Guadalcanal. He dispatched a task force under Rear Admiral C. H. ("Bosco") Wright to intercept and wreck this latest "Tokyo Express."

Admiral Wright's force (designated TF 67) as eventually constituted contained five cruisers—heavies MINNEAPOLIS (flagship), NEW ORLEANS, PENSACOLA, and NORTHAMPTON, and light cruiser HONOLULU—and six destroyers.

Admiral Wright, just arrived in the South Pacific, inherited this mission from Rear Admiral Kinkaid, who had been ordered to Pearl Harbor to take over another command. Kinkaid had already devised the operational plan, and Wright carried on with it.

Speed was imperative, and to save time Wright led his force from Espiritu Santo *via* Indispensable Strait into Lengo

Channel and on westward into Savo Sound. His ships were formed in an extended column, destroyers FLETCHER, PERKINS, MAURY, and DRAYTON in the van, followed by cruisers MINNEAPOLIS, NEW ORLEANS, PENSACOLA, HONOLULU, and NORTHAMPTON, with DD's LAMSON and LARDNER bringing up the rear.

The column reached Lunga Roads about 2225 in the evening of November 30. Simultaneously "Tenacious Tanaka" with a force of eight Japanese destroyers steamed down into the channel between Savo Island and Cape Esperance. Japs racing east and Americans racing west met in a head-on crash.

Not only was the American force prepared for action, but it had a good set of operational plans. The van destroyers were positioned to use their radar to best advantage. They were instructed to hit the enemy upon encounter with a fast torpedo attack (provided the range was closed to 6,000 yards or less); then they were to haul out to the sidelines to give the cruisers a clear field. The cruisers were not to open fire until the DD's had launched their "fish" and pulled aside— the idea being to give the torpedoes a chance before gunfire alarmed the enemy.

Thus Wright's ships went into action forewarned, forearmed, and rid of many of the wrenches that had fouled the machinery for the earlier battle-teams which had blazed the way at Savo. They had radar, and the Japanese had none. Above all, they had a tremendous weight advantage over the oncoming foe—five cruisers and six destroyers versus eight destroyers (of which six were encumbered with troops and cargo).

A word of recognition is due here for Japan's DD's and the Japanese Destroyer Service. They were rugged little warships manned by rugged little sailors with plenty of know-how in their sea bags.

For many months they had done the dirty work for Yamamoto's Imperial Fleet, going into waters where such mighty giants as KONGO and YAMATO feared to tread. If they were worn by hard usage, they were also as combat-hardened as alley-cats, and they had learned some of the grimalkin's canny techniques for survival—how to make best use of cover; how to hit and run; and particularly, how to fight at night.

And so, like tigerish alley cats, Tanaka's destroyers came prowling down into Savo Sound in the night. They were in column, NAGANAMI (flagship) in the van followed by MAKANAMI, OYASHIO, KURASHIO, KAGERO, KAWAKAZE, and SUZUKAZE. On NAGANAMI's port bow the TAKANAMI steamed as scout to feel out the way ahead. As the column entered Savo Sound, Tanaka slowed the pace to 12 knots and set a course to follow the Guadalcanal coastline down to Tassafaronga.

Meantime Wright had steered his American column northward toward the center of the Sound, then ordered a simultaneous ships' turn left which put his cruisers in line of bearing, and placed the van destroyer column on the starboard flank and the rear destroyer column on the flank to port. With a wide front the formation thus swept westward toward Cape Esperance.

The Sound was as black and silent as a pond at the bottom of a coal mine. The very air seemed dead. Then it livened up. At 2306 the radar watch on flag cruiser MINNEAPOLIS snared a suspicious "pip," range 23,000 yards, directly ahead. Wright immediately ordered a right turn which put his formation back into single column. The "pip" multiplied into a number of "pips," and there was the enemy. Swinging the column leftward, Wright set a course which was almost parallel to Tanaka's.

The van destroyers readied their torpedoes. FLETCHER, in the lead, probed the dark with acute radar. At 2316 the targets showed up on her port bow, range 7,000 yards. Over TBS FLETCHER's skipper, Commander Cole, asked permission to launch torpedoes. The Force Commander, dubious about the range, asked Cole if he considered it short enough. When Cole replied in the affirmative, Admiral Wright (time: 2320) ordered Cole to open torpedo fire. Cole instantly passed the word to the other van destroyers, and by 2321 FLETCHER's "fish" were unleashed in two salvos that sent a spread of ten torpedoes racing.

But neither time nor Tanaka had waited for Admiral Wright to issue the firing order. And while Commander Cole was waiting, the enemy targets slid past FLETCHER's beam, necessitating a rapid readjustment of the fire-control set-up. The range was lengthened, and when Cole finally received permission to shoot, the targets were going away on FLETCHER's quarter. Instead of broadside torpedo-fire with a favorable track-angle, she was compelled to get off a more difficult "up-the-kilt" shot.

Directly astern of FLETCHER, destroyer PERKINS flung eight torpedoes at the passing enemy. Destroyer MAURY, equipped with inferior radar, could not detect the Jap ships against the Guadalcanal coastline, so held her "fish" in check. DRAYTON also had weak radar; nevertheless, she got off two torpedo shots at a range of about 7,000 yards.

Twenty torpedoes went humming through the water in an undersea barrage at the enemy. And FLETCHER missed. PERKINS missed. DRAYTON missed. Not a single American torpedo found a mark. And worse still, lookouts on Tanaka's flagship sighted two oncoming wakes, and the foaming ribbons touched off the Japanese alarm.

Meantime, FLETCHER and the other DD's in the American van did their best to haul out (in accordance with plan) and give the cruisers a clear field. However, the cruisers opened fire within seconds of FLETCHER's final torpedo shot. Some of the cruisers fired starshells, and the battle was on. When the big guns started booming, FLETCHER, PERKINS, MAURY, and DRAYTON joined in with 5-inch gunnery. So did destroyers LAMSON and LARDNER at the tail-end of the column. Under all this heavy and medium fire Tanaka's eight destroyers should have been battered into trash.

Instead, they slipped out of the trap. Tanaka ordered a counter-attack with torpedoes. Aiming at the American gun flashes, the Jap destroyermen let fly. But the Japs were expert at this game.

TAKANAMI, the scout destroyer, unleashed her "fish" and swung hard right, reversing course. As she was out in front of the Jap column, she was exposed to the American gunnery, and she took a concentrated pounding. In a few minutes her own guns were out of action, her superstructure was thrashed to a shambles, she was afire and going down.

But TAKANAMI served as a decoy duck. While the Americans were hammering at this target, the other Jap ships were dodging. There was some confusion among them when the Squadron Commander signaled for a mass torpedo attack that required a column movement by each of the three divisions. Some of them steamed on toward Tassafaronga, their sailors busily tossing overside the floating cargo-drums. One or two missed the turn. But Tanaka reformed his column quickly, and in jig-time his ships were heading out of Savo Sound, getting away. And getting away with murder.

For the Japanese torpedoes were running "true, hot, and normal" in a fashion only too fatal for the targets. FLETCHER and the other van destroyers, swinging around Savo Island in accordance with the battle plan, were out of danger. But at 2327 flagship MINNEAPOLIS was hard hit by two torpedoes.

As she sheered off to avoid collision with the damaged flagship ahead of her, NEW ORLEANS was hit in the port bow by a torpedo. Her bow was blown away.

Then PENSACOLA, maneuvering past the damaged ships, was hit. The blast ignited a horrible oil fire which cremated many of the crew.

HONOLULU, next cruiser in column, zigzagged off to starboard and evaded the torpedo barrage. She was the only one of Wright's cruisers to escape unscathed. For, a few minutes later, NORTHAMPTON, last cruiser of the column, received the hardest blow of all. She was struck by two torpedoes. The blasting tore a tremendous gash in her port side, burst her fuel tanks, and drenched her with blazing oil. With her mainmast burning like an enormous torch and her boat deck a mass of flame, NORTHAMPTON reeled out of action.

Steaming toward this pile-up of disaster and devastation, rear destroyers LAMSON and LARDNER were left to fend for themselves. LAMSON had endeavored to follow NORTHAMPTON's right turn, and while doing so, she had been shot at by one of the crippled cruisers. Whereupon her skipper had sagely decided to "get the hell out of there." LARDNER, too, was fired upon by the damaged American ships. She also evacuated at best speed.

It was now the first day of December, 1942. Admiral Raizo Tanaka, with seven of his eight destroyers intact, was high tailing up the "Slot." In the dark passage between Savo Island and Cape Esperance, three United States cruisers were fighting serious damage and disablement, and a fourth was going down. The Battle of Tassafaronga was over.

Nowhere in the Pacific would the Navy's combat leaders encounter a surface adversary tougher than "Tenacious" Tanaka.

Yet still another ship was to go down in the battle for "Cactus"— the USS DEHAVEN.

Loss of USS DEHAVEN

To block the enemy at Cape Esperance, General Patch dispatched an infantry battalion to Verahue Beach. The troops were carried to the beachhead by five LCT's and a seaplane tender under escort of Captain Briscoe's "Cactus Striking Force" from Tulagi—destroyers FLETCHER, RADFORD, NICHOLAS, and DEHAVEN. Fighters from Henderson Field covered the landings, which were handily made in the early hours of February 1, 1943.

As luck would have it, the Japs had decided to begin their evacuation on this date. And their scout planes, looking down on Marovovo, evidently took the "Cactus Striking Force" for a group lying in ambush to intercept. The word was enough to bring a squadron of Aichi dive-bombers to the scene.

Winging over the horizon on the afternoon of February 1, the Jap airmen caught a glimpse of two destroyers and several LCT's about two miles southeast of Savo Island. The destroyers were NICHOLAS and DEHAVEN shepherding a trio of unloaded landing craft back to Tulagi. To the northwest of Cape Esperance, FLETCHER and RADFORD were coming with the rest of the unloaded LCT's, but they were not spotted by the Japs.

The destroyers had been warned by Guadalcanal radio that the enemy was in the air and on the hunt. Radars and lookouts were watching the sky, and the destroyer and LCT gunners were waiting at hair-trigger. Unfortunately the American fighter planes had remained with the RADFORD-FLETCHER group. This neglect, whatever its cause, exposed NICHOLAS and DEHAVEN to a cyclonic aerial attack.

Some 14 "Vals" were in the sky. Nine of these were counted by DEHAVEN as the flight roared in at 5,000 feet. The ship's clocks timed the attack at 1457. Down came the lightning as six of the planes plummeted on the target destroyer.

DEHAVEN's anti-aircraft batteries rattled, banged, and flamed, smearing the sky with flak. The barrage was unable to stop the bombers. The screaming planes ripped through the AA curtain, and dropped three bombs squarely on the ship.

One bomb, smashing the destroyer's bridge, killed her captain, Commander C. E. Tolman. Men, guns, and deck gear were blown high in the air. A near miss, exploding near the bow, crushed in a section of the hull. With fires leaping from her mangled superstructure, DEHAVEN wallowed in agony, settling by the head. She went down as her frantic engineers were fighting their way topside out of the inferno, and sailors topside were desperately striving to launch rafts.

The battle ended as abruptly as it had begun, and the planes winged away to report another United States warship on the floor of "Ironbottom Bay." Nearby LCT's circled in to rescue the DEHAVEN survivors. There were deplorably few to be rescued.

Of the ship's 14 officers, only four were found alive. One of the four was painfully wounded. And 146 men—38 of them wounded—were recovered. Altogether, 167 of the destroyer's complement had perished with the ship.

Adding DEHAVEN's name to the long, lugubrious list, the United States Navy could count her as the 15th destroyer lost in the Guadalcanal campaign.

Guadalcanal Conclusion

On the night of February 1, 1943, the Japs began their evacuation of Guadalcanal.

The loss of Tulagi and defeat on Guadalcanal had cost the Japanese all chance of gaining control over the South Pacific, and had pulled a bastion out from under Rabaul and citadels west. *"I look upon the Guadalcanal and Tulagi Operations,"* said Admiral Nagano in gloomy postwar confession, *"as the turning point from offense to defense, and the cause of our setback there was our inability to increase our forces at the same speed that . . . (the Americans) did."*

The American victory was purchased at a high price in life, limb, and material. Naval losses were particularly high. Ship for ship, the Japanese came out on the easier end of the bill, as the following table shows:

U. S. Navy and Imperial Navy
LOSSES
in the Guadalcanal Campaign
AUGUST 7, 1942 TO FEBRUARY 7, 1943

TYPE OF CRAFT	AMERICAN	JAPANESE
Battleships	0	2
Aircraft Carriers	2	1
Heavy Cruisers	5	2
Light Cruisers	2	2
Destroyers	15	12
TOTAL	24	19

The 15 American destroyers which went down in the Guadalcanal campaign were TUCKER, JARVIS, BLUE, DUNCAN, MEREDITH, O'BRIEN, PORTER, CUSHING, MONSSEN, LAFFEY, BARTON, WALKE, PRESTON, BENHAM, and DEHAVEN. All did not go down in Savo Sound. But it might be said that this squadron is permanently based on the bottom of "Ironbottom Bay." Every ship, with the exception of TUCKER, was a victim of enemy fire, and all contributed their services to the sinking of the Rising Sun in the Lower Solomons.

Chapter 17

Central Solomons Sweep

(Part 1)

☆ ☆ ☆

Destroyers Versus "Operation I"

Ainsworth — Moosbrugger — Burke —three DesPac names to be indelibly enscribed on the waters of the Solomons Archipelago. Coincident with their ascendancy was the setting of the Rising Sun in the Solomons.

"Operation Watchtower" did not end with the American occupation of Guadalcanal. Capture of that strategic island was only a beginning. Often described as a ladder, the Solomon Islands extend northwestward to the gateway of the Bismarcks. Guadalacanal was only a "bottom rung."

After eviction from Guadalcanal, the enemy did not sit idly by in despair. Admiral Yamamoto promised Emperor Hirohito that the Americans would be stopped dead in the Central Solomons.

How was this to be accomplished? By air power. Concentrate the Japanese air forces at Papua, New Guinea. Bring in Ozawa's Third Fleet with carriers ZUIKAKU, ZUIHO, JUNYO, and HIYO to put the head on a mighty sledgehammer with which to pound the Americans in the Lower and Central Solomons. Land-based aircraft from Rabaul in the Bismarcks, from Bougainville, Buka, and other Solomons bases, would weight the sledge.

On March 25, 1943, the Imperial War Council put the Japanese ideograph of approval on Yamamoto's aerial offensive. It was designated "Operation I."

Destroyermen working under Burke, Ainsworth and Moosbrugger—and Rear Admiral A. S. ("Tip") Merrill—went far to hammer the "I" into a costly Japanese zero. Meantime—

175

FLETCHER and Naval Aircraft Kill RO-102

On February 11, 1943, destroyer FLETCHER (Lieutenant Commander F. L. Johnson) was steaming as a unit in an A/S screen working with Task Force 67. The force was maneuvering about 100 miles south of Rennell Island when one of HELENA's planes sighted and bombed a Jap submarine about nine miles distant from FLETCHER. The sub was 75 feet under when the airmen dropped a 100-pounder, and in the wake of this blast it went deeper.

The plane planted a smoke pot to mark the spot, and FLETCHER was ordered to the scene to take a hand in the affair. The destroyer's sonar soon registered a clear, firm contact at a range of 2,900 yards. Johnson conned the ship in to launch a deliberate attack, and the deystroyer let go with a 9-charge pattern. The charges were accurately placed, and all detonated.

Six minutes after the attack two deep-bellied explosions boomed under the sea. The turbulent rumble brought up a large air-and-oil bubble. Then a glistening slick. Five minutes later the FLETCHER was rocked by a stupendous undersea blast. For a moment the jolted destroyermen believed their ship had been torpedoed. The detonation, however, echoed from an exploding submarine.

Up came the ghastly trash—shattered deck-planking, chunks of cork, bits of jigsaw debris, and particles of this and that which bore undisputable evidence to the demolishment of submersible and submariners.

Johnson and company could now paint a Japanese naval flag on FLETCHER's scoreboard. And the Japanese Submarine Force could erase RO-102 from its roster.

O'BANNON *Kills* RO-34

Early in the morning of April 5, 1943, "Pug" Ainsworth's task force was up the "Slot," hunting contact with a reported convoy. The contact, tipped off, had made itself scarce. But destroyers STRONG and O'BANNON of the task force screen made radar contact at 0218 with an enemy sub.

Initial range was 7,000 yards. O'BANNON reported the suspicious "pip," and her captain, Lieutenant Commander D. J. MacDonald, was ordered to conduct an immediate investigation. It took MacDonald about ten minutes to get his ship within sighting range and identify the submarine's silhouette as "made in Japan."

That was all the destroyermen needed. O'BANNON passed ahead of the sub at a distance of about 90 yards. Before the Jap deep-sea sailors knew what hit them, a hot 5-inch salvo was punched down the submarine's throat. The K-guns barked, lobbing charges at the wallowing undersea boat. A flash from the destroyer's searchlight showed the sub going under by the stern.

At 0319 O'BANNON's sonarmen obtained sound contact with the submerged target, and MacDonald conned the ship for a depth-charge run. An 8-charge pattern was dropped. It was noted that *"all charges functioned properly."* This was a technical way of saying that eight timed detonations were heard by the destroyermen, not to mention the submariners in the target submersible. Also, *"There was one particular very heavy explosion quite different in effect from a normal depth-charge explosion."* Evidently something bigger than a light bulb had popped within the submarine.

Flying over that locale the following day, American aviators sighted a large, undulant oil slick drifting on the surface of the "Slot." It was the last earthly remnant of RO-34.

Loss of the USS AARON WARD

About noon of April 7, 1943, Ainsworth's task force set out from Tulagi on mission to bombard Munda. The ships were just getting under way when Ainsworth received an air alarm broadcast from Guadalcanal. Turning his formation eastward, he headed for Indispensable Strait at high speed. This move was highly discreet on Ainsworth's part. Down the "Slot" were coming 67 "Val" dive-bombers and 110 "Zeke" fighters, most of them from Ozawa's Carrier Force. Yamamoto had pulled the big trigger on "Operation I."

Up from Henderson soared a flock of 76 U.S. fighter planes to intercept the aerial armada. The warning, "Condition Red!", had sent shipping in the area running for cover, alerted. Then, shortly after 1400, came the alarming broadcast, "Condition very Red!" The aerial storm broke about an hour later when a horde of "Zekes" flew into a crowd of American fighters over "Ironbottom Bay." During the wild dogfight that ensued, a number of "Vals" penetrated the American screen and struck at targets in the Sound.

One of their targets was destroyer AARON WARD (Lieutenant Commander F. J. Becton), veteran of the Guadalcanal campaign. With an ocean-going landing craft under her wing, she was headed for Lengo Channel.

As the destroyer and the LST ran eastward, tugs VIREO and ORTOLAN and several small craft tagged along, eager to avail themselves of the DD's anti-aircraft cover. Then at 1512 three "Vals" burst from a cloud bank and came plummeting down a blinding shaft of sunlight.

Before Lieutenant Commander Becton could order an

evasive maneuver, the bombers were on top of the ship. Becton called for flank speed and left full rudder. The portside automatic guns blazed at ranges between 1,500 and 2,000 yards. Three bombs, perhaps 500-pounders, came thunderbolting down. Two were near misses which showered the destroyer with jagged fragments. The third rocked the ship with a deafening blast.

AARON WARD was fatally injured.

The destroyermen fought the battle damage with every available means. Tugs ORTOLAN and VIREO took the ship in tow and started her toward Tulagi. Six hours after the bombing AARON WARD was still afloat, but she was now far over on her starboard beam. Despite desperate efforts to beach her, she sank that evening at 2135, going down three miles offshore in 40 fathoms of water. Down with her she took 27 dead. The remainder of her crew, including 59 wounded, were picked up by the accompanying tugs.

Bombed under with AARON WARD that day were a New Zealand corvette and the tanker KANAWHA. The Japanese paid for this success with 12 "Vals" and numerous "Zekes." Apparently Yamamoto was not too pleased with the assessment, for on April 16 he canceled "Operation I" and sent Ozawa's planes back to the flat-tops.

Two days later Yamamoto himself was canceled.

Brief Obituary of Japanese Admiral

This is not an incident of destroyer history. It is, however, an incident that was of more than passing interest to all DesPac destroyermen.

About the time of the "Operation I" strike at Guadalcanal, a tense conference took place in CinCPac's headquarters at Pearl Harbor. Subject of discussion was none other than Isoroku Yamamoto, Commander-in-Chief of the Japanese Combined Fleet.

It seemed that Yamamoto was planning to visit Bougainville in the Solomons. As Admiral Halsey subsequently wrote (in *Admiral Halsey's Story*), *"The Navy's code experts had hit a jackpot."* Unraveling a Japanese dispatch, they not only learned of Yamamoto's intended junket, but they discerned the time and place of his arrival.

Here was a chance to take one of Japan's top War Lord's on the wing. And aircraft from Henderson Field were assigned the role of executioner. The Admiral's plane was a little late, but not late enough to win him a reprieve. At 1135 in the morning of April 18, 1943, he was intercepted and shot down by American Lightning fighters over Buin, Bougainville.

Admiral Mineichi Koga replaced Yamamoto as Commander-in-Chief of the Imperial Navy's Combined Fleet.

RADFORD *Kills* RO-101

Late in June '43, the Americans drove to New Georgia Island.

While Army forces were digging in at Rendova, Marines were carried to Viru by destroyer-transports HOPKINS, KILTY, and CROSBY, and troops were landed on Vangunu and other islands of the New Georgia group. Destroyers WOODWORTH and JENKINS supported the Vangunu landings with a bombardment of Japanese trenches which flanked the beach. Rendova proved the only worthwhile prize in this grab-bag, but the troops did not think it a fit bog for crocodiles.

Reinforcements, the second section of Turner's transport fleet, arrived with a rainstorm early in the morning of July 1. By nightfall the transports were unloaded and on their way out of Blanche Channel. Some Jap float planes attempted a twilight attack, but were driven off. Then, as darkness deepened, another threat materialized in the form of a Japanese submarine. It was soon dematerialized by destroyer RADFORD.

A unit of the transport screen, RADFORD was at that hour conducting a sweep on the eastern side of Rendova. At 1948 the destroyer's SG radar registered contact with an unknown vessel about six miles distant. Deftly conning his DD, Commander Romoser closed range to 2,000 yards.

Time: 2008. The destroyermen snapped on a searchlight which caught a surfaced submarine full in the face. Instantly the silhouette was recognized as enemy, and in the same instant RADFORD's marksmen opened fire with all guns. A torpedo was also fired at the sub, but it was the shelling which did her in.

Right on target, the first three salvos whisked away the conning tower. Five-inchers and 20 mm. riddled the pressure hull. RADFORD closed the range to 1,500 yards. The sub lay in the sea like a waterlogged tree trunk, slowly foundering. Then it went under.

Romoser maneuvered his ship into position to ram if the sub happened to broach. It didn't happen. At 2012 he conned RADFORD over the submerged target, and an 11-charge pattern was deposited in the sea. Three minutes later the water was roiled by an undersea thunderclap that vibrated the cookpots in RADFORD's galley. Inquisitive searchlights were turned on the channel. The lights discovered lakes of dark oil, and a variegated clutter of debris which contained such items as strips of wood, hunks of cork, rags of fabric or clothing, and human remains.

Put them all together, they spelled RO-101. Another enemy removed from the Rendova area by destroyer warfare.

Bombardment of Vila and Bairoko Harbor

Early in the morning of July 5, 1943, American troops were landed at Rice Anchorage on the northwest coast of New Georgia. Halsey dispatched a task group under Rear Admiral Ainsworth to support the landings by bombarding Vila-Stanmore and shelling the Jap defenses at Enogai and Bairoko.

About 0000, July 5, the American bombardment group arrived off Visuvisu Point, the northernmost tip of New Georgia. As the ships rounded the point and steamed into Kula Gulf, Ainsworth formed them in column. Destroyers NICHOLAS and STRONG moved up into the van, NICHOLAS about 3,000 and STRONG about 1,500 yards ahead of HONOLULU, HELENA, and ST. LOUIS. O'BANNON and CHEVALIER covered the cruiser column's rear.

The night was humid and overcast, and drenched by sporadic rainsqualls. Under cover of this weather the bombardment ships made the run to Vila undetected, and at 0026 the cruisers began hurling shells at the enemy shore.

NICHOLAS and STRONG opened fire at Bairoko Harbor at 0030. Meantime, the transports quietly approached Rice Anchorage. They were off the Anchorage when the radar watch in RALPH TALBOT reported two "pips" on the screen. That was at 0031. The contacted vessels were coming westward. Nine minutes later they showed up as two unidentifiable ships steaming at 25 knots out of the Gulf on a northwest course.

Suddenly STRONG's Gunnery Officer sighted a torpedo wake sizzling toward his destroyer. "Torpedo!" No time to order an evasive maneuver. The torpedo struck home with a thunder-blast, and STRONG staggered out of line in mortal hurt.

All hands in the task group believed the ship had been torpedoed by an undetected submarine. Ainsworth detached destroyers O'BANNON and CHEVALIER to stand by the disabled STRONG, stationed near NICHOLAS as picket, and led the cruiser column out of the Gulf to cover the entrance to the northward, prior to a fast retirement.

Loss of USS STRONG

The torpedo which struck STRONG had burst her hull from port to starboard and left her sagging amidships like a hammock. The blast wiped out her forward fireroom, and water plunged into her engineering spaces, quickly swamping her vital machinery. The dead swirled uncaring through the flooded compartments as the living fought their way topside.

This doom had struck STRONG about two miles off Rice Anchorage. There she was found by CHEVALIER and O'BANNON. The rescue ships immediately stood in to her assistance. Commander Wellings, expecting aid, held his crew on board.

Closing in on the disabled destroyer's port side, CHEVALIER thrust her bow into the wreckage. The thrust damaged the rescue ship's bow, but it enabled the CHEVALIER men to throw a web of nets and lines to STRONG's battered hull. The sea was flat, and the STRONG's survivors were able to crawl across the span of cables and hemp. A number of the badly wounded were handed to safety, and all of the survivors might have gotten across had not the Jap gunners ashore suddenly spied the sinking ship.

The battered ship went under at 0122. As the wreckage sank, several 300-pound depth charges exploded in the water, killing and maiming swimmers. Pursued by Jap salvos, CHEVALIER and O'BANNON retired up the Gulf. In passing they asked the destroyers at Rice Anchorage to search for survivors.

The DD's of the transport group combed the water where STRONG went down. Among the lucky few recovered was Commander Wellings. But in the darkness which followed the shore gunnery, a huddle of swimmers drifted away to southward. Most of this group failed to reach land.

The torpedo which struck the ship was a Model 93 specimen fired by one of the two Japanese destroyers fleeing out of the Gulf to escape the bombardment group. It was an unbelievably long shot—another example of crack torpedo-work with a superior torpedo.

Survival Story: The Stamina of Lieutenant Miller

When the depth charges exploded as the stricken STRONG went down, Lieutenant Hugh Barr Miller, USNR, was among those injured by the undersea blasts. Badly hurt though he was, he managed to tread water and remain afloat. Some 23 men were in a little huddle around him, clinging to life nets and pieces of raft.

The night was stygian—not a star visible—and it was

easy for rescuers to miss this little group in the blind darkness. A current carried them away from their shipmates, and morning found them drifting in an empty world of gulf and sky. One after another men lost their hold on the flotsam which supported them, and slipped away into eternity. Four days after the torpedoing, when the flotsam drifted ashore on Arundel Island, about midway between New Georgia and Kolombangara, only six of the group remained. Lieutenant Hugh Barr Miller was among the six.

Two of these six survivors died of their injuries after they crawled ashore. The lieutenant and three bluejackets started to work their way through the coastal jungle. Miller was so weakened by internal bleeding that he thought he was going to die. On July 14 he suffered a severe hemorrhage which convinced him that his life was ebbing.

He told the three sailors with him that they would have to leave him and try to reach friendly territory. He gave one lad his shoes; pressed his rainproof parka on the second; directed the third to take other articles of his clothing. Emergency rations were divided, and Miller kept for himself a broken pocket knife. The three men were reluctant to leave him in such fashion. Miller sent them on. Orders were orders.

But Lieutenant Miller didn't die. For a time he was in a semi-comatose state, but on the 17th a tropical downpour bathed and revived him. A few gulps of rainwater brought him to his feet, and he stumbled on through the jungle that fringed the beach.

Another night—another day—he found and broke open a coconut and chewed its meat. This was his first meal on Arundel Island, the first substantial food he had been able to swallow in two weeks.

Then he found an old Japanese Navy blanket in the underbrush. Scouting forward on the alert, Miller found something else. He found a dead Japanese infantryman, complete with uniform, rations, and hand grenades.

Costumed, armed, and provided with solid food, Miller went on. On August 5, or thereabouts, he sighted a Jap patrol coming up the beach, evidently on the hunt for the party who had stripped the dead man. Miller ambushed the five-man patrol and killed the lot with a volley of grenades.

The battle provided him with more weapons and implements for survival. Also with more impetus to keep going. He built a lean-to in the jungle and set out to locate and raid the enemy camp. From his solitary base he staged a series of forays. When he was finally picked up after 43 days of existence on Arundel Island, he had lost 40 pounds, grown a scraggy reddish beard, and acquired the look of a wolf. But he was decidedly alive. And he had waged a one-man offensive against the Japanese occupants, killed about 30 Jap soldiers, and obtained a dossier of valuable military information. He was picked up by Luck—Major Goodwin R. Luck, USMRC, who flew over the Arundel beach in a seaplane. Not long after that he was in hospital at Nouméa, where Admiral Halsey shook his hand, and he was recommended for the Navy Cross.

As a story of survival Miller's can scarcely be equalled. Appropriately he served in a destroyer named STRONG.

The Battle of Kula Gulf

After the Vila-Stanmore bombardment and the brush with the enemy near Rice Anchorage, Admiral Ainsworth led his task group down the "Slot" to Savo Sound and eastward to Indispensable Strait. He was heading for a fueling rendezvous with a tanker south of San Cristobal Island. But before this rendezvous could be made, he received orders from Halsey directing him to reverse course. A fast "Tokyo Express" had been sighted on the southbound run from Bougainville, steaming for Vila-Stanmore with reinforcements. Ainsworth was to return to Kula Gulf on the double and intercept this train load of Japs.

At once he swung the column in a 180-degree turn, and headed back for Kula at 29 knots. As CHEVALIER had gashed her bow in going alongside the sinking STRONG, she was ordered to drop out with the STRONG survivors at Tulagi. Destroyers JENKINS (Commander H. F. Miller) and RADFORD (Commander W. K. Romoser), at that time loading fuel and ammunition at Tulagi, were hitched on to Ainsworth's formation as replacements. Full gun, Task Group 36.1 went racing northward up the "Slot" in pitchy midnight.

And coming down the "Slot" was the Jap reinforcement group, ten destroyers under command of Rear Admiral Teruo Akiyama. The enemy DD's were moving tandem in three groups. In the lead was a support unit composed of destroyers NIIZUKI, SUZUKAZE, and TANIKAZE. Next came a transport unit: destroyers MOCHIZUKI, MIKAZUKI, and HAMAKAZE. Then came a second transport unit: destroyers AMAGIRI, HATSU-YUKI, NAGATSUKI, and SATSUKI. About 0025 in the morning of July 6, at the very time Ainsworth's ships were off Visu-visu Point, the Jap destroyers swung down into the Gulf.

Admiral Akiyama sent the first transport unit inshore to hug the Kolombangara coast on the run down the Gulf to Vila. The rest of the "Express" took down the Gulf in column on a course farther out. The Americans were not acquainted with the fact that flag destroyer NIIZUKI carried new Japanese radar gear. Nor did they know the Jap DD's were equipped with enormous 24-inch torpedoes and special apparatus for the handling and re-loading of these three-ton whales.

With the clock nearing 0136, cruiser HONOLULU made the first radar contact with the Japanese ships at 22,000-yard range. Ainsworth immediately aligned his ships in single-column battle formation. In the van were destroyers NICHOLAS and O'BANNON. They were followed by HONOLULU, HELENA, and ST. LOUIS. Destroyer JENKINS steamed in ST. LOUIS's wake, and RADFORD was "tail-end Charlie."

At 0142, with radar "pips" multiplying on the screens, Ainsworth shifted course to come to grips with the enemy. One minute later Akiyama detached the second Jap transport unit and sent it in to Vila while he turned the support destroyers northward. Between Jap and American ships the range rapidly closed. Studying the radar picture, the Americans were momentarily baffled by the separation of Akiyama's column into two groups. When the Vila-bound group showed up as the larger of the two, Ainsworth ordered his rear DD's to join the three cruisers in gunning for this target. Van destroyers NICHOLAS and O'BANNON were directed to tackle the nearer, smaller group which was heading up the Gulf.

Ainsworth directed his ships to concentrate on the oncoming target-group. They were then to make a simultaneous turn and *"get the others on the reverse course."*

At 0157, with the range closed to about 7,050 yards, Ainsworth snapped the order to fire. Steaming at 30 knots, the Japs were broad on the port beam. But they were not taken by surprise. NIIZUKI's lookouts had sighted and reported the American column. Admiral Akiyama had instantly rushed his crews to battle stations.

Even so, the American gunners got the jump. Squarely on target, the first cruiser salvo struck NIIZUKI a stunner. Holed, afire, her steering gear disabled, Admiral Akiyama's flagship floundered off course and started to settle.

Destroyers SUZUKAZE and TANIKAZE had better luck. Neither was stopped by the blizzard of heavy shells, and both were able to fling torpedoes at the American column—those supersize torpedoes with the double dose of dynamite in their war heads.

HELENA was hit by one of the long-range Jap torpedoes. Then she was hit by another! Then another! When the thunder echoed away and the smoke cleared, the cruiser was *in extremis.*

Meantime, Ainsworth had ordered the countermarch, aiming to engage the second target-group. Although Ainsworth succeeded in capping the "T" of both enemy groups, the Japs dodged the American salvos and escaped destruction.

As usual, the Jap torpedoes had scored heavily whereas the American "fish" had flubbed. As they swung up the Gulf several of the U.S. destroyers hurled shell at the sinking NIIZUKI. She was the only Jap warship killed in this round of the battle—poor recompense for HELENA. But Round Two was coming up. And in this climax two of the American DD's distinguished themselves.

The two DD's were NICHOLAS and RADFORD, detached to rescue HELENA's survivors. The ship had gone down when the destroyers hove to at 0341 and lowered whaleboats to pick up the cruisermen. Shouts from the black water guided the rescuers to clusters of floats and swimming men. The sea was clotted with rafts and flotsam, and smeared with thick carpets of oil that gagged the swimmers and made them as hard to clutch as eels.

At 0515 the American destroyers were alerted by a radar contact, range 13,000 yards. The enemy contacted was the Japanese destroyer AMAGIRI, which had come up the Gulf from Vila in search of the NIIZUKI survivors. The Japs had just begun recue operations when their lookouts sighted the American ships. AMAGIRI put on steam to deliver a torpedo attack at the very moment NICHOLAS and RADFORD were doing the same.

At 0522 NICHOLAS fired a spread at 8,000 yards. AMAGIRI got off her torpedoes eight minutes later. Both spreads missed the marks. The Americans sent up starshells, and opened fire on the Jap's silhouette at 0534. They plunked a shell into AMAGIRI which demolished her radio room and knocked out her fire-control gear. Spouting a smoke screen, the damaged Jap fled. The Americans thought they had destroyed her. Actually they put a *finis* to some 300 of NIIZUKI's survivors. These hapless sailors were never picked up, and lost with them was Admiral Akiyama.

Two other Jap destroyers at Vila Roads saw the gunfire to the north, and, having unloaded their troops, made haste to retire through Blackett Strait, the southern exit of Kula Gulf. A third destroyer, the MOCHIZUKI, tried to haul out through Kula Gulf.

Once again NICHOLAS and RADFORD broke off rescue operations and made for the enemy. Reporting this action, Squadron Commander McInerney wrote: *"No better description can be given than the words of the Commanding Officer of the* NICHOLAS *as he stood toward the enemy ship at full speed.* IF THE SON-OF-A-BITCH WANTS TO FIGHT, I'LL GIVE HIM A FIGHT!"

MOCHIZUKI did not particularly want a fight, but she got one anyway. She unleashed a torpedo at the American ships at 0615, and they opened fire with 5-inch almost simultaneously. When several shells smacked the Jap, she laid smoke and ran for it. As daylight was making, and there was threat of air attack, McInerney also ordered a smoke screen to cover a retirement up the Gulf by NICHOLAS and RADFORD.

"Captain," someone reports, "we've picked up over 700 of HELENA's men, but there are still several hundred in the water."

"We'll leave four boats to get them! Call for volunteers."

On board NICHOLAS and RADFORD volunteers were not lacking. The four boats circled off in the morning gloom as the two destroyers steamed on out of Kula Gulf. All told, the DD's carried 745 cruiser survivors out with them. As will be seen, the volunteer lifesavers picked up many of the remaining HELENA men, and DD's returned to recover a large party which drifted in to a hostile beach—one of the more heroic rescue exploits of the war.

TAYLOR *Kills* I-25

While the Munda push rolled forward, Admiral Ainsworth's task group revisited Kula Gulf, supporting a reinforcement convoy bound for Rice Anchorage. Ainsworth's warships did not get into action on this night of July 11-12, but one of the two destroyers screening the transports did.

The screen destroyers were TAYLOR and WOODWORTH. Their run up the "Slot" and down the Gulf to Rice was uneventful, and so were the early morning landings. Uninterrupted, the landings were completed by 0430 in the morning of the 12th. And the emptied transports were heading northward up the Gulf, homebound for Guadalcanal, before trouble eventuated.

Action was sparked by a radar "pip" which showed up on the scope at 0450. TAYLOR sliced away from the convoy to investigate.

Four minutes later her lookouts spied the silhouette of a Jap conning tower 2,500 yards distant. Skippering the destroyer, Lieutenant Commander Benjamin Katz ordered on a searchlight and told the gunners to open fire. Down went the submarine and into the disappearing conning tower went several of TAYLOR's 5-inch shells.

Bursts of debris went swirling, the water churned and frothed; the sub sloughed under. A pattern of nine depth charges was spread in the sea where the mangled sub had submerged. Two more depth charges were dropped at 0510. They raised a hubbub under the surface, and then all was still.

Daylight was diluting the dark, and TAYLOR's skipper hauled

away, satisfied he had bashed the enemy to the bottom. His satisfaction was warranted. The Japanese submarine I-25 had gone beyond the range of human vision and, for that matter, any kind of detection gear.

Chapter 18

Central Solomons Sweep

(Part 2)

☆ ☆ ☆

The Battle of Kolombangara

To the Solomon Islanders, Kolombangara means "King of the Waters." The American sailors who fought the Japs off this island called it other descriptive names.

About 0530 in the morning of July 12 the "Tokyo Express" set out from Rabaul with reinforcements and supplies for the Jap garrison at Vila-Stanmore.

The "Express" had a new driver. Removed by jealous deskadmirals in High Headquarters, Tenacious Tanaka had been replaced by Rear Admiral Shunji Izaki—typical substitution of routine mediocrity for efficient non-conformity. Tanaka had not been a yes-man.

But the "Express" was still powerful materially. On this occasion, it was composed of a support group containing the light cruiser JINTSU (flagship), and destroyers MIKAZUKI, YUKIKAZE, HAMAKAZE, KIYONAMI, and YUGURE. Passengers and freight were carried by destroyer-transports SATSUKI, MINAZUKI, YUNAGI, and MATSUKAZE.

Coast watchers and aircraft spied the Jap ships, and Halsey was tipped off. Out went a dispatch to Admiral Ainsworth; his ships were to make another dash to Kula Gulf to intercept. Ainsworth's Task Group 36.1 was expanded by the addition of six destroyers. The force roster is listed on the next page.

Ainsworth received the order to head for Kula in the afternoon of July 12, and the task group stood northward from Tulagi at 1700. At 2300, when the force was about an hour's run from Visuvisu Point, the Admiral sent all hands to battle stations. Tonight there was a bright moon gilding the seascape and silhouetting the ships. With radar Ainsworth planned to beat the enemy to the punch.

At 0036 in the morning of July 13, a "Black Cat" search

TASK GROUP 36.1
Rear Admiral Ainsworth

DESTROYER SQUADRON 21
Captain Francis X. McInerney

NICHOLAS	*Lt. Comdr. Andrew J. Hill*
Flagship	
O'BANNON	*Lt. Comdr. D. J. MacDonald*
TAYLOR	*Lt. Comdr. Benjamin Katz*
JENKINS	*Lt. Comdr. Madison Hall*
RADFORD	*Comdr. W. K. Romoser*

CRUISER DIVISION 9
Rear Admiral Ainsworth

HONOLULU	ST. LOUIS

H.M.N.Z.S. LEANDER
Replacement for HELENA

DESTROYER SQUADRON 12
Capt. T. J. Ryan

GWIN	*Lt. Comdr. J. B. Fellows*
	Flagship of
Comdr. J. M. Higgins, COMDESDIV 23	
RALPH TALBOT	*Comdr. J. W. Callahan*
BUCHANAN	*Lt. Comdr. F. B. T. Myhre*
MAURY	*Comdr. G. L. Sims*
WOODWORTH	*Comdr. V. F. Gordinier*

plane contacted the Jap ships some 26 miles northwest of Ainsworth's force. The "Cat" reported a Jap cruiser and five DD's rat-racing toward Kula. Ainsworth immediately formed his night battle column—McInerney's destroyers in the van; cruisers next; Ryan's destroyers in the rear. He headed the column on a course that took it directly across the mouth of Kula Gulf.

At 0059 flag cruiser HONOLULU made first radar contact with the enemy, and at 0103 the lookouts on lead destroyer NICHOLAS spied the enemy's silhouette. Three minutes later Ainsworth swung his ships on a simultaneous 30° turn to the right to close the Jap warships. Suddenly the second ship in the Jap column laid a searchlight on the American DD's. Snapping the word over the TBS, Ainsworth ordered the destroyers to fire torpedoes at discretion.

McInerney's van destroyers let go at once, range about 10,000 yards. So did New Zealand cruiser LEANDER. Ryan's rear DD's had been crowding on steam to get in column formation when the firing order came, and they were badly bunched astern of ST. LOUIS. These rear destroyers were all newcomers, drawn from three unacquainted squadrons, and had never worked in harness with each other. Yet with the exception of GWIN, all unleashed torpedo salvos. In spite of dense smoke from flashless powder, they avoided collision and made the turn safely. The trouble that came was the handiwork of the Japs.

Unbeknownst to Ainsworth, the Jap ships carried radar-detectors. Admiral Izaki had seen the Americans coming, and about 0108 he had ordered a DD torpedo attack, thereby beating Ainsworth's by some 60 seconds. By jumping the gun, the Japs might have had a considerable advantage.

When the American destroyers in the van loosed their torpedoes, Jap cruiser JINTSU flashed a searchlight at them and opened fire with gun and torpedo batteries. Answering with rapid fire, Ainsworth's cruisers pumped shell after shell at JINTSU. In the action the Allied column had swung northwest, then southward on a wide loop. While it was swinging on this loop, the early-launched Jap torpedoes began to nip in. Cruiser LEANDER, overrunning the southward turn, was struck hard. Disabled by the blast, she fell out of action with 28 of her crew lying dead.

The Japs paid for this blow. As they looped around to the southward, the American warships, one and all, flailed at JINTSU with shellfire. Centered in a tempest of flame and steel, JINTSU was literally melted down. While the cruiser was melting she was stsuck by a torpedo from the American van group.

Admiral Izaki's flagship disintegrated. So did Admiral Izaki. So did some 483 Japanese cruisermen. JINTSU broke in two, and the flaming, exploding wreckage disappeared. Nearly all hands were either drowned, blown to pieces, or cremated.

Meanwhile, Ainsworth (at 0126) had ordered his van destroyers to peel away and pursue the Jap DD's reported by the Black Cat to be breaking off the action.

Heading northward in NICHOLAS, Captain McInerney shouted to Captain Ryan over TBS: WE FOUR ARE ON COURSE 325 CHASING THE ENEMY DON'T THROW ANYTHING AT US.

Ryan replied: I WOULDN'T DO IT FOR THE WORLD—GO TO IT AND GET THE BASTARDS X GOOD LUCK.

Language to shock nice old ladies. But the ladies for whom this epithet was intended were neither old nor nice. Their names were MIKABUKI, YUKIKABE, HAMAKAZE, KIYONAMI, and YUGURE.

However, the order which sent McInerney's destroyers in pursuit of these Japanese destroyers proved unfortunate. The van DD's tnus became separated from Ainsworth's main body. Confusion resulted at 0156 when the American cruiser column was running northwest up the "Slot," and HONOLULU made radar contact with a group of ships on her port bow, range 23,000 yards. Were they Japs, or were they McInerney's?

Ainsworth was compelled to hold his fire until he could find out. The investigation cost time and a lot of talk over the TBS. Seven minutes ticked by. Then Ainsworth ordered his cruisers to fire starshells. When the eerie light flooded the seascape, the target ships were seen retiring at high speed. The retirement meant they were enemy. Ainsworth swung his cruisers on a right turn to bring their batteries to bear. But the Japs had fired first—and they had fired a barrage of Model 93 torpedoes.

HONOLULU sighted one of the poisonous wakes. She flashed the alarm, but it was too late. Astern of her, ST. LOUIS was hit. The "fish" struck forward, and bent her stem sideways like a broken nose. HONOLULU was also struck on the nose, and a dud smacked her in the stern. Each with a nose out of joint, the two American cruisers went floundering. Then GWIN, leading HONOLULU, caught a torpedo amidships. Instantly she was writhing in a bramble bush of fire. Those death-dealing Jap torpedoes had killed again.

A destroyer sinking, three cruisers severely damaged, two destroyers bruised by collision—these were stiff casualties in exchange for the JINTSU.

Slowly and painfully, cruisers LEANDER, HONOLULU, and ST. LOUIS and destroyers WOODWORTH and BUCHANAN made their homeward way down the "Slot." Astern, they left destroyer GWIN sinking under the evil eye of Kolombangara, "King of the Waters."

The Battle of Vella Gulf (Moosbrugger in Action!)

On July 15, 1943, Rear Admiral T. S. Wilkinson relieved Admiral Turner as Commander Amphibious Forces South Pacific. At that time Army and Marine troops were slugging their way toward Munda on New Georgia, fighting hard for that Central Solomons rung. The enemy was being driven back. But the disablement of three cruisers had almost left Ainsworth's task group on the beach, and the Japs had taken to running barges down the "Slot" to reinforce their Central Solomons front. Early in August Wilkinson received word that such a Japanese train was coming. He lacked heavy ships for the wrecking job in prospect, but there were some new destroyers in Tulagi. And with those destroyers was an officer named Moosbrugger.

Commander Frederick Moosbrugger had been sent to Tulagi to serve as ComDesDiv 12. His division consisted of destroyers DUNLAP (Lieutenant Commander Clifton Iverson), CRAVEN (Lieutenant Commander F. T. Williamson), and MAURY (Commander G. L. Sims).

On August 5 Munda fell. While it was falling Admiral Wilkinson sent Moosbrugger a dispatch ordering him to Vella Gulf to intercept the new "Tokyo Express." Moosbrugger was ordered to proceed by the southern route and enter the gulf via Gizo Strait between Kolombangara and Gizo Islands. Upon entering the Gulf he was to assume complete command of the operation and adopt whatever tactics he chose. He was to have daylight fighter cover, and cooperation of PT-boats in the Blackett Strait area. His force would include three DD's of Destroyer Division 15. These destroyers were LANG (Commander J. L. Wilfong), flying the pennant of Commander R. W. Simpson, ComDesDiv 15; STERETT (Lieutenant Commander F. G. Gould); and STACK (Lieutenant Commander R. A. Newton).

Here was the opportunity the DesPac captains had been waiting for. And Moosbrugger's outfit, DesDiv 12, had operated as a unit since May 1941. Further, their specialty was night torpedo attack under radar control.

Moosbrugger's plan was for the two destroyer divisions to steam up the Gulf in separate columns about two miles apart, Simpson's a little astern of Moosbrugger's. If the target proved to be a destroyer group, Moosbrugger's DD's would hit the first blow with torpedoes. If barges were encountered, Simpson's DD's, armed with new 40 mm. batteries, would open up with shells. Understood? Let's go!

At 1130 the six destroyers steamed out of Tulagi. As his ships entered Vella Gulf, Moosbrugger ordered them into battle formation. After probing the waters off Blackett Strait they headed due north, following the Kolombangara coast, with Simpson's DD's in the inshore position and Moosbrugger's on the outside track. The rainy night was as thick as liquid shoe blacking.

At 2333 DUNLAP made the first radar contact, a target in the mouth of the Gulf about ten miles distant. On the radar screen the "pip" quickly multiplied itself into four distinct "pips" which meant four enemy ships heading southward.

The enemy destroyers which had steamed into radar view were IJN HAGIKAZE, ARASHI, and KAWAKAZE, chock-a-block with troops and supplies for the Emperor's garrison on Kolombangara, supported by SHIGURE, crammed with ammunition and torpedoes to be fired in the event of interference. These Jap ships did not carry radar, and they were unaware of Commander Moosbrugger and his destroyer team.

The range closed swiftly to good torpedo range. Moosbrugger had tuned his torpedoes up by deactivating the cranky magnetic exploder device. Also his torpedo batteries were equipped with flash-hiders. These improvements were now to pay off.

At 2336 Moosbrugger passed the word over TBS to his leading division, "Stand by to fire torpedoes!" As DesDiv 12 came to course 335° T, the computed course to the torpedo firing point, Simpson's destroyers took station clear of the van division and headed for the enemy. Moosbrugger barked the torpedo-firing order. DUNLAP, CRAVEN, and MAURY let go with spreads—eight torpedoes to a spread. As the "fish" raced off across the mouth of the Gulf, Moosbrugger swung his ships hard right to dodge Jap torpedoes, if any. Surface visibility was less than 4,000 yards, and no ship had as yet been sighted.

And now the Japs, having belatedly sighted the foaming torpedo wakes, were frantically trying to fire their own big "fish." All was uproar and confusion on HAGIKAZE's bridge. ARASHI and KAWAKAZE were also unprepared for action. Cracking the whip at the tail end of the column, SHIGURE was equally unready.

Only the rear Jap destroyer escaped a blasting. HAGIKAZE blew up. Ditto for ARASHI. Double ditto for KAWAKAZE.

The SHIGURE, sole survivor of this pogrom, had fired eight aimless torpedoes and taken to her heels. Moosbrugger led his destroyers in a footless chase of the fugitive, then circled back and headed southward down the "Slot" astern of DesDiv 12.

In the Battle of Vella Gulf, as this engagement came to be called, the enemy had not laid a hand on the American ships. The only casualty among these last was a broken feed pump in a destroyer. On board LANG a loader's hand was accidentally crushed. On the Japanese side three destroyers went down, two of them almost the latest thing in Jap construction. With them went some 1,500 Jap sailors and their soldier passengers.

PATTERSON *Kills* I-178

In the evening of August 25, 1943, destroyer PATTERSON (Lieutenant Commander A. F. White) was steaming along in the screen of Task Unit 32.4.7, at that hour on the road between Espiritu Santo and the Lower Solomons. At 1912 she picked up something on her radarscope and was promptly ordered to investigate.

Eleven minutes later, the range having closed to 4,000 yards, the "pip" suddenly vanished from the radar screen. This abrupt disappearance had all the ear-marks of a diving sub. Sonar substantiated the evidence by registering with the submerged target at 3,800 yards.

Maneuvering in on the run, PATTERSON steamed across the water, dropping depth charges. Follow-up attacks were made for the next two hours. At 2147 the last pattern went down. The TNT thumped far beneath the surface. Then (time: 2153) the destroyermen heard a deep undersea *boom* which sounded like blasting in a tunnel under a distant subway.

The detonation was too remote for accurate analysis, and PATTERSON "pinged" around on the usual search, but the contact was gone. She had never actually sighted the submarine; it was just a flicker on a screen, a whisper in the sound gear, and that final echo from deep under.

That—and a notation in the records of the Japanese Sixth (Submarine) Fleet, examined after the war. The notation disclosed that the submarine I-178 had disappeared on the night in question at the point where PATTERSON's depth charges, going deep, produced the deep-going *boom!*

ELLET *Sinks* I-168

On September 3, 1943, the I-168 made the fatal mistake of nosing to the South Pacific surface in the vicinity of lat. 13 S., long. 165 E.

The sub's presence in the area was detected, and an A/S sweep was ordered by the naval authorities at Espiritu Santo. Evening of the 3rd found destroyer ELLET (Lieutenant Commander T. C. Phifer) on the job. Sweeping through the cobwebby gloom, ELLET snared a radar pip at 1935, range 13,000 yards.

ELLET's skipper closed the range to about 5,000 yards. As the "pip" was unidentifiable, the destroyer challenged at that point with a blinker-gun. When the stranger made no reply, tie destroyermen lit up the seascape with a starshell spread. The target disappeared at 3,400 yards, and the chase was on.

ELLET obtained sonar contact at 3,000 yards, and Lieutenant Commander Phifer conned the ship for a depth-charge attack. The first pattern was dropped at 2012, and the last one splashed into the sea at 2038. At 2040 sonar contact was reestablished; then it was lost for good at 2059.

Hunt as she would, ELLET could find no further trace of the submarine. The destroyermen, trained to be skeptical in such matters, could not readily believe they had slain a sub in a depth-charge effort of only 26 minutes' duration. But at daylight an extensive oil slick was sighted by a plane. Oil bubbles were seen, and a few scraps of debris were sighted.

The slick, the bubbles, the hrifting scraps were the last earthly remains of Japanese submarine I-168. After the war her obituary was found in the Imperial Navy's records.

SAUFLEY *and Aircraft Down* RO-103

In company with the old minelaying "four-stacker" MONT-
GOMERY, the SAUFLEY (Commander B. F. Brown) was steaming southward from Port Purvis on September 15, 1943, with
two merchantmen in convoy. About 11 o'clock in the morning
the convoy was waylaid by a submarine at the lower end of
Indispensable Strait.

First warning came when a torpedo whisked past one of the
merchantmen in a near-miss. Apparently the Japs, over-hasty,
had tried a long-range "browning shot." To the convoy the
miss was as good as the proverbial mile. To the submarine it
was fatal.

All hands on the alert, SAUFLEY began a search that found
the target at 1251, range 3,000 yards. Maneuvering in on the
attack, the destroyer steamed over the submarine, and pelted
the target with teardrops and ashcans.

Up came an RO-boat to be riddled and blasted under.
Evidence of this particularly futile Jap submarine effort
bobbed to the surface in the form of oil slicks, shattered gratings, splintered planks, and kindling wood.

The submarine was eventually identified as the RO-103.

EATON *Kills* I-20

EATON (Lieutenant Commander E. F. Jackson) was a member of Captain W. R. Cooke's Striking Force which steamed
up the "Slot" on the night of October 1-2, 1943, to intercept
Jap traffic. As the group passed the mouth of Kula Gulf, the
radar screens began to shimmer like television flaked with
"snow." At 2248 EATON opened fire at a plump "pip" which
blossomed on her radar, range 3,000 yards.

A barrage of starshells shed light on the target which was
promptly identified as a Japanese submarine running on the
surface. It did not run fast enough to escape EATON's gunnery.
The first salvos were right on. And the next three nailed the
conning tower and pressure hull of the hapless submersible.
The submarine rolled over on her back and put her propellers
in the air.

EATON's gunners planted a few more shells in the vessel's
belly. For a minute or two the sub drifted like a dead whale.
At 2251 the carcass sank from view. It had taken the killers
exactly three minutes to slay this specimen. They went on to
exterminate a few barges for good measure.

The submarine blown to the bottom was the I-20, a veteran
of the Guadalcanal campaign.

The Battle of Vella Lavella

The task of evacuating the remnant Japanese garrison on Vella Lavella was detailed to Admiral Matsuji Ijuin. The Rabaul command scraped up a sizable force for this emergency job—nine or ten DD's and a flotilla of small boats and sub chasers. A train reminiscent of the heyday of the "Tokyo Express." Early in the morning of October 6, 1943, this force stood southward from Rabaul. It skirted the northern coast of Bougainville, and by twilight it was steaming down the "Slot."

The progress of Ijuin's train was duly reported by search planes. Only three DD's were flying the American flag in the Vella Lavella vicinity. Admiral Wilkinson dispatched these immediately to the waters off the northwest coast of the island, and then detached three more destroyers from a convoy below New Georgia and ordered them to rush northward to reinforce the first three.

The first destroyers to reach an intercepting position were units of Captain Frank R. Walker's Squadron 4—destroyers SELFRIDGE (Lieutenant Commander G. E. Peckham), CHEVALIER (Lieutenant Commander G. R. Wilson), and O'BANNON (Lieutenant Commander D. J. MacDonald). The destroyers racing up from New Georgia were under Commander H. O. Larson—RALPH TALBOT (Lieutenant Commander R. D. Shepard), TAYLOR (Commander Benjamin Katz), and LAVALLETTE (Lieutenant Commander R. L. Taylor). Six American destroyers could have given Ijuin's nine or ten a good run for their money. But three against the Japanese gang was not such a happy circumstance. Yet that was the circumstance Captain Walker found himself up against when the "Tokyo Express" came over the dark horizon.

At 2231 SELFRIDGE, leading Walker's three-ship column, made radar contact with the enemy up the "Slot." Walker headed his DD's toward the targets to investigate. By 2240 the enemy was in binocular range—six destroyers in two groups.

Walker must have been a little worried about the odds. A moment after sighting the enemy, he put in a call for Larson's ships over the TBS. Some 20 miles away, Larson was beyond range of radio-telephony, and the call drew a blank.

Walker then might have hauled away to stall for time. Instead, he pressed forward to strike while the iron was hot. As Ijuin's support group came steaming southward in two columns, the four-ship column—AKIGUMO, ISOKAZE, KAZEGUMO, and YUGUMO—missed a chance to cap Walker's "T." To the starboard of Ijuin's main column, SHIGURE and SAMIDARE were on the disengaged side when the Americans, racing in at 33 knots, opened torpedo fire. Range was 7,000 yards, and the

Japs were swinging sharp left in line of bearing when Walker ordered his ships to launch torpedoes. A barrage of 14 went leaping from the American tubes at 2255, and a split minute later Walker snapped the order for gunnery.

Put on the inside track by Ijuin's maneuver, the destroyer YUGUMO was not only presenting her beam to the American torpedoes, but she was also interfering with counterfire from her companions. Then at the crucial moment she veered off to deliver a torpedo attack on her own hook, swinging northward to close this range. By so doing she jaywalked right into a barrage of torpedoes and shells from SELFRIDGE, CHEVALIER, and O'BANNON.

Ijuin pulled out of the muddle by ordering his ships back into column and swinging them southward behind a smoke screen. KAZEGUMO got in a couple of salvos on the turn, but ISOKAZE and AKIGUMO were as yet unable to fire a shot. As for YUGUMO, she was out of it. Having collected an American torpedo and a swarm of 5-inchers, she was squatting disabled in the water and vomiting flames that were seen by Larson's destroyers miles to the south.

Now Ijuin was running westward in fast retreat. The flotilla of Jap small-craft was legging it in to Vella Lavella. And Walker still had five Jap DD's and a mess of Jap "fish" to deal with.

In an effort to deal with the DD's, he sent his column westward in enthusiastic pursuit. In the lead, SELFRIDGE was firing at SHIGURE and SAMIDARE. CHEVALIER and O'BANNON, after pegging shots at YUGUMO's blazing hulk, also shifted attention to the two-ship column. The gun smoke was dense, and O'BANNON, astern of CHEVALIER, was racing through acrid fog. CHEVALIER was on the point of illuminating the targets ahead when her captain was notified that a pair of small craft were making a high-speed approach from starboard.

On CHEVALIER's bridge Lieutenant Commander Wilson ordered a swing to the left. Evidently the small craft were motor torpedo-boats from the Jap group to the north. Wilson intended to bring his 1.1-inch guns to bear on these vicious speedboats while keeping his 5-inchers trained on the two DD's in the west.

Just as CHEVALIER was swinging she was struck in the port bow by a torpedo. Then she was rammed by O'BANNON. Then SELFRIDGE up ahead was torpedoed. All this in a matter of moments.

Loss of USS CHEVALIER

It was Japanese destroyer YUGUMO that flung the torpedo which struck CHEVALIER. The warhead smashed into a portside magazine, and the resulting blast ripped off the destroyer's bow as far aft as the bridge.

All hands on the bridge were thrown from their feet by the thunderclap explosion. Lieutenant Commander Wilson was knocked momentarily unconscious. When he dragged himself upright, he found himself clutching the rail and staring, dazed, at a yawn of swirling water where the destroyer's forecastle should have been.

Then men on the fantail were yelling. Someone squalled, "We're going to be raaaamed!" Before the decapitated vessel could be turned or backed, she was struck amidships by O'BANNON. When his lookouts cried the warning, Commander MacDonald of the O'BANNON tried desperately to swing his destroyer aside. Too late. Momentum carried O'BANNON squarely into CHEVALIER's starboard side.

There was the crunch of metal chewing metal. The disabled destroyer shuddered and heeled. Some of her crew were spinning and somersaulting across the deck. In the dark after passageways wounded men cried out. Smoke gushed from the wreckage, and bluejackets came climbing topside, coughing.

O'BANNON's screws had been churning to pull her back when her stem gnashed into CHEVALIER. The bite was not deep, but it was deep enough to let the sea into the disabled ship's after engine-room and start copious leakage in both firerooms. With her forecastle torn away, her hull gashed, her powerplant half wrecked, and water rising to swamp her boilers, CHEVALIER leaned on her side, mortally injured. O'BANNON backed off, and MacDonald lowered boats to pick up CHEVALIER stretcher cases.

While O'BANNON was jockeying about, destroyer SELFRIDGE, five miles up the "Slot," had run into a fan of torpedoes spread by SAMIDARE and SHIGURE. Swinging to comb the wakes, she caught another Model 93. When the thunder and smoke ebbed away, SELFRIDGE had lost most of her bow.

The SELFRIDGE blast put an exclamation point finish to the Vella Lavella destroyer battle. The Japs raced north, leaving mayhem and manslaughter behind them.

Larson's three destroyers raced to the scene. It was all over but the damage control when they got there.

Destroyer TAYLOR moved up to take off the SELFRIDGE crew. As her engines were unharmed, the ship was able to move through the water at about 10 knots. Lieutenant Commander Peckham, determined to stick it out, remained on board with a salvage party. Most of the crew and Squadron Commander Walker were taken off by the TAYLOR. With gun crews manning her undamaged weapons, SELFRIDGE steamed slowly down the "Slot" under her own power. She was screened by RALPH TALBOT and TAYLOR.

LAVALLETTE was ordered to sink wrecked CHEVALIER. At the range of one mile she fired a single torpedo. A great balloon of fire rolled up into the sky, and then nothing was left of the broken warship.

Lost with CHEVALIER were 53 bluejackets and an officer.

Bougainville Invaded ("Operation Shoestring 2")

With New Georgia, Kolombangara, and Vella Lavella in Allied hands, only Bougainville remained as a major barrier to the "Watchtower" drive on Rabaul. Dominating the Upper Solomons, Bougainville is the largest of the Solomon Isles. Given bases on Bougainville for fighters and light bombers, the Allies would have Rabaul in an aerial nut-cracker. Halsey planned an offensive against Bougainville for the express purpose of acquiring these advanced airfields.

The first troops put ashore on Bougainville were some 13,300 Marines, and the convoy of 12 transports was screened by 11 destroyers under Commander Ralph Earle, ComDesRon 45. The destroyers were: FULLAM, GUEST, BENNETT, HUDSON, ANTHONY, WADSWORTH, TERRY, BRAINE, SIGOURNEY, CONWAY, RENSHAW.

At Cape Torokina the Japs had one 75 mm. artillery piece and a company of less than 300 men. For a short time this force put up savage resistance, but it was soon whittled down and chased into the jungle. A few Jap aircraft from Rabaul struck at 0735, D-day morning. During D-day afternoon about 100 Jap carrier planes roared down from the Bismarcks. They, too, were intercepted by American fighter planes. The Americans were coached into position by a fighter-director team in destroyer CONWAY. No ships or landing craft were hit by the attacking Japs. Wilkinson pulled his transports out of Empress Augusta Bay before nightfall, anticipating a furious reaction from Japanese air and surface forces at Rabaul. General MacArthur's claim that Rabaul had been knocked out by Army Air was soon to be exploded by Navy anti-aircraft guns.

The Battle of Empress Augusta Bay (Arleigh Burke in Action!)

When word reached Admiral Koga at Truk that the Americans had dared to put foot on Bougainville, he radioed instructions to strike the interloper and strike hard. Rabaul's air strength was mustered, and with air power to back him up, Rear Admiral Sentaro Omori set out from Rabaul late in the afternoon of November 1 with a bloodthirsty surface force. Mission: to blast the Americans off the Bougainville beachheads at Cape Torokina.

In Omori's force were heavy cruisers MYOKO and HAGURO, light cruisers SENDAI and AGANO, and six destroyers. Five troop-carrying assault transports sortied with the force. Omori sent them home. He wanted freedom for fast maneuver.

He needed it. Halsey had the word on the sortie, and ComSoPac had lost no time in dispatching Rear Admiral Merrill's task force to intercept the southbound Japs. When "Tip" Merrill received this flash assignment his cruisers were off Vella Lavella, enjoying a breather after the strenuous bombardment work of the previous day. Commander B. L. ("Count") Austin was on hand with DesDiv 46. Captain Arleigh Burke's DesDiv 45 was refueling in Hathorn Sound at the entrance of Kula Gulf. These destroyers topped off with dizzy speed, and by 2315 in the evening of November 1, Merrill's force was racing headlong to meet the warships of Admiral Omori.

Omori did not expect to encounter a cruiser-destroyer force. He expected, perhaps wishfully, to encounter a transport group. Bearing down on Empress Augusta Bay, he had his Imperial naval vessels disposed in a simple formation with heavy cruisers MYOKO (flagship) and HAGURO in the center; light cruiser SENDAI and destroyers SHIGURE, SAMIDARE, and SHIRATSUYU to port; light cruiser AGANO and destroyers NAGANAMI, HATSUKAZE, and WAKATSUKI to starboard.

Merrill's force was disposed in line-of-bearing of unit guides. In column to starboard were Burke's van destroyers: CHARLES AUSBURNE (Commander L. K. Reynolds); DYSON (Commander R. A. Gano); STANLY (Commander R. W. Cavenagh); and CLAXTON (Commander H. F. Stout). In center column steamed cruisers MONTPELIER (flagship), CLEVELAND, COLUMBIA, and DENVER. To port steamed Austin's rear destroyers: SPENCE (Commander H. J. Armstrong); THATCHER (Commander L. R. Lampman); CONVERSE (Commander D. C. E. Hamberger); and FOOTE (Commander Alston Ramsay).

Omori's force suffered the first blow when an American plane, detecting the Jap approach, planted a bomb in the superstructure of heavy cruiser HAGURO. Lamed by the hit, HAGURO reduced the formation's speed to 30 knots. Then one of that cruiser's planes reported Merrill's task force coming up. The airmen erroneously notified Omori that one cruiser and three destroyers were in the offing. When, a few minutes later, he was informed (again erroneously) that a fleet of transports was unloading in Empress Augusta Bay, he sent his formation racing southeastward, hot for a massacre.

The night was black as carbon. Several of Omori's warships carried radar apparatus, but he put more reliance on binoculars. American "Sugar George" radar was to out-see Japanese vision on this occasion.

Merrill's cruisers made the initial radar contact at 0227. He had already decided to maintain his ships in a position that would block the entrance to Empress Augusta Bay. His destroyers were to open proceedings with a torpedo attack, and the cruisers were to hold their fire until the "fish" had opportunity to strike the foe.

These plans, carefully laid, were known, chapter and verse, by Captain Arleigh Burke, leader of DesDiv 45. Commander Austin and DesDiv 46 were not so well versed in the detail. They were new to Task Force 39, and Austin was not thoroughly acquainted with Merrill's battle techniques.

As soon as radar contact was established, Merrill headed his formation due north. After a brief run, Burke's van destroyers sliced away northwestward to deliver a torpedo strike as planned. Merrill then ordered a simultaneous turn to reverse course. Austin's destroyers were instructed to countermarch, and then hit the enemy's southern flank with torpedoes as soon as they could reach firing position.

While Merrill's cruisers were swinging around the hairpin turn, Burke's destroyers were tacking in on Omori's portside column. At 0246 Burke shouted the word over TBS, *"My guppies are swimming!"* But the Japs had sighted Merrill's cruisers, and Omori was turning his formation southwestward. Because of this sudden turn, the barrage of 25 "guppies" sailed on into silence and oblivion, and Burke's briskly executed attack failed to score.

Meanwhile, the SENDAI column launched torpedoes at the American cruisers. But Merrill had not waited for this counterfire. When C.I.C informed him of Omori's southwestward turn, he ordered his cruisers to let go with gunnery. IJN SENDAI was chief target for this booming fusillade. She caught a cataract of shells just as she was swinging to starboard, and the explosions blew her innards right out through the overhead.

SENDAI's abrupt come-uppance threw her column into a jumble. In the ensuing confusion, destroyers SAMIDARE and SHIRATSUYU collided full tilt, and went reeling off in precipitous retirement. That left the SHIGURE all by herself, and she chased southward to join the Jap cruiser column.

MYOKO and HAGURO made a blind loop that tangled them up with the AGANO column. Although Jap starshells had turned the night into a dazzle, the heavy cruisers failed to sight Merrill's ships, and they maneuvered right into a tempest of American shellfire. Steaming in a daze, MYOKO slammed into destroyer HATSUKAZE and ripped off a section of that DD's bow.

Meantime, Burke's "Little Beavers," having launched torpedoes, became separated. And they did not get back into battle until 0349, when AUSBURNE spotted SENDAI and hurried the vessel under with a volley of shots. Then SAMIDARE and SHIRATSUYU, the two DD's which had collided, showed up on the radar screen. Burke took off after these departing enemies at top speed.

Commander Austin's DesDiv 46 destroyers had run into hard luck. Destroyer FOOTE misread Merrill's signal to turn, and fell out of formation. While racing to rejoin Austin's column, she was hit in the stern by a Jap torpedo. Swinging hard right to give the cruiser column a clear line of fire, destroyer SPENCE sideswiped destroyer THATCHER. The 30-knot brush sent sparks and sweat-beads flying, and removed a wide swath of paint, but both DD's kept on traveling at high speed. Then at 0320 a Jap shell punctured SPENCE's hull at the waterline. Salt water got into a fuel tank, contaminating the oil, and this slow poison soon reduced the destroyer's speed.

However, SPENCE made contact with cruiser SENDAI. The Jap vessel was staggering merry-go-round, but her guns were still firing, and she was as dangerous as a wounded leopard. Austin maneuvered for torpedo fire, and SPENCE and CONVERSE flung eight "fish" at the cripple. They did not sink her—Burke's destroyers would presently perform that chore. Austin's three DD's raced on northwestward in an effort to catch SAMIDARE and SHIRATSUYU.

By 0352 SPENCE, THATCHER, and CONVERSE had overhauled the two Jap DD's, and 19 American torpedoes were fanning out. The 19 torpedoes scored a perfect zero. The zero probably had its source in defective mechanisms.

In counterattack, SAMIDARE and SHIRATSUYU flung shells and "fish" at Austin's three destroyers. If the Jap "fish" missed, the marksmen at least had an excuse for poor torpedo work—the two Jap DD's were dodging to escape a tempest of shell fire, and both ships had been badly damaged by collision.

Now SPENCE was running low on fuel, and what little she had was contaminated by salt water. Austin relinquished tactical command to THATCHER's skipper, Commander Lampman, and veered away with SPENCE to disengage. The maneuver brought his flag destroyer into line for a salvo from Arleigh Burke's fast-shooting division. At 0425 a pack of projectiles slammed into the sea around SPENCE.

Over the TBS Commander Austin shouted a plea to Burke: WE'VE JUST HAD ANOTHER CLOSE MISS HOPE YOU ARE NOT SHOOTING AT US.

Captain Burke's answer was a classic of Navy humor:

SORRY BUT YOU'LL HAVE TO EXCUSE THE NEXT FOUR SALVOS
THEY'RE ALREADY ON THEIR WAY.

Austin made haste to get SPENCE out of the vicinity. In
dodging Burke's ebullient fire, SPENCE picked up a good target
in Jap destroyer HATSUKAZE.

HATSUKAZE was the DD which MYOKO had rammed, and
she was in no condition to dodge well-aimed salvos. SPENCE
closed the range to 4,000 yards while her gunners pumped
shells into the disabled Jap. HATSUKAZE was soon flaming and
wallowing, her engines dead. Austin yearned to finish off this
foe, but SPENCE's ammunition was running low, so he put in
a call for Burke's destroyers to complete the execution. Thereupon an avalanche of 5-inchers from DesDiv 45 buried HAT-
SUKAZE. The ship rolled over and descended into the grave.

SPENCE joined up with DesDiv 45 as Burke ordered a retirement. Unable to catch SAMIDARE and SHIRATSUYU, destroyers THATCHER and CONVERSE were also retiring. As day was
making, Admiral Merrill had already headed his cruiser
column eastward. While his DD's were trying to tag fleeing
Japs, Merrill's cruisers had been maneuvering across the seascape in a duel with the Jap heavies. For over an hour the
opposing formations had dodged about like gamecocks in a
pit, neither side able to score a death-dealing blow. Convinced
that he had tangled with no less than seven heavy cruisers,
Omori pulled out at 0337 and fled northwest up the coast of
Bougainville. The American cruisers chased until daybreak,
then Merrill turned back, anticipating aircraft from Rabaul.

Around 0500 Burke's voice came cheerfully over the TBS.
His destroyers were still to the west of Merrill's cruisers, and
he requested permission to pursue the fleeing Japs. According to Captain Briscoe, Merrill's answer to this was: ARLIE
THIS IS TIP FOR GODS SAKE COME HOME WE'RE LONESOME.

So Burke came steaming south with his seven DD's to keep
the cruisers company.

About 0800 the Jap aircraft attacked the retiring ships.
Merrill had the force disposed in a circular AA formation.
As the bombers came over, he maneuvered to bring main
batteries to bear, and the destroyers opened up with AA fire
at about 14,000 yards.

Merrill described it in his Action Report:

> The scene was of an organized hell in which it was impos-
> sible to speak, hear, or even think. As the ships passed the first
> 90 degrees of their turn in excellent formation, the air seemed
> completely filled with bursting shrapnel and, to our great glee,
> enemy planes in a severe state of disrepair. . . . Planes were in
> flames as they passed over the flagship, exploding outside the
> destroyer screen. . . . Ten planes were counted in the water at

one time, and seven additional were seen to crash well outside the formation.

At the height of the battle, Merrill ordered a 360° turn which kept the warship carousel steaming clockwise. All the gunners seemed to be catching prizes from the air. Three Japs bailed out in parachutes and landed almost in the center of the wheeling formation. "Bettys" blew up in the sky and exploded in the water. Of the 70 or 80 planes which attacked, perhaps two dozen were shot down. The Japs landed only two hits, both on cruiser MONTPELIER, damaging a catapult and wounding one man. At 0812 they broke off the attack and ran northward.

The Battle of Empress Augusta Bay and its aerial epilogue were over. On the sea and in the air the enemy had taken a colossal thrashing.

Augusta Bay Aftermath

With the Allies holding a grip on Bougainville, the Japanese war effort in the South Pacific was all but paralyzed. They were virtually ousted from the Solomons, and they were checkmated at Rabaul.

A number of factors had contributed to Japan's South Pacific defeat. One was the VT proximity-fused projectile. Introduced in the South Pacific by cruiser HELENA the preceding January, this item of ammunition was widely distributed in Halsey's fleet by November, 1943. (A word about the VT device. In effect it worked as a miniature radio transmitter-receiver. Affixed to an anti-aircraft shell, the contrivance sent out radio waves which were reflected back from a plane when it passed within 70 feet of it. The returning impulse exploded the shell. Shrapnel did the rest. Deadly for AA work, the projectile could also be used against surface targets.)

Destroyers carrying fighter-director teams were another big help at Empress Augusta Bay.

And so was the initiative a help. By the time Merrill reached Cape Torokina, the whole Pacific Fleet was going on the offensive. The top of the Solomons ladder had been reached. A new, aggressive spirit spurred the Allies.

The Japanese were inspired by no such spirit.

In the afternoon of November 10 Merrill's Task Force 39 was operating in an area west of Treasury Island. Six of Burke's destroyers were working with the force, and as usual the "Little Beavers" stirred up something. On this occasion destroyer SPENCE did the stirring. Here is the story as recorded in her Action Report by her skipper, Commander H. J. Armstrong:

> At 1545 the SPENCE sighted and, as requested, was ordered to investigate a life float. On approaching, several bodies were noted in the float as it passed close aboard down starboard side. Seven men who had been feigning death sat up and started talking in Japanese. One, apparently an officer and pilot, broke out a 7.7 mm. machine-gun (evidently salvaged from a plane). Each man in succession placed the muzzle of the gun in his mouth, and the Jap officer fired a round, blowing the back of the man's head out. The Jap first to be killed showed great reluctance to be included in the suicide pact. One man held him while another wielded the machine-gun. All of the bodies toppled over the side and sank, followed closely by sharks. The Jap officer, alone on the raft, gave a short farewell speech or harrangue to the Commanding Officer, then shot himself. Total time was only about five minutes.

The Japanese pilot's farewell address makes a fitting curtain-line for the last act of the Solomons drama.

Chapter 19

Aleutian Conclusion

☆ ☆ ☆

The Battle for Attu

The spring of 1943 was selected as the season for expelling the Japs from Attu in the Aleutians. Rear Admiral Kinkaid directed the operation, and the job was assigned to Allied troops and to an attack force commanded by Rear Admiral F. W. Rockwell.

Rockwell's force contained battleships PENNSYLVANIA, NEVADA and IDAHO, escort carrier NASSAU, four transports, two seaplane tenders, five minecraft and 12 DD's.

On May 10 the attack force was off Attu. Recapture of the island is largely an Army story—GI's locked in wicked combat with rabid Japs bent on *banzai* charges and suicide. Destroyers supported the landings with shore bombardments, reconnaissance, escort work and A/S patrols.

Fog was the destroyermen's worst enemy. Blinded, a minesweeper rammed and disabled MACDONOUGH. Other DD's had close calls. But the little ships drove in with the amphibs, and did a job. PHELPS, one of the busiest, led eight boats carrying scouts to Red Beach in the Holtz Bay area.

The DD gunners hurled tons of shells at the evil island. By May 15 PHELPS was almost out of 5-inch ammunition. Destroyer ABNER READ covered a landing at Holtz Bay the following day. On the 19th PHELPS delivered a bombardment that helped to clear the enemy from the bay's East Arm. After the amphibious work was completed, PHELPS, MEADE, and destroyer AYLWIN stood by to lend fire support to the Army's advance.

The Attu operation cost 552 American lives. Some 1,140 Americans were wounded. About 2,200 Japs were slain.

Navy personnel casualties were limited to minor injuries, and not a warship was lost.

Frazier *Kills* I-31

After the capture of Attu, the U.S. Navy clamped a tight blockade on Kiska. Bent on secretly evacuating Kiska, the Japs determined to run the blockade with submarines. Fifteen I-boats were assigned to this extraordinary evacuation.

On June 13, destroyer Frazier was plodding on patrol off Point Sirius, Kiska. At 1758 her radar picked up a miniscule "pip" at a range of 7,000 yards. Frazier headed for the contact at 20 knots. It faded from the radar screen, then was regained at 3,000 yards. The "pip" looked like business, and Lieutenant Commander E. M. Brown rushed the crew to battle stations and slowed down to 15 knots. At 1809, Sound reported contact, at 1,500 yards. The DD held radar contact as the range closed to 600 yards. At 1815 the destroyer's lookouts sighted twin periscopes close aboard, range 100 yards.

The destroyermen let fly with two starboard projectors, and then opened fire with main battery and machine-guns. As explosions dug holes in the smooth sea, and 5-inch shells struck the periscopes, the sub went under. The ashcans went down and fountains of water erupted. At 1825, the destroyermen unleashed still another depth-charge attack. The explosions trailed off in watery thunder, and a streak of oil and a large bubble appeared on the heaving surface.

Five minutes later Brown directed a final depth-charge onslaught. The ashcans raised an undersea rumpus, and brought up a gurgling gusher of oil. Combing the area, Frazier's destroyermen noted a spreading carpet of Diesel fuel and a great clutter of oil-scummed debris—splintered gratings, chunks of cork, scraps of paper, human residue.

The demolished submarine was the I-31.

Monaghan *Kills* I-7

Three days prior to the sinking of I-31, an American patrol craft (PC 487) had downed the I-9 in Kiska's waters. And nine days after Frazier's kill off Point Sirius, the destroyer Monaghan (Lieutenant Commander P. H. Horn) took a hand in wrecking the I-boat effort to evacuate Kiska.

Early in the morning of June 22, Monaghan was patrolling south of Kiska Island. At 0135 she made contact with her "Sugar George" radar, picking up a "pip" at range of 14,000 yards. Horn sent his destroyer steaming forward to investigate.

After about an hour's tracking, Monaghan had closed the range to 2,300 yards. The night was thicker than coagulated ink; the target remained invisible. Time: 0230. Horn snapped the order to commence firing. As Monaghan's guns flashed and roared, the unseen foe replied with a chattering automatic. The blind duel lasted for ten minutes, then DD and the enemy ceased firing.

Ensued a swift game of blindman's bluff. At 0310, with the range closed to 2,030 yards, Horn ordered MONAGHAN's gunners to resume fire. The enemy answered with a pugnacious fusillade. Such duelling was reckless on the part of a thinskinned I-boat. After eight minutes of shooting, MONAGHAN's bridge personnel saw a crimson glow mushroom in the darkness where the target was positioned. The hot flush waxed and waned as though some spectral stoker had opened and closed a furnace door in the night sky.

Kiska Recovered (Disaster Strikes ABNER READ)

August 15, 1943, was set for Kiska D-Day. Allied leaders believed the Japs would make a *hari-kiri* stand, and a bloody campaign to root them out—another Attu battle—seemed in prospect.

So a large invasion force was assembled.

At dawn of the 15th the armada lay off Kiska, and the landing forces moved in to selected beachheads while battleships, cruisers, and destroyers blasted the island's ominous coasts with a covering bombardment. Japanese shore batteries remained mute.

Not a single, solitary Jap was to be found on Kiska. Nineteen days before the Americans landed, the Japs had pulled up bag and baggage and abandoned!

The price the occupation forces might have paid had the enemy resisted is suggested by the token payment made by the destroyer ABNER READ. The Japs collected this gratuitous toll on August 18, long after their abandonment of Kiska.

Early in the morning of the 18th, ABNER READ was steaming along on A/S patrol off Kiska's dark coast. At 0150 the destroyer was executing a turn when a stupendous explosion jolted the ship with a gigantic leverage that drove her bows deep in the tide. A deafening blast. A fountain of flame and water. With that fiery thunderclap the destroyer's fantail heaved, and she fell back with a tremendous shudder, disabled. A floating mine had blown up her stern.

Plates, decks, and framework ruptured and broke as the ship's stern section settled. Many survivors on the fantail found the deck almost too hot to stand on barefooted. Worse was the smudge that enveloped the stern. Choking officers reported to the bridge that the fumes were becoming unbearable. Men staggered blindly through this suffocating vapor, stumbling, gagging, with hands to throat.

Veterans shouted to tell the rookies that the fog was not

enemy gas, but chemical smoke—the destroyer's smoke generators were damaged and the FS tanks were fuming. FS liquid, a compound of sulphur trioxide and chlorsulphonic acid, combines immediately and violently with water or moisture in the air. If consistently inhaled, the fumes can prove toxic and painful. Spraying from ABNER READ's damaged smoke generators, these fumes enveloped the ship with a vapor that was almost as anguishing as phosgene. Commander Burrows described the ordeal in his report:

> The FS smoke was the most depressing single defect of the disaster that the men had to cope with. It blinded them, but worse yet it strangled them. It appeared to immobilize their respiratory muscles, so that they could neither breathe in nor out. After a few whiffs of smoke, their mental outlook became one of forlorn abandon. They lay down and waited for the ship to sink. Some leaned fruitlessly over the lifelines desperately gasping for air. About four climbed up on top of No. 5 gun mount, where they caught not over one or two whiffs of fresh air before the stern sank. Sinking of the stern brought great relief to all men on it by way of escape from FS smoke. Water was cold and covered with fuel, but such was a minor consideration compared to the terrifying effects of the smoke.

It was a silent crew of destroyermen who took ABNER READ from Adak to the States for ultimate repairs. Seventy-one of their shipmates had been lost in the mine explosion, and 34 others had been injured. The ABNER READ was the only warship casualty in the Kiska operation.

GILMORE *Sinks* I-180

In the summer of 1943 the Japanese frantically began strengthening their Kurile Island defenses, certain that the American assaults on Attu and Kiska were but preliminary to a great northern offensive via the Aleutians.

Throughout the winter of 1943–44 the Japs in the Kuriles remained on tenterhooks. To obtain information, the intelligence-hungry Japanese Fifth Fleet commander dispatched a submarine or two to scout the Aleutian Islands. And late in April '44 the submarine I-180 was prowling in the waters east of Dutch Harbor.

This I-boat was intrepid, if nothing else. On April 25 she reached a position off the south coast of the Alaskan peninsula, about 120 miles from Kodiak Island. And in the evening of that day she was coolly charging batteries on the surface.

On that same evening destroyer-escort GILMORE, in company with destroyer-escort EDWARD C. DALY, was engaged in convoy duty escorting a cargoman from Dutch Harbor to

Kodiak. A monotonous run. On GILMORE's bridge, her captain, Lieutenant W. D. Jenckes, USNR, was bored by the tedium. Below decks the men off watch yawned over cards, wrote letters, or idled in their bunks. Then radar picked up a "pip" at 2230, range four miles.

At 2235, range two miles, the target disappeared from the radar screen.

"Wow! That looks like a diving submarine!"

The anwser reached the bridge at 2238. Sound contact at 2,600 yards!

At 2252 GILMORE's destroyermen opened fire with a hedgehog salvo. At 2307 they again fired hedgehogs. They sent another hedgehog salvo splashing into the sea at 2336.

No hits, and it was twelve o'clock, and all wasn't well. Jenckes decided to dig out the deep-submerged enemy with depth charges. At 0027, the destroyermen distributed 13 depth charges in a barrage calculated to obtain results. But the underwater blasts failed to produce visual or sonic evidence of a hit.

Shortly before one o'clock GILMORE made a run over the target, and obtained a fathometer reading of 47 fathoms. At 0107, Jenckes ordered another barrage of 13 depth charges. Six minutes later, a volcano seemed to explode deep in the sea, violently shaking the DE.

After the war, that disillusioned Japanese Fifth Fleet staff officer, Commander Hashimoto, recalled that five I-boats were lost in the Aleutians. He based the failure of the I-boat effort on the fact that the boats were unwieldy, the skippers lacked aggressiveness, and the evasion tactics were poor. Hashimoto's memory was short one boat—the I-180. (Which raised the casualties to six.)

Chapter 20

South Seas Mop-up

☆ ☆ ☆

Destroyer Operations, New Guinea (DD's with the Seventh Fleet)

In 1942 the Japs had triumphantly invaded New Guinea. January 1943 found the invaders retreating through Buna, and by February American-Anzac forces were in possession of that advance New Guinea base.

Given Milne Bay and Buna for springboards, MacArthur plotted an offensive aimed to clear the Japs from the northeast coast of New Guinea. The offensive was to consist of a series of amphibious drives that would go leap-frogging westward along the coast and scoop up such enemy bases as Lae, Salamaua, Finschhafen, and Wewak. The sea offensive was to be carried by the Navy—meaning the U.S. Seventh Fleet. Or, more specifically, the Seventh Amphibious Force under command of Rear Admiral D. E. ("Uncle Dan") Barbey.

MacArthur and Admiral Barbey (who commanded all Seventh Fleet naval units in the operation) readied their forces. In August 1943 the drive for Lae was launched.

Ahead of the Lae Task Force, destroyer REID (Commander H. H. McIlhenny) was dispatched to take station as a radar picket off Cape Cretin. On board REID was a fighter-director team prepared to vector Allied aircraft into combat with enemy planes. A new duty for destroyers.

Salamaua fell to the Allies on September 11. Five days later Yanks and "Aussies" skirmished into Lae. The securing of Lae blighted the last Japanese hope of conquering eastern New Guinea. Outnumbered at sea and in the air, and unable to reinforce their New Guinea garrisons with anything more than driblets, the Japs pulled back to Finschhafen.

The American-Australian offensive followed hard on the

211

enemy's heels. Assault date for Finschhafen was advanced to September 22.

It was during operations to secure this New Guinea strong point that the Seventh Fleet suffered its first destroyer loss of the war.

Victim was the USS HENLEY.

Loss of USS HENLEY

Steaming from Buna on the morning of September 21, 1943, the USS HENLEY (Commander Carleton R. Adams) was one of five DD's accompanying a herd of sixteen LCI's bound for a Finschhafen beachhead. Off the target beachhead the amphib group ran into some savage aircraft opposition.

HENLEY emerged from this hot engagement unscathed. And throughout the ensuing week the destroyer was a busy unit in the amphibious machine that maintained and sustained the Australian troops battling southward from the beachhead.

On October 3, in company with destroyers REID and SMITH, the HENLEY was ordered to conduct an offensive A/S sweep off Cape Cretin. The three destroyers commenced the sweep late that afternoon.

The destroyers were moving at 20 knots. REID and SMITH were able to work their echo-ranging gear at this speed, but HENLEY's sonar equipment was ineffective at 20 knots, and she was not "pinging." So it happened that in HENLEY's path a Japanese submarine remained undetected. Apparently chance placed it in an intercepting position. In any event the sub was there. For destroyer HENLEY this was zero hour.

Abruptly SMITH sheered out of column with a sudden swerve to starboard. As the ships had previously been ordered to form a scouting line at sunset, HENLEY, following the directive, swung to port to form the line. And just as his destroyer heeled, Commander Adams, on HENLEY's bridge, sighted two foaming torpedo trails whipping through the sea like streaks of underwater lightning, aiming for his DD.

Jap submarine torpedoes were practically wakeless—no more than a glimpse, and the thunderbolts would strike. Adams responded instantly, snapping a "Left full rudder!" that swung the ship on the arc of a tight circle. As the destroyer swerved to comb the wakes, the first torpedo whisked by, clearing the bow by some 30 yards. The second missed close astern. But a third torpedo, centered in the spread, struck the vessel a shattering smash on the port side, amidships.

Bursting in at the No. 1 fireroom, the torpedo exploded with a blast that stopped the ship dead in her tracks with a broken back. Spouting smoke and steam, the destroyer im-

mediately began to settle. In less than four minutes the main
deck was awash. At 1818 Commander Adams ordered the
ship abandoned.

Destroyers REID and SMITH searched for the submarine,
dropped depth charges, lost contact, and turned to the task
of recovering the HENLEY survivors—18 officers and 225 men.
Eight of the surviving officers and 44 of the men were
wounded. Two of the wounded men died after they were
picked up. One officer and 14 men went down with the
stricken ship.

HENLEY's loss left a hard-to-fill gap in the destroyer roster
of the Seventh Fleet.

Loss of USS PERKINS

She was not a battle casualty. Hers was the fate perhaps
hardest on heroes—to survive the storm's vortex and the fury
of battle, only to go down through freakish mishandling.

Tassafaronga—Gifu—Lae—Finschhafen—those were the
names on PERKINS' war record. From those actions she
emerged with colors flying, wearing only some scars from the
battle off Finschhafen.

Disaster struck in the early-hour darkness of November
29. An hour as black as the New Guinea coastline to port,
smudged by the ink of bad weather. Bound from Milne Bay
to Buna, and proceeding independently, PERKINS was steaming through the gloom when, around 0145, her radar picked
up a ship about six miles dead ahead. PERKINS' Executive Officer, who was navigator, kept tabs on the contact as radar
tracked the target to within 8,000 yards. The "Exec" then
went to the pilot-house and asked the Officer of the Deck
(whom he was about to relieve) if he could see the oncoming
ship, which was obscured in the murk. Somehow the nearing
vessel faded from view—there was one of those strange moments of physical or psychological blindness which seem to
precede such catastrophes—then the "Exec" suddenly sighted
the ship bearing down close aboard. Steep as a cliff the vessel's
prow loomed out of blackness—a churn of froth at the cut-
water—iron eyes looking down. And exactly at four bells the
destroyer was rammed full tilt by the Australian troopship
HMAS DUNTROON.

Twenty-five minutes after the ramming, PERKINS sank. She
broke in two just before going down. Nine of her crew were
lost with her. Squadron Commander Jesse H. Carter, Commanding Officer Ketchum, and 228 others of the ship's company were saved.

A Court of Inquiry found the captain, the navigator, and
the Officer of the Deck at fault for the collision. A tragic blow

for brave men who had risked their lives in combat. Reminder that sea duty is relentlessly exacting.

The Christening of "31-Knot" Burke

No *nom de guerre* originating in World War II will be better established in legend than the one conferred on Captain Arleigh Burke, extraordinary leader of extraordinary Destroyer Squadron 23.

This is the story behind that famous nickname.

During the third week in November 1943, Burke's DD's, busiest destroyers in the Solomons, were engaged in offensively sweeping the Bougainville area. As of this date DesRon 23 was composed of flag destroyer CHARLES AUSBURNE (Commander L. K. Reynolds); CLAXTON (Commander H. F. Stout); DYSON (Commander R. A. Gano); CONVERSE (Commander D. C. E. Hamberger), flying the pennant of Commander B. L. Austin, ComDesDiv 46; and SPENCE (Commander H. J. Armstrong).

On the 24th the five destroyers put in for fuel at Hathorn Sound in Kula Gulf, New Georgia Island. They were loading their tanks to capacity ("topping off," in Navy parlance) when Intelligence dispatched the interesting information that the Japs planned to evacuate important aviation personnel from the battered Buka-Bonis airfields. As Jap destroyers and high-speed transports would probably attempt the evacuation, it semed logical that American destroyers, if they also moved at high speed, could frustrate the evacuation effort. Halsey's flagship advised Burke's flag destroyer accordingly.

Burke was directed to finish topping off at top speed, then to steam to "Point Uncle"—a point off the southwest coast of Bougainville. There he was to report his time of arrival. And if the evacuation eventuated, DesRon 23 was to "take care of it."

Burke was away from Hathorn Sound with a celerity that let no moss grow under keel. He reported that his squadron would arrive at "Point Uncle" about 2200, via a route south of Treasury Island. This and a subsequent report indicated that his destroyers were making 31 knots—a fact which brought an exclamation from Captain R. H. Thurber, Halsey's Operations Officer and one-time squadron mate of the fast-moving Burke. According to one story, Thurber cried:

"Thirty-one knots! And he recently advised us he could make only 30 knots formation speed!"

When Halsey's next order was dispatched it was worded as follows:

THIRTY-ONE KNOT BURKE GET ATHWART THE BUKA-RABAUL

EVACUATION LINE ABOUT 35 MILES WEST OF BUKA X IF NO
ENEMY CONTACTS BY 0300 . . . 25TH . . . COME SOUTH TO
REFUEL SAME PLACE X IF ENEMY CONTACTED YOU KNOW WHAT
TO DO.

Historic message! Flashing from ComSoPac to ComDes-
Ron 23, it sent Burke's destroyers steaming into the waters
between Buka and New Ireland to fight the classic Battle of
Cape St. George. And it endowed Captain Burke with a
sobriquet destined to stay with him for the duration of naval
history—"31-Knot" Burke.

The Battle of Cape St. George

About 0130 in the morning of November 25 the five destroyers of "31-Knot" Burke began their fateful patrol in the
waters between Buka and New Ireland. Burke had his two
divisions ranged in two-column echelon formation—CHARLES
AUSBURNE in the lead, followed by DYSON and CLAXTON, with
CONVERSE and SPENCE trailing on parallel course to port.

The night was overcast and moonless, its 3,000-yard visibility blurred by sporadic rainsqualls. Burke ordered a patrolling speed of 23 knots through warm seas that were
greasy-smooth and heaving. *"An ideal night,"* he noted, *"for
a nice quiet torpedo attack."*

At 0141 through the propitious quietude came the first
tally-ho—radar contact by destroyer DYSON on a target 22,000
yards to the northeast. Commander Gano passed the word
over voice radio, and Burke's reply by TBS was as informal
as it was informative.

HELLO DS 23 HANG ON TO YOUR HATS BOYS HERE WE GO.

The Squadron Commander's next order was:

DIVISION CORPEN 85 COMDESDIV 46 HOLD BACK UNTIL YOU GET
YOUR PROPER BEARING . . . THAT IS 225.

This order headed the squadron for the enemy, the DesDiv
45 column in the lead, and the DesDiv 46 column trailing to
starboard in backfield position.

As the destroyers sprinted toward Target No. 1, a second
"pip" showed up on the radar screen. Then, as the range decreased, a third "pip" glimmered into view on the scope, and
the radar watch thought they had three Jap ships in the immediate offing. Actually one of these "pips" was an electronic
phantom—an illusion. The squadron was bearing down on two
Jap men-of-war which were serving as a screen for the evacua-

tion ships astern and to the east. These other ships were detected in due time—three more "pips" snared by the Americans' radar to make a total of five goodly targets in all. Although Burke formed no positive opinion as to the type of enemy ships ahead, some of the destroyermen believed they were cruisers, and Burke counted the enemy force as six. Perhaps it was just as well that the Jap ships numbered five, and that they proved to be destroyers instead of cruisers.

As it was, the combatants were evenly matched as to weight; and for Burke's scrappy destroyers an even match was tantamount to a sizable advantage. Given radar's all-seeing eye, the American advantage became overwhelming. Deployed in two columns (screening pair, and trio astern), the Japs were taken completely by surprise, and forced to fight blindly against a foe with long-range vision.

Failing to detect the approaching Americans, the two Jap DD's in screening position were steaming on a steady course when Burke's van destroyers closed the range to 5,500 yards. The Japs were blissfully unaware of what was coming. AUSBURNE, CLAXTON, and DYSON had time to maneuver into position for a sharpshooting torpedo set-up. "31-Knot" Burke drew a bead, so to speak, and ordered his DesDiv 45 DD's to let fly.

Five port torpedoes were fired by each attacking destroyer —a barrage that sent fifteen deadly "fish" in a school toward the Japanese targets. A lengthening wait stretched suspense to the limit of endurance, and then the TNT thunderstorm exploded across the distance. Orange flame spouted against the sky as detonations boomed across the seascape. One target sent up a ball of fire 300 feet in height. Explosions hurled up burning towers of debris. In that livid climax one of the Japanese destroyers crumpled in ruination and sank. The other staggered about in solitary desolation, a burning wreck.

Immediately after the torpedoes were fired Burke's DD's had executed a 90-degree right turn to side-step any counter torpedo-attack. The defensive tactic proved unnecessary in this instance, but while it was being made the radar watch picked up the second Jap column, 13,000 yards astern of the first. AUSBURNE, CLAXTON, and DYSON promptly wheeled to attack these new targets.

Alarmed by the blasting of Column No. 1, the second Jap column ran. Ordering CONVERSE and SPENCE to demolish the enemy cripple, Burke sent DesDiv 45 in hot pursuit of the fugitives—targets that finally materialized as three destroyers.

The three Jap destroyers hiked for home base with their fantails between their legs. Racing northward, they built up a speed of 32 knots. Ordering all the turns the engineers could make, "31-Knot" Burke coaxed 33 knots out of his pursuing DD's.

The Japs had a long head start, however, and DesDiv 45 could not overhaul for torpedo attack. A stern chase is invariably a long one, and this one seemed interminable to the sweating American destroyermen. For a time it seemed as though it might go on until the whole "kit and boiling" ended up in a Jap backwater of Simpson Harbor. No matter—DesDiv 45 kept on going.

At 0215 Burke, acting on a sudden hunch, ordered a radical course-change to the right to avoid a possible salvo of Jap torpedoes. The division steadied, and a moment later came back to its base course. Intuition—whatever it was—Burke's hunch-move apparently paid off. As he reported it:

> No sooner had the . . . division come to course . . . than three heavy explosions were felt by all ships. The explosions were so heavy the ships were badly jarred and the Squadron Commander could not resist the temptation to look at the bow to see whether or not it was still there. CHARLES AUSBURNE did not slow, and it was felt that at least one of the ships astern had been hit by torpedoes. Each one of the ships astern thought that one of the other ships had been hit. Fortunately the explosions were merely Japanese torpedoes exploding at the end of their runs or as they crossed our wakes.

At 0222 the pursuing DD's were within gun-range, and Burke snapped the order to open fire. The destroyers opened up with their forward guns at a range of about 8,000 yards. Burke penned a colorful description of the action which ensued.

> The enemy from this time on made several changes of course and also returned our fire. A large amount of smoke covered the retreating Japanese force which was either a smoke screen purposely laid or powder and stack smoke resulting from incidental operations. As soon as enemy fire was observed the Division started to fishtail, weaving back and forth within 30° of the base course. The enemy salvos were well grouped. Patterns were small and they came close, but for some unaccountable reason there were no direct hits. The nearness of the enemy projectiles is best demonstrated by the fact that there were two inches of water on the CLAXTON's bridge caused by the splashes of the shorts. Some of the enemy salvos landed short, some over. They were not consistent in their missing.
>
> Hits were observed on the targets almost at once, but they seemed to have no effect. There were no fires in the beginning, the targets did not slow, and in spite of the magnificent efforts of the gunners of the 45th Division, we seemed to be conducting a futile gun-practice.

As the American 5-inchers continued to blaze and bark, the Jap destroyers, zigzagging like jackrabbits, took divergent courses. The fastest raced ahead on a base course of 350°T, and the other two tangented on either side. This split-up occurred at 0225, three minutes after the Americans opened fire. And presently it was apparent that the American gunnery was not as futile as Burke had feared. Shots from DesDiv 45, flashing and twinkling through the smoke which shrouded the fleeing ships, had hit the enemy some savage blows. At 0300 one of the jackrabbiting Jap destroyers burst into flame and went reeling.

Burke led his pursuing division in a column past this disabled warship. In passing, AUSBURNE, CLAXTON, and DYSON punched shell after shell into the target. Soon the assailed vessel was flaring like a fireworks display. To complete the destruction, Burke brought his division circling back on the exploding hulk. Destroyer DYSON was directed to sink the wreck with a torpedo salvo, but before the torpedoes could strike the mark the Jap DD went down of its own accord.

Meanwhile, CONVERSE and SPENCE were attending to the vessel previously crippled. Five torpedoes from CONVERSE and multiple shell-hits from both DD's laid this Jap warship on the sea floor. While engaged in this endeavor, CONVERSE was struck by a malignant torpedo, but the enemy war head was a dud.

By dawn it was all over but the obituaries. Although two of the five Jap ships had managed to escape, Burke's DesRon 23 had every right to hoist the broom of victory. To the bottom (at 31 knots) it had sent Jap destroyers YUGIRI, MAKINAMI, and ONAMI. A Jap sub from Rabaul rescued YUGIRI's survivors. But down in MAKINAMI and ONAMI had gone a large passenger complement of that important aviation personnel whose evacuation from Buka had incited this water carnival. More important, of course, was the destroyer destruction which seriously impoverished the enemy force hanging on by the skin of its teeth at Rabaul. All this without a single American fatality, and no casualties other than a few ruptured eardrums and several cases of battle fatigue.

Well might the "Little Beavers" of "31-Knot" Burke claim a lion-sized victory. They had fought an engagement to be characterized by the Naval War College as *"the almost perfect surface action."*

Loss of USS BROWNSON

In company with DD's HUTCHINS, DALY, and BEALE, the BROWNSON (Lieutenant Commander J. B. Maher) escorted a troop and supply convoy from Cape Cretin, New Guinea, to the Cape Gloucester objective.

After reaching the landing area BROWNSON was ordered to conduct an independent patrol outside the reefs. For two hours, nothing to report. Then, at 1419, with the ship about eight miles north of Cape Gloucester, BROWNSON's radar picked up several enemy planes. The DD's squared away to meet the attack, and they were maneuvering to do so when two "Val" dive-bombers swooped down on BROWNSON's stern.

BROWNSON's gunners lashed at the planes with 40 mm. and 20 mm. fire. One of the "Vals," scorched by tracer, went floundering off on a tangent. But the other ripped through the AA fusillade. Two bombs struck the BROWNSON near the base of her No. 2 stack. The destroyer staggered under a cloud of smoke and debris, then slumped in the sea mortally injured and afire.

Stunned bluejackets clung to the fantail and forecastle, and others struggled out of the wreckage amidships as the flood poured in below decks. Through smoke-choked hatches the wounded were dragged to safety. Rafts and floats were flung overside to swimming men.

Destroyers DALY and LAMSON moved in to rescue survivors. They found the sea a bloodstained welter where BROWNSON had gone under. Huddled on floats and clinging to rafts were the remnants of the destroyer's crew—those lucky enough to live through a blasting which exacted a final-count death toll of some 108 lives. Among the survivors there were men blinded, maimed, sick; men suffering from burns and shock.

One of the survivors was the ship's doctor, Lieutenant C. F. Chandler, USNR. Among the last to leave the BROWNSON, Chandler was picked up by the destroyer DALY. He had been struck by flying shrapnel which lacerated his right forearm—a searing wound that left him partially incapacitated.

"You've got to take it easy," someone told him.

But the lieutenant who wore a doctor's insignia refused to take it easy. In spite of his crippled arm he worked throughout that afternoon and late into the night, tending the emergency cases on board DALY.

Chandler's performance was indicative of the fine practitioner skilled in the arts of medicine and surgery and dedicated to the service of his fellow man in the hour of need. Such devotion to duty was, and is, typical of the profession many concede to be the finest in the world. For the Chandlers who saw action in the Navy during World War II the citation valued even above any medal or ribbon was the one voiced by the ship's company itself.

"He was a good Doc."

BUCHANAN *Kills* RO-37

GO TO THE ASSISTANCE OF USS CACHE TORPEDOED LAT 12-08 S LONG 164-33E

That, in substance, was the message flashed to the destroyer BUCHANAN as she was proceeding from Purvis Bay to Espiritu Santo in the morning of January 22, 1944. Her skipper, Commander F. B. T. Myhre, immediately called for top speed, and the destroyer headed for the disaster scene with her engines humming. The CACHE had been ambushed by a submarine not far from San Cristobal Island.

At 2005, when BUCHANAN was about 25 miles from the torpedoed ship's reported position, the destroyer's SG radar registered a "pip" at 12,750 yards. The shimmering indication was bright and sharp, and there was good reason to believe it was "enemy."

Commander Myhre sent the DD's gunners scrambling to their mounts as BUCHANAN sprinted on through the moonless and murky tropic dark. When the range closed to 2,000 yards Myhre determined to identify the unknown craft, which might conceivably be friendly. So he ordered the searchlight crew to open up with a 36-inch.

The white light swept across the seascape and caught the target, bull's eye. A conning tower nestling down into the sea. Astern of this Japanese silhouette there was the froth of churned water and a luminous, curving wake, broad as an avenue. Before the destroyermen could open fire the target had sunk from view; the submarine was burrowing deep.

At 1,250 yards, BUCHANAN's sonar instruments gained contact. Myhre jockeyed the destroyer into attack position and directed the launching of a depth charge pattern. The first charge splashed into the sea exactly 30 minutes after the radar contact that instigated the search. Two hours later the destroyer circled in a final attack. The depth charges walloped the water, and after this booming turmoil subsided BUCHANAN's sonarmen were unable to locate the sub.

Combing the area, the BUCHANAN discovered a great spread of floating oil. Sunrise confirmed this evidence of a submarine's liquidation by revealing a seascape strewn with kindling, chunks of cork, and nondescript debris.

Post-war inquest divulged the "name and serial number" of BUCHANAN's victim. Myhre and his men had accounted for the RO-37.

GUEST *and* HUDSON *Down* I-171

On January 31, 1944, destroyers HUDSON and GUEST were

operating with a task group which landed a raiding party in the Green Islands above Bougainville.

On February 1, this group was engaged in evacuating the raiders, when, at 0411 of that morning, a radar "pip" revealed the presence of a strange vessel in the waters off the Green Islands. Target range: 10,500 yards.

Task Group Commander Earle ordered GUEST (Lieutenant Commander E. K. McLaren) and HUDSON (Lieutenant R. R. Pratt) to peel off and investigate. The two DD's closed in on the stranger. As the range closed, GUEST's destroyermen made a flash sweep with a searchlight. Nothing in view. Then, at 3,500 yards, the target glimmered out on the radar scope. A diving submarine!

A few minutes later both HUDSON and GUEST picked up the sub's trail with their sound gear. Tracking swiftly, GUEST was first to reach attack position. Lieutenant Commander McLaren directed two depth charge runs. Four minutes after the last charge was dropped, the destroyermen heard two muffled, tumultuous explosions that blended in a prolonged, rolling road. Not the basso boom of depth charges, but the tympanic din of a bursting pressure hull, collapsing framework, and tearing steel.

Then HUDSON's destroyermen heard a deep-sea explosion in the near-by depths, and Lieutenant Commander Pratt ordered a depth-charge salvo. Evidently the two charges dropped by HUDSON gave the submarine the *coup de grace*. So another I-boat was erased from the roster of the Imperial Navy.

Japanese records verified the kill. The submarine downed by GUEST and HUDSON was the I-171.

Rabaul Knockout

Allied strategy had called for the elimination of Rabaul. But as the Central Pacific offensive was rolling westward in high gear, Allied leaders decided to by-pass the already checkmated bastion.

In by-passing, U.S. destroyers took a final crack at the island fortress. Under Squadron Commander R. W. Simpson, DesRon 12 steamed to Rabaul on the night of February 17-18. Some 4,000 shells were lobbed into the enemy harbor.

Kavieng was simultaneously treated to a similar final by "31-knot" Burke and his "Beavers."

Off the northwest coast of New Ireland the indefatigable "Beavers" shot up a Jap auxiliary and a small minelayer-destroyer. AUSBURNE captured 73 prisoners, most of them aviation personnel—a good catch for Intelligence to catechize.

"Not all of the Japs wanted to be taken prisoner," Burke

reported later. *"Many of them cut their throats in the water. Some deliberately bashed their heads against wreckage. Others tried to drown themselves."* Oddly enough, a number who preferred life to *harikiri* were presently offering to pass ammunition when AUSBURNE, DYSON, and STANLY moved in on the night of February 22-23 to bombard Duke of York Island off New Ireland.

While the "Beavers" were gnawing the foundations out from under Kavieng, two American destroyer divisions were threshing the wreckage at Rabaul. The final shellings were delivered by Destroyer Squadron 45 (Captain Ralph Earle, Jr.). When the shooting was over, Rabaul was not only neutralized, it was virtually pulverized. The knockout previously claimed by MacArthur was now factually accomplished by Navy "cans."

PART FOUR

Coming of the Hunter-Killers

☆ ☆ ☆

Howl, Ye ships of Tarshish
For your strength is laid waste.
ISAIAH XXIII.i

Chapter 21

Holding the Trans-Atlantic Line
(January-April 1943)

☆ ☆ ☆

U-Boat Counter Offensive

New Year's 1943—and to most Americans on the home front the eastward horizon seemed promisingly bright. Even in naval circles some of the more hopeful were encouraged to think that the U-boat menace was nearly liquidated.

But withdrawing from the Western Atlantic, the U-boat Force was merely gathering muscle for offensive blows at Allied shipping in mid-ocean. During the winter of 1942-43, the Nazi wolfpacks struck Allied convoys some of the hardest smashes of the war—torpedoings which climbed to dismal summits on secret statistical graphs in Allied naval headquarters.

Within five winter months' time, almost 2,000,000 tons of shipping were torpedoed and sunk, most of it by wolfpack submarines operating in North Atlantic Convoy Areas. Balanced against the loss of 334 torpedoed ships, Nazi sub losses in the Atlantic for that period totaled less than 50, from all causes. If the wolfpacks were not squelched in the near future, Hitler would win the Battle of the Atlantic.

But the wolfpacks *could* be squelched—that was the conclusion drawn by Captain P. R. Heineman, U.S. Navy. Former captain of the destroyer MOFFETT, and veteran escort commander, Captain Heineman was thoroughly acquainted with anti-submarine warfare. In February 1943, when Ocean Escort Unit A-3 took the field, Heineman was in command. Fighting a four-day North Atlantic U-boat battle, "Heineman's Harriers" set a pattern for the A/S task groups of the future.

Heineman's Harriers

When Ocean Escort Unit A-3 formed up for convoy duty, one of the stormiest winters in history was lashing the North Atlantic into a state of chronic fury. In this heaving wilderness of wind and froth, merchantmen were rolling their beam ends under—and sometimes failing to regain even keel. Some 166 Allied merchantmen were lost through accident and wreck that winter.

But the cargoes had to reach England; the trans-Atlantic convoys had to go across. Then the ships had to return to the States for another load—and getting back was as perilous as going over.

Appointed guardian of west-bound Convoy ON-166 (United Kingdom to Halifax), Captain Heineman's Ocean Escort Unit joined the convoy train at "Eastomp" around noon on February 12, 1943. The convoy numbered 63 merchant ships. Ocean Escort Unit A-3 was eventually composed of eight naval vessels.

But the eight escorts were not simultaneously on hand with the convoy. Heineman's force contained but one destroyer, and this DD did not join the escort group until the 22nd. Two United States Coast Guard cutters were the only American ships in the little task group. One British and four Canadian corvettes constituted the remainder of the escort force.

"Heineman's Harriers," then, lined up as follows:

The 1540-ton Polish destroyer Burza *(which did not join the group until February 22).*

USCGC Spencer	Comdr. H. S. Berdine, USCG
USCGC Campbell	Comdr. J. A. Hirschfield, USCG
HMS Dianthus	HMCS Rosthern
HMCS Chilliwack	HMCS Trillium
HMCS Dauphin	

For the first three days the convoy bucked into a nor'wester which slowed the advance to an average 4-knot pace. However, the escorts managed to fuel from three tankers in spite of a 50-knot wind, and there were only two stragglers during the first week. Then, on February 18, "Huff-Duff" bearings indicated that submarines were in the offing. "Heineman's Harriers" tightened their belts, adjusted their lifejackets, and prepared for combat.

By midnight of the 20th all hands knew that zero hour had arrived.

SPENCER *Kills* U-225

Shortly after midnight, radar contact was reported. SPENCER, in the convoy's van, ran forward to investigate. At 0038, the Coast Guard cutter's lookout sighted a conning tower, range 5,000 yards. At 0045, the submarine dived. A few moments later, Sound reported contact at 1,500 yards. Then contact evaporated at 200 yards. The U-boat was within 600 feet of the Coast Guard cutter, and SPENCER was forced to strike at a vanished target. Blind-man's-buff in the dark!

SPENCER's skipper, Commander Berdine, reacted immediately. Just three seconds after contact was lost, he ordered a depth-charge attack. Firing on "recorder time," the Coast Guard cutter dropped a 9-charge pattern that blew up tons of water in her wake.

After the thunder of this barrage faded out, Sound was unable to regain contact. A "box search" was promptly conducted, but contact remained unobtainable. Estimating the submarine's probable position, Berdine ordered the dropping of two 600-pound charges, set for 100-foot depth. The explosions blasted up a mound of water. The foam-topped mound collapsed. After a few minutes' futile probing with detection gear, SPENCER steamed off to rejoin the convoy.

Berdine and his Coast Guard crew were not certain of a kill. Subsequently they learned they had finished off U-225.

Convoy Under Fire

SPENCER's fray with U-225 was only a curtain raiser. While Berdine and his Coast Guardsmen were scuffling with the undersea foe, the convoy was stalked by other invisible assailants. "Huff-Duff" gave the escorts several fixes, and U.S. Coast Guard cutter CAMPBELL made two or three attacks after sound contact.

CAMPBELL was no novice at this deadly game of hide and seek. Early in the war she had steamed into dangerous waters off Greenland, and in November 1941 she had served as ocean escort with Convoy HX-159. Her skipper, Commander Hirschfield, was an experienced Coast Guardsman. Aboard CAMPBELL was an all-Negro 20 mm. gun crew that had won a reputation for marksmanship and was all-out All-American. A tough little craft, the CAMPBELL.

Late in the afternoon of February 21 SPENCER and DIAN-THUS ran a 10-mile race to team up with an RAF Liberator that was attacking a trio of submarines off the convoy's starboard quarter. Assailed by the two escort vessels and the plane, the U-boats were driven down. And while this scrimmage was taking place, the corvette ROSTHERN made radar contact with two surfaced U-boats. ROSTHERN tried to run them down, but the U-boats made off at top speed and escaped.

But the worst was yet to come, for Convoy ON-166 had now voyaged beyond the range of air cover by the land-based Liberators.

The U-boats were waiting. Ghostly and vengeful, they closed in around the convoy, cloaked spectres creeping through the blackout. The opening assault came at 2135, perhaps seven Nazi submarines ganging up on the convoy's van. At that hour on the evening of February 21, only four escorts were near at hand. The Polish destroyer BURZA had not yet joined Heineman's team. SPENCER was eight miles on the starboard quarter, rejoining. CAMPBELL was eight miles astern, rejoining, And DIANTHUS was 10 miles astern, rejoining. The four corvettes in the convoy's vicinity had a battle on their hands.

Outnumbered though they were, the Canadian corvettes dispersed the attacking U-boats. Only one of the wolves managed to get its fangs into prey. This U-boat fired a spread of torpedoes at the lead ship in the convoy's second column, the SS EMPIRE TRADER. The warheads struck the target; the merchantman staggered to a halt, disabled.

Early the following morning came another torpedo attack. The escorts bunched forces to fight off the wolfpack, but a second freighter was stricken. At 0151 this vessel was torpedoed in the stern by a U-boat which penetrated the screen. Carrying out a night search, the escorts illuminated the seascape with starshells, but the U-boat escaped detection. CAMPBELL closed the sinking ship, and picked up all survivors. The battle's hide-and-seek went relentlessly on. About 0530, two submarines were sighted dogging the convoy's stern, and DIANTHUS peeled off to drive away this pair with hedgehog salvos.

By that hour "Heineman's Harriers" were taut-nerved and red-eyed from lack of sleep. It had been necesary to detach the corvette DAUPHIN and send her to escort the disabled EMPIRE TRADER back to British waters—a futile effort, for the TRADER was so badly damaged that the Admiralty ordered her abandoned and sunk before she made port. To add to Heineman's worries the weather was too rough for fuelling at sea, and the corvette HMS DIANTHUS reported her fuel tanks running low. And a three-day run through open seas without air cover remained to be logged.

But the day of February 22 brought some relief. Over the horizon came ORP BURZA, running to join the escort group. Wind and seas shifted a little, and the convoy was able to make 9 knots. And the U-boats, following the familiar *Rudeltaktic,* kept their distance that day.

The respite, however, was the lull before the storm. BURZA (the name means "Squall") joined up that afternoon, and the "Harriers" were cheered by the destroyer's arrival. But darkness promised more U-boats, and the Coast Guard and corvettemen tightened their belts for another night of it.

They did not have long to wait. About an hour and a half after sundown the attack exploded.

CAMPBELL *and* ORP BURZA *Kill* U-606

All day U-606 had been trailing the convoy like a shark trailing a lonely group of dories. By nightfall she was closing in for the strike. Nightfall—the hour between sundown and moonrise when the dusk had gone and the seas were all but invisible. Time: around 2000. Closing on the convoy's port flank, U-606 planed to the surface and ran in for the strike.

Accounts vary as to the details of the action that followed. The submarine pumped torpedoes into three ships on the convoy's flank. The explosions flared in the night, and merchant seamen died in fiery engine-rooms and drowned in a muddle of capsized lifeboats and tangled lines. "Heineman's Harriers" immediately counterattacked. Apparently the corvette HMCS CHILLIWACK sighted the retiring U-boat and went after it with depth charges. CHILLIWACK lost contact, and at that juncture, according to some reports, BURZA stepped in with a depth-charge attack.

According to CAMPBELL's War Diary and Commander Hirschfield's action report, the Coast Guard cutter's radar screen picked up the enemy "pip" at 2016, range 4,600 yards. Not long after contact, the U-boat silhouette was sighted off the Coast Guardman's starboard bow.

Ordering right full rudder and 18 knots on the line, Hirschfield set a collision course to ram the enemy. At about 200 yards, the CAMPBELL gunners manning the forward 3-incher opened fire.

After it was over some of the Nazi submariners stated they had come to the surface because of battle damage received from depth charges a few minutes before CAMPBELL's attack. Whether previously damaged or no, the submarine was due for a bashing from CAMPBELL. Guns blazing, the cutter loomed over the U-boat's flank. Nazi gunners fell riddled on the cigarette desk; the conning tower was drilled. All that in a flash of time, and then *crash!* Under the impact of collision, the submarine rolled and floundered, mortally hurt.

CAMPBELL herself was damaged by the smash. At the moment before collision, the U-boat veered, and the submarine's diving planes knifed into the cutter's side, slashing a deep gash in CAMPBELL's hull. Water spurted through the incision, flooding the engine-room. At 2025 the engines were stopped, and the engineers scrambled topside.

On deck, CAMPBELL's gunners were pouring a withering fire at the wallowing U-boat, and Hirschfield had ordered two 600-pound ashcans rolled from the racks. At 2028, he gave the "cease-fire" order—the sub was lying helpless, her conning tower knocked all acockbill. Two minutes later, all of CAMPBELL's electrical power went out, short-circuited in the flooded engine-room.

About this time the submariners decided to abandon. CAMPBELL saw the flutter of water-lights off to starboard, but the cutter was too busy with her own trouble to go to the assistance of the U-boat crew. Once the damage was under control, however, Hirschfield sent a boarding party to inspect the disabled submarine and pick up survivors.

High seas prevented the rescue of those still in the submarine. U-606 was slowly foundering, settling sluggishly as swooping waves slopped over her conning tower and poured successive Niagaras down into her control room.

At 2220 (according to CAMPBELL's report) the destroyer BURZA arrived to screen the damaged cutter. At 2255 CAMPBELL's small boat returned with five of the U-606 survivors. Meantime BURZA lowered a boat and picked up some half dozen shivering Germans. Some time around midnight the punished U-boat sank with the remainder of her Nazi crew.

The Long Voyage Home

The following morning, CAMPBELL transferred some of her crew and all of her German prisoners to BURZA. HMCS DAUPHIN had rejoined the group, and this hard-working corvette relieved BURZA of the duty of screening crippled CAMPBELL. Hirschfield and a skeleton crew kept their cutter going, and on February 26 the tug TENACITY showed up out of the West and took CAMPBELL in tow. On March 3, the battle-weary Coast Guardsmen reached St. Johns, Newfoundland.

CAMPBELL's disablement left "Heineman's Harriers" seriously shorthanded, and the abbreviated escort group had a lot of fighting on its hands after the sinking of U-606. Early in the morning of February 23 the wolfpack struck again. Corvettes ROSTHERN and TRILLIUM beat off that attack, and the U-boats failed to score.

The seas roughened that day, slowing the convoy again, and prevented fueling operations. HMS DIANTHUS reported that her tanks were nearing the empty point, and Heineman was compelled to order the corvette to proceed ahead on her own, lest she run out of oil while maneuvering with the convoy and became an encumbrance. Shortly before midnight of the 23rd the British corvette pulled away. As it was, she had to make a tight squeeze to reach St. Johns. *"We emptied 120 gallons of Admiralty Compound into Number 6 tank,"* the corvette's captain reported later. *"Also all gunnery oil, paint mixing oil, and two drums of special mineral oil. This increased fuel remaining by approximately half a ton, and eventually enabled me to get in."*

The U-boats struck again in the dark before dawn of February 24. Torpedoes smashed into another merchantman, and the convoy suffered its sixth ship-loss.

Still another ship was torpedoed in the darkness of the following morning when the U-boats made their sixth attack on the convoy. And the U.S. Coast Guard cutter SPENCER three times narrowly missed being torpedoed.

"Heineman's Harriers" were a haggard company when Convoy ON-166 finally gained the shelter of air cover and home water. For five days running, the wolfpack battle had been touch and go. The iron-nerved escort group had fought off six attacks and downed two U-boats. And only seven ships of the slow convoy had been torpedoed and sunk. But seven lost were seven too many, and the one-sided battle had worn Ocean Escort Unit A-3 down to the nub.

Captain Heineman summarized the experience of Ocean Escort Unit A-3 in a report which contained a number of pertinent suggestions and recommendations. Excerpts:

> *Great value of long-range aircraft as demonstrated by excellent air coverage given to convoy as far out as 1,000 miles from the British Isles by planes of the 4-engine type, such as are lacking in the Western Atlantic. . . .*
>
> *Great handicap in escort operations due to lack of high-speed escorts. . . .*

Captain Heineman concluded with a recommendation that convoys be accompanied by tankers properly equipped for fueling escorts at sea—a rarity at that period of the war.

SPENCER *Kills* U-175

On April 12, 1944, Ocean Escort Unit A-3 picked up a Western Atlantic-to-British Isles convoy off St. Johns. The seas had flattened somewhat after an equinoctial rampage, and a forecast of fair weather promised a fast and successful voyage.

Convoy HX-233 contained 57 ships disposed in 11 columns.

The merchantmen were steaming in good order, and the convoy's tight front facilitated the screening job.

Heineman's group was composed of the following eight escorts:

USCGC Spencer	*Comdr. H. S. Berdine, USCG*
USCGC Duane	*Capt. H. B. Bradbury, USCG*
HMCS Skeena	HMS Bergamot
HMCS Wetaskawin	HMS Bryony
HMS Dianthus	HMCS Arvida

First indication of wolfpack activity came on April 15 when four U-boat transmissions were intercepted. The next day Spencer made sound contact with a sub, and attacked with depth charges, with negative results. Convoy course was shifted to evade a nearing wolfpack, and these anti-sub measures frustrated attack on the 16th.

On the 17th the convoy was steaming due south of Reykjavik, vicinity of lat. 48-00 N., long. 21-00 W. Four British destroyers joined the escort in this submarine zone—formidable protection that might be expected to give the convoy a breathing spell.

The breathing spell proved illusory. About 0505, the freighter Fort Rampart staggered out of line. At 0530, a near-by merchantman saw the freighter displaying a red light. Fort Rampart's davits were outboard, lines were down, and her boats were in the water. In the gloaming of 0505 she had been torpedoed. Curiously enough, the stealthy attack had been as silent as a dagger blow in a featherbed.

Captain Heineman reported:

No explosion was heard, no signal made nor rocket fired at the time, and no report received from Commodore or the ships. Escorts present considered at the time that the ship was falling out due to defects. Accordingly, no search was ordered or conducted by escorts.

Later that day Fort Rampart broke in two. The derelict sections were sunk by destroyers of the support force.

About the time this ship was torpedoed, Spencer, patrolling in the convoy's van, sighted a dark object off the bow, ahead. She passed the word to Dianthus, and the two peeled off to investigate. That was the beginning of a busy morning for Ocean Escort Unit A-3.

For Spencer and her veteran crew the morning proved particularly busy. At 1050 she was patrolling along as usual when Sound reported another contact—range 1,500 yards. Berdine's Coast Guardsmen sprang into action. At exactly 1052 Spencer's depth charges started rolling. Eleven charges exploded in a thundering pattern. And then another 11-charge pattern was dropped at 1058. Ten minutes later SPENCER, maneuvering between columns 6 and 7 of the convoy, was working to regain sound contact. While she probed with her detection gear, she coached her sister Coast Guard cutter DUANE into the hunt.

At 1117 the contact was reestablished; range 1,700 yards. Berdine ordered a mousetrap barrage. The rocket projectiles soared away and silently plunged into the pellucid sea.

About 15 minutes later the submarine broached, breaking water astern of the convoy and some 2,500 yards from SPENCER. The sub was U-175, a 750-ton specimen. Badly hurt by the depth-charge barrage, she had plunged to 38 fathoms before regaining depth control, and then, blowing all ballast, she had surfaced like a bale of cork. With decks awash she turned to run. SPENCER rushed her with blazing guns.

The crippled U-boat circled about helplessly. DUANE opened fire. Armed Guard crews on the merchantmen open fire. SPENCER's gunners were knocking the U-boat's conning tower into junk. Somehow a submarine gun crew got topside and fired a few rounds in return. During this savage exchange a shrapnelburst raked SPENCER's deck and eight of her crew were struck. J. T. Petrella, Radioman Third, was mortally wounded.

Berdine set a collision course to ram. But the assailed submariners had had enough, and they were seen abandoning as the Coast Guard cutter closed in. At 1145 SPENCER's gunners were ordered to hold their fire. With DIANTHUS screening, SPENCER and DUANE moved in to recover survivors. Forty-one of the Nazi undersea warriors were recovered.

Captain Heineman dispatched a SPENCER boarding party to examine the U-boat with an eye to possible salvage. Especially trained for such duty by Lieutenant Commander John B. Orem, USCG, the boarding party went alongside the wallowing submarine. Salvage was found to be impossible. U-175's conning tower had been punctured like a tin can on a boy's rifle range; her pressure hull was ruptured and leaking. At 1220 (five minutes after the boarding party was ordered off) the damaged submersible began to sink. At 1227 the sub's bow angled skyward, and the hulk slid down under the sea, stern first. Another U-boat done for.

Convoy HX-233 was about 600 miles off Land's End when this battle occurred. Aircraft from England soon arrived on the scene, and from there on in the convoy marched along under a canopy of planes. With aircraft aloft, the U-boats went under and stayed under.

The Ordeal of Convoy UGS-6

The second week in March, 1944, Convoy UGS-6 was trudging eastward on the main line, New York-to-Casablanca. The ships had reached that lap of the voyage which entered hot submarine water in the vicinity of the Azores. Consisting of 45 vessels, all laden to the Plimsoll-mark with military supplies, the slow convoy must have looked appetizing to enemy periscopes observing its heavy-footed advance.

And the periscopes were watching. However, the greedy-eyed U-boats took a second look before endeavoring to attack these tempting targets. Convoy UGS-6 was under escortage of seven destroyers. This escort group, under the leadership of Captain Charles Wellborn, Jr., contained the following DD's:

WAINWRIGHT *(Flagship)*	*Comdr. R. H. Gibbs*
TRIPPE	*Lt. Comdr. R. C. Williams*
CHAMPLIN	*Lt. Comdr. C. L. Melson*

Flagship of
Comdr. B. R. Harrison, COMDESDIV 32

MAYRANT	*Comdr. E. K. Walker*
ROWAN	*Lt. Comdr. R. S. Ford*
RHIND	*Lt. Comdr. O. W. Spahr, Jr.*
HOBBY	*Lt. Comdr. E. Blake*

These destroyers carried the latest in radar gear. Each was equipped with SG, SC, and FD radar, plus the QC projector.

However, as the convoy neared the Azores Islands it came under submarine surveillance. The scouting U-boats relayed the word to pack leaders, and the subs farther eastward ganged up to intercept. Then, on the evening of March 12, the U-boat onslaught began.

CHAMPLIN *Sinks* U-130

The evening twilight had faded into darkness, and Convoy UGS-6 had reached the vicinity of lat. 37-00 N., long. 40-00 W., when the destroyer CHAMPLIN obtained an SG radar contact on an enemy submarine. Time: 2150. Range: 4,020 yards. CHAMPLIN's skipper, Lieutenant Commander Melson, sounded "General Quarters," and drove the destroyer for the target.

At 2158 the submarine's phosphorescent wake was sighted about 2,000 yards off. A moment later the conning tower was visible. Melson gave the order to open fire. CHAMPLIN's gunners opened up, but were unable to spot hits. CHAMPLIN was almost on top of the U-boat—150 yards—when the Nazi skipper "pulled the plug." Squarely into the bull's-eye of the swirling water CHAMPLIN dropped two depth charges.

The sea heaved skyward and crashed in a spreading sprawl of foam. Melson and crew followed through with four more depth-charge attacks, the last at 0158 of March 13. Thereafter the destroyer was unable to contact the submarine. A vigorous search plan was adopted and continued until daylight. At 0645, CHAMPLIN's lookouts sighted a number of oil slicks. Examination disclosed them to be the lifeblood of a submarine, and CHAMPLIN was able to report a kill.

CHAMPLIN's victim, identified by post-war records, was the U-130. This was the submarine that had got in under the screen at Fedala Roads on March 12, 1942, and torpedoed the transports HUGH L. SCOTT, EDWARD RUTLEDGE, and TASKER H. BLISS, with a consequent loss of 108 American lives. CHAMPLIN had killed a killer.

UGS-6 Versus Wolfpack

While CHAMPLIN was finishing off U-130, the other destroyers were busy driving off other submarines. The wolfpack continued to shadow the convoy throughout the daylight hours of March 13. Around 2030 of that evening a straggler was torpedoed and sunk about 50 miles astern of the convoy. The destroyers made high-speed sweeps from bow to quarter —tactics which were employed just before the twilight faded, and which may have disrupted a wolfpack attack.

Similar sweeps were made on March 14, and the convoy made several course changes to throw off the trailing wolfpack. But that night the U-boats loped forward on the surface, to strike at the convoy's rear. Again the DD's radar screen proved effective, and the pack was driven off. The following day Cominch reported that at least four U-boats were trailing UGS-6. That afternoon HOBBY and MAYRANT made high-speed sweeps to a distance of 10 miles off the convoy's port and starboard flanks to drive the U-boats away.

At 1830 on the evening of the 15th, WAINWRIGHT's hydrophone picked up the whisper of a stalking sub. The trace was evanescent, and after a fruitless 15-minute search of the immediate area, WAINWRIGHT resumed her normal patrol station. At 1852, the SS WYOMING was torpedoed by a U-boat which slipped under the screen from ahead. Executing a short-range, submerged attack, the sub opened fire at about 650 yards to slam two deadly fish into the target vessel. CHAMPLIN picked up survivors while HOBBY screened and simultaneously made a sweep for the killer. At 2304 HOBBY gained an SG radar contact, range 9,000 yards, but the sub escaped as the DD sent up starshells. Late in the afternoon of the next day, more U-boat contacts were made—this time ahead of the convoy—

and at sunset another merchantman was torpedoed and sunk. Other ships in the convoy were narrowly missed by torpedoes. At 1903, RHIND had sound contact; she veered to avoid a torpedo, and thrashed the water with depth charges, but failed to kill her assailant.

On March 17, at sunset, a fourth merchantman was torpedoed and sent down. The stricken vessel, the SS MOLLY PITCHER, was struck by one torpedo in the port bow—the lucky shot of what appeared to be a four-torpedo spread fired by a sub at extreme range on the convoy's port quarter. The destroyer ROWAN searched astern of the convoy for the U-boat, but the slippery foe escaped. The next day the convoy made large, evasive course-changes in the late afternoon to frustrate ambush. Patrolling well ahead of the convoy's front a (tactic employed to force down lurking U-boats), one of the destroyers put up an effective screen. Since the evening of March 17, however, UGS-6 had been provided with continuous air cover, and from there on in the voyage was untroubled. Loss of four ships was serious, but fatalities were unusually light. Only six men were lost in the ships sunk while steaming with the formation. Loss of life aboard the straggler was considerably heavier.

Admiral Jonas H. Ingram tersely summarized the A/S situation in a report submitted some months later to Naval Secretary Forrestal.

"In early 1943, when the Germans had as many as 450 submarines available, it was just nip and tuck, and if they had kept on at the rate of sinkings of early 1943 for the remainder of that year, I doubt if there would have been any invasions in the Mediterranean or Normandy, or any Great Britain."

But the Germans did not keep on at that rate. By April 1943, strong destroyer reinforcements were emerging from American shipyards, and air umbrellas for convoys in mid-ocean were coming into being. These new A/S teams would turn the tide in the Battle of the Atlantic.

Chapter 22

The Gang Busters

(May 1943-December 1943)

☆ ☆ ☆

The Coming of the Hunter-Killers

The answer to the mid-ocean wolfpack was the escort-carrier (CVE) and the destroyer-escort (DE)—warships which were relatively inexpensive; which could be constructed on a mass production basis; and which could be rushed into the Battle of the Atlantic to supplement the hard-working destroyer and other A/S forces engaged in the war against the U-boat.

But the construction of escort-carriers and destroyer-escorts took time. So did the training of crews which were to specialize in the hunting and killing of submarines. Not until the summer of 1943 did the "hunter-killer" campaign go into high gear.

However, during the second quarter of 1943, German Admiral Doenitz's wolfpacks failed to equal their success of the year's first quarter. In April '43 the Atlantic U-boats sank only 44 Allied and neutral ships—less than half the number downed in March. In May the figure dwindled to 41—a significant score. In that same month exactly 41 U-boats were downed, even-Stephen. And no one knew better than Doenitz that the U-boat Force could not afford to fight it out on a 50-50 basis.

Of that Maytime score two U-boats were downed by Destroyers Atlantic. The first was sunk by the USS MACKENZIE.

MACKENZIE *Kills* U-182

On May 16, 1943, the destroyer MACKENZIE (Commander D. B. "Dan" Miller) was en route to Casablanca in company with destroyer LAUB. At 0350 MACKENZIE had a radar contact on her SG radar, range 7,800 yards. At 2,700 yards the radar contact was lost, but a good sound contact was established at 1,600 yards.

MACKENZIE made a run on the submarine, dropping a 10-charge pattern at 0439. While the destroyer turned to make a second attack, Sound reported contact at 500 yards. Miller ordered five more depth charges dumped upon the enemy. The barrage raised the usual geyser followed by a spreading maelstrom, then silence.

For some time thereafter MACKENZIE and LAUB searched in the vicinity. But attempts to regain contact with the target proved futile. However, at 0458 and at 0503 both destroyers heard marine explosions, similar to the blast of deep depth charges.

The destroyers searched for wreckage—found nothing. No scraps of submarine; no oil slicks. Turning their bows for Casablanca, the destroyers proceeded on their way.

The wreck left by MACKENZIE's handiwork was not located until after the war, when it was found in the vicinity of lat. 33-55 N., long. 20-35 W.—in the German Navy's records. The submarine that disappeared in that locale early in the morning of May 6, 1943, was the one sunk by MACKENZIE.

The records identified the victim as U-182.

MOFFETT, JOUETT, *and Aircraft Kill* U-128

In May 1943, destroyers MOFFETT and JOUETT, veterans of the South Atlantic Force (recently designated the Fourth Fleet), took care of a U-boat in the warm waters off the hump of Brazil, about 200 miles southeast of Recife.

About sundown on the evening of the 16th two patrolling aircraft of Squadron VP-74 sighted a Nazi sub charging its batteries on the surface. Out went the call, and destroyers MOFFETT (Commander J. C. Sowell) and JOUETT (Commander F. L. Tedder) were rushed to the reported position.

The DD's had a long run of it. While they were on the way, the two planes bombed, strafed, and hounded the undersea invader. The scrimmage between airmen and submariners continued throughout the early hours and tropical morning of the following day. At 1246 of the 17th, the destroyers sighted the U-boat on the surface, 10 miles distant. They opened fire at 1303, range 5,500 yards.

Two minutes later the DD's ceased firing. Under a storm of shell bursts the submarine had disappeared. But a moment later the U-boat's conning tower was again in view, and the MOFFETT and JOUETT gunners were immediately on target. Straddles were observed, and several smashing hits were seen.

At 1309 the punctured submarine went under, leaving a cluster of frantic swimmers in her wake.

Jouett covering Moffett, the DD's ran forward to pick up the survivors. They found most of the submarine's crew paddling and splashing around in an otherwise clean sea. No debris—no litter—no mess of oil. Fifty live U-boaters and one dead man were taken aboard the destroyer Moffett. The sunken submarine was identified as U-128. The German commander reported only three of the crew missing.

Introducing the Escort-Carrier

The vessel's christened name was SS Mormacmail. She was a Diesel-powered, C-3 type freighter which the Navy had acquired from the Maritime Commission for experimental purposes. The experiment? Conversion of this cargo ship into a small flat-top—a "baby" aircraft carrier which could be employed as an A/S escort for convoy duty, or as an aircraft transport, or, if need arose, as a substitute for a first-line carrier.

For the special training of aviators and crews, two Great Lake steamers were converted into CVE's, and the CVE Charger, commissioned early in March 1942, was assigned to training duty. Then the first new escort-carrier on A/S duty in the Atlantic was USS Bogue (Captain G. E. Short). Launched in Puget Sound, and commissioned in September 1942, Bogue steamed eastward through the Canal in November of that year, and early 1943 found her on the Newfoundland-Iceland run in the North Atlantic. She was trailed through the Canal by USS Card (Captain A. J. "Buster" Isbell). These two were presently followed into the Atlantic by Core, Block Island, Santee, Croatan, and other "baby flat-tops."

The U-boats were hard to find that June. Alarmed by mounting casualties from air attack, Commander-in-Chief Doenitz was calling home his *unterseebooten* to arm them with anti-aircraft guns. On April 11, Admiral Doenitz had reported to Hitler, *"I fear that the submarine war will be a failure if we do not sink more ships than the enemy is able to build."* And in June 1943 the U-boats sank only 19 merchantmen!

Anti-aircraft batteries or no, a surfaced U-boat was hardly able to cope with a group of Grumman Wildcats or Avengers flying from a baby flat-top. Nor could U-boats hope to shoot it out with gunning DD's. Put together, the aircraft-destroyer combination was a submarine Nemesis against which the Nazis had no countermeasure.

BADGER *Kills* U-613 *(With a Footnote by Edgar Allan Poe)*

On July 23, 1943, while serving as screen for BOGUE, the BADGER (Lieutenant T. H. Byrd, USNR) made sound contact with a submarine. The time: 1106. The place: lat. 35-31 N., long. 28-40 W. Range was 1,100 yards.

BADGER did not have much opportunity for preliminary sparring. Lieutenant Byrd drove the destroyer in a rush at the enemy, and with great skill and alacrity gave the submarine a going-over.

BADGER's first depth-charge attack brought up nothing but the usual tons of salt water. Byrd maneuvered the old four-piper back into position for other barrages at a different level. Ashcans and teardrops splashed the sea, the TNT volleyed and thundered, the water thrashed and calmed. Evidently the submarine had gone deeper than the usual dive.

Lieutenant Byrd determined to dig out the U-boat, whatever its depth. Ordering a new setting on the charges, he directed the firing of a fourth barrage. In BADGER's wake the sea erupted with a roar, and with the upheaval a swirling litter of wreckage, debris, and human remains gushed to the surface.

Searching through this residue of destruction and death, the destroyermen managed to identify their victim as the U-613. One of BADGER's crew delved into the ghastly flotsam and came up with a dripping book. Appropriate volume for the scene and the occasion, it was a German translation of *The Murders in the Rue Morgue.*

MOFFETT *and Aircraft Kill* U-604

This aircraft-destroyer versus U-boat contest began in South American waters on July 30, 1943, when the U-185 was sighted off the Brazilian coast by a PV-1 plane. Destroyers soon arrived on the scene, and they teamed up with the planes to conduct one of the war's most persistent U-boat hunts. U-185 and her pack-mate, U-604, were spotted early in the first week of August. Thereafter the pair were marked submarines.

For five days the two Nazi subs were kept on the run by bombs, gunfire and ashcans. They could hardly make a daylight periscope exposure without inviting attack, and when they surfaced at night to charge batteries they were spotted by radar's all-seeing eye.

By the evening of August 5 the fugitive U-boats had retreated far to the west of Fernando de Noronha. But hard on their weary heels came the pursuit—long-range aircraft and the destroyer MOFFETT. The destroyer, captained by Lieutenant Commander G. H. Richards, was finding the chase exciting enough for any DD. Twice, while running through the night, she was mistaken for a U-boat by friendly planes and subjected to a lively strafing.

Fortunately the aircraft found the right target on August 6, and U-604 was put on the receiving end of a strafing by two sharpshooting planes. The planes also dropped bombs on the exhausted foe, and MOFFETT raced into the fray in time to sight the submarine before the U-boaters were able to take her down.

Rushing to the spot where the sub went under, the destroyermen followed through with a series of depth-charge attacks. Staggering out from under the depth-charge barrage, the U-boat managed to elude the finger of MOFFETT's detection gear. But it was a severely injured submarine that eventually struggled to the surface and opened its hatches to gasp for air.

Not long after that, U-604 got off a message to U-185, urgently requesting assistance. A rendezvous was eventually arranged. On the 11th of August, U-185 and U-172 managed to meet U-604 at the designated point some 800 miles off the Brazilian coast. The men in U-604 were a haggard company of Germans. By dint of desperate damage-control measures they had kept the submarine afloat. But the pressure hull was leaking dangerously. The battered submersible was at the end of her rope, and the German pack-commander ordered the crew to scuttle.

And the full price was yet to be paid. Playing host to the U-604 crew, U-185 was an overcrowded submarine. Overcrowding in a submarine can create numerous difficulties— bad air, short rations, jarred elbows, jangled nerves. And in the event of emergency the escape hatches can be too narrow and too few.

Jammed like "sardines in a tin." The phrase is hackneyed, but it best describes the crews of U-185 and U-604 all in the same boat. Running home, the crowded submarine got as far as the waters off the Azores. There, on August 24, it was caught and sunk by aircraft from the escort carrier CORE.

BORIE *Kills* U-405 (*"Scratch One Pig Boat—"*)

BORIE was one of those old flush-deck four-pipers the sailors referred to as "cans." High-ranking naval officers frowned at the term as "undignified." But what's dignified about a knock-down drag-out fight? BORIE was just such a ship. A fighter.

In the autumn of 1943 BORIE was a unit of the task group built around the escort-carrier CARD. On CARD's bridge stood Captain A. J. ("Buster") Isbell. On BORIE's bridge stood

Lieutenant Commander Charles H. Hutchins, USNR. But they stood as one in the resolution to sink U-boats whenever and wherever found.

On the evening of November 1, the task group was cruising in high water some 700 miles north of the Azores. In came word from one of CARD's scout planes—submarine! BORIE was off on the scent, steaming on ahead of the group through seas that mounted higher as the hour grew late and the night thickened.

Then a "pip" appeared on the radar screen—and another. Two U-boats in the offing! Hutchins sent BORIE boring in on the attack. Sighting the nearer U-boat, the destroyermen opened up with an accurate fire that promptly drove the enemy under. Hutchins followed through with a depth-charge onslaught. Hard to tell in those jumping seas whether shells and ashcans were on target, but explosions sounded like hits and the submarine seemed to evaporate. Hutchins sent CARD a terse report: SCRATCH ONE PIG BOAT AM SEARCHING FOR MORE.

The search turned out to be a chase. Loping away in the night, the second U-boat had run for the cover of a blinding rainsquall that swirled through the darkness like blowing ink. The ink failed to impair radar's all-seeing eye. Hutchins drove his old four-piper in top-speed pursuit. Swinging uphill and down dale through 15-foot seas, the veteran BORIE—an oldtimer from the days of World War I—overhauled one of Doenitz's new submarines, and caught the enemy on the surface! Not only caught the big U-boat, but spotted her in the white glare of a searchlight. A second later the livid breath of gunfire scorched the darkness, and the battle was on!

This U-boat was one of the specimens equipped with heavy deck-batteries. Her guns spat in the night, and BORIE was shaken by two hits, one amidships and one on the bridge.

For nearly an hour the gun battle continued, the destroyer and the submarine circling each other "like tomcats in the dark," as a commentator expressed it. Now the U-boat's gunners were driven from their mounts by a fusillade of machinegun fire from BORIE. Now the destroyermen were under the fire of salvos and bursts of tracer from the submarine.

Finally Hutchins saw the opening he wanted. Stepping up the speed to 25 knots, he drove BORIE in to ram. There was a crash and then a grinding din as the old DD slammed into the U-boat and rode up on the submarine's afterdeck, shearing through the pressure hull as though it were so much cardboard. Her own bow damaged by the collision, BORIE was for the moment held fast, even as she pinned the enemy's stern under water. For a full ten minutes the thrashing destroyer and struggling submarine were locked together—a panther with teeth fastened in the hindquarters of a crocodile.

The Nazis came boiling up from below. Forward of the conning tower, the submarine's deck-gunners clung to their mounts, and the U-boat's bridge personnel sniped wildly at the destroyer's bow. BORIE's searchlight poured down its blinding glare. At such close quarters the destroyermen were unable to bring their big guns to bear, and they bore down with every other weapon available.

Pistols barked and rifles spanged. Hot-shell men flung empty shell cases. A German gunner sprinted down the submarine's sloped foredeck—someone hurled a sheath knife at him from the destroyer's bridge. Other Nazis had Lugers shot out of their hands. A BORIE man opened fire with a Very pistol, and the U-boat's bridge was showered with pyrotechnic stars. Rifle volleys riddled the submarine's conning tower; a burst from a machine-gun brought smoke spurting from the structure, and a moment later it was spouting flame.

As an American described it afterward, *"That battle was like a riot in a shooting gallery. The boys hit that Nazi U-boat with everything but the kitchen range. They didn't need to throw that when the sub's conning tower took fire. Why carry coals to Newcastle?"*

So the submarine was a burning wreck when the heavy seas, which had wedged the vessels firmly together, suddenly washed them apart, permitting DD and sub to break their death-grip. As the U-boat slithered away, mortally hurt, Hutchins learned that his own ship was severely injured, her forward engine-room taking water. But the foe was not yet downed, and Hutchins drove the damaged destroyer in dogged pursuit.

Unable to dive, the sub remained on the surface. BORIE, painfully crippled, hung on the trail. Tracking with radar, Hutchins tried to stop the fugitive with a torpedo attack. Again, he closed in to ram, and BORIE missed the submarine by the width of her paint. Then the U-boat turned with guns snapping and barking, and tried to ram the lamed destroyer. With a salvo of shallow-set depth charges, the destroyer stopped the U-boat's wild rush, and once more the gunners were firing pointblank. Again the sub slipped away, and again the destroyer failed to hit the enemy with torpedoes.

The end came suddenly when the BORIE gunners got on target with their main battery. A salvo hit the U-boat's charred conning tower, reducing it to a shattered mangle. The exhausted Nazis fired pyrotechnic stars in signal of surrender. When BORIE's searchlight spotted the submarine, the Germans were going overside in rubber boats and the U-boat was going down.

"Scratch one pig boat," Hutchins had advised at the end of the action with the first U-boat. As it turned out, he had been

overly optimistic; he had damaged but not finished off that first one, and it got away. But BORIE did not miss on the second one, the U-405. Shell fire—machine-gun fire—rifle fire —empty shell-cases—a sheath knife—Very stars—depth charges. And, of course, old BORIE herself, veteran destroyer, DD 215, "can," or whatever one chose to call her—BORIE delivered the kayoe.

Loss of USS BORIE

After the battle BORIE rolled all night long in the rising seas, barely able to keep her screws turning. She had conquered the U-boat, but she could not beat back the Atlantic. By morning, when CARD's planes found her, the old four-piper was in sore distress.

The Task-group Commander, Captain Isbell, dispatched the destroyers GOFF (Lieutenant Commander H. I. Smith, USNR) and BARRY (Lieutenant Commander H. D. Hill, USNR) to assist the wounded warship. Throughout the daylight hours of November 2, BARRY and GOFF, themselves oldtimers, stood by while Hutchins and crew fought BORIE's battle-damage.

It was a losing fight. The maimed engines were beyond first aid, and the destroyer's hull, crushed at the bow below the waterline, was letting in the sea at a rate which pumps and bucket brigades were unable to contend with. As the afternoon grayed into dusk, 20-foot waves were crashing over BORIE's fantail, and it was all she could do to keep her stern to the gale.

At nightfall it was evident that the vessel was sinking. Commander Hutchins signalled his intention to abandon, and summoned the men up from below. As though determined not to be cheated of this victim, the seas climbed higher as BARRY and GOFF closed in to take off BORIE's crew. Tragically enough, 27 of BORIE's crew were lost in the rabid seas. Expert rescue work by GOFF and BARRY, and the superb courage of all hands from BORIE, prevented a greater loss.

The destroyer went down, but she had sent U-405 ahead of her.

BADGER, CLEMSON, DuPONT, INGRAM, *and* BOGUE *Kill* U-172

On December 12-13, 1943, a CVE-DD team fought an antisub battle that was to stand as a prototype for cooperative effort between the surface and air units of a hunter-killer group. Here was synchronized teamwork as successful as it was exemplary.

The group (Task Group 21.13) was composed of the escort-carrier BOGUE (Captain J. B. "Joe" Dunn) and the veteran destroyers GEORGE E. BADGER (Lieutenant E. M. Higgins, USNR), DuPONT (Commander J. G. Marshall), CLEMSON (Lieutenant W. F. Moran, USNR), and OSMOND INGRAM (Lieutenant Commander R. F. Miller, USNR). Led by Commander E. W. Yancey, the quartet of old four-pipers teamed with BOGUE to form a crack hunter-killer outfit under over-all command of Captain Dunn.

Conducting an offensive anti-sub patrol, the group was steaming en route from Casablanca to the States, and it had reached the vicinity of lat. 26-19 N., long. 29-58 W., when December 12 came up on the calendar. The date was not all that came up on that day.

Action began when BOGUE'S scouting aircraft spotted a skulking U-boat. The enemy submerged, and the hunt was on. Racing to the area where the sub had been discovered, CLEMSON made sound contact with the U-boat and promptly spread a pattern of depth charges over the appropriate spot. While the water boiled, a plane from BOGUE took station overhead to watch for bubbles or debris.

Meanwhile, BADGER, DuPONT, and INGRAM steamed forward to join CLEMSON in the hunt.

Following the oil slick, CLEMSON and INGRAM thrashed the adjacent and subjacent waters with a steady rain of depth charges. Then, just as American patience was giving out along with the anti-sub ammunition, the U-boat climbed to the surface and ran for it. One of BOGUE'S aircraft spied the sub as she broke water, and the aviator shouted the word over voice radio. Two Wildcats zoomed from BOGUE'S flight deck and bulleted to the target, whipping machine-gun fire at the U-boat. With three planes strafing the conning tower, and the destroyers closing in, the Nazi submariners opened the hatches and dived overside. The aircraft held their fire and veered off, believing the U-boaters were abandoning ship.

But not all of the U-boaters abandoned. The Nazi captain and some of the crew rushed to man the deck guns, and the U-boat gunners opened fire. One shell struck INGRAM'S quarter-deck. The explosion killed a destroyerman and wounded eight others of the crew.

The DD's answered the Nazi's fire with deadly gunnery that soon had the U-boat wheeling helplessly in circles. Six minutes of this shooting match, and the submarine's decks were awash. As the Germans flung themselves from her bridge, the battered U-boat plunged for the last time. The captain, executive officer, and 33 other survivors were fished from the littered sea by the American hunter-killers.

The submarine destroyed by Task Group 21.13 was the U-172, one of Nazi Germany's largest and newest specimens.

Hunter-killer teamwork had achieved a great success. But perhaps the moral which highlights this A/S episode concerns persistence.

If the U-boat was stubborn, the hunter-killers were more so. The patience and perseverance which moves mountains had removed from the Atlantic another Nazi submarine.

SCHENCK *Kills* U-645

While the BOGUE hunter-killers were patrolling the convoy route to Casablanca, other A/S groups were making the North Atlantic unsafe for the wolfpacks. One of these was Task Group 21.14 built around escort-carrier CARD and Captain A. J. ("Buster") Isbell. They were out on the hunt the week before Christmas 1943.

On the night of December 23-24, SCHENCK (Lieutenant Commander E. W. Logsdon) was operating as screen on CARD's port bow. At 0216 on the morning of the 24th the destroyer picked up a radar contact, range 10,100 yards. As SCHENCK rushed for the submarine, the "pip" faded on the radar screen. But at 2,500 yards the U-boat was sighted in the act of submerging, her stern toward the DD.

Logsdon ordered a swift change of course to avoid a possible homing torpedo, then shifted rudder after swinging 50°, and slowed to 15 knots to probe with sonar where the U-boat had gone under. Sound reported contact at 800 yards, and at 0250 SCHENCK dropped the first depth charge of a pattern. The destroyer rolled and veered as fountains boomed in her wake. The battle was on.

Thirty minutes of this, and then a "pip" showed up on the radar screen, range 4,000. As Logsdon drove his destroyer at this target (probably the U-boat which had been depth-charged), radar contact was lost at 2,500 yards. But Sound regained contact at 1,900, and at 0327 SCHENCK sowed another depth-charge pattern across the sea.

About two minutes after the last charge exploded, a rumbling blast welled up from the deep with a detonation that shook the destroyer. Up came a great billow of oil that spread a dark carpet across the water. There could be no doubt of a kill, and postwar records verified the U-boat's destruction. However, SCHENCK's destroyermen were unable to make immediate verification. As Logsdon was preparing to get a sample of the Nazi sub's lifeblood, a call came in over the TBS. The destroyer LEARY had been torpedoed!

Loss of USS LEARY

LEARY had been bucking along through the December seas

with a crew hair-triggered for action. The night of the 23rd-24th was typical of the season—frosty whitecaps leaping in the dark, and a boreal wind brooming up gusts of spume and spray that stung a lookout's face like shots of salt.

Midnight on the clock, and LEARY was driving along in the blackout, making radar sweeps. Then the monotony was jolted by a sharp report from the radar watch. Contact! Submarine off the bow!

Time: 0158. LEARY's captain, Commander James E. Kyes, rushed all hands to battle stations, and the destroyer went after the U-boat. While tracking, she momentarily established a sound contact at close range. Before her crew could unlimber depth-charges, the destroyer was struck and staggered by two torpedoes that smote her on the starboard flank, well aft. The rapid explosions blended into a single roar. Men were thrown from their feet as the LEARY lurched and veered, hard hit. Twelve minutes had elapsed between the time of radar contact and this mortal blow.

LEARY's men fought her battle-damage with the quiet desperation of seamen who know their ship is *in extremis*. There was no holding back the icy seas that plunged with a roar through the breach in the destroyer's hull. About 0225, Commander Kyes gave the order to abandon. The men lined up in their kapok jackets and went over the side.

About 0237, the sinking destroyer was convulsed by two more explosions. Survivors believed that LEARY was struck by a third torpedo which hit her amidships, causing the internal blasts. A moment before this volcanic eruption, LEARY's captain, Commander Kyes, was glimpsed in the act of handing his kapok life-jacket to a mess attendant. He refused to abandon ship until those who served under him were safely off, and this valiant conduct was to cost him his life. Her hull ruptured by those two final explosions, LEARY sank almost immediately, taking her captain down with her.

Thanks to Captain Isbell and the good work of SCHENCK and other units of the task group, many of LEARY's crew were saved. By final count, some 97 of the stricken destroyer's complement were lost. It was a painful blow for the DesLant Force on that day before Christmas, but one that left in memory the silhouette of a fighting ship and the name of two valiant captains—Commander Kyes, who gave his life-jacket to a messman, and Captain Isbell, who risked an escort-carrier to rescue a good company of destroyermen.

LEARY was the third United States destroyer to go down to U-boat torpedoes in the Battle of the Atlantic. And she was the last.

Inventory 1943

Grand Admiral Karl Doenitz, Commander-in-Chief of the German Navy, must have been a worried Nazi on New Year's Eve, 1943. His troubles were as obvious as the simple arithmetic of profit and loss.

SUBMARINE WAR STATISTICS

In 1939 (four months of war): 9 U-boats lost, 810 Allied ships sunk.
In 1940: 22 U-boats lost; 4,407 Allied ships sunk.
In 1941: 35 U-boats lost; 4,398 Allied ships sunk.
In 1942: 85 U-boats lost; 8,245 Allied ships sunk.
In 1943: 237 U-boats lost; 3,611 Allied ships sunk.

But Doenitz promised himself a comeback. Under construction in German yards were new and formidable submarines—prefabricated jobs that could be mass produced. Of the new U-boat types projected, Type XXI, a 1,600-tonner, was a submersible calculated to put all previous models in the shade. Radically streamlined, this 251-foot submarine was powered by a stepped-up drive that gave it a submerged speed of approximately 18 knots. It was reported that the craft could dive to the unheard-of depth of 700 feet.

Another surprise Doenitz had up his sleeve was *Schnorkel*. In fact, this famous "breather device" was already emerging from his cuff.

But *Schnorkel* would not go into action until 1944, and Type XXI did not enter the war until 1945. And neither of these submarine innovations could turn the war-tide.

Speaking of U-boats, Secretary of the Navy Frank Knox had observed, *"Each time they go out, there will be a sharply increasing likelihood that they will not come back."*

Chapter 23

The Gang Busters (Continued)

(January 1944-April 1944)

☆ ☆ ☆

Schnorkel

Probably the most important submarine innovation of the war was the variously spelled *"Schnorkel"* device which permitted a submarine to operate its Diesels (and thus charge its batteries) while submerged. Aptly described as a "breather tube," it served as an air intake and an exhaust for the Diesel engines, and the U-boat equipped with the device might remain under water for weeks at a time, presumably beyond the easy reach of radar discovery.

The *Schnorkel* stack was Dutch in origin. It was invented in the early 30's by Commander J. J. Wichers of the Royal Netherlands Navy. By 1939 the *"Snuiver,"* as the Dutch termed the device, was being installed in all new Netherlands Navy submarines.

When the Nazis invaded Holland in May, 1940, the invading Germans found some scuttled *Snuiver* submarines in Dutch construction yards. The *Snuiver* apparatus was promptly salvaged, and Doenitz had an ace card in his U-boat deck. Fortunately for the Allied A/S effort, matériel priorities were hard to obtain for German naval purposes, and *Schnorkel* did not appear on German submarines until 1944.

The *Schnorkel* gear was hard to sight, but it did not provide the submarine with an invisible cloak. Aircraft spotted the *Schnorkel* "feather," even as they spied the wake of a slinking periscope. And, of course, the U-boat's pressure hull was still vulnerable to air bombs and depth charges. So *Schnorkel* was not in time to overcome the Allies' head start in scientific submarine detection and destruction.

Loss of USS TURNER

Early in the morning of January 3, 1944, the USS TURNER maneuvered into an assigned anchorage off Ambrose Light, and dropped the hook. The destroyer swung quietly in the darkness—all the usual routine.

Then, at 0616, just as the night was graying to eastward, TURNER was shaken by a violent explosion. Men were jostled from their feet and thrown from their berths. As all hands rushed to emergency stations, some thought the ship had been hit by a torpedo, or had been struck by a drifting mine. But the blast had hurled up a fan of light in the vicinity of No. 2 mount; the explosion was internal, probably caused by defective ammunition. Flames leapt up through open hatches, exposing deck and turret in holocaustal light. TURNER had been badly damaged, and she was burning fiercely.

Having sighted the blast, the destroyer SWASEY and other vessels of Task Force 64 closed in to aid TURNER, and pilot boats and small boats were soon standing by for the rescue. TURNER's decks were hot when the rescuers reached her anchorage. Neither foamite nor bulkheads seemed able to contain the flames, and flash after flash turned the destroyer into a floating inferno.

She burned until 0742, when the fire evidently reached her magazines and a volcanic eruption burst her smoke-wrapped hull. TURNER went down almost immediately, rolling over to starboard and sinking stern-first in a shroud of lethal fumes and steam. As the waters closed over the stricken vessel, the rescuers ran in to pick up survivors.

TURNER's captain, Commander H. S. Wygant, Jr., went down with the ship. Two officers and about 165 men were saved. Fatalities were unusually heavy, and the violence of the initial explosion and subsequent flash fire consumed evidence as to the exact cause of the disaster.

Enter the Destroyer-Escort

The destroyer-escort was a tough little warship. Averaging 1,140 to 1,450 tons, she was designed to do the A/S work of the full-sized destroyer and was given sufficient punch to enable her to trade hard blows with surface and air attackers if necessary. Although the DE lacked the speed, fire power, and armor of the DD, her depth charges were equally as destructive, and anti-submarine warfare was specifically the destroyer-escort's business. To that end she was equipped with the latest detection devices and the newest of A/S weapons.

All DE's were in one of six different design groups. Their

armament varied from three 3-inch 50-caliber dual-purpose guns and one 40 mm. quad to two 5-inch 38-caliber dual-purpose guns, one 40 mm. quad, and three 40 mm. twin mounts. They were variously powered by turbo-electric plants, Diesel engines, or geared-turbines. Their shaft horsepower ran from 6,000 to 12,000; their speed from some 20 to 24 knots —slower than the average DD. But the horsepower was not destroyer-escort's big talking point. As a submarine hunter she enjoyed one considerable advantage over the DD—the advantage of a tight "turning circle" that gave the DE an agility or maneuverability which was envied by veteran destroyermen and feared by enemy submariners.

Like destroyers newly commissioned, many of the Navy's new DE's were named after naval heroes, officers and men who had lost their lives in heroic action during the opening months of World War II as well as legendary Navy figures.

It was not until the autumn of 1943 that DE's appeared in the Atlantic in anything like the desired number. But by December of that year destroyer-escorts were showing up on the flanks of trans-Atlantic convoys and as screens for baby flat-tops leading groups of hunter-killers on offensive A/S missions.

The CVE-DD-DE teams would knock the ultimate bottom out of the Nazi U-boat effort.

THOMAS, BOSTWICK *and* BRONSTEIN *Kill* U-709

March 1944 was the month in which the DE's made their first U-boat kill. Sharing honors were the destroyer-escorts THOMAS (Lieutenant Commander D. M. Kellogg, USNR), flying the pennant of Commander G. A. Parkinson, USNR, ComCortDiv 48; BOSTWICK (Lieutenant Commander J. H. Church, Jr., USNR); and BRONSTEIN (Lieutenant S. H. Kinney). These DE's were units of Task Group 21.16, built around the new escort-carrier BLOCK ISLAND, under the driving command of Captain Logan C. Ramsey. The baby flat-top's screen included the destroyer CORRY and the DE BREEMAN, but these two did not get into the action which exploded late in the evening of February 29.

Action had been brewing for several days, for BLOCK ISLAND and her team of hunter-killers were operating in wolfpack water, vicinity of lat. 49-00 N., long. 26-00 W., where at least 18 Nazi submarines were reported to be holding rendezvous.

Steaming as screen on the port bow of BLOCK ISLAND, destroyer-escort BRONSTEIN made the radar contact, range 6,500 yards, at 2208. Then, as BRONSTEIN raced for the target, the flare of a depth-charge marker lit up the seascape. DE's THOMAS and BOSTWICK, developing their own contacts, were silhouetted by one of their markers as they bore in on a coordinated attack. The three destroyer-escorts boxed the target, but the submarine remained unsighted until 2213, when BRONSTEIN fired an illumination spread. The light sprayed a downward glare that caught the enemy full in the face—a surfaced U-boat.

Kinney ordered his gunners to open fire. As BRONSTEIN's guns roared and spat, the sub captain called for a dive, and "pulled the plug."

BRONSTEIN made two hedgehog attacks, pelting the sea with pattern after pattern. Then BOSTWICK and THOMAS followed through with runs, spattering the submerged enemy with hedgehog barrages and deep-thundering depth-charge bombardments.

For five hours the DE's kept at it, tracking and bombing, tracking and bombing. There was no respite for the Nazi submarine, no let-up.

It was all up with the U-709. About 0320 of that March morning, destroyer-escort THOMAS was laying a pattern of depth-charges set for a deep barrage. Down went the ashcans. Up came the rumble of explosions deep under. Then, at 0324, the surface heaved with the detonation of a blast that left a maelstrom in the DE's wake. The eruption could have had but one meaning—a U-boat had blown up.

But U-709 (identified by post-war records) was not the only U-boat sunk by the DE hunters on that spot and date. While THOMAS and BOSTWICK had been concentrating on their quarry, BRONSTEIN had found other fish to fry.

BRONSTEIN *Sinks* U-603

Commissioned on December 13, 1943, BRONSTEIN had completed her shakedown period only three weeks before this North Atlantic U-boat battle. But lack of experience did not prevent her sonar operator from recognizing a brand new echo in his gear as distinctly different from the intermittent depth-bombing THOMAS and BOSTWICK were giving the U-709.

Skipper Kinney of BRONSTEIN immediately went to work—and high time, for when contact was made at 0137, the range was a perilously short 450 yards. In exactly one minute Kinney had the depth charges going. After the TNT went overside, Kinney sent the DE veering about in an effort to regain sound contact. Fifteen minutes of patient searching by the DE followed, with the U-boat somewhere down below, playing "it" in this lethal game of tag.

At 0155, with all hands in a vise of tension, Kinney directed the dropping of a pattern of 18 depth-charges, set to go deep. The barrage was still thundering down under when a tremendous explosion boomed in the sea. There could be little doubt that the submarine's pressure hull had burst, but Kinney was taking no chances. At 0236 he ordered a full 18-charge pattern. The echoes of this barrage died away into a silence which convinced the DE's Sound crew that the submarine under fire had also died away.

Post-war records revealed that BRONSTEIN's target on this occasion was U-603. Score two for BRONSTEIN. And her maiden cruise was not yet over.

Loss of USS LEOPOLD

In March 1944, Convoy CU-16 was trudging across the North Atlantic under escort of Task Group 21.5. Among the units of TG 21.5 were the destroyer-escorts LEOPOLD and JOYCE. Both comparative newcomers, the pair were running along on the convoy's flank like shepherd dogs guarding a plodding herd.

On the 9th of March the convoy was in the vicinity of 58-00 N., 25-00 W., about 540 miles southwest of Iceland. No waters of the Atlantic were more dangerous.

Now, treading the path across this submarine zone, destroyer-escort LEOPOLD picked up a radar contact at 1950 in the evening. The DE's skipper, Lieutenant Commander K. C. Phillips, USCG, rushed all hands to battle stations, and drove LEOPOLD forward to investigate.

About 1955, LEOPOLD's TBS excitedly voiced the message: THIS LOOKS LIKE THE REAL THING

Destroyer-escort JOYCE (Lieutenant Commander Robert Wilcox, USCG) was ordered to assist her sister DE. But before JOYCE could get there, the battle was on. About 2000, two starshells soared from LEOPOLD's deck, and as the pyrotechnic bursts illuminated the seascape, the DE's guns opened fire at the enemy's silhouette.

The U-boat fired a spread of torpedoes. Before Phillips could swing his ship to comb the wakes, two of the deadly fish smote the DE, blasting her portside compartments B-1 and B-2. Bounced by the explosions, the destroyer-escort staggered to a halt. There was a dreadful rending of metal, the creak and crunch of buckling plates. LEOPOLD's back was broken.

When JOYCE reached the scene at 2015, LEOPOLD was dead in the water, jackknifed, with bow and stern up-angled, and screws in the air. After a fruitless search for the enemy sub, JOYCE began rescue operations.

At 0045 of the following morning, a gush of sea rode over the half-swamped vessel, and LEOPOLD's stern section tore loose and sank. Going under, the DE's depth charges exploded. Men died wretchedly in this eruption of fire and water, and JOYCE had a difficult time locating swimmers in the littered swirl.

LEOPOLD was gone. She was the first destroyer-escort downed in the war.

But only two more destroyer-escorts would go down to U-boat torpedoes in the Atlantic Battle—a remarkable record for the months of unceasing A/S warfare that engaged the DE's in the Atlantic until VE-Day.

HOBSON, HAVERFIELD, PRINCE RUPERT, *and Aircraft Kill U-575*

The pseudo-science of numerology endows the number 13 with influential properties, mostly unlucky.

But to the officers and men of Task Group 21.11, the 13th of March must have seemed a fortuitous date, whereas the Nazi captain and crew of U-575 must have considered it precisely the opposite. Much depends on a point of view.

Task Group 21.11 was a hunter-killer group led by escort carrier BOGUE under Captain J. B. Dunn. It included the destroyer HOBSON (Lieutenant Commander K. Loveland), the destroyer-escort HAVERFIELD (Lieutenant Commander J. A. Mathews, USNR), HMCS PRINCE RUPERT, and three aircraft squadrons—British 172 and 206 and American VC-95.

Action began in the morning of the 13th when one of BOGUE's planes sighted an oil slick off the Azores. The plane sent out a call for surface craft, and dropped a sonobuoy. The buoy signalled the presence of a submarine in the vicinity, and the hunt was under way.

At 1151, destroyer-escort HAVERFIELD arrived on the scene. After searching for about two hours, she made sonar contact at 1,700 yards, and at 1417 she fired a hedgehog salvo. She followed through with a second and third hedgehog attack, and at 1447 she unleashed a depth-charge barrage. The explosions brought a cluster of black oil bubbles to the surface.

Meantime, HMCS PRINCE RUPERT arrived on the field of battle. The Canadians delivered a depth-charge attack and let fly with a hedgehog pattern. HAVERFIELD laid still another depth-charge pattern at 1538, and followed through with a full pattern of hedgehogs at 1551. PRINCE RUPERT continued the depth-charging. The Canadian remained "to the left of contact" to conn HAVERFIELD into firing position. At 1632 HAVERFIELD dumped 13 depth charges down on the target when PRINCE RUPERT signalled on bearing.

At this juncture destroyer HOBSON steamed onto the scene of action. She stood by as HAVERFIELD made a run at 1704, dropping a deep barrage. At 1732 HAVERFIELD tried yet again. Then at 1759 HOBSON opened fire with a full depth-charge pattern, following through with another barrage at 1833, on a bearing given by HAVERFIELD.

No submarine could survive this sort of bombardment, and the Nazi specimen in question was not the exception. Two minutes after HOBSON's second attack, the U-boat broached. As the submarine's hull broke water, HAVERFIELD opened fire.

By 1843 the submarine's conning tower was in flames, fire was spouting from a forward hatch, and frantic Germans were fighting for a chance to leap overside. Settling slowly on an even keel, the U-boat gradually submerged. Then, with the water lapping over her decks, she suddenly thrust her bow at the sky and slid under the sea, stern-first.

HAVERFIELD picked up seven survivors. HOBSON recovered sixteen, including the U-boat captain "and one corpse."

Thus sub, the U-575, was the first *Schnorkel*-submarine killed by American A/S forces. But it was too late for *Schnorkel*. The hunter-killers already had the U-boat Force by the throat.

CORRY *and* BRONSTEIN *Kill* U-801

For some months the Nazis had been stationing big cargo subs to fuel the Atlantic wolf-packers in the vicinity of the Azores. The Allies called these fuel-carriers "milk cows."

The "milk cows" were back on the job that March, and TG. 21.16 got the word. Their morale high from their recent victories in the North Atlantic, the USS BLOCK ISLAND (now under command of Captain F. M. Hughes) and her associate hunter-killers steamed at top speed for the target area, which was located northwest of the Cape Verdes.

Scouting ahead, aircraft from BLOCK ISLAND went ranging over the enemy's refuelling ground. And on the morning of St. Patrick's Day the BLOCK ISLAND scouts spotted a U-boat, vicinity of lat. 16-42 N., long. 30-28 W.

The attack fell to the destroyer CORRY (Lieutenant Commander G. D. Hoffman) and destroyer-escort BRONSTEIN (Lieutenant S. H. Kinney). BRONSTEIN was the same DE that had won distinction on the night of March 1 by single-handedly sinking one U-boat and participating in the destruction of another. CORRY was an old hand in the Atlantic Battle, with experiences ranging all the way from service stripes with the British Home Fleet to icy North Atlantic and humid Caribbean patrols. With her and BRONSTEIN and BLOCK ISLAND that March day were THOMAS, BREEMAN, and BOSTWICK.

Promptly on word from the BLOCK ISLAND, BRONSTEIN and CORRY peeled off and made for the target. Guided by the tracking aircraft, they maneuvered to box the U-boat in. Earlier that morning, while conducting an independent search,

CORRY had made radar contact with what turned out to be radar decoy balloons. After shooting up these futile novelties, the destroyermen had continued the sub-hunt with whetted appetite. When BRONSTEIN joined the search at 0705, an oil slick was visible on the surface. Ensued the usual game of tag, the two hunters veering this way and that as the submarine dodged down below, and contact was lost, regained, lost again, and again regained. Down went the ashcans and teardrops, to be followed by thunderous upheavals of water and a flotsam of dead fish.

Then, at 1318, U-801 came plunging to the surface like a wounded whale. As the submarine broached, both CORRY and BRONSTEIN opened fire. For about five minutes the DD and DE flung 5-inch and 20 mm. fire at the struggling sub. Hits struck the U-boat's deck and conning tower, scattering the sea with debris. Then the submarine's hatches burst open and the crew came up from below.

The Nazi submariners were given no chance to man the deck guns. They had only time to abandon ship. At 1326 CORRY was closing in to ram, when the battered U-boat went abruptly down, stern first. Forty-seven of the crew of U-801 were picked up.

That afternoon of March 17, 1944, there was jubilation aboard the BRONSTEIN. Within 17 days she had participated in three U-boat kills, a record which many a veteran A/S vessel might well envy.

CHAMPLIN *and* HUSE *Down* U-856

Only a few U-boats were sent westward across the Atlantic that spring. One of these was U-856. Early in April 1944 she was roaming the sea lanes about 500 miles south of Halifax, and risking her life every time she ran up her periscope.

On April 7, DesDiv 32 (Commander C. L. Melson in flagship BOYLE), accompanied by destroyer-escort HUSE, was on the hunt. At dawn the sub had been spotted in the vicinity of lat. 40-00 N., long. 62-00 W. The destroyer group spent the morning combing the area. Contact was not made until 1542 when destroyer CHAMPLIN (Commander J. J. Schaffer) detected the deep-sea intruder with sound gear.

A veteran with one U-boat already to her credit, CHAMPLIN was joined by the destroyer-escort HUSE, and the pair made several depth-charge and hedgehog attacks. The onslaught went on for a little over an hour. Then the tormented U-boat lunged to the surface to fight it out.

And in the heat of the battle, a 20 mm. projectile from the CHAMPLIN's port bridge mount had struck the open top of the near-by ready-box and exploded. The shrapnel-burst felled

CHAMPLIN's captain and injured three men. The Pharmacist's Mates were carrying the captain below when a shout went up from the destroyer's deck—the U-boat was sinking.

The submarine plunged at 1714, and a moment later CHAMPLIN and HUSE were shaken by a deep-sea explosion. U-856 had blown up.

Destroyers NIELDS and ORDRONAUX recovered 28 German survivors. The sole American fatality was CHAMPLIN's captain, Commander John J. Schaffer, who died of his wounds the following morning.

In the time-old tradition of the Navy his body was commended to the deep.

PILLSBURY, POPE, CHATELAIN, FLAHERTY *and Aircraft Kill* U-515

Captain D. V. ("Dan") Gallery's new escort carrier GUADALCANAL had her prow pointed for Madeira that first week of April 1944. Nazi submarines were foregathering in those familiar waters, and Gallery intended to be in on the rendezvous.

So Task Group 21.12, consisting of GUADALCANAL, plus destroyer-escorts PILLSBURY (Lieutenant G. W. Casselman, USNR), POPE (Lieutenant Commander E. H. Headland), CHATELAIN (Lieutenant Commander J. L. Foley), and FLAHERTY (Lieutenant Commander M. Johnston, Jr.), steamed for the area at top speed. The DE's were under group leadership of Commander F. S. Hall, riding in PILLSBURY.

Gallery's task group introduced a new feature into the book of anti-submarine warfare tactics. GUADALCANAL's pilots had been doing some experimental night flying. Hazardous enough on a full-size carrier, night take-offs and landings on a baby flat-top called for aviation of a high order. And on the night of April 8-9 the aviators who flew by starlight produced results.

About half an hour before midnight, searching aircraft sighted a U-boat loitering on the surface. The planes attacked, and the U-boat made a dive to duck a rain of bombs.

Gallery dispatched destroyer-escorts PILLSBURY and FLAHERTY to the scene. The DE's commenced searching with their sound gear around 0710, and PILLSBURY made contact about five minutes later. Lieutenant Casselman ordered two hedgehog attacks. The water was figuratively boiling when CHATELAIN steamed up to lend a hand. Not long after that, POPE arrived. Boxed by the four DE's, the U-boat was trapped.

At 1405 there was a gush of white water close aboard CHATELAIN, and the U-boat snorted to the surface. The sub, determined to fight it out, was no novice. Hatches snapped open, gunners spilled out on deck, and German bullets were flying almost as soon as CHATELAIN's gunners opened fire.

FLAHERTY opened fire as soon as she had a clear bearing. She also launched a torpedo at 1,200 yards, which missed ahead of the dodging submarine. The U-boat gunners directed a savage fire at FLAHERTY, but were unable to score hits. CHATELAIN and FLAHERTY were on target, however, and several shell bursts staggered the U-boat. At 1408 an internal explosion shook the sub; smoke poured from her conning tower hatch; the crew came fighting up from below. Eight minutes after the explosion, the U-boat sank in a swirl of water strewn with struggling Germans.

Of the U-boat's complement of six officers and 53 men, 37 men and all the officers were picked up. They identified the downed submarine as U-515.

Among the submariners captured was the U-boat's skipper, Herr Kapitan Werner Henke, complete with Knight's Cross of the Iron Cross, plus oak leaves.

Henke's capture seems to have given Captain Gallery an idea. If a CVE-DD-DE team could bag a U-boat skipper who wore the Knight's Cross of the Iron Cross, plus oak leaves, why couldn't it bring an entire U-boat back alive?

The dramatic upshot of Captain Gallery's thinking will be related presently.

GANDY, JOYCE *and* PETERSON *Kill* U-550

Early in the morning of April 16, 1944, the merchant tanker PAN PENNSYLVANIA was ambushed and torpedoed about 100 miles off New York. Units of Task Group 21.5, the destroyer-escorts GANDY (Lieutenant Commander W. A. Sessions, USNR), JOYCE (Lieutenant Commander Robert Wilcox, USCG), and PETERSON (Lieutenant Commander S. M. Hay, USCGR) were at that time engaged in escorting the ships of a convoy which was forming in the area. The three DE's were ordered to get the submarine invader and rescue the crew of the stricken tanker.

At top speed the DE's raced to the tanker's aid.

JOYCE soon made sound contact with the enemy. Lieutenant Commander Wilcox directed a depth-charge attack, and the DE sowed her teardrops and ashcans with such speed and accuracy that the first pattern disabled the submarine and brought it lunging to the surface.

The U-boat broached and made a lame run for it. All three DE's opened fire. The submarine gunners tumbled topside and fired back. A shell-burst sprayed shrapnel across GANDY's foredeck, wounding four of her men. In answer Lieutenant

Commander Sessions ordered the DE full speed ahead, and sent her charging at the foe. Hot on the heels of her shells the DE rammed the U-boat and sent her reeling.

JOYCE picked up the swimming survivors—a dozen Germans, all told, including the Commanding Officer. He identified the sunken submersible as U-550.

The fight with U-550 was the GANDY's baptism of fire. She had completed her shakedown cruise less than two weeks before, and had been on duty no more than eight days when she went into battle.

"That," observed a captain in Atlantic Fleet destroyers, *"was going to war in a hurry."*

FROST, HUSE, BARBER, *and* SNOWDEN *Kill* U-488

Along came another baby flat-top—the CVE CROATAN under Captain J. P. W. ("Johnny") Vest. She led another group of sharpshooting hunter-killers: Task Group 21.15, composed of the destroyer-escorts INCH (Commander C. W. Frey, USNR), FROST (Lieutenant Commander J. H. McWhorter, USNR), HUSE (Lieutenant Commander R. H. Wanless, USNR), BARBER (Lieutenant Commander E. T. B. Sullivan), and SNOWDEN (Lieutenant Commander N. W. Swanson, USNR).

West of the Cape Verdes, in the morning mists on April 26, 1944, HUSE and FROST were investigating a sound contact with inquisitive detection gear. At 0555 FROST fired a hedgehog salvo that was presently echoed by three muffled deep-sea explosions. Then silence. The DE "ping jockies" worked their instruments as the destroyer-escorts roamed the area. The Sound men at the phones were all ears. No answer. Straining lookouts and CROATAN's sharp-eyed planes searched the seascape for signs of U-boat flotsam. Nothing. Was it a kill?

Two days later a persistent CROATAN hunter spied a dark carpet of oil floating on the sea's warm surface. Destroyer-escorts SNOWDEN, FROST, and BARBER raced to the spot to conduct a hunt.

The DE trio probed the deep, and dropped depth charges. After several attacks, two undersea explosions were heard. Then a silence that drifted off into nothing. If a U-boat had been down there, it was no longer operating.

Post-war inquiry revealed that U-488 had vanished somewhere west of the Cape Verdes late in April 1944. Doenitz's headquarters had written her off as *Sperlos Versenkt*—"sunk without a trace." But evidence indicates that she was sunk in the vicinity of lat. 17-54 N., long. 38-05 W., by action of destroyer-escorts FROST, HUSE, BARBER, and SNOWDEN.

From Menace to Problem

By the spring of '44 the tide of the Atlantic Battle had turned. Its turn was registered in Tenth Fleet Headquarters by a set of simple statistics.

For each U-boat destroyed in 1941, about 16 Allied vessels went down. For each U-boat destroyed in 1942, the Allies lost about 13 vessels. In 1943, the Allied figure was reduced to 2. And by the spring of 1944, a U-boat was going down for almost every Allied vessel sunk.

Chapter 24

Sweeping the Western Ocean

(May 1944-September 1944)

☆ ☆ ☆

Loss of USS PARROTT

There was something of brutal irony in the fate that befell the destroyer PARROTT. She was one of the five old Asiatic Fleet four-stackers to survive the whirlwind Japanese offensive and reach Australia after the fall of the Malay Barrier. Scarred and salty from long duty on the Pacific front, a veteran of many battles, and brushed by many a close shave, she returned to the States for repairs and recuperation.

In the spring of 1944 she was at Norfolk, Virginia. With her was her veteran skipper, Commander J. N. Hughes, and many of her original complement—men of the old Asiatic Fleet who had fought the war under Admiral Hart and shot it out pointblank with the invasion forces from Tokyo.

On the afternoon of May 2, the destroyer received orders to move. She was backing clear of her berth at the Naval Operating Base, Norfolk, when at 1636 there was a shout; a shadow loomed over her like a cliff rising out of fog, and a crash shook the old DD from stem to stern. She had been rammed by the merchant ship SS JOHN MORTON.

Three of her men dead. Seven wounded. And PARROTT, her hull half buckled, fatally hurt.

At 1655 the disabled destroyer was beached by tugs. Later she was towed to the Navy Yard at Portsmouth, Virginia. Repair crews looked her over, and reported extensive damage. She was decommissioned on June 16, 1944. An old war horse victimized by collision.

BUCKLEY *and Aircraft Kill* U-66 (*"Stand By To Repel Boarders!"*)

Here is the story of a DE-submarine battle that featured

a command the like of which had not been heard in the Navy for many years. The destroyer-escort was the BUCKLEY, commissioned as recently as April 30, 1943. The submarine was a Nazi model, the U-66. The battle occurred in the Central Atlantic on May 6, 1944. And the command, quoted in the above heading, had not been heard by United States Navy men since the day of cannon and cutlass.

But the story's beginning is modern enough—a hunter-killer team (Task Group 21.11) led by the new escort-carrier BLOCK ISLAND (Captain F. M. Hughes) in a foray to the Cape Verdes area. There, in the Arquipélago de Cabo Verde, the wolfpacks had been reported again, with their migrant "milk cows" driven far south of Madeira and the Azores. Sailing from Norfolk on April 22, the BLOCK ISLAND team was to relieve the CROATAN group which had been operating in the Cape Verdes area.

Including the escort-carrier, the BLOCK ISLAND group was composed of four 24-knot "black oil" DE's: the destroyer-escorts AHRENS (Commander M. H. Harris, USNR), BARR (Lieutenant Commander H. H. Love, USNR), BUCKLEY (Lieutenant Commander B. M. Abel, USNR), and EUGENE E. ELMORE (Lieutenant Commander G. L. Conkey, USNR).

At 1555 on April 29, the BLOCK ISLANDers relieved the CROATAN team on station, and the offensive sub-hunt was under way. Two days later the group was given a "Huff-Duff" fix on a submarine in the offing. A search plane made radar contact and attacked the U-boat with depth charges. When the sub evaded, the BLOCK ISLAND team commenced intensive hold-down tactics which continued for the next five days.

Under that sort of pressure the U-boaters usually made a desperate rise for air and a battery-charge. Exactly what occurred in this case.

On the fifth day of the hunt the DE's AHRENS and ELMORE were sent to a position some 60 miles ahead on the submarine's projected track. Destroyer-escorts BUCKLEY and BARR remained behind on the projected track. By the evening of May 5, the hunter-killers were some 500 miles to the west of the Cape Verdes, making radar sweeps for the hidden submarine. BUCKLEY was steaming along as screen for BLOCK ISLAND.

A fine night for cruising on a sea laved with silver from a full May moon. Flying fish and phosphorus twinkling in the water and all the rest of it. Were it not for the blackout and the drone of scouting aircraft, a sailor standing lookout might think the world at peace.

But at 0216 the next morning one of BLOCK ISLAND's night-flying scouts reported radar contact. Some 20 miles from BUCKLEY the U-boat was prowling along on the surface.

Aided by a stream of information voice-radioed from the

plane, BUCKLEY ran the contact down. The DE's lookouts sighted the sub at about 2,500 yards, sharply silhouetted in the moon-path and making no apparent effort to avoid detection. To the surprise of Lieutenant Commander Abel and others on the destroyer-escort bridge, the U-boat defied both convention and BUCKLEY by making herself more conspicuous with a pyrotechnic display of three red flashes.

Whether the flares were a challenge, a signal to some companion submarine, or a Nazi trick, Abel had no time to learn. At 2,200 yards he ordered his gunners to open fire. Washed with carmine light, the target was a set-up for the DE marksmen and they were on it with first salvo. Replying with deck batteries, the U-boat returned the salvo and pulled away to open the range. Abel called for high speed, and the DE raced in.

There was a moment wherein BUCKLEY and U-66 were running neck and neck, leaving parallel wakes that streamed astern in the moonlight like silver railroad tracks. Not 20 yards apart, the American and Nazi gunners were firing hammer-and-tongs. Then, at Abel's order BUCKLEY's helmsman threw her over. Veering sharply, the DE swung at top speed and rammed the submarine.

The collision sent BUCKLEY's bow riding high over the U-boat's deck, and the two were locked in a tight embrace. It was the BORIE-U-405 battle all over again, with a few unusual refinements. Neither BUCKLEY nor U-66 could bring their guns to bear. But the Nazis in this instance showed more pugnacity than the U-405 crew. Scrambling out of the hatches and mounting the conning tower, they let fly with a fusillade of small-arms and rifle fire. For a moment those on BUCKLEY's bow and bridge were forced to take cover. And then the destroyermen were astounded to see the submariners clambering up the DE's bow, coming hand over fist in a squalling assault to board.

"STAND BY TO REPEL BOARDERS!"

Above the tumult and shouting, the crackle of pistol fire, the din and clang, that command seemed to linger in the gunsmoke as an echo from the past.

A man on BUCKLEY's bow saw a Teutonic face in the smoke, and struck it with a knotty fist. The Nazi foemen kept coming. The infuriated destroyermen hurled empty shell-cases, coffee mugs, spitkits, anything and everything that could serve as missiles. Rifles and hand grenades reached the defenders up forward just as the DE broke away and slid clear of the submarine's hull. A splash and a roll, and BUCKLEY and U-66 were grappling beam to beam, frigate-fashion.

A grenade curved like a baseball from the DE's bow and exploded in a submarine deck-hatch. The U-boat veered to port, then swung hard right to ram the destroyer-escort. Jarred by a glancing blow, BUCKLEY swayed and veered away, then swung back toward the submarine. Another pitched grenade hurtled from the DE's deck and curved into the enemy's conning tower hatch. A savage explosion, a fiery glare, and a gush of smoke—and the U-boat went sloughing down under the sea.

Abel followed up with the usual A/S maneuvers. BUCKLEY was a little prankish about answering her helm, for her bow below the waterline was bent a bit to port, in the shape of a plowshare. The U-66, too, must have been cranky about answering her helm—unless the steersman in her control room was deliberately following a course to Valhalla. The silence in her wake was the hush of extinction. The sea swept away the watery swirl where she had plunged, and she was erased.

Damaged, but far from disabled, BUCKLEY was detached from the BLOCK ISLAND group at midnight on the 7th, and directed to proceed independently to New York *via* Bermuda. She carried with her a unique distinction. She was the first U.S. naval vessel in modern history obliged to repel boarders.

ELMORE *and* AHRENS *Kill* U-549 (BLOCK ISLAND's *Last Battle*)

On May 23 the BLOCK ISLAND group, reinforced by destroyer-escort ROBERT I. PAINE (Lieutenant Commander D. Cochran, USNR) was out again. With Captain F. M. Hughes on her bridge, BLOCK ISLAND led her team straight to the troubled Canary area—the vicinity of Monaco Deep, where the bottom lies at 3,441 fathoms—and where U-boats were known to be foregathering.

For four days the cruising task group conducted routine search operations. Then, shortly after midnight on May 28, one of BLOCK ISLAND's Grummans made a radar contact which the pilot interpreted as a surfaced sub. The CVE-DE team raced to the spot, and hold-down tactics were begun.

Battle exploded in the evening of May 29 with the suddenness of chain lightning. The gloaming had thickened into darkness, the hunter-killers were on the alert, but the U-boat lying in ambush was not spotted until a moment too late. Unseen, the submarine upped a furtive periscope, and opened fire. Time: 2015. Two torpedoes struck BLOCK ISLAND, their explosions melting into a single thunderclap and a volcanic blast of orange flame.

Destroyer escort ELMORE spotted the enemy's periscope at 2022, and started a full-gun dash for the sub. One minute later a third torpedo struck BLOCK ISLAND. Within the following sixty seconds, ELMORE let go a depth-charge barrage, a full pattern that tossed up foaming haystacks of sea, but failed to destroy the enemy beneath. Now AHRENS came running in. And the PAINE. About 3,000 yards from BLOCK ISLAND, the destroyer-escort BARR headed in on the attack. At 2033 BARR was struck in the stern by a torpedo.

All this in less than 20 flying minutes—an escort-carrier mortally stricken and a DE torpedoed and disabled. BARR would remain afloat, but "FIGHTING BLOCK ISLAND" was going under. About 40 minutes after she was struck, the escort-carrier sank, a smoking mass of buckled steel and wreckage. But AHRENS saved 674 survivors, and PAINE rescued 277.

Meantime the destroyer-escort ELMORE was battling it out with the enemy. At 2038 she dodged a torpedo, and at 2110 she picked up a sound contact previously made by AHRENS. At 2113 ELMORE's captain, Lieutenant Commander G. L. Conkey, ordered a hedgehog salvo. He followed through with another. And another. Thrashing the water into a miniature storm, the hedgehog barrage scored a hit. The sea tumbled and boomed from the U-boat explosions. Four minutes later the destroyermen heard the crackly, tearing noises and prolonged rumble that mean a submarine is breaking up like a crushed bushel basket.

The battle was over—a murderous action for the record. BLOCK ISLAND sunk—BARR disabled so that she had to be towed to Casablanca.

But the "FIGHTING BLOCK ISLAND" did not go down alone. With her in Monaco Deep went her attacker, sunk by ELMORE—the U-549.

FRANCIS M. ROBINSON *Kills* RO-501 *(Thereby Downing a U-Boat)*

German Vice Admiral Paul H. Weneker arranged a deal in Tokyo. Weneker was in charge of blockade-running by submarines between Japan and Germany. A number of U-boats reached the Java Sea and Singapore late in the war, and several made Japan. One or two Japanese submarines managed to run from Japan to Germany for training.

However, one Axis sub failed to run this global blockade. Instead, she ran into destroyer-escort FRANCIS M. ROBINSON.

The DE was a screening unit for BOGUE in Task Group 22.2, the hunter-killers who had relieved the BLOCK ISLAND team in the Cape Verdes area where BUCKLEY had won her memorable battle. Not to be outdone by their predecessors, on the very day they took over from the BLOCK ISLANDERS the BOGUE team stirred up a submarine.

The date was May 13. The play fell to the FRANCIS M. ROBINSON.

The seascape was painted with sunset (time: 1900) when

ROBINSON made sound contact at 825 yards. In a flash the hedgehogs fired. As the scattered projectiles splashed the water, a salvo of depth charges went lobbing overside—Mark 8 magnetics set to blow the moment they were "influenced."

Seven seconds after the projectiles were fired, two distinct explosions indicated a couple of hedgehog hits. Then came the deep-throated thundering of three depth-charge explosions, booming with a rumpus of upthrown water. Two or three minutes after the last depth charge explosion there was a muffled roar that sounded like a bursting pressure hull. This was followed by a deep-sea blast that must have killed fish a quarter of a league away.

The destroyermen presumed they had polished off a U-boat. As indeed they had—the U-1224. It was not until after the war that they learned that the selfsame U-boat was also the RO-501.

Records in Doenitz's German Navy Headquarters and the testimony of Admiral Weneker in Tokyo explained the paradox. The U-1224 had been turned over to a Japanese crew in Germany, renamed the RO-501, and entered into the service of the Emperor. So it was that destroyer-escort FRANCIS M. ROBINSON, operating in the Atlantic, sank a Japanese submarine that was a German U-boat.

CHATELAIN, JENKS, PILLSBURY, *and Aircraft Capture* U-505 *("Away Boarders!")*

Ever since the capture of the much decorated Kapitan Henke, the idea had intrigued "Dan" Gallery. If you could bag a U-boat skipper caparisoned with medals, why not an entire U-boat? And at this stage of the war, when Doenitz was equipping his submarines with all manner of highly secret gadgets, a specimen U-boat would provide the United States Tenth Fleet with a wealth of valuable information.

The captain of the escort-carrier GUADALCANAL had little difficulty in justifying an enterprise to capture a U-boat. When the GUADALCANAL hunter-killers (Task Group 22.3) sailed from Norfolk late in May '44, the group had special permission to "bring one back alive."

Task Group 22.3 contained the following units:

CVE GUADALCANAL	Capt. D. V. Gallery
DE PILLSBURY	Lt. Comdr. G. W. Casselman, USNR
DE FLAHERTY	Lt. Comdr. M. Johnston, Jr.
DE POPE	Lt. Comdr. E. H. Headland
DE JENKS	Lt. Comdr. J. F. Way
DE CHATELAIN	Lt. Comdr. D. S. Knox, USNR

*The five DE's were under division
leadership of Comdr. F. S. Hall*

All hands were instructed on the "Frank Buck" objective of the enterprise, and it loaned an exciting flavor to a hunt which might otherwise have followed tedious routines.

On June 4 the hunters were about 100 miles off the African coast, on the parallel that marks the boundary of Rio de Oro and French Mauretania.

The date—two days before the Normandy landings—was propitious for this high enterprise. Day broke with a pleasant sky; the sea was rumpled and touched here and there with lazy whitecaps. At 1110 in the morning the destroyer-escort CHATELAIN made the first sound contact that touched off the action.

The DE's had been steaming ahead and off both bows of the escort-carrier. At the middle of the right flank, CHATELAIN was about a mile from the GUADALCANAL when she picked up the contact. Evidently the submarine was trying to slip through the screen for a headlong torpedo strike at the CVE. CHATELAIN'S captain, Lieutenant Commander Knox got off the report: AM STARTING TO ATTACK.

Upon receiving CHATELAIN'S report, Captain Gallery launched GUADALCANAL'S planes as fast as they could take off. Skimming over the seascape in a Wildcat, Ensign J. W. Cadle, USNR, sighted the sub running under the surface. A moment later a brother Wildcat pilot, Lieutenant W. W. Roberts, USNR, glimpsed the shadowy U-boat. Splashing the sea with machine-gun fire, the two pilots pointed out the quarry to CHATELAIN and to DE's JENKS and PILLSBURY rushing to the spot.

The submarine glided in a roundabout turn to present its stern tubes toward the flat-top. This scorpion-like maneuver, the prelude for a stern torpedo shot, cost the submarine the initiative. Following directions given by the aircraft, and tracking by sound, CHATELAIN dashed to an intercepting position and lambasted the U-boat with a full pattern of shallow-set depth charges. The submarine immediately broached within 800 yards of ready CHATELAIN. This was fast action. From salvo to barrage, it had taken the DE less than 13 minutes to gouge the subbmarine out.

Fast as was that piece of work, the ensuing action was even faster. As the U-boat floundered to the surface, the CHATELAIN gunners opened fire with a small caliber fusillade hot enough to make Jerry keep his head down, but not so withering as to wreck the submarine. Scrambling up out of the hatches, the U-boaters were able to snap back with a few wild shots. But when PILLSBURY and JENKS joined the shooting match with long-range (but light) gunnery, the Nazis promptly threw up the sponge. With bullets whistling across the slender decks and ricochetting off the conning tower, the submariners went overside like bullfrogs. Division Commander Hall in PILLS-BURY had opportunity to count the jumpers and ascertain the fact that the U-boaters had summarily abandoned. Amazingly enough the U-boats screws were still churning, and the expected thunder of demolition charges failed to come.

Yet the Nazis might have left the submarine fused and set to blow up like a mammoth time-bomb. Or one or two of the crew might have remained below to open flood valves and go down with the U-boat. Wallowing on the surface, the sub was a thing of mystery and menace not to be taken lightly. There were some quickened pulses among the destroyermen when Commander Hall gave the "Go get 'er" order.

To CHATELAIN and JENKS: PICK UP SURVIVORS.

To PILLSBURY: WE ARE GOING TO BOARD. AWAY BOARDING PARTIES. LOWER AWAY WHALEBOATS.

Here was another drama reminiscent of old Navy days— a small boat hauling away to come alongside the prize and put a boarding party on the enemy's deck. Not an easy task under the immediate circumstances. The abandoned U-boat was making about 7 knots, and traveling in a circle. The PILLS-BURY men had a time of it trying to overhaul and catch the vagrant craft. When the DE closed in and made an effort to get lines aboard, the sub swung alongside and slashed PILLS-BURY's hull with sharp bow planes. The destroyermen might have been trying to lasso a giant shark.

But at length the boarding party managed to overhaul, and the party's leader, Lieutenant (jg) A. L. David, USNR, accompanied by S. E. Wdowiak, Radioman Second, and A. W. Knispel, Torpedoman Third, clambered up the slippery hull. They were met on deck by a dead man who watched them with a sightless stare.

"All right, boys. Let's go."

Down through the open conning tower hatch. Down to the evacuated control room. The murky atmosphere redolent of oil, grease, and body smell; the periscope shaft and complex instrument panels; the passageways that were a jungle of water and air lines, pipes, cables—to Lieutenant David, an old submariner, at least these things were familiar. He found the right controls, and managed to stop the Diesel engines. With the engines stopped, the submarine went logy; evidently the 7-knot pace was all that had kept her from sinking by the stern. Another lurch and she might head for the bottom. The boarders rushed to the seacocks and shut out the flood just in time.

And so it was done. The U-boat neither sank nor exploded.

GUADALCANAL sent a boarding party to take over the sub; a tow line was passed to the CVE; Captain Gallery boarded the prize to examine her interior and adjust her jammed steering mechanism. Minor repairs were managed then and there; the submarine was battened down and prepared for a journey.

There remained for the victors the long voyage home, a 2,500-mile haul to Bermuda, with U-505 trailing meekly on the end of a tow line. Tenth Fleet experts at Bermuda were waiting in a high pitch of excitement and curiosity.

While U-boat skipper *Oberleutnant zur See* Harald Lange and his crew were interrogated by Intelligence officers, the U-505 was gone over by trained examiners. The U-505 divulged some of Doenitz's most cherished secrets. Needless to say, this inside knowledge greatly enhanced the Navy's A/S effort.

For this invaluable contribution to that effort Captain Gallery's CVE-DE group was awarded the Presidential Unit Citation.

FROST, INCH, HUSE, *and Aircraft Down* U-490

Concentrating on the wolfpacks was an A/S team led by the escort-carrier CROATAN. It included the destroyer-escorts FROST (Lieutenant Commander J. H. McWhorter, USNR), INCH (Lieutenant Commander D. A. Tufts, USNR), and HUSE (Lieutenant J. H. Batcheller, Jr.).

On June 10 the group received word that a U-boat was in the Azores vicinity. "Huff-Duff" fixes were obtained at 1231 that afternoon and at 2236 in the evening. Hot on the trail went the CROATAN team.

FROST picked up the first sound contact on the morning of the 11th. Thereafter sonar contact was made intermittently until 2000 that evening. Synchronizing their efforts, FROST, HUSE, and INCH made numerous runs in an effort to blast out the submarine. All day they kept the ashcans crashing, trying to catch the U-boat with a neat "tic-tac-toe" of patterns. They blew up tons of salt water, but could find nothing to indicate a blown-up submarine.

Evidently the sub had found a foxhole, and was lying low. With midnight approaching, the DE hunter-killers decided to try a new game. The play called for a ruse—a simulated retirement.

FROST, INCH, and HUSE had hardly withdrawn to a distant point when the U-boat's "pip" was registered by FROST's radar. Lieutenant Commander McWhorter sent the DE steaming for the target. As the range closed, he fired starshells, and at 3,000 yards FROST had the submarine silhouetted in the glare of her searchlight. The DE opened fire with all batteries.

INCH, racing up, followed suit. Wildly zigzagging, the U-boat ran for it. By stepping up speed and changing course, the DE's remained on target and held range to about 1,600 yards. At 1,200 yards, the target vanished from the radar scope.

A few minutes later, the racing destroyer-escorts were at the spot where the U-boat had disappeared. The water seemed to be alive with screaming men. A searchlight sweep revealed floundering swimmers and yellow rubber rafts. No sign of the submarine. But as the destroyermen maneuvered to pick up survivors, a stupendous deep sea explosion was heard. The blast was followed by the crunching sound of buckling metal and disintegrating machinery. Far under the surface, sea pressure was tearing the U-boat to fragments. The hour was 2210 in the evening of June 11.

The submarine thus demolished was the U-490. She had been in commission no more than six months. Loaded with Diesel oil and provisions, she had arrived at the appointed rendezvous, only to make a rendezvous with death. In an effort to elude the continuous depth-charging, her skipper had taken her down to a depth below 700 feet. At this whale-hole level she had escaped the ashcans. But after the deep dive for cover, and after 17 hours' submergence under fire, both her oxygen and the nerve of her crew had reached the point of exhaustion. It was this critical state of affairs that caused the U-boaters to surface as soon as they thought the hunter-killers had left the vicinity.

It might be said that the DE men put a new twist on an old axiom. "Whatever goes down must come up." For U-490 the rise was fatal.

INCH *and* FROST *Kill* U-154

In July the CROATAN hunter-killer group was again in action, beating the oceanic bushes to the east of the Azores. Captain J. P. W. Vest was on CROATAN's bridge; Commander F. D. Giambattista was in charge of the DE's; FROST (Lieutenant Commander J. H. McWhorter, USNR) and INCH (Lieutenant Commander D. A. Tufts, USNR) were there on the team.

At 0911—a typical day—INCH made sound contact with a submarine. At 0914 FROST hustled forward to assist. At 0916 INCH's lookouts sighted two torpedoes coming, and the DE veered with neatness and dispatch to let the "fish" race by. At 0917 INCH let fly with hedgehogs.

Meantime FROST made several sonar contacts; lost them; came back on the hunt. At 1026 INCH attacked with a depth-charge barrage. FROST followed through with more depth charges at 1039. The team was working like a precision machine, and the submarine was caught. At 1050 the DE's were shaken by a stunning underseas explosion. That was it!

Half an hour later the two destroyer-escorts sighted a great mess of oil and floating debris. Combing through this rummage, they picked up life-jackets, coats, shattered wood, cork, and other bits of wreckage. Realistic American hunter-killer commanders were reluctant to credit a kill unless anatomical remains were in evidence. In this particular case there was no lack of that sort of evidence.

Post-war records identified the victim of INCH and FROST as the U-154. The gang busters had scored again.

BAKER *and* THOMAS *Sink* U-233

Indicative of the jeopardy risked by a U-boat when it ventured to trespass in American waters in the summer of 1944 was the end which overtook U-233.

This Nazi submarine was a minelayer, newly equipped with some of the latest undersea novelties. Across the North Atlantic she came *Schnorkeling* to sow her lethal fields in the shipping lanes of the Eastern Sea Frontier. As she sowed, so would she reap.

For all her new apparatus and *Schnorkel* gear U-233 was detected in the Gulf Stream off Cape Sable. The detectors were units of the CARD hunter-killer group (Task Group 22.10) under Captain R. C. Young. This group included the destroyer-escorts BAKER (Lieutenant Commander N. C. Hoffman, USNR) and THOMAS (Lieutenant Commander D. M. Kellogg, USNR).

Steaming about 100 miles south of Sable Island, BAKER made sound contact at 1907 in the afternoon of July 5. The DE dropped her first depth-charge pattern at 1913, and dropped a second at 1920. Caught in the thundering barrage, the U-boat pitched and rolled down under. Then at 1931 the submarine came up like a snorting hippopotamus.

As the U-boat's bow broke water in a foaming broach, BAKER'S gunners let go with all batteries, flaying the target with a scorching fusillade. Dashing forward, BAKER passed ahead of the sub, and as she did so, the destroyermen let fly with K-guns. This U-boat was tough. As she kept on coming, BAKER launched a full pattern of 13 depth charges squarely in the submarine's path. The blast hurled up a hill of water that fell down with the roar of an earthquake. The submarine, half swamped but still under way, came ploughing through this avalanche.

However, the U-boaters were not quite so obdurate as the U-boat. As the conning tower pitched and rolled, a number of submariners dived overside and others were seen struggling to get out of the hatches. Destroyer-escort THOMAS was now bearing down, peppering U-233 with shells and bullets. Damaged, punctured, bleeding oil, the undersea minelayer tried to drag herself out of range. But she was boxed. Driving his DE forward at top speed, Lieutenant Commander Kellogg set a collision course, and THOMAS rammed the sub, slicing into the pressure hull about 20 feet abaft the conning tower. A rending of metal, a bedlam of swirling sea and screaming men—and the U-boat plunged for the bottom.

The destroyermen rescued 30 half-drowned, wholly wretched Germans. Thirty-nine of the submarine's crew went down to those depths which lie beyond the reach of rescue.

The U-boaters were learning that the way of the transgressor (especially in the Western Atlantic) remained hard.

Loss of USS FISKE

The second destroyer-escort lost in the Battle of the Atlantic, the USS FISKE (Lieutenant J. A. Comly, USNR) was operating in the summer of 1944 as a unit in Task Group 22.6, a hunter-killer team led by the escort-carrier WAKE ISLAND.

On the morning of August 2, the group was combing a North Atlantic area about midway between Newfoundland and the British Isles. *Schnorkel* subs had been reported on this old battleground, and the WAKE ISLANDERS (group included five DE's) were on the hunt. At 1157 the destroyer-escort FISKE, accompanied by her companion DE DOUGLAS L. HOWARD, peeled off to investigate a contact.

Racing across a seascape burnished with noon, the two DE's reached the vicinity of lat. 47-11 N., long. 33-29 W. With the chronometers at 1223, the contact was identified as a submarine. At 1235, sonar range 1,075 yards, FISKE was suddenly stunned by a tremendous underwater explosion. The blast shattered her hull amidships, left her listing and disabled. No torpedo had been heard by the sonarmen, the lookouts had seen no telltale wake. It is possible that FISKE was hit by a "wakeless" electric, a model that could sometimes strike like a bolt from the blue.

At 1240 the disabled DE was convulsed by an internal explosion somewhere forward. Through a haze of steam and smoke the men below decks groped their way topside. Lieutenant Comly gave the order to abandon, for the vessel's back was broken, her forward engine-room flooding. Although many of the crew were badly injured, the men went overside in good order. Close at hand, the destroyer-escort FARQUHAR moved in to pick up survivors.

In the heaving sea FISKE broke in two. The flooded bow

section sank. With screws awash, the stern section remained afloat until sunk by gunfire from the HOWARD later in the afternoon.

FISKE suffered painful losses: 33 dead, and 52 injured among the 183 survivors. By 1620 all survivors were recovered by FARQUHAR, and the injured were in the good hands of doctors and Pharmacist's Mates.

A/S Assessment

By the end of summer, 1944, the U-boat effort was practically squelched.

Admiral Doenitz would make a final desperate try with the long-range, streamlined Type XXI's and improved *Schnorkels*. The try was a submarine swan song.

The *Rudeltaktik* was done for. Sunk by search radar and hunter-killer teams composed of CVE's, DD's, and DE's.

PART FIVE

Destroyers to Europe

☆ ☆ ☆

*The trident of Neptune
is the sceptre of the world.*
JOHN ADAMS

Chapter 25

Destroyers to Sicily

(DD Support of "Operation Husky")

☆ ☆ ☆

Destination Sicily

After the successful landings in North Africa, Allied strategists cast an eye on Italy, the midriff of what Churchill called the "soft underbelly of Europe." A smash at Italy had a good chance of knocking the Fascists out of the war; also a large German army might be trapped on the Italian boot. Seizure of Italy would place the Allies at the back door of occupied France. And it would give them control of the Mediterranean Sea—the vital passage to Suez.

But Sicily, the stumbling block at the toe of the Italian boot, had first to be taken care of. Capture of this mountainous island would remove a barrier lying athwart the sea road from North Africa to Italy, and at the same time it would give the Allies a strategic base on Italy's southwest flank. Sicily, then, became item No. 1 on the 1943 invasion agenda.

The Germans in North Africa had yet to be contended with. Cornered in northeast Tunisia, the Nazi-Fascist African Army finally surrendered on May 11.

During May and June the Allies rushed preparations for the invasion of Sicily. Tunisia provided them with front-line ports for the staging and maintenance of a drive across the narrow waist of the Mediterranean. From Algerian and Moroccan bases came parades and processions of troop and supply convoys that had steamed down from the British Isles or made the Atlantic passage from America. All this war-shipping meant convoy duty for destroyers; screening duty for destroyers; an escort program, and an A/S campaign, and anti-aircraft work that grew hotter and heavier as the calendar approached the target date.

The escort of Allied invasion convoys through the Straits of Gibraltar to points east in the Mediterranean was no easy task.

Mussolini had striven to turn the great sea into an Axis lake. Aided by Nazi might and the connivance of Franco Spain, this project had almost been realized. In the spring of 1943 U-boats roamed the waters below Gibraltar; German torpedo-planes flew from nests on the Azure Coast, Sicily, and the Italian boot; and *Il Duce's* naval forces struck when and where they could.

The Italian Navy was represented, even by the Nazis, as a "fleet-in-being," remarked for its menace value rather than its fighting qualities. Whether this Nazi scorn for Italy's surface fleet was warranted or not, such derision for the Italian submarine service would not have been justifiable. Italian subs undoubtedly torpedoed a fairly sizable tonnage of Allied shipping, and they joined the U-boats in the Axis effort to hold the Mediterranean.

American destroyers fought Italian submarines during the build-up for the Sicilian invasion. So far as is known, the Fascist submariners did not sink any American ships during this period. But American destroyermen operating off the coast of Algeria demolished an Italian submarine.

NIELDS *Kills Submarine* GORGO

Early in the afternoon of May 21, 1943, seven destroyers of Captain T. L. Wattles' DesRon 16 steamed out of Mers-el-Kebir, Algeria, and headed for patrol sectors off Oran Harbor. A member of this busy squadron, destroyer NIELDS (Lieutenant Commander A. R. Heckey) was assigned the easternmost station of the patrol area.

NIELDS reached her station at 1515. The patrol was so much routine until 1650, at which time Heckey's destroyer received a "sub sighted" signal from a British observation plane. The aircraft led NIELDS to the point where the submarine was spotted, and at 1710 the plane dropped a depth charge. Then flares were dropped by this and a second plane. Six minutes later the destroyer made a sound contact with the target at 400 yards.

At 1718 NIELDS attacked, spreading a pattern of nine depth charges. Sound contact was again established at 1723, and Heckey and company treated the target to another 9-charge pattern at 1724. Maneuvering for a third attack, the destroyermen fired two forward K-guns on sound contact at 1731. They followed through with three portside K-guns at 1741, firing at a contact that was dim and whispery. The barrage thunder ebbed off into silence—the quietude of a deep-sea grave.

Circling the area, NIELDS continued the sonar search until 0700 of the following morning, when she moved to take up station off Oran to cover the sortie of a convoy. By that hour the submarine's destruction was confirmed by splintered deck planking and oil streaking the sea's surface over a three-mile expanse—and by the Italian records, after the war.

The records identified the victim as the Italian submarine GORGO. She was one of the two Fascist subs sunk by United States ships during the war. The second sinking would come during the Sicilian invasion. That, too, was the work of an American destroyer.

"Operation Husky"

By July over 3,200 Allied ships, craft, and boats, 4,000 air craft, and 250,000 troops were assembled in staging areas for the Sicilian invasion. The operation, appropriately titled "Husky," called for a simultaneous attack on Sicily by British and American task forces. The American Western Task Force would put General Patton's American army ashore on the southwestern coast of the island. The British Eastern Task Force would land an army division on Sicily's east coast. D-Day was set for July 10, 1943.

Vice Admiral Hewitt's United States task force—the naval complement of the Western Task Force—was composed of three separate attack forces which were to land American invasion troops on beachheads at Licata, Gela, and Scoglitti. These attack forces were given the code names "Joss," "Dime," and "Cent."

Upon departing from Tunis on July 8, the Allied armada headed southward from Cape Bon on a deceptive course calculated to baffle enemy observers. In the van was the British Eastern Task Force. To the rear were American attack forces "Cent," "Joss," and "Dime." The great fleet's formation was more than a mile wide and 60 miles long.

The following morning radio listeners intercepted a Nazi broadcast concerning the invasion fleet. So the enemy was alerted. Even so, he could not be certain of the fleet's destination.

As the ships steamed toward the objective, they bucked high winds and foam-bearded seas. Nasty weather could not delay "Operation Husky," however. Already Allied saboteurs had parachuted into Sicily, Allied planes were bombing Sicilian and mainland-Italian airfields, paratroopers were taking off for a drop behind enemy lines.

By 0000 D-Day the American attack forces were maneuvering into position off Licata, Gela, and Scoglitti. H-Hour was set for 0245. Foul weather delayed the assault, but by dawn of July 10 the "Joss," "Dime," and "Cent" troops were all fighting their way across Sicilian beachheads, and the Allied fist had landed on Europe's "soft underbelly."

But there was nothing soft about Sicily.

"Husky was a rugged deal," a destroyerman said afterward. "We went in through a gale; we shot it out with shore batteries; we traded punches with the *Luftwaffe*. We had plenty to do. We even got called on to do business with some enemy tanks. The cans worked their heads off at Sicily."

"Joss" at Licata

The "Joss" Attack Force (TF 86) was led by Rear Admiral R. L. Conolly, an officer who had climbed to the top on destroyer ladders. The force contained the amphibious force flagship BISCAYNE, cruisers BROOKLYN and BIRMINGHAM, two ocean-going LSI's (Landing Ships, Infantry), over 200 ocean-going landing craft of other types, eight mine vessels, 33 patrol craft, several auxiliaries, and the following DD's of Destroyer Squadron 13:

BUCK	*Lt. Comdr. M. J. Klein*
	Flying the pennant of
	Comdr. E. R. Durgin, COMDESRON 13
WOOLSEY	*Lt. Comdr. H. R. Wier*
LUDLOW	*Lt. Comdr. L. W. Creighton*
EDISON	*Lt. Comdr. H. A. Pearce*
BRISTOL	*Comdr. J. A. Glick*
WILKES	*Lt. Comdr. F. Wolsieffer*
	Flying the pennant of
	Comdr. V. Huber, COMDESDIV 26
NICHOLSON	*Comdr. L. M. Markham, Jr.*
SWANSON	*Lt. Comdr. E. L. Robertson, Jr.*
ROE	*Lt. Comdr. R. L. Nolan, Jr.*

Mission of the "Joss" Attack Force was to place assault troops ashore on beaches near Licata, and capture and secure that port with its local airfield. About 0200 on D-Day morning the landing craft started in through darkness that was bituminous-black and pitching, but all landings were made successfully on the proper beaches according to the planned time-interval schedule.

The enemy in the "Joss" area opened up about 0400, and the American fire-support ships let go at coastal targets. At dawn the sea and shore in Licata's vicinity were roaring. There was trouble at Red Beach where enemy guns were lashing at the boat waves going in. Two destroyers were ordered close inshore to screen the boat lanes with smoke.

Excerpt from Admiral Conolly's Battle Report:

At 0725 WOOLSEY and NICHOLSON commenced laying smoke screen on Red Beach as directed. At 0728 Beachmaster Red Beach reported fire support excellent, that no enemy fire had landed on the beach for fifteen minutes. Situation was clearing on Red Beach. Fire support and smoke screen laid by destroyers was very effective in supporting and screening the landing of the LCT's.

The most notable use of smoke during the operation was made in the Joss Area during the early hours of daylight on D-Day. The destroyer WOOLSEY placed a very effective smoke screen on the left flank of one of the beaches using 5"-38 white phosphorous projectiles, thus hiding the beach and craft from shore batteries fiiring from Licata.

As the morning advanced, DesRon 13 destroyers on bombardment detail added their 5-inch 38 salvos to the cruiser barrage hammering the Licata batteries. One after another the enemy guns were silenced. Admiral Conolly noted that the fire-support groups performed their missions most efficiently and the gunnery was excellent.

Equally efficient was the anti-aircraft defense put up by destroyer and other warship gunners when Axis aircraft struck at the "Joss" force.

By 1605 in the afternoon of D-Day the Sicilian port of Licata was in American hands. Naval casualties were unexpectedly light: a few landing craft damaged; 23 sailors lost; 118 wounded.

"Cent" at Scoglitti

The "Cent" Attack Force (TF 85) was commanded by Rear Admiral A. G. Kirk, USN. It was the largest of the three American attack forces in "Operation Husky." "Cent" contained the amphibious force flagship ANCON, U.S. cruiser PHILADELPHIA and British monitor ABERCROMBIE, 18 transports (APA's and AKA's), 28 ocean-going landing craft of various types, 16 mine vessels, four patrol craft, several auxiliaries, and 19 destroyers.

Mission of the "Cent" Attack Force was to put assault troops ashore on beaches near Scoglitti, to secure the beachhead area, and to capture the near-by airfields of Comiso and Biscari.

A good picture of destroyer work in "Operation Husky" is limned in the following sketch by Captain T. L. Wattles, briefly recording the activity of Squadron 15 and 16 before, during, and immediately after the "Cent" attack.

On 5 July DesRons 15 and 16 sortied from Mers el Kebir with ships of NCF-1 (TF 85). At 2215, 9 July, the transports of TF 85 divided into two Assault Units, screened by DesRons 15 and 16, and approached the landing beaches off Scoglitti. At 2255 heavy AA fire was noticed ashore.

At 2330 DD's shifted from screening to approach stations. Friendly planes passed overhead. Fires burned along the beach as a result of earlier bombing attacks. Flares and AA fire were sighted, probably directed at our transport and bombing planes. Many tracers were observed, red, green, white, and blue, producing a 4th of July fireworks effect. A flight of our own bombers passed overhead at a low altitude, probably less than 600 feet, heading south. These planes turned on their running lights, and fortunately all ships withheld their fire—they were so close we could have hit them with spuds. Three large AA searchlights on the beach swept to seaward periodically, but apparently the beams extended beyond the vision of the operators because no action was taken by the shore batteries against the assembled ships. H-Hour was delayed one hour.

At 0330, 10 July, boat waves left the transports. H-Hour was at 0345 at which time fire-support ships commenced shore bombardment according to plan. The searchlights and an air beacon were knocked out. No naval opposition materialized. DesRon 15 performed mostly fire-support duties while DesRon 16 screened the transport area; some ships of the latter—LAUB, MACKENZIE, and CHAMPLIN—relieved DesRon 15 DD's when their ammunition supply ran low. Enemy aircraft dropped bombs on the Cent transport area at various times and dogfighting took place overhead; sneak bombing attacks were made on the beaches. The enemy air effort, however, was too weak to disrupt proceedings. . . . At about 1220, 13 July, PARKER, COWIE, and MACKENZIE conducted A/S operations against a reported sub about eight miles from Cape Scalambri Light with no apparent results. At 1800 Convoy CNF-3, consisting of remaining transports, escorted by remaining DD's, left the area for Oran.

During the amphibious assault on the Scoglitti beachheads, the "Cent" fire-support ships were notably successful in knocking out enemy shore batteries. The destroyer and cruiser barrages reached several miles inland to blast enemy battery emplacements.

Scoglitti fell at 1415, D-Day afternoon. As at Licata, naval casualties were unexpectedly light: 12 men lost; 164 wounded. Most of the injuries were caused by shell and bomb fragments. It would seem that expert seamanship and marksmanship paid off.

"Dime" at Gela

Commander of the "Dime" Attack Force (TF 81) was Rear

Admiral J. L. Hall, Jr., USN. This attack force consisted of eight transports (APA's and AKA's) including Admiral Hewitt's flagship MONROVIA, force flagship SAMUEL CHASE, two ocean-going LSI's, cruisers BOISE and SAVANNAH, 35 ocean-going landing craft of various types, eight mine vessels, ten patrol craft, several auxiliaries, and the following destroyers:

NELSON	*Lt. Comdr. M. M. Riker*
	Flying the pennant of
	Capt. D. L. Madeira, COMDESRON 17
MURPHY	*Lt. Comdr. L. W. Bailey*
GLENNON	*Comdr. F. C. Camp*
JEFFERS	*Lt. Comdr. W. T. McGarry*
MADDOX	*Lt. Comdr. E. S. Sarsfield*
BUTLER	*Lt. Comdr. M. D. Matthews*
GHERARDI	*Lt. Comdr. J. W. Schmidt*
	Flying the pennant of
	Comdr. J. B. Rooney, COMDESDIV 34
HERNDON	*Lt. Comdr. G. A. Moore*
SHUBRICK	*Lt. Comdr. L. A. Bryan*
McLANAHAN	*Lt. Comdr. H. R. Hummer, Jr.*
	Relief flagship for Vice Admiral Hewitt
	Operating in "Dime" area.
ORDRONAUX	*Lt. Comdr. R. Brodie, Jr.*
	Operating with "Dime" area screen

Mission of the "Dime" Attack Force was to land assault troops on beachheads near Gela, expand the captured area and seize the near-by airfield at Ponte Olivo. Gela, "center beach" of the Western Task Force assault sector, was flanked on the left by the "Joss" area and on the right by the "Cent" area.

The first assault waves struck the Gela beaches about 0245 on D-Day morning. Plunging in through the breakers, the shock troops encountered negligible opposition. But the follow-up waves were raked by furious shellfire.

As soon as troops were ashore, destroyers SHUBRICK and JEFFERS opened counterfire on the offending batteries. Hurling accurately-aimed salvos, they blasted the shore guns and blew out searchlights. Cruisers SAVANNAH and BOISE began harassing fire on designated targets at 0400. The cruisers catapulted spotting planes at dawn (around 0430), and about the same time all fire-support ships plugged into communication with shore fire-control parties. An earthquaking naval barrage smote the beaches of Gela.

As darkness waned, Axis aircraft joined the battle. Flying

out of the Acate River valley on the eastern border of the "Dime" area, they winged along the coast, bombing and strafing ships, landing craft, and beaches. One of these dive-bombers, flitting over the "Dime" transport area, loosed fateful lightning on an American destroyer.

Loss of USS MADDOX

Death came for the destroyer MADDOX with thunderbolt suddenness at 0458 in the morning of July 10, 1943. One minute before the fatal moment she was serving in a screen for American vessels off Gela. Two minutes after death struck she was deep under the sea.

Her captain, Lieutenant Commander E. S. Sarsfield, and those at battle stations topside heard the plane. A penetrating drone overhead, faint, loudening. The aircraft was unseen.

Then a bomb came hurtling down; there was a deafening crash of a near miss which showered the ship with water and flying iron. An instant later she was struck by one or two bombs on the fantail. In a gust of flame, smoke, and debris the destroyer's stern was blown open.

Evidently the ship's watertight integrity was immediately dissolved. Her after compartments were inundated before many of the men below decks could escape. She went down in less than two minutes, sinking in a whirlpool of smoke, fire, and steam.

Few warships stricken in action went under with such instantaneous finality. A nearby tug, racing in to the rescue, could find but 74 survivors. Lost with the detroyer were 202 men and eight officers, including Lieutenant Commander Sarsfield, who went down with his ship.

Destroyers Versus German Tanks

In the American sector of southwest Sicily the Germans had available some 60 tanks. Around 0830 of D-Day morning about 30 of these crawling armored monsters—members of the famous Hermann Göering Panzer Division—were spotted on the upland roads above Gela, lumbering down from the foothills, eager to gore and chew their way across the "Dime" area beachheads.

Spotting planes flashed the alarm. And "alarm" was the word for it. At that hour the assault forces had not yet landed their anti-tank guns or the heavy artillery to cope with such tanks. Nor did the Army at that date possess weapons which could readily demolish these Hermann Göering models. In the path of this rumbling herd, troops of the American 1st

Division were directly threatened. Something had to be done to stop the enemy tanks, and stop them soon. The call went out for Navy gunfire.

Cruiser BOISE and destroyer JEFFERS took the leading tanks under fire at 0830. The cruiser's salvos ruined at least one tank and perhaps disabled others. However, some of them, scattering, nosed steadily forward until they reached Gela's outskirts, and others debauched across the coastal plain at the mouth of the Acate Valley.

Then destroyer SHUBRICK (Lieutenant Commander L. A. Bryan) hurled shells at a tank column on the Gela-Ponte Olivo road. Other "Dime" destroyers, moving to firing positions some 800 yards off the beach, blazed away at the Herman Göering specimens. Not long after the destroyers opened fire, the tanks turned tail and retired, leaving several burned out hulks behind them.

They were back again the morning after D-Day. To the destroyers BOISE relayed the word from her spotter, and the DD's once more squared off for a tank-shoot.

This time the anti-tank gunnery featured the marksmanship of destroyers LAUB (Commander J. F. Gallaher) and COWIE (Commander C. J. Whiting). On fire-support mission in the joint "Dime-Cent" fire-support area, the two DD's flung pinpoint salvos at the Göerings as they came snorting across the Gela plain.

Scorched by shellfire, the tank group turned this way and that in a desperate effort to find cover. Several tanks were exploded by hits. Others, disabled, sat down on their haunches and burned. Fourteen demolished tanks were counted on the field by the time the enemy retreated and the cruiser-destroyer barrage was over.

LAUB was credited with the destruction of at least four tanks. COWIE was also commended as a big-game hunter. And "Nimrod" honors were divided among the other destroyers in on the shooting.

So Gela, in American hands by D-Day afternoon, remained in American hands in spite of the Nazi tanks. Excerpt from the Action Report of Admiral Hewitt:

> The destruction of this armored force by naval gunfire delivered by U.S. cruisers and destroyers, and the recovery of the situation through naval support, was one of the most noteworthy events of the operations.

Action off Palermo (Damaging of MAYRANT and SHUBRICK)

By the evening of July 12 the Americans had a solid foothold on southwest Sicily, the British "Husky" forces were equally well established on the island's eastern coast, and the emptied transports were starting the return run to North Africa. A wing of Patton's army drove westward along the coast to Marsala. Another wing pushed directly northward into Sicily's mountainous interior. And a third raced all the way across the island to seize the strategic port of Palermo on the north coast. When the troops reached Palermo on July 22 they slammed shut an Axis escape-hatch, and American destroyers were rushed to the port to keep it locked.

Off Palermo in the afternoon of July 25 arrived Task Group 80.2 under command of Captain C. Wellborn, Jr., ComDesRon 8. The task group contained destroyers WAINWRIGHT (Commander R. H. Gibbs); MAYRANT (Commander E. K. Walker); ROWAN (Lieutenant Commander R. S. Ford); and RHIND (Lieutenant Commander O. W. Spahr, Jr.). The group's roster included 12 mine vessels and four patrol craft, the "miners" assigned to the important task of sweeping the approaches to Palermo.

In the morning of July 26 the storm broke. MAYRANT saw it coming at 0931 when her radar picked up aircraft five miles distant. In a few minutes the planes were in view—three Junker 88's.

As the destroyer steamed across the water her gunners opened fire with two ready 5-inch 38's. One of the Junkers broke up into shards. Another flew off at a tangent, dragging a long tail of smoke. The third plane came on.

MAYRANT'S Action Report vividly describes the destroyer-versus-Junker battle that ensued.

Speed was changed to flank speed 25 knots, and the rudder was put over to full right. Before the ship had even begun to swing, a stick of 3 or 4 bombs was dropped on the starboard side, distance about 150 yards, by a plane approaching from astern, which had not been previously sighted. This was immediately followed by a plane attacking from the port quarter, which had also not been previously sighted. This was followed by a stick of one or two bombs dropped approximately 500 yards ahead of the ship by one of the three planes in the initial contact group. At this time it is believed that all guns which were manned were firing on the initial contact on the port bow. However, one of these planes dropped his stick of 4 bombs which straddled the MAYRANT. One bomb landed approximately 5 feet off the port beam at frame 102½. A second bomb landed off the starboard beam at a distance of about 40 yards. At that instant the ship was accelerating and had swung through approximately 50 degrees of her turn. The ship listed heavily to port and nearly all personnel were thrown to the deck or against bulkheads.

In spite of severe damage, MAYRANT remained stubbornly

afloat. Her battle casualties were two men lost, 13 wounded. Among the wounded was a young lieutenant, Franklin D. Roosevelt, Jr. A large segment of the American public remained unaware of the fact that the President's son had been injured while serving as a two-striper in a destroyer off Palermo.

USS SHUBRICK was the second American DD to undergo a severe blasting at Palermo.

During a raid delivered on August 1, enemy bombs set fire to an ammunition ship, blew up a cargo of gasoline drums stored on the wharf, and damaged destroyer MAYRANT under repair at the dock. Another raid hit the port about 0400 in the morning of August 4th. At that date and time the warships of Task Force 88 were anchored in the outer harbor. Among those present was destroyer SHUBRICK (Lieutenant Commander L. A. Bryan).

When the alert was sounded, Bryan got his ship under way to occupy a screening station on the starboard bow of cruiser SAVANNAH as the latter headed for open sea. As related in SHUBRICK'S Action Report, here is the account of her ordeal:

At 0430 a plane was heard diving from the starboard side, and was accordingly taken under fire. Immediately after it passed over, a stick of three bombs landed, one short, one hit, one over. The ship shook violently and it was at once apparent that the hit was a serious one. The bomb, estimated to be either 500 pounds or 1,000 pounds, struck just aft of the torpedo tube.

All light and power was lost immediately. Due to split-plant operations, the flooding of the two engineering spaces and the intense heat of the escaping steam, it was impossible to effect sufficient repairs to use the port engine. The ship was therefore dead in the water, although the bulkheads held water out of the forward fireroom and after engine-room and steam was bottled up in boilers one and two. No further air attack on this ship developed.

When the blockbuster struck, the SHUBRICK'S after fireroom was transformed into a torture chamber. Live steam, invisible and murderous, spurted from broken pipes. Men slipped, slid, and floundered in blindness . . . sea water rushed in with a roar . . . they were trapped, suffocating, drowning.

Chief Water Tender J. W. Daugherty, USNR, went to their assistance. A blackout device blocked his way. He cut down this gear, and forced an entry in to the fast-flooding, steamfogged compartment. Shouting orders and encouragement, he reached the imprisoned men.

Daugherty was joined in the rescue effort by Chief Water Tender J. J. Dennison, and Machinist's Mate W. W. Pemberton. Together these men braved scalding and drowning to fight their way into the fireroom and release their shipmates.

This rescue might have been impossible but for the action of Chief Machinist's Mate F. M. Borcykowski, whose quick-thinking and damage-control work met emergency requirements immediately after SHUBRICK was bombed.

And all of the 14 critically wounded might have died but for the skill and professional acumen of Lieutenant G. M. Caldwell, USNR, ship's Medical Officer. The destroyer's light had been extinguished. Sterile water was lacking. There were no hospital anesthetists . . . no laboratory facilities . . . no operating room. Caldwell improvised. Someone fetched blankets. Someone held lights. Someone scrubbed a shipmate's arm, preparing it for injection. Quickly and expertly he treated the burned, the maimed, those suffering from shock. Medical assistance was finally rushed from cruiser PHILADELPHIA and destroyer KNIGHT. Seven of the desperately wounded pulled through. So did the ship.

The foregoing episodes were related to give an inside picture of destroyer damage and ship-saving which was typical rather than exceptional. Typical of the ships and the men in the Destroyer Service.

BUCK *Kills Submarine* ARGENTO

On August 2 destroyer BUCK (Lieutenant Commander M. J. Klein), a member of Task Force 86, was engaged in patrolling the approaches to Licata. About 1400 that afternoon she took station with destroyer NICHOLSON as escort for a convoy of six Liberty ships, bound for Algiers from Sicily.

Off the Island of Pantelleria that evening, BUCK'S radar detected a sharp little "pip" indicating an intruder on the seascape some 5,500 yards distant. The "pip" vanished at 2257, range 2,800 yards. At the conn, Lieutenant Commander Klein took appropriate steps to investigate this phenomenon, which had all the aspects of a diving submarine.

By 2300 the submersible was identified as such by sonar contact at 700 yards. Klein and BUCK pitched in to dig out the undersea rover. Klein maneuvered the destroyer to the target, and BUCK unleashed a depth-charge barrage.

Circling off, the destroyer squared away for a second attack which was delivered at 2311. Contact was lost during the deep-sea upheaval, and not recovered until after midnight. BUCK made a third depth-charge attack at 0019 in the morning of August 3. One minute later, her radar registered a "pip" at short range. The sub had broached and was blundering around on the surface.

Three minutes after the "pip" came in, BUCK'S lookouts glimpsed the enemy's silhouette. That was all the destroyermen needed. Klein snapped the order, and the gunners opened fire with all batteries, lambasting the target with everything in the book.

For 24 minutes BUCK blazed away like a shooting gallery; then the sub was observed to be sinking, and the crew abandoning her in haste.

Klein ordered a whaleboat overside, and 46 prisoners, including the submarine captain, were fished from the sea. One of the men died of wounds after he was taken on board the destroyer.

These hapless submariners were Italians. They informed BUCK's Commanding Officer that he had sunk the Italian submarine ARGENTO. This was the second Fascist sub downed by American depth charges in World War II.

Chapter 26

Destroyers to Italy

(Supporting Operations "Avalanche" and "Shingle")

☆ ☆ ☆

"Operation Avalanche"

Invasion of Italy began in the dark before dawn of September 3, 1943, when two divisions of Montgomery's British Army jumped across the Messina Strait and landed without opposition on the point of Italy's toe.

The main invasion assault was aimed at the Gulf of Salerno, where a British-American naval force was to land the Fifth Army of Lieutenant General Mark Clark. Once Salerno was secured, the invaders were to make a swift thrust to Naples—one of the largest seaports of southern Europe—35 miles to the northward. The Salerno operation was given the code-name "Avalanche."

To "Operation Avalanche" the Navy assigned many of the warships which had been engaged in Sicilian "Husky." Vice Admiral Hewitt headed the Salerno invasion fleet, which was divided into a Northern Attack Force and a Southern Attack Force.

The Southern Attack Force was under Rear Admiral Hall, whose flag was in the USS SAMUEL CHASE. Admiral Hewitt was with this force, flying his flag in ANCON. The Force contained a Fire-Support Group under Rear Admiral Davidson. Mission of this force was to land and support the Army on an eight-mile stretch of foreshore which extended from the south bank of the Sele River to Agropoli.

United States destroyers which operated with the Southern Attack Force listed on the following page.

The Northern Attack Force contained four British cruisers, an anti-aircraft ship and a monitor, 18 destroyers, about 40 minecraft of various types, and over 300 landing craft. A Support Carrier Force built around five aircraft carriers, and

DESTROYERS IN SCREEN

PLUNKETT	*Lt. Comdr. E. J. Burke*

Flying pennant of
Comdr. G. L. Menocal, COMDESRON 7

NIBLACK	*Lt. Comdr. R. R. Connor*
BENSON	*Lt. Comdr. R. J. Woodaman*
GLEAVES	*Lt. Comdr. B. L. Gurnette*
MAYO	*Lt. Comdr. F. S. Habecker*
WAINWRIGHT	*Lt. Comdr. R. H. Gibbs*

Flying pennant of
Capt. C. Wellborn, Jr., COMDESRON 8

ROWAN	*Lt. Comdr. R. S. Ford*
KNIGHT	*Lt. Comdr. J. C. Ford, Jr.*

Flagship of
Capt. C. L. Andrews, Jr., COMMANDER DIVERSION GROUP

COLE	*Lt. Comdr. B. Chipman*
BERNADOU	*Lt. Comdr. B. L. E. Talman*
DALLAS	*Comdr. A. C. Roessler*

DESTROYERS IN SCREEN AND
FIRE-SUPPORT GROUPS

WOOLSEY	*Lt. Comdr. H. R. Wier*

Flying pennant of
Comdr. E. R. Durgin, COMDESRON 13*

BRISTOL	*Comdr. J. A. Glick*
EDISON	*Lt. Comdr. H. A. Pearce*
LUDLOW	*Comdr. L. W. Creighton*
NICHOLSON	*Comdr. L. M. Markham, Jr.*
TRIPPE	*Lt. Comdr. R. C. Williams, Jr.*
RHIND	*Lt. Comdr. O. W. Spahr, Jr.*

* Relieved on 15 September by Comdr. Harry Sanders.

a Covering Force containing eight British battleships and screen, operated with the Salerno invasion fleet, which was loaned a United Nations complexion by the inclusion of two Polish destroyers, a Greek destroyer, and a couple of Dutch gunboats.

D-Day was scheduled for September 9. From Oran, from Algiers, from Bizerte, from Tripoli, from ports as far east as Alexandria, and from Palermo, the ships of the "Avalanche" armada set out.

At 0630 in the evening of September 8, while the armada was off the Gulf of Salerno, General Eisenhower broadcast the stunning announcement that Italy had capitulated. But the Germans had already disarmed many Italian garrisons and were preparing to fight to the last Italian ditch.

Apparently well informed on the "Avalanche" objective,

German Field Marshal Albert von Kesselring had rushed
reinforcements to the Sele estuary, installed strong defenses
on the neighboring beaches, and planted artillery on the ridges
dominating Salerno Gulf. The Gulf was a lion's mouth waiting to snap when the Allied invasion fleet arrived.

Bloody Salerno

On some of the Salerno beaches the American and British
troops, enfiladed, were driven back to water's edge. On several, the combat teams were slaughtered to a man. Nazi aircraft swept over to bomb and strafe the reeling landing forces.
By mid-morning of D-Day the Salerno shallows were a crimson sludge, and it appeared as though the invaders might be
literally blown from the beachhead.

At this point Admiral Davidson's First Support Group
stepped in. They were just in time.

By noon the Salerno beaches looked like deathtraps. Nazi
artillerymen had rolled forward big batteries which included
88 mm. guns, and these rifles, emplaced on ridges, were pounding the sands with a devastating barrage. Then the fire-support
ships opened up. Nazi machine-gun emplacements were wiped
out. Mobile guns were blown off their wheels, and heavy artillery units were put out of action. A railway battery was
either knocked out or silenced. Crashing in from the sea,
naval shellfire stopped Nazi tanks in their tracks, blowing a
goodly number out of existence.

By D-Day evening the Nazis were falling back.

No less an authority than the German military savant,
Sertorious, attributed the loss of Salerno to General Von
Kesselring's inability to cope with naval bombardments.

By the end of September, Salerno had been won. But the
Allies had paid a heavy price for the prize. Some 7,000 British
and 5,000 American soldiers had been slain in the fighting.
And two United States destroyers had been downed in action.
First victim was the USS ROWAN.

Loss of USS ROWAN

Late in the evening of September 10, 1943, the destroyer
ROWAN (Lieutenant Commander R. S. Ford) took station in
the screen which was forming around the empty transports
and cargo vessels of Convoy SNF-1, bound from Salerno to
Oran.

Over the inner reaches of Salerno Gulf the night sky was
flushed by the crimson breath of angry guns. The distant foreshore resembled a dark grid on which embers smoldered,

while smoke coiled and fumed over the glowing coals.

ROWAN had joined the convoy screen at 2240. At midnight she was pacing along—nothing to report. A moment later her startled lookouts glimpsed a phosphorescent streak racing through the water on the ship's bow. Torpedo!

The alarm sent all hands to battle stations. The torpedo passed harmlessly ahead. Lieutenant Commander Ford turned the destroyer on the proverbial dime, and drove her down the torpedo's track.

As ROWAN charged across the water, a flicker of "pips" appeared on her radar screen—enemy torpedo-boats (E-boats) in the offing. Firing by full radar control, the destroyer opened up on the enemy. Guns blazing, she closed the range on one target to 2,000 yards. Then, while swinging in a fast turn, she was apparently struck in the port quarter by a torpedo.

Crash of the explosion was instantly followed by a ship-shattering blast that ripped open the destroyer's stern and blew segments of deck and superstructure skyward. The first detonation had exploded the after magazine.

Men and officers were hurled into the sea. Gunners who had been standing at their mounts found themselves clinging to mats of wreckage. Sailors found themselves swimming desperately through glutinous oil in a fog of steam. ROWAN was nowhere in sight. The destroyer had vanished. Forty seconds after the explosion, the ship was under the sea.

Heroic lifesaving work by destroyer BRISTOL could not prevent a tragic death toll. She picked up 72 of ROWAN's complement.

Was ROWAN torpedoed by an E-boat? One of her signal-men declared that he sighted the killers through a spyglass, but no one else saw or heard them. Although an E-boat torpedoing seemed highly probable, there remained the possibility that the ship had struck a mine.

ROWAN was the first American destroyer lost in "Operation Avalanche." In the embattled seas off Salerno she was to have company.

Loss of USS BUCK

Not far from the spot where ROWAN went down, destroyer BUCK was patrolling the approaches to Salerno. This was the night of October 8-9, 1943. The Americans had entered Naples on October 1, only to find the harbor a shambles. Re-treating, the Nazis had blown up wharves, demolished docks and marine machinery, and blocked the bay with a sargasso of sunken ships.

Midnight, and all was well on board the Buck. Then suddenly all was changed. A surface radar contact. Buck's captain, Lieutenant Commander M. J. Klein, sounded General Quarters. And whatever the preoccupation of those on or off watch at that hour—coffee, or sleep, or odd job, or reminiscence— all hands sprang as one man to battle stations. These were the same men who had taken the measure of Italian submarine Argento.

But while Buck was tracking the enemy that morning of October 9, the foe drew a deadly bead on the destroyer. Destroyermen thought they saw a dim silhouette across the water —a ghostly conning tower. Two torpedoes struck the destroyer's bow with killing violence. Smashing explosions burst the ship's hull plates, wrecked her forward compartments, and let in the flood.

In a turmoil of smoke, flame, and steam, the ship sloughed to a halt. Four minutes after she was hit, Buck plunged for the bottom.

Steaming to the rescue, destroyer Gleaves and British LCT 170 picked up 75 survivors. Lieutenant Commander Klein was not among the rescued. In an action that had taken the lives of some 150 of Buck's good company, the captain had gone down with his ship.

On the chart Rowan's grave is marked at lat. 40-07 N., long. 14-18 E. Near-by, within 15 miles, lies Buck. Two destroyers lost in the Salerno campaign. Within a fortnight the effort would claim still another American DD.

Loss of USS Bristol

In mid-October, 1943, all roads led to Rome. In particular, all transport highways in the Western Mediterranean were leading to Rome.

On the night of October 12, 1943, Bristol (Commander J. A. Glick) was with a destroyer squadron steaming as screen for a transport division. The convoy was on a Mediterranean road which followed the coastline of Algeria. The evening was fine—clement weather and placid seascape under a sky powdered with stars.

At 0400 in the morning the convoy was off Cape Bougaroun, about midway between Algiers and Tunis. Patrolling at 15 knots on the port side of the formation, Bristol paced like a restless lion.

At 0423 the destroyer's sonar watch heard the hydrophone effect of a torpedo. The low, rushing whistle of an oncoming 88 mm. shell might have given the ship more warning. Scarcely was the alarm flashed topside when, ten seconds after it first was heard, the torpedo struck BRISTOL.

Smashing in on the ship's port side at the forward engine-room, the blast stopped the destroyer dead with a broken back. Men, guns, fragments of gear and machinery were strewn by the violent explosion. Mortally stricken, BRISTOL sagged in the moon-washed sea, and began to settle under a surge of smoke.

There was time to launch life rafts, to give the wounded a hand, to get overside in "Mae Wests." Not much time. A few minutes after she was struck, BRISTOL broke in two and sank. WAINWRIGHT and TRIPPE soon arrived to rescue survivors. Dawnlight presently aided the rescue work, and the lifesaving went swiftly forward. All told, 241 men were saved. But in spite of brave work by survivors and rescuers, casualties were heavy. Fifty-two of the crew were lost with the ship.

Onslaught on Ship-Train for Naples

Bound for Naples in the first week of November was a great Allied ship-train, Convoy KME-25A, transporting tons of war supplies and thousands of troop reinforcements for the Army of General Mark Clark. Assembled in the United Kingdom, the convoy contained 15 American and eight British transports. These heavy-laden vessels were screened by a powerful destroyer task group, TG 60.2 under command of Captain C. C. Hartman, ComDesRon 15. American destroyers in the screen were:

DAVISON	*Lt. Comdr. J. D. Collett*
	Flagship of Capt. Hartman
BEATTY	*Lt. Comdr. W. Outerson*
MERVINE	*Lt. Comdr. D. R. Frakes*
TILLMAN	*Lt. Comdr. C. S. Hutchings*
PARKER	*Comdr. J. W. Bays*
	Flying pennant of
	Capt. C. J. Carter, COMDESRON 16
LAUB	*Lt. Comdr. A. G. Hay*
MCLANAHAN	*Lt. Comdr. N. C. Johnson*

In addition to the seven American DD's, the screen in-cluded three British destroyers, two Greek destroyers, and the anti-aircraft vessel HMS COLOMBO. After the convoy entered the Mediterranean and headed eastward for the Tunisian War Channel, the task group was augmented by two American destroyer-escorts from Mers-el-Kebir. The DE's were FRED-ERICK C. DAVIS (Lieutenant Commander O. W. Goepner,

USNR), and HERBERT C. JONES (Lieutenant Commander
A. W. Gardes).

On November 6, as the ships, having left Algiers far astern,
were approaching Philippeville. Traveling at 12 knots, they
had reached a point on the road not far from Cape Bougaroun, the scene of the BRISTOL ambush, when the enemy
struck. Time: 1800. Visibility poor. Diving out of the dark
and the daylight, the *Luftwaffe* descended like a flock of vultures on unsuspecting game.

During this aerial onslaught on Convoy KME-25A the
Germans unleashed a new killer.

At first glimpse, destroyer gunners who had never seen it
before took the thing for a midget airplane. Then, at close
range, it resembled a winged rocket, a streak of red light with
a flaring green tail. Released from a high-flying bomber, these
phantasmal comets would swoop across the sky, then abruptly
plummet down on a target in a screaming dive. Radio-controlled glider bombs!

First employed on Allied invasion shipping at Salerno, the
glider bombs had appeared as a lethal menace to anchored
vessels. Now they gave Captain Hartman's task group some
spine-chilling moments. They did not strike any ships, but
they came devilishly close.

Dangerous as were the glider bombs in the battle off Cape
Bougaroun, aircraft torpedoes were the weapons which
wrought the havoc. Before the Nazi planes were finally beaten
off, two Allied transports were fatally torpedo-stabbed and
destroyer BEATTY was sunk.

Loss of USS BEATTY

When BEATTY was hit, she was maintaining her position in
the convoy formation. Stationed on the starboard quarter of
the rear ship in the right-hand column, and about 3,000 yards
out, the destroyer was target for the first attack which roared
in through the twilight.

Lieutenant Commander W. Outerson and others topside
scarcely had time to set their teeth before the killing torpedo
struck the ship. With a stunning blast the warhead burst
against the starboard side at the after engine-room. BEATTY
shuddered to a halt and sagged in the water with a broken
keel.

With a sudden lurch the ship broke in two. Under a pall
of smoke the fore and aft sections sank. The time was about
2305.

BEATTY's crew had abandoned smartly, with opportunity to
launch rafts and floats, and to make good use of lifesaving

gear. Casualties were consequently few. Eleven bluejackets were lost with the ship, and a wounded man died after rescue. The other wounded—an officer and six enlisted men—recovered from their injuries.

WAINWRIGHT *and* HMS CALPE *Kill* U-593

By December 1943 the Mediterranean was no longer an Axis lake. But the Nazis were doing their best to keep the Swastika flying over (and under) its waters. While they concentrated on the Tyrrhenian storm center, they did not neglect Algiers and Gibraltar traffic lanes.

In mid-December destroyer A/S teams killed two U-boats in the Western Mediterranean. The first was downed on the 13th by USS WAINWRIGHT and British destroyer CALPE.

The two DD's were conducting a sub-hunt in company with destroyers NIBLACK and BENSON. They were sweeping an area northwest of Algiers and about midway between the North African coast and the coast of Spain when WAINWRIGHT left the group to investigate a "sub sighted" report. That was at 0120 in the morning of December 13. At 0229 HMS CALPE arrived on the scene to team up on the hunt.

The search continued through daybreak and sunrise—no success. Doggedly the two destroyers kept at it while the clock ticked through the morning, through noon, into afternoon. Persistence paid off. At 1408 WAINWRIGHT's sonar instruments registered a contact. Her captain, Commander W. W. Strohbehn, directed a booming depth-charge attack. CALPE picked up the contact at 1423 and promptly let go with depth charges. WAINWRIGHT regained sound contact at 1435, and coached her British team-mate up to the target. CALPE distributed a pattern of depth charges at 1440, and this blasting rang the bell.

Seven minutes after the last depth charge was dropped, a U-boat came spouting to the surface some 1,800 yards from WAINWRIGHT.

As the Nazi crew sprang overside, Strohbehn ordered the destroyer gunners to cease fire. Then he sent a party across the water to pick up survivors. The destroyermen had time to board the damaged U-boat and bring out men who were calling, "*Kamerad!*" CALPE joined in the rescue of these frantic submariners who preferred a Prisoner-of-War camp to entombment in a sunken U-boat—the U-593.

WOOLSEY *and* TRIPPE *Kill* U-73

On the afternoon of December 16, 1943, a U-boat ambushed a convoy off Cape Falcon, Algeria. Torpedoes smashed into the SS JOHN S. COPLEY, and there was death in the afternoon. Then American destroyers steamed out of Mersel-Kebir to track down the sub.

Under command of Captain H. Sanders, ComDesDiv 13, the destroyers were WOOLSEY, TRIPPE, and EDISON.

They reached the vicinity of the torpedoing about 1715, and started the A/S search about 1730. Within 45 minutes of the hunt's beginning WOOLSEY's sonar put the finger on the skulking enemy.

Thundering around the submarine, WOOLSEY's depth charges dished in the hull, pulverized light bulbs, and knocked out various electrical fixtures. The blasting also caused leakage, a casualty obviously fatal to a submarine if not soon mended. The captain of leaking U-73 ordered the crew to blow all ballast and take her to the surface.

Whereupon WOOLSEY's SG radar snared a "pip" dead ahead at a range of 1,900 yards—precisely what WOOLSEY and TRIPPE had been waiting for. They shot the ray of a powerful searchlight across the water. As the spotlight fastened on the submarine, the Nazi gunners opened fire. Hot steel whistled across WOOLSEY's deck; two bluejackets were wounded. The submariners were to regret this folly, for both destroyers immediately replied with a hot and accurate fusillade that lashed the U-boat into sinking wreckage. The destroyermen picked up 34 survivors.

The Battle for Anzio ("Operation Shingle")

Sicily had been tough. Italy was a lot tougher. Nazi General Kesselring pulled his troops out of the southern end of the peninsula and established the rock-ribbed "Gustav" and "Adolf Hitler" lines athwart the peninsula to block the Allied drive for Rome. Fighting northward from Naples, the American Army crashed into the defenses at Monte Cassino. To outflank the German positions, the Allies planned an amphibious landing on the Tyrrhenean coast at Anzio. The Anzio operation was given the code-name "Shingle." D-Day was set for January 22, 1944.

The landings were to take place on beaches in a sector which extended from Nettuno, a holiday resort some 30 miles south of Rome, to a point just below the Tiber estuary. Bull's-eye in this target sector was the little port of Anzio.

The American naval forces (Amphibious Task Force 81) were commanded by Rear Admiral F. J. Lowry. American destroyers and destroyer-escorts which operated with Task Force 81 are listed on the next page.

PLUNKETT	*Comdr. E. J. Burke*

Flying the pennant of
Capt. J. P. Clay, COMDESRON 7

WOOLSEY	*Comdr. H. R. Wier*

Flying the pennant of
Capt. H. Sanders, COMDESRON 13

WAINWRIGHT	*Comdr. W. W. Strohbehn*
TRIPPE	*Comdr. R. C. Williams*
NIBLACK	*Comdr. R. R. Connor*
GLEAVES	*Comdr. B. L. Gurnette*
EDISON	*Comdr. H. A. Pearce*
LUDLOW	*Comdr. L. W. Creighton*
MAYO	*Comdr. A. D. Kaplan*
*CHARLES F. HUGHES	*Lt. Comdr. J. C. G. Wilson*

Flying the pennant of
Comdr. V. Havard, Jr., COMDESDIV 14

*HILARY P. JONES	*Comdr. F. M. Stiesberg*
*MADISON	*Comdr. D. A. Stuart*
*LANSDALE	*Lt. Comdr. D. M. Swift*
H. C. JONES	*Lt. Comdr. R. A. Soule, III, USNR*
FREDERICK C. DAVIS	*Lt. Comdr R. C. Robbins, Jr., USNR*

* *Arrival off Anzio between 7-19 February.*

Mission of Task Force 81 was to establish Army Forces ashore on beaches near Cape D'Anzio for an attack on the rear of the enemy's right flank. The warships were to cover the landings, furnish all necessary fire-support, and bolster the attack wherever possible.

Sufficient evidence of the able fire-support loaned the "Shingle" effort by the destroyers may be found in the records of the USS EDISON (Commander H. A. Pearce). In action at Anzio this destroyer fired 1,854 rounds of 5-inch 38 ammunition at 21 separate targets.

On the evening of January 24, destroyer MAYO was disabled by an underwater explosion. Mine or torpedo? No one could say. The severe damage sent MAYO home to the States.

Air Raids at Anzio (Damaging of USS PLUNKETT)

Bombardment missions were not the only ones deftly accomplished by destroyers at Anzio. As was usual in an amphibious operation, they did all sorts of jobs, some routine, some odd. For instance, some were conducting A/S sweeps around the transport area, and keeping an eye out for possible E-boats. Some were escorting empty convoys over the seaward horizon. A paramount duty was the covering of invasion shipping with anti-aircraft protection. Most of the destroyers participated in this effort at one time or another.

Destroyers watched the sky with vigilant radar, hammered the raiders with flak, and rushed about laying smoke screens to cloak threatened shipping. Early in the battle against the *Luftwaffe,* destroyer PLUNKETT was hit. The ship, which was skippered by Commander E. J. Burke, was sorely wounded.

The attack occurred on January 24 in the shadows of evening—the *Luftwaffe's* favorite hour. It was one of those triple-threat onslaughts which featured torpedo-planes, dive-bombers, and glider bombs. Some eight or ten aircraft participated. The planes sighted were identified as Junker 88's. PLUNKETT's Action Report describes the attack's development:

> The action opened when two glider bombs were observed coming in on the port beam. They were identified by a pale green light which marked their trajectory. Almost simultaneously two Junker 88's were observed at a 50 foot altitude, one to port and one crossing ahead from starboard to port. Fire was opened and speed increased to 27 knots. A turn was made toward the glider bombs. These bombs hit the water about 200 yards astern of the ship.
>
> From this time on the ship was turned so as to keep pointed at the low flying planes. . . . The silhouette of the ship must have been outlined by the continuous firing at the low level planes. One enemy plane was seen to crash about 1,000 yards on the port beam and another 1,000 yards on the starboard bow. . . . About twelve minutes after the action started this ship was hit on the 1.1-inch gun mount by a bomb. . . .

While desperate hands fought fire and explosion, the gunners at the forward 5-inch and 20 mm. mounts blazed away at the attacking aircraft. For five more minutes the ferocious battle continued; then the holocaust aft was brought under control, and simultaneously the planes sped off in the night. Barbarously mutilated, PLUNKETT limped out of the battle area. Some 53 destroyermen had lost their lives in the blasting; 20 were wounded. Under escort of destroyer NIBLACK the maimed warship was sent to Palermo.

PLUNKETT was not the only *Luftwaffe* victim at Anzio. But losses were relatively light when balanced against the weight of air bombs, torpedoes, and glider bombs which the Nazi aircraft flung at Allied shipping in the first three weeks of "Shingle." And it was at Anzio that a pair of DE's nipped the glider bomb menace in the bud.

DE's Versus Glider Bombs ("Frau Maier" Squelches the Robots)

Hatched in dark secrecy in the recesses of Nazi Germany,

the glider bomb—it might have been more appropriately called a robot jet—was a dwarf descendant of the murderous "buzz bomb." It did not have the "buzz bomb's" range, nor carry as big an explosive charge, but militarily it was far more dangerous, and its potentialities were appalling. In effect, it operated as a small "buzz bomb" having rocket propulsion and a sentient control-mechanism which answered the directives of a radio signal. Launched by a high-level bomber, it could be guided by remote control, and sent into a meteor-like dive straight for the target.

Like comets the robots came rocketing down the sky, too fast for accurate AA fire, too small for snaring in a net of flak. At Salerno the only antidote seemed to be an aircraft counterattack on the high-level bombers which launched the glider bombs. Convoy KME-25A, without air cover, had been compelled to sweat out the robot onslaught.

Then someone in the Allied camp came up with an idea. Since radio was the "brain" which worked the glider bomb's steering mechanism, why not jam the air waves with radio signals that would knock out the bomb's brains?

Enter destroyer-escorts HERBERT C. JONES and FREDERICK C. DAVIS, each equipped with radio specialists and radio-jamming gear. Stationed off Anzio, JONES and DAVIS were assigned the special mission of squelching the glider bombs.

No one was certain that jamming would do the trick, but all hands involved in the effort were determined to make the try.

So "Shingle" found the two destroyer-escorts stationed at the anchorage off Anzio beachhead. Day after day, raid after raid, they were there on duty with their peculiar equipment. Other ships flung up spectacular screens of AA fire. DAVIS and JONES were in there firing, too, but their most effective barrages were invisible. And while the TNT was bringing down Nazi aircraft, the radio transmissions from DE's JONES and DAVIS were bringing down glider bombs.

WOOLSEY also participated in this special work, but her DD equipment was not as effective as that on board the DE's. JONES and DAVIS fought the lion's share of the weird battle.

Excerpts from the battle reports of Task Group Commander Sanders:

> During the period 22 January-2 February, 1944, there were some 26 bombing attacks by the German Air Force. Radio-controlled bombs were dropped during four of these attacks. . . . The efficiency with which F. C. DAVIS and H. C. JONES jammed radio-controlled bombs is an outstanding achievement on the part of these vessels.
> During the period of this report (2-7 February, 12-14 Febru-

ary, 1944) there were some thirteen bombing attacks in the Anzio area. . . . Radio-controlled bombs were noted in two of these attacks. No ships were hit. . . . A feature of the glider bombs attacks was the effective deflection of the bombs by jammers in F. C. DAVIS and H. C. JONES and to a lesser extent by WOOLSEY.

Between the foregoing lines one may discern some nerve-wracking drama: the tense moment when the DE's first tried the jamming gear—the cheering when a glider bomb was deflected—the sober faces of men who realized that a DE with her radio prattling could stand out like a sore thumb. What if those Nazi bombers got the idea these little ships were throwing a wrench in the robot machinery?

One day when the *Luftwaffe* was in the sky, a radioman of the DAVIS team overheard an enemy pilot call to a squadron mate, *"Let's all concentrate on Frau Maier."* A knowledge of colloquial German sent the listener's hair up. "Frau Maier" is German slang for "old gossip." The listening radioman had an idea that "old gossip" was the FREDERICK C. DAVIS.

And no sooner had the intercepted message been reported to the bridge than four enemy planes peeled off and made for the DE. Thirteen bombs fell around her in a tight circle, ringing the ship with geysers. DAVIS rolled and shook. Not a bomb hit her, but flying shrapnel left her with the only casualty she was to suffer during 142 days of "Operation Shingle."

"Frau Maier" continued her gossiping. She was attacked by torpedo planes; she was dive-bombed; she was strafed. She was jolted by near-misses. She was given a close shave by practically every aircraft weapon except one—the glider bomb. FREDERICK C. (*"Frau Maier"*) DAVIS simply talked the robot down.

Excerpt from endorsement on F. C. DAVIS Action Report by Captain J. P. Clay, Commander Destroyers Eighth Fleet:

After the Anzio landing, [either] the F. C. DAVIS or H. C. JONES remained at the anchorage off the beachhead most of the time. Many enemy aircraft bombing and radio-controlled missile attacks were delivered on the convoys and beachhead anchorage while these destroyer-escorts were present. Their work in investigating frequencies and jamming the radio bombs has been outstanding.

Then the punch line:

As a result of the counteraction against the weapon, the Germans practically ceased using it in this area after February.

Last Mile to Rome

The Allied armies marched into Rome on June 4. Fall of the first Axis capital shook the world. For the Allies, ultimate victory was now within sight. For Nazi Germany and Samurai Japan, defeat loomed on the horizon. As for Italy, Fascism was in its grave.

American destroyers and destroyermen had played no small part in bringing about that dramatic victory.

Chapter 27

Destroyers to Normandy

(Fire Support for the Drive on Fortress Europe)

☆ ☆ ☆

Festung Europa, 1944

The downfall of the Italian Axis capital filled Berlin with a cold fear matched only by the chill from the eastern front where the Russian steamroller was steadily advancing. And now in the spring of 1944 the Allies threatened Normandy. The Nazis could defend the beaches for a time, perhaps. But they lacked the air and naval power to block amphibious invasion and prevent landings. They had lost the Battle of the Atlantic, and Eisenhower's armies were mustered on France's threshold.

Afterwards Grand Admiral Doenitz blamed it all on *Der Fuehrer*. "*Germany was never prepared for a naval war. . . .*" Doenitz complained in rueful retrospect. "*A realistic policy would have given us a thousand U-boats at the beginning.*"

"Operation Overlord"

The drive designed to break the Nazi grip on Europe was given the code name "Overlord." Eisenhower's armies were to be landed on the beaches of Normandy by a massive amphibious operation unmatched by any in previous history. The naval program was given the code name "Neptune."

More than 4,000 ships were assembled for "Operation Neptune." The huge armada contained five task forces—three British and two American. The U.S. naval forces were under Rear Admiral A. G. Kirk. Some 33 destroyers and six DE's served with the "Neptune" assault forces.

Targets for the American landings were "Utah Beach" and "Omaha Beach." German defenses were known to include tricky barriers, mines and heavy coastal batteries. A wild storm threatened to wreck "Neptune" at the outset. But the operation was begun despite the storm.

June 6, 1944.

And there ahead was Normandy. The clock was ticking toward H-Hour. With the vanguard at "Utah Beach," destroyers HOBSON, FITCH, and CORRY moved in.

Action of HOBSON, FITCH, and CORRY

They were DD's of Commander L. W. Nilon's DesDiv 20—flagship HOBSON (Lieutenant Commander K. Loveland); FITCH (Commander K. C. Walpole); and CORRY (Lieutenant Commander G. D. Hoffman). Assigned as Fire-Support Unit 3 in Task Force "U," the trio sortied from Tor Bay, England, about noon on June 5.

They found the Channel baring its white teeth to the whip of ill-tempered weather, but they plodded stubbornly through the chop to take up screening positions with a convoy bound for the Cotentin Peninsula. Despite the ugly weather and surly seas they made the crossing on schedule.

USS HOBSON, FITCH, and CORRY reached the Transport Area at 0110 in the morning of June 6. There they lay to for three hours while the mine-sweeping of the Transport Area was completed.

At 0410 the three DD's maneuvered into the boat lane to lead the first boat wave in to the offshore Line of Departure. This shoreward procession moved at slow speed, "walking softly to go far." Evidently because of low visibility and unpreparedness, the Germans had not yet sighted the advancing ships.

At 0530 the trio of lead destroyers turned away from the boat lane and headed for their assigned fire-support stations, which were located some 4,000 yards off "Utah Beach" at a point about two miles from the St. Marcouf Islands. Just as they were clearing the boat lane, FITCH and CORRY were fired upon by shore batteries.

At once FITCH and CORRY answered the challenge. Noting the location of the flashes, the two destroyers replied in unison, firing what were probably the first defensive naval shots of "Operation Neptune." Apparently the destroyer gunners found the target, for at 0550 the offending batteries went silent.

Meantime, flag destroyer HOBSON had opened up on scheduled targets. FITCH followed suit at 0550, and CORRY entered the bombardment program at 0600.

At this hour the "Neptune" battering-ram struck full force against the entire Normandy sector. As dawn dispelled the darkness, dozens of combat ships unleashed a barrage that

shook the French coast from the Cotentin shore to Deau-
ville. Flight after flight of Allied aircraft stormed across the
sky to join in the bombardment. At "Utah Beach" the Allied
bombers and Force "U" warships delivered a steel hurricane
that seemed to blow the shoreline loose.

While CORRY was jockeying about, her guns and those of
her companion DD's blazed away at enemy batteries which
hurled sudden salvos in their direction. The clocks touched
H-Hour. At 0631 a swarm of landing craft let go with a
rocket barrage. The sands of "Utah" erupted, exploded,
churned, founted, and roared. Seaward rolled drifts of acrid
smoke and dust, and under this hot fog the shock troops
streamed shoreward. The landings were under way.

The Naval Fire Support Group covered the landings with
salvo after salvo. HOBSON, FITCH and CORRY joined in the
shore bombardment.

At 0633 CORRY struck a mine.

Loss of USS CORRY

The mine let go under CORRY's engineering spaces, crushing her bottom plates as though they were cardboard, and
rending her hull. *"There was a fearful explosion,"* one of her
officers remembered. *"We seemed to jump clear of the water."*

The sea plunged into the forward engine-room and forward
fireroom, swamping vital machinery and flooding fires. A moment later the after fireroom was inundated. All electric power
went out, and the ship's compartments were in darkness. As
engineers raced topside, beating the rush of water and deadly
steam, the destroyer traveled the arc of a tight circle with
her rudder jammed at hard right.

At 0637—four minutes after the blast—all steam was lost
in the after engine-room, and the ship's propulsion power expired. Drifting, she slowed to a stop. It was evident that her
case was desperate; she was still under enemy fire, and the
mine explosion, which had stifled her turbines, had also
snapped her keel and opened a great fissure in her main deck
and hull. Still, there seemed a chance of saving her. Boats
were lowered, and men stood ready to rig a tow to prevent her
from drifting ashore into enemy hands. As the boats went
overside, CORRY hoisted the distress signal: *"This ship needs
help."*

She needed more than help. At 0639 the waves were lapping
her main deck, and she lolled sway-backed in helpless paralysis.

For those who escaped the flooded destroyer, the ordeal
was only beginning. As she settled slowly, her stacks leaned
together, her bow and fantail made the "V" of a folding jack-

knife, and the Nazi gunners continued a wicked fire that maimed survivors in the water, and slashed at the broken ship. A hit ruptured the smoke-screen generator on CORRY's fantail, releasing a torrent of FS vapor that swirled out over the flotsam, blinding and choking the swimmers and boat crews. Another shell struck one of the 40 mm. gun tubs, exploding the projectiles that were at ready stowage.

In the midst of carnage, CORRY's survivors hung on, fighting through blood and oil and debris. One raft was carried in a complete circle around the drowned ship. As the survivors passed between wreck and shore, a near-miss from a German salvo lashed them with shrapnel, creating fresh casualties. Water temperature was 54°F., and several men died of exposure. But in spite of shellfire, toxic fog, adverse currents, and bitter immersion, most of CORRY's complement remained alive.

Ordered by Admiral Deyo to pick up CORRY's survivors, destroyer FITCH made a fast run to the scene.

By 0900 the last of CORRY's survivors were picked up. Lost with CORRY were 21 men and an officer.

Destroyers to "Omaha Beach"

For the amphibs the "Omaha" landings were a hell of fire and water. That was the place where, as Field Marshal Montgomery phrased it, *"the American troops held on by their eyelashes."*

All morning the Germans held the Americans pinned down to the water's edge. It appeared that the "Omaha" invasion might be thrown back.

That was the critical hour when the Germans should have seized the initiative, throwing every tank, every Panzer gun, every machine-gun squad in the area to the fore. Indeed, at that hour the roads to "Omaha" were crawling with Panzers, with infantry caravans, with all manner of military traffic. But much of this traffic could not get through. Nearing the coast, it jammed.

It jammed because of a stupendous naval bombardment which struck the Nazi front at "Omaha" on D-Day afternoon. That bombardment would never be forgotten by the Nazis who lived to remember it. Or by the Navy men who delivered it—particularly the destroyermen who shared in its delivery.

Time: about noon. Admiral Deyo's Fire Support Group had been standing inshore, blasting at the Nazi positions with everything. Battleships ARKANSAS and TEXAS heated their turrets now. So did the Allied cruisers working with Force "O." As for the Fire-Support destroyers, they pushed so close inshore that, as Admiral Kirk expressed it, *"they had their bows against the bottom."*

The American destroyers which had their "bows against the bottom" at "Omaha" were the USS DOYLE, FRANKFORD, McCOOK, THOMPSON, BALDWIN, CARMICK, and EMMONS. Throughout noon hour and the rest of the afternoon the destroyermen kept up a pointblank bombardment, sweeping the enemy's beach guns and bluff guns with shellfire. Dealing out salvo after salvo, they blasted pathways for the invasion troops to follow from water's edge to bluffs.

By 1700 the Nazi reinforcements bound for "Omaha" were stalled on roads blocked with wrack and ruin. Nazi guns no longer dominated the coast, and the American Army was going steadily ashore. The situation at "Omaha Beach" was in hand.

After it was over, Field Marshal Von Rundstedt glumly attributed the German defeat on the Norman coast to *"the power of the Allies' naval guns, which reached deep inland . . . making impossible the bringing up of reserves needed to hurl Allied invasion forces into the Channel."* To an interrogator who questioned him after his capture, he said bluntly, *"Your naval artillery was terrific."*

Loss of USS MEREDITH

At about 0110 in the morning of June 8 the destroyer MEREDITH, serving with the Force "U" Fire Support Group, arrived in her assigned screening area near the cruiser TUSCALOOSA off "Utah Beach." These ships were units of a task group working in the northwest waters of "Utah." MEREDITH's skipper, Commander George Knuepfer, set the destroyer on course for a vigorous patrol, screening to the northward of numerous heavy ships on locale.

The dark was lively with spray and choppy water. A fresh breeze blowing under low, wet clouds occasionally unravelled them to reveal a pallid moon.

About five minutes after the ship commenced screening operations, a covey of planes droned into view. That the planes were German "miners" was almost a certainty. The Nazi airmen had taken to the mission with enthusiasm, making it a practice to drop their magnetic and contact specimens after dark. And it was a good night for such an endeavor. With the clock no later than 0152, MEREDITH struck a mine.

Hearing the thunder, men on destroyer JEFFERS, a mile away, thought MEREDITH had been hit by a guided missile.

When the mine struck, Chief Machinist's Mate Brady L. Bryan was in charge of the watch in MEREDITH's after engine-room. Bryan and the men about him were hurled off their feet and the engine-room went into complete darkness.

Then all hell broke loose. Before a man could get his bearings he was struck in the face by a steel bar, or a scalding jet of steam, or a flash of hot grease or oil. He was struggling in a swirl of water that swept him across tilted floor-plates, perhaps sucked him through a hatch, or smashed him against a bulkhead. He might be trapped under a grating, or wedged in a vise of shattered machinery; might find his arm pinned behind him by an invisible hook, or his pants leg caught in a snare.

Deafened, stunned, Chief Machinist's Mate Bryan groped through the dark, found the portside ladder. Dimly aware of the effort, he scrambled up the greasy rungs. He went through the after engine-room hatch with a lunge, and stumbled along the portside passageway to the fantail.

Out in the open—fresh air; a reassuring glimpse of men and officers hurrying about the business of seamanship and damage-control; the exhilarating feel of safety. Brisk commands. Crews at their stations. Boats, gear, and sea in familiar order. Perhaps Bryan's first thought was, *"I made it!"*

Perhaps not. But if it was, his next thought was for his shipmates. The hands who had stood watch with him down there in the after engine-room—they weren't here on the fantail! They hadn't made it!

That was all Bryan needed. That, and a flashlight. He retraced his journey through that dark portside passageway to the engine-room hatch, and down that slippery ladder to the inky limbo below.

The flood had climbed to within four feet of the overhead, and the whirling water was scummed with oil and clots of grease, and littered with bits of flotsam. But in that swirling cistern, Bryan found four injured men. Badly wounded, they were clinging to handholds, fighting for breath, treading water. Working his way through the topsy-turvy of murk and shadow, the Chief went after them. He got them.

Recommending Brady L. Bryan for the Navy Cross, Commander Kneupfer noted that had it not been for Bryan's act the four injured men might have died in the ship.

MEREDITH did not go down that morning. Heroic salvagers got alongside. Some of the crew returned on board. By dint of desperate effort, the crippled vessel was moved to an offshore anchorage.

But early in the following morning (June 9) a flock of Nazi aircraft raided the "Utah" area. These Swastika planes roared over MEREDITH's anchorage, dropping 2,000-pound bombs. One of the blockbusters landed about 800 yards off the port bow. The blast shook the ship, jarring her stern.

At 1010 of that morning, without preliminary warning, the MEREDITH broke in two amidships, and went down with a plunge. The BANNOCK cut her lines to clear the side, and stood off to recover survivors. All hands of the security watch jumped or lowered themselves from the sinking ship, and were rescued.

MEREDITH was the third ship to carry that name on the Navy's roster—and the second MEREDITH to be sunk during World War II.

Loss of USS GLENNON

While MEREDITH was drifting in mortal disablement off Cape Barfleur, a second American destroyer was blasted by a mine in the "Utah" area. The destroyer was the USS GLENNON (Commander C. A. Johnson). The date: June 7.

Disaster smote GLENNON off Quineville, a clutter of cottages and fishing smacks on the Cotentin coast about ten miles below Barfleur. Crash! She had struck a mine.

As described in Commander Johnson's Action Report:

> The effect was violent throughout the ship. All power was lost due to the tripping of circuit breakers, but regained in about three minutes. The force of the explosion had been of such magnitude as to throw two men, who were standing on the fantail, 40 feet in the air, landing them in the water. One of these men was later recovered with both legs broken and possible internal injuries. A 600-pound depth charge was torn from the stern racks and thrown 50 feet, landing on the torpedo platform abreast No. 3 5-inch gun-mount. A 150-pound cement dan buoy anchor was thrown 125 feet from the fantail to the port 20 mm. gun nest, torpedo platform. Water rose to a height of 25 feet about equally on the port and starboard quarters.
>
> General Quarters was sounded. A boat was lowered to pick up 16 men who had been thrown into the water. Repair parties assembled for rescue and salvage work. After an immediate report of damage, word was passed over the loudspeaker circuit: "The ship will not sink, all hands remain on board, repair parties proceed with rescue and salvage work." . . .

Commander Johnson and all able hands pitched in to save their disabled ship. About 0830 mine-sweepers STAFF and THREAT maneuvered ahead to sweep a path, and GLENNON prepared for a haul to the Transport Area.

While the tow was being rigged, the destroyer-escort RICH approached from eastward, to inquire if assistance were needed. The reply was sent immediately: NEGATIVE X CLEAR AREA CAUTIOUSLY DUE MINES

The DE circled astern of GLENNON, and headed away at five knots.

Commander Johnson appealed for a salvage tug. Tug KIOWA came alongside about 1100. KIOWA's journey was useless; strive and sweat as she would, the powerful tug could not move the inert destroyer. GLENNON's stern had settled to the bottom and was holding her fast like a massive anchor.

Next day (June 9) Johnson and his destroyermen worked with the salvage crew to get GLENNON off. But time and tide were against them, and so were the Germans.

About sunrise on June 10 the Nazi shore guns at Quineville opened up. Their second salvo hit GLENNON aft, wrecking the after engine-room.

At 2145 that evening the destroyer leaned over on her beam with a list of exhaustion. She had taken a lot of punishment. She was done. The dark waters presently closed over her, and she was under.

Lost with GLENNON at the time of her mining were 25 men. Some 267 officers and bluejackets—among them 38 wounded —survived the mine blast and subsequent shelling.

Loss of USS RICH

When destroyer-escort RICH steamed to the aid of the disabled destroyer GLENNON on that ill-omened morning of June 8, her skipper, Lieutenant Commander E. A. Michel, knew the DE was entering dangerous water. However, the DE's skipper did not hesitate. In the dry, official language of the Navy he *"proceeded in his vessel with utmost dispatch, with disregard of the danger from enemy gunfire and possible mines, and stood by close aboard the stricken ship to render assistance."*

As she neared the GLENNON, the destroyer-escort lowered a motor whaleboat which headed for the disabled ship. At that point, as related in the GLENNON story, the destroyer signalled RICH that her assistance was unnecessary, and warned her to beware of mines.

Observing that the GLENNON was in no need of immediate help, Lieutenant Commander Michel turned the DE close under the destroyer's stern, and, passing GLENNON's starboard side, headed away.

RICH's captain took every precaution—slow speed; the ship squared away for emergency; all hands topside instructed to maintain a sharp lookout for enemy planes and drifting mines. But there were undersea mines which a lookout could not detect—mines which drifted deep under in the tidal currents, and were set to explode by "influence" when they entered a ship's magnetic field.

Time: about 0920. A stunning explosion burst the sea about

50 yards off RICH's starboard beam. The seaquake shook the DE from stem to stern; sent sailors stumbling from their stations; tripped the circuit breakers, and knocked out the ship's light and power. Some gauge lines had suffered injury, and instrument glasses had been shattered. Nothing worse.

But that was only a beginning. About three minutes after the offside blast, a mine exploded directly under the ship.

Then she was blasted by a third mine. That did it!

RICH was the last DesLant ship to go down to Nazi mines off Normandy. The little DE's losses were very heavy. Of a complement of 215, some 89 officers and men were lost with the ship; 73 survivors were wounded.

Torpedoing of USS NELSON

As the Navy had learned in the Mediterranean, the German E-boat could be a thorn in the side of an invasion force. Similar to a PT-boat, it was speedy, agile, hard-hitting, and hard to hit. Its strategy and tactics were those of surprise raid—night attack. Its arms were 40 mm. machine-guns and torpedoes.

It was a good night for E-boating—water calm; wind negligible; sky darkly overcast, with visibility about 2,000 yards; the seascape as black as carbon.

The date was June 12, 1944. The hour: 0100. At that time the destroyer NELSON (Lieutenant Commander T. D. McGrath) was anchored at her screening station on the "Dixie Line" boundary of the "Omaha Beach" assault area. Other units of the Area Screen in NELSON's vicinity were destroyers LAFFEY (Commander F. J. Becton) and SOMERS (Commander W. C. Hughes).

NELSON was not at her best, for she could not use her port engine for propulsion. Her port shaft and propeller had been removed after she had fouled a buoy at Plymouth, England. Despite this handicap she had steamed across the Channel to carry on in "Operation Neptune."

The following terse account is from the destroyer's Action Report:

> At 0105 C.I.C. reported contact bearing 358°T at six thousand yards. Shortly thereafter reported target course 190°T, speed twenty. . . . As required by operation order, signalman challenged, and about fifteen seconds later ship opened fire at four thousand yard range, with entire battery in full radar control. Contact slowed, turned away and separated into three distinct targets. Anchor had been heaved in and chain was up and down. About ten salvos had been fired when at about 0109 ship was hit. There was an explosion aft and the ship heeled sharply to port and then resumed an even keel. Electric power was lost momentarily but regained in a short time. Chain was veered;

repair parties rescued personnel and checked flooding. Ship was reported in no danger at 0122. The next day she was towed to Portsmouth, England.

The destroyer's lookouts never saw the E-boat. Evidently it had fired at the challenging signal light.

NELSON was harder hit than the above summary would suggest. The torpedo blast blew off the stern and No. 4 mount; the starboard shaft was bent downward and, with propeller attached, it dragged water at a depth of 52 feet. Crew casualties were severe. Some 24 of the ship's complement were lost; nine were wounded.

"Neptune" Postscript

After participating in the battles for "Utah" and "Omaha Beach," the destroyermen off Normandy had a brief breather. Then, on June 25, eleven of the "Neptune" DD's served in a Task Group which bombarded Cherbourg. During the bombardment, destroyer BARTON was hit by an 8-incher and LAFFEY was slugged by a dud. But the Nazi Krupp batteries were hammered into junk. The naval smash at Normandy was over.

It had been a costly effort for the DesLant Force. Spearheading "Operation Neptune," the Destroyer Service had suffered the only major combat-ship losses inflicted by the enemy during the Battle for the Beachheads. CORRY, MEREDITH, GLENNON, and destroyer-escort RICH were warships from truck to keel, and they would not be easily replaced.

But the landings had been successfully made and the beachheads secured. By early July Allied troops, guns, and war supplies were pouring into France through Cherbourg like floodwater through a breach in a dyke. Eisenhower's armies were on their way to Germany.

Chapter 28

Winning the Mediterranean

(Destroyers to Southern France)

☆　☆　☆

War in the Mediterranean

During the prolonged Anzio dead-lock, which lasted from January until June, 1944, Allied convoy escorts had fought life-and-death battles on that sea-going road which entered the Mediterranean through the Straits of Gibraltar, trailed along the coast of North Africa, squeezed through the Tunisian War Channel, and swung northward through the Tyrrhenian Sea. These Mediterranean battles did not make front-page news, but they were all part and parcel of the effort that loosened the Nazi grip on Italy and Southern Europe. Typical were the onslaughts on Convoys UGS-37, UGS-38, and GUS-38—onslaughts which sank Allied cargoes, killed Allied sailors, and cost the Navy's Destroyer Force three hard-fighting warships.

Attack on Convoy UGS-37

Convoy UGS-37, bound from Norfolk for Bizerte, consisted of 60 merchant vessels and six LST's. It was escorted by Task Force 65, under command of Captain W. R. Headden. This task force contained the naval vessels listed on the next page.

The convoy needed every gun of this heavy guard. As usual, the Germans were informed of this shiptrain's arrival in the Mediterranean, and the *Luftwaffe* struck late in the evening of April 11, 1944, when the convoy was about seven miles off Cape Bengut, Algeria.

The night was as fine as good weather could contrive—sky cloudless, sea as calm as a millpond, water silvered by the light of a three-quarters moon. Steaming at 7.5 knots, the ships were in good formation, aligned in 12 columns, 600 yards between columns, each ship in column 400 yards from the next.

The escorts were disposed around the convoy in positions

3,000 yards from the convoy's perimeter. DesDiv 66 had the stations astern on the "down moon" side. Destroyer LANSDALE, equipped with glider-bomb jamming gear, and four DE's of CortDiv 58 were on the port side of the convoy. Four escorts were to starboard. Cruiser DELHI was stationed on the port quarter between the convoy and CortDiv 58 ships. Destroyer-escorts HOLDER and FORSTER paced ahead of the convoy's front.

At 2245 one aircraft was reported in the convoy's vicinity. Twenty minutes later some five to ten aircraft were hovering in the offing. The clan was gathering.

At 2318 a white flare was dropped about five miles ahead of the convoy. More flares were dropped ahead and to port. Watching in sweaty fascination, destroyer lookouts gripped their binoculars, and gunners waited tight-nerved.

TASK FORCE 65
ESCORT FOR
CONVOY UGS-37

DESTROYER-ESCORTS
Temporarily assigned to DesDiv 66

STANTON	*Lt. Comdr. P. J. Tiffany, USNR*

Flagship of Task Force Commander Headden

SWASEY	*Lt. Comdr. H. M. Godsey, USNR*

DESTROYERS (DESDIV 66)

BRECKENRIDGE	*Lt. Comdr. F. R. Arnold*

Flying pennant of
Comdr. A. M. Kowalzyk, Jr., COMDESDIV 66

BLAKELEY	*Lt. Comdr. R. J. Brooke, USNR*
BIDDLE	*Lt. Comdr. R. H. Hopkins, USNR*
BARNEY	*Lt. H. D. Sprenger, USNR*

DESTROYER-ESCORTS (CORTDIV 58)

PRICE	*Lt. Comdr. J. W. Higgins, Jr., USNR*

Flying pennant of
Comdr. E. E. Garcia, COMCORTDIV 58

STRICKLAND	*Lt. Comdr. A. J. Hopkins, USNR*
FORSTER	*Lt. Comdr. I. E. Davis, USNR*
STOCKDALE	*Lt. Comdr. R. W. Luther, USNR*
HISSEM	*Lt. Comdr. W. W. Low, USNR*
HOLDER	*Lt. Comdr. W. P. Buck, USNR*
Destroyer LANSDALE	*Lt. Comdr. D. M. Swift*
HMS DELHI	HMS. NADDER
(*AA Cruiser*)	(*Escort vessel*)
HMS JONQUIL	HMS MINDFUL
(*Escort vessel*)	(*Rescue tug*)

HMS VAGRANT
(*Rescue tug*)

At 3232 Captain Headden ordered various escorts to make smoke. Two minutes later, about a dozen planes were in the vicinity, and flares blazed over the convoy. At 2335, flag DE STANTON opened fire on a plane which came in from port and crossed her bow. The battle was on.

The escorts in Task Force 65 put up a formidable barrage. That the *Luftwaffe* had its first team in the field was evident from the cool deliberation with which the onslaught was launched, and the determination with which it was pushed. Some 15 to 26 aircraft delivered the assault. The planes were Dornier 217's and Junker 88's.

Early in the battle, destroyer-escort HOLDER was torpedoed by one of the low-flying bombers.

Loss of USS HOLDER

Destroyer-escort HOLDER (Lieutenant Commander W. P. Buck, USNR) was one of the UGS-37 escorts ordered to make smoke just before the *Luftwaffe* attacked. HOLDER was on her first operational voyage after a shakedown, but she went into battle like a veteran.

Between 2323 and 2332 her radar picked up two enemy planes. At 2335 she let go with her smoke generators as directed, and began to build a wall of fog across the convoy's menaced front. A few minutes later she sighted a Nazi plane skimming across the water.

As reported by HOLDER's skipper:

> At 2339 a plane of a type not positively identified was sighted off the port beam and fire was opened with all guns that could bear. As plane approached, flying very close to the water, it was observed to launch a torpedo at a range estimated at 300-400 yards. The torpedo wake was clearly visible and strong hydrophone effect was picked up and reported from the Sound Hut. As soon as torpedo was sighted, flank speed was ordered and full left rudder applied. At 2340, before the order to increase speed had taken effect, the torpedo struck amidships on the port side below the waterline with two distinct heavy explosions. They were a fraction of a second apart and seemed of almost equal intensity. A yellow flash accompanied the explosions. The ship settled and took on a four degree list to starboard.

The destroyer-escort FORSTER (Lieutenant Commander I. E. Davis, USNR) was ordered to go to the disabled DE's assistance. At 0113 she edged up alongside HOLDER and took off twelve critically injured men. Sixteen of the crew had perished in the torpedoing.

Destroyer-escort PRICE (Lieutenant Commander J. W. Higgins, Jr., USNR) transferred a doctor to the battered DE.

At 0230 in the morning of April 12 the ship was taken under tow by the rescue tug MINDFUL. About eight hours later she reached the harbor of Algiers. Later she was sent to New York Navy Yard.

On September 13, 1944, the USS HOLDER was placed out of commission.

Attack on Convoy UGS-38

The convoy consisted of 85 merchant vessels, two Navy tankers, and the Coast Guard cutter DUANE. It was escorted by Task Force 66 under command of Captain W. H. Duvall. The warships which composed this escort force are enumerated below.

TASK FORCE 66
ESCORT FOR
CONVOY UGS-38

CGC TANEY	Comdr. H. J. Wuensch, USCG

Flagship of Task Force Commander Duvall

DESTROYER-ESCORTS (CORTDIV 21 AND CORTDIV 46)

JOSEPH E. CAMPBELL	Lt. Comdr. J. M. Robertson

Flying the pennant of
Comdr. L. M. Markham, Jr., COMCORTDIV 21

LANING	Lt. Comdr. E. A. Shuman, Jr., USNR
FECHTELER	Lt. C. B. Gill
FISKE	Lt. J. A. Comly, USNR
MOSLEY	Lt. Comdr. J. A. Alger, Jr., USCG
PRIDE	Comdr. R. R. Curry, USCG
FALGOUT	Comdr. H. A. Meyer, USCG
LOWE	Comdr. R. H. French, USCG
MENGES	Lt. Comdr. F. M. McCabe, USCG

Flying the pennant of
Capt. R. E. Wood, USCG, COMCORTDIV 46

NEWELL	Comdr. R. J. Roberts, USCG
CHASE	Lt. Comdr. G. O. Knapp, II, USNR
FESSENDEN	Lt. Comdr. W. A. Dobbs, USNR
Destroyer LANSDALE	Lt. Comdr. D. M. Swift*
HNMS HEEMSKERCK	HMS SUSTAIN*
AA Cruiser*	(Minesweep)
HMS SPEED*	HMS VAGRANT*
(Minesweep)	(Tug)

* Joined convoy in Mediterranean

Approaching Cape Bengut on the evening of April 20, 1944, the convoy was steaming in 10-column formation. Three destroyer-escorts were stationed in the outer screen. Other DE's formed the inner screen which covered the front and both flanks of the convoy. One DE was in "caboose position" astern.

The code word for an aircraft alarm was "Whoopee." There were several daytime "whoopees" as the ship-train, steaming at 7.5 knots, approached Cape Bengut. But after dark the attackers were not detected until they were almost on top of the ship-train.

The attack came from ahead on a bearing about 100° true, the planes barely skimming the water and employing the dark shoreline as background to blur their silhouettes and to frustrate radar. Destroyer-escort LOWE sighted five of the oncoming aircraft at 2103. In the gloaming they had appeared with the suddenness of a flight of bats. It was "Whoopee!" then, and no mistake.

The onslaught was delivered in three waves.

Obviously the *Luftwaffe* scored heavily in this foray. While an estimated six planes were shot down in the battle and five more damaged, these shootings hardly compensated for the casualties suffered by the convoy. Torpedoed and sunk were two merchant vessels and destroyer LANSDALE.

Loss of USS LANSDALE

Nazi aircraft struck Convoy UGS-38 off Cape Bengut at 2103. About 2104 the third attack wave—a group of Heinkel 111's—swept in on the convoy's port bow. In the center of this onslaught, LANSDALE was assailed from both port and starboard. Her AA guns put up a double-barreled defense, but she could not fend off the two-sided attack. At 2015 a Heinkel torpedo smashed into the destroyer.

The blast wrecked the ship's forward fireroom and broke her back. Valiantly the LANSDALE crew fought her battle-damage, but with her vital machinery swamped, the destroyer leaned helplessly in the sea, smoke and steam pouring from her breached hull. About 2122, fearing that the vessel might capsize, Lieutenant Commander Swift ordered the ship abandoned.

Not long after the destroyermen went overside, the ship tore apart amidships, and the wreckage sank. Some 235 survivors (two fatally injured) were picked up by destroyer-escorts NEWELL and MENGES. Forty-seven of the crew were not recovered.

PRIDE, J. E. CAMPBELL, SUSTAIN, L'ALCYON, SENEGALAIS, *and* HMS BLANKNEY *Kill* U-371

Task Force 66, steaming westward with Convoy GUS-38, had reached the dangerous waters below the southeast coast of

Spain by morning of May 3, 1944. In this area, where the Mediterranean bottle narrows into a neck, the Nazi enemy was ready and waiting for GUS-38. And in the early hours of May 3 a submarine torpedo crashed into destroyer-escort MENGES, flagship of Captain R. E. Wood, USCG, ComCortDiv 46.

MENGES had been patrolling 3,000 yards astern of the convoy. Shortly after midnight her radar spotted a target six miles astern. Captain Wood ordered the DE to investigate. MENGES' skipper sent the crew to battle stations, and the ship streamed "foxer" (false targets) to outfox acoustic torpedoes. About 0050 the DE began to zigzag. At 0104 she increased speed to 20 knots to close the range. The target disappeared, but a new spatter of "pips" flickered on the radar screen to confuse the issue. At 0115 MENGES' speed was slowed to 15 knots to facilitate sonar search. And three minutes after that a torpedo hit her in the stern.

The blast carried away both propellers and rudders, and wrecked the after compartments of the ship. Thirty-one of the crew were slain in the explosion, and 25 were injured. The DE wallowed logily in the sea, paralyzed and almost defenseless. With the exception of her forward batteries and four 20 mm's. near the stack, all her weapons had been put out of commission.

At 0140 Task Force Commander Duvall ordered two destroyer-escorts to leave the convoy screen, go to MENGES' assistance, and hunt down her assailant. These DE's were PRIDE (Commander R. R. Curry. USCG) and JOSEPH E. CAMPBELL (Lieutenant J. M. Robertson), flagship of Commander L. M. Markham, Jr., ComCortDiv 21.

At 0255 PRIDE picked up the submarine contact near MENGES, and the two able-bodied DE's closed in to trap and exterminate the U-boat. It was soon apparent they were up against a wily customer.

For more than 24 hours the U-boat evaded the DE's. HMS BLANKNEY, U.S. mine vessel SUSTAIN, and French destroyers L'ALCYON and SENEGALAIS joined the hunt.

Finally the desperate U-boat came to the surface. SENEGALAIS tagged her with radar, sighted her, and blazed away with ready guns. Meantime, CAMPBELL and PRIDE were closing in at full speed, and maneuvering to block the sub's escape to the north. BLANKNEY and SUSTAIN blocked escape to the west. Moving at about 12 knots, the sub headed southwest. At 0359 the U-boat submerged. Five minutes later SENEGALAIS was struck in the stern by a torpedo. The blast smashed her fantail, but she remained afloat, more durable than her mortal enemy.

At 0433 some shouting Germans were glimpsed in the water by lookouts on board the SUSTAIN. The mine vessel steamed forward to investigate. In all, 41 men and seven officers were picked up. Five of their fellows had gone down with the submarine, which had been abandoned at 0409. She was the U-371—one of the toughest Nazi subs to be sunk in the Mediterranean.

Unfortunately the killing of this U-boat did not end the attack on Convoy GUS-38. The following day, destroyer-escort FECHTELER was torpedoed.

Loss of USS FECHTELER

One of the escorts for westbound Convoy GUS-38, destroyer-escort FECHTELER (Lieutenant C. B. Gill) plodded on with the slow ship-train which took an evasive course after the submarine attack on USS MENGES. The convoy swung southward toward Oran, then headed west. Early in the morning on May 5, 1944, it was approaching the island of Alboran, a Spanish flyspeck in the center of the Mediterranean's bottleneck.

About 0315, destroyer-escort LANING (Lieutenant Commander E. A. Shuman, Jr., USNR) made sonar contact with a strange vessel 13 miles distant. Presently the "pip" disappeared; the vessel had submerged. The submarine alarm was flashed, and the convoy made several course-changes, maneuvering to evade ambush.

At 0345 FECHTELER, covering a sector between the convoy and the sub's reported position, was swinging right to follow a new course. The ship was still turning when she was rocked by a thunderclap explosion. On the topside men were thrown from their footing on the bridge and at gun mounts. In the compartments below decks engineers and firemen were hurled against bulkheads or pitched into a jungle of shattered machines. Water spouted in through the smashed hull, and the destroyer-escort wallowed in helpless disablement.

All hands abandoned at 0415. Then the ship snapped amidships and folded until bow and stern were almost perpendicular. About 0500 the wreckage exploded and sank.

Some 186 survivors were picked up by the destroyer-escort LANING and a rescue tug. The rest of FECHTELER's crew either perished in the torpedo blast or went down with the wreckage.

U.S. DD's and British Aircraft Kill U-616 ("Operation Monstrous")

Determined to squelch the marauders operating in the waters between Spain and Algeria, Commander in Chief Mediterranean (CinCMed) instituted one of the biggest submarine hunts ever staged in that sea—a hunt appropriately designated "Operation Monstrous."

Launching the campaign, Allied commanders in the area tightened the A/S defenses and accelerated the A/S sweeps. British Coastal Command aircraft flew needle-eyed patrols, and American warships from Algiers and Mers-el-Kebir beat the undersea bushes for a trace of the enemy. It was a reckless U-boat commander who would dare to prowl in these precincts while this heat was on.

Such a boat was the U-616.

No sooner was the submarine detected on May 14, 1944, than the wheels of the hunt went into motion. The search brought into action the aircraft of British Squadron 36. The destroyers, teamed up under squadron command of Captain A. F. Converse, included the following ships:

ELLYSON	*Comdr. E. W. Longton*
Flagship of Capt. Converse	
NIELDS	*Comdr. A. R. Heckey*
GLEAVES	*Comdr. B. L. Gurnette*
HILARY P. JONES	*Lt. Comdr. F. M. Stiesberg*
MACOMB	*Lt. Comdr. George Hutchinson*
HAMBLETON	*Comdr. H. A. Renken*
RODMAN	*Comdr. J. F. Foley*
EMMONS	*Comdr. E. B. Billingsley*

All of these DD's were veterans. And one of them, Commander Renken's HAMBLETON, had a particularly long U-boat score to settle. She, it may be recalled, was the destroyer torpedoed in Fedala Roads during "Operation Torch"—the DD that, having been cut in two, foreshortened, and sewn together again, had gone home under her own power to be overhauled and re-lengthened.

ELLYSON took first crack at the foe. She made a high-speed run to the point of first contact, which the aviators had marked with flares. After picking up sonar contact, ELLYSON pitched in with a depth-charge attack. She treated the target to a full pattern, set to explode at "shallow."

In ELLYSON's wake the sea vomited and heaved, but it failed to disgorge any submarine.

From morning until midnight of the 15th the destroyer squadron pursued the trail, hunting in two groups. The DD's swept in to the Spanish coast the following day, combing the waters off Cap de Santa Pola. U-616 was not there. Her skipper had decided to run northeast, and that evening of the 16th the sub was loping along on the surface, heading toward the Riviera.

At 2356 the U-boat was sighted by a British Wellington bomber about 50 miles distant from Converse's destroyers. The airmen passed the word, and the contact report was intercepted by both hunter-groups. They headed for the target at once, steaming at top speed on converging courses.

At midnight the sub was racing for her life, with the two groups of huntsmen in hot pursuit.

MACOMB was the first DD to sight the target. Opening up with her searchlight, she speared the gray conning tower at 2,400 yards. Mistaking the destroyer's light for that of an aircraft, the submariners opened fire with 20 mm. deck guns. MACOMB'S 5-inch 38's answered with an authoritative roar. The sub made a running dive, and MACOMB was on top of the target with depth charges at a rush. She dropped them deep, and followed with a pattern set to explode at 600 feet.

Now GLEAVES arrived on the spot, and a creeping attack was begun, with MACOMB coaching. As sonar contact could not be regained, the attack went uncompleted.

At 0145 NIELDS stepped in to drop a pattern. EMMONS followed suit. Contact petered out entirely after these attacks, and another box search was set in motion, seven DD's participating. It was now May 17.

For four days the enemy had led the hunters in a chase all around Robin Hood's Barn. And now, although they had him in the barn, he succeeded in hiding somewhere in the hay.

Around and around the hunters circled, determined to smoke out the quarry. Somewhere deep under, the sub glided and drifted with motors cut off, then ran for a moment to regain momentum, then slid silently to another level. But coast and fishtail as he would, the enemy could not shake the pursuit overhead.

At 0645, with daylight on the seascape, HAMBLETON made the electrifying sonar contact about ten miles south of the point where contact had been lost at 0230. Commander Renken conned the ship through two fast depth-charge runs, laying deep patterns set for 500-600 feet. ELLYSON and RODMAN closed in for a go at the target, and the other destroyers formed a circle with a four-mile radius encompassing the three DD's at the hub.

About 0710, while HAMBLETON, ELLYSON, and RODMAN were probing for contact, there was a swirl of water at the center of the circle. With a swoosh of spray the U-boat came up right in the bull's-eye. At once the three ships opened fire, range 2,500 yards. As 5-inchers hit the U-boat's conning tower, the Nazi submariners hit the deck. Wildly waving dungarees and shirts, the U-boat crew dived overside in one of the fastest abandonments ever beheld. As the Diesel engines were in high gear, the sub raced on across the water, leaving the survivors strewn astern.

The destroyer gunners lashed at the deserted sub. They were somewhat more humane than the U-616's skipper who, it appeared, had made a "crash dive" the previous night, leaving a crew of deck-gunners on the surface of the Mediterranean to sink or swim. The rest of the crew—53 in all—were fished from the water by destroyers ELLYSON and RODMAN. Only one of their number was injured—a man with a shrapnel wound in his hip.

U-616 went down, punctured by a score of direct hits. About three minutes later the water echoed to a thunderous boom. A few items of debris swirled to the surface. "Operation Monstrous" was over.

NIBLACK, LUDLOW, *and British Aircraft Kill* U-960 *("Monstrous 2")*

Sequel to the establishment of U-616 was the pursuit and punishment of U-960, a fellow member of the Doenitz Mediterranean mob.

If the actions of U-616 had been reckless, those of U-960 were positively suicidal. For this undersea-boat had the nerve to fire at several of the destroyers of Captain Converse's killer squadron, even as those DD's were returning in triumph from the U-616 kill. Among the targets was Captain Converse's flag destroyer ELLYSON. The spread of three torpedoes missed, but the wakes were arrows pointing to the enemy's whereabouts. Destroyer GLEAVES sighted something that looked like a periscope, and the spot was marked for immediate reference.

Presently DesDiv 25—WOOLSEY, MADISON, BENSON, and LUDLOW—arrived on the scene to relieve Captain Converse's destroyer. Division Commander R. B. Ellis in WOOLSEY took charge of the proceedings. Then another DD joined the hunt.

Top speed from the vicinity of Mers-el-Kebir raced destroyer NIBLACK (Commander R. R. Connor). To the area flew aircraft of British Squadrons 36 and 500.

The enemy was lurking in that favorite U-boat haunt, the waters about midway between Ténès, Algeria, and Cartagena on the southeast coast of Spain. At 0240 in the morning of the 19th a plane reported suspicious radar contact some ten miles from NIBLACK. The British flyers tagged the spot with a marker.

NIBLACK and LUDLOW highballed over to investigate. They sighted the marker at 0251. Thirty minutes later LUDLOW's sonar instruments registered the presence of a submarine in the vicinity. NIBLACK made sonar contact a few minutes after that, and the two DD's pitched in to dig out the U-boat.

As senior officer present, Commander Connor in NIBLACK directed the blasting, and the two destroyers roiled the water with a total of eleven depth-charge attacks. The barrage was right on target. The sun came up, and so did the U-boat.

At 0708 the submbarine broached, popping to the surface, stern first. The U-boat's tail was still silhouetted against the sky when the destroyermen opened fire. At 0712 a British plane dived on the floundering sub, pelting the water with bombs that landed close. A moment later shells from NIBLACK and LUDLOW smashed into the conning tower. Centerpiece in a bouquet of shrapnel-bursts, the U-boat sank.

NIBLACK sprinted forward to treat the sinking sub to a 10-charge pattern. Once again the U-boat was blown to the surface. Then, with stern thrust skyward, the submarine made a final dive. At 0721 NIBLACK and LUDLOW moved in to pick up the 20 survivors of the U-960—another Nazi submarine that was *kaput*. The participating destroyermen called the operation "Monstrous 2."

Spearheading "Operation Anvil" (The Cans Create a Diversion)

By July 1944 the Axis naval effort in the Mediterranean was virtually on the bottom. On the Allied agenda was "Operation Anvil—Dragoon," a power drive calculated to hurl the Nazis out of Southern France. Amphibious forces were prepared to land liberation armies on the Riviera. Beachhead battles were in prospect. But enemy naval defenses were known to be sketchy—E-boats, mine plants, some indescriminate torpedo craft.

D-Day was set for August 15. "Anvil" landings were scheduled for 0830, D-Day morning. All through the night of August 14-15 the Allied invasion ships were closing in on the French Riviera. Three main target beaches were located near the resort towns of St. Tropez, St. Maxime, and St. Raphael. Meantime, action developed on the flanks of the target area where, on the one hand, enemy surface craft were unexpectedly encountered, and on the other, a diversion was intentionally created.

A few miles south of Port Cross and Levant Islands, destroyer SOMERS (Commander W. C. Hughes, Jr.) conducted a patrol, on the lookout for enemy submarines and surface craft. She was also on duty as a fire-support ship for an advance force which had gone ashore on the Isles d'Hyeres and on the mainland near Toulon. It was hoped the landings would take the local defense by surprise at H-Hour. But at 0347 SOMERS' radar spotted two unidentified craft in the offing.

While SOMERS was discreetly shooting up these corvettes, a United States destroyer and consorts a few miles west of Toulon were indulging in some purposely indiscreet gunnery. This destroyer was the USS ENDICOTT. In her company were British gunboats APHIS and SCARAB and several rambunctious PT-boats.

If silence and blackout were imposed on the "Anvil" forces waiting for H-Hour to the east, there were no such restraints to inhibit this little group to the west. Their mission called for an excursion in the coastal waters midway between Toulon and Marseilles, and when they reached a point off the beach at La Ciotat they were to create a five-alarm disturbance with no sounds barred.

The purpose of this naval charivari was, of course, to attract attention, rattle the local area command, and convince the enemy that landing forces were about to swarm ashore at this point. While this storm in a teacup was diverting the Nazis, the real hurricane would strike the Riviera to the eastward.

In over-all command was Captain H. C. Johnson of Rear Admiral Davidson's staff. Skippering destroyer ENDICOTT was Lieutenant Commander John D. Bulkeley, who had starred as a PT-boater in the Philippines. The two British gunboats were under command of another well-known star, Lieutenant Commander Douglas Fairbanks, Jr. Serving as Special Operations Officer on Admiral Hewitt's staff, Fairbanks had himself written the plan for the La Ciotat diversion. Now, on board HMS APHIS, he was to act in the dynamic skit he had authored.

The group went in to raise a rumpus, and they raised it. As ENDICOTT and the gunboats smashed the quietude with a beach bombardment, the PT's raced shoreward in a frenzy, making all the motions of an assault.

The local reaction was immediate—wild volleys from startled sentinels, and a general view-halloo. To keep the pot boiling, ENDICOTT and her consorts moved in the following night to plaster the Ciotat beach with another barrage. But the enemy did not counterattack until early in the morning of the 17th, when two large Nazi corvettes arrived on the scene just as the "invaders" were retiring from the area. In the dusk before daybreak the British gunboats were intercepted, and there was nothing sham about the battle that ensued.

The corvettes were ugly specimens—an ex-Egyptian craft by name of KEMID ALLAH, and an ex-Italian, the CAPRIOLO. Both out-weighed the British gunboats, and the CAPRIOLO carried torpedo tubes and 4.7-inch guns.

The scrimmage promptly went against Fairbanks and his Britons. APHIS and SCARAB were outgunned to begin with, elderly to go on with, and low on ammunition to end with. Raked by shellfire, they fled soutward. The corvettes chased. At 0545 the ENDICOTT received a call for help.

Bulkeley headed the destroyer for the scene of action at 35 knots, and soon began throwing salvos at KEMID ALLAH, the larger of the two enemy vessels.

ALLAH was fast, pugnacious, and fairly powerful. Still she would have been easy prey for ENDICOTT had the destroyer's main batteries been in working order. But only one 5-inch 38 was working. ENDICOTT's other three 5-inchers were out of kilter with jammed breech-blocks—casualties caused by over-heating from fast and furious fire during the simulated assault on La Ciotat.

There was also CAPRIOLO to be dealt with. Both corvettes hurled shells at ENDICOTT, and she dodged through numerous straddles. A dud drilled through her hull, whistled into a for-ward compartment, and set fire to some bedding.

But in spite of close shaves, dud-damage, and handicapped batteries, ENDICOTT pressed forward to close the range and keep the corvettes engaged.

At 0648 the ex-Egyptian, slopping along with a port list, began to explode. The Nazi crew abandoned forthwith. CAPRIOLO now shot her bolt by firing two torpedoes at the ENDICOTT. As Bulkeley maneuvered his ship to avoid, two of the PT-boats, which had been screening ENDICOTT, dashed in to launch torpedoes at CAPRIOLO.

The ALLAH sank at 0709. A few minutes later CAPRIOLO was foundering in a fiery shellstorm. Overside scrambled as many Nazis as could make it, and the vessel sank at 0830. The destroyermen picked up 169 prisoners; the gunboats grabbed 41.

The Nazis were certainly looking in the wrong direction when "Anvil" struck the beaches east of Toulon. It could be that they were watching the drama at La Ciotat—a British-American production directed by Henry C. Johnson, starring John D. Bulkeley and Douglas Fairbanks Jr., with a cast of Royal Navy gunboat sailors, American PT-boaters, and Des-Lant destroyermen.

Destroyers Versus Human Torpedoes

What induces a man to become a human torpedo? The question is not entirely academic, for this suicidal stunt was of more than passing intrest to the Navy when the perform-ance was staged during "Operation Anvil."

Was it a desperate measure of bankrupt defense forces turning to last resorts? Or was it the manifestation of a bank-rupt Nazidom indulging the psychology of *Götterdammerung*?

In any event the German twilight had set in, and out of this twilight came the human torpedo. One of the earliest encounters with these fantastic freaks involved the American destroyer LUDLOW (Lieutenant Commander W. R. Barnes).

On the morning of September 5, 1944, LUDLOW and the French light cruiser LE MALIN were patrolling off Cape Forrat near Monte Carlo. Operating as a fire-support group, the two warships were waiting for calls from shore fire-control parties advancing with American troops along the Riviera toward Menton.

Then, about 0810, a lookout on board LE MALIN spied a queer-looking object rippling along through the sun-glazed water. An object that looked incredibly like a bubble containing a human head.

The captain of LE MALIN fixed fascinated binoculars on the object. The thing was now about 1,200 yards away, moving through the water at 6 or 7 knots, and leaving a thin, lacy wake. *"It was,"* stated Captain Ballande, *"a glass—or plexiglass—dome, about 20 inches long and 20 inches high. . . . We identified this object as the lookout station of a human torpedo."*

The object was demolished. But LUDLOW soon captured one named Seaman Joseph Schwartz of the Nazi Navy. On September 10 HILARY P. JONES sighted and sank a similar specimen.

But the Nemesis of the human torpedoes that day was destroyer MADISON (Commander D. A. Stuart). Operating off Cape Martin in the Menton area, she ran into a school of these queer fish. The first was sighted at 0718. The fish-eye globe was only 500 yards distant, and Commander Stuart directed speedy maneuvering to avoid. Then MADISON's gunners sprayed 40 mm. and 20 mm. fire at the target. A nearby PT-boat simultaneously shot at the glass dome. The torpedo went under, and the PT-boat captured the half-drowned operator.

At 0743 a scouting plane from the cruiser BROOKLYN sighted another human torpedo south of Cape Martin. MADISON and the PT-boat raced to the spot. Gunfire from the PT and depth charges from MADISON disposed of this item.

An hour or so later, while MADISON was delivering a shore bombardment, a third human torpedo was sighted. At 0900 MADISON opened fire at about five-mile range. Two salvos were seen to straddle. The target disappeared, and was scored as a "probable."

Eight minutes after that, another of these contrivances showed up on the seascape. MADISON attacked with depth charges and gunfire, sank the torpedo, and picked up the injured pilot.

She nailed a fifth human torpedo shortly after noon, having sighted the "bubble" some 1,000 yards distant to starboard. A few 5-inch salvos and a couple of depth charges put an end to the affair.

The human torpedoes were menacing enough, and their freakish effort could not be discounted as one primarily designed for a spectacular display of *hari-kiri*. Potentially the torpedo contraption was dangerous. His head in a plexiglass cupola, the pilot crouched in a watertight housing or cabin astride the torpedo. Literally riding the torpedo, he could aim it, then detach it from the housing and let it rip.

According to the captured operators, the torpedoes were electric, and left no wake. They could dive to 100 feet (if the pilot had the nerve), and in effect they were miniature midget submarines.

The pilots complained that they couldn't aim the torpedoes at fast-moving targets. To aim at anything they had to get their glass domes above the surface, and a single machine-gun bullet could smash the dome.

The captured operators confessed to a fear of gunfire, but claimed they were unafraid of depth charges—an assertion hardly substantiated by their hasty surrenders when depth charges or shells were thrown.

There remains the question of what induces a man to become a human torpedo to begin with. Consider one of the characters captured by the USS LUDLOW. Hauled to the deck, he is seen as a young man wearing blouse and shorts, swimming shoes, life jacket, and some sort of rescue breather. On his thigh is the holster of a fine Luger pistol which he has readily surrendered along with himself. He is exhausted; dripping. But when presented to LUDLOW's Commanding Officer, he stands rigid, heels together, eyes front.

Name? He answers to the absolutely improbable name of Parsival Heller.

Rank? *"Steurmaun's Obergefreiter."*

Serial number? "W18894/42."

Other questions, too, he answers willingly enough—about the number of human torpedoes in the area; their make-up, speed, diving depth, and so on. His testimony contributes to the evidence that the German commanders were desperately using last-resort measures against the ships off the Riviera.

But as to why such characters volunteered for the duty—who knows?

Destroyers in "Anvil" Chorus (Featuring MADISON *and* H. P. JONES)

The destroyers in "Operation Anvil" did not spend all or even a great part of their time chasing corvettes and freakish human torpedoes. Covering the landings and the movements of the forces ashore, the fire-support DD's were particularly busy with shore bombardments.

Perhaps one of the best examples of destroyer-work in an invasion operation comes from the industrious DD which was skippered by Lieutenant Commander F. M. Stiesberg. Here is a page from the war diary of the HILARY P. JONES.

During period 8-30 September, 1944, a total of 38 success-ful fire-support missions were fired for the First Airborne Task Force.

Ammunition Expended: 3,450 AA Common; 80 Common; 22 Smoke; 11 Star—Total 3,563 rounds.

It is clear the men in HILARY P. JONES were not sitting on their hands. Neither were any of the destroyermen who worked in "Operation Anvil." It was over by October 1944.

PART SIX

Destroyers to Asia

☆　☆　☆

Perhaps more valid Armes,
Weapons more violent when next we meet,
May serve to better us, and worse our foes,
Or equal what between us made the odds.
In Nature none: . . .

PARADISE LOST

Chapter 29

Central Pacific Push

(From the Gilberts to Saipan)

☆ ☆ ☆

DD's to the Gilberts (Battle for Tarawa)

While the destroyers of Burke, Moosbrugger, Simpson, and their contemporaries were chasing Japanese warships, *marus*, and barges out of the Upper Solomons Admiral Nimitz had decided that the time had come to excise the Gilbert Islands in the Central Pacific from the Japanese Empire.

By September, 1943, Navy and Marine forces were set for the invasion of the Gilberts. The operation was designated "Galvanic." Landings on Makin, Tarawa, and Apamama were scheduled for the morning of November 21.

Altogether some 54 DesPac destroyers and six DE's served with the forces dispatched to the Gilberts. For the most part the destroyermen had little to do. At the southern end of the Gilbert group, Apamama fell easily into the hands of a small company of Marines landed on the beach by submarine NAUTILUS and the destroyer GANESVOORT (Lieutenant Commander J. M. Steinbeck). At the northern end Makin was swiftly taken. Tarawa, in the center, was tough—a story to be told by the Marines.

FRAZIER *and* MEADE *Sink* I-35

Six Japanese I-boats, dispatched to the Gilberts, did not arrive in time to intercept the invasion forces, but two of them managed to get themselves intercepted.

In the afternoon of November 22, while screening the heavy units of a cruiser division about nine miles northwest of Betio, destroyer MEADE (Lieutenant Commander J. Munholland) put a "pinging" finger on an undersea target. MEADE's report brought destroyer FRAZIER (Commander E. M. Brown) on the run to join the hunt.

The destroyers jockeyed into attack position; the "ashcans" were sent rolling; patterned explosions thudded under the sea. The sub, when detected, was at shallow depth, and the blasting must have hampered her diving capacity. Up came a great swirl of oil which clogged the air with fumes. The DD's immediately deposited four more depth charges on the fringe of the oil slick.

Results were prompt. The sub came thrashing to the surface, and Japs scrambled out of the conning tower. Both destroyers opened fire as the I-boat broached. Pummeled by 5-inch and 40 mm. fire, the submarine pitched and rolled in a torment of TNT. Then FRAZIER raced in to ram. Like a ploughshare, the destroyer's bow sliced into the sub's pressure hull just aft of the conning tower. FRAZIER backed off, and the I-boat, with the sea pouring into its vitals, plunged to the bottom.

Two survivors, fished from the sea, identified the sunken sub as the I-35.

RADFORD *Kills* I-19

The submarine which had torpedoed WASP on September 15, 1942, and which may have been responsible for the torpedoing of NORTH CAROLINA on that same date, was the Imperial Navy's I-19. This ship-killer met her match on the evening of November 25, 1943, when she surfaced in the waters off Tarawa. At that hour she ran into destroyer RADFORD (Commander G. E. Griggs).

The time was 2049. The radar range was about eight miles. At 2130 the "pip" disappeared from the screen—meaning submarine. Ten minutes later RADFORD tagged the submerged target with her sonar gear, and her skipper conned the destroyer for seven runs over the target. Several of the runs were "dry," but enough of them were of the type which liquidates submarines. Down went the "ashcans" and up came the rubbish. The destroyermen smelled Diesel oil for the rest of the night, and an expansive oil slick was sighted. The following morning, aircraft noted a great strew of flotsam which included wood, cork, and various indefinable remnants of submarining.

A post-war examination of Japanese records disclosed the number of RADFORD's victim—I-19.

DD's *to the Marshalls* (WALKER *Kills* RO-39)

In February 1944 Nimitz pulled the trigger on "Operation

Flintlock," a massive naval-air drive designed to blast the Japs out of the Marshall Islands. Kwajalein was the big bull's-eye. Roi, Namur, Wotje and Taroa were in for a blasting.

Some 54 DD's and six DE's had participated in the Gilbert seizure. Now 83 destroyers and three DE's served in the naval power-house that swept into the Marshalls.

While Kwajalein was being blown out of the Japanese Empire, Task Unit 50.15.2 was operating in the eastern Marshalls, hammering Jap airfields on Wotje and Taroa. Working as a screen for SALT LAKE CITY were destroyers ABBOT and WALKER. The ships concluded a shelling of Wotje at 0327 in the morning of February 2, 1944. At 0418 WALKER's radar picked up a surface target at 13,300 yards range. Her skipper, Commander H. E. Townsend, closed the range to 6,000 and ordered a starshell spread. Silhouetted in the eerie light was the conning tower of a Jap submarine.

The sub dived before WALKER's gunners could open fire. But the sonar crew had the contact directly at 2,500 yards. Townsend conned the ship for a depth-charge run. Five charges were dropped. The ship circled off, maneuvering to start a second run. A second was unnecessary. Under the sea there was a clap of thunder that trailed off into the valleys of the deep. After the thunder ebbed away, sonar contact could not be regained.

WALKER searched the area, and her lookouts sighted a large carpet of oil on the water. Ordinarily a destroyer did not sink an ocean-going submarine with a single depth-charge run, but WALKER's was the exceptional performance that proved the rule. After the war the sunken sub was located in the records of the Japanese Sixth (Submarine) Fleet. She was the RO-39.

CHARRETTE *and* FAIR *Down* I-21

The Japanese submarine I-21 had an interesting, and to the Jap point of view, distinguished career. She was in the vanguard of Vice Admiral Nagumo's Striking Force at Pearl Harbor. And she was the sub which probably sank the destroyer PORTER during the Battle of the Santa Cruz Islands. But her own destiny overtook her on February 4, 1944.

On that date destroyer CHARRETTE (Commander E. S. Karpe) was operating with Rear Admiral F. C. Sherman's Task Group 58.3 (built around the carriers BUNKER HILL, MONTEREY, and COWPENS). At 2203 in the evening of the 3rd, battleship NEW JERSEY reported radar contact with an enemy vessel 21 miles distant. CHARRETTE was ordered to leave her station in the Sound screen and track down the target. The "pip" disappeared at 10,300 yards.

At 0003 in the morning of February 4 the destroyer put a "pinging" finger on the sub. Running in, CHARRETTE dropped an 8-charge pattern. She followed through with several approaches, but lost sonar contact as the sub went deep. Destroyer-escort FAIR (Lieutenant Commander D. S. Crocker, USNR) was sent to the scene to aid the hunt.

The DD and the DE worked like a long-practiced team. Nine minutes after FAIR reported for duty CHARRETTE coached her into position for a hedgehog attack. The DE let fly at 0040. The projectiles splashed in the sea, and a moment later four detonations were counted. These hits were followed by a roulade of explosions which signalled the farewell of the enemy submersible. About three minutes after the hedgehog salvo, the roulade was concluded by a deep-sea thunderclap. The war had caught up with I-21.

PHELPS *and* SAGE *Sink* RO-40

PHELPS (Lieutenant Commander D. L. Martineau) was one of th escort vessels assigned to the Southern Group of the Eniwetok Expeditionary Group which Rear Admiral H. W. Hill rushed westward. The group steamed out of Kwajalein at daylight on February 15, 1944. At 1742 of the following day, PHELPS made sonar contact with a target at 1,700 yards.

The destroyer executed a deliberate attack, dropping a full pattern of depth charges. While the destroyer was attacking, Captain E. R. McLean, Commander of the Southern Group, riding in PHELPS, turned the formation away. Two ships joined the sub-hunt—destroyer MACDONOUGH and minesweeper SAGE. The SAGE (Lieutenant F. K. Zinn, USNR) was a little 700-tonner, but she followed up the contact and launched a depth-charge attack on the undersea foe.

The contact evaporated after SAGE made her attack. The ship searched until sunset, and then PHELPS and SAGE were ordered to rejoin the formation. MACDONOUGH continued the hunt for some time with negative results. An oil slick was sighted by other vessels in the area, but the destroyermen and the "miners" could not believe they had downed a sub in an action which lasted only a few minutes.

But there the RO-40 was on the bottom, and her obituary was found in the records of the Japanese Submarine Force at the end of the war.

NICHOLAS *Kills* I-11

Early in the morning of February 17, 1944, destroyer NICHOLAS (Commander R. T. S. Keith) was escorting three merchantmen from Pearl Harbor to Kwajalein. The convoy was about halfway between Hawaii and the Marshalls when NICHOLAS picked up a radar contact with a surface target 24,000 yards distant.

Commander Keith sent the DD racing to close the range. At 2,800 yards the target vessel appeared to be submerging—obviously a submersible. NICHOLAS immediately opened fire with main battery guns, and flashes indicated several hits. The 5-inch salvos hurried the submarine's dive, but she did not go down fast enough to escape sonar detection.

Conning the ship deftly, Commander Keith ran NICHOLAS in for an urgent depth-charge attack. She followed through with three deliberately laid patterns. About ten minutes after the third attack a basso explosion boomed in the deep. The blast sent to the surface a swirl of oil and a litter of shattered planking. This residue was all that remained to mark the grave of the Imperial Navy's I-11.

MANLOVE *and* PC-1135 *Kill* I-32

After blasting the Marshall out of the Japanese Empire, the Navy's power-house smote other Jap strongholds in the Central Pacific. By March '44 the Jap bastion at Truk was neutralized. Eniwetok was in American hands. Jap bases in the Marianas had been flogged by an iron hurricane.

DesPac destroyers and DE's worked with the task forces that lambasted these Jap outposts and sank the Rising Sun in the middle of the Pacific Ocean.

For reasons best known to the strategists of the Imperial High Command, the Japs tried to maintain a foothold on some of the atolls of the eastern Carolines. By so doing they provided the U.S. Navy with some excellent gunnery and anti-submarine practice.

On March 24 a hunter-killer team was dispatched to waters east of the Marshalls to intercept a Japanese transport submarine bound with supplies for the garrison on Wotje. The team contained destroyers HALSEY POWELL and HULL, and destroyer-escort MANLOVE. Operating with these ships was PC-1135.

Rendezvousing at Erikub Atoll on March 23, the team searched around Wotje for three nights. At 0422 on March 24 the DE and PC moved to investigate a target detected by radar. The range was about five miles. The night was moonless, but apparently the destroyer-escort and her companion were sighted by Jap eyes at 3,000 yards. At any rate the "pip" vanished, and MANLOVE promptly acquired sound contact. Skippering the DE, Lieutenant Commander J. P. Ingle, USNR, jockeyed in for a hedgehog barrage. The PC, captained by Lieutenant W. S. O'Kelly, USNR, was coached in for a one-two attack. This coordinated attack produced results.

MANLOVE fired four hedgehog salvos, and rolled an ashcan pattern. The PC let fly with four mousetrap salvos. This was one of the few instances in the war wherein American mousetraps caught a rat. A few seconds after the fourth mousetrap snapped, there were several explosions. Four minutes later the hunters heard two distant, deep explosions. After this final blasting neither ship was able to regain contact. With their usual methods, the hunter-killer team continued the search. To no avail. Daylight provided an answer—the seascape was smeared by an oil slick that extended for five miles. From the waters off Wotje the destroyer-escort MANLOVE and PC-1135 had removed one submarine, the I-32.

Punch at Palau

Late in March, 1944, Task Force 58 struck at the Pelews (sometimes called the Palau Islands) in the western Carolines. This strike took Navy planes within 500 miles of the Philippines. Meantime, Nimitz and Spruance were planning an invasion of the Marianas similar to "Operation Flintlock." With the invasion of Saipan the Japanese sun would go down to the western horizon.

Admiral Koga saw disaster coming, but he died in a plane smash somewhere off Palau before he could do anything about it. His epaulets passed to Admiral Soemu Toyoda, who had no better success at stopping the sunset.

Chapter 30

Gang Busters, Pacific

(April 1944-June 1944)

☆ ☆ ☆

Sinking the Emperor's Subs

The Japanese submarine effort was in some respects like buckshot. It went off with a great, thundering bang, and then sprayed all over the place, losing force through dispersal.

There was no Japanese wolfpack campaign comparable to the German; no attrition offensive dedicated to the destruction of Allied merchant or naval shipping. The Jap submarines were kept busy running erands for the Army, or hauling oil from some remote Borneo port to the homeland.

In consequence the American A/S forces in the Pacific were not called upon to fight such an undersea war as engaged their counterparts in the Atlantic. As fighting units, the I-boats and RO-boats were decidedly inferior to the U-boats. Jap Submarine Admiral Miwa boasted that the Japanese had invented a "breather" device similar to *Schnorkel,* but material bottlenecks impeded its production. Radar was not installed in Japanese submarines until June 1944. The large plane-carrying I-boats were slow divers, and the smaller I- and RO-specimens were not as sturdy as their Nazi accomplices.

However, the Japanese sub could be a dangerous foe, and there was nothing buckshot about the Jap torpedo. The Emperor's Submarine Force maintained the menace of a "fleet in being." And U.S. Navy hunter-killer teams were organized in the Pacific to reduce the menacing "being." The spring of '44 would be an unhappy season for Jap submariners.

SAUFLEY *Kills* I-2

After the Battle of Cape Esperance (October 11-12, 1942), a Jap submarine had attacked the destroyer McCALLA, which was combing the waters north of Savo for survivors. The sub which had made that frustrated effort was the I-2.

The I-2 was still in the Solomons area in the spring of 1944. That was her last season on that or any front. On April 7, DesDiv 43 (RENSHAW, SAUFLEY, PRINGLE, and PHILIP) was patrolling in the vicinity of Mussau and Emirau Islands. At 0630 SAUFLEY's sonar tagged a submarine 1,350 yards distant. Lieutenant Commander D. E. Cochran conned the ship for a depth-charge run.

At 0645 SAUFLEY dropped a conventional 9-charge pattern. Thirty minutes later she dropped another of the same. Eight minutes after that a couple of heavy deep-sea explosions shook the ship. Sonar contact evaporated. SAUFLEY "pinged" all over the seascape to no avail. Then, at 1120, an expanding oil slick was located about four miles from the scene of the last depth-charging. The oil was analyzed and found to be Diesel. By sunset the slick was 14 miles long. It marked the grave of I-2, SAUFLEY's No. 2 submarine.

MACDONOUGH, STEPHEN POTTER, and *Aircraft Down* I-174

Late in April '44, while the Navy's forces solidified their positions in the Marshalls and MacArthur's troops swept across Hollandia, U.S. Task Force 58 dealt a final smash at Truk. Among the numerous smashers were the light aircraft carrier MONTEREY (Captain S. H. Ingersoll) and the destroyers MACDONOUGH (Commander J. W. Ramey) and STEPHEN POTTER (Commander C. H. Crichton).

As with the previous strike, this one was an air show. The island was given a monstrous blasting. Meanwhile, MONTEREY, MACDONOUGH, and STEPHEN POTTER, on picket station 60 miles south of Truk, bagged an I-boat.

MACDONOUGH made the contact at 0621 in the morning of April 30—a radar indication, range 12,600 yards. Commander Ramey rushed the destroyer for an intercepting position. At 1,760 yards the target vanished from the screen in a fast dive. Sonar took up where radar left off.

Ramey directed the dropping of a depth-charge pattern. Overside went the ashcans and teardrops. Up came the water-thunder. A few minutes later the DD's lookouts sighted a glistening oil slick. The I-boat was bleeding.

At this juncture STEPHEN POTTER steamed up to lend a hand. And down from the distance came a Grumman to join the proceedings. The POTTER made a run, depositing a pattern of depth charges. Then the aircraft got in its licks at the slicks, after which MACDONOUGH made a second depth-charge attack.

When the barrage quieted down and the waters calmed, a great patch of oil spread across the sea and a litter of debris came bobbing to the surface. Deep-bellied rumblings were heard. After these explosions, the sonar operators were unable to regain contact with the submarine. Like Truk, it had been blown out of the war.

Japanese records indicated later that this victim was the I-174.

HAGGARD, FRANKS, and JOHNSTON *Kill* I-176

Another highly efficient I-boat hunt began on May 12, 1944, when DesDiv 94 (Commander J. H. Nevins, Jr.) steamed out of Blanche Harbor in the Treasuries to track down a Jap sub spotted by a plane off Buka.

The hunting division consisted of DD's HAGGARD (Commander D. A. Harris), HAILEY (Commander P H. Brady), FRANKS (Commander N. A. Lidstone), and JOHNSTON (Commander E. E. Evans).

Early in the morning of May 16 the hunters arrived in the waters northwest of Buka where the I-boat had been spotted. The search was begun. Not long after sunrise, four destroyers of DesDiv 93 (Captain I. H. Nunn) arrived on the scene. Under Captain Nunn's direction the search intensified.

To the submarine crouching in the depths the whisper of screws loudening, fading, and coming back with a roar of static, and the hour-after-hour tension of waiting in helpless inertia, must have created an accumulation of nerve-strain approaching the unbearable. All the sweating, stupefied Japanese crew could do was to wait for their hour to come.

For I-176 that fatal hour arrived at 2145, twenty hours after the beginning of the "holddown," when the destroyer HAGGARD, after making sound contact, dropped a full depth-charge pattern on the hiding submersible. The stunned submariners got their I-boat out from under, but they could not escape the trap.

Destroyers JOHNSTON and FRANKS closed in. At 2213 HAGGARD's sonar again picked up the I-boat, and Commander Harris immediately treated the sub to another full depth-charge pattern.

At midnight JOHNSTON turned over contact to destroyer FRANKS. Down upon the target FRANKS dropped a full depth-charge pattern. When the thunder finally died away, the silence in the sea was that of a grave. Duly inscribed in Imperial Navy records, the obituary of the I-176 was found by American investigators after the war.

ENGLAND *and the RO-Boats (Prologue to a Six-Part Serial)*

In the spring of 1944, Admiral Soemu Toyoda assembled

the Japanese Combined Fleet in the Philippines at the old American fleet anchorage of Tawi Tawi. There he sat down to wait. For what? Toyoda himself was not sure.

In the Central Pacific a United States armada was gathering muscle in the Marshalls. In the Southwest Pacific MacArthur's troops were firmly installed on the New Guinea coast at Hollandia and Aitape. Would the American fleet drive from the Marshalls to strike Guam and Saipan in the Marianas? Or would MacArthur's forces drive from New Guinea to strike the Japanese stronghold of Palau in the western Carolines? At Tawi Tawi in the Philippines, Admiral Toyoda would have given a good deal to know the answer.

Studying charts, piecing together intelligence reports, Toyoda finally concluded that the island of Manus in the Admiralties was being rigged by the Americans as the springboard for a great drive at Palau. The Admiral did not risk a jump at this conclusion. Convinced though he was, he sought substantiating evidence. For an American drive at the Marianas still remained a possibility, and Toyoda wanted to know with absolute certainty which way the cat was going to leap.

So Admiral Toyoda appealed to Headquarters Japanese Submarine Force. What the Admiral wanted was a submarine scouting line to cover the southern approaches to the Pelews; a line that would extend from the waters south of Truk to the waters some distance west of Manus. He wanted the submarines so placed along this line that an invasion fleet moving westward would inevitably be detected.

The subs were provided. Assigned to the vital mission was a select division of war-built RO-boats: RO-104, RO-105, RO-106, RO-108, RO-116, and RO-117. Southward they went in mid-May to take their stations in the scouting line. No doubt Toyoda realized they were flimsy pickets in a precarious fence. But they were the only pickets available.

Now it happened that while Toyoda and other Japanese naval heads were juggling grand strategy, a little DE was fussing around in the far-off eastern Solomons—on May 18, to be specific, she was at Purvis Bay, Florida Island. The destroyer-escort ENGLAND, commissioned on December 10, 1943, was a newcomer in the Southwest Pacific.

ENGLAND was captained by Lieutenant Commander Walton B. Pendleton. Her Executive Officer was Lieutenant Commander John A. Williamson. They were trained naval officers and experienced shiphandlers, but in common with the rest of ENGLAND's crew, they had as yet to hear the explosion of hedgehog projectiles against an enemy submarine's pressure hull.

At Purvis Bay ENGLAND was assigned to Escort Division 39, which included destroyer-escorts GEORGE (Lieutenant Commander Fred W. Just, USNR), and RABY (Lieutenant Commander James Scott, II). Commander Hamilton Hains, the Officer in Tactical Command, rode in GEORGE. Commander C. A. Thorwall, USNR, the second escort division commander in the group, rode in ENGLAND. The three DE's were attached to the new escort-carrier HOGGATT BAY for A/S duty.

On the morning of May 18 there were no indications of high drama in the making for destroyer-escort ENGLAND. No star fell across her bow, nor did an albatross visit her as a sign. A Jap submarine was reported heading south from Truk with supplies for Bougainville, and the DE division was ordered out to intercept. Just another job—nothing to suggest that in future histories of the Destroyer Service, the name ENGLAND would assume the glow of a first-magnitude constellation.

ENGLAND *Kills* I-16 *(First Installment)*

Report of the I-boat from Truk had reached the U.S. Third Fleet flagship on the evening of May 17. Ever since Bougainville had been cut off and by-passed, Jap submersibles had been trying to supply the large garrison isolated at Buin. Obviously the sub in question was Buin bound. Accordingly, ENGLAND, GEORGE, and RABY were dispatched to waters northwest of Bougainville to waylay this undersea supply boat.

The DE's employed the familiar technique of plotting the submarine's assumed course from start to destination, and then proceeding on this course to meet the advancing sub. Spaced 4,000 yards apart, the three ships steamed in a line, making sonar sweeps calculated to detect the I-boat if it passed anywhere in the vicinity. By a blend of estimate and algebra, the destroyermen deduced they would meet the enemy submarine sometime in the afternoon of May 20. But the sun was high on the 19th when ENGLAND made sound contact in the vicinity of lat. 05-10 S., long. 158-17 E.—a point not far from the passage between Bougainville and Choiseul. The time was 1325. The sub was seven miles east of the expected point, and 24 hours ahead of schedule!

The Sound man reported an "underwater object." He was an inexperienced hand, but ENGLAND's skipper would not risk a delay to replace him. Commander Pendleton ordered an immediate attack. Executive Officer Williamson and crew snapped into action. A cautious trial run—a "dry run"—convinced Sound the "object" was a submarine. Then Pendleton ordered a hedgehog salvo. ENGLAND maneuvered into firing position. The projectiles soared away and spattered the surface.

No luck on the first attack. But the DE's second attack produced results. Somewhere under water there was a sharp explosion, not much louder than a door-bang. ENGLAND's captain and crew had heard their first hedgehog hit. Up came a cluster of bubbles. The turbulence subsided; the ship swung around; Pendleton drove ENGLAND on another run. The sub was fishtailing, and the destroyer tried again with hedgehog. Altogether ENGLAND made five runs, firing hedgehog. On the fifth run—time: 1433—she hit the winning combination.

Twelve seconds after the projectiles splashed water, the depth re-echoed the thud of several muffled explosions. A flash at 54 fathoms was registered on the fathometer as the ship passed over the submarine. About two minutes later came the deep-sea climax, a blast that jolted the ship.

Executive Officer Williamson stated, *"This explosion was so violent that it knocked men off their feet throughout the ship. At first we thought we had been torpedoed."*

About 20 minutes later the destroyermen sighted the evidence of a kill. Up came a slow seepage of oil which gradually developed into a gusher that spread across acres of the ocean's surface. Up with the oil came kindling wood and other items of debris. I-16 was an ex-submarine. And ENGLAND was on her way to stardom.

ENGLAND *Kills* RO-106 (Second Installment)

The sinking of I-16 puzzled the hunter-killers. According to calculations, the supply sub from Truk should not have shown up until the following afternoon. On the assumption that they had bagged a Japanese "stray," the hunters continued on the line they had originally set out to follow. So they headed toward Truk.

Then a plane from Manus sighted a sub in the area. The plane flashed the word to Halsey's flagship. Since his big board showed ENGLAND, RABY, and GEORGE in the suspected scouting line's vicinity, Halsey immediately dispatched the DE trio to the area where the RO-boat had been sighted.

Early in the morning of May 22, destroyer-escort GEORGE reported radar contact, range 14,000 yards. The three DE's headed for the target. ENGLAND picked up the "pip" at 15,000 yards, and closed in with GEORGE on the attack.

At 0410 GEORGE swept the seascape with her searchlight. ENGLAND's bridge personnel glimpsed the sub—a ghostly shadow in the offing. GEORGE's bridge gang failed to spot the ghost, but ENGLAND's had a good look at 1,400 yards. The phantom immediately faded, and its "pip" vanished from the radar screen. But as the enemy submerged, GEORGE made sound contact and Commander Just fired hedgehog.

The salvo missed. GEORGE lost contact. However, ENGLAND

obtained a clear sound contact at 2,500 yards. Pendleton maneuvered in, and the hedgehogs soared. No hits! The sub was fishtailing. But ENGLAND got another 'bead," and at 0444 Pendleton ordered another hedgehog salvo. Eighteen seconds later came three sharp explosions. At 0451, while ENGLAND was making a third run, all hands heard a thunderstorm under the sea. The rumbling shook the DE and vibrated the teeth of her sister ships. The booming came from an exploding submarine.

In the morning an oil slick was sighted. Also scraps of debris. This was the residue of RO-106.

ENGLAND *Kills* RO-104 *(Third Installment)*

Twenty-four hours after ENGLAND scored her second sinking, the group picked up a new contact. Time: 0604 in the morning of May 23. Destroyer-escort RABY caught the "pip" on her radar screen, and dashed forward as the target disappeared. Promptly RABY obtained sound contact; and Commander Scott directed a hedgehog attack. The salvo missed. RABY tried again. Another miss. For the next half hour she made runs and attacks, relaying ranges and bearings as she did so to let the other DE's plot positions. She riddled the water with a hedgehog barrage, but she failed to hit the detected submarine.

For this Jap sub was skippered by an artful dodger. Foxy, he "pinged" back at the "pinging" DE's to muddle the electronic recorders. Having expended 50 minutes and most of her hedgehog ammunition, frustrated RABY gave over to GEORGE.

GEORGE picked up the contact, ran in, and let fly with hedgehog. The salvo missed. Then ENGLAND stepped up to bat. Sound had difficulty obtaining distinct echoes, so ENGLAND's marksmen held their fire to let GEORGE do it. GEORGE executed four more attacks—no hits. She retired again to the sidelines, and ENGLAND took over.

At 0819 ENGLAND fired a full hedgehog salvo. She followed through with another at 0834. About 22 seconds after this salvo went rocketing, the adjacent water boiled and boomed like a witch's cauldron.

Apparently a dozen projectiles had found the mark, for the undersea din was prodigious. So was the eventual silence. Pendleton sent his DE running over the spot, and the submarine's destruction was certified by a pattern of 13 depth charges set to blow deep. They blew, and the fragmentary rummage of RO-104 swam to the surface.

Score another kill for ENGLAND.

ENGLAND *Kills* RO-116 *(Fourth Installment)*

About an hour after ENGLAND slew her third Jap submersible, Hains' hunter-killer group made still another submarine contact. The DE's were unable to run this one down. But it assured Hains that the Japanese had indeed established a scouting line southwest of Truk. And the group leader was in something of a quandary. His ships were running low on fuel and hedgehog ammunition. Should they chance it toward Truk, or head for Manus? The decision was to head for Manus on the line they were already following. They could not have taken a more fortuitous tack.

They were patrolling down the line—interval eight miles—when they made their next contact. Early in the morning of May 24 GEORGE caught the "pip" on her radar screen, range 14,000 yards. The "pip" soon vanished, but at 0150 ENGLAND had Sound contact with the submerged submarine.

ENGLAND at once headed for the sub. But the enemy executed some cagey evasion tactics. *"This submarine was by far the trickiest we had encountered,"* Pendleton noted. *"We were forced to make two dry runs before our firing run, on which we hit."* Projector Mark-10 charges were thrown. At least three struck the target. No undersea uproar at this time. Nothing more than a muffled grumble followed by deep silence. But the silence had the sound of extinction. The echo-rangers could find nothing to "ping" on.

And in the morning ENGLAND's whaleboat, searching a sea burnished with sunrise, discovered several small ponds of oil in which drifted shattered pieces of deck-planking. The next afternoon extensive oil slicks were sighted. The oil and the planking were all that was left of RO-116—another submarine deleted from the Japanese scouting line.

ENGLAND *Kills* RO-108 *(Fifth Installment)*

May 26, 1944—by that day ENGLAND's reputation had soared to a point that embarrassed her modest captain and crew. Modesty, however, would not restrain her from pursuing her sensational career—which she did on the evening of May 26.

Spaced at 16,000 yards, ENGLAND, GEORGE, and RABY were patrolling across dark seas toward Seeadler Harbor. At 2303 RABY picked up radar contact, range 14,000 yards. One minute later ENGLAND had the contact. She headed for the target. The Jap sub submerged when the range closed to 4,100 yards. Too late. At 2315 ENGLAND's sonar crew reported contact, range 1,700 yards. The DE slowed to 10 knots; maneuvered into position; fired a hedgehog salvo at 2323. The salvo was echoed by basso explosions.

ENGLAND moved to the sidelines, and her teammates took over the detection gear. RABY and GEORGE conducted a retiring search to the sub's "7-hour circle," but they were unable to locate the target. Reason: there was no target left to locate.

At daybreak the destroyermen discovered evidence of ENGLAND's deadly marksmanship. Greasy bubbles were blubbering to the surface at the spot where the sub had broken up. Boating through the bubbles, RABY's men found a piece of mahogany with a brass fitting (perhaps part of a chronometer case), deck planking, some hunks of cork, and other nondescript items of debris. One item found was a meat chopping block—a grim *memento mori*. The victim was eventually identified as RO-108.

So ENGLAND had done it again. Five submarines within a week! Toyoda's scouts were suffering like the Ten Little Indians in the nursery rhyme. No. 1 had been ousted by the plane from Manus. ENGLAND had carried on as recounted. And then, as in the rhyme, that left only one.

ENGLAND, GEORGE, RABY, HAZELWOOD, and SPANGLER *Kill* RO-105 *(Last Installment)*

At this stage of the ENGLAND campaign, Halsey decided to send HOGGATT BAY to the scene. On May 30 the escort-carrier was in the waters off Manus. With her were destroyers HAZELWOOD (Commander V. P. Douw) and McCORD (Commander W. T. Kenny).

The destroyer-escort SPANGLER (Lieutenant Commander D. J. McFarlane, USNR), had already been dispatched from Tulagi for a rendezvous with ENGLAND, GEORGE, and RABY at Manus. She was waiting with a supply of hedgehog ammunition when Hains' hunter-killer group came in on the afternoon of the 27th.

So the three DE's found a sizable reception committee on hand at Seeadler Harbor. They stayed overnight; loaded; took on fuel. Late afternoon of the 28th they were out again, SPANGLER included.

Early in the morning of May 30 the destroyer HAZELWOOD, sweeping with radar, picked up a "pip" at 15,000 yards. Time: 0144. At 0153 the "pip" evaporated, but the destroyer immediately obtained sonar contact. HAZELWOOD attacked with depth charges. Damage was probable, but she failed to flush the sub. She maintained contact until 0435, at which time she was relieved by GEORGE and RABY, called in to assist. The two DE's had been echo-ranging in formation with ENGLAND and SPANGLER. The latter pair, under Commander C. A. Thorwall,

USNR. (ComCortDiv 40, riding in ENGLAND), continued the search.

GEORGE established contact; made several attacks: finished off with a run at 0630, firing a full hedgehog pattern. Three explosions indicated hits. RABY followed through with several attacks. These the wounded sub evaded. The two DE's spent the rest of the day trying to track the sub. By evening it was apparent that she was playing 'possum in a foxhole.

Shortly after sunset three underwater blasts thundered in the sea. But evidence of destruction did not bob to the surface. The explosions were baffling. Had a tricky submarine skipper detonated torpedoes to deceive the hunters? So it seemed, for the DE's presently regained contact with the submersible. RABY and GEORGE were ordered to maintain the contact. The following morning they renewed the attack.

Meanwhile, ENGLAND and SPANGLER, overhearing TBS dialogue between RABY and GEORGE, steamed to the attack area. Arriving on the scene at 0500, they took position on the 5,000 yard circle. SPANGLER presently maneuvered in to add her hedgehogs to the barrage. Her salvos missed. And at that juncture the DE's were warned by Halsey's flagship that they might be attacked by air and had better clear out.

Pull out and let the cornered submarine escape? *"Oh, hell,"* Commander Hains exclaimed over the TBS, *"Go ahead, ENGLAND!"*

So ENGLAND went ahead. At 0729 she obtained sonar contact. Six minutes later Pendleton ordered the firing of a full salvo. The hedgehogs soared, dug in, and hit. Initial explosions were climaxed by a ship-shaking blast.

Soon the surface was blotched by a spew of debris. Reporting the matter, Lieutenant Commander Pendleton wrote: *"It is believed this submarine was destroyed. It seems that practice does make perfect."* He need not have qualified these statements. RO-105 had come to the end of the line. And ENGLAND had polished off her sixth submarine.

ENGLAND *and the RO-Boats (Epilogue)*

Six enemy submarines in 12 days! In recognition of a feat unparalleled in Navy history, destroyer-escort ENGLAND was awarded the Presidential Unit Citation.

But ENGLAND's phenomenal A/S score was by no means the sum total of her accomplishment. Pendleton and his crew had done something more than annihilate six Japanese subs. They had wiped out a scouting line—one of the more important scouting lines of the Pacific War.

Even in the barest of summaries the record is impressive. She killed I-16.

She killed RO-106.
She killed RO-104.
She killed RO-116.
She killed RO-108.
And she finished off RO-105.

With that Toyoda's scouting line was abolished. In consequence, the Commander-in-Chief of the Japanese Combined Fleet at Tawi Tawi failed to get word which might have made all the difference between victory and defeat in the Battle of the Philippine Sea.

For the word he did get was the gloomy intelligence that his scouting line had been sunk. Not unnaturally he assumed that a great armada was assembling in the Manus area and that his undersea scouts had been obliterated by a horde of Allied warships. This assumption was never officially admitted, but in post-war statements Toyoda acknowledged that he thought the Allies were aiming their next drive at Palau. It would seem he based this deduction on the A/S activity south of Truk.

In any event, Toyoda bobbled a command decision and rushed 71 Jap planes from Guam to the Pelews. If Toyoda's decision *was* influenced by the destruction of his Truk-Manus scouting line, ENGLAND and her companions had indeed done something more than sink six RO-boats. All unknowing, they had achieved what amounted to a major feint—a strategic feint that threw Toyoda's defenses off base two weeks before the American drive for Saipan.

Chapter 31

Western Pacific Push

☆ ☆ ☆

Destroyers Westward Ho! (Down Go More Imperial Subs)

By the late spring of 1944 the bastions of Japan's inner Pacific defense line were crumbling like rotten ice. Like a tidal wave the war was rushing westward toward Japan, toward the Philippines, and toward the Netherlands East Indies. Allied A/S teams were sinking Jap submarines in droves. And Allied fleets, including American destroyers and destroyer-escorts, were priming for a showdown.

In the South Pacific, Seventh Fleet forces swept the Admiralty Islands into the Allied bag. American and Australian troops drove the Japs toward the western end of New Guinea, and MacArthur's vanguard stormed into Hollandia. In June '44 the Navy's Central Pacific powerhouse crashed over the Marianas and gained Saipan and Tinian. Teams of destroyers and DE's contributed A/S screens, AA gunnery and shore bombardments to these drives. Some 138 DD's and 21 DE's participated in the Marianas assault. Miraculously enough no DD's nor DE's were lost in these giant amphibious operations. And only a few suffered battle damage.

But June 1944 was a bad month for the Imperial Japanese Navy. Jap carrier forces took a stupendous beating in the Battle of the Philippine Sea which was triggered off by Admiral Toyoda's faulty assumption concerning Allied intentions (an assumption due in part, at least, to the rampage staged by DE ENGLAND). And in addition to disastrous losses suffered by Japanese forces afloat, the Jap Submarine Force was hard hit.

Nine of the Emperor's subs were abolished by Allied A/S teams that June. American destroyermen accounted for six of the nine.

On June 10 destroyer TAYLOR (Commander N. J. F. Frank)

sank the I-5 off the Admiralties. Depth-charges blew the I-boat to the surface. Gunfire buried the remains.

That same night destroyer-escort BANGUST (Lieutenant Commander C. F. MacNish, USNR) caught and sank the RO-111 off Kwajalein. Hedgehog did the job.

Destroyer MELVIN (Commander W. R. Edsall) killed an RO-boat off Saipan on the 13th. Depth-charges. The victim: RO-36.

On the 16th destroyer-escort BURDEN R. HASTINGS was nearing Eniwetok. Lookouts sighted something on the surface. The DE's skipper, Lieutenant Commander E. B. Fay, USNR, challenged by Aldis lamp. No answer. So the DE pitched in, and summarily sank the RO-44.

On the 17th destroyer MELVIN contacted another enemy sub off Saipan. Destroyer WADLEIGH (Commander W. C. Winn) joined the deadly game of tag. Depth charges killed RO-114.

On June 22 destroyer NEWCOMB (Commander L. B. Cook) and destroyer mine-sweeper CHANDLER (Lieutenant Commander H. L. Thompson, Jr.) were screening transports bound for Saipan. Between them they caught the I-185. When the blasting was ended so was the I-boat.

July '44 was another bad month for the Japanese Submarine Fleet.

Destroyer-escort RIDDLE (Lieutenant Commander R. H. Cramer, USNR) and destroyer DAVID W. TAYLOR (Commander W. H. Johnson) celebrated the Fourth by winning an A/S engagement off the Marianas. Hedgehog and depth-charge patterns spelled doom for the I-10.

On the 13th destroyer-escort WILLIAM C. MILLER (Lieutenant Commander D. F. Francis, USNR) caught the I-16 off Saipan. Two thirteen-charge patterns got the I-boat's number.

On July 19 destroyer-escort WYMAN (Lieutenant Commander E. P. Parker, USNR) tracked down a sub in the waters between Eniwetok and Saipan. Parker dealt two hedgehog patterns. Down went RO-48. Up came oil and debris. While WYMAN's whaleboat was combing the debris for evidence, the boaters were strafed by friendly aircraft. Two destroyermen were wounded before recognition was made.

On the evening of July 28 the WYMAN and destroyer-escort REYNOLDS (Lieutenant Commander E. P. Adams, USNR) steamed away from a group screening the carrier HOGGATT BAY. They were bent on bagging a sub spotted by the lookouts. After a long, fast run, WYMAN picked up sonar contact. Parker fired a hedgehog pattern. The pattern raised a deep-sea roar. Up came oil and rubbish—the remains of a Jap sub later identified as the I-55. WYMAN had earned sharpshooter laurels. In two A/S actions she had fired a total of three hedgehog patterns. And killed two enemy subs.

Jap subs were hard to find in August 1944. Late in September the DE McCoy Reynolds (Lieutenant Commander E. K. Winn, USNR) caught and killed the I-175 on the run between Palau and Guam. Conventional hedgehog and "ashcan" attack.

On October 3, DE Samuel S. Miles (Lieutenant Commander H. G. Brousseau, USNR) was steaming with the Hoggatt Bay hunter-killer group off Palau. At 0440 a surfaced sub was sighted. Jap! Miles ran in to peg hedgehog as the I-boat made a hasty dive. A second hedgehog salvo was trailed by an underwater thunderclap. At daybreak a mess of flotsam was sighted. End of the I-364.

But on the very day that Miles killed the I-364, hard-hitting destroyermen scored a ghastly error. Victim was an American submarine.

Loss of USS Shelton (and Sinking of Seawolf)

Always dangerous for the surface, air, and undersea forces were areas of joint operation where safety lanes and attack zones were frequently shifted with the tide of battle, and security from friend and foe alike depended on a rapid relay of accurate information. In such a joint operational area two factors placed friendly forces in constant jeopardy. First, the enemy might invade the defined safety lane, thereby obtaining temporary sanctuary. Second, someone might fail to "get the word," an open fire on a friendly unit detected in an area designated as safe. Early in October, 1944, these two adverse factors linked up to produce for the Seventh Fleet forces a tragic hour that cost the Navy a hard-working destroyer-escort and an ace submarine.

In the morning of October 3, 1944, a Seventh Fleet Task Group was steaming in the seascape off Morotai, on the road between New Guinea and the Philippines. The task group, built around the carriers Midway and Fanshaw Bay, was screened by destroyer-escorts Eversole, Edmonds, Richard M. Rowell, and Shelton.

A new submarine safety lane, wherein American submarines would presumably be immune from attack by friendly forces, had recently been established in that area. On the morning in question, four American subs were working in these "safe waters." So was a Japanese submarine.

Here was the set-up for dire trouble. The American hunter-killers on the surface and in the air were prohibited from attacking any sub detected in the safety lane because it presumably would be "friendly." In consequence, the I-boat invader had that temporary sanctuary which at least would have compelled the hunters to make a positive identification before opening fire. The Japanese I-boat skulking off Morotai took advantage of this situation, and ambushed the hunter-killers.

At 0807 the sub fired a long-range spread. Target was destroyer-escort SHELTON (Lieutenant Commander L. G. Salomon, USNR). The ship's lookouts glimpsed an oncoming wake at 900 yards, but before the DE could veer away, a second "fish" struck the ship astern, blasting her starboard screw. Two officers and 11 men were killed by the explosion, and 22 of the crew were wounded.

Destroyer-escort ROWELL was directed to stand by the disabled DE and search for the submarine. While ROWELL was circling SHELTON, the injured ship's listening gear heard the whisper of a submarine propeller. The word was passed to ROWELL. At once ROWELL's skipper ordered a depth-charge salvo, and a pattern of "ashcans" went booming down into the sea.

At 1130 two planes took off from the escort-carrier MIDWAY to search the area. One of these planes sighted and dived on a submarine, bombing the submersible as it went down. The sighted sub was well within the saftey lane, but the pilot who made the attack had not been properly informed on this detail.

The plane marked the spot with dye, and destroyer-escort ROWELL was sent racing to the scene—a run which took her 18 miles from the spot where SHELTON had been torpedoed. At 1310 ROWELL made sound contact with the submarine. The DE let fly with hedgehogs. As she circled off after this unsuccessful attack, she heard faint signals from the submarine. The stuttering bore no resemblance to friendly recognition signals. ROWELL's skipper decided that an enemy sub was trying to "jam" the DE's sound gear.

So the DE made a second pass, throwing hedgehog projectiles. In the wake of this attack, four or five explosions were heard. A large air bubble ballooned to the surface. Up came a small scatter of debris, and the DE's lookouts saw what appeared to be a section of periscope. ROWELL was convinced she had downed a Jap submarine.

Meanwhile, the disabled SHELTON had assumed a list, and efforts to stem the flood proved unavailing. Her crew, transferred to ROWELL, was certain their fellow destroyermen had killed SHELTON's assailant. Affairs took a bad turn that evening when destroyer LANG arrived to take SHELTON in tow. With destroyer STEVENS screening, the long trek to port was begun. But SHELTON was too far gone for salvaging. At 2145, while under tow, the damaged vessel capsized.

As the hull remained adrift, Captain J. L. Melgaard, ComDesDiv 4, in LANG, ordered the destroyer to sink the DE. About 2200 the destroyer's guns roared, and the SHELTON sank under a storm of fire.

This brought the curtain down on a tragic drama. For the submarine sunk by RICHARD M. ROWELL was not Japanese. The story emerged when the USS SEAWOLF, which had been en route from Manus to Samar with a group of Army specialists, failed to arrive in the Philippines. Eventually it was learned that the famous SEAWOLF had been passing through the safety area at the fatal hour of the ROWELL attack. Bucking heavy seas, the American submarine had been running a day behind schedule. She had informed the Commander of Task Force 72 of that fact, and the information had been promptly relayed to the Commander of the Seventh Fleet. But someone failed to get the word. The A/S forces off Morotai never received this vital information. And, as has been related, the aviator from the MIDWAY was unaware that he had bombed a sub in a safety lane.

In view of the grim evidence, the Submarine Force could only draw the unhappy conclusion that SEAWOLF had been sunk by the aircraft bombing or by the hedgehog attacks delivered by RICHARD M. ROWELL. A Board of Investigation held it unlikely that a submarine would try to jam the sound gear of an A/S vessel by transmitting signals. ROWELL's Commanding Officer was censured for failing to make an effort to identify the signalling submarine. However, the Board recommended that no disciplinary action be taken, as the DE captain's action was considered *"due to over-zealousness to destroy an enemy."* And the major error was obviously a blunder in the communications system. Repeat: Somebody failed to get (or pass) the word.

What of the submarine that torpedoed SHELTON? She was identified after the war as Japanese submarine RO-41. After delivering the attack off Morotai, this RO-boat eventually returned to Japan. But the RO-41 herself was not on hand at war's end to testify in her own behalf. As will be seen, in the spring of 1945 she would encounter one DE too many.

Chapter 32

Return to the Philippines

(Leyte Gulf, Surigao)

☆ ☆ ☆

"King Two" Versus "Sho-Go"

During September 1944 Halsey's Third Fleet flyers bombed Jap installations in the Philippines and obliterated about 900 enemy planes and some 70 Japanese ships. Convinced that enemy defenses were crumbling, Halsey recommended that the Philippine "return" be scheduled at once. Nimitz concurred. Halsey went on to propose that the invasion forces should by-pass Mindanao (where MacArthur wanted to land) and go ashore on Leyte in the central Philippines. The Joint Chiefs of Staff readily approved. Thereupon "Operation King Two" was advanced on the Allied agenda. The landings were set for October 20.

For "King Two" the Allies mustered the largest invasion armada yet assembled in the Pacific. The operation called for a drive from the south by MacArthur's forces, which included Admiral Kinkaid's Seventh Fleet. Simultaneously Halsey's Third Fleet would strike at the northern Philippines and support the Leyte invasion with Navy Air. Under Halsey's command were 9 heavy and 8 light carriers, 5 battleships, 14 cruisers, and 58 destroyers. Admiral Kinkaid's Seventh Fleet contained 6 old battleships, 18 escort-carriers, 11 cruisers, 86 destroyers, 25 destroyer-escorts, and scores of smaller vessels.

To meet this massive invasion threat, Admiral Soemu Toyoda, Japanese Commander-in-Chief, could muster 9 battleships, 23 cruisers, 63 destroyers, and 4 carriers. The carriers were manned by green airmen.

The Japanese battle plan for the defense of the Philippines —"Plan Sho-Go"—was another halfbaked affair. It called for a do-or-die stand by Kurita's weary Second Fleet. It called for a suicidal feint by Ozawa's crippled Carrier Force. And it called for a *hari-kiri* effort by Imperial airmen.

As of October, 1944, the Imperial Navy's forces were at both ends of the shrinking Empire. Ozawa's Carrier Force was at home base in Japan. Kurita's Second Fleet (built around the twin giantesses, MUSHASHI and YAMATO) was at Lingga, near Singapore. In the Pescadores, off Formosa, lay a cruiser squadron under Admiral Shima. "Sho-Go" was to bring Ozawa down from the north; to bring Kurita up from the south; and to leave Shima in a fog. But the general idea was the defense of Leyte Gulf.

Kinkaid's vanguard landed several Ranger battalions on the beaches of Leyte Gulf on October 17. Before the defenders could recover from this surprise, minesweepers, Underwater Demolition Teams, and a covering force of battleships, cruisers, and destroyers under Rear Admiral J. B. Oldendorf moved in. For three days the local beaches were bombarded. On the morning of the 20th the landing ships went in through storm-tossed water, and the Army waded ashore. MacArthur took the microphone to say, "I have returned!"

Somewhat belatedly Admiral Toyoda now put "Plan Sho-Go" into effect, sending Kurita's Second Fleet steaming up the South China Sea, and bringing Ozawa's carriers chugging down from Japan. Ozawa was under orders to play decoy duck in the north while Kurita barged through the Central Philippines to strike at the Leyte invaders.

Kurita put in at Brunei, Borneo, to pick up fuel. He left Brunei on the 22nd to make a northeast run past Palawan Island, then swing east through San Bernardino Strait. Kurita split his fleet after leaving Brunei. Detaching a squadron under Admiral Shoji Nishimura, he sent these ships across the Sulu Sea to strike at Leyte Gulf through Surigao Strait. The American invasion fleet in the Gulf was thus to be caught in a pincer composed of Nishimura's Southern Force and Kurita's Main Body, while Halsey's fleet was lured far afield by decoy-duck Ozawa. This triple threat was supposed to confuse the United States Navy, and for a time it did. It also confused the Imperial Japanese Navy.

While the "Sho-Go" forces were steaming into play, the "King Two" invasion and covering forces were disposed off the Philippines with the Seventh Fleet ranged across the Gulf mouth between Mindanao and Samar and the Third Fleet off Samar and Luzon. On October 23 the Third Fleet carrier groups of Rear Admiral Davison, Bogan, and Sherman were located at their proper stations. Ozawa had by that time reached the marge of the Philippine Sea, and Kurita's Main Body was off Palawan.

Early in the morning of the 23rd two American submarines ambushed Kurita's force off Palawan, and Kurita's Main Body lost the services of three heavy cruisers. This was an ominous beginning for the "Sho-Going" Japs. American submarines off Japan had also detected and reported Ozawa's sortie.

For their part, Japanese submarines rushed to the Leyte area did not do so well. Through the efforts of U.S. DE's and other energetic sub-hunters, the Imperial Navy lost five of the ten Jap submarines dispatched to Leyte Gulf.

Jap Subs Squelched at Leyte

Providing air support for the Leyte landings during the morning of October 24 was a carrier group under Rear Admiral T. L. Sprague. Serving in the group's screen was DE RICHARD M. ROWELL (Commander H. A. Barnard, Jr.). Jap I-boats were expected in the area, and at 0833 ROWELL's exploratory "pinging" caught an undersea target. ROWELL tracked and fired a hedgehog pattern at 0908. One did it. Up came watery thunder and debris. Down to extinction went I-362.

Four days later destroyers HELM (Commander S. K. Santmyers) and GRIDLEY (Commander P. D. Quirk) tagged a sub off Leyte. The DD's were units of Admiral Davison's carrier group. Contact was made at 1228. Soon the "ashcans" struck oil. At 1414 the battered sub exploded under the sea. Among items blown to the surface were *"three pieces of teak deck planking and two fresh human lungs."* All that was left of the I-54.

These sinkings bracketed a naval showdown that tore loose the Japanese grip on Asia.

PRINCETON-BIRMINGHAM *Disaster*

Rear Admiral F. C. Sherman's Task Group 38.3 was sighted by a Japanese search plane shortly after daybreak of October 24. As a result, Imperial aircraft took to the sky from most of the strips on Luzon, and Ozawa's carriers launched bombers.

The first enemy attack wave arrived just as Sherman's planes were warming up for a take-off. The U.S. Hellcats were outnumbered, but they clawed into the enemy hawks and chased them all over the sky.

Then a single "Judy" dropped out of the clouds to strike at carrier PRINCETON. A bomb hit squarely amidships, plumping into the hangar. Fire and explosions ravaged the carrier. By mid-morning she was swaddled in dense smoke, and dead in the water.

Working with PRINCETON were cruisers BIRMINGHAM and RENO and destroyers MORRISON (Commander W. H. Price), GATLING (Commander A. F. Richardson), IRWIN (Com-

mander D. B. Miller), and CASSIN YOUNG (Commander E. T. Schreiber). At once they moved in to aid the flat-top. With luck she might have been saved.

But at 1002 a thunderous explosion convulsed the carrier, bursting the flight deck and turning the vessel into a furnace. CASSIN YOUNG closed the stern to rescue men who were struggling in the water, while RENO, IRWIN, and GATLING circled the ship, maintaining air guard. Three minutes later another fiery explosion ruptured the carrier's bow. Going alongside to port, IRWIN took off some of the carriermen and stood by to fight the flames. Pounding against PRINCETON's hull, the destroyer suffered topside damage which soon forced her to stand clear. The two light cruisers were also prevented from standing alongside by the searing heat and ugly sea. At 1245 destroyer MORRISON snugged against the burning ship, only to become wedged fast. Just in time she managed to escape. BIRMINGHAM was ordered alongside to give PRINCETON a tow.

But a rising wind fanned the flames. And while PRINCETON's hands were passing several lines to BIRMINGHAM, a huge explosion shattered the carrier's stern. BIRMINGHAM was engulfed by an avalanche of fire and raked by enormous chunks of torn steel. When the cruiser staggered away, her decks seemed to be bleeding, and her starboard-side superstructure was perforated as though by a barrage. Some 233 dead sailors lay in the wreckage.

Fearing that another explosion would smite the rescue vessels, Captain W. H. Buracker finally ordered the carrier abandoned. On orders from Admiral Sherman, cruiser RENO and destroyer IRWIN fired torpedoes into the molten hulk. After PRINCETON went down, destroyers MORRISON, GATLING, and IRWIN escorted BIRMINGHAM to Ulithi.

The Battle of Surigao Strait

When Kurita's elephantine main body lumbered into San Bernardino Strait, the wheels of Toyoda's "Sho-Go" machine clashed into high gear. Down from Formosa Strait steamed Admiral Shima's so-called Fifth Fleet—three cruisers and four destroyers. Around the northern end of Borneo went Admiral Nishimura's Southern Force—battleships YAMASHIRO (flagship) and FUSO; heavy cruiser MOGAMI; and destroyers MICHISHIO, ASAGUMO, YAMAGUMO, and SHIGURE. The mission of this Southern Force was to penetrate Surigao Strait and strike at the American invasion shipping in Leyte Gulf. Shima's "fleet" was supposed to join Nishimura's in this endeavor. But Shima's orders seem to have been fuzzy. Steaming southward, he was under the impression that he would encounter and mop up the left-overs of a disastrous sea-air battle.

Shima's first surprise came by way of a radio message from Nishimura, who stated that he was already in Surigao Strait engaging strong American forces. At that hour Shima's ships were some 30 miles from the scene of action—another nasty surprise, for Nishimura was to have waited for Shima to join up.

Speeding into Surigao Strait at 0245 in the morning of October 25, 1944, Nishimura had rushed into a trap. The trap was the work of Rear Admiral Jesse B. Oldendorf. Informed by submarine and air scouts that the Japs were headed eastward, Admiral Kinkaid's Seventh Fleet flagship had a good idea of what was coming, and Oldendorf, operating in Leyte Gulf, was forewarned and fore-armed. On October 24 he sent a flotilla of 30 PT-boats down to the southern entrance of Surigao Strait to act as reception committee. Across the Leyte Gulf end of the Strait he "deployed the force in battle disposition with guide in center of battle line."

On the right flank (off the coast of Leyte) were stationed destroyers HUTCHINS (flagship of Captain K. M. McManes, ComDesRon 24), BACHE, DALY, HMAS ARUNTA, BEALE, and KILLEN. Cruisers HMAS SHROPSHIRE and USS BOISE and PHOENIX were stationed on this flank. Also off the Leyte coast were three DD's CLAYTON, THORN, and WELLES.

Directly in the center were destroyers NEWCOMB (flagship of Captain R. N. Smoot, ComDesRon 56), RICHARD P. LEARY, and ALBERT W. GRANT, with destroyers ROBINSON (flagship of Captain T. F. Conley, Jr., ComDesDiv 112), HALFORD, and BRYANT located to the north, and destroyers HEYWOOD L. EDWARDS, LEUTZE and BENNION to the south. Farther south, and athwart the passage, were destroyers REMEY (flagship of Captain J. G. Coward, ComDesRon 54), MELVIN, MCGOWAN, MCDERMUT (flagship of Commander R. H. Phillips, ComDesDiv 108), and MONSSEN.

Due north of Hibuson Island were cruisers LOUISVILLE (flagship of Admiral Oldendorf), PORTLAND, MINNEAPOLIS, DENVER, and COLUMBIA. Positioned north of these cruisers were destroyers AULICK, CONY, and SIGOURNEY.

In the backfield were the six battleships—the PENNSYLVANIA, CALIFORNIA, TENNESSEE, MISSISSIPPI, MARYLAND, and WEST VIRGINIA.

Advancing northward in Surigao Strait, impetuous Nishimura was charging right into the jaws of disaster. Even with the support of Shima's three cruisers and four destroyers, his force would have been overwhelmingly outnumbered. As it was, he was throwing two aged battleships, a reconditioned cruiser, and four DD's against six battleships, eight cruisers, and 26 DD's.

Late in the evening of the 24th the Japs were ambushed by the PT-boats. They brushed off this attack. Then, around 0300 next morning, Nishimura's van destroyers ran into Captain Coward's eastern attack group, and the main fight was on. By 0301 the American DD's of DesRon 54 had fired a total of 27 torpedoes at the enemy, and had retired, zigzagging and making smoke. The Japs snapped on searchlights, and opened fire. Near-by shoreline blurred their radar, and they failed to get on target, although they managed a number of straddles.

About 0309 destroyers McDERMUT and MONSSEN on the western attack group launched 20 torpedoes at the oncoming foe. Again Jap salvos futilely straddled the retiring American ships.

Meanwhile, American torpedoes ploughed into the enemy. Old battleship Fuso, struck hard by two "fish," floundered in mortal hurt. Also fatally struck in this opening round was Jap destroyer MICHISHIO. Score two for DesRon 54!

Nishimura plugged doggedly forward—straight into a torpedo and gunfire barrage from the DD's of DesRon 24 strung along the Leyte coast. The Japs answered with furious but inaccurate gunnery. For their part, the Americans punched four torpedoes and a fusillade of 5-inch into battleship YAMASHIRO.

Apparently the torpedoes which struck the venerable battleship were launched by destroyer KILLEN. Her skipper, Commander H. G. Corey, had recognized the Jap battleship and quickly ordered a torpedo depth of 22 feet. After the war, the captain of IJN SHIGURE stated that YAMASHIRO was hit by deep-running torpedoes which blasted her keel and broke her back. Corey's fast readjustment of the firing set-up evidently accomplished this execution. Blasted at 0400, YAMASHIRO sank in about 15 minutes. Scouting to the bottom ahead of her went Jap destroyer YAMAGUMO, torpedoed at 0330. Shortly before YAMASHIRO went down, Nishimura issued his last order from the battleship's bridge: YOU ARE TO PROCEED AND ATTACK ALL SHIPS. But with battleships YAMASHIRO and FUSO and two destroyers now out of the battle, there was not much Southern Force left to do the specified "proceeding and attacking."

Nevertheless, cruiser MOGAMI and destroyers ASAGUMO and SHIGURE plodded ahead. By so doing, they waded into gunfire and torpedo fire from Captain Smoot's DesRon 56. These centrally positioned destroyers attacked in three sections. Section 2 (destroyers ROBINSON, HALFORD, and BRYANT) and Section 3 (H. L. EDWARDS, LEUTZE, and BENNION) launched their torpedoes at 0355 and 0358 respectively. The ships ran through a storm of Jap salvos, but none was hit. Retiring smartly behind smoke, the two sections cleared the channel.

Now destroyers NEWCOMB, R. P. LEARY, and A. W. GRANT, led by Captain Smoot in NEWCOMB, steamed in to launch torpedoes. Attacking from ahead, these DD's were in sizzling water. Smoke billowed in the narrows between Dinagat Island and Leyte; ships were here, there, and everywhere, and target identification was almost impossible. Radio crackling—shells banging—radar "pips" from all directions—in this bedlamite confusion, sorting out enemy targets was on a par with selecting hornets from a swarm of honey-bees. However, when flashes of gunfire indicated the position of Jap warships turning from a northerly to a westerly course, Captain Smoot turned his DD's westward to parallel. At 0405 he ordered torpedoes fired to port at targets 6,300 yards distant. Evidently the spreads were not fired in vain, for Jap destroyer ASAGUMO was struck by a "fish" soon after these were launched.

Having come under heavy fire from the Japs, Smoot's ships were faced with a Hobson's choice for retirement. They could turn directly away from the enemy and retire up the middle of the Strait—a tactic which would present the enemy with the smallest target angle, would open the range fastest, and would afford best smoke-cover. But such a mid-channel run would bring them spearing into the American ships maneuvering to the north, and would expose them to fire from the heavy ships athwart the northern end of the Strait. Yet a westward dash across the Strait and a run up the Leyte shoreline, while clearing the American line of fire in short order would expose the DD's to Jap fusillades.

NEWCOMB's skipper, Commander L. B. Cook, decided to turn directly away from the Japs. With Captain Smoot's advice and approval, he swung the flagship northward. Destroyer LEARY followed the swing. A storm of Jap and American shells descended on the wheeling ships. Last in column, ALBERT W. GRANT was hit before she could make the turn.

At 0403—three minutes before NEWCOMB swung up the channel—GRANT had fired a half-salvo of torpedoes at the enemy. A shell struck her at 0407. Several more hit her just as she was on the point of heading northward to follow NEWCOMB and LEARY. GRANT's skipper, Commander T. A. Nisewaner, now realized she would have been hit whether she had started to turn north or had continued westward. Aware that GRANT might be sunk, he ordered the rest of her torpedoes flung at the enemy. By the time these spreads were fired, the DD was sorely hurt.

Excerpt from GRANT's Action Report:

Additional shell hits began to riddle ship. Hit forward at waterline flooded forward storeroom and forward crew's berthing compartment. Hit in 40 mm. No. 1 exploded 40 mm. ammunition and started fire. Hit through starboard boat davit exploded, killing ship's Doctor, Lieutenant C. A. Methieu, five radiomen, and almost entire amidships repair party. Other hits in forward stack, one hit on port motor whaleboat, one hit and low-order explosion in galley. One hit in scullery room, one hit in after crew's berthing compartment, and one additional hit in forward engine-room. All lights, telephone communications, radars, and radios out of commission. Steering control shifted aft.

Struck by no less than seven Japanese 4.7-inch projectiles and eleven American 6-inch armor-piercing shells, GRANT was a floating catafalque. Desperately Commander Nisewaner flashed a call for help over blinker gun: WE ARE DEAD IN WATER TOW NEEDED.

Ravaged by fire and explosion, the ship drifted helplessly. Topside and below decks the dead lay everywhere, and the agonized cries of the wounded penetrated the roar of combat, the screech of shells, the blast-splash of near misses, and the clangor of broken machinery.

When a companion Pharmacist's Mate was killed, burden of tending the injured fell upon First Class Pharmacist's Mate W. H. Swaim, Jr. Swaim did the work of a full-fledged physician, surgeon, and specialist. Maintaining his own battle dressing station in the "head" aft, he also supervised the sick bay amidships and the dressing station forward. He was aided by Chief Commissary Steward L. M. Holmes, who labored in the wardroom, and by a Sonarman, J. C. O'Neill, Jr., who skillfully administered morphine and tended several sailors who had fallen at their posts with an arm or leg shot away.

Almost every officer and man in the shell-butchered vessel was cited in GRANT's Action Report for valiant conduct. And no man in the GRANT, at least, would ever forget Radioman First Class, W. M. Selleck. His obituary was written as follows by the ship's Executive Officer:

"Both legs blown off, and near death from loss of blood, Selleck went out a hero. His last words as he lay on the wardroom table . . . were 'There's nothing you can do for me, fellows. Go ahead and do something for those others.'"

Held on the surface by little more than the courage of brave men, ALBERT W. GRANT remained afloat. Word of her predicament reached the flagship at 0410, and the Officer in Tactical Command immediately ordered the heavy ships to cease fire. At 0515 NEWCOMB and LEARY steamed back down the channel to aid the crucified ship. NEWCOMB's Medical Officer and two Corpsmen were placed on board the GRANT, and by 0630 the crippled vessel, towed by NEWCOMB, was on her way out of Surigao Strait.

Death made one last swipe at the GRANT—and missed. While the destroyermen were struggling to rig the tow, torpedo-wakes came streaking up the dark channel. These shots had been fired by the warships of Admiral Shima, the ambiguous Japanese Fifth Fleet which had at last arrived on the scene.

Shima crashed into the ruin of Nishimura's force like an automobile smashing into a wrecked truck. Before Shima could turn tail, one of his cruisers was torpedoed by a PT-boat. Then cruisers MOGAMI and NACHI collided on the turn.

That was enough for Shima. Recalling his four destroyers, he headed southward to get out of Surigao at best speed. Best speed wasn't fast enough. Both ABUKUMA and MOGAMI were caught and finished off in the Mindanao Sea by American aircraft. On November 5 NACHI was sighted and sunk by Navy planes. Only the ASHIGARA and two of Shima's destroyers managed to reach Japan. They, with destroyer SHIGURE, lone survivor of Nishimura's force, were the only Jap ships to escape the Surigao debacle. Surigao Strait was registered in history as a smashing American victory.

When Toyoda heard the news he must have been stunned. At the cost of ten warships, the maladjusted Nishimura-Shima team had failed to sink a single American man-of-war. All told, they had landed no more than seven hits, and those, in company with American shells, had fallen on battered ALBERT W. GRANT. Even so, the GRANT had remained unsinkable. She was the only United States warship damaged in the five-hour engagement.

Chapter 33

Battle Off Samar

Small Boys versus Giants

☆ ☆ ☆

Battle Off Samar

While Nishimura's force was racing eastward across the Sulu Sea en route to disaster, Kurita's main body entering the Sibuyan Sea barged into trouble. It was discovered, about midmorning of the 24th, by scout planes from the U.S. carrier groups of Admirals Davison and Bogan. By nightfall Kurita's five battleships were bomb-scorched and smoking. Heavy cruiser MYOKO, disabled, was crawling down the South China Sea. A destroyer had been sent to the bottom. And monster battleship MUSHASHI was a monster junk-pile on the sea floor.

Down, too, had gone Kurita's enthusiasm for "Plan Sho-Go." With darkness setting in, he reversed course. This retrogression seems to have been directly contrary to Toyoda's previous battle order. When Toyoda heard of it, he directed Kurita to turn about and head once more for San Bernardino Strait. The Commander-in-Chief's directive was couched in poetic terms. It read: ADVANCE, COUNTING ON DIVINE ASSISTANCE.

Obediently Kurita ordered a turn-about, and headed his punished force eastward. The force was six hours behind schedule as it debouched in the Philippine Sea and steamed southward along the east coast of Samar. By 0600 in the morning of October 25, the ships were about halfway between the San Bernardino exit and the Gulf of Leyte. Had Kurita but known it, he could indeed have thanked Providence for permitting his advance. He could also have thanked Admirals Ozawa and Halsey.

For Ozawa, in the north, had been wandering around with his "decoy ducks" doing everything possible to invite attention. And Halsey was of course unaware that the enemy carriers off Cape Engano were deliberate lures. Convinced that the Jap flat-tops had to be kept away from Leyte at all cost, he had drawn off the task groups of Bogan and Davison and sent them on a top-speed run to intercept.

Halsey's move left the San Bernardino gateway open at the very time Kurita was hoping to slip through. Someone failed to inform Admiral Kinkaid of the Third Fleet's northward run. In consequence, Kinkaid did not know that the Samar approaches to Leyte Gulf were left wide open. His first intimation of this dangerous gap came when Rear Admiral C. A. F. Sprague's Northern Carrier Group called for help from the waters off southern Samar.

Sprague's group was composed of escort-carriers FANSHAW BAY (flagship), SAINT LÔ, WHITE PLAINS, KALININ BAY, KITKUN BAY, and GAMBIER BAY, screened by three destroyers and four DE's. The destroyers were HOEL (Commander L. S. Kintberger), flagship of Commander W. D. Thomas, Screen Commander; HEERMANN (Commander A. T. Hathaway), and JOHNSTON (Commander E. E. Evans). The destroyer-escorts were DENNIS (Lieutenant Commander S. Hansen, USNR), JOHN C. BUTLER (Lieutenant Commander J. E. Pace), RAYMOND (Lieutenant Commander A. F. Beyer, USNR), and SAMUEL B. ROBERTS (Lieutenant Commander R. W. Copeland, USNR).

At 0645 Kurita's force detected the exposed American ships. About the same time, the Japs were detected by American aircraft.

ENEMY SURFACE FORCE OF FOUR BATTLESHIPS SEVEN CRUISERS AND 11 DESTROYERS SIGHTED 20 MILES NORTH OF YOUR TASK GROUP AND CLOSING AT 30 KNOTS.

Shouted down from the sky, this message sent a shock through FANSHAW BAY. Unable to believe this foul intelligence, Admiral Sprague demanded verification. He was informed that the ships had pagoda masts. A splatter of AA fire above the northern horizon convinced him. At once he ordered a course-change, flank speed, and the launching of all aircraft.

A moment later the Japs opened fire at 17 miles. Sprague's ships, which had been on a northerly course, ran eastward, laying smoke. Planes buzzed away from the "jeep carriers" to strike at the oncoming Japanese battleships and cruisers. Justifiably alarmed, Sprague reported the situation in plain language, urgently requesting help.

Help was not immediately available. Halsey's Third Fleet was far to the north. In Leyte Gulf, Oldendorf's force was low on fuel, weary from the Surigao battle, and almost out of ammunition. Southeast of Sprague's group Rear Admiral F. B. Stump's escort-carrier group was stationed. Stump alone could be counted on for ready aid. And the two escort-carrier groups were the only American naval forces standing between Kurita's battleship force and Leyte Gulf.

So the immediate defense-burden fell like an avalanche on Sprague's escort-carriers. On them, too, like an avalanche would fall shellfire from the Japanese heavy ships. Those ships included the KONGO, the HARUNA, the NAGATO, and the monster battleship YAMATO, sister-ship of the dead MUSHASHI. The giantess was out for revenge, and no American baby flat-top would be able to endure her 18-inch salvos. As for de-stroyers, the American DD's were never made to withstand normal battleship fire, much less the shells of a super BB. Such shots, of course, would burst a DE as a pistol-volley would burst an egg.

Sprague could only run hell-for-leather, and run he did. With most of his planes in the air, he raced toward Leyte Gulf.

It was Kurita himself who provided the desperate Americans with a break. Instead of sending his ships due south to cut off the approach to Leyte Gulf, he split his force three ways in an effort to box Sprague's formation on three sides. Piling on best speed, the Jap cruisers raced across the rear of the American formation, and then closed in from the east. The Jap destroyers swung westward to take the Americans from that direction. Down through the center boomed the Imperial battlewagons.

Kurita's tricky maneuvering gave Sprague a momentary breathing spell. But the cruiser threat from the east proved mortally dangerous, for it prevented the carriers from turning into the wind to launch planes. And as the Jap cruisers gained, the threat of a "box" compelled drastic counteraction. The action was taken by Sprague's destroyers and destroyer-escorts, and it remains an epic in the drama of destroyer warfare. Never anywhere had little DE's presumed to exchange blows with cruisers and battleships. Never, anywhere, had DE's *or* DD's faced such a mastodon as the 63,000-ton super battle-ship YAMATO.

First destroyer to attack the nearing enemy was the USS JOHNSTON (Commander E. E. Evans). At 0720 she peeled away to rush a heavy cruiser. Evans and his men got off a full torpedo salvo. A cyclone of enemy shells hit the attacking JOHNSTON and she reeled through the water with her speed reduced to 17 knots. Then, taking one hit after another, she maintained a hot fire on the Jap cruisers, shooting at ranges as short as 5,000 yards.

Meanwhile, Sprague ordered the DD's and DE's to spread smoke, and his flat-tops were soon covered by a cotton-thick screen. As the Jap fire slackened, Sprague ordered the screening ships to form up for two torpedo attacks.

At 0727, destroyer HOEL (Commander L. S. Kintberger) rushed out of the smoke to launch a half-salvo at a battleship 9,000 yards distant. She was hammered by shells, but she managed to get off another half-salvo at 0735—a spread that apparently damaged a heavy cruiser. And the fight was just beginning.

Destroyer HEERMANN (Commander A. T. Hathaway) made her attack at 0754. Racing out of the smoke-fog, she flung seven torpedoes at a heavy cruiser. Six minutes later she threw three torpedoes at a battleship. Then, bold as brass, she exchanged gunfire with a pair of heavy cruisers. Lucky HEERMANN! With tons of projectiles crashing in the sea around her, she came through the action only slightly damaged.

The relatively slow destroyer-escorts had been instructed to launch their torpedo attack after the three destroyers stepped out. Rainsquall swept the seascape as the DE's squared away to tackle the enraged enemy. Maneuvering in sheeting rain and dense smoke, the DE's were unable to coordinate their torpedo strikes. Blinded, they dashed across the water, and several of them nearly collided. But they threw the Japs off stride.

Closing to within 4,000 yards of a heavy cruiser, destroyer-escort SAMUEL B. ROBERTS (Lieutenant Commander R. W. Copeland, USNR) unloosed a spread of torpedoes at a heavy cruiser. Between 0805 and 0855, the ROBERTS engaged the Jap heavies, firing pointblank at ranges as short as 6,000 yards. The little DE was struck by a shell at 0851—the first lash of a terrible flogging.

At 0759 destroyer-escort DENNIS (Lieutenant Commander S. Hansen, USNR) closed the enemy and fired three torpedoes at a range of 8,000 yards, after a gun-battle begun at 0740. After throwing torpedoes, she continued to blaze away with her gun batteries until 0920 when she reeled out of action, savagely mauled.

Destroyer-escort JOHN C. BUTLER (Lieutenant Commander J. E. Pace) did not launch a torpedo attack. After engaging a heavy cruiser and a destroyer with gunfire, she was ordered ahead of the carriers to lay smoke.

DENNIS retired behind JOHN C. BUTLER's smokescreen.

Destroyer-escort RAYMOND (Lieutenant Commander A. F. Beyer, USNR) opened fire on the foe at 0730. Closing the Jap cruiser column to within 5,700 yards, she slammed something like 16 shells into the superstructure of one vessel. At 0808 she flung three torpedoes at the enemy ships. Hers was a charmed life. In the thick of battle for two hours and 20 minutes, she would emerge without a scratch.

JOHNSTON, HOEL, HEERMANN, SAMUEL B. ROBERTS, DEN-

NIS, JOHN C. BUTLER, RAYMOND—the names of these warships were indelibly written that morning in the Navy's Log of Fame. The history of naval warfare contains few actions which match the battle fought by these DD's and DE's against the heavyweight men-of-war of the Imperial Navy.

"*Small boys,*" Admiral Sprague had called them, ordering them to cover his carriers. "*Small boys form for our second attack!*"

Small boys, they pitched in—literally no bigger than midgets against the giants of the Japanese Navy. Five-inch guns against 8- and 16- and 18-inchers. Unarmored ships against capital vessels clad in coats of steel.

Despite their suicidal efforts, they were unable to save all the carriers. The Japs got close enough to land four 8-inch shells on the FANSHAW BAY. The KALININ BAY was rocked by 15 shells. And GAMBIER BAY, hit below the waterline and disabled, was torn to pieces and sunk by Jap cruiser fire. But these blows serve to indicate what could have happened to Sprague's force if the DD's and DE's had not intervened.

That intervention fended off Kurita's force and gave Admiral Stump's aircraft time to arrive on the scene. It also gave Sprague's aircraft time to reload and refuel on Leyte and fly back into the battle. It also gave Seventh Fleet bombers from the waters off Mindanao a chance to reach the battle area in time. These air reinforcements convinced Kurita that the American flat-tops were not worth the risk of further pursuit, and the way into Leyte Gulf was barred. Their defense had been so magnificent that he thought he had encountered ESSEX-class carriers with cruiser escorts!

But, as was expected, the DD's and DE's took a frightful beating. Ships that suffered untold agony were destroyers JOHNSTON and HOEL, and destroyer-escort SAMUEL B. ROBERTS. All three were riddled. All three went down. And each went down fighting.

First to go was the USS HOEL.

Loss of USS HOEL

About 0725, while Commander Leon Kintberger was maneuvering his ship in an effort to get in a torpedo attack, the HOEL took her first hit, a smash on the director platform. She kept on going at high speed. Targets were hard to distinguish in the surging fogs of white and black smoke and the torrential downpours which blotted the seascape. But HOEL's C.I.C. team had its multiple eye on the leading Jap battleship, which happened to be the IJN KONGO. Closing the range to 9,000 yards, Kintberger ordered a half-salvo of five torpedoes thrown at this booming menace. The "fish" were away at 0727. About 0728 a 14-inch shell thunderbolted into the ship's after engine-room, blowing the port engine to scrap. A moment later another 14-incher struck aft, uprooting guns and damaging the electric steering apparatus.

HOEL shifted to hand steering, and plugged ahead on one engine as Kintberger aimed a torpedo strike at the Jap cruiser column. Loss of electrical power forced the Torpedomen to train their batteries by hand, but at 0735 another half-salvo was launched. Geysers jumped around the target cruiser, possibly IJN KUMANO. The ship roared and turned away. If she were indeed the KUMANO, brave HOEL could be credited with striking a blow that crippled the vessel and set in motion a chain of events which ultimately resulted in her death.

For this valiant blow, HOEL was to pay dearly. "With our ten 'fish' fired," one of her officers stated afterward, "we decided to get the hell out of there." But getting out proved many times harder than getting in. Eight thousand yards on the port beam loomed Kurita's battleships. On the starboard quarter at 7,000 yards loomed the Jap heavy cruisers. A rain of heavy shells fell on the little ship as she zigzagged madly to escape the gantlet. Five-inchers, 8-inchers, and 14-inch sledgehammers struck the ship aft and amidships. Flame burst from her fantail. Her superstructure was torn, chewed, and pulverized by successive explosions. Still the forward gunners kept firing. They fired to the end.

It came at 0855 in the morning of October 25, 1944, after two excruciating hours in which the HOEL had been pounded by some forty hits. Only a few of her crew survived this crimson thrashing. And almost every man who escaped the molten vessel was wounded. On the bridge Screen Commander William D. Thomas and Destroyer Captain Kintberger were with her to the last. Around them the disintegrating decks were strewn with dead and crawling with wounded. Men had to be sent forward to compel the gun crews to leave their mounts and abandon the sinking ship. Already listing and down by the stern, HOEL was a fiery skeleton when she capsized to port and went under. Lost with the ship were 253 destroyermen. Fifteen of the wounded later succumbed.

Loss of USS SAMUEL B. ROBERTS

SMALL BOYS FORM FOR OUR SECOND ATTACK.

When the order from Admiral Sprague rasped over the TBS, the DE's—smallest of the "small boys"—were racing through the smoke and rain, some of them pegging shots at the enemy. SAMUEL B. ROBERTS (Lieutenant Commander

R. W. Copeland, USNR) had opened fire at 0655. Now at about 0800, she dashed toward a dimly seen heavy cruiser; closed the range to less than 4,000 yards; swung, and threw a spread of three torpedoes at the pagoda-masted foe. One war head struck home—a flash and a waterspout. The cruiser's guns flamed, and straddles raised fountains around the little ship. Other cruisers roared at ROBERTS. Like a terrier barking at mastiffs, the DE dodged in to fire 5-inch at these monster, steel-clad opponents.

At 0851 ROBERTS was struck by the first shell of a fusillade that was to batter her into a blind and bleeding wreck. But staggering through a tornado of flame and steel, she struck fierce blows in return. For 50 minutes she endured hit upon hit. Enduring, she threw shell after shell at her tormentors. Ranges shifted between 7,500 and 6,000 yards as DE and enemy cruisers zigzagged across the smoky seas in death-battle. Against the massive batteries of the enemy, the assailed destroyer-escort had but two 5-inch guns—and one of these was presently silenced by a crushing salvo. With one hand thus figuratively tied behind her, this "small boy" fought on.

Out of the thunder, the smoke, the incinerating blast of shells, the clangor and outcry of the ship's ordeal, came another saga of men who met that definition of heroism which describes it as "the accomplishment of the impossible." Typical was the fight put up by Gunner's Mate Third, Paul Henry Carr, gun captain of the DE's No. 2 mount. His story was told by ROBERTS' Action Report and by Lieutenant W. S. Burton, one of the ship's surviving officers.

According to Lieutenant Burton:

> That gun in less than an hour expended something in excess of 300 rounds of 5-inch ammunition, including star-shells when all Common and AA projectiles were gone. . . . The rapid and continuous fire from Gun 2 was an inspiration to every man on the ship. . . . Carr was able to obtain a great many hits on a Japanese cruiser.

Excerpt from ROBERTS' Action Report:

> After all power, air, and communications had been lost, and before the word to abandon ship was passed, the crew of No. 2 gun, who as a crew distinguished themselves throughout the entire action, loaded, rammed, and fired six charges entirely by hand and with a certain knowledge of the hazards involved due to the failure of the gas-ejection system caused by the air supply having been entirely lost.

While attempting to fire the seventh round, the powder charge cooked off before the breech closed, wrecking the gun and killing or wounding all but three crew members, who were critically injured and two of whom were blown clear of the mount and the ship as a result of the explosion.

The first man to enter the mount after the explosion found the gun captain, Carr, on the deck of the mount holding in his hands the last projectile available to his gun. He was completely torn open and his intestines were splattered throughout the inside of the mount. Nevertheless, he held in his hand the 54-pound projectile, held it up above his head and begged the petty officer who had entered the mount to help him get that last round out . . . The petty officer, who entered the mount, took the projectile from Carr and removed one of the other men, who was wounded and unconscious, to the main deck in order to render him first aid. When he returned to the mount, there was Gunner's Mate Carr again with the projectile in his hand, still attempting, although horribly wounded, to place the projectile on the loading tray. . . .

Carr died a few minutes after he was dragged from the gun mount. All told, he and the other marksmen who served in the SAMUEL B. ROBERTS fired 608 rounds from the ship's 5-inch 38's. But by 0907 some 20 Jap heavy shells had smitten her, and the vessel herself was disemboweled.

About 0935, Lieutenant Commander Copeland shouted the order to abandon. The SAMUEL B. ROBERTS sank at 1005.

Lost with the ship were some 89 of the crew. The Navy would always remember her as the destroyer-escort that fought like a battleship.

Loss of USS JOHNSTON

First destroyer into action, USS JOHNSTON (Commander E. E. Evans) was the last "small boy" to go down in the Battle off Samar. Like HOEL and ROBERTS, she fought until her hull was riddled, her engines were wrecked, her superstructure was chopped to a shambles, and her guns knocked out.

She was hit just after she unleashed a spread of ten torpedoes at the nearest Jap cruiser, range 8,000 yards. Launched at 0720, the torpedo salvo was answered by a stupendous barrage. Three 14-inch shells struck the leaping destroyer. The monstrous blows sent the little ship stumbling through the sea, and they were echoed by the minor blasts of three 6-inch shells.

About this time Admiral Sprague ordered the destroyers to form up for a coordinated torpedo attack. Although her tor-

pedoes were gone and she was crippled by damage that slowed
her to 17 knots, JOHNSTON swung in astern of HOEL and
HEERMANN in an effort to support them with gunfire. And
support them she did. Driving in on the enemy's flank, Commander Evans closed the range to 5,000 yards while the
JOHNSTON gun crews pumped 5-inch at the Japanese cruiser
column.

For over an hour JOHNSTON blazed away at the Jap heavies,
trading 5-inch salvos for 6-inch barrages that gradually
hammered her superstructure to rubbish and turned her hull
into a stove. Below decks men were cremated in clogged
passages, or roasted in red-hot compartments. Topside, they
vanished in incandescent splurts of high explosive. By 0830
only two of JOHNSTON's guns were fully operative. From
forecastle to fantail the decks were littered with wreckage.
And in whatever shelter they could find, the wounded and
dead huddled together in pitiful companionship.

Through the battle's din came Sprague's order over the
hoarse TBS: SMALL BOYS ON MY STARBOARD QUARTER INTER-
POSE WITH SMOKE BETWEEN MEN AND ENEMY CRUISERS.

The "men" in reference were the escort-carriers. The "small
boys" were the DD's and DE's ripping this way and that
across the seascape in the path of the oncoming Jap men-of-
war. The "small boys" laid smoke—funnel smoke, and FS
fumes. JOHNSTON was trailing smoke when she was hit by
a fatal salvo.

The destroyer died hard. On her bridge Commander Ernest
Evans fought his ship to the last. Struck by a burst of shrapnel,
he was bleeding as though from the volley of a firing squad.
A cuff of his jacket had been slashed away. He refused to
quit his post.

Lunging out of the smoke, destroyer HEERMANN passed
close to JOHNSTON. HEERMANN's skipper, Commander A. T.
Hathaway, later reported: *"It was obvious that the* JOHNSTON
*was badly damaged and couldn't make the speed we could.
The radar was hanging down on her yardarm, and Evans sent
me a signal, 'Only one engine, no radar, and no gyros.'"* It
was evident that JOHNSTON could not last long.

She fought until 0945. Then the order to abandon was
spoken, and the survivors struggled to get overside. At 1010
the shattered destroyer sank. Adrift in her wake she left 101
wounded men. Lost with the ship were 184 of the crew and
Commander Evans.

Writing of the JOHNSTON sacrifice, Admiral Kinkaid commented: *"This ship did not go down in vain; largely through
its efforts and those of the other ships the Japanece force
was slowed down and turned back. What the Japanese had*

planned as an American naval disaster was turned into a Japanese rout. The part played by the JOHNSTON *in this cannot be over-estimated."*

Samar Aftermath

When Kurita turned northwestward at 0920 in that morning of October 25, his leviathans had taken a few hits, but the only warship seriously damaged was the heavy cruiser KUMANO, struck by a destroyer torpedo. Before him Sprague's force lay practically helpless, and beyond it the whole fleet of American transports and landing craft. Yet monster YAMATO, KONGO, NAGATO, and HARUNA turned tail.

Miles to the north, off Cape Engano, Halsey's Third Fleet airmen rained death and destruction on Ozawa's "decoy-duck" carrier force. When all was over, the Japanese Imperial Navy was virtually a skeleton.

So the naval gambit of "King Two" checkmated "Operation Sho." In Japanese the word "Sho" means "conquer." At Leyte the U.S. Navy hammered the meaning out of the word.

"After that battle," mourned Vice Admiral Ozawa, "the Japanese surface force became strictly auxiliary."

Fighting desperately to retain a hold on the upper Philippines and on the islands close to Japan, the Japs now looked to air and submarine defenses to hold the naval line.

In the wake of the Leyte battle a Jap sub fired a killing shot.

Loss of USS EVERSOLE

EVERSOLE (Lieutenant Commander George E. Marix) cleared Leyte Gulf in the evening of October 27, 1944, to rendezvous with Rear Admiral Sprague's task force at daylight the following morning. At 0210 in the morning of the 28th, the destroyer-escort made radar contact with a vessel five and a half miles distant.

About 18 minutes later the ship's sonar watch reported contact with a target at 2,800 yards. Thirty seconds after contact was made, EVERSOLE was struck by a torpedo. The ship staggered and canted in a 15° list. A moment later she was struck by a second torpedo which crashed inboard through the hole blasted by the first torpedo. The explosion dealt death and destruction below decks, and the mortally stricken DE assumed a 30° list. Lieutenant Commander Marix ordered the ship abandoned at 0240.

The EVERSOLE sank within 15 minutes. About 0300 the Japanese submarine opened fire on the survivors. For 20 minutes the desperate men were target for this ruthless gunnery; then the sub submerged. A few minutes later the sea was erupted by a murderous blast which killed or wounded everyone in the water. Casualties exacted by torpedo explosions, strafing, and underwater blast were tragically high.

Undoubtedly fatalities would have been close to total had not destroyer-escorts RICHARD S. BULL and WHITEHURST soon arrived on the scene. With the following results—

WHITEHURST Sinks I-45

Shortly after EVERSOLE went down, destroyer-escort WHITEHURST received over the TBS word from destroyer-escort BULL that their sister DE had been torpedoed and sunk.

After relaying the word on EVERSOLE, destroyer-escort BULL requested a DE to act as A/S screen while she rescued survivors. WHITEHURST was thereupon dispatched to the scene of the sinking. Her skipper, Lieutenant J. C. Horton, USNR, took the ship through a search pattern around the area. The search had almost been complete when WHITEHURST picked up a sonar contact at 0545. Ten minutes later she reached firing position. She delivered hedgehog attacks. Eleven seconds after the fourth salvo splashed into the sea, a series of explosions echoed up from below.

Making a daylight search of the area, the destroyermen discovered some submarine residue. After the war these items were attributed the submarine 1-45, the sub which probably sank EVERSOLE. Grim echo from the Battle for Leyte.

Chapter 34

Enter the Suiciders

☆ ☆ ☆

DD's Versus Death-Divers at Leyte

On November 1, 1944, the Japanese Air Force made an effort to blast the Seventh Fleet's Covering Forces out of Leyte Gulf. Covering Leyte on that date was Task Group 77.1 under Rear Admiral G. L. Weyler. With the group were 19 DD's, among them BUSH, BRYANT, NEWCOMB, LEARY, KILLEN, CLAXTON, AMMEN, ANDERSON, and ABNER READ. With "bogies" in the offing, the ships had maintained an all-night air alert. Lull before storm. The thunderbolts came in mid-morning.

BUSH (Commander R. E. Westholm) bore the brunt. Between 0940 and 1115 she beat off six aerial onslaughts, shot down two planes. CLAXTON was brutally damaged by a downed plane that exploded close aboard. KILLEN was disabled by a bomb.

The Jap "Bettys," "Zekes" and "Vals" seemed intent on diving into the assailed ships. Early in the afternoon a plane deliberately crashed into ABNER READ. Now the tactic was obvious. The Navy's Pacific destroyermen realized they were up against something new in the grim book of warfare—the suicider.

Loss of USS ABNER READ

Screening damaged CLAXTON, ABNER READ (Commander A. M. Purdy), was conducting a circular patrol. About 1339 the radar watch reported two enemy aircraft 11 miles distant, and coming fast. ABNER READ opened fire with main battery and automatic guns. Down from the sky plunged a "Val" dive-bomber, dragging a tail of smoke. Evidently hit by ABNER READ's scorching fire, the plane was burning, but the pilot drove straight for the destroyer.

It happened fast—three minutes after the initial radar contact. ABNER READ's guns were slamming, chattering, and roaring. It seemed impossible that an aircraft could penetrate the lacework of flame, machine-gun lead, and flak. All hands on the bridge watched in a freeze of dread as the dive-bomber came on, nearer and nearer.

Someone shouted, "Oh, my God!"

Men were thrown to the deck as the "Val" crashed into the destroyer's starboard side, smashing in a splatter against the after stack. A wave of fire blew across the superstructure. Blazing gasoline showered the wreckage with flame. At once the ship was an inferno topside. Then the conflagration ignited a magazine. Ready ammunition exploded near a gun mount. Sailors were struck down by flying shrapnel and whistling scraps of debris. The flames ran below decks and touched off a series of explosions. ABNER READ, listing and shaken by interior blasting, lay dying in the sea. Thirty-six minutes after the plane crash, ABNER READ plunged for the bottom of Leyte Gulf. Lost with the ship were 19 men and three officers.

More Death for the Emperor's Subs

While American destroyermen fought against suicide planes at Leyte, Jap submarines made suicidal appearances elsewhere in the Pacific. Perhaps the I-boats did not deliberately court death in November 1944. But for a number the outcome was definitely fatal.

In the evening of November 12, destroyer NICHOLAS (Commander R. T. S. Keith) made radar contact with a sub in the waters between Ulithi and the Pelews. The sub went under. NICHOLAS delivered two depth-charge attacks. Up came a mess, flotsam and human remains. End of the I-37.

From Ulithi on November 4 sailed a hunter-killer team built around escort-carrier ANZIO. Action developed early in the morning of the 18th when an ANZIO plane reported radar contact with a surfaced sub. Destroyer-escorts LAWRENCE C. TAYLOR and M. R. NAWMAN raced to attack. On target, TAYLOR (Commander R. Cullinan, Jr.) fired hedgehog salvos. Morning found the seascape strewn with oil and debris. The demolished sub proved to be the I-26, the killer that had torpedoed the SARATOGA and sunk the light cruiser JUNEAU in 1942.

In the morning of November 19, destroyer-escorts CONKLIN (Lieutenant Commander E. L. McGibbon, USNR) and McCOY REYNOLDS (Lieutenant Commander E. K. Winn, USNR) were ordered out of Kossol Passage, Palau, on a sub hunt. The DE's put a "pinging" finger on the sub at 1500 in the afternoon. The ships launched a coordinated hedgehog attack that lasted for two hours. And ended with a stupendous undersea explosion. Upwelling oil, a litter of flotsam and human remains spelled the end of the I-177.

Late in November the remnant Imperial Navy tried to run supplies from northern Philippine bases down to invaded Leyte. Naval convoys steamed down to Ormoc Bay on Leyte's west coast. To put a stop to this traffic, DesDiv 43 was dispatched to Ormoc Bay with guns loaded for bear. The division included destroyers WALLER, RENSHAW, SAUFLEY and PRINGLE.

The ships charged into Ormoc Bay on November 27. Shore installations were pounded with 5-inchers. Then the DD's swept across the Camotes Sea. Early in the morning of the 28th WALLER snared radar contact with an enemy sub.

The sub elected to stay on the surface for a gun duel. WALLER's skipper, Commander H. L. Thompson, Jr., obliged by closing in to 50-yard range with his gunners pumping 40 mm. into the I-boat's conning tower. Spouting smoke and flame, the sub slid under the sea, stern first. A few Jap swimmers remained on the surface. As several of them gestured hand grenades, the survivors were not picked up. The extinguished submarine was the I-46.

Loss of USS COOPER

Entering Ormoc Bay with destroyers ALLEN M. SUMNER and MOALE, the COOPER made surface contact with a target at 12,200 yards range just minutes after midnight of December 2. Commander M. A. Peterson gave the order to open fire. For nine minutes the destroyer's guns pumped 5-inch at the target. Evidently a large destroyer, target was seen to be burning—sinking under a cloud of flame. This was the Jap DD KUWA. She had been transporting reinforcements for the Japanese Leyte garrison. Many of those infantrymen never made it. About 250 of them floated in to the Ormoc beaches for hasty burial.

COOPER immediately shifted fire to a second target, but was unable to learn the results of her gunnery, for only a minute or two later she was struck by an undersea weapon just as she completed a turn.

A hugh explosion heeled the COOPER on her side. Fire and water swept over her superstructure, and within 30 seconds of the blast she broke in two. The survivors swam in swirling oil and hot foam under a fog of smoke. Division Commander Zahm on SUMNER was faced with a bitterly difficult decision—to risk air attack and fire from shore batteries in an effort to save COOPER's men, or pull out to assure the safety of his two remaining ships. Reviewing the case, an experienced destroyer officer wrote: *"It was a tough decision. But, in deciding not to make the rescue attempt, the Division Commander did the right thing."*

COOPER survivors were picked up between mid-afternoon and dusk of that day by U.S. Navy "Black Cat" planes. While swimming in the Bay, the afflicted destroyermen saw several submarines sneak out through the entrance. The presence of subs in Ormoc Bay suggested that COOPER might have been the victim of a giant "Long Lance" torpedo. Down with the ship went 10 officers and 181 men. Some 168 of COOPER's crew were saved.

Battle for Ormoc Bay

By the opening days of December, Yamashita's garrison on Leyte had been increased by some 30,000 troops, but this transport effort had cost the Japs eight destroyers, a cruiser, six smaller warships, and at least ten transports.

Soon after the loss of COOPER, the Navy was called upon to undertake an amphibious landing at Ormoc. On short notice, Read Admiral A. D. Struble was ordered to Ormoc Bay with Task Group 78.3. The group consisted of eight fast transports and 43 landing craft, carrying General A. D. Bruce's 77th Division. Admiral Struble flew his flag in the destroyer HUGHES (Commander E. B. Rittenhouse). Twelve destroyers screened the task group. They were: BARTON, WALKE, LAFFEY, O'BRIEN, FLUSSER, DRAYTON, LAMSON, EDWARDS, SMITH, REID, CONYNGHAM, and MAHAN.

The way into the harbor was cleared by a minesweeping unit, and a Control and Fire-Support Unit abetted the amphibious work. Opposition to the landings was *nil*. But the retiring ships were attacked by enemy aircraft.

The air assault began about 0820. U.S. fighters flew to intercept the Jap planes, but a number of Japs broke through the CAP cover and dodged the AA barrage. By midday several ships had been hit by crash-diving suicide planes. Among those struck were destroyer MAHAN (Commander E. G. Campbell), destroyer-transport WARD (Commander R. E. Farwell, USNR), and destroyer-transport LIDDLE (Lieutenant Commander L. C. Brogger, USNR).

The attacks continued throughout the day. About 1400 a plane plummeted on destroyer LAMSON (Commander J. V. Noel, Jr.), and crashed forward of the stack. Twenty-one men were killed by the smash and 50 were wounded. As flames roared through LAMSON's superstructure, destroyer FLUSSER (Commander T. R. Vogeley), stood by to cover the stricken vessel. While FLUSSER's gun crews hurled flak at enemy aircraft, a rescue tug finally succeeded in extinguishing the flames, and LAMSON was saved. FLUSSER picked up about 20 men (most of them wounded) who had jumped off the bridge and director platform when the plane ploughed into the ship. Later beating off an air attack, she shot down a "Dinah."

The suiciders hit a savage blow that day. The old WARD of Pearl Harbor fame was fire-gutted and had to be sunk. And the MAHAN was mortally blasted.

Loss of USS MAHAN

MAHAN was one of the two fighter-director ships in Task Group 78.3. MAHAN's fighter-director team had gone to work the moment the Jap planes appeared on the radar screen. She was joined in this work by the team on board destroyer SMITH (Commander F. V. List).

About 0948, MAHAN's gunners opened fire on a flight of nine enemy bombers escorted by four fighter planes. Four Jap planes were shot down by MAHAN's guns. But the enemy airmen, launching a coordinated suicide assault, penetrated the defense. Skimming in across the water, three of the Jap planes crashed into MAHAN.

The ship shuddered and reeled under the impact. Drenched with burning gasoline, the destroyer's wrecked superstructure was enveloped in flames. Fire vomited from the exploding forward magazine. Thirteen minutes after the third crash, Commander E. G. Campbell, MAHAN's skipper, ordered the crew to start abandoning.

Nothing could be done to save the wrecked and exploding destroyer, and at 1150 MAHAN was sunk by gun and torpedo fire from destroyer WALKE.

Loss of USS REID

Ormoc Bay claimed still another Seventh Fleet destroyer, the USS REID (Commander S. A. McCornock). On December 11, the REID was operating with a re-supply echelon which was dispatched to the Ormoc beachhead. The task unit, under command of Captain J. F. Newman, Jr., ComDesRon 14, contained 13 landing craft and destroyers CALDWELL (flagship of Captain Newman), REID, CONYNGHAM, SMITH, COGHLAN, and EDWARDS.

Carrying vital and urgently needed supplies to the land forces in the Ormoc area, the ships hauled out of Tarraguna and raced through Surigao Strait. About 1700 in the evening of the 11th a flight of 12 "Jills" attacked. Newman's ships had fighter cover of only four Corsairs. Guided by fighter-director ship SMITH, they shot down two planes. But the leading planes broke through the defense and swooped down at REID and CALDWELL. The assailed DD's lashed at the "Jills" with AA fire. In the ensuing scrimmage four planes were shot down by the destroyer barrage, and at least four others were damaged. But five of the "Jills" crash-dived.

A plane crashed into CALDWELL's radio room. Twenty-nine sailors died in the explosion, 40 were wounded. Disabled, afire, the ship limped out of action.

Four of the diving planes concentrated on the REID. One "Jill" raced in and hooked a wing on the destroyer's starboard whaleboat, then collided at the waterline abreast of the No. 2 gun, the smash detonating the aircraft's bomb. A moment later a second plane caromed off the No. 3 gun, skidded into a 40 mm. tub, and exploded. The explosions set off the after magazines. Her superstructure aflame, her lower compartments gutted by internal blasts, the REID heeled over and went down by the stern. The ship sank swiftly. Two minutes after she was hit by the first plane, she was rumbling down under the sea. Loss of life, heavy in this action, was typical of the toll exacted by suicide crashes. Some 152 of REID's crew escaped death.

REID was the last destroyer lost in the battle for Ormoc. But elsewhere in the Philippines, American DD's were maimed by suicide planes. Early that month MUGFORD was hard hit in Surigao Strait. So was DRAYTON. Later HUGHES and GANSEVOORT were crashed in Philippine waters.

And for the duration of the war American destroyermen in the Pacific were going to need all the stamina and courage they could muster. Leyte and Ormoc composed only the curtain-raiser of a horror drama that had no previous equal in all the bloody history of warfare.

Chapter 35

Typhoon – Manila Bay Conclusion

☆ ☆ ☆

Typhoon!

While the Mindoro invasion was going forward, the Third Fleet stood off the Philippines ready for a series of strikes at the Manila area. Halsey planned to fuel his ships on December 17 and to launch the strike series on the 19th. But the day chosen for fuelling operations proved one of the darkest in Third Fleet history. When the calendar turned on December 19, the Third Fleet had lost three ships, 790 men, and about 200 planes. Twenty-eight ships were damaged, and nine of the damaged were so badly battered they had to be sent into port for major overhauls. The enemy was that "Ole Devil Sea."

On the morning of the 17th the ships were about 500 miles east of Luzon. Begun during the forenoon watch, fuelling work was made increasingly difficult by rising winds.

Upon receiving word that the weather would worsen, Halsey ordered the fuelling operation suspended, and headed the Fleet northwestward to evade the storm, which was advancing from the east. Later that afternoon the storm changed course, and so did Halsey in another effort to evade. That night the Third Fleet ran southwest. But the storm, strangely vindictive, refused to take the expected tack, and gradually caught up with the retiring ships. During the morning of December 18 the glass fell steadily, and by 0830 the storm had grown into a monster typhoon, its center only 150 miles from the ocean-blown Third Fleet. At 1358 the typhoon's center was only 35 miles distant, and the sea and sky were berserk.

Rough on battleships and carriers, the typhoon was unmitigated hell for the destroyers, some of which, low on fuel, had pumped out water ballast preparatory to fuelling and were consequently riding high in the water. During the peak of the storm, a number of the DD's were rolled on their beams and

376

pinned down with their stacks almost flat against the sea. In such a roll to leeward, destroyer DEWEY lay over in a cant which registered 75° on the ship's inclinometer. The AYLWIN, another FARRAGUT-class destroyer, rolled 70°. With their beam ends buried and giant waves sweeping over forecastle and superstructure, the destroyers endured excruciating moments of jeopardy. Water plunged into ventilators and intakes. Electrical installations were swamped and short-circuited. With loss of electric power, lights gave out, steering gear failed, and the ships, without means of communication, were left to wallow feebly in deaf-and-dumb desolation. The destroyermen could only batten down, lash such items of unstable gear as could be captured and hogtied, and cling to handholds and bulkheads.

Loss of USS HULL, USS SPENCE, *and* USS MONAGHAN

They come under the same heading, for theirs was a common grave.

HULL	*Lt. Comdr. J. A. Marks.*
SPENCE	*Lt. Comdr. J. P. Andrea.*
MONAGHAN	*Lt. Comdr. F. B. Garrett, Jr.*

Somewhere in the immediate vicinity of lat. 14-57 N., long. 127-58 E., they were erased by mountainous seas—battered under by a foe more relentless than any human agency.

The storm came howling down from the north; the ocean surged up to meet the sagging sky; the seascape blurred out in a gray-white opacity of flying spume. And somewhere in that screaming limbo of wind and water the three ships went down. Apparently first to go, SPENCE capsized after her rudder jammed full right shortly after 1100. Only 23 of her crew lived to tell the story of her final hour. Lost with his ship was Lieutenant Commander Andrea.

HULL went down during the noon hour. The wind had driven her over on her starboard side until her inclinometer went "out of sight." A sudden gust forced her beyond the point of recovery; a hill of water avalanched across her decks; she rolled over and sank. Fifty-five men and seven officers, among them Lieutenant Commander Marks, managed to escape the vessel and survive the raving ocean.

The exact moment of MONAGHAN's end is unknown, but she went down at midday in company with HULL and SPENCE. About 300 officers and men went down with the ship when it capsized. Lost with the destroyer was Lieutenant Commander Garrett. Only six of the crew survived.

About 1400 of that dark day the weather began to mend.

By 1600 the wind had decreased to 35 knots and the barometer had climbed to 29.46. Halsey had word of the missing ships, and a search for survivors was begun.

Throughout that night and the ensuing two days, the ships and planes of the Third Fleet conducted what Halsey described as *"the most exhaustive search in Navy history."* Four ships were believed lost, for the destroyer-escort TABBERER had disappeared and did not answer radio calls. Here and there a few swimmers were picked up, and several rafts were located. Then word came in from the TABBERER. The little DE had lost her foremast. Her radio had been knocked out and her radar ruined. But she was very much afloat, and she was bringing with her 55 destroyermen, survivors she had rescued from the typhoon's wrath. A number of these survivors—men from the HULL—said they had never seen such seamanship as that exhibited by TABBERER's skipper (Lieutenant Commander Henry L. Plage, USNR) when he jockeyed his ship through giant seas to snatch drowning men from the water. Recalling the rescues in *Admiral Halsey's Story*, the leader of the Third Fleet remarked that he expected to learn that Plage was a veteran mariner who had "cut his teeth on a marlinspike." Halsey was overwhelmed to discover that Plage was a Reserve Officer at sea for his second cruise—a sailor who had "cut his teeth" in the ROTC at Georgia Tech.

From the survivors rescued by TABBERER, by destroyer-escort SWEARER, destroyer BROWN, and other lifesavers, the Navy learned details of the HULL, SPENCE, and MONAGHAN sinkings. Typical were the stories told by Lieutenant (jg) A. S. Krauchunas, USNR, sole surviving officer of SPENCE, and Water Tender Second Class Joseph C. McCrane, USNR, highest ranking of the six MONAGHAN survivors.

Krauchunas told a grim story of nine men adrift on a floater net.

> The men began to suffer from the hot sun that burned any exposed areas of the skin. The floater net had two kegs of water, no flare, no medicine kit, and no food kits, all of which broke off during the vicious typhoon. Water was given out once every three hours in order that it would last longer. A can of vegetable shortening was picked up and spread over the men's sunburned areas. Two search planes flew overhead but did not see us. One of the men became unconscious and slipped from the net several times before he was missed. Of the three men to die, he was the first. His name was Ensign George W. Poer. At midnight, December 20, 1940, Lieutenant (jg) John Whalen slipped from the net. The other man had become unconscious some time before, but was held on the net by Charles

Wohlleb, Water Tender Third Class. But it became necessary to let him go.

At 0300 on the morning of December 20, an aircraft carrier slipped into view on the horizon.

The men on the carrier shouted, whistled, and waved.

The carrier heard us and dropped smoke bombs and flares to mark our approximate position, and it continued on its way. Within a half an hour, a destroyer appeared from the other direction but we were not successful in attracting its attention. Shortly another ship appeared and it found the flares which the carrier had dropped. This ship was the USS Swearer, *which eventually picked us up. . . .*

William Keith, Seaman First, was picked up by the USS Gatling *after he had been floating by himself for two days and nights. He was delirious, and his . . . experience . . . was interesting. He claimed that drowning was not his way of dying . . . and that a Japanese torpedo was floating by, and he chased it for some time. He wanted to set it off and blow up with it. . . .*

Water Tender McCrane of the Monaghan related this stark story:

. . . I went back to the engineers' compartment and the ship was rolling so heavy that all of us decided to go topside into the after gun shelter. . . .

I managed to work myself to within about ten feet of the door on the port side. There were about 40 men in the shelter. One of the fellows was praying aloud. Every time the ship would take about a 70 degree roll to starboard, he would cry out, "Please bring her back, dear Lord, don't let us down now." We must have taken about seven or eight rolls to the starboard before she went over on her side. When the ship went over some of the fellows tried to get the door open on the port side. It was a difficult job because the wind was holding and the waves were beating up against it, but they did get it opened and we started out. All the fellows kept their heads and there was no confusion or pushing and everyone was trying to help the other fellow. A Gunner's Mate by the name of Joe Guio, with absolutely no thought of his own safety, was standing outside of the hatch pulling everyone out. . . .

McCrane, himself, was knocked off the shelter into the churning sea. Swimming through the watery smother, he finally reached a raft. Guio also got to the raft. The Gunner's

Mate was injured and shivering—suffering from shock. His clothing had either been discarded or torn from his body, and McCrane held him in his arms to keep him warm. The wounded man lapsed into unconsciousness, while McCrane chafed his wrists and hands. Then—

> *Guio awoke and asked me if I could see anything, and when I told him I could see the stars, he said that he couldn't see anything. He then thanked Melroy Harrison, Seaman Second, for pulling him aboard the raft and then he thanked me for trying to keep him warm. He laid his head back on my shoulder and went to sleep. About a half-hour later I had a funny feeling come over me and I tried to wake him up only to find that he was dead. I told the rest of the fellows and we decided to hold him a little longer before we buried him. In about 20 minutes we had our first burial at sea. We all said the Lord's Prayer as he was lowered over the side. . . .*

McCrane and his five companions were finally picked up by the destroyer BROWN.

In rescuing the survivors of HULL and SPENCE, the TABBERER men risked their own lives in more ways than one. At one point the ship, struggling to make 10 knots, was caught in the deep valley of a trough, and forced over on her beam in a roll of 72 degrees. They sighted an exhausted swimmer who, unable to reach a life ring, was treading water. Suddenly an enormous shark slid down a wave and glided toward the man. Sighting the deadly fin, TABBERER's sailors opened fire with rifles. The shark passed within six feet of the swimmer, then was driven off by the sharpshooting destroyermen. The DE's "Exec," Lieutenant Robert M. Surdam, USNR, plunged overside to secure a line around the fainting man. The exhausted swimmer was hauled aboard and quickly revived.

Another TABBERER lifesaver, L. A. Purvis, Bos'n's Mate, First Class, almost lost his life while struggling in the water with a half-drowned swimmer. Too much slack was left in his line, and a bight caught on the underwater sound dome when the DE rolled. Purvis was dragged under the ship. Realizing what had happened, he wrenched off his kapok jacket, swam under the ship, and came up on the other side. Only his presence of mind and his skill as a swimmer saved him from a fatal keel-hauling.

Concerning kapok jackets, TABBERER's Commanding Officer noted that *"Out of the 55 men rescued, 54 had kapok jackets. It is believed many were drowned during the storm because of the inadequate support given by the belt-type life jacket."*

The typhoon of December 18 was one of the worst encountered in the Pacific. No oceanic tantrum struck the Navy a harder blow than the one which downed HULL, SPENCE, and MONAGHAN. Only two other destroyers were storm-sunk during the war; TRUXTUN, driven aground by a North Atlantic, blizzard-blinded gale, and WARRINGTON, swamped by a Caribbean hurricane.

There were contributing factors to the December 18 tragedy. The typhoon was not accurately predicted, the immediate signs of it in the operating area were not heeded early enough, and it traveled a capricious path. In reviewing the disaster, Admiral Nimitz noted that the three ships lost had been maneuvering to the last in an attempt to maintain station. It might have been better had they disregarded station-keeping in an effort to ride out the storm. *"The time for taking all measures for a ship's safety is while able to do so,"* wrote Admiral Nimitz. *"Nothing is more dangerous than for a seaman to be grudging in taking precautions lest they turn out to be unnecessary. Safety at sea for a thousand years has depended on exactly the opposite philosophy."*

In conclusion, Admiral Nimitz stated that the December 18 typhoon caused *"the greatest loss that we have taken in the Pacific without compensatory return since the First Battle of Savo."*

Goodbye to More Japanese Subs

By war year 1945 the Imperial Navy's submariners must have said goodbye with doleful sincerity when they left home base to go out on cruise or special mission.

First submarine kill of 1945 was scored for the DesPac Force by destroyer-escort FLEMING (Lieutenant Commander K. F. Burgess, USNR). Victim was RO-47 caught in the path of a tanker convoy bound for Eniwetok from Ulithi. FLEMING drove the target under, blasted the sub with four hedgehog salvos. Date: January 18.

Early in the morning of the 23rd, destroyer-escorts CONKLIN (Lieutenant Commander E. L. McGibbon, USNR), CORBESIER (Lieutenant H. V. Jones, USNR) and RABY (Lieutenant J. L. Slade, USNR) blasted the I-48 out of existence. The kill climaxed a two-day hunt in waters off Ulithi. Hedgehog downed the sub with an explosion that kicked a 1400-pound safe eight feet across CONKLIN's deck.

The next submarine sinking in Philippine waters was a prime example of the streamlined teamwork now exhibited by the DD's and DE's.

The destroyers involved were the BELL (Commander J. S. C. Gabbert), O'BANNON (Lieutenant Commander J. A. Pridmore), and JENKINS (Commander P. D. Gallery). The destroyer-escort was the ULVERT M. MOORE, captained by Lieutenant Commander Franklin D. Roosevelt, Jr., USNR.

Date: January 31, 1945. On that day BELL and O'BANNON were steaming in the screen of Rear Admiral F. B. Stump's Task Force 77.3, which was operating to the west of Mindoro on mission to intercept Jap transports on the run to Luzon.

Action began that evening as dusk darkened the South China Sea.

Time: 1955: Cruiser BOISE reported a surface radar contact.

1956: BELL snared same contact at 9,250 yards.

2000: BELL and O'BANNON were ordered to investigate.

2001: Radar contact disappeared at 5,500 yards.

2005: BELL obtained sound contact at 2,900 yards.

2012: Making depth-charge run, BELL dropped pattern.

2020: O'BANNON attacked with depth charges.

2034: BELL reported to ComTaskGroup that contact was temporarily lost, and requested a DE be sent to assist. (A DE, because that type carried superior A/S equipment.)

2035: ULVERT M. MOORE was detached for job. Peeling off, she joined BELL and O'BANNON.

2041: Meanwhile, O'BANNON reported passing through an oil slick.

2042: BELL regained sonar contact with target.

2050: BELL launched depth-charge attack.

2051: ComTaskGroup ordered JENKINS to relieve BELL and take charge of sub-hunt operation.

2122: JENKINS joined hunter-killers conducting "Operation Observant."

2223; BELL sighted oil slick, and noted strong smell of same. (Evidently BELL and O'BANNON had wounded the quarry before JENKINS and U. M. MOORE arrived on scene.)

2225: While the three destroyers circled the bull's-eye, destroyer-escort MOORE stepped into the ring and fired hedgehog.

2228: MOORE delivered another hedgehog attack. The projectiles soared and splashed. Three explosions crackled under the sea.

2259: MOORE let fly with a third hedgehog barrage. The projectiles sank in silence, but bubbling noises and muffled detonations continued to echo the previous salvo.

2319: MOORE's Sound men heard still another gruff explosion. (Obviously things were cooking in a smitten submarine.)

2337: Maneuvering into attack position, the DE unleashed another hedgehog salvo. Two loud detonations boomed up from below.

0015: With the calendar 15 minutes into February, MOORE made her fifth hedgehog attack. The projectile barrage produced two more smacking explosions. (If the sub were not already dimpled, dented, and dished in, these last shots dealt the damage.)

0019: The hunting ships were jolted by a prodigious deep-sea blast. Goodbye Japanese submarine!

In the wake of that final bombilation, Sound contact was permanently lost. So was the RO-115.

Commenting on the kill, a DesPac officer wrote: *"The Commanding Officer of* JENKINS *was smart in letting the DE do the attacking with hedgehogs, while the three DD's circled the area of attack to prevent the sub's escape."*

A week later destroyer-escorts THOMASON and NEUENDORF spotted a Jap submarine's periscope. THOMASON (Lieutenant Commander C. B. Henriques, USNR) attacked with hedgehog. The salvo ended in rumbling explosions and watery lightning that was like a thunderstorm under the sea. That was the end of RO-55.

Late in February, destroyer-escort FINNEGAN (Lieutenant Commander H. Huffman, USNR) was one of four ships escorting a convoy of nine transports from Iwo Jima to Saipan. Just before daybreak of the 26th, when the convoy was about midway between the Volcano Islands and the Marianas, FINNEGAN's radar registered a contact with a surfaced submarine. The sub dived as the DE closed in.

Presently FINNEGAN had sonar contact, and at 0659 she let fly with hedgehog. The projectiles missed. Four more hedgehog patterns were fired in vain. At 0800 Comamnder Huffman realized the sub must have gone deep. So he tried for her with a pattern of 13 depth charges.

The charges boomed down, but nothing came up. Then the DE's fathometer indicated that the sub was swimming at varying levels between 20 and 30 fathoms. At 0925 FINNEGAN fired another hedgehog barrage. Silence. At 1000 she maneuvered in and dropped a full pattern of depth charges set to blow at "medium." About five minutes after the first "ashcan" rolled from the rack, a thunder-blast roared under the sea. It was echoed by muffled rumbling and regurgitative bubbling sounds. The explosion was way down under, and the ocean's surface remained unruffled. FINNEGAN had really reached for that one.

Oil and debris kept coming up for the rest of the day. The oil smeared an area four miles long and two miles wide. Thirty-one pieces of shattered timber and shattered Jap were picked up. Miwa's records identified the sub as the I-370.

Unlocking Luzon (The Drive to Lingayen Gulf)

Japanese Vice Admiral Shigeru Fukudome, Commander

Imperial Second Air Fleet, headquarters Manila, was surprised when the American invasion force by-passed Manila Bay and landed at the Lingayen Gulf back door instead.

For the Lingayen operation Admiral Kinkaid had mustered an attack force of some 850 vessels—an armada that could have mowed down the Japs even in their heyday.

The Lingayen landings were scheduled for January 9. Kinkaid's forces expected little trouble from the Imperial Navy, but they frowned apprehensively at the sky. With increasing frequency one word was uttered with grim emphasis by ship captains and muttered uneasily by gun crews. The word was "suicide." Destroyers and DE's were particularly vulnerable to Japanese suicide plane attack, and all hands were acutely aware of that vulnerability.

Steaming with an escort-carrier group that was a part of the Luzon Attack Force, STAFFORD (Lieutenant Commander V. H. Craig, Jr., USNR) was one of five DE's screening the carrier TULAGI. In the afternoon of January 5, 1945, the group was struck by Jap aircraft off Mindoro. The Jap planes broke through the tired Combat Air Patrol (CAP) defenses. Five suiciders were shot down by AA gunnery, but six made good their *hari-kiri* dives, and destroyer-escort STAFFORD was struck in this meteor-rain of crashing planes. Fortunately crew casualties were light—two killed; 12 wounded—and the little DE, although crippled, limped gamely along in the wake of the Lingayen-bound group.

Approaching the objective, the Attack Force encountered only a shadowy surface opposition. There were, however, a number of submarine alarms. And on January 5, destroyer TAYLOR (Commander N. J. F. Frank), patrolling in advance of the San Fabian Attack Force, put the finish to the minor career of a midget. This undersized sub discharged two torpedoes at light cruiser BOISE. The torpedoes missed. TAYLOR saw the wakes, and maneuvered to avoid. Later the destroyer's lookouts spied a periscope, lobbed depth charges at close range, then rammed the damaged midget hard amidships. The midget submarine went down with a drowning gurgle.

As they steamed northward toward Lingayen Gulf, the destroyers of DesRons 60 and 56 experienced one air attack after another. On one day, January 6, the assaults were almost continuous, and the Jap suiciders scored a total of 16 scorching hits or near-misses.

Patrolling isolated stations off the beachhead that day, the destroyers were target set-ups for the hell-divers. WALKE (Commander G. F. Davis) was attacked simultaneously by four Jap planes. Her desperate gun crews shot down two suiciders, and, after she was crashed by a third, they got the fourth with an AA burst. The smashing plane blasted the ship's superstructure, killed 12 of the crew, and wounded 35. Among the mortally wounded was Commander Davis.

After disabling WALKE, the suiciders fell upon the ship which relieved her—destroyer O'BRIEN (Commander W. W. Outerbridge).

The plane struck like a lightning bolt. O'BRIEN reeled from the blow and crawled out of action with a section of her superstructure knocked all acockbill. Luckily her crew escaped with few casualties. Meanwhile, destroyer SUMNER was crashed by a plane that blasted her deck and left her disabled. With 14 dead and 29 wounded, the ship endured the day's heaviest casualties.

On that same day RICHARD P. LEARY was damaged by a suicider which grazed her forward 5-inchers; NEWCOMB was blistered by a near miss, the blast of which killed two men and wounded 15; and LOWRY, jolted by a near miss, was damaged by friendly fire.

On January 10 destroyer-escort LERAY WILSON was struck by a suicider. The blast killed six men, injured seven, and wrecked half the vessel's superstructure. Although charred by a gasoline fire, the DE remained on patrol until evening, when she joined a task unit bound for Leyte. On the 12th destroyer-escort GILLIGAN was struck by a "Betty" which her sharpshooting AA gunners had turned into a blowtorch. The flaming plane struck a 40 mm. mount aft, killed 12 men and injured 13. About 30 minutes later, RICHARD W. SUESENS was damaged by a suicider as she was searching the water for men blown overside from GILLIGAN. Riddled by SUESEN's automatic guns, the plane skimmed over the DE and plunged into the sea close aboard.

For a suicide variation, Jap speedboats made a try in Lingayen Gulf in the dark before dawn of January 10. Destroyer PHILIP (Commander J. B. Rutter, Jr.) drove off several of these suicide boats with gunfire, and blew one of them to smithereens.

Philippine Sundown

March, 1945—the Philippines were liberated. Coincident with the liberation was the finish of the Japanese Empire. Here and there in the Netherlands East Indies the Emperor's troops clung to patches of ground, but these troops were marooned. The Co-Prosperity Sphere was bankrupt. The Japanese Merchant Marine was wrecked. Most of the Imperial Navy was rusting on the floor of the Pacific. What was left of it lay at anchor for want of fuel.

Yet the hardest battle of the whole Pacific War was still in store for the United States Navy. Ahead of the Navy's destroyermen was perhaps their most gruelling ordeal.

Over the dark northern horizon lay Okinawa.

Chapter 36

Prelude to Okinawa

The Background—Including Iwo Jima

☆ ☆ ☆

The Coming of the Kamikazes

In the Mediterranean, American destroyermen encounted human torpedoes. In the closing months of the Pacific War, they encountered the deadly *Kamikaze* suicide-plane, and the wicked *Oka,* a jet-propelled, human bomb. These diabolical weapons, in which a man was deliberately sacrificed as a part of the infernal machine, measured the barbarism and desperation of the Japanese war leaders who sponsored such devices. The *Kamikaze-Oka* onslaught gave the United States Navy what many consider its worst hour of World War II.

When Admiral Toyoda ordered Kurita's Second Fleet to turn about and head back into the Leyte battle, his order read: ADVANCE, COUNTING ON DIVINE ASSISTANCE.

Evidently the divinity in reference had to do with the Imperial Navy's Special Attack Corps—its newly devised *Kikusui* program featuring the suicide attack and the *Kamikaze* plane. *Kamikaze* means "Divine Wind."

But at Leyte the promised wind failed to blow with drastic force. The "Divine Wind" was no more than a preliminary puff. As the calendar entered 1945 the *Kamikaze* campaign was only getting under way.

The *Kamikaze* plane was in effect a huge projectile in which the pilot served as fire-control device and exploder mechanism. The *Oka* (Americans called it *Baka*—Japanese for "idiot") was even more in the order of a projectile. Powered by jet propulsion, it was a winged rocket with a warhead that contained 1,135 pounds of high explosive. Like the German glider-bomb, the *Oka* was carried to the scene of action by a mother plane, usually a medium bomber. But the Jap *Oka* was controlled by a human robot who rode the rocket down to the target. There was no turning back once the flying bomb was launched from the release gear of the plane which carried it. The rocket ride was suicide.

So it was that skies around and above Okinawa were fairly seared by the *Kamikazes*. And from the naval standpoint, the story of "Operation Iceberg"—the Okinawa campaign—is the story of the DD's and DE's that fought in the epicenter of the "Divine Wind" hurricane. That "Iceberg" did not melt away under the hot "Divine Wind" was largely due to the fight put up by those little gray ships that were called "small boys" and "tin cans." Against the champions of suicide, they fought a battle which has no equal in the annals of warfare—a battle described by no less an authority than Winston Churchill as *"the most intense and famous of military history."*

"Operation Iceberg"

Located midway between Formosa and Kyushu, Okinawa is the largest of the 55 Nansei islands. It is shaped something like a salamander, about 60 miles in length, 18 miles wide in the narrow strip which joins the lengthy northern head to the splayed southern tail. The mountainous northern terrain is thickly forested; the hilly southern terrain is under green-thumb cultivation.

Strategically, Okinawa's relation to Japan was similar to that of Cuba to the southeast seaboard of the United States; and as a bastion in Japan's inner defense perimeter, the island had been made a honeycomb of fortifications.

Allied Intelligence considerably underestimated the island's strength. It was realized, however, that the campaign would not be a mere picnic. The home-based Japanese Air Force was considered a major problem. And it was recognized that before the Okinawa invasion could be attempted, the Japanese air defenses would have to be whittled down.

Iwo Jima Overture

In the public mind Iwo Jima means Mount Suribachi and the Marines. But the dramatic capture of Suribachi was the peak-high point of the battle; there was fierce fighting before, and ferocious fighting afterward. And the Marines had to be transported, landed, supported, and maintained on the island.

In the pre-invasion preliminaries of heavy air raids, shore bombardments, and the establishment of a blockade, U.S. Navy destroyers participated all around the clock. They were on duty as lifesavers ready to race to the rescue of downed aviators. They steamed with bombardment groups which shot at the island and its Volcano neighbors. They supplemented the submarine blockade with surface sweeps for supply and reinforcement shipping. As early as the first week in January, destroyers were operating in the Iwo area, paving the way for the big assault.

On January 5, destroyers DUNLAP, FANNING, CUMMINGS, ELLET, ROE, and DAVID W. TAYLOR were in the area on bombardment mission.

During the bombardment of Chichi Jima, DAVID W. TAYLOR (Commander W. H. Johnsen) fouled an enemy mine. The blast flooded a forward compartment; four men were drowned; the ship staggered out of action. FANNING (Commander J. C. Bentley) was holed by an enemy shell. Both ships were detached and sent in company to Saipan; from there the TAYLOR went home for a Navy Yard overhaul. Destroyers TERRY and PORTERFIELD were also clawed by enemy fire during the Iwo drama. But the DD's had it relatively easy.

Task Force Off Japan (DD's to the Rescue of FRANKLIN)

The Ides of March found Task Force 58 steaming up from Ulithi to deliver a series of strikes on the Japanese home islands. The blows were calculated to clear the northern air for the "Iceberg" invasion. Approaching Kyushu, Navy planes flew in to bomb the daylights out of the Emperor's airdromes. The carrier airmen turned one field after another into a junkyard, and in the bargain wrecked a number of Jap warships which were lurking in the Inland Sea.

Hitting back in the morning of March 19, Jap bombers caught Admiral Marc Mitscher's task force about 50 miles off the Kyushu coast and dropped two 500-pounders on the carrier FRANKLIN just as her planes were taking off. One bomb went through the flight deck and burst in the hangar. FRANKLIN's aircraft began to blaze like blowtorches. Bombs and rockets started to explode. The detonations ruptured the ship's gasoline lines, and 40,000 gallons of high octane fed the flames. A magazine erupted. In a few minutes the vessel was a floating blast furnace.

Destroyers HICKOX, HUNT, MARSHALL, TINGEY, and MILLER, along with cruiser SANTA FE, stood in to the carrier's assistance. At 0800 MILLER (Lieutenant Commander D. L. Johnson) moved alongside the burning ship to take off Admirals Davidson and Bogan and their staffs for transfer to the carrier HANCOCK. While TINGEY mounted guard, the other DD's maneuvered around the FRANKLIN, rescuing men in the water.

Although FRANKLIN's predicament worsened by every

minute of the morning, her skipper, Captain L. E. Gehres, rejected the idea of abandonment.

At 1130 destroyer HICKOX was ordered to go alongside FRANKLIN's stern to rescue men trapped on the fantail.

During the afternoon destroyer MILLER went alongside the FRANKLIN to fight fires and take off wounded survivors. Jap aircraft put in an appearance, but the enemy bombers were driven off by fighter planes and an ack-ack barrage. The rescue work went steadily forward, with HUNT, TINGEY, and the other destroyers grabbing carriermen from the sea. All told, the DD's recovered about 850 of the FRANKLIN crew. Skippered by Commander J. D. McKinney, destroyer MARSHALL alone plucked 212 survivors from the water.

By evening the carrier's fires were almost smothered, the explosions were fizzling out, and cruiser PITTSBURGH had the charred ship in tow. The Navy and the American public would be thrilled by the story of FRANKLIN's survival—how she reached Ulithi, and from there traveled to Pearl and on to New York Navy Yard under her own steam. Fatalities were high, but the DD's prevented a wholesale charnel.

"Iceberg" Opening Gun (DD's versus Kamikazes Off Kerama Retto)

"Operation Iceberg" was bearing down on the Nansei Shoto archipelago throughout the last week in March, 1945. Six days before invasion D-Day, an advance U.S. detachment under Admiral I. N. Kiland skirted the southern tip of Okinawa to seize Kerama Retto and the Keise Group, island clusters lying west of Naha. No more than 20 miles from Okinawa, Kerama Retto would provide the Navy with a seaplane base on the enemy's southern flank, and a sheltered anchorage for backfield invasion shipping.

Kiland's detachment steamed in with the 77th Infantry Division, and the local garrison, taken completely by surprise, burrowed into the hills and remained "underground" like a prairie dog colony—a situation which at once gave the invaders the upper hand. But the capture of Kerama Retto was not easy. That morning the "Divine Wind" blew. Its hot breath scorched the destroyer KIMBERLY, the first DD to be thus blistered in the "Iceberg" campaign.

At 0615 in the morning of March 26, the KIMBERLY (Commander J. D. Whitfield) was proceeding to her radar picket station off Kerama Retto. As she steamed through the morning twilight, her lookouts sighted two Jap "Vals" apparently headed for the transport area. The destroyer opened fire on the planes, and they turned away. Commander

Whitfield gave the order to cease fire. His Action Report goes on:

> Almost simultaneously with "cease firing," one of the Vals peeled off and began to close the range on a converging but nearly opposite course. Fire was immediately reopened and the rudder put over hard right to maintain all guns bearing as the relative target-bearing rapidly dropped aft. During this phase of the approach, the fire control problem was one of an extremely high deflection rate which the Japanese pilot further complicated by resorting to radical maneuvers including zooming, climbing, slipping, skidding, accelerating, decelerating, and even slow rolling. He continued to close the range on a circling course indicating his intention to get on "our tail."
>
> By this time the range had closed to 4,000 yards and all bearing 40 mm. mounts opened fire. The plane was now in a vertical right bank, circling to come in from astern. The target seemed to be completely surrounded with 5-inch bursts and 40 mm. tracers. At about 1,500 yards range on relative bearing 170° he leveled off and came straight in at an altitude of about 150 feet, performing continuous right and left skids. . . .
>
> Now only the after guns would bear, and each 5-inch salvo blasted the after 20 mm. crews off their feet. In spite of this difficulty, at the instant the Val passed over the stern, the 20 mm. guns had managed to empty one complete magazine. The plane was now about 100 feet in the air and apparently headed for the bridge, with 40 mm. guns No. 3 and No. 5 still firing at maximum rate. Just as the plane reached a point above 40 mm. gun No. 5, it went out of control and fell nearly vertically between 5-inch mounts No. 3 and No. 4, crashing into the still rapidly firing guns of 40 mm. mount No. 5.

Intensity of the resulting explosion and nature of the damage indicated that the plane was armed with a bomb, perhaps a 200-pounder, fitted with a virtually instantaneous fuze. Commander Whitfield summarized the blast-damage as follows:

> Ship's complement reduced by 18%. Two 5-inch 38 guns put out of commission; one 40 mm. gun missing; effectiveness of 20 mm. battery reduced by at least 30% (Mark 14 sights inoperative). All radar and fire control spare parts destroyed. Two K-guns and five roller-loaders out of commission, Smokescreen generator controls and air supply demolished. Two fuel oil service tanks pierced and buckled.

All fires were extinguished within five minutes of the crash —fast work by damage controlmen. And half a minute after the *Kamikaze* hit the deck, the KIMBERLY gunners at undamaged batteries were training their weapons on the second "Val," which failed its mission.

KIMBERLY acquitted herself well in this *Kamikaze* battle. In the afternoon of March 31 she steamed southward, Ulithi-bound for repairs. With her went destroyer O'BRIEN, another *Kamikaze* victim.

The O'BRIEN (Commander W. W. Outerbridge) was struck on the day after the Kerama Retto landings. Both ship and captain were hardened battle veterans, and some of the crew had been in the war since pioneer days. The *Kamikaze* off Kerama Retto was the toughest antagonist the destroyer had yet encountered.

At 0545 in the morning of March 27, O'BRIEN was attacked by a suicider. The plane was shot down.

At 0624 a second plane plummeted at the O'BBIEN and smashed into the destroyer's port side just above the main deck and aft of the No. 1 stack. The blast, evidently the work of a 500-pound bomb, sent the ship reeling. Flames lunged from the wrecked superstructure. All radars were put out of commission. The TBS was knocked out. The starboard twin 40 mm. was shattered; the port twin was crushed; the forward fireroom had to be abandoned by the steaming watch. The ship's sonar gear went out, as did the two torpedo directors. All facilities in the C.I.C. were thus incapacitated. Fifty of the ship's crew were killed, and 76 were wounded. Nothing short of miraculous damage-control work contained the fires topside and kept O'BRIEN going.

Other "small boys" were struck by the mad suiciders off Kerama Retto.

So the "Divine Wind" howled at Kerama Retto. But the first destroyer lost in "Operation Iceberg" was downed by an undersea weapon. Victim was the USS HALLIGAN.

Loss of USS HALLIGAN

Destroyer HALLIGAN (Lieutenant Commander E. T. Grace) was a member of Fire Support Unit 2 working along the southwest coast of Okinawa.

At dusk on March 26, HALLIGAN had orders to take a night patrol station located off the coast. Minesweeping was still in progress, between Kerama Retto and Okinawa, and all ships had been warned to give unswept areas a scrupulous avoidance. But doom struck HALLIGAN as she moved to her patrol station. At 1835 the destroyer was lifted half out of the tide by a monstrous explosion that sent a pillar of fire towering in the twilight. Men and scraps of deck machinery were hurled overside, and the ship's hull was split open by the blast. Below decks officers and men were slain outright, and many more were drowned as the sea engulfed the stricken vessel. So swiftly did HALLIGAN go down that nearly half her crew went under with her. With the exception of two ensigns, the ship's entire officer complement perished in the disaster. One hundred and sixty-six men survived the sinking.

Available evidence suggested a moored mine as the destructive agent. The area in which the ship was steaming when she was blasted had not been declared swept.

There remained the question of why HALLIGAN steamed headlong into an unswept area. Was she there through navigational error? Investigating something? Somebody failed to get the word? The answer will never be known. All officers in a position to know were lost.

Chapter 37

Okinawa Invasion

☆ ☆ ☆

(Iceberg: Destroyer's Hottest Mission!)

D-Day for Okinawa fell on Easter Sunday. But to the men in "Operation Iceberg" the day was just April 1, 1945—ironically designated "Love Day."

As has been stated, from a naval standpoint the story of the Okinawa campaign is the story of the 148 American DD's and DE's that bore the brunt of the sea-air battle. Allied carrier groups stood far offshore; bombardment groups came and went. On blockade duty, American submarines met practically no opposition. But the destroyer forces on the "Iceberg" front were in there fighting for days and weeks on end. The "small boys" got the man-size job at Okinawa. And they put up a giant-size effort to accomplish that job.

Most of the destroyers and destroyer-escorts on the "Iceberg" front worked as radar pickets or patrol vessels in the area screen. Covering the approaches to Okinawa, they mounted guard at radar picket stations positioned in a ring encircling the island, or patrolled the convoy approaches and served as A/S and anti-aircraft guards on a perimeter which embraced the transport area. These picket and patrol ships constituted Task Flotilla 5, under command of a veteran destroyerman, Commodore Frederick Moosbrugger.

Twenty-three destroyers worked with the fire-support groups which bombarded the Okinawa beaches in the interval between dawn and H-Hour of D-Day. At 0830 the troops began to land on the designated six-mile stretch of Hagushi foreshore.

There was virtually no opposition. By nightfall of April 1 the advance guards had seized the Yontan and Kadena airfields. About 50,000 soldiers and Marines were ashore. "Love Day" had been practically bloodless. But by morning of April

2, General S. B. Buckner's troops were clashing with the outposts of the tough Shuri Line. During the next three days the land battle steadily developed. And on April 6 the *Kamikaze* hurricane broke over the sea in full fury.

Down from Kyushu and the upper Nansei Shoto islands came the planes—"Vals" and "Zekes," "Bettys" and "Oscars" and "Jills." Some were new and some had been modernized, but many were old-timers, aged and battle-scarred, rigged especially for suicide jobs and carrying just enough gas for a one-way trip to doom. As they approached Okinawa on April 6, many of these *Kikusui* pilots were shot down by intercepting planes. However, about 200 broke through the screen. Not to live, but hoping to die.

Weaving and skidding, barrel-rolling and looping, they descended on the "Iceberg" forces at Hagushi Beach.

The ordeal began on that day of April 6—a day which might well have been designated DD-Day—"Destroyer Day." At Okinawa the shore was afire. The sky was afire. The sea was afire. Plane after plane was blown to extinction by destroyer gunners fighting for their lives. One ship after another was blasted by the mad aviators of the Mikado, seeking death for the glory of the god-Emperor. Destroyer MULLANY was hit. NEWCOMB was hit. LEUTZE was hit. HOWORTH was hit. HYMAN was hit. MORRIS was hit. HAYNSWORTH was hit. Destroyer-escort FIEBERLING was hit. HARRISON was scorched by a near miss. And in this one day's hell of fire and death, two destroyers, each struck by two or more *Kamikazes,* went flaming and exploding to the bottom.

The destroyers slain were the USS BUSH and the USS COLHOUN.

Loss of USS BUSH

Destroyer BUSH (Commander R. E. Westholm) occupied No. 1 Picket Station, which was located 51 miles north of Okinawa. On April 2, the destroyer PRICHETT reported to relieve her, and BUSH proceeded to Kerama Retto for fuel. On the next day, word was received that the PRICHETT had been seriously damaged by a suicide plane. BUSH was at once ordered back on station.

From April 3 to April 5 the Japs gave BUSH a nasty time. She succeeded in repelling the air attacks and in warning the task force of impending strikes. Her luck ended on April 6.

Shortly after 1500, just when the third raid in half an hour was driven off, a lone Jap suicider came streaking in about 30 feet above the water. The pilot ran into a streak of bullets and shells. Fragments broke away from his plane. But accurate fire could not deter him. The *Kamikaze* crashed with a huge explosion at deck level on the ship's starboard side between No. 1 and No. 2 stacks. A torpedo or bomb exploded in the forward engine-room with such force that a six-foot section of engine-room blower, weighing about 4,000 pounds was flung into the air high enough to knock off the radar antenna and land on the port wing of the bridge. The bursting plane scattered firebrands across the deck, and flame spurted from the wreckage.

The fires were beaten down by damage-control crews, and water-tight integrity was preserved sufficiently to keep the vessel afloat. Destroyer COLHOUN came in from a near-by picket station to offer assistance. Then, at 1700, while all hands were battling to save the BUSH, a flight of 10 to 15 Jap planes swept in. The COLHOUN was hit immediately, and the BUSH received her second smash 25 minutes later. This *Kamikaze* crash nearly cut her in two. At 1745 a third *Kamikaze* plummeted into the blazing destroyer. That was the end of BUSH. The ship broke up and sank about 1830.

Eighty-seven officers and men were killed in the murderous action, and 42 were wounded. Among those who died in BUSH was Commander J. S. Willis, ComDesDiv 48.

Loss of USS COLHOUN

About 1600 in that volcanic afternoon, while destroyer COLHOUN was steaming to the aid of stricken BUSH, the suicide onslaught crescendoed to its height. All up and down the Okinawa coast the rabid *Kamikazes* were striking.

In the C.I.C. the team sweated through a bedlam of calls, signals, orders, reports. "Sparks" could not keep up with the frantic radio. On the radar screen was a hailstorm—"bogies" and "bandits" appearing from all directions. Over TBS came a shouting babel, insanely frenzied by sporadic interjections of static. Voices from the air: "Lamppost, this is Lovebird. I see bogey one four zero. Do you concur? Over." Answer: "Hello, Lovebird. This is Lamppost. Affirmative. Raid coming in. Out."

COLHOUN was attacked as she stood by BUSH, offering what little help she could. Down came the suiciders in screaming power dives.

They picked on two tough ships—BUSH, a veteran with a fine combat record; COLHOUN, skippered by Commander G. R. Wilson—that same George Rees Wilson who had captained hard-bitten CHEVALIER in the Solomons.

On board wounded BUSH the AA guns blazed with unstinted fury. Injured though she was, BUSH probably got several suiciders. And COLHOUN blew five *Kamikazes* to blazes. But four of the planes smashed into Wilson's ship in a mass murder-and-suicide assault that no destroyer could withstand.

One crashing plane threw a searing sheet of fire across COL-HOUN's superstructure. Another struck on the bow with a dazzling burst that opened up the forecastle as a hammer-smash would open a melon. Skimming in low, *Kamikazes* three and four exploded against the ship's side, showering the vessel with fire, water, blazing gasoline, and debris.

COLHOUN was still afloat when the ship she had tried to save went under.

About five hours later COLHOUN, herself, went under. Wilson fought to save her as he had fought to save CHEVALIER. But the battle proved hopeless. CASSIN YOUNG stood off to bury the abandoned hulk with gunfire. About 2330 the hull broke up, and COLHOUN went down, wrapped in a shroud of steam. Down with her she took the bodies of one officer and 34 men. Some 295 of the crew, including 21 wounded, survived.

Loss of USS MANNERT L. ABELE

Six days later death stalked destroyer MANNERT L. ABELE. April 12, 1945. That was the day Franklin D. Roosevelt died, and the enemy thought to make capital of the tragedy which stunned the Allied world. *Banzai!* A monster suicide assault to celebrate the death of the American President.

So the *Kamikazes* came, about 200 strong. With them they brought the *Oka*—the madman's idiot little brother. The noon-day sky was blue, and sunshine flecked the sea with gold. Then, all in a breath, the sky was spattered with shrapnel bursts and the seascape was gouged by explosions, smudged with smoke, streaked with oil, and cluttered with debris.

Seventeen times the suiciders struck. Seventeen raids in which crazed *Kamikazes* and idiot *Okas* flung themselves upon the American ships off the Okinawa shore. In that fiery tempest battleship TENNESSEE was struck. So was battleship IDAHO. So were smaller vessels working near the beach. As usual, destroyers were in the vortex of this *Kamikaze* tornado.

Destroyer-escort WHITEHURST was hit. Destroyer STANLY was hit by a demented *"Baka."* Destroyer-escort RIDDLE was hit. Destroyer CASSIN YOUNG was hit. Destroyer-escort RALL was hit. Destroyer PURDY was hit. And one of the first to be struck was destroyer MANNERT L. ABELE.

She was hit by two suiciders. The first, a *Kamikaze,* came screaming at her about 1445. Plunging through fusillades of AA fire, the plane smashed into the destroyer's starboard side. The blast wiped out the after engine-room, hurling men and machinery skyward. Sixty seconds later, what was believed to be a *"Baka"* smashed into the ship's starboard side, forward, blowing up the forward fireroom. The vessel's main deck was awash almost immediately after the *Oka* smash. Three minutes later she went under.

A Jap plane dropped a bomb squarely in the center of a large group of swimming survivors, and those who lived through this blasting found themselves struggling in a sludge of oil and blood. Lieutenant (jg) John E. Hertner, ship's Medical Officer, worked valiantly over the wounded on the rafts and in the water. Seventy-three of the destroyer's crew were lost in the sinking. The ship's survivors would never forget an indebtedness to Lieutenant Hertner.

Loss of USS PRINGLE

April 16 was another nightmare day for "The Fleet That Came to Stay." On that day the carrier INTREPID was damaged by a suicide plane, and destroyer McDERMUT, working in the flat-top's screen, was badly slashed by friendly AA fire. Destroyer LAFFEY was hit by a *Kamikaze*. Destroyer-escort BOWERS was hit. Destroyer BRYANT was hit. And destroyer PRINGLE was fatally struck by a suicider. This, in spite of reinforcements—VT ammunition; fighter cover of two CAP planes for each picket station; a companion destroyer or ship of comparable AA fire-power to support each picket destroyer.

The PRINGLE (Lieutenant Commander J. L. Kelley, Jr.) was patrolling Radar Picket Station No. 14 in company with destroyer-minelayer HOBSON and two landing craft. About 0900 down came a "Zeke." As the plane roared in, making a shallow dive, PRINGLE's AA batteries paved the aircraft's road with fire and iron. The "Zeke" suddenly skidded, turned over on a broken wing, and plunged into the sea with a haystack splash. One *Kamikaze* down!

Ten minutes later, three "Vals" came winging across the seascape. Skimming the water, they began to stunt around the PRINGLE, dipping and weaving and alternately opening and closing the range at distances between 11,000 to 9,000 yards—bat-like tactics calculated to baffle the destroyer's gunners.

Although the wild maneuvering drew a steady fire that wore loaders and hot-shell men to a frazzle, PRINGLE's gunners were not entirely baffled. One of the outside "Vals"—the plane lowest to the water—flew smack into a shell-splash and crashed.

But the middle "Val" got in. Suddenly peeling off to make a shallow dive, the *Kamikaze* rushed at the ship with the velocity of a comet. At the "con" Lieutenant Commander Kelley tried to swing the ship away. The destroyer couldn't make it. There was a blinding crash as the plane struck the ship's superstructure just abaft the No. 1 stack. The blast up-rooted both smokestacks, wrecked the superstructure from pilot house to No. 3 gun mount, gutted the vessel amidships, and buckled her keel.

PRINGLE broke in two. Bluejackets and officers smeared with oil, grease, and blood struggled out of the sinking wreck-age. The sea swiftly closed over the fore and after sections of the ship.

Valiant rescuers, destroyer-minelayer HOBSON and the two landing craft were immediately on the job. Before noon most of the destroyer's 258 survivors were picked up. Almost half of these were suffering from burns, fractures, shock, or minor injuries. They considered themselves lucky. Sixty-two of their shipmates were gone.

Loss of USS LITTLE

As the Battle for Okinawa raged into May, all hope of a quick wind-up of "Operation Iceberg" expired. May brought no rest to the destroyermen off Okinawa. Alert followed alert. Lookouts, radar watch, all hands waited in tension for the next hour's raid, or the surprise assault of the next moment. It was only a question of time before the *Kamikazes* would come.

They came for destroyer LITTLE (Commander Madison Hall, Jr.) early in the evening of May 3. She was on radar picket station with the new minelayer AARON WARD and four smaller ships—an LSM and three LCS's. Such a group of land-ing craft stationed in company with a picket destroyer was commonly referred to as "The Pall Bearers." Typical destroy-erman humor—the wry humor that carried many a small "small boy" through the ordeal of Okinawa.

On the evening in question all the humor that could be mustered was neded. About 1415 the first "pips," deadly as smallpox, were on the radar screen. Over TBS went the warn-ing. Into action went the C.I.C. In housings and tubs the gun crews adjusted their helmets; fingered their weapons, waited with stomach muscles taut.

"Here they come!"

A growing roar—a flock of Jap planes streaking through the sky.

At 1843 they struck at the picket destroyer.

Excerpt from LITTLE's Action Report: "*One was vertical dive, one was low level, and one was gliding in. That such coordination could be achieved is almost unbelievable, but such was the case.*"

LITTLE's gunners got two of them. But four of them got LITTLE. Like a chain of thunderbolts they smashed into the destroyer, shattering her superstructure, crushing her hull, wrecking her vital machinery. It was all over in two minutes of volcanic eruption—four shattering explosions. Then the broken ship was reeling in a turmoil of fire and smoke. The dead were vanishing in floodwater and flame. The living were going overside.

"The Pall Bearers" closed in. At 1855 LITTLE sank into an Okinawa grave. Down with her she took 30 of her crew.

Loss of USS LUCE

May 4th was the last day for 149 of the crew of USS LUCE and 152 of the crew of USS MORRISON. The "Divine Wind" blew foul for the American Destroyer Force that morning!

Destroyer LUCE (Commander J. W. Waterhouse) was stationed as fighter-director ship in the radar picket line. At 0740 —the tag-end of the morning watch, when haggard crews were gulping coffee before "going on," and weary hands were sighing with what little relief could be had from "going off"—at 0740 the enemy bat-men were sighted. Then nobody went off watch. *Bong! Bong! Bong!* General Quarters! A concerted dash for battle stations. Gunners scrambling to their mounts. Talkers hitching into their gear. The C.I.C. team pitching in. Babel on the radio-telephone. The CAP fighter planes vectored out to intercept. Back-talk between ship and sky.

"Bugeye One, this is Bugeye! Five bandits at Angel six! Vector six zero. Buster! Over!"

"Bugeye, this is Bugeye One! Tallyho! Splashed one Emily and one Judy! Out!"

The CAP fighters intercepted. But two of the Japs escaped the aerial melee. Down the sky they came as though in grooves, straight for destroyer LUCE.

Her guns rattled and banged, flaying the air with flak, but the planes ripped in through the blazing curtain. One smashed into the ship's starboard side abreast of the No. 1 stack. The explosion showered the superstructure with fire, spreading flames over a mangle of men, guns, and machinery. The second plane roared in on the port quarter to crash the hull near the after engine-room. Framework gave under the blast; water plunged into the engineering spaces; LUCE was done for.

An inrush of water carried the ship down, stern first, and under a fog of smoke she was gone. "Pall Bearers" closed in to rescue the survivors. Of the 186 who were picked up, 57 were severely wounded.

Referring to the sudden death which struck LUCE, a destroyer officer wrote grimly, *"This action shows the virtual impossibility of stopping a determined suicide-plane attack."*

Loss of USS MORRISON

Destroyer MORRISON (Commander J. R. Hansen) had Radar Picket Station No. 1. She was on duty as fighter-director ship with a unit which included destroyer INGRAHAM and four landing craft. This group was representative of the "double-banking" which Spruance employed in an effort to shore up each picket station. Supporting each other, the two destroyers could raise a parasol of flak that would unnerve the average aviator. But the *Kamikaze* pilot was not an average aviator. Determined on suicide, he cared nothing for the dangers of combat and would face any fire with the indifference of madness.

A case in point was the MORRISON blasting. The carnage occurred shortly after LUCE was blown to the bottom. The "pips" snowed across her radar screen, and the Corsairs covering the station were coached in to meet the approaching Japs. The Corsairs shot down two of the enemy, but they were unable to block the onslaught. As in the assault on LUCE, the *Kamikazes* broke through the CAP defense, singled out their target, and launched a multiple, coordinated suicide attack.

They struck MORRISON one at a time in something like two-minute intervals—one, two, three, four!

There was no time to abandon. The wreck sank so swiftly that most of the men below decks were lost. Out of a total complement of 331 men, only 179 were recovered. And 108 of those rescued were wounded.

Loss of USS OBERRENDER

OBERRENDER's is an unusual story. To begin with, the ship —skippered by Lieutenant Commander Samuel Spencer, USNR—was patrolling off the western coast of Okinawa not as a radar picket, but as an anti-submarine sentinel. She was the only destroyer-escort to be done in by a *Kamikaze*. Yet she was not sunk by the suicide plane; her gunners practically shot the plane to pieces before it struck. Finally, through the foresight of her captain, the ship had been well prepared for a suicide onslaught, and his intelligent provisions paid off in the saving of lives. Only eight men perished in the blasting which wrecked OBERRENDER. Here is the story, a condensation of her Action Report, prepared by a destroyer officer who made a study of this ship's performance.

On 9 May OBERRENDER *was patrolling on A/S Screening Station No. A-34-A off Okinawa. At 1844 an enemy plane was reported 34 miles away.* OBERRENDER *picked it up on her SA radar at 16 miles and plotted it in to 1.5 miles. At 1850 flank speed of 24 knots was rung up. At 1852 the plane was picked up visually, bearing about 260°, range about 9,000 yards, altitude 18,000 feet, position angle 35°. At about the time* OBERRENDER *sighted the plane, it started a power dive for her at an angle of descent of about 35°. The ship was put in a hard left turn and fire was opened with both 5-inch guns. The 40 mm. guns opened fire at about 4,000 yards range. Almost immediately after these guns opened fire, a 40 mm. shell hit the engine of the plane at a range of about 3,000 yards and 40 mm. shells appeared to be registering hits from there in. At about 2,000 yards a 5-inch burst seemed to loosen the port wing. It was flapping from there in to about 250 yards, when it came off the plane altogether. When the wing came off, the plane swerved somewhat to the right, but not quite enough to miss the ship. It hit the gun platform of Gun 25 a glancing blow. The port wing, which was floating clear of the plane, hit the after fireroom uptake just below the stack, doing slight damage. The plane itself did little damage other than demolish the gun bucket of Gun 25. What is believed to have been a 500-pound delayed-action bomb apparently went through the main deck a few inches inside the starboard gunwale, and the bomb went off in the forward fireroom, causing very heavy damage in the amidships area of the ship. At 2045 the tug* TEKESTA *passed a line and towed* OBERRENDER *in to Kerama Retto.*

At Kerama Retto the DE's battle damage was carefully examined. Naval technicians shook their heads. OBERRENDER was beyond all hope of repair. On July 25, 1945, she was stricken from the Navy's roster.

Eight of OBERRENDER's crew were the ship's only fatalities. Of the 53 in the ship's company who were wounded by the blasting, a number might have died but for the foresight of the vessel's captain.

Here is an explanatory paragraph taken verbatim from the ship's Action Report:

Where a large number of persons are injured at a single stroke, as was the case here, the normal Pharmacist's Mate complement is of course unequal to handle the situation. Moreover, on such occasions the services of repair party personnel are apt to be urgently needed to combat fires, etc., so that they are not available to assist the Pharmacist's Mates. With this possibility in mind, we had developed a group of about six men with considerable first-aid experience, had

*given them battle stations which were not of a vital nature
for ship operation or gunnery, and had trained them to take
the lead in first-aid-work if needed. Also we had emphasized
first-aid for all hands in our training program. Both of these
policies paid dividends.*

Loss of USS Longshaw

Longshaw was one of the two American destroyers
downed off Okinawa by some agent other than *Kamikaze*.
(Lost in a minefield, Halligan was the first non-*Kamikaze*
fatality.)

On May 14, 1945, the Longshaw stepped into action as
a fire-support ship on call to bombard designated beach-
targets. For an unrelieved four days and four nights the destroyer worked along the molten coast, supporting the American forces ashore with constant shell fire.

All hands were bleary-eyed and haggard by the morning
of the 18th. So someone erred in plotting the ship's position on the chart, or gave the wrong order to the helmsman.
Or someone failed to take action in time. At 0719 there was
a shocking growl under her keel; the ship jolted to a halt
like a locomotive which had lumbered through a broken
switch. Longshaw was jammed hard aground.

She had ridden up on Ose Reef, right in the maw of a
Japanese shore battery. Desperately the ship's skipper, Lieutenant Commander C. W. Becker, and all hands tried to get
her off. Backing engines strained and propellers churned up
a fury of froth. Weights were jettisoned—everything that
could go to lighten ship. The destroyer could not be moved.

A call for help brought the tug Arikara racing up. The
little tug worked with main and could not budge the destroyer.

Then, at 1100 of that morning, gruff thunder rumbled out
from the beach, and deadly shell geysers spurted on the reef.

So Longshaw's hour came in a rush of salvos that splashed
close aboard, then reached out to straddle, then fell upon the
ship with homicidal violence. The destroyermen answered
with four rounds of counter-battery fire, but there was no
chance to make it a shooting match. From the start Jap shells
were thrashing the destroyer's superstructure, pounding her
decks, and uprooting her batteries. Fixed as she was, the ship
could neither fight nor run away. In a matter of moments
she was afire and burning, her deck a shambles, her interior
a slaughter-house.

From the bridge Longshaw's captain shouted orders to
abandon. But abandonment under artillery fire was to leap
from an exploding deck into exploding water.

In that tempest of blood, flame, and iron, Lieutenant Commander Becker disappeared. Ten companion officers vanished in the inferno—half the ship's officer complement. Sixty-six bluejackets perished in the LONGSHAW's massacre. Of the 225 who escaped, 95 were wounded, and seven would die of their wounds.

Late in the afternoon of May 18 LONGSHAW's charred and shattered remains were sunk by friendly naval fire.

Loss of USS DREXLER

On the 28th of May the suiciders delivered another all-out onslaught on the picket line.

Skippered by Commander R. L. Wilson, destroyer DREXLER was standing Okinawa radar picket duty. On station with her was destroyer LOWRY and two picket support craft. DREXLER had totaled 15 days as an Okinawa radar picket, in which time she had become only too well acquainted with the all-or-nothing *Kikusui* program.

Influence type ammunition, "double-banking," and CAP cover were exterminating more and more of the aerial suiciders. But not enough for the saving of USS DREXLER on this savage day. During the later part of the morning watch six *Kamikazes* broke through the screen shielding the DREXLER-LOWRY group. This suicide squad made a coordinated attack on DREXLER.

Riddled by DREXLER's fire, two of the planes plunged into the sea. And two failed to strike the ship. But the remaining two, power-diving, rammed the destroyer full-gun. The blast of the second-strike opened DREXLER's deck to the sky, and threw her over on her beam. She never returned to an even keel.

Nearly all hands below decks were imprisoned in the vessel. The "Pall Bearers" stood in to the rescue. About 170 officers and men were picked up, 51 of their number wounded. One hundred and fifty-eight men and eight officers died with the ship.

Loss of USS WILLIAM D. PORTER

By the first of June victory for the American forces on Okinawa was dimly in sight. Over Shuri Castle, citadel of the Japanese defense line, a tattered Stars and Stripes slatted in the wind. Some 50,000 corpses, one-time men of the 32nd Imperial Army, lay dead in the crumbled fortifications of the Shuri Line. The troops of General Simon Buckner were slugging relentlessly forward.

On June 4 the *Kamikazes* struck in a series of 18 raids.

They were shot down in flocks; no picket line destroyers were so much as damaged.

On June 5, battleship MISSISSIPPI and cruiser LOUISVILLE were struck by *Kamikaze* planes. On the 7th the raids continued, and more suicide pilots died in flames. But the *Kamikazes* got a ship on the 10th of June. Victim was the WILLIAM D. PORTER.

Captained by Commander C. M. Keyes, the destroyer was on radar picket duty at Station No. 15. The *Kamikaze* showed up early in the forenoon watch. At a distance of four miles the plane was identified as a "bandit," and as it hove into near view it turned out to be a "Val."

WILLIAM D. PORTER and the four LCS "Pall Bearers" with her splotched ack-ack on the plane, but it still came on.

Diving at the destroyer, the *Kamikaze* struck the sea close aboard, and blew up with a shattering blast. The tremendous concussion had the effect of a mine explosion, crushing the underside of PORTER's hull and opening her stern to the flood. The inrush could not be stemmed, and in a short time the entire after part of the ship was swamped.

Moving up alongside, the four "Pall Bearers" joined in the destroyer's battle for buoyancy. All available pumping facilities were rushed into action. But the flooding could not be controlled.

The men had time to go overside with care. The badly wounded were handled gently, and those suffering from minor injuries—sprains, lacerations, a few burns—were not compelled to endure long immersion in salt water. All 61 of the wounded were thus enabled to recover. And the entire crew was removed from the WILLIAM D. PORTER before she sank.

WILLIAM D. PORTER was the eleventh American destroyer melted down in the crucible of Okinawa. Her crew was the only one to come through without a single fatality.

Loss of USS Twiggs

During the evening of June 16 the rabid airmen struck again. One of them struck at a destroyer which was standing offshore for bombardment duty—the USS TWIGGS, captained by Commander George Philip.

Time: about 2030. The plane, a "Jill" torpedo-bomber, dropped down out of the dusk like a thunderbolt. When detected, it was less than 1,000 yards from the destroyer, and coming with the velocity of a bullet. An unleashed torpedo knifed into the water and raced at the ship. Before TWIGGS could be swung away, the torpedo ripped into the No. 2 magazine. Then the plane crashed into the ship, aft.

Torpedo explosion—magazine explosion—aircraft explosion—the triple blasting tore the destroyer's frame and sent sheets of fire flagging through her superstructure. Damage controlmen never had a chance. All in a gust the ship was a furnace, with men fighting their way topside to escape roasting heat and suffocating smoke, only to find the deck a burning griddle.

Thirty minutes after the *Kamikaze* smash, the ship's after magazine blew up with a shattering detonation. The vessel plunged immediately. Down with her she took 18 of her 22 officers. One hundred and sixty-five men were lost with the ship. Down with the destroyer went her captain, Commander Philip.

The survivors drifted in clots on the sea, and waited for help to come. Presently destroyer PUTNAM arrived to pick up these latest victims of the "Divine Wind." Many of the 131 who were recovered needed surgery and hospitalization. The three surviving officers were among the wounded; the TWIGGS disaster was one of the few in which every officer in the embattled ship was either killed or injured.

Loss of USS UNDERHILL

On June 21, 1945, Japanese resistance on Okinawa collapsed in a horror of *banzai* charges and *hari-kiri*.

Off Okinawa the line of radar pickets maintained vigilant watch. By all indications the "Divine Wind" hurricane had blown itself into history, but there remained suicidal undercurrents in the sea.

Late in July, 1945, one of those undercurrents proved fatal for destroyer-escort UNDERHILL. Captained by Lieutenant Commander R. M. Newcomb, USNR, the DE was serving as a unit in a group escorting a convoy of seven LST's and a merchantman on the Okinawa-to-Philippines run.

In the afternoon of July 24 the ships were steaming in formation some 150 miles northeast of Luzon. UNDERHILL was marching along in the convoy's van, her engines drumming their smooth rhythm. The convoy was bound for Leyte, after eight days at Okinawa. It was always a relief to leave Okinawa astern.

Yet at sea one never could tell, one never knew. And on that afternoon Destiny placed her invisible finger on UNDERHILL, and the little destroyer-escort was a marked ship. Lieutenant E. M. Rich, USNR, described the action as he saw and heard it evolve:

> *We had just changed course and were all prepared to start a new patrol plan for the escorts when we got a sound contact just about 1400. We started an attack on the sound*

contact, were all set to drop our depth charges, but the contact did not look good. The ASW officer said it was mushy and advised the captain, since we were directly ahead of the convoy, not to drop any charges.

Shortly thereafter the DE's lookouts sighted a floating mine. The account continues:

> *We maneuvered around the mine . . . and then began firing on the mine. We still had the sound contact and as we lay there maneuvering around, the contact . . . seemed to be firmer.*
>
> *We sent one of the PC's, the other escorts, over to see if he could pick up the contact. . . . The PC went ahead and dropped charges.*
>
> *Just a few seconds afterwards, we saw a periscope come up aft of the place where the charges had exploded. . . . We turned anud headed for the periscope. . . . The word was passed over the phones and over the Public Address system to stand by to ram. Immediately afterwards it was changed to set a shallow pattern of depth charges.*
>
> *We went on for a short period of time and then we heard the depth charges explode. . . . I heard the captain report, "We got one Jap midget submarine. We can see oil and debris on the surface."*
>
> *We . . . sighted another periscope, and immediately started for that one. . . . A short time later I heard the range given from somewhere as 700 yards. Then the word was passed again to stand by to ram.*
>
> *Shortly after that I heard the talker say, "He's looking right at us." Then I got braced ready for the collision. I felt two sharp jars so we just hit something—had gone over the top of it. Then right after that came an explosion. I lost my phones. Everything went dark in the log room, and in feeling around trying to find my phones I discovered water coming in. I thought the ship was sinking. . . . I tried to phone Control, and someone told me we didn't have any Control. Then I realized that the whole forward end of the ship had been blown off up to the forward fireroom bulkhead; all forward of that was gone. All the bridge area, the bridge structure and the mast . . . all had been blown off.*

There was no Action Report left by UNDERHILL. The officers who could have written it were gone.

Loss of USS CALLAGHAN

During the last fortnight of July, 1945, destroyer CAL-

LAGHAN (Commander C. M. Bertholf) was on radar picket station off Okinawa. With her on station were destroyers PRICHETT and CASSIN YOUNG and three LCS's.

CALLAGHAN had seen her share of the Pacific War. More than her share. Now she was due to go *home*—overhaul for the ship; recuperation for the crew. As the mid-watch came on and the ship's log entered the 29th, the crew could hardly bear the anticipation. Destroyer LAWS was coming to relieve the CALLAGHAN; this was to be her last hour on station at Okinawa.

It was to be her last hour—period.

At 0030 a "bogey" was reported.

At 0031 the crew was rushed to General Quarters.

An instant later the 5-inch batteries opened fire, smearing the night sky with splashes of flame.

Then the plane was seen as a *Kamikaze* heading straight for CALLAGHAN.

At 0041 the plane crashed into the ship near the No. 3 upper handling-room.

A thunderclap blast rocked the destroyer, and then, at 0045, the handling-room exploded.

The "Pall Bearers" closed in to pick up the survivors. Forty-six bluejackets and an officer were lost with the ship in this most unlucky sinking. CALLAGHAN had 12 Jap planes painted on her director; the *Kamikaze* that killed her would have been the 13th. And, dying, she was the thirteenth and last American destroyer to go down in the battle of Okinawa.

Chapter 38

The Battle Scarred

☆ ☆ ☆

Okinawa Crash Bill

Eighty-eight destroyers and 30 destroyer-escorts were damaged in the Battle for Okinawa. Those figures sum up to nearly a third of the total for all warship types damaged in the "Iceberg" operation.

Not all of the wounded DD's and DE's were injured by *Kamikazes*. Several were struck by *"Baka"* rockets. Several were hit by suicide boats; a few were struck by the fire of enemy shore batteries. But *Kamikaze* wounds were by far in the majority and by far the worst; some of the DD's and DE's disabled by the suicide planes suffered worse punishment than the ships which were sunk by *Kamikaze* strikes. Destroyer WILLIAM D. PORTER, for example, went down without a single fatality, whereas destroyer HAZELWOOD, disabled by a *Kamikaze* smash, reeled out of action with 46 dead, including her captain and "Exec." Similarly disabled, destroyer BRAINE made port with 50 dead and 78 wounded. Destroyer-escort BOWERS came out of a suicide crash with half her crew lying dead or injured.

Wounded in the "Divine Wind" tornado of April 6, eight DD's and a DE were *Kamikaze* victims.

Destroyers NEWCOMB and LEUTZE were at adjacent screening stations that day. Positioned off Okinawa, they were covering the heavy ships of Task Force 54. Down the afternoon sky came the suicide squadrons; the CAP fighters intercepted; the battle splintered into a bewildering free-for-all of aerial dogfights and crash-dive attacks. At 1759 NEWCOMB's radar spotted a nearing enemy. A moment later the destroyer's lookouts saw the aircraft skimming in across the water. The AA guns roared; fragments of metal were flicked from the plane; but the aircraft came on like a streaking shadow and smashed into the destroyer's after stack. The ship slowed rapidly as steam whistled from ruptured boilers. Fire broke out in the upper handling room of a 5-inch battery.

As NEWCOMB's crew was fighting battle damage, a second Jap plane came in on the starboard bow. This menace was shot down at a range of 6,000 yards. Then a third plane, which had followed the first one in from the west, crashed the destroyer amidships near the torpedo workshop. The explosion stopped the destroyer dead in the sea. Both engine-rooms and the after fireroom were blown into scrap. The after stack, both torpedo mounts, all of the amidship superstructure, 40 mm. mounts, and magazines disintegrated in crimson eruption. And at that critical moment a fourth *Kamikaze* slammed into the forward stack, showering the molten wreckage with gasoline.

Within 11 short minutes NEWCOMB had been reduced from a warship to a wallowing crematorium. But her captain, Commander I. E. McMillian, and his equally stout crew hung on.

Destroyer LEUTZE (Lieutenant L. Grabowsky) steamed to NEWCOMB's aid, boldly going alongside the burning wreck. Hoses were passed forward, and preparations were being made to pass them aft when a fifth *Kamikaze* hurtled down from the sky. An accurate VT projectile burst under the plane's left wing and tilted it just enough to send it skidding across LEUTZE's fantail, where it exploded with a huge detonation. The ship immediately lost steering control, and her torn stern settled in the water. *"Am in serious danger of sinking,"* she signalled NEWCOMB, *"am pulling away."*

While LEUTZE was limping away, destroyer BEALE (Commander D. M. Coffee) moved alongside the flaming NEWCOMB. BEALE passed six hoses to the fiery vessel, and the conflagration was then brought under control in less than 30 minutes. The smolder was finally extinguished by bucket brigades, and by 1930 NEWCOMB was out of immediate danger.

In his Action Report Commander McMillian paid high tribute to the members of his crew. *"Never,"* he stated, *"was there any hint that the ship would be abandoned. . . . This, although all officers and men were suffering from severe shock not lessened in any degree by the grim presence of dead and dying throughout the ship, along with the distinctly audible cries of those suffering from severe burns and shrapnel wounds."*

Both NEWCOMB and LEUTZE were to be on the binnacle list for many days, but they would sail again. So would many another DD disabled by the berserk *Kamikazes* at Okinawa. Destroyer MULLANY (Commander A. O. Momm) was struck at almost the same moment NEWCOMB was hit. Fire and explosion followed the aircraft blast. A number of the depth charges exploded, ripping great segments from the ship's superstructure. Then two more *Kamikazes* attacked the burning destroyer. Both planes were shot down by MULLANY's desperate gunners. As friendly vessels closed in to aid, the ship was convulsed by internal explosions which slung men overside and spread fire below decks. Advised that a magazine bulkhead was glowing like a stove lid, and that the heat threatened to set off a disastrous ammunition blast, Commander Momm ordered MULLANY abandoned.

That evening destroyer PURDY (Commander F. L. Johnson) moved up to hose the burning ship. When the fires were subdued Commander Momm led a salvage party back to the fuming destroyer. Every man who went below decks risked his life, but at 0030 in the morning of the 7th a watch was set in the forward fireroom and forward engine-room. No 1 and No. 2 boilers were lighted off, and at 0145 the ship got under way. At 0936 the MULLANY crawled into the Kerama Retto anchorage.

Destroyer HYMAN (Commander R. N. Norgaard) was somewhat luckier than NEWCOMB, LEUTZE, and MULLANY. Her turn came while she was steaming to a picket support station northeast of Ie Shima. Attacked by *Kamikazes*, she shot down four of the suicide crates, and destroyers STERETT and ROOKS, in her vicinity, joined the shooting to blast three more.

But a Jap plane broke through the barrage. There was the usual smash, followed by explosions and fire as bombs and torpedoes blew their red breath through the ship's superstructure.

HYMAN came out of it with an ugly mangling. But she made port under her own power, was patched up by the tender OCEANUS, and steamed south for the repair yards of Saipan.

Destroyer HOWORTH (Commander E. S. Burns) was struck by a *Kamikaze* that same afternoon as she steamed independently toward an A/S patrol station off the Hagushi beaches. Coming in from the north and east, flocks of Japanese planes were bearing down on the beachhead. HOWORTH paused to shoot at a *Kamikaze* which was diving at the cruiser ST. LOUIS. While running at 25 knots, HOWORTH shot down another "Val"—a plane that gave her a nerve-wracking shave by banking between her two stacks, slashing the radio antenna, and crashing close aboard. Reaching her picket station at 1700, HOWORTH immediately went into action to shoot down an attacking "Zeke." At 1703 she downed a second "Zeke." This suicider brushed the destroyer's fantail, carrying away several lifelines before plunging into the water.

Two minutes later the HOWORTH riddled a third "Zeke" which was diving on a nearby minesweeper. The *Kamikazes* were now coming so fast that HOWORTH's ammunition passers could hardly keep up with the guns. Then, swooping down in a long glide, another "Zeke" struck home. The plane flew squarely into the main-battery director on HOWORTH's bridge. The crash drenched the bridge with burning gasoline, and knocked out the ship's steering control. Repair parties quickly extinguished the fire; steering control was taken over aft; the ship was conned from the secondary conning station; and still another "Zeke" was killed by 40 mm. fire from the destroyer's guns.

"Once again," HOWORTH's Commander Burns observed, *"Lady Luck was on board ship. The plane that crashed could have caused considerably more damage. The contributing factors in stopping these suiciders proved to be high speed, a large volume of accurate fire, and radical maneuvers."*

Skippered by Lieutenant Commander R. V. Wheeler, Jr., destroyer MORRIS, was patrolling Station A-11, Sector C, that same day. Down roared an attacking *Kamikaze*. As the plane approached, the destroyer sprinted at 30 knots to evade, while her gunners pumped steel into the enemy. The plane's wings were clipped, and its underbelly took a *hari-kiri* slashing from the DD's guns. The *Kamikaze* should have come apart like a dropped jig-saw puzzle, but by some weird adhesion its body remained intact. It sloughed into MORRIS, crashing between her No. 1 and No. 2 five-inch guns.

Explosion! Fire! Damage control! Emergency repairs! MORRIS went through the harrowing routine. The ship was a furnace when rescuers arrived, but by 2030 the conflagration was extinguished, the wounded had been transferred to BATES and R. P. LEARY; and MORRIS, her power plant undamaged, was on her way to Kerama Retto.

One other destroyer was maimed by a suicider on April 6—HAYNSWORTH (Commander S. N. Tackney). She got it during the noon hour while she was operating in the screen of Task Group 58.3 off Okinawa. Down the sky came a "Judy," chased by two Corsairs. The Jap plane headed away from the destroyer, then winged over in an Immelmann turn, and dived at the ship. Tackney swung his destroyer hard left while her automatic guns raked the plane. The "Judy," afire, crashed into the main radio-transmitter room. Up went an enormous gasoline fireball—an incandescent balloon that floated for a second, then splattered HAYNSWORTH's superstructure with flame. Topside, the ship became an inferno. Fighting the fire with water, fog, and CO_2, the crew quelled the conflagration in about 10 minutes. But HAYNSWORTH, her radio ruined, her C.I.C. and plotting rooms wrecked, and a number of guns junked, was another candidate for the repair yards.

Early in the morning of April 9, destroyer CHARLES J. BADGER (Commander J. H. Cotten) took a bad mauling from a suicider. After delivering a harassing barrage from a fire-support station off Kezu Saki, Okinawa, the ship was lying to in the pre-dawn dark. The morning watch had just come on when a high-powered boat engine was heard to starboard, close aboard. About seven seconds later a stunning under-water blast shook the destroyer; evidently the strange craft had dropped a depth charge. The enemy escaped before BADGER's gunners could fire a shot. And the destroyer was sorely hurt. Buckled and ruptured, her leaking after fireroom let a flood into the after engine-room. Live steam spurted from broken lines, filling the after fireroom with a scalding fog. The starboard main shaft, jolted out of alignment, held the starboard main engine inoperative, and the ship was unable to get under way. Her SC radar, sonar gear, and gyro compass were scotched. All pumps in the after fireroom were damaged, and the available fire and bilge pumps, rushed into emergency service, could barely cope with the swirling flood that poured in through the ruptured plates.

By 0715 the BADGER, on a tow line, was en route to Kerama Retto. One of the few destroyers disabled by a suicide boat, she was out of the war for the duration.

Here is the story of an *Oka* attack—one of the few instances wherein the idiot *"Baka"* hit the mark. Target for this weird weapon was the destroyer STANLY (Lieutenant Commander R. S. Harlan). In her company was destroyer LANG (Lieutenant Commander J. T. Bland, III), flagship of Commander W. T. McGarry, ComDesDiv 4.

During the afternoon of the 12th the two DD's were fighting off a hot *Kamikaze* attack aimed at CASSIN YOUNG, then holding the fort at Radar Picket Station No. 1. STANLY and LANG shot down a "Val," and they were training their guns on other enemy aircraft when a *"Baka"* suddenly rocketed out of the aerial melee and made a hell-bent dive at STANLY. The destroyer's gunners pumped a fusillade into the robot, but they might as well have tried to stop a meteor. Striking STANLY's starboard bow, the *"Baka"* burst like a giant grenade. Parts of the rocket went clean through the ship, as did the rocket's bomb, which was kind enough to refrain from ex-ploding until it passed through the destroyer's port side. Afterward, the *"Baka"* pilot was found splattered against a bulkhead in the wrecked forward compartment.

Shortly after this attack, a second *"Baka"* zoomed down at the STANLY. Sharp gunnery sheared off one of the rocket's wings, and the human robot missed the ship, flitting over the superstructure just aft of the No. 2 stack, and ripping the ensign. Then, hitting the sea about 2,500 yards to port, the *"Baka"* bounced once and exploded.

One of the DE's hard hit at Okinawa was champion sub-killer ENGLAND, now skippered by Lieutenant J. A. Williamson, USNR. On March 27 she was given an Okinawa welcome by a *Kamikaze* which struck close aboard. But ENGLAND's black-letter day was May 9. About sundown of that day, while she was on screening duty at a station midway between Kerama Retto and Tonachi Shima, she was hit by a suicide "Val." Her radar spotted this enemy at seven miles—one of three bumblebees in a melee with fighter hornets. Two of the Jap raiders were eventually shot down by the CAP fighters, but the fatal "Val" broke through to dive at ENGLAND. The DE maneuvered at flank speed to evade, while her 3-inch 50's, 20 mm.'s, and 1.10 automatic flailed at the oncoming suicider. A wheel flew from the plane; fire rushed from the cockpit; the pilot was riddled. He had been heading for ENGLAND's bridge, and for a moment it seemed as though the "Val" would miss. But the "Val's" port wing snagged in the forward boat davit, and the plane went spinning into the passageway just abaft the ship's office.

Crash! Bomb explosion! Fire! ENGLAND was blitzed. The blast cloaked her superstructure with flame and smoke. Wardroom, captain's cabin, ship's office, pilothouse and C.I.C. were turned into incinerators. Flames bushed up around the flying bridge and signal bridge. Clutching wounded shipmates, men on the signal bridge leaped overside. Hands on the main deck manned hoses to spray comrades who came fighting down out of the wreckage with their clothing afire. Within twenty seconds of the *Kamikaze* smash the ship's damage controlmen were battling the conflagration, but the vessel was an inferno for the next hour. Some of the deep-rooted fires were not extinguished until midnight.

Destroyer-minesweeper GHERARDI, minesweeper VIGILANCE, and tug GEAR steamed to ENGLAND's *aid*. GEAR towed the fire-blackened DE to Kerama Retto. Patched up there and at Leyte, in June she set out on the long voyage home. She was decommissioned on October 15, 1945.

A remarkable performance of ship-saving was staged by the destroyermen of USS HAZELWOOD. "She was one of the greats to get home from Okinawa," veteran destroyer Admiral Tisdale observed, recalling an inspection of the damaged ship at Mare Island Navy Yard. "She took one hell of a beating from the *Kamikazes*. About a quarter of her complement, including her Captain and Exec, were killed in the smash. Her bridge and much of her superstructure were reduced to scrap. A young Reserve Officer—a lieutenant (jg)—assumed immediate command, and he handled the ship like a Farragut. Then she was taken down to Ulithi and brought home by another Reserve Officer—a lieutenant. With officers like HAZELWOOD's in the line, the Navy never had to worry."

No study of the ordeal endured by the destroyer forces at

Okinawa would be complete without mention of the ships which came through unscathed, and a comparison of destroyer and *Kamikaze* casualties.

Some of the unscathed—vessels which were on the firing line over a long period of time—merit special mention. In "Iceberg" waters from March 21 to July 28, destroyer HEYWOOD L. EDWARDS (Commander A. L. Shepherd) came through without a scratch. So did VAN VALKENBURGH (Commander A. B. Coxe, Jr.). After weeks on the Okinawa picket line, BROWN (Commander R. R. Craighill) and BRADFORD (Commander W. W. Armstrong) retired without a scar. WADSWORTH (Commander R. D. Fusselman), in action from April to June 24, worked like a miniature dreadnaught. Her masterful performance at Okinawa won her the coveted Presidential Unit Citation. BARTON (Commanders E. B. Dexter and H. P. McIntire) fought through the worst of April, May, and June, and did not have an enemy hand laid on her. She arrived on the "Iceberg" front on March 25—an Okinawa pioneer, and one of the first on the scene. Between that date and June 30, the BARTON fired a total of 26,789 rounds of 5-inch ammunition for an average of 4,465 rounds per gun. Between March 26 and June 21, she fired 22,057 rounds without accident and almost without incident.

BARTON'S record hints something in regard to Japanese casualties. In many instances it was impossible to discern the burst which felled the suicider. Planes shot down by AA fire may have been previously damaged in dogfight. Firing severally as well as singly, destroyers dissected many a *Kamikaze* crate. So the exact figure scored by the DD's and DE's at Okinawa remains an unknown. Altogether the Japs lost some 7,830 aircraft in the Okinawa debacle. It is estimated that over 3,000 of these were shot down by Navy and Marine planes, and that about 410 were shot down by Navy guns. Perhaps two-thirds of those guns were in the "small boys"—the destroyers and destroyer-escorts.

Probably the champion *Kamikaze*-killers in the Okinawa death struggle were destroyers EVANS and HUGH W. HADLEY. On May 10 this pair were teamed up at Radar Picket Station No. 15. Although EVANS' Captain, Commander R. J. Archer, was senior, he turned over the duties of Officer in Tactical Command to HADLEY's skipper, Commander B. J. Mullaney, as HADLEY was a fighter-director ship.

On the morning of May 11 the *Kamikazes* came over in force. About 0740 the "bogies" were reported thick as swarming bees in the northeast mist. Five minutes later a Jap float plane zoomed out of the murk, diving at HADLEY. She and EVANS opened fire. End of *Kamikaze* at 1,200 yards.

That was the beginning of an action which was a miniature of the entire Okinawa sea-air battle. For the next hour and a half the Jap planes kept coming in a series of waves that rumbled across the sky much as successive combers sweep across an expanse of sea. In the first wave there were 36 Jap planes; in the second 50; in the third 20; in the fourth about 25; in the last about 20. EVANS, HADLEY, and the CAP planes fought it out with a total of some 150 Jap aircraft.

Excerpt from HADLEY's Action Report:

HADLEY and the EVANS were attacked continuously by numerous enemy aircraft coming at us in groups of four to six planes on each ship. During the early period, enemy aircraft were sighted trying to pass our formation headed for Okinawa. These were flying extremely low on both bows and seemingly ignoring us. The HADLEY shot down four of these. . . .

The tempo of the engagement and the maneuver of the two destroyers at high speed was such as to cause the HADLEY and the EVANS to be separated by distances as much as two and three miles. This resulted in individual action by both ships. . . . From 0830 to 0900 the HADLEY was attacked by groups of planes coming in on both bows. Twelve enemy planes were shot down by the HADLEY's guns during this period, at times firing all guns in various directions. The EVANS . . . to the northward, was seen fighting off a number of planes. . . . At 0900 the EVANS was hit and put out of action. . . .

From this time on the HADLEY received the bulk of the attacks and action became furious with all guns firing at planes on all sides of the ship. . . . For 20 minutes the HADLEY fought off the enemy singlehanded. . . . Finally, at 0920, ten enemy planes which had surrounded the HADLEY—four on the starboard bow . . . four on the port bow . . . and two astern— attacked the ship simultaneously. All ten planes were destroyed . . . and each plane was definitely accounted for.

This remarkable exhibition of gunnery was performed in the face of dire adversity. Early in the action HADLEY was struck by a bomb. Then a low-flying "Betty" released a *"Baka"* which rocketed into the ship. Next she was struck aft by a suicide plane. And then another *Kamikaze* smashed into her rigging. Badly holed, with both engine-rooms and a fireroom flooded, the ship listed over and settled rapidly. Ammunition explosions raged on deck, and the vessel was engulfed in a turmoil of flame and dense black smoke. But the gun crews that were living stuck it out at guns that were undamaged, and the Jap planes fell like shot crows.

Meantime, EVANS had put up a battle-royal to carry out her end of the mission. With "bandits" swarming around her, this destroyer's marksmen staged a *Kamikaze*-shoot no less remarkable than HADLEY's.

Few ships at Okinawa were hit harder than HADLEY and EVANS. Both ships kept on fighting. Both were saved.

But the big feature of the HADLEY-EVANS drama was the amazing target score of this team. All told, the two destroyers accounted for 46 enemy aircraft—a massacre which must have given the Japanese Special Attack Corps a surfeit of suicide.

As a superb destroyer effort on the Okinawa picket line, the sharpshooting of EVANS and HADLEY had its match in the ship-saving endeavor which brought destroyer LAFFEY out of the Valley of the Shadow of Death.

April 16, 1945—one of the darkest days at Okinawa, and LAFFEY (Commander F. J. Becton), with a fighter-director team on board, patrolling Radar Picket Station No. 1. At 0744 she drove off a "Val." It was soon followed by others—a few at first, and then a swarm of them flitting across the radar screen.

On station with LAFFEY were two LCS's—sturdy ships, but hardly able to cope with the coming onslaught. Converging from north, northeast, and northwest were some 50 "bandits."

Two "Judy's" launched a coordinated attack on the destroyer. Both were brought down by 40 mm. and 20 mm. fire to port and starboard. The port plane exploded close aboard, and the blast put LAFFEY's fire-control radar out of kilter. Then the ship was grazed by a "Val" which burst in the sea a few yards from the destroyer's fantail. Another "Judy" was shot down close aboard. Then LAFFEY was hit.

Down came the planes like vultures trying to get their talons into a crippled wildcat. Some of the Japs were shot down by CAP fighters which trailed them until they splashed. Several were blown apart by LAFFEY's forward guns. However, two more *Kamikazes* crashed the ship, Striking in quick succession, they ploughed into the after deckhouse, feeding the flames with more firebrands and gasoline.

As LAFFEY stumbled out from under this blasting an "Oscar" broke away from a dogfight and headed for the ship's forecastle, a Corsair in close pursuit. Machine-gunners on the bow riveted the enemy plane with bullets as it pancaked over the ship. "Oscar" and Corsair both hit the mast—a one-two that tore off the SC antenna, the port yardarm, and the SG wave guide. Raising a huge waterspout, the Jap plane plunged into the sea to starboard. The Corsair pilot was seen to bail out as his damaged plane went looping down the sky.

Meanwhile, a "Judy" struck the water close aboard to port, showering LAFFEY with burning scrap. Still another "Judy," zooming up on the starboard quarter, was shot down 800 yards from the ship. Struck by a 5-inch shell, an "Oscar" blew up about 500 yards from the ship. Another "Oscar," driving from ahead, caught a VT burst and crashed 500 yards off the bow. Then LAFFEY was struck by a bomb dropped by a "Val" which sideswiped the starboard yardarm. The bomb exploded in the ship's fiery superstructure, while the *Kamikaze* crashed in the sea. Yet another "Val" came in to drop a bomb which erased a 20 mm. battery. Riddled by 5-inch and 40 mm. fire, and scorched by the fire of a chasing CAP fighter, this plane hit the sea off LAFFEY's port quarter. The last assault was made by a "Judy" which came in from the port with a pursuing CAP fighter pouring tracer into her tail. LAFFEY's port 40's and 20's blazed at the plane, which blew up close aboard. The attack was over.

And, incredibly, the USS LAFFEY remained afloat. During the 80-minute action she had been attacked by 22 planes, of which nine had been shot down by the destroyermen.

But the real story of LAFFEY has to do with fortitude. Progressive damage finally brought LAFFEY to a dead stop as her crew—or what was left of it—fought fire and flood. Eventually she was towed to safe anchorage off Okinawa. But— marvel no less—in six days she was steaming for Saipan under her own power. After nine plane crashes and four bomb hits!

"Iceberg" Battle Below

Nine Jap submarines were sunk in the Okinawa maelstrom. Five of these were downed by American destroyermen holding the "Iceberg" A/S line.

Destroyer HAGGARD (Lieutenant Commander V. J. Soballe) scored the first kill. HAGGARD was a unit in the screen of a fast carrier task group steaming toward Okinawa late in March '45. Scouting 12 miles in the van, she snared a sonar contact. After a brief midnight search, HAGGARD spread a depth-charge pattern. The explosions blasted an I-boat to the surface. HAGGARD raked the target with 40 mm. With shells lashing her conning tower, the sub went down by the stern. From the deep echoed a thunderous roar. Up came the trash and human residue. When ultimately bashed by a *Kamikaze* on April 29, HAGGARD proved she could take it as well as give it. The sub she gave it to off Okinawa on March 23 was the I-371.

Eight days after the HAGGARD exploit, destroyers STOCKTON (Lieutenant Commander W. R. Glennon) and MORRISON (Commander J. R. Hansen) teamed up to blast an I-boat. On the night of March 30-31, STOCKTON spotted the enemy by radar while screening a task group off Kerama Retto. STOCK-TON drove the sub under and delivered seven depth-charge attacks. Then MORRISON stepped into the arena while STOCK-TON took the backfield. Boxed by the two DD's, the sub was trapped. Eleven depth charges from MORRISON brought the I-boat to the surface, spouting like a narwhal. At 900 yards

Morrison opened pointblank fire. Punched by shot after shot, the sub eventually burst open and sank. One survivor was fished from the flotsam. When asked the name of his submarine, this durable individual replied, "If your ship were sunk, would you reveal the name?" But it was found in Admiral Miwa's revealing records. Stockton and Morrison had abolished the I-8.

On April 5, 1945—the day before the "Divine Wind" hurricane—destroyer Hudson (Commander R. R. Pratt)— trapped an enemy sub near Radar Picket Station No. 1, west of Okinawa. Radar contact and sonar tracking followed routine methods. So did the delivery of six depth-charge attacks. But the eventual upsurge of oil and flotsam embraced a notable feature. The debris marked the grave of the RO-41, the sub which had sunk destroyer-escort Shelton and indirectly caused the loss of USS Seawolf.

The RO-41 soon had netherworld company. On April 9, destroyers Monssen (Lieutenant Commander E. G. Sanderson) and Mertz (Commander W. S. Maddox) blasted the RO-46 out of Okinawa's coastal waters. The two DD's were in the screen of the fast carrier task group which had been spearheaded by the Haggard. The sub made the mistake of penetrating this high-powered A/S screen. Making sonar contact at 900 yards, Monssen delivered an urgent attack, laying three depth-charge patterns. Mertz ran in to spread three more. A final two from Monssen produced a series of underwater explosions that obliterated the RO-46.

On April 17 the same task-group screen closed in on still another enemy sub. Late in the evening destroyer Heermann (Commander A. T. Hathaway) snared the radar contact. Destroyer Uhlmann (Commander S. C. Small) stepped in around midnight to track with sonar and attack with depth charges. In the morning destroyer McCord (Commander F. D. Michael), Collet, skippered by Commander J. D. Collet, (the ship had been named after his brother, Lieutenant Commander J. A. Collet, a Navy flyer killed in 1943) and Mertz entered the roundelay, as did two aircraft from carrier Bataan. Hour after hour the hunters probed with "pinging" sonar and took turns in blasting the undersea target. Only the luckiest sub in creation could have escaped such a coordinated attack. The I-56 was not that lucky. Early in the afternoon of April 18 the undersea boat burst its seams. Up with the usual swirl of oil came the usual miscellany of wood, cork and human fragments.

Okinawa Conclusion

At Okinawa the Rising Sun went down for the last time.

History's almanac would record the date as June 21, 1945. The brief twilight that followed was no more than a crepuscular after-glow; Imperial Japan was finished on that 21st of June. On that day General Ushijima, commander of the Japanese 32nd Army, and his Chief of Staff, Lieutenant General Isamu Cho, committed *hari-kiri* rather than surrender. Some 100,000 Japanese troops had already died. The Battle of Okinawa—the "Last Battle"—was over.

For the Americans Okinawa had been a costly campaign, won at a price of over 12,000 dead. Buckner's Tenth Army paid the lion's share of this fatality toll, the General himself being among the slain. But U.S. Navy losses were well over a third of the total—about 5,000 fatalities, and a like number of wounded. At Okinawa the Navy suffered a death-toll greater than that suffered in the four years of the Civil War.

Destroyers and DE's footed most of the bill, but warships of all classes took savage punishment.

It is not difficult to conceive of the odds accepted by destroyers when they entered combat with an enemy capable of injuring steel-coated battleships and crippling such powerful carriers as BUNKER HILL and HANCOCK. The length of those odds has its measure in the DD and DE casualty list, and in the roll call of the "Fleet that stayed permanently." HALLIGAN, BUSH, COLHOUN, MANNERT L. ABELE, PRINGLE, LITTLE, LUCE, MORRISON, OBERRENDER, LONGSHAW, DREXLER, WILLIAM D. PORTER, TWIGGS, UNDERHILL, and CALLAGHAN—twelve of these 15 ships were downed by the *Kamikazes*. The consensus was that coördinated and sustained suicide air assault spelled disastrous damage, if not doom, for the unarmored American destroyer or DE of World War II classes.

PART SEVEN

Small Boys Finish Big Job

☆   ☆   ☆

No thought of flight, none of retreat;
no unbecoming deed that argued fear;
each on himself relied as only in his arm
the moment lay of victory.

PARADISE LOST

Chapter 39

DesLant Scours the Atlantic

(September '44 to VE-Day)

☆　☆　☆

Undersea Tidal Turn

In April, 1944, Rear Admiral Francis S. Low, Chief of Staff of the Tenth Fleet, declared, "The German U-boat today is sinking considerably less than one half of one percent of the ships being convoyed across the Atlantic."

The percentage figure must have inclined Admiral Doenitz's Headquarters to pessimism. The Germans had pinned high hopes on the *Schnorkel* stack. It was now apparent that the "breather tube" would not, of itself, save the U-boat's day.

Demanded was a submarine which could not only elude radar, but could go deeper than the reach of sonar detection— a U-boat which could cruise at a depth far below the 1943 operating level, and which could lie for many hours inert on the bottom in some deep foxhole. Such a boat—the previously mentioned Type XXI—was under construction in 1944. This long-winded, deep-going submarine was Grand Admiral Doenitz's last trump. But Type XXI's would not get to sea in any number until 1945.

Meanwhile the U-boat campaign almost dead-stalled as Doenitz called in the submarines for *Schnorkel* refits and scraped the bottom of the Nazi barrel for personnel. In consequence American destroyermen in the Atlantic found poor hunting in the autumn of '44.

But one of the DD's was engaged by an enemy tougher and more dangerous than any U-boat ever launched by Doenitz. The enemy? That "Ole Devil Sea."

Loss of USS WARRINGTON

Early in September, 1944, the destroyer WARRINGTON (Commander S. F. Quarles) was escorting the USS HYADES from Norfolk, Virginia, to the Canal Zone. Commissioned in February, 1938, WARRINGTON was a destroyer of the SOMERS class, a one-stacker of 1,850 tons. The HYADES was a refrigerated provision ship of the type known to bluejackets as "beef boats." Senior officer present was aboard HYADES.

Normally the neo-tropic seas off Florida and the Bahamas provide some of the finest cruising weather in the world. Abnormally they kick up some of the worst. And on September 12 the bottom fell out of the glass, and the blow fell with it.

By the afternoon of that day WARRINGTON and HYADES were ploughing through high water off the northern Bahamas. Hell came with the evening—a screaming, discolored sky; blinding rain; wind-whipped, rip-roaring seas. Struggling against rising winds and climbing waves, the two ships were slowed to a 4-knot pace.

WARRINGTON was an old hand at storm fighting, but she had never experienced anything like this. At 1810 Commander Quarles gave the order to heave to, in deference to the mountainous seas.

Wind velocity went from 5 to 100 miles. By midnight the ships were driven off course and apart, and at about 0100 in the morning of September 13 HYADES lost radar contact with WARRINGTON. The destroyer was in trouble. The terrific beam-sea pounding had sprung her port bulwarks in two places, and her deck gear was wrenched, distorted, and bruised as though battered by gunfire.

Unable to cope with the main force of the hurricane, WARRINGTON reversed course. An emergency request for help was flashed on all circuits at 0417. She gave her position as lat. 25-57 N., long. 73-44 W. By estimate the disabled warship was at that time only 60 miles southwest of the storm center. HYADES, some 75 miles distant, was riding out the wild night. With house-high seas, visibility zero, and a wind that could uproot the Bahamas, there was nothing she could do to aid the imperiled destroyer.

By noon of the 12th the helpless DD was going logy. Staggering through the hurricane like a derelict adrift, she could no longer bring her head up when battered by a collapsing hill of water.

At 1345 she sent her last distress message—an S-O-S and the three words: WE NEED ASSISTANCE.

The urgent appeal brought into action all the available rescue forces of the Navy.

By late afternoon WARRINGTON was beyond all mortal help. Commander Quarles and his "Exec," Lieutenant Wesley U. Williams, USNR, stared grimly into the bleak prospect as the seas sluiced over her. A moment later a great sea crashed over the foredeck and swept the bridge-wing. Commander Quarles and Lieutenant Williams were whirled outboard and away like chips on a millrace. The captain went deep under the foam, then fought his way to the surface, and glimpsed the destroyer's ghostly silhouette yards distant. She was over—far over. Then she was gone. Some of the men who saw her go said that at the last she capsized.

Quarles swam to a raft, and hauled bluejackets out of the swirling water.

Quarles and the survivors with him had a two-day wait for rescue. About 0900 of the 15th HYADES steamed over the horizon, followed by a number of search planes. The CROATAN task group had been ordered to the disaster scene.

The airmen spotted a little flotsam of rafts and destroyermen. HYADES located five life rafts and floats. Before rescue operations were concluded, some 68 destroyermen had been saved. But the disaster exacted a most tragic toll of 251 offcers and men. Aircraft flying over the area sighted at least a hundred bodies adrift on the sea's desolation.

FESSENDEN *Kills* U-1062

The U-boat Force pulled in its horns, that autumn of 1944, and American destroyermen made but one kill—a score held down by lack of game. Doenitz was rebuilding his undersea navy at this time, and only a relatively few U-boats were in the Atlantic, chiefly for their "nuisance value."

In September such a "nuisance" pack was operating in the Cape Verdes area. There it was detected by Task Group 22.1, a hunter-killer group built around the new escort-carrier MISSION BAY. Steaming southwest of the Cape Verdes, the group's scouts made contact with a submarine on the morning of September 30th. At 1120 the destroyer-escort FESSENDEN (Lieutenant Commander W. A. Dobbs, USNR) peeled off with the DE's DOUGLAS L. HOWARD and J. R. Y. BLAKELEY to investigate the aircraft report.

FESSENDEN picked up sonar contact at 1610. At 1628 her destroyermen fired a full pattern of Mark X projectiles. Fourteen seconds after the projectiles splashed into the sea, four explosions rumbled up from below. FESSENDEN followed through with a full pattern of depth charges. The water heaved and flattened over an outburst of deep-sea thunder. Thereafter the DE's heard nothing but the silence of extinction.

Post-war records named FESSENDEN's victim as the U-1062.

U-boats to Bombard New York

Revealed at war's end was the news that the Navy had received intelligence reports disclosing a German plan to attack New York City with robot bombs. The bombardment was to have been unleashed by submarines.

But the robot bombardment failed to materialize. Apparently it was to have been delivered by the new deep-sea *Schnorkels*—the Type XXI's.

Admiral Ingram got the word on these ultra-modern U-boats. In a post-war report to Navy Secretary Forrestal he stated: *"We knew they had put a lot of fancy gadgets on them. Increased them in size, increased their radius, increased their effectiveness, and made it difficult to get them. But they were pressed for time. The Russian offensive drove them out of the Baltic, and the heavy bombings in their shipbulding places put their offensive back."*

The new XXI's did not come. Not then. But something else and quite unusual did turn up—a German weather-reporting submarine.

HAYTER, OTTER, VARIAN, *and* HUBBARD *Sink* U-248

When Von Rundstedt's mid-winter counterdrive developed into the "Battle of the Bulge," Allied leaders knew "this was it." If the Ardennes break-through was not contained, the war would be prolonged for many months.

And oddly enough, at the climax of the Bulge campaign, success or failure for either side hinged on the weather. Days of icy drizzle, snow, and fog had screened the German advance and kept Allied aircraft grounded. So long as this weather front persisted, Von Rundstedt's driving legions retained the advantage. Imperative, then, that his headquarters be informed by accurate forecasts. So the U-248 was dispatched to a station in the North Atlantic about midway between France and Newfoundland, where the submarine was to play weather prophet.

Operating north of the Azores at this time was Escort Division 62, and the express mission of this DE division was the hunting and killing of any weather-reporting U-boat. The division consisted of the destroyer-escorts OTTER (Lieutenant Commander J. M. Irvine, USNR), HAYTER (Lieutenant Commander Fred Huey, USNR), VARIAN (Lieutenant Commander L. A. Myhre, USNR), and HUBBARD (Lieutenant Commander L. C. Mabley, USNR). The four-ship team was working with HF/DF, and on January 16 "Huff-Duff" bearings on German sub transmissions put the finger on this nervy U-boat's position—vicinity of lat. 47-00 N., long. 26-00 W.

HAYTER made the first sound contact at 0910. The DE's swung into action with the usual team work, first one, then another, sowing lethal depth-charges.

The ashcans and teardrops blew up tons of sea water, and finally they blew up tons of submarine.

The Nazi forces in Europe would receive no more weather reports from the aerographers of U-248.

FOWLER *and* L'INDISCRET *Kill* U-869

Slow Convoy GUS 74 steamed westward through the Pillars of Hercules late in February 1945, and in the morning of the 28th the convoy reached a point about 100 miles due west of Port Lyautey. At that same date and time the German submarine U-869 reared its ugly head in those waters off the *"Iron Coast."*

KNOXVILLE (flagship, ComCortDiv 30), and DE's FOWLER and ROBINSON went into action against the sub. At 0648, FOWLER (Lieutenant Commander S. F. Morris) made sound contact on the stalking submarine, range 2,900 yards. Six minutes later the DE let fly with a magnetic pattern, and two explosions banged in the water at the 12th and 20th seconds after firing. FOWLER dropped another pattern of magnetics at 0718. Within 120 seconds, two voluminous but ambiguous explosions bellowed up from down under.

Enter French escorts L'INDISCRET and LE RESOLUTE. Taking a hand in the game the two French vessels conducted a *coup de grace* attack. The action put a period to the career of U-869. Under the circumstances it would seem it was the submarine which should have borne the name of *"Indiscreet."*

LOWE, MENGES, PRIDE, *and* MOSLEY *Kill* U-866

American destroyermen scored their third U-boat kill of the year in March. The laurels in this case went to the Coast Guard's A/S warriors serving in Escort Division 46. The division consisted of destroyer-escorts LOWE (Lieutenant Commander Herbert Feldman, USCGR), MENGES (Lieutenant Commander F. M. McCabe, USCG), MOSLEY (Lieutenant Commander E. P. MacBryde, USCGR), and the flagship PRIDE (Lieutenant Commander W. H. Buxton, USCG). This was the first hunter-killer group manned by Coast Guardsmen, and the hunters went all out to fulfill the high traditions of that veteran sea-going organization.

They also went all out to track down and destroy a Nazi submarine reported in Nova Scotian coastal waters about 100 miles east of Halifax. Mid-morning of March 18, 1945, LOWE picked up sound contact. Time: 1027. Commander Feldman rushed the DE through fast investigative maneuvers, and at 1105 LOWE made two depth-charge attacks. Oil burbled to the surface and spread across a wide area, and the Coast Guardsmen sighted splintered wood and other fragments and flotsam.

Post-war records verified the kill, and the victim was identified as the U-866.

Doenitz's Last Bid (The Supersubs)

Grand Admiral Doenitz had no unrealistic illusions. A deep-sea armada, much less a small flotilla of Type XXI U-boats, could hardly have turned the war tide as of springtime 1945. The Anglo-American forces were across the Rhine. The Russians were in East Prussia. Nazi Germany was through. Nevertheless, the streamlined *Schnorkel* super-submarines might accomplish a little something. They might bombard the eastern seaboard of the United States, might even hurl a vengeful rocket barrage into Boston or New York.

So, late in March 1945, Admiral Doenitz sent the *Schnorkel* super-submarines speeding westward across the Atlantic. Mission: to attack the United States coast in a supreme, final effort for Adolf Hitler.

This was the raid Admiral Ingram had warned of.

To beat back the new U-boat drive, Admiral Ingram mustered a powerhouse A/S task force which included four escort carriers and a total of 75 destroyers and destroyer-escorts. Dispatched to mid-Atlantic, the CVE-DD-DE teams maintained a vigilant ocean patrol that began early in the year and went into action when the first super-sub came along. One by one the streamlined *Schnorkels* were tracked down in mid-ocean and obliterated.

"Two or three got through to the coast," Admiral Ingram wrote later. *"They torpedoed five ships and sank two, and we got them close to the coast, one right off Newport Harbor . . ."*

But the Nazi try at Boston and New York ended in a grand *kaput.*

Gustafson *Sinks* U-857

Only a few informed officers on duty in the First Naval District knew, that first week in April, 1945, that a U-boat was operating within 20 miles of Cape Cod.

Of course Washington was informed, and Admiral Ingram's forces afloat knew what was up. So did most of the ships at sea in the area. Submarine warning! U-boat almost within range of Boston Light.

Also almost within range of that famous light was a fast-moving hunter-killer group composed of the frigates Knoxville (flagship) and Eugene, and DE's Gustafson and Micka. Early in the morning of April 7 this A/S team was sweeping the vicinity of lat. 42-15 N., long. 69-52 W. As a result GUSTAFSON (Lieutenant Commander A. E. Chambers, USNR) swept up a Sound contact, and the hunter-killers got on the track of the deep-sea invader.

At 0226 GUSTAFSON reached attack position and opened fire with hedgehogs. A basso explosion came rumbling up out of the sea.

GUSTAFSON circled off and waited. There was no upsurge of debris. The destroyermen were disappointed. They sighted a good-sized oil slick which exuded strong oil fumes. But GUSTAFSON's skipper was not convinced of a kill, and the outcome was evaluated as a "possible."

Not until after the war did investigators learn that the U-857 had expired in New England waters as of April 7, '45. Score one against the Nazi Submarine Force in its big finale.

Super-Sub Götterdammerung (End of Four More U-boats)

Destroyer-escort GUSTAFSON set the pace for April '45. A fatal month for the Nazi U-boat Force. Sending the Super Men in their super subs across the Atlantic into American waters, Grand Admiral Doenitz signed their death warrants. The executioners were ready and waiting.

For example, destroyer-escorts FROST and STANTON, operating with the CROATAN Killer Group (Task Group 22.5). The DE's were in Escort Division 13 under Commander F. D. Giambattista, with pennant in FROST. On the evening of April 15, the group was working in mid-ocean almost exactly midway between Newfoundland and the British Isles. STANTON (Lieutenant Commander J. C. Kiley, Jr., USNR) snared a radar contact that spelled U-boat.

Shortly after midnight, the FROST (Lieutenant Commander A. E. Ritchie, USNR) stepped in with a hedgehog salvo. For another hour the two DE's hounded the submarine, probing, tracking, attacking in turn. At 0114 two thunder-blasts rolled up from the deep. The explosions shook the hulls of DE's ten miles away. End of super sub U-1235.

About half an hour after the deep-sea thunder was heard, FROST's radar spotted a surfaced U-boat at 500 yards. Giambattista ordered the DE to "close the target, illuminate, fire and ram." Spraying the night with starshells, FROST charged. As her searchlight caught the U-boat full in the face, the DE smashed the enemy conning tower with 3-inch shells. The sub burrowed under.

For the next three hours FROST and STANTON gave the target a working over. Destroyer-escort HUSE entered the deadly game of tag. And at 0410 a headhog salvo from STANTON touched off an undersea thunderclap that shook the CROATAN,

15 miles away. Up came a thick carpet of oil that smelled of sunken Diesels and sudden death. Score two for FROST and STANTON. Eventually captured in Germany, Doenitz' records revealed that the second sub downed that night by the two DE's was the U-880.

A few days later another hard-hitting American hunter-killer team erased the U-879. The killers were destroyer-escorts BUCKLEY (Lieutenant R. R. Crutchfield, USNR) and REUBEN JAMES (Lieutenant Commander Grant Cowherd, USNR), units of Task Group 22.10. On the morning of April 19 the group was en route from Halifax to New York, combing the sea for a reported U-boat. At 0348 BUCKLEY picked up sonar contact. REUBEN JAMES steamed in to tag the target. DE's SCROGGINS and JACK W. WILKE played the back-field, conducting a four-mile box search around the arena's perimeter. The U-boat was trapped. And sunk.

Two days after U-879 was sunk, U.S. hunter-killers holding a line between the Azores and Argentia, Newfoundland, erased the U-518. The kill was wrought by destroyer-escorts CARTER (Lieutenant Commander F. J. T. Baker, USNR) and NEAL A. SCOTT (Lieutenant Commander P. D. Holden). CARTER swept up the lethal contact on the night of April 21-22. SCOTT joined in tracking, and opened fire with hedge-hog. Two muffled explosions indicated hits at a depth of 400 feet. To deliver a sure thing, CARTER followed through with a hedgehog attack. Up came a volcanic roar.

"There goes your old U-boat!"

The obituary, written in floatsam, spelled the finish of U-518.

Loss of USS FREDERICK C. DAVIS

On April 23, 1945, in mid-Atlantic about halfway between Newfoundland and the Azores, several escort-carriers and a parade of destroyer-escorts were strung out in a 100-mile north-south barrier patrol. This CVE-DE flotilla, one of the largest hunter-killer forces yet assembled, formed another segment of the "net" spread to catch the super-*Schnorkels* swimming across the Atlantic to invade America's Eastern Sea Frontier.

The A/S barrier was composed of two CVE task groups (TG. 22.3 and TG. 22.4) and a large detachment of DE's. The force was operating under Captain G. J. Dufek, in BOGUE. The DE's included the PILLSBURY, KEITH, OTTERSTETTER, POPE, FLAHERTY, CHATELAIN, FREDERICK C. DAVIS, NEUNZER, HUBBARD, VARIAN, OTTER, HAYTER, JANSSEN, and COCKRILL. Spaced five miles apart, the 14 DE's were ranged across 70 miles of seascape.

At 1322 in the afternoon of April 23, a search plane sighted a submarine about 70 miles from the destroyer-escort PILLS-BURY. The ships formed a scouting line (normal to base course, speed 16.8 knots, ships spaced 3,000 yards apart), and steamed for the spot where the enemy had been glimpsed. The sub went down and stayed down. All afternoon the hunters combed the vicinity with their detection gear. All through the evening. Midnight, and they were still searching. Into the early hours of April 24 the hunt went on.

Destroyer-escort FREDERICK C. DAVIS (Lieutenant J. R. Crosby, USNR) worked her way across the dark water, sweeping with her acute radar, fingering the depths with her sensitive "pinging" gear. The men standing lookout saw the night begin to pale. Sunrise. Another day. Routine change of watch. Routine reports. And then—

Time: 0829. Sonar contact. Range 2,000 yards. The contact dropped rapidly aft and was lost in a muddle of other noises.

Sound contact was regained at about 0834. At 0839 DAVIS had reversed course. Range closed to 650 yards. And at that instant, with the ship's clock at 0840, FREDERICK C. DAVIS was struck by a torpedo, a stern-tube shot that smashed home like a thunderbolt.

A blast on the DE's port side. A sheet of fire climbing the hull and tossing on its searing wings a scatter of debris. Men died instantly in the molten vortex of that eruption. A number were flung overside. Others, trapped in a mangle of bulkheads and machinery, went down with the ship.

Companion DE's of the scouting line ran in to pick up survivors. But casualties were heavy. Although most of the men had on lifejackets and were able to reach rafts and floating nets, cold water and heavy sea took a high toll. Lieutenant Crosby and about two-thirds of the crew died in this torpedoing.

FREDERICK C. DAVIS was the second and last American destroyer-escort to go down to enemy torpedo-fire in the Battle of the Atlantic.

Death of U-546

The U-boat skipper who fired at the FREDERICK C. DAVIS must have known he was courting suicide. The DE scouting line closed around the U-boat like a noose. PILLSBURY (Lieutenant Commander G. W. Casselman, USNR)—FLAHERTY (Lieutenant Commander H. C. Duff, USNR)—NEUNZER (Lieutenant Commander V. E. Gex, USNR)—CHATE-LAIN (Lieutenant Commander D. S. Knox, USNR)—VA-

RIAN (Lieutenant Commander L. A. Myhre, USNR)—
HUBBARD (Commander L. C. Mabley, USNR)—JANSSEN
(Lieutenant Commander S. G. Rubinow, Jr., USNR)—
KEITH (Lieutenant W. W. Patrick, USNR)—these eight
soon formed a "ring" around the undersea enemy.

A rain of hedgehog, "ashcans" and teardrops descended
on the deep-running submarine. Again contact was lost.
Again it was regained. Hour after hour the hunting and
depth-charging went on. By mid-afternoon all eight DE's of
the scouting line were concentrating on the target.

The U-boat tried to evade at 580-foot depth. Again it
drifted at 420-foot level. Late in the afternoon it was tagged
at a depth of 220 feet. It began to bleed oil and exhale bubbles. Then, at 1838, it suddenly lunged to the surface.

As the U-boat's conning tower broke water, all ships that
had a clear range opened fire. Frantic submariners fought
their way out of the hatches. Under a storm of hits the sub
plunged and rolled. At 1844 its bridge knocked all acock-
bill, the U-546 went under with her *Schnorkel* throat severed.

The killer of the FREDERICK C. DAVIS had been executed.
The destroyermen moved in to capture the survivors. Thirty-
three U-boaters, including the submarine's Commanding Officer, *Herr Kapitan Leutnant* Paul Just, were taken prisoner.

End of U-548 and U-881

By April 1945 the Navy's hunter-killer teams had U-boat
extermination down to something like an exact science. The
U-boat that poked up its *Schnorkel* snout in the path of a
convoy 100 miles from the entrance of Chesapeake Bay on
April 30 was asking for it. And got it from frigate NATCHEZ
and DE's COFFMAN (Lieutenant Commander J. C. Croker,
USNR), BOSTWICK (Lieutenant J. R. Davidson, USNR) and
THOMAS (Lieutenant Commander D. M. Kellogg, USNR).

The U-boat tried to escape by going deep and releasing
Pillenwerfer. The hunters' sonar was not deceived and the
TNT was soon on target. Up came a great blotch of oil. Down
with all hands went U-548.

U-548 was the seventh Nazi sub downed by American destroyermen in April '45. On May 6 the U-881 met a death
that was becoming routine.

Killer was destroyer-escort FARQUHAR (Lieutenant Commander D. E. Walter, USNR), serving with the MISSION BAY
group at that date off the southeast reaches of the Grand
Banks.

Time: 0313 of a starlit morning. FARQUHAR was right on
top of the U-boat before the sonar registered contact. The

DE launched an urgent depth-charge barrage. And hit the target first crack. End of U-881, killed the day before VE-Day.

ATHERTON *and* MOBERLY *Kill* U-853 *(Finale's End)*

The waters between Point Judith, Rhode Island, and Block Island were decidedly unhealthy for German undersea boats during World War II.

The *Schnorkel* submarine that invaded this area on May 5, 1945, was a marked U-boat. Reckless, the captain of this submersible took her within four miles of Point Judith (near Newport Naval Base). Then, instead of torpedoing a liner or a warship, this super-sub torpedoed a little 5,300-ton coal collier, the SS BLACK POINT. All that naval science, marine engineering and Prussian training to sink a small, unarmed merchantman.

Certainly the torpedoing wasn't worth it to the crew of the U-853. The submarine had hardly begun evasive action before the S-O-S was on the air, and all the A/S forces in the area were alerted.

Those forces were considerable. Coast Guardsmen from Point Jude, Block Island, Montauk. Destroyers, destroyer-escorts, corvettes, frigates, armed yachts. Land-based aircraft.

Thus the destroyer-escort ATHERTON (Lieutenant Commander L. Iselin, USNR), the destroyer ERICSSON, and the frigate MOBERLY (Lieutenant Commander L. B. Tollaksen, USCG) were soon combing the seascape off Point Judith. ERICSSON's hunt was fruitless. But, probing with their detection gear, both the ATHERTON and the frigate made contact with a submerged vessel lying about five miles from the scene of the torpedoing.

ATHERTON attacked. MOBERLY attacked. Down went the TNT.

Up came mounds of water and the thunder of sea-smothered explosions. The assailed U-boat made no move. Blasting continued through the early hours of May 6, a din that roused the fishermen on distant Block Island and rattled the windows of the island post office.

In their pressure hull the U-boaters were as confined as meats in a nut. A sledge-hammer depth-charge came down—slam!—and the nutshell cracked. *Slam! Slam! Slam!* The shell was crushed.

The men aboard ATHERTON and MOBERLY saw bubbles cluster on the surface. Up came a gurgling gush of oil. A great litter of cork spread out across the heaving sea.

Boating through this flotsam some time later, the destroyermen picked up escape lungs, some pieces of German equipment, and other items bearing visible evidence of a kill. That afternoon divers from New London found the dead submarine. No survivors were recovered.

Downed the day before VE-Day the U-853 was the last German submarine demolished by American destroyermen in World War II. So the super-sub threat was sunk. The Battle of the Atlantic was finally and definitely over.

Atlantic Battle Summary

VE-Day—the radio operators of DesLant could not believe their ear-phones. Hitler cremated, Nazi Germany *Kaput*. Destroyermen, incredulous, took it at first for scuttlebutt. Then the word came over the squawk-boxes:

ATTENTION ALL HANDS AT TWO FORTY-ONE IN THE MORNING OF MAY SEVEN THE SURRENDER INSTRUMENT WAS SIGNED BY FIELD MARSHAL JODL

All hostilities ceased at midnight on May 8. Doenitz, wearing *Der Fuehrer's* tattered mantle, had capitulated.

Like woodchucks emerging en masse from their holes on some mythical Ground-Hog Day, German submarines in the Atlantic began surfacing and surrendering. Seven surfaced in the western Atlantic. One of these, the U-805, came up off Delaware Bay early in the morning of May 9, to haul down the flag to an A/S force which took the sub as a prize to Philadelphia. Another, the U-234, made its appearance off the New England coast. A prize crew hauled this *Schnorkeler* into Portsmouth, N.H., where it was learned that the U-boat had been bound for Japan with a cargo of two Japanese officers—both of whom, just before the submarine's surrender, had ceremoniously committed *hari-kiri*.

With the U-boat war at an end, Navy statisticians promptly set to work on summarizations, percentages, and totals. To the American destroyermen who had fought the hot Atlantic Battle, some of these cold figures proved most interesting.

German submarines fighting in World War II to cut the Allies' trans-Atlantic lifelines, had sunk some 3,000 Allied and neutral vessels for a staggering loss of more than 14,000,000 tons of shipping.

But after the U.S. Navy entered the Atlantic Battle, the ratio of ships sunk to U-boats sunk was drastically altered in favor of the Allies. About 26 Allied vessels went down for each U-boat destroyed in 1940. By 1942 the ratio was 13 Allied vessels per U-boat. In 1943 the exchange was 2 for 1, and in the second half of that year more enemy subs were sunk than Allied vessels were torpedoed. In 1944 the Allies whittled the exchange and in 1945 it was reduced to more than two U-boats sunk for every Allied vessel torpedoed.

Altogether the Nazi Germans lost some 768 U-boats. Entering the war in 1939, and bearing the brunt thereafter, British A/S forces downed a total of 561. American A/S forces accounted for 177. Allied A/S forces accounted for 30.

Of the 177 U-boats destroyed by American forces, Army aircraft demolished 48 in air raids on enemy-held seaports, and sank 14 at sea. The remaining 115 were downed by Navy. DD's, DE's, Coast Guard cutters, and other A/S craft, operating singly and in hunter-killer teams, downed 48 U-boats—43 in the Atlantic and 5 in the Mediterranean. They also accounted for 2 Italian submarines.

The American A/S forces opposed a deadly foe, superbly trained, magnificently equipped, supremely dangerous. But the U-boats were able to torpedo and sink but ten American A/S vessels—the escort-carrier BLOCK ISLAND, the destroyers JACOB JONES and LEARY, destroyer-escorts FISKE and FREDERICK C. DAVIS, and five Coast Guard cutters.

Schnorkel and the capacity to dive to depths approaching 700 feet might have swung the balance in the U-boat's favor. But these submarine innovations were not developed in time. The U-boats that fought the Battle of the Atlantic were no match for the CVE-DD-DE hunter-killer teams.

Chapter 40

Destroyers to Japan

☆ ☆ ☆

Exit Last Axis Partner

The Pacific War went on to its tragic end because the militarists on the Japanese Imperial Council refused to acknowledge defeat in a senseless effort to "save face"—and perhaps their own skins.

Japan was on the rocks by April 1945, and the Emperor wanted peace.

As the wrangling in Japan's Supreme War Council went on in secret, the Allied leaders were unaware of Hirohito's peace moves. Nor were they accurately informed on the paralysis of Japan. Accordingly plans went forward for "Operation Olympic"— the invasion of Kyushu, which was scheduled to take place five months after the securement of Okinawa.

Meanwhile, American hunter-killers were relentlessly fighting the A/S campaign. In the third week of July a DesPac DE teamed up with carrier aircraft to score the last major submarine kill, destroyer-wise, in the Pacific. The job was done by the L. C. TAYLOR and planes from the carrier ANZIO.

L. C. TAYLOR *and Aircraft from* ANZIO *Kill* I-13

Steaming from San Pedro Bay in the Philippines on July 6, 1945, the escort-carrier ANZIO and five DE's headed seaward for a rendezvous with a fuelling group. By July 16 the task group was cruising in an assigned area off Honshu.

At 0747 in the morning of the 16th, an ANZIO plane sighted and bombed a Jap sub which had dared daylight exposure on the surface. Trailing oil, the sub submerged. The wounded I-boat was tracked and attacked by a relief plane. At 1140 the LAWRENCE C. TAYLOR (Lieutenant Commander J. R. Grey) was guided into position by the plane. The DE let fly with a hedgehog barrage. A spatter of small explosions indicated hits. Two deep-bellied blasts echoed the rataplan.

To the oil-streaked surface bobbed a miscellany of rubbish which included shattered desk planks, cork, sponge rubber, candles, Jap magazines, paper money, a snapshot (candid camera), and some soggy mail. The contents of this correspondence was not recorded; evidently it was not as interesting as some. (For instance, a postcard found on the body of a *Kamikaze* pilot, from a feminine admirer who praised him for joining the Suicide Corps and somewhat inconsistently "hoped that he would have a long and prosperous life.")

The submarine which fell afoul of the ANZIO aircraft and LAWRENCE C. TAYLOR off Honshu had a short life and an impecunious one. But it did have the distinction of being the last big Jap sub downed by destroyermen in the Pacific War. It also had a numerological distinction similar to that which haunted destroyer CALLAGHAN. Its number was I-13.

Imperial Finish

The atom bombs fell. Hiroshima was obliterated on August 6. Nagasaki was pulverized on the 9th. Soviet Russia declared war, in accordance with Yalta agreements, and Japan was at Death's door.

On August 14, 1945, the "Cease fire" order flashed through the United States Fleet.

Tell It to the Destroyermen

Fought at a cost of four trillion dollars and 40 million lives, the global war that ended in Japan in September, 1945, was unquestionably the greatest tragedy in human history. Never in the past had civilian populaces been scourged by such cruel punishment as was inflicted upon them by invasion, starvation, and genocide. Never had armed forces waged campaigns of such scope, or fought battle as furious with weapons as devastating.

Seen in panoramic perspective, United States losses were relatively light compared with those suffered by Allied and enemy powers. Although United States battle deaths did not approach the millions lost by Russia, Germany, China, and Japan, the American death toll of 293,000 was sufficiently grievous.

The Navy's fatalities were proportionately high. Ship losses (from all causes) during World War II included 2 battleships, 5 aircraft carriers, 6 escort-carriers, 7 heavy cruisers, 3 light cruisers, 71 destroyers, 11 destroyer-escorts, 52 submarines, and several hundred other vessels of various types.

The Pacific War cost the Japanese 11 battleships, 15 aircraft carriers, 5 escort-carriers, 36 heavy and light cruisers, 126 destroyers, approximately 130 submarines, and innumerable vessels of other types. The Japanese started the war with the world's third largest navy. When they sued for peace, the entire Imperial Navy was strewn across the bottom of the Pacific from the Aleutians to Australia, from Australia to the Philippines, and from the Philippines to Tokyo Bay. Most of that strewing was the work of the United States Navy.

The 49 U-boats and 68 Japanese subs sunk by American destroyers and destroyer-escorts, operating singly and in hunter-killer teams, would have been enough to justify a Force which at war's end contained approximately 438 destroyers and 374 destroyer-escorts. Anyone who thought this fleet over-expanded and some of the squadrons superfluous could "tell it to the destroyermen." For answer, those sailors would point to the many and various missions undertaken and accomplished by DD's and DE's.

No type of ship afloat served in as many capacities as did the DD. No type fought harder or took it harder on the chin. "Poor devils," a submarine admiral recalled the plight of the DD sailors in the early days of the war. They put up a rugged battle in the North Atlantic and in the South Pacific."

They put up a rugged fight everywhere. Just where they found the going toughest might be hard to say. For all, and everywhere, combat was tough—bullets were tough; shells were tough; bombs, mines, and torpedoes were tough. *Kamikazes*, rockets, robot jets, E-boats, and human torpedoes were tough. The sea itself was on occasion a savage adversary, as the sailors who battled fog, blizzard, tempest, hurricane, and typhoon could testify. What could be said of one battle area or another, one amphibious beach or another, one action or another, one sinking or another, except that anywhere Death was striking, the battle was toughest?

All who participated in the war knew the degree at its superlative when they entered combat.

How they acquitted themselves, and to what purpose, are questions answered by the war record built by the men who manned the "cans."